THE
DEVIL IN THE
WHITE CITY

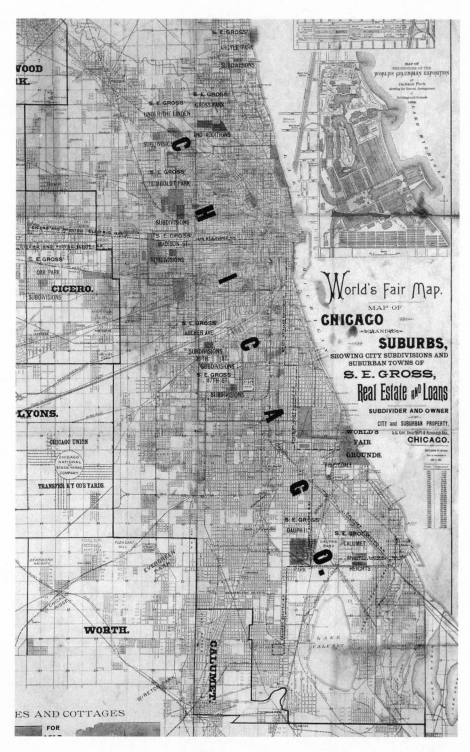

Chicago, 1891.

ALSO BY ERIK LARSON

Isaac's Storm

Lethal Passage

The Naked Consumer

THE
DEVIL IN THE
WHITE CITY

MURDER, MAGIC, AND MADNESS
AT THE FAIR THAT CHANGED AMERICA

ERIK LARSON

Crown Publishers • New York

Endpapers: Rand, McNally and Art Institute of Chicago;
courtesy of the Art Institute of Chicago

Illustration credits appear on page 433.

Published by Crown Publishers, New York, New York.
Member of the Crown Publishing Group, a division of Random House, Inc.
www.randomhouse.com

CROWN is a trademark and the Crown colophon is a registered trademark of
Random House, Inc.

Printed in the United States of America

Design by Leonard W. Henderson

Library of Congress Cataloging-in-Publication Data
Larson, Erik.
The devil in the white city : murder, magic, and madness at the fair that changed
America / Erik Larson.—ed.
Includes bibliographical references and index.
1. Mudgett, Herman W., 1861–1896. 2. Serial murderers—Illinois—Chicago—
Biography. 3. Serial murders—Illinois—Chicago—Case studies. 4. World's
Columbian Exposition (1893 : Chicago, Ill.) I. Title.
HV6248.M8 L37 2003
364.15'23'0977311—dc21
2002154046

ISBN 0-609-60844-4

10 9 8 7 6

First Edition

To Chris, Kristen, Lauren, and Erin,
for making it all worthwhile

—and to Molly, whose lust for socks
kept us all on our toes

CONTENTS

EVILS IMMINENT

(A NOTE)

IN CHICAGO AT THE END of the nineteenth century amid the smoke of industry and the clatter of trains there lived two men, both handsome, both blue-eyed, and both unusually adept at their chosen skills. Each embodied an element of the great dynamic that characterized the rush of America toward the twentieth century. One was an architect, the builder of many of America's most important structures, among them the Flatiron Building in New York and Union Station in Washington, D.C.; the other was a murderer, one of the most prolific in history and harbinger of an American archetype, the urban serial killer. Although the two never met, at least not formally, their fates were linked by a single, magical event, one largely fallen from modern recollection but that in its time was considered to possess a transformative power nearly equal to that of the Civil War.

In the following pages I tell the story of these men and this event, but I must insert here a notice: However strange or macabre some of the following incidents may seem, this is *not* a work of fiction. Anything between quotation marks comes from a letter, memoir, or other written document. The action takes place mostly in Chicago, but I beg readers to forgive me for the occasional lurch across state lines, as when the staunch, grief-struck Detective Geyer enters that last awful cellar. I beg forbearance, too, for the occasional side journey demanded by the story, including excursions into the medical acquisition of corpses and the correct use of Black Prince geraniums in an Olmstedian landscape.

Beneath the gore and smoke and loam, this book is about the evanescence of life, and why some men choose to fill their brief allotment of time engaging the impossible, others in the manufacture of sorrow. In the end it is a story of the ineluctable conflict between good and evil, daylight and darkness, the White City and the Black.

ERIK LARSON
SEATTLE

Make no little plans; they have no magic to stir men's blood.
DANIEL H. BURNHAM
DIRECTOR OF WORKS
WORLD'S COLUMBIAN EXPOSITION, 1893

I was born with the devil in me. I could not help the fact that I was a murderer, no more than the poet can help the inspiration to sing.
DR. H. H. HOLMES
CONFESSION
1896

PROLOGUE

Aboard the Olympic

1912

The architects *(left to right)*: Daniel Burnham, George Post, M. B. Pickett,
Henry Van Brunt, Francis Millet, Maitland Armstrong, Col. Edmund Rice,
Augustus St. Gaudens, Henry Sargent Codman, George W. Maynard,
Charles McKim, Ernest Graham, Dion Geraldine.

Aboard the *Olympic*

THE DATE WAS APRIL 14, 1912, a sinister day in maritime history, but of course the man in suite 63–65, shelter deck C, did not yet know it. What he did know was that his foot hurt badly, more than he had expected. He was sixty-five years old and had become a large man. His hair had turned gray, his mustache nearly white, but his eyes were as blue as ever, bluer at this instant by proximity to the sea. His foot had forced him to delay the voyage, and now it kept him anchored in his suite while the other first-class passengers, his wife among them, did what he would have loved to do, which was to explore the ship's more exotic precincts. The man loved the opulence of the ship, just as he loved Pullman Palace cars and giant fireplaces, but his foot problem tempered his enjoyment. He recognized that the systemic malaise that caused it was a consequence in part of his own refusal over the years to limit his courtship of the finest wines, foods, and cigars. The pain reminded him daily that his time on the planet was nearing its end. Just before the voyage he told a friend, "This prolonging of a man's life doesn't interest me when he's done his work and has done it pretty well."

The man was Daniel Hudson Burnham, and by now his name was familiar throughout the world. He was an architect and had done his work pretty well in Chicago, New York, Washington, San Francisco, Manila, and many other cities. He and his wife, Margaret, were sailing to Europe in the company of their daughter and her husband for a grand tour that was to continue through the summer. Burnham had chosen this ship, the R.M.S. *Olympic* of the White Star Line, because it was new and glamorous and big. At the time he booked passage the *Olympic* was the largest vessel in regular service, but just three days before his departure a sister ship—a slightly longer twin—had stolen that rank when it set off on its maiden voyage. The twin, Burnham knew, was at that moment carrying one of his closest friends, the painter Francis Millet, over the same ocean but in the opposite direction.

As the last sunlight of the day entered Burnham's suite, he and Margaret set off for the first-class dining room on the deck below. They took the elevator to spare his foot the torment of the grand stairway, but he did so with reluctance, for he admired the artistry in the iron scrollwork of its balustrades and the immense dome of iron and glass that flushed the ship's core with natural light. His sore foot had placed increasing limitations on his mobility. Only a week earlier he had found himself in the humiliating position of having to ride in a wheelchair through Union Station in Washington, D.C., the station he had designed.

The Burnhams dined by themselves in the *Olympic*'s first-class salon, then retired to their suite and there, for no particular reason, Burnham's thoughts returned to Frank Millet. On impulse, he resolved to send Millet a midsea greeting via the *Olympic*'s powerful Marconi wireless.

Burnham signaled for a steward. A middle-aged man in knife-edge whites took his message up three decks to the Marconi room adjacent to the officer's promenade. He returned a few moments later, the message still in his hand, and told Burnham the operator had refused to accept it.

Footsore and irritable, Burnham demanded that the steward return to the wireless room for an explanation.

Millet was never far from Burnham's mind, nor was the event that had brought the two of them together: the great Chicago world's fair of 1893. Millet had been one of Burnham's closest allies in the long, bittersweet struggle to build the fair. Its official name was the World's Columbian Exposition, its official purpose to commemorate the four hundredth anniversary of Columbus's discovery of America, but under Burnham, its chief builder, it had become something enchanting, known throughout the world as the White City.

It had lasted just six months, yet during that time its gatekeepers recorded 27.5 million visits, this when the country's total population was 65 million. On its best day the fair drew more than 700,000 visitors. That the fair had occurred at all, however, was something of a miracle. To build it Burnham had confronted a legion of obstacles, any one of which could have—*should* have—killed it long before Opening Day. Together he and his architects had conjured a dream city whose grandeur and beauty exceeded anything each singly could have imagined. Visitors wore their best clothes and most somber expressions, as if entering a great cathedral. Some wept at its beauty. They tasted a new snack called Cracker Jack and a new breakfast food called Shredded Wheat. Whole villages had been imported from Egypt, Algeria, Dahomey, and other far-flung locales, along with their inhabitants. The Street in Cairo exhibit alone employed nearly two hundred Egyptians and contained twenty-five distinct buildings, including a fifteen-hundred-seat theater that introduced America to a new and scandalous form of entertainment. Everything about the fair was exotic and, above all, immense. The fair occupied over one square mile and filled more than two hundred buildings. A single exhibit hall had enough interior volume to have housed the U.S. Capitol, the Great Pyramid, Winchester Cathedral, Madison Square Garden, and St. Paul's Cathedral, all at the same time. One structure, rejected at first as a "monstrosity," became the fair's emblem, a machine so huge and terrifying that it instantly eclipsed the tower of Alexandre Eiffel that had so wounded America's pride. Never before had so many of history's brightest lights, including Buffalo Bill, Theodore Dreiser, Susan B. Anthony, Jane Addams, Clarence Darrow, George Westinghouse, Thomas Edison, Henry Adams, Archduke Francis Ferdinand, Nikola Tesla, Ignace Paderewski, Philip Armour, and Marshall Field, gathered in one place at one time. Richard Harding Davis called the exposition "the greatest event in the history of the country since the Civil War."

That something magical had occurred in that summer of the world's fair was beyond doubt, but darkness too had touched the fair. Scores of workers had been hurt or killed in building the dream, their families consigned to poverty. Fire had killed fifteen more, and an assassin had transformed the closing ceremony from what was to have been the century's greatest celebration into a vast funeral. Worse had occurred too, although these revelations emerged only slowly. A murderer had moved among the beautiful things Burnham had created. Young women drawn to Chicago by the fair and by the prospect of living on their own had disappeared, last seen at the killer's block-long mansion, a parody of everything architects held dear. Only after the exposition had Burnham and his colleagues learned of the anguished letters describing daughters who had come to the city and then fallen silent. The press speculated that scores of fairgoers must have disappeared within the building. Even the street-hardened members of the city's Whitechapel Club, named for the London stalking grounds of Jack the Ripper, were startled by what detectives eventually found inside and by the fact that such grisly events could have gone undiscovered for so long. The rational explanation laid blame on the forces of change that during this time had convulsed Chicago. Amid so much turmoil it was understandable that the work of a young and handsome doctor would go unnoticed. As time passed, however, even sober men and women began to think of him in less-than-rational terms. He described himself as the Devil and contended that his physical shape had begun to alter. Enough strange things began happening to the men who brought him to justice to make his claim seem almost plausible.

For the supernaturally inclined, the death of the jury foreman alone offered sufficient proof.

Burnham's foot ached. The deck thrummed. No matter where you were on the ship, you felt the power of the *Olympic*'s twenty-nine boilers transmitted upward through the strakes of the hull. It was the one constant that told you—even in the staterooms and dining chambers and smoking lounge, despite the lavish efforts to make these rooms look as if they had been plucked from the Palace of Versailles or a Jacobean mansion—that you were aboard a ship being propelled far into the bluest reaches of the ocean.

Burnham and Millet were among the few builders of the fair still alive. So many others had gone. Olmsted and Codman. McKim. Hunt.

Atwood—mysteriously. And that initial loss, which Burnham still found difficult to comprehend. Soon no one would remain, and the fair would cease to exist as a living memory in anyone's brain.

Of the key men, who besides Millet was left? Only Louis Sullivan: embittered, perfumed with alcohol, resenting who knew what, but not above coming by Burnham's office for a loan or to sell some painting or sketch.

At least Frank Millet still seemed strong and healthy and full of the earthy good humor that had so enlivened the long nights during the fair's construction.

The steward came back. The expression in his eyes had changed. He apologized. He still could not send the message, he said, but at least now he had an explanation. An accident had occurred involving Millet's ship. In fact, he said, the *Olympic* was at that moment speeding north at maximum velocity to come to her aid, with instructions to receive and care for injured passengers. He knew nothing more.

Burnham shifted his leg, winced, and waited for more news. He hoped that when the *Olympic* at last reached the site of the accident, he would find Millet and hear him tell some outrageous story about the voyage. In the peace of his stateroom, Burnham opened his diary.

That night the fair came back to him with extra clarity.

Part I

Frozen Music

Chicago, 1890–91

Chicago, circa 1889.

The Black City

How easy it was to disappear:

A thousand trains a day entered or left Chicago. Many of these trains brought single young women who had never even seen a city but now hoped to make one of the biggest and toughest their home. Jane Addams, the urban reformer who founded Chicago's Hull House, wrote, "Never before in civilization have such numbers of young girls been suddenly released from the protection of the home and permitted to walk unattended upon the city streets and to work under alien roofs." The women sought work as typewriters, stenographers, seamstresses, and weavers. The men who hired them were for the most part moral citizens intent on efficiency and profit. But not always. On March 30, 1890, an officer of the First National Bank placed a warning in the help-wanted section of the *Chicago Tribune*, to inform female stenographers of "our growing conviction that no thoroughly honorable business-man who is this side of dotage ever advertises for a lady stenographer who is a blonde, is good-looking, is quite alone in the city, or will transmit her photograph. All such advertisements upon their face bear the marks of vulgarity, nor do we regard it safe for any lady to answer such unseemly utterances."

The women walked to work on streets that angled past bars, gambling houses, and bordellos. Vice thrived, with official indulgence. "The parlors and bedrooms in which honest folk lived were (as now) rather dull places," wrote Ben Hecht, late in his life, trying to explain this persistent trait of old Chicago. "It was pleasant, in a way, to know that outside their windows, the devil was still capering in a flare of brimstone." In an analogy that would prove all too apt, Max Weber likened the city to "a human being with his skin removed."

Anonymous death came early and often. Each of the thousand trains that entered and left the city did so at grade level. You could step from a curb and be killed by the Chicago Limited. Every day on average two people were destroyed at the city's rail crossings. Their injuries were grotesque. Pedestrians retrieved severed heads. There were other hazards. Streetcars fell from drawbridges. Horses bolted and dragged carriages into crowds. Fires took a dozen lives a day. In describing the fire dead, the term the newspapers most liked to use was "roasted." There was diphtheria, typhus, cholera, influenza. And there was murder. In the time of the fair the rate at which men and women killed one another rose sharply throughout the nation but especially in Chicago, where police found themselves without the manpower or expertise to manage the volume. In the first six months of 1892 the city experienced nearly eight hundred violent deaths. Four a day. Most were prosaic, arising from robbery, argument, or sexual jealousy. Men shot women, women shot men, and children shot one another by accident. But all this could be understood. Nothing like the Whitechapel killings had occurred. Jack the Ripper's five-murder spree in 1888 had defied explanation and captivated readers throughout America, who believed such a thing could not happen in their own hometowns.

But things were changing. Everywhere one looked the boundary between the moral and the wicked seemed to be degrading. Elizabeth Cady Stanton argued in favor of divorce. Clarence Darrow advocated free love. A young woman named Borden killed her parents.

And in Chicago a young handsome doctor stepped from a train, his surgical valise in hand. He entered a world of clamor, smoke, and steam, refulgent with the scents of murdered cattle and pigs. He found it to his liking.

The letters came later, from the Cigrands, Williamses, Smythes, and untold others, addressed to that strange gloomy castle at Sixty-third and Wallace, pleading for the whereabouts of daughters and daughters' children.

It was so easy to disappear, so easy to deny knowledge, so very easy in the smoke and din to mask that something dark had taken root.

This was Chicago, on the eve of the greatest fair in history.

"The Trouble Is Just Begun"

ON THE AFTERNOON OF MONDAY, February 24, 1890, two thousand people gathered on the sidewalk and street outside the offices of the *Chicago Tribune,* as similar crowds collected at each of the city's twenty-eight other daily newspapers, and in hotel lobbies, in bars, and at the offices of Western Union and the Postal Telegraph Company. The gathering outside the *Tribune* included businessmen, clerks, traveling salesmen, stenographers, police officers, and at least one barber. Messenger boys stood ready to bolt as soon as there was news worth reporting. The air was cold. Smoke filled the caverns between buildings and reduced lateral visibility to a few blocks. Now and then police officers cleared a path for one of the city's bright yellow streetcars, called grip-cars for the way their operators attached them to an ever-running cable under the street. Drays full of wholesale goods rumbled over the pavers, led by immense horses gusting steam into the murk above.

The wait was electric, for Chicago was a prideful place. In every corner of the city people looked into the faces of shopkeepers, cab drivers, waiters and bellboys to see whether the news already had come and whether it was good or bad. So far the year had been a fine one. Chicago's population had topped one million for the first time, making the city the second most populous in the nation after New York, although disgruntled residents of Philadelphia, previously in second place, were quick to point out that Chicago had cheated by annexing large expanses of land just in time for the 1890 decadal census. Chicago shrugged the sniping off. Big was big. Success today would dispel at last the eastern perception that Chicago was nothing more than a greedy, hog-slaughtering backwater; failure would bring humiliation from which the city would not soon recover, given how heartily its leading men had boasted that Chicago would prevail. It was this big talk, not the persistent southwesterly breeze, that had prompted New York editor Charles Anderson Dana to nickname Chicago "the Windy City."

In their offices in the top floor of the Rookery, Daniel Burnham, forty-three, and his partner, John Root, newly forty, felt the electricity more keenly than most. They had participated in secret conversations, received certain assurances, and gone so far as to make reconnaissance forays to outlying parts of the city. They were Chicago's leading architects: They had pioneered the erection of tall structures and designed the first building in the country ever to be called a skyscraper; every year, it seemed, some new building of theirs became the tallest in the world. When they moved into the Rookery at La Salle and Adams, a gorgeous light-filled structure of Root's design, they saw views of the lake and city that no one but construction workers had seen before. They knew, however, that today's event had the potential to make their success so far seem meager.

The news would come by telegraph from Washington. The *Tribune* would get it from one of its own reporters. Its editors, rewrite men, and typesetters would compose "extra" editions as firemen shoveled coal into the boilers of the paper's steam-driven presses. A clerk would paste each incoming bulletin to a window, face out, for pedestrians to read.

Shortly after four o'clock, Chicago standard railroad time, the *Tribune* received its first cable.

———

Even Burnham could not say for sure who had been first to propose the idea. It had seemed to rise in many minds at once, the initial intent simply to celebrate the four hundredth anniversary of Columbus's discovery of the New World by hosting a world's fair. At first the idea gained little momentum. Consumed by the great drive toward wealth and power that had begun after the end of the Civil War, America seemed to have scant interest in celebrating its distant past. In 1889, however, the French did something that startled everyone.

In Paris on the Champ de Mars, France opened the Exposition

Universelle, a world's fair so big and glamorous and so exotic that visitors came away believing no exposition could surpass it. At the heart of the exposition stood a tower of iron that rose one thousand feet into the sky, higher by far than any man-made structure on earth. The tower not only assured the eternal fame of its designer, Alexandre Gustave Eiffel, but also offered graphic proof that France had edged out the United States for dominance in the realm of iron and steel, despite the Brooklyn Bridge, the Horseshoe Curve, and other undeniable accomplishments of American engineers.

The United States had only itself to blame for this perception. In Paris America had made a half-hearted effort to show off its artistic, industrial, and scientific talent. "We shall be ranked among those nations who have shown themselves careless of appearances," wrote the *Chicago Tribune*'s Paris correspondent on May 13, 1889. Other nations, he wrote, had mounted exhibits of dignity and style, while American exhibitors erected a mélange of pavilions and kiosks with no artistic guidance and no uniform plan. "The result is a sad jumble of shops, booths, and bazaars often unpleasing in themselves and incongruous when taken together." In contrast, France had done everything it could to ensure that its glory overwhelmed everyone. "Other nations are not rivals," the correspondent wrote, "they are foils to France, and the poverty of their displays sets off, as it was meant to do, the fullness of France, its richness and its splendor."

Even Eiffel's tower, forecast by wishful Americans to be a monstrosity that would disfigure forever the comely landscape of Paris, turned out to possess unexpected élan, with a sweeping base and tapered shaft that evoked the trail of a skyrocket. This humiliation could not be allowed to stand. America's pride in its growing power and international stature had fanned patriotism to a new intensity. The nation needed an opportunity to top the French, in particular to "out-Eiffel Eiffel." Suddenly the idea of hosting a great exposition to commemorate Columbus's discovery of the New World became irresistible.

At first, most Americans believed that if an exposition honoring the deepest roots of the nation were to be held anywhere, the site should be Washington, the capital. Initially even Chicago's editors agreed. As the notion of an exposition gained shape, however, other cities began to see it as a prize to be coveted, mainly for the stature it would confer, stature being a powerful lure in this age when pride of place ranked second only to pride of blood. Suddenly New York and St. Louis wanted the fair. Washington laid claim to the honor on grounds it was the center of government, New York because it was the center of everything. No one cared what St. Louis thought, although the city got a wink for pluck.

Nowhere was civic pride a more powerful force than in Chicago, where men spoke of the "Chicago spirit" as if it were a tangible force and prided themselves on the speed with which they had rebuilt the city after the Great Fire of 1871. They had not merely restored it; they had turned it into the nation's leader in commerce, manufacturing, and architecture. All the city's wealth, however, had failed to shake the widespread perception that Chicago was a secondary city that preferred butchered hogs to Beethoven. New York was the nation's capital of cultural and social refinement, and its leading citizens and newspapers never let Chicago forget it. The exposition, if built right—if it topped Paris—might dispel that sentiment once and for all. The editors of Chicago's daily newspapers, upon seeing New York enter the contest, began to ask, why *not* Chicago? The *Tribune* warned that "the hawks, buzzards, vultures, and other unclean beasts, creeping, crawling, and flying, of New York are reaching out to get control of the fair."

On June 29, 1889, Chicago's mayor, DeWitt C. Cregier, announced the appointment of a citizens committee consisting of 250 of the city's most prominent men. The committee met and passed a resolution whose closing passage read: "The men who have helped build Chicago want the fair, and, having a just and well-sustained claim, they intend to have it."

Congress had the final say, however, and now the time for the big vote had come.

A *Tribune* clerk stepped to the window and pasted the first bulletin. The initial ballot put Chicago ahead by a big margin, with 115 votes to New York's 72. St. Louis came next, followed by Washington. One congressman opposed having a fair at all and out of sheer cussedness voted for Cumberland Gap. When the crowd outside the *Tribune* saw that Chicago led New York by 43 votes, it exploded with cheers, whistles, and applause. Everyone knew, however, that Chicago was still 38 votes shy of the simple majority needed to win the fair.

Other ballots followed. Daylight faded to thin broth. The sidewalks filled with men and women leaving work. Typewriters—the women who operated the latest business machines—streamed from the Rookery, the Montauk, and other skyscrapers wearing under their coats the customary white blouse and long black skirt that so evoked the keys of their Remingtons. Cab drivers cursed and gentled their horses. A lamplighter scuttled along the edges of the crowd igniting the gas jets atop cast-iron poles. Abruptly there was color everywhere: the yellow streetcars and the sudden blues of telegraph boys jolting past with satchels full of joy and gloom; cab drivers lighting the red night-lamps at the backs of their hansoms; a large gilded lion crouching before the hat store across the street. In the high buildings above, gas and electric lights bloomed in the dusk like moonflowers.

The *Tribune* clerk again appeared in the newspaper's window, this time with the results of the fifth ballot. "The gloom that fell upon the crowd was heavy and chill," a reporter observed. New York had gained fifteen votes, Chicago only six. The gap between them had narrowed. The barber in the crowd pointed out to everyone in his vicinity that New York's additional votes must have come from congressmen who previously had favored St. Louis. This revelation caused an army lieutenant, Alexander Ross, to proclaim, "Gentlemen. I am prepared to state that any person from St. Louis would rob a church." Another man shouted, "Or poison his wife's dog." This last drew wide agreement.

In Washington the New York contingent, including Chauncey Depew, president of the New York Central and one of the most celebrated orators of the day, sensed a tide change and asked for a recess until the next day. On learning of this request the crowd outside the *Tribune* booed and hissed, correctly interpreting the move as an attempt to gain time to lobby for more votes.

The motion was overruled, but the House voted for a brief adjournment. The crowd remained in place.

After the seventh ballot Chicago was only one vote short of a majority. New York had actually lost ground. A stillness settled on the street. Cabs halted. Police ignored the ever-longer chains of grip-cars that stretched left and right in a great cadmium gash. Passengers disembarked and watched the *Tribune* window, waiting for the next announcement. The cables thrumming beneath the pavement struck a minor chord of suspense, and held it.

Soon a different man appeared in the *Tribune* window. He was tall, thin, and young and wore a black beard. He looked at the crowd without expression. In one hand he held a paste pot, in the other a brush and a bulletin sheet. He took his time. He set the bulletin on a table, out of sight, but everyone in the crowd could tell what he was doing by the motion of his shoulders. He took his time unscrewing the paste pot. There was something somber in his face, as if he were looking down upon a casket. Methodically he painted paste onto the bulletin. It took him a good long while to raise it to the window.

His expression did not change. He fastened the bulletin to the glass.

Burnham waited. His office faced south, as did Root's, to satisfy their craving for natural light, a universal hunger throughout Chicago, where gas jets, still the primary source of artificial illumination, did little to pierce the city's perpetual coal-smoke dusk. Electric bulbs, often in fixtures that combined gas and electricity, were just beginning to light the newest buildings, but these in a sense added to the problem, for they required basement dynamos driven by coal-fired boilers. As the light faded, gaslights on the streets and in the buildings below caused the smoke to glow a dull yellow. Burnham heard only the hiss of gas from the lamps in his office.

That he should be there now, a man of such exalted professional stature in an office so high above the city, would have come as a great and satisfying surprise to his late father.

Daniel Hudson Burnham was born in Henderson, New York, on September 4, 1846, into a family devoted to Swedenborgian principles of obedience, self-subordination, and public service. In 1855, when he was nine, the family moved to Chicago, where his father established a successful wholesale drug business. Burnham was a lackluster student: "the records of the Old Central show his average scholarship to be frequently as low as 55 percent," a reporter discovered, "and 81 percent seems the highest he ever reached." He excelled, however, at drawing and sketched constantly. He was eighteen when his father sent him east to study with private tutors to prepare him for the entrance exams for Harvard and Yale. The boy proved to have a severe case of test anxiety. "I went to Harvard for examination with two men not as well prepared as I," he said. "Both passed easily, and I flunked, having sat through two or three examinations without being able to write a word." The same happened at Yale. Both schools turned him down. He never forgot it.

In the fall of 1867, at twenty-one, Burnham returned to Chicago. He sought work in a field where he might be successful and took a job as a draftsman with the architectural firm of Loring & Jenney. He had found his calling, he wrote in 1868, and told his parents he wanted to become the "greatest architect in the city or country." The next year, however, he bolted for Nevada with friends to try his hand at mining gold. He failed. He ran for the Nevada legislature and failed again. He returned to Chicago broke, in a cattle car, and joined the firm of an architect named L. G. Laurean. Then came October 1871: a cow, a lantern, confusion, and wind. The Great Chicago Fire took nearly eighteen thousand buildings and left more than a hundred thousand people homeless. The destruction promised endless work for the city's architects. But Burnham quit. He sold plate glass, failed. He became a druggist, quit. "There is," he wrote, "a family tendency to get tired of doing the same thing very long."

Exasperated and worried, Burnham's father in 1872 introduced his son to an architect named Peter Wight, who admired the young man's skill at drawing and hired him as a draftsman. Burnham was twenty-five. He liked Wight and liked the work; he liked especially one of Wight's other draftsmen, a southerner named John Wellborn Root, who was four years younger. Born in Lumpkin, Georgia, on January 10, 1850, Root was a musical prodigy who could sing before he could talk. During the Civil War, as Atlanta smoldered, Root's father had smuggled him to Liverpool, England, aboard a Confederate blockade-runner. Root won acceptance into Oxford, but before he could matriculate, the war ended and his father summoned him back to America, to his new home in New York City, where Root studied civil engineering at New York University and became a draftsman for the architect who later designed St. Patrick's Cathedral.

Burnham took to Root immediately. He admired Root's white skin and muscular arms, his stance at the drafting table. They became friends, then partners. They recorded their first income three months before the Panic of 1873 snuffed the nation's economy. But this time Burnham stuck with it. Something about the partnership with Root bolstered him. It filled an absence and played to both men's strengths. They struggled for their own commissions and in the meantime hired themselves out to other more established firms.

One day in 1874 a man walked into their office and in a single galvanic moment changed their lives. He wore black and looked ordinary, but in his past there was blood, death, and profit in staggering quantity. He came looking for Root, but Root was out of town. He introduced himself instead to Burnham and gave his name as John B. Sherman.

There was no need to amplify the introduction. As superintendent of the Union Stock Yards, Sherman ruled an empire of blood that employed 25,000 men, women, and children and each year slaughtered fourteen million animals. Directly and indirectly nearly one-fifth of Chicago's population depended on the yards for its economic survival.

Sherman liked Burnham. He liked his strength, his steady blue gaze, and the confidence with which he conducted the conversation. Sherman commissioned the firm to build him a mansion on Prairie Avenue at Twenty-first Street among homes owned by other Chicago barons and where now and then Marshall Field, George Pullman, and Philip Armour could be seen walking to work together, a titanic threesome in black. Root drew a house of three stories with gables and a peaked roof, in red brick, buff sandstone, blue granite, and black slate; Burnham refined the drawings and guided construction. Burnham happened to be standing in the entrance to the house, considering the work, when a young man with a mildly haughty air and an odd strut—not ego, here, but a congenital fault—walked up to him and introduced himself as Louis Sullivan. The name meant nothing to Burnham. Not yet. Sullivan and Burnham talked. Sullivan was eighteen, Burnham twenty-eight. He told Sullivan, in confidence, that he did not expect to remain satisfied doing just houses. "My idea," he said, "is to work up a big business, to handle big things, deal with big business men, and to build up a big organization, for you can't handle big things unless you have an organization."

John Sherman's daughter, Margaret, also visited the construction site. She was young, pretty, and blond and visited often, using as her excuse the fact that her friend Della Otis lived across the street. Margaret did think the house very fine, but what she admired most was the architect who seemed so at ease among the cairns of sandstone and timber. It took a while, but Burnham got the point. He asked her to marry him. She said yes; the courtship went smoothly. Then scandal broke. Burnham's older brother had forged checks and wounded their father's wholesale drug business. Burnham immediately went to Margaret's father to break the engagement, on grounds the courtship could not continue in the shadow of scandal. Sherman told him he respected Burnham's sense of honor but rejected his withdrawal. He said quietly, "There is a black sheep in every family."

Later Sherman, a married man, would run off to Europe with the daughter of a friend.

Burnham and Margaret married on January 20, 1876. Sherman bought them a house at Forty-third Street and Michigan Avenue, near the lake but more importantly near the stockyards. He wanted proximity. He liked Burnham and approved of the marriage, but he did not entirely trust the young architect. He thought Burnham drank too much.

Sherman's doubts about Burnham's character did not color his respect for his skill as an architect. He commissioned other structures. In his greatest vote of confidence, he asked Burnham & Root to build an entry portal for the Union Stock Yards that would reflect the yards' growing importance. The result was the Stone Gate, three arches of Lemont limestone roofed in copper and displaying over the central arch the carved bust—Root's touch, no doubt—of John Sherman's favorite bull, Sherman. The gate became a landmark that endured into the twenty-first century, long after the last hog crossed to eternity over the great wooden ramp called the Bridge of Sighs.

Root also married a daughter of the stockyards, but his experience was darker. He designed a house for John Walker, president of the yards, and met Walker's daughter, Mary. During their courtship she became ill with tuberculosis. The disease rapidly gained ground, but Root remained committed to the engagement, even though it was clear to everyone he was marrying a dead woman. The ceremony was held in the house Root had designed. A friend, the poet Harriet Monroe, waited with the other guests for the bride to appear on the stairway. Monroe's sister, Dora, was the sole bridesmaid. "A long wait frightened us," Harriet Monroe said, "but at last the bride, on her father's arm, appeared like a white ghost at the halfway landing, and slowly oh, so hesitatingly dragging her heavy satin train, stepped down the wide stairway and across the floor to the bay window which was gay with flowers and vines. The effect was weirdly sad." Root's bride was thin and pale and could only whisper her vows. "Her gayety," Harriet Monroe wrote, "seemed like jewels on a skull."

Within six weeks Mary Walker Root was dead. Two years later Root married the bridesmaid, Dora Monroe, and very likely broke her poet-sister's heart. That Harriet Monroe also loved Root seems beyond dispute. She lived nearby and often visited the couple in their Astor Place home. In 1896 she published a biography of Root that would have made an angel blush. Later, in her memoir, *A Poet's Life,* she described Root's marriage to her sister as being "so completely happy that my own dreams of happiness, confirmed by that example, demanded as fortunate a fulfillment, and could accept nothing less." But Harriet never found its equal and devoted her life instead to poetry, eventually founding *Poetry* magazine, where she helped launch Ezra Pound toward national prominence.

Root and Burnham prospered. A cascade of work flowed to their firm, partly because Root managed to solve a puzzle that had bedeviled Chicago builders ever since the city's founding. By solving it, he helped the city become the birthplace of skyscrapers despite terrain that could not have been less suited to the role.

In the 1880s Chicago was experiencing explosive growth that propelled land values to levels no one could have imagined, especially within the downtown "Loop," named for the turn-around loops of streetcar lines. As land values rose, landowners sought ways of improving the return on their investments. The sky beckoned.

The most fundamental obstacle to height was man's capacity to walk stairs, especially after the kinds of meals men ate in the nineteenth century, but this obstacle had been removed by the advent of the elevator and, equally important, by Elisha Graves Otis's invention of a safety mechanism for halting an elevator in free-fall. Other barriers remained, however, the most elemental of which was the bedeviling character of Chicago's soil, which prompted one engineer to describe the challenge of laying foundations in Chicago as "probably not equaled for perverseness anywhere in the world." Bedrock lay 125 feet below grade, too deep for workers to reach with any degree of economy or safety using the construction methods available in the 1880s. Between this level and the surface was a mixture of sand and clay so saturated with water that engineers called it gumbo. It compressed under the weight of even modest structures and drove architects, as a matter of routine, to design their buildings with sidewalks that intersected the first story four inches above grade, in the hope that when the building settled and dragged the sidewalks down with it, the walks would be level.

There were only two known ways to resolve the soil problem: Build short and avoid the issue, or drive caissons down to bedrock. The latter technique required that workers excavate deep shafts, shore the walls, and pump each so full of air that the resulting high pressure held water at bay, a process that was notorious for causing deadly cases of the bends and used mainly by bridge builders who had no other choice. John Augustus Roebling had used caissons, famously, in building the Brooklyn Bridge, but their first use in the United States had occurred earlier, from 1869 through 1874, when James B. Eads built a bridge over the Mississippi at St. Louis. Eads discovered that workers began experiencing the bends at sixty feet below ground, roughly half the depth to which a Chicago caisson would have to descend. Of the 352 men who worked on the bridge's notorious east caisson, pressure-related illness killed twelve, left two crippled for life, and injured sixty-six others, a casualty rate of over 20 percent.

But Chicago's landowners wanted profit, and at the city's center, profit meant height. In 1881 a Massachusetts investor, Peter Chardon Brooks III, commissioned Burnham & Root to build the tallest office building yet constructed in Chicago, which he planned to call the Montauk. Previously he had brought them their first big downtown commission, the seven-story Grannis Block. In that structure, Burnham said, "our originality began to show. . . . It was a wonder. Everybody went to see it, and the town was proud of it." They moved their offices into its top floor (a potentially fatal move, as it happens, but no one knew it at the time). Brooks wanted the new building to be 50 percent taller "if," he said, "the earth can support it."

The partners quickly grew frustrated with Brooks. He was picky and frugal and seemed not to care how the building looked as long as it was functional. He issued instructions that anticipated by many years Louis Sullivan's famous admonition that form must follow function. "The building throughout is to be for use and not for ornament," Brooks wrote. "Its beauty will be in its all-adaptation to its use." Nothing was to project from its face, no gargoyles, no pedimenta, for projections collected dirt. He wanted all pipes left in the open. "This covering up of pipes is all a mistake, they should be exposed everywhere, if necessary painted well and handsomely." His frugal glare extended to the building's bathrooms. Root's design called for cabinets under sinks. Brooks objected: A cabinet made "a good receptacle for dirt, mice too."

The trickiest part of the Montauk was its foundation. Initially Root planned to employ a technique that Chicago architects had used since 1873 to support buildings of ordinary stature. Workers would erect pyramids of stone on the basement slab. The broad bottom of each pyramid spread the load and reduced settlement; the narrow top supported load-bearing columns. To hold up ten stories of stone and brick, however, the pyramids would have to be immense, the basement transformed into a Giza of stone. Brooks objected. He wanted the basement free for the boilers and dynamo.

The solution, when Root first struck it, must have seemed too simple to be real. He envisioned digging down to the first reasonably firm layer of clay, known as hard-pan, and there spreading a pad of concrete nearly two feet thick. On top of this workers would set down a layer of steel rails stretching from one end of the pad to the other, and over this a second layer at right angles. Succeeding layers would be arranged the same way. Once complete, this *grillage* of steel would be filled and covered with Portland cement to produce a broad, rigid raft that Root called a floating foundation. What he was proposing, in effect, was a stratum of artificial bedrock that would also serve as the floor of the basement. Brooks liked it.

Once built, the Montauk was so novel, so tall, it defied description by conventional means. No one knows who coined the term, but it fit, and the Montauk became the first building to be called a skyscraper. "What Chartres was to the Gothic cathedral," wrote Thomas Talmadge, a Chicago architect and critic, "the Montauk Block was to the high commercial building."

This was the heyday of architectural invention. Elevators got faster and safer. Glassmakers became adept at turning out ever larger sheets of plate glass. William Jenney, of the firm Loring & Jenney, where Burnham started his architectural career, designed the first building to have a load-bearing metal frame, in which the burden of supporting the structure was shifted from the exterior walls to a skeleton of iron and steel. Burnham and Root realized that Jenney's innovation freed builders from the last physical constraints on altitude. They employed it to build taller and taller buildings, cities in the sky inhabited by a new race of businessmen, whom some called "cliff-dwellers." These were men, wrote Lincoln Steffens, "who will not have an office unless it is up where the air is cool and fresh, the outlook broad and beautiful, and where there is silence in the heart of business."

Burnham and Root became rich men. Not Pullman rich, not rich enough to be counted among the first rank of society alongside Potter Palmer and Philip Armour, or to have their wives' gowns described in the city's newspapers, but rich beyond anything either man had expected, enough so that each year Burnham bought a barrel of fine Madeira and aged it by shipping it twice around the world on slow freighters.

As their firm prospered, the character of each partner began to emerge and clarify. Burnham was a talented artist and architect in his own right, but his greatest strength lay in his ability to win clients and execute Root's elegant designs. Burnham was handsome, tall, and strong, with vivid blue eyes, all of which drew clients and friends to him the way a lens gathers light. "Daniel Hudson Burnham was one of the handsomest men I ever saw," said Paul Starrett, later to lead construction of the Empire State Building; he joined Burnham & Root in 1888 as an all-purpose helper. "It was easy to see how he got commissions. His very bearing and looks were half the battle. He had only to assert the most commonplace thing and it sounded important and convincing." Starrett recalled being moved by Burnham's frequent admonition: "Make no little plans; they have no magic to stir men's blood."

Burnham understood that Root was the firm's artistic engine. He believed Root possessed a genius for envisioning a structure quickly, in its entirety. "I've never seen anyone like him in this respect," Burnham said. "He would grow abstracted and silent, and a faraway look would come into his eyes, and the building was there before him—every stone." At the same time he knew Root had little interest in the business side of architecture and in sowing the relationships at the Chicago Club and Union League that eventually led to commissions.

Root played the organ every Sunday morning at the First Presbyterian Church. He wrote opera critiques for the *Chicago Tribune*. He read broadly in philosophy, science, art, and religion and was known throughout Chicago's upper echelon for his ability to converse on almost any subject and to do so with great wit. "His conversational powers were extraordinary," a friend said. "There seemed to be no subject which he had not investigated and in which he was not profoundly learned." He had a sly sense of humor. One Sunday morning he played the organ with particular gravity. It was a while before anyone noticed he was playing "Shoo, Fly." When Burnham and Root were together, one woman said, "I used always to think of some big strong tree with lightning playing around it."

Each man recognized and respected the other's skills. The resultant harmony was reflected in the operation of their office, which, according to one historian, functioned with the mechanical precision of a "slaughterhouse," an apt allusion, given Burnham's close professional and personal association with the stockyards. But Burnham also created an office culture that anticipated that of businesses that would not appear for another century. He installed a gym. During lunch hour employees played handball. Burnham gave fencing lessons. Root played impromptu recitals on a rented piano. "The office was full of a rush of work," Starrett said, "but the spirit of the place was delightfully free and easy and human in comparison with other offices I had worked in."

Burnham knew that together he and Root had reached a level of success that neither could have achieved on his own. The synchrony with which they worked allowed them to take on ever more challenging and daring projects, at a time when so much that an architect did was new and when dramatic increases in the height and weight of buildings amplified the risk of catastrophic failure. Harriet Monroe wrote, "The work of each man became constantly more necessary to the other."

As the firm grew, so did the city. It got bigger, taller, and richer; but it also grew dirtier, darker, and more dangerous. A miasma of cinder-flecked smoke blackened its streets and at times reduced visibility to the distance of a single block, especially in winter, when coal furnaces were in full roar. The ceaseless passage of trains, grip-cars, trolleys, carriages—surreys, landaus, victorias, broughams, phaetons, and hearses, all with iron-clad wheels that struck the pavement like rolling hammers—produced a constant thunder that did not recede until after midnight and made the open-window nights of summer unbearable. In poor neighborhoods garbage mounded in alleys and overflowed giant trash boxes that became banquet halls for rats and bluebottle flies. Billions of flies. The corpses of dogs, cats, and horses often remained where they fell. In January they froze into disheartening poses; in August they ballooned and ruptured. Many ended up in the Chicago River, the city's main commercial artery. During heavy rains, river water flowed in a greasy plume far out into Lake Michigan, to the towers that marked the intake pipes for the city's drinking water. In rain any street not paved with macadam oozed a fragrant muck of horse manure, mud, and garbage that swelled between granite blocks like pus from a wound. Chicago awed visitors and terrified them. French editor Octave Uzanne called it "that Gordian city, so excessive, so satanic." Paul Lindau, an author and publisher, described it as "a gigantic peepshow of utter horror, but extraordinarily to the point."

Burnham loved Chicago for the opportunity it afforded, but he grew wary of the city itself. By 1886 he and Margaret were the parents of five children: two daughters and three sons, the last, a boy named Daniel, born in February. That year Burnham bought an old farmhouse on the lake in the quiet village of Evanston, called by some "the Athens of suburbs." The house had sixteen rooms on two floors, was surrounded by "superb old trees," and occupied a long rectangle of land that stretched to the lake. He bought it despite initial opposition from his wife and her father, and did not tell his own mother of his planned move until the purchase was complete. Later he wrote her an apology. "I did it," he explained, "because I can no longer bear to have my children in the streets of Chicago. . . ."

Success came easily to Burnham and Root, but the partners did have their trials. In 1885 a fire destroyed the Grannis Block, their flagship structure. At least one of them was in the office at the time and made his escape down a burning stairway. They moved next to the top floor of the Rookery. Three years later a hotel they had designed in Kansas City collapsed during construction, injuring several men and killing one. Burnham was heartbroken. The city convened a coroner's inquest, which focused its attention on the building's design. For the first time in his career Burnham found himself facing public attack. He wrote to his wife, "You must not worry over the affair, no matter what the papers say. There will no doubt be censure, and much trouble before we get through, all of which we will shoulder in a simple, straightforward, manly way; so much as in us lies."

The experience cut him deeply, in particular the fact his competence lay exposed to the review of a bureaucrat over whom he had no influence. "The coroner," he wrote Margaret three days after the collapse, "is a disagreeable little doctor, a political hack, without brains, who distresses me." Burnham was sad and lonesome and wanted to go home. "I do so long to be there, and be at peace again, with you."

A third blow came in this period, but of a different character. Although Chicago was rapidly achieving recognition as an industrial and mercantile dynamo, its leading men felt keenly the slander from New York that their city had few cultural assets. To help address this lack, one prominent Chicagoan, Ferdinand W. Peck, proposed to build an auditorium so big, so acoustically perfect, as to silence all the carping from the East and to make a profit to boot. Peck envisioned enclosing this gigantic theater within a still larger shell that would contain a hotel, banquet room, and offices. The many architects who dined at Kinsley's Restaurant, which had a stature in Chicago equal to that of Delmonico's in New York, agreed this would be the single most important architectural assignment in the city's history and that most likely it would go to Burnham & Root. Burnham believed likewise.

Peck chose Chicago architect Dankmar Adler. If acoustically flawed, Peck knew, the building would be a failure no matter how imposing the finished structure proved to be. Only Adler had previously demonstrated a clear grasp of the principles of acoustical design. "Burnham was not pleased," wrote Louis Sullivan, by now Adler's partner, "nor was John Root precisely entranced." When Root saw early drawings of the Auditorium, he said it appeared as if Sullivan were about to "smear another façade with ornament."

From the start there was tension between the two firms, although no one could have known it would erupt years later in a caustic attack by Sullivan on Burnham's greatest achievements, this after Sullivan's own career had dissolved in a mist of alcohol and regret. For now, the tension was subtle, a vibration, like the inaudible cry of overstressed steel. It arose from discordant beliefs about the nature and purpose of architecture. Sullivan saw himself as an artist first, an idealist. In his autobiography, in which he always referred to himself in the third person, he described himself as "an innocent with his heart wrapped up in the arts, in the philosophies, in the religions, in the beatitudes of nature's loveliness, in his search for the reality of man, in his profound faith in the beneficence of power." He called Burnham a "colossal merchandiser" fixated on building the biggest, tallest, costliest structures. "He was elephantine, tactless, and blurting."

Workers began building the Auditorium on June 1, 1887. The result was an opulent structure that, for the moment, was the biggest private building in America. Its theater contained more than four thousand seats, twelve hundred more than New York's Metropolitan Opera House. And it was air-conditioned, through a system that blew air over ice. The surrounding building had commercial offices, an immense banquet hall, and a hotel with four hundred luxurious rooms. A traveler from Germany recalled that simply by turning an electric dial on the wall by his bed, he could request towels, stationery, ice water, newspapers, whiskey, or a shoe shine. It became the most celebrated building in Chicago. The president of the United States, Benjamin Harrison, attended its grand opening.

Ultimately these setbacks proved to be minor ones for Burnham and Root. Far worse was to occur, and soon, but as of February 14, 1890, the day of the great fair vote, the partners seemed destined for a lifetime of success.

———

Outside the *Tribune* building there was silence. The crowd needed a few moments to process the news. A man in a long beard was one of the first to react. He had sworn not to shave until Chicago got the fair. Now he climbed the steps of the adjacent Union Trust Company Bank. On the top step he let out a shriek that one witness likened to the scream of a skyrocket. Others in the crowd echoed his cry, and soon two thousand men and women and a few children—mostly telegraph boys and hired messengers—cut loose with a cheer that tore through the canyon of brick, stone, and glass like a flash flood. The messenger boys raced off with the news, while throughout the city telegraph boys sprinted from the offices of the Postal Telegraph Company and Western Union or leaped aboard their Pope "safety" bikes, one bound for the Grand Pacific Hotel, another the Palmer House, others to the Richelieu, Auditorium, Wellington, the gorgeous homes on Michigan and Prairie, the clubs—Chicago, Century, Union League—and the expensive brothels, in particular Carrie Watson's place with its lovely young women and cascades of champagne.

One telegraph boy made his way through the dark to an unlit alley that smelled of rotted fruit and was silent save for the receding hiss of gaslights on the street he had left behind. He found a door, knocked, and entered a room full of men, some young, some old, all seeming to speak at once, a few quite drunk. A coffin at the center of the room served as a bar. The light was dim and came from gas jets hidden behind skulls mounted on the walls. Other skulls lay scattered about the room. A hangman's noose dangled from the wall, as did assorted weapons and a blanket caked with blood.

These artifacts marked the room as headquarters of the Whitechapel Club, named for the London slum in which two years earlier Jack the Ripper had done his killing. The club's president held the official title of the Ripper; its members were mainly journalists, who brought to the club's meetings stories of murder harvested from the city's streets. The weapons on the wall had been used in actual homicides and were provided by Chicago policemen; the skulls by an alienist at a nearby lunatic asylum; the blanket by a member who had acquired it while covering a battle between the army and the Sioux.

Upon learning that Chicago had won the fair, the men of the Whitechapel Club composed a telegram to Chauncey Depew, who more than any other man symbolized New York and its campaign to win the fair. Previously Depew had promised the members of the Whitechapel Club that if Chicago prevailed he would present himself at the club's next meeting, to be hacked apart by the Ripper himself—metaphorically, he presumed, although at the Whitechapel Club could one ever be certain? The club's coffin, for example, had once been used to transport the body of a member who had committed suicide. After claiming his body, the club had hauled it to the Indiana Dunes on Lake Michigan, where members erected an immense pyre. They placed the body on top, then set it alight. Carrying torches and wearing black hooded robes, they circled the fire singing hymns to the dead between sips of whiskey. The club also had a custom of sending robed members to kidnap visiting celebrities and steal them away in a black coach with covered windows, all without saying a word.

The club's telegram reached Depew in Washington twenty minutes after the final ballot, just as Chicago's congressional delegation began celebrating at the Willard Hotel near the White House. The telegram asked, "When may we see you at our dissecting table?"

Depew sent an immediate response: "I am at your service when ordered and quite ready after today's events to contribute my body to Chicago science."

Although he was gracious in acknowledging defeat, Depew doubted that Chicago really understood the challenge that lay ahead. "The most marvelous exhibit of modern times or ancient times has now just closed successfully at Paris," he told the *Tribune*. "Whatever you do is to be compared with that. If you equal it you have made a success. If you surpass it you have made a triumph. If you fall below it you will be held responsible by the whole American people for having assumed what you are not equal to.

"Beware," he warned. "Take care!"

Chicago promptly established a formal corporation, the World's Columbian Exposition Company, to finance and build the fair. Quietly officials made it clear that Burnham and Root would be the lead designers. The burden of restoring the nation's pride and prominence in the wake of the Paris exposition had fallen upon Chicago, and Chicago in turn had lodged it firmly, if for now discreetly, on the top floor of the Rookery.

Failure was unthinkable. If the fair failed, Burnham knew, the nation's honor would be tarnished, Chicago humiliated, and his own firm dealt a crushing blow. Everywhere Burnham turned there was someone—a friend, an editor, a fellow club member—telling him that the nation expected something tremendous out of this fair. And expected it in record time. The Auditorium alone had taken nearly three years to build and driven Louis Sullivan to the brink of physical collapse. Now Burnham and Root were being called upon to build what amounted to an entire city in about the same amount of time—not just any city, but one that would surpass the brilliance of the Paris exposition. The fair also would have to make a profit. Among Chicago's leading men, profitability was a matter of personal and civic honor.

By traditional architectural standards the challenge seemed an impossible one. Alone neither architect could have done it, but together, Burnham believed, he and Root had the will and the interlocking powers of organization and design to succeed. Together they had defeated gravity and conquered the soft gumbo of Chicago soil, to change forever the character of urban life; now, together, they would build the fair and change history. It could be done, because it had to be done, but the challenge was monstrous. Depew's oratory on the fair quickly grew tiresome, but the man had a way of capturing with wit and brevity the true character of a situation. "Chicago is like the man who marries a woman with a ready-made family of twelve," he said. "The trouble is just begun."

Even Depew, however, did not foresee the true magnitude of the forces that were converging on Burnham and Root. At this moment he and they saw the challenge in its two most fundamental dimensions, time and money, and these were stark enough.

Only Poe could have dreamed the rest.

The Necessary Supply

ONE MORNING IN AUGUST 1886, as heat rose from the streets with the intensity of a child's fever, a man calling himself H. H. Holmes walked into one of Chicago's train stations. The air was stale and still, suffused with the scent of rotten peaches, horse excrement, and partially combusted Illinois anthracite. Half a dozen locomotives stood in the trainyard exhaling steam into the already-yellow sky.

Holmes acquired a ticket to a village called Englewood in the town of Lake, a municipality of 200,000 people that abutted Chicago's southernmost boundary. The township encompassed the Union Stock Yards and two large parks: Washington Park, with lawns, gardens, and a popular racetrack, and Jackson Park, a desolate, undeveloped waste on the lakeshore.

Despite the heat Holmes looked fresh and crisp. As he moved through the station, the glances of young women fell around him like wind-blown petals.

He walked with confidence and dressed well, conjuring an impression of wealth and achievement. He was twenty-six years old. His height was five feet, eight inches; he weighed only 155 pounds. He had dark hair and striking blue eyes, once likened to the eyes of a Mesmerist. "The eyes are very big and wide open," a physician named John L. Capen later observed. "They are blue. Great murderers, like great men in other walks of activity, have blue eyes." Capen also noted thin lips, tented by a full dark mustache. What he found most striking, however, were Holmes's ears. "It is a marvelously small ear, and at the top it is shaped and carved after the fashion in which old sculptors indicated deviltry and vice in their statues of satyrs." Overall, Capen noted, "he is made on a very delicate mold."

To women as yet unaware of his private obsessions, it was an appealing delicacy. He broke prevailing rules of casual intimacy: He stood too close, stared too hard, touched too much and long. And women adored him for it.

He stepped from the train into the heart of Englewood and took a moment to survey his surroundings. He stood at the intersection of Sixty-third and Wallace. A telegraph pole at the corner held Fire Alarm Box No. 2475. In the distance rose the frames of several three-story homes under construction. He heard the concussion of hammers. Newly planted trees stood in soldierly ranks, but in the heat and haze they looked like desert troops gone too long without water. The air was still, moist, and suffused with the burned-licorice scent of freshly rolled macadam. On the corner stood a shop with a sign identifying it as E. S. Holton Drugs.

He walked. He came to Wentworth Street, which ran north and south and clearly served as Englewood's main commercial street, its pavement clotted with horses, drays, and phaetons. Near the corner of Sixty-third and Wentworth, he passed a fire station that housed Engine Company no. 51. Next door was a police station. Years later a villager with a blind spot for the macabre would write, "While at times there was considerable need of a police force in the Stock Yards district, Englewood pursued the even tenor of its way with very little necessity for their appearance other than to ornament the landscape and see that the cows were not disturbed in their peaceful pastures."

Holmes returned to Wallace Street, where he had seen the sign for Holton Drugs. Tracks crossed the intersection. A guard sat squinting against the sun watching for trains and every few minutes lowered a crossing gate as yet another locomotive huffed past. The drugstore was on the northwest corner of Wallace and Sixty-third. Across Wallace was a large vacant lot.

Holmes entered the store and there found an elderly woman named Mrs. Holton. He sensed vulnerability, sensed it the way another man might capture the trace of a woman's perfume. He identified himself as a doctor and licensed pharmacist and asked the woman if she needed assistance in her store. He spoke softly, smiled often, and held her in his frank blue gaze.

He was good with conversation, and soon she revealed to him her deepest sorrow. Her husband, upstairs in their apartment, was dying of cancer. She confessed that managing the store while caring for him had become a great burden.

Holmes listened with moist eyes. He touched her arm. He could ease her burden, he said. Not only that, he could turn the drugstore into a thriving establishment and conquer the competition up the block.

His gaze was so clear and blue. She told him she would have to talk to her husband.

———

She walked upstairs. The day was hot. Flies rested on the window sill. Outside yet another train rumbled through the intersection. Cinder and smoke drifted like soiled gauze past the window. She would talk to her husband, yes, but he was dying, and she was the one who now managed the store and bore its responsibilities, and she had come to a decision.

Just thinking about the young doctor gave her a feeling of contentment she had not experienced in a long while.

———

Holmes had been to Chicago before, but only for brief visits. The city impressed him, he said later, which was surprising because as a rule nothing impressed him, nothing moved him. Events and people captured his attention the way moving objects caught the notice of an amphibian: first a machinelike registration of proximity, next a calculation of worth, and last a decision to act or remain motionless. When he resolved at last to move to Chicago, he was still using his given name, Herman Webster Mudgett.

As for most people, his initial sensory contact with Chicago had been the fantastic stink that lingered always in the vicinity of the Union Stock Yards, a Chinook of putrefaction and incinerated hair, "an elemental odor," wrote Upton Sinclair, "raw and crude; it was rich, almost rancid, sensual and strong." Most people found it repulsive. The few who found it invigorating tended to be men who had waded in its "river of death," Sinclair's phrase, and panned from it great fortunes. It is tempting to imagine that all that death and blood made Mudgett feel welcome but more realistic to suppose it conveyed a sense that here at last was a city that allowed a broader range of behavior than was tolerated in Gilmanton Academy, New Hampshire, the town in which he was born and where he drifted through childhood as a small, odd, and exceptionally bright boy—and where, as a consequence, in the cruel imaginations of his peers, he became prey.

The memory of one episode stayed with him throughout his life. He was five, wearing his first boy's suit, when his parents sent him off to begin his education at the village schoolhouse. "I had daily to pass the office of one village doctor, the door of which was seldom if ever barred," he wrote in a later memoir. "Partly from its being associated in my mind as the source of all the nauseous mixtures that had been my childish terror (for this was before the day of children's medicines), and partly because of vague rumors I had heard regarding its contents, this place was one of peculiar abhorrence to me."

In those days a doctor's office could indeed be a fearsome place. All doctors were in a sense amateurs. The best of them bought cadavers for study. They paid cash, no questions asked, and preserved particularly interesting bits of diseased viscera in large clear bottles. Skeletons hung in offices for easy anatomical reference; some transcended function to become works of art so detailed, so precisely articulated—every bleached bone hitched to its neighbor with brass, under a skull grinning with slap-shoulder bonhomie—that they appeared ready to race chattering down the street to catch the next grip-car.

Two older children discovered Mudgett's fear and one day captured him and dragged him "struggling and shrieking" into the doctor's office. "Nor did they desist," Mudgett wrote, "until I had been brought face to face with one of its grinning skeletons, which, with arms outstretched, seemed ready in its turn to seize me.

"It was a wicked and dangerous thing to do to a child of tender years and health," he wrote, "but it proved an heroic method of treatment, destined ultimately to cure me of my fears, and to inculcate in me, first, a strong feeling of curiosity, and, later, a desire to learn, which resulted years afterwards in my adopting medicine as a profession."

The incident probably did occur, but with a different choreography. More likely the two older boys discovered that their five-year-old victim did not mind the excursion; that far from struggling and shrieking, he merely gazed at the skeleton with cool appreciation.

When his eyes settled back upon his captors, it was they who fled.

⸻

Gilmanton was a small farming village in New Hampshire's lake country, sufficiently remote that its residents did not have access to a daily newspaper and rarely heard the shriek of train whistles. Mudgett had two siblings, a brother and sister. His father, Levi, was a farmer, as was Levi's own father. Mudgett's parents were devout Methodists whose response to even routine misbehavior relied heavily on the rod and prayer, followed by banishment to the attic and a day with neither speech nor food. His mother often insisted he pray with her in her room, then filled the air around him with trembly passion.

By his own assessment, he was a "mother's boy." He spent a good deal of time alone in his room reading Jules Verne and Edgar Allan Poe and inventing things. He built a wind-powered mechanism that generated noise to scare birds from the family fields and set out to create a perpetual motion machine. He hid his most favored treasures in small boxes, among them his first extracted tooth and a photograph of his "twelve-year-old sweetheart," although later observers speculated these boxes also contained treasures of a more macabre sort, such as the skulls of small animals that he disabled and then dissected, alive, in the woods around Gilmanton. They based this speculation on the hard lessons learned during the twentieth century about the behavior of children of similar character. Mudgett's only close friend was an older child named Tom, who was killed in a fall while the boys were playing in an abandoned house.

Mudgett gouged his initials into an old elm tree at his grandfather's farm, where the family marked his growth with notches in a doorjamb. The first was less than three feet high. One of his favorite pastimes was to hike to a high boulder and shout to generate an echo. He ran errands for an "itinerant photographer" who stopped for a time in Gilmanton. The man had a pronounced limp and was glad for the help. One morning the photographer gave Mudgett a broken block of wood and asked him to take it to the town wagon maker for a replacement. When Mudgett returned with the new block, he found the photographer sitting beside his door, partly clothed. Without preamble, the photographer removed one of his legs.

Mudgett was stunned. He had never seen an artificial limb before and watched keenly as the photographer inserted the new block into a portion of the leg. "Had he next proceeded to remove his head in the same mysterious way I should not have been further surprised," Mudgett wrote.

Something about Mudgett's expression caught the photographer's eye. Still on one leg, he moved to his camera and prepared to take Mudgett's picture. Just before he opened the shutter, he held up his false leg and waved it at the boy. Several days later he gave Mudgett the finished photograph.

"I kept it for many years," Mudgett wrote, "and the thin terror-stricken face of that bare-footed, home-spun clad boy I can yet see."

At the time Mudgett described this encounter in his memoir, he was sitting in a prison cell hoping to engineer a swell of public sympathy. While it is charming to imagine the scene, the fact is the cameras that existed during Mudgett's boyhood made candid moments almost impossible to capture, especially when the subject was a child. If the photographer saw anything in Mudgett's eyes, it was a pale blue emptiness that he knew, to his sorrow, no existing film could ever record.

At sixteen Mudgett graduated school and, despite his age, took a job as a teacher, first in Gilmanton and then in Alton, New Hampshire, where he met a young woman named Clara A. Lovering. She had never encountered anyone quite like Mudgett. He was young but poised and had a knack for making her feel good even when she was inclined to feel otherwise. He spoke so well and with such warmth, always touching her in small affectionate ways, even in public. His great flaw was his persistent demand that she allow him to make love to her, not as a lover in formal courtship but in that way that was supposed to come only after marriage. She held him off but could not deny that Mudgett aroused within her an intensity of desire that colored her dreams. Mudgett was eighteen when he asked her to elope. She agreed. They married on July 4, 1878, before a justice of the peace.

At first there was passion far beyond what the dour gossip of older women had led Clara to expect, but their relationship chilled rapidly. Mudgett left the house for long periods. Soon he was gone for days at a time. Finally he was just gone. In the wedding registry of Alton, New Hampshire, they remained married, their contract a legal if desiccated thing.

At nineteen Mudgett went to college. Initially he set his sights on Dartmouth but changed his mind and instead went directly into medical school. He enrolled first in the medicine program at the University of Vermont in Burlington but found the school too small and after only one year moved to the University of Michigan in Ann Arbor, one of the West's leading scientific medical schools, noted for its emphasis on the controversial art of dissection. He enrolled on September 21, 1882. During the summer of his junior year he committed what he called, in his memoir, "the first really dishonest act of my life." He took a job as a traveler for a book publisher, assigned to sell a single book throughout northwestern Illinois. Instead of turning in the proceeds, he kept them. At the end of the summer he returned to Michigan. "I could hardly count my Western trip a failure," he wrote, "for I had seen Chicago."

He graduated in June 1884 with a lackluster record and set out to find "some favorable location" in which to launch a practice. To do so he took another job as a traveler, this time with a nursery company based in Portland, Maine. His route took him through towns he might otherwise never have encountered. Eventually he came to Mooers Forks, New York, where, according to the *Chicago Tribune*, the trustees of the grade school, "impressed with Mudgett's gentlemanly manners," hired him as the school principal, a post he held until he at last opened a medical practice. "Here I stayed for one year doing good and conscientious work, for which I received plenty of gratitude but little or no money."

Wherever he went, troubling things seemed to occur. His professors in Michigan had little to say about his academic talents but recalled that he had distinguished himself in a different way. "Some of the professors here recollected him as being a scamp," the university said. "He had a breach of promise with a hairdresser, a widow, who came to Ann Arbor from St. Louis, Mich."

In Mooers Forks there were rumors that a boy seen in his company had disappeared. Mudgett claimed the boy had returned to his own home in Massachusetts. No investigation took place. No one could imagine the charming Dr. Mudgett causing harm to anyone, let alone a child.

At midnight, many nights, Mudgett would pace the street outside his lodging.

———

Mudgett needed money. Teaching had paid a poverty wage; his medical practice yielded an income only slightly larger. "In the fall of 1885," he wrote, "starvation was staring me in the face."

While in medical school he and a fellow student, a Canadian, had talked about how easy it would be for one of them to buy life insurance, make the other the beneficiary, then use a cadaver to fake the death of the one insured. In Mooers Forks the idea came back to Mudgett. He paid a visit to his former classmate and found that his financial condition was no better. Together they devised an elaborate life insurance fraud, which Mudgett described in his memoir. It was an impossibly complex and gruesome plan, likely beyond the powers of anyone to execute, but his description is noteworthy for what it revealed, without his intention, about his astigmatic soul.

Broadly stated, the plan called for Mudgett and his friend to recruit a couple of other accomplices, who together would fake the deaths of a family of three and substitute cadavers for each person. The bodies would turn up later in an advanced state of decomposition, and the conspirators would divide the $40,000 death benefit (equivalent to more than one million dollars in twenty-first-century valuation).

"The scheme called for a considerable amount of material," Mudgett wrote, "no less than three bodies in fact," meaning he and his friend somehow had to acquire three cadavers roughly resembling the husband, wife, and child.

Mudgett foresaw no difficulty in acquiring the cadavers, although in fact a national shortage of corpses for medical education had by then driven doctors to raid graveyards for the freshly dead. Recognizing that even a doctor could not secure three bodies at once without raising suspicion, Mudgett and his accomplice agreed that each should contribute toward "the necessary supply."

Mudgett claimed to have gone to Chicago in November 1885 and there to have acquired his "portion" of the bodies. Unable to find a job, he placed his portion in storage and left for Minneapolis, where he found work in a drugstore. He remained in Minneapolis until May 1886, when he left for New York City, planning to take "a part of the material there," and to leave the rest in Chicago. "This," he said, "necessitated repacking the same."

He claimed to have deposited one package of dismembered cadaver in the Fidelity Storage Warehouse in Chicago. The other accompanied him to New York, where he lodged it "in a safe place." During his train journey to New York, however, he read two newspaper articles about insurance crime, "and for the first time I realized how well organized and well prepared the leading insurance companies were to detect and punish this kind of fraud." These articles, he claimed, caused him to abandon the plan and to jettison all hope of ever succeeding at such a scheme in the future.

He was lying. In fact, Mudgett was convinced that the fundamentals of the approach had merit—that by faking the deaths of others, he could indeed fleece life insurance companies. As a physician, he knew no means

existed for establishing the identities of burned, dismembered, or otherwise disfigured corpses. And he did not mind handling bodies. They were
"material," no different from firewood, although somewhat more difficult to dispose of.

He was lying too about needing money. The owner of the house in
Mooers Forks where he boarded, D. S. Hays, noticed Mudgett often displayed large sums of cash. Hays grew suspicious and watched Mudgett
closely—albeit not closely enough.

Mudgett left Mooers Fork at midnight, without paying his lodging bill
to Hays. He made his way to Philadelphia, where he hoped to situate
himself in a drugstore and eventually to become a partner or owner. He
found nothing suitable, however, and instead took a job as a "keeper" at
the Norristown Asylum. "This," he wrote, "was my first experience with
insane persons, and so terrible was it that for years afterwards, even now
sometimes, I see their faces in my sleep." Within days he quit.

Eventually he did find a position at one of Philadelphia's drugstores.
Soon afterward a child died after taking medicine acquired at the store.
Mudgett immediately left the city.

He caught a train for Chicago but quickly found that he could not
work as a druggist in Illinois until he passed a licensing examination in
the state capital in Springfield. There, in July 1886, the year Sir Arthur
Conan Doyle introduced his detective to the world, Mudgett registered
his name as Holmes.

Holmes understood that powerful new forces were acting upon
Chicago, causing a nearly miraculous expansion. The city was growing
in all available directions, and where it abutted the lake, it grew skyward,
sharply increasing the value of land within the Loop. Everywhere he
looked he saw evidence of the city's prosperity. Even the smoke was
proof. The city's newspapers loved to crow about the startling increase in
the number of workers employed by Chicago's industries, especially

meat-packing. Holmes knew—everyone knew—that as skyscrapers soared and the stockyards expanded their butchery, the demand for workers would remain high, and that workers and their supervisors would seek to live in the city's suburbs, with their promise of smooth macadam, clean water, decent schools, and above all air untainted by the stench of rotting offal from the Union Yards.

As the city's population swelled, demand for apartments turned into "flat fever." When people could not find or afford apartments, they sought rooms in private homes and boardinghouses, where typically the rent included meals. Speculators thrived and created eerie landscapes. In Calumet a thousand ornate streetlamps stood in a swamp, where they did nothing but ignite the fog and summon auras of mosquitoes. Theodore Dreiser reached Chicago about when Holmes did and was struck by this landscape of anticipation. "The city had laid miles and miles of streets and sewers through regions where perhaps one solitary house stood out alone," he wrote in *Sister Carrie*. "There were regions, open to the sweeping winds and rain, which were yet lighted throughout the night with long, blinking lines of gas lamps fluttering in the wind."

One of the fastest-growing suburbs was Englewood. Even a newcomer like Holmes could tell that Englewood was booming. Real estate advertisements were full of testimonials to its location and appreciating values. Englewood in fact had been growing quickly ever since the Great Fire of 1871. One resident recalled how immediately after the fire "there was such a rush for homes in Englewood and the population increased so rapidly that it was impossible to keep up with it." Old railroad men still called it Chicago Junction or Junction Grove or simply the Junction, for the eight railroad lines that converged within its borders, but after the Civil War residents grew weary of the industrial resonance of the name. In 1868 a Mrs. H. B. Lewis suggested a new one, Englewood, the name of a New Jersey town in which she previously had lived and which had taken its name from a forest in Carlisle, England, legendary for having sheltered two outlaws of Robin Hood stripe. It was here, in what Chicagoans called a "streetcar" suburb, that stockyard supervisors chose to settle, as did officials of companies headquartered in the skyscrapers of the Loop. They acquired big houses on streets named Harvard and Yale that were lined with elm, ash, sycamore, and linden and posted with signs barring all but essential wagon traffic. They sent their children to school and went to church and attended meetings of the Masons and of forty-five other secret societies having lodges, kingdoms, and hives in the village. On Sundays they wandered among the velvet lawns of Washington Park and, if in the mood for solitude, the wind-blasted ridges of Jackson Park at the easternmost end of Sixty-third Street, on the lakeshore.

They took trains and streetcars to work and congratulated themselves on living upwind of the stockyards. The developer of a large Englewood parcel touted this asset in a catalog promoting the auction of two hundred residential lots called the Bates Subdivision: "To the business men of the Union Stock Yards it is particularly convenient and accessible, and free from the odors that are wafted by the prevailing winds to the most fashionable localities of the City."

Dr. Holton did die. Holmes made his widow an offer: He would buy the store, and she could continue to reside in the second-floor apartment. He couched his offer in prose that made it seem as if he were proposing the purchase not to benefit himself but solely to free the grieving Mrs. Holton from the burden of work. He touched her arm as he spoke. After she signed the deed over to him, he stood and thanked her with tears in his eyes.

He financed the purchase mainly with money he raised by mortgaging the store's fixtures and stock, agreeing to repay the loan at a rate of one hundred dollars a month (about three thousand dollars in twenty-first-century value). "My trade was good," he said, "and for the first time in my life I was established in a business that was satisfactory to me."

He put up a new sign: H. H. HOLMES PHARMACY. As word spread that a young, handsome, and apparently unmarried young doctor now stood behind the counter, an increasing number of single women in their twenties began to patronize the store. They dressed nicely and bought things they did not need. Longtime customers also liked the new proprietor, although they missed the comforting presence of Mrs. Holton. The Holtons had been there when their children were sick; had comforted them when these illnesses proved mortal. They knew Mrs. Holton had sold the place. But why had they not seen her around town?

Holmes smiled and explained that she had decided to visit relatives in California, something she had long wanted to do but could never find the time or money to accomplish and certainly could not have done with her husband on his deathbed.

As time wore on and the inquiries dwindled, Holmes modified the story a bit. Mrs. Holton, he explained, liked California so much she had decided to settle there permanently.

"Becomingness"

Nothing. There had been so much energy, so much bravado, but now—nothing. It was July 1890, nearly six months since Congress had voted to give the World's Columbian Exposition to Chicago, but the forty-five men on the exposition's board of directors still had not decided where within the city the fair should be built. At the time of the vote, with the city's pride at stake, all Chicago had sung with one voice. Its emissaries had boasted to Congress that the city could deliver a grander and more appropriate setting than anything New York, Washington, or any other city could propose. Now, however, each quarter of Chicago was insisting on a location within its own boundaries, and the squabbling had stymied the board.

The fair's Committee on Grounds and Buildings had asked Burnham, quietly, to evaluate a number of locations in the city. With equal discretion, the committee assured Burnham and Root that ultimately they would direct the design and construction of the fair. For Burnham, each lost moment was a theft from the already scanty fund of time allotted to build the exposition. The final fair bill signed in April by President Benjamin Harrison established a Dedication Day for October 12, 1892, to honor the moment four hundred years earlier when Columbus had first sighted the New World. The formal opening, however, would not occur until May 1, 1893, to give Chicago more time to prepare. Even so, Burnham knew, much of the fair would have to be ready for the dedication. That left just twenty-six months.

A friend of Burnham's, James Ellsworth, was one of the board's directors; he too was frustrated by the stalemate, so much so that on his own initiative, during a business trip to Maine in mid-July, he visited the Brookline, Massachusetts, office of Frederick Law Olmsted to try and persuade him to come to Chicago and evaluate the sites under consideration and perhaps take on the task of designing the fair's landscape. Ellsworth hoped that Olmsted's opinion, backed by his reputation as the wizard of Central Park, would help force a decision.

That Ellsworth, of all people, should be driven to this step was significant. Initially he had been ambivalent about whether Chicago should even seek the world's fair. He agreed to serve as a director only out of fear that the exposition was indeed at risk of fulfilling the meager expectations of the East and becoming "simply a fair as the term generally implies." He believed it imperative that the city protect its civic honor by producing the greatest such event in the world's history, a goal that seemed to be slipping from Chicago's grasp with each sweep of the clock's hands.

He offered Olmsted a consulting fee of one thousand dollars (equivalent to about thirty thousand today). That the money was his own, and that he lacked official authority to hire Olmsted, were two points Ellsworth failed to disclose.

Olmsted declined. He did not design fairs, he told Ellsworth. He doubted, moreover, that enough time remained for anyone to do the fair justice. To produce the kind of landscape effects Olmsted strived to create required not months but years, even decades. "I have all my life been considering distant effects and always sacrificing immediate success and applause to that of the future," he wrote. "In laying out Central Park we determined to think of no result to be realized in less than forty years."

Ellsworth insisted that what Chicago had in mind was something far grander than even the Paris exposition. He described for Olmsted a vision of a dream city designed by America's greatest architects and covering an expanse at least one-third larger than the Paris fair. Ellsworth assured Olmsted that by agreeing to help, he would be joining his name to one of the greatest artistic undertakings of the century.

Relenting slightly, Olmsted said he would think about it and agreed to meet with Ellsworth two days later, on Ellsworth's return from Maine.

━━━

Olmsted did think about it and began to see the exposition as an opportunity to achieve something for which he had fought long and hard but almost always with disappointing results. Throughout his career he had struggled, with little success, to dispel the perception that landscape architecture was simply an ambitious sort of gardening and to have his field recognized instead as a distinct branch of the fine arts, full sister to painting, sculpture, and brick-and-mortar architecture. Olmsted valued plants, trees, and flowers not for their individual attributes but rather as colors and shapes on a palette. Formal beds offended him. Roses were not roses but "flecks of white or red modifying masses of green." It irked him that few people seemed to understand the effects he worked so long and hard to create. "I design with a view to a passage of quietly composed, soft, subdued pensive character, shape the ground, screen out discordant elements and get suitable vegetation growing." Too often, however, he would "come back in a year and find destruction: why? 'My wife is so fond of roses;' 'I had a present of some large Norway spruces;' 'I have a weakness for white birch trees—there was one in my father's yard when I was a boy.' "

The same thing happened with large civic clients. He and Calvert Vaux had built and refined Central Park from 1858 through 1876, but forever afterward Olmsted found himself defending the park against attempts to tinker with its grounds in ways he considered tantamount to vandalism. It wasn't just Central Park, however. Every park seemed subject to such abuse.

"Suppose," he wrote to architect Henry Van Brunt, "that you had been commissioned to build a really grand opera house; that after the construction work had been nearly completed and your scheme of decoration fully designed you should be instructed that the building was to be used on Sundays as a Baptist Tabernacle, and that suitable place must be made for a huge organ, a pulpit and a dipping pool. Then at intervals afterwards, you should be advised that it must be so refitted and furnished that parts of it could be used for a court room, a jail, a concert hall, hotel, skating rink, for surgical cliniques, for a circus, dog show, drill room, ball room, railway station and shot tower?" That, he wrote, "is what is nearly always going on with public parks. Pardon me if I overwhelm you; it is a matter of chronic anger with me."

What landscape architecture needed, Olmsted believed, was greater visibility, which in turn would bring greater credibility. The exposition could help, he realized, providing it did rise to the heights envisioned by Ellsworth. He had to weigh this benefit, however, against the near-term costs of signing on. His firm already had a full roster of work, so much, he wrote, that "we are always personally under an agitating pressure and cloud of anxiety." And Olmsted himself had grown increasingly susceptible to illness. He was sixty-eight years old and partly lame from a decades-old carriage accident that had left one leg an inch shorter than the other. He was prone to lengthy bouts of depression. His teeth hurt. He had chronic insomnia and facial neuralgia. A mysterious roaring in his ears at times made it difficult for him to attend to conversation. He was still full of creative steam, still constantly on the move, but overnight train journeys invariably laid him low. Even in his own bed his nights often became sleepless horrors laced with toothache.

But Ellsworth's vision was compelling. Olmsted talked it over with his sons and with the newest member of the firm, Henry Sargent Codman—"Harry"—an intensely talented young landscape architect who had quickly become a trusted adviser and confidant.

When Ellsworth returned, Olmsted told him he had changed his mind. He would join the venture.

⌀━━━⌀

Once back in Chicago, Ellsworth secured formal authority to hire Olmsted and arranged to have him report directly to Burnham.

In a letter to Olmsted, Ellsworth wrote: "My position is this: The reputation of America is at stake in this matter, and the reputation of Chicago is also at stake. As an American citizen, you have an equal interest in furthering the success of this great and grand undertaking, and I know from talking with you, that on an occasion like this you grasp the whole situation and will be confined to no narrow limits."

Certainly that seemed to be the case when, during later contract negotiations, Olmsted at Codman's urging requested a fee of $22,500 (about $675,000 today) and got it.

On Wednesday, August 6, 1890, three weeks after Ellsworth's Brookline visit, the exposition company telegraphed Olmsted: "When can you be here?"

Olmsted and Codman arrived three days later, on Saturday morning, and found the city ringing from the news that the final census count had confirmed the earlier, preliminary ranking of Chicago as America's second largest city, even though this final tally also showed that Chicago's lead over Philadelphia was a skimpy one, only 52,324 souls. The good news was a salve for a difficult summer. Earlier, a heat wave had brutalized the city, killing seventeen people (including a man named Christ) and neatly eviscerating Chicago's boasts to Congress that the city possessed the charming summer climate—"cool and delicious," the *Tribune* had said—of a vacation resort. And just before the heat wave, a rising young British writer had published a scalding essay on Chicago. "Having seen it," Rudyard Kipling wrote, "I desire never to see it again. It is inhabited by savages."

To Burnham, Codman seemed amazingly young, late twenties at the most. To be so young and have the trust of America's greatest landscape architect, Codman must have been very bright indeed. He had obsidian eyes that looked as if they could punch holes in steel. As for Olmsted, Burnham was struck by the slightness of his frame, which seemed structurally insufficient to support so massive a skull. That head: Bald for most of its surface, trimmed at bottom with a tangled white beard, it resembled an ivory Christmas ball resting on a bed of excelsior. Olmsted looked worn from his travels, but his eyes were large, warm, and bright.

He wanted to start work immediately. Here at last, Burnham saw, was a man who understood the true cost of each lost minute.

Burnham of course knew of Olmsted's achievements: Central Park in Manhattan, Prospect Park in Brooklyn, the grounds of Cornell and Yale, and scores of other projects. He knew also that before launching the field of landscape architecture, Olmsted had been a writer and editor who had journeyed throughout the antebellum South exploring the culture and practice of slavery. Olmsted had a reputation for brilliance and tireless devotion to his work—but also for an acerbic candor that emerged most predictably in the presence of men who failed to understand that what he sought to create were not flower beds and ornamental gardens but expanses of scenery full of mystery, shadow, and sun-stippled ground.

Olmsted, for his part, knew that Burnham had been a leading force in driving buildings into the clouds. Burnham was said to be the business genius of his firm, Root the artist. It was with Burnham that Olmsted felt the greatest kinship. Burnham was decisive, blunt, and cordial; he spoke under a level blue gaze that Olmsted found reassuring. In private communication Olmsted and Codman agreed that Burnham was a man they could work with.

The tour began at once, but it was hardly an objective one. Burnham and Root clearly favored one location in particular: Jackson Park, on Chicago's South Side, due east of Englewood on the lakeshore. As it happened, Olmsted knew this ground. Twenty years earlier, at the request of Chicago's South Park commissioners, Olmsted had studied both Jackson Park and, to its west, Washington Park, and the broad boulevard that connected them, called Midway. In the plans he had produced for the commissioners, he envisioned transforming Jackson Park from a desert of sand and stagnant pools into a park unlike any other in the nation, focused on water and boating, with canals, lagoons, and shady coves. Olmsted finished those plans shortly before the Great Fire of 1871. In the rush to rebuild, Chicago never got around to realizing his vision. The park became part of Chicago during the 1889 annexations, but otherwise, Olmsted saw, little had changed. He knew its flaws, its *many* flaws, but believed that with a lot of deft dredging and sculpting, the park could be transformed into a landscape unlike any that had ever seated an exposition.

For he recognized that Jackson Park had something no other city in the world could equal: the spreading blue plain of Lake Michigan, as comely a backdrop for a fair as anyone could hope for.

⟡════⟡

On Tuesday, August 12, just four days after he and Codman arrived in Chicago, Olmsted filed a report with the exposition directors, who then to his chagrin made the report public. Olmsted had intended the report for a professional audience, one that would take for granted Jackson Park's fundamental acceptability and value the report as an unflinching guide to the challenges ahead. He was surprised to find the report put to use by opposing cliques as evidence that the fair could not possibly be placed in Jackson Park.

The directors asked for a second report. Olmsted delivered it on Monday, August 18, six days after the first. Burnham saw to his delight that Olmsted had given the directors somewhat more than they perhaps had wished to receive.

⟡════⟡

Olmsted was no literary stylist. Sentences wandered through the report like morning glory through the pickets of a fence. But his prose revealed the depth and subtlety of his thinking about how landscape could be modified to produce an effect in the mind.

First he had set down a few principles and done a little chiding.

Rather than squabbling over sites, he lectured, the different factions needed to recognize that for the exposition to succeed, everyone had to work together, no matter which location the directors selected. "It is to be desired, let us say, that it should be better understood than it yet seems to be by some of your fellow citizens, that the Fair is not to be a Chicago Fair. It is a World's Fair, and Chicago is to stand before the world as the chosen standard bearer for the occasion of the United States of America.

All Chicago can afford to take nothing less than the very best site that can be found for the fair, regardless of the special local interests of one quarter of the city or another."

Every landscape element of the fair, he argued, had to have one "supreme object, viz., the becomingness: the *becomingness* of everything that may be seen as a modestly contributive part of a grand whole; the major elements of which whole will be in the towering series of the main exhibition structures. In other words, the ground, with all it carries, before, between, and behind the buildings, however dressed with turf, or bedecked with flowers, shrubs or trees, fountains, statues, bric-a-brac, and objects of art, should be one *in unity of design* with the buildings; should set off the buildings and should be set off, in matters of light and shadow and tone, by the buildings."

Clearly certain sites were endowed more richly than others. More would be gained by associating the exposition with some feature of striking natural beauty "than by the most elaborate and costly artificial decorations in the form of gardening features, terraces, fountains and statues, than it is possible for the mind of man to devise or the hand of man to carry out." What the many factions in the battle for the fair seemed to ignore was that Chicago had "but one natural object at all distinctively local, which can be regarded as an object of much grandeur, beauty or interest. This is the Lake."

The lake was beautiful and always changing in hue and texture, but it was also, Olmsted argued, a novelty capable of amplifying the drawing power of the exposition. Many visitors from the heart of the country "will, until they arrive here, never have seen a broad body of water extending to the horizon; will never have seen a vessel under sail, nor a steamboat of half the tonnage of those to be seen hourly passing in and out of Chicago harbor; and will never have seen such effects of reflected light or of clouds piling up from the horizon, as are to be enjoyed almost every summer's day on the lake margin of the city."

Olmsted next considered four specific candidates: a site on the lakeshore above the Loop; two inland sites, one of which was Garfield Park on the western perimeter of the city; and of course Jackson Park.

Although Olmsted himself preferred the northernmost site, he insisted Jackson Park could work and "produce results of a pleasingly becoming character, such as have not hitherto been aimed at in World's Fairs."

Olmsted dismissed the inland sites out of hand as being flat and monotonous and too far from the lake. In critiquing Garfield Park, he again took a moment to express his annoyance at Chicago's inability to select a site, a failure he found all the more exasperating given the elaborate boasts issued by the city's leading men back when they were lobbying Congress for the fair:

"But considering what has been so strenuously urged upon the attention of the country in regard to the number and excellence of sites which Chicago has to offer; considering what advantages the Centennial Fair in Philadelphia possessed in the neighboring scenery; considering what advantages of the same order would have been possessed by the Fair if it had been given a site in the beautiful Rock Creek Valley at Washington, of which the Nation is just taking possession for a Park; considering what superb views were presented of the Palisades and up the valley of the Hudson on the one hand, and the waters and varied shores of Long Island Sound on the other, from the site offered for the Fair by New York; considering all this, we cannot but fear that the choice of a site in the rear of the city, utterly without natural landscape attraction, would be found a disappointment to the country, and that it would give occasion for not a little ironical reference to the claims of an endless extent of *perfect* sites made last winter before Congress."

The emphasis was Olmsted's.

Burnham hoped this second report would at last compel a decision. The delay was maddening, absurd, the hourglass long ago upended. The board seemed unaware that Chicago now risked becoming a national, even global, embarrassment.

Weeks passed.

At the end of October 1890 the site question remained unresolved. Burnham and Root tended to their fast-growing practice. Contractors had begun erecting two of the firm's newest, tallest Chicago skyscrapers, the Women's Christian Temperance Union Temple and the Masonic Fraternity Temple, at twenty-one stories the tallest building in the world. The foundations of both were nearly finished and awaited the installation of cornerstones. With architecture and construction such a fascination in Chicago, cornerstone ceremonies became extravagant affairs.

The Temperance celebration took place at the corner of La Salle and Monroe, beside a ten-ton boulder of dark New Hampshire granite seven feet square by three feet thick. Here Burnham and Root joined other dignitaries, including Mrs. Frances E. Willard, president of the Union, and Carter Henry Harrison, a former mayor who, with four terms already under his belt, was again running for the office. When Harrison appeared, wearing his usual black slouch hat, his pocket quilled with cigars, the crowd roared a welcome, especially the Irish and union men who saw Harrison as a friend of the city's lower classes. The presence of Burnham, Root, and Harrison beside the Temperance stone was more than a bit ironic. As mayor, Harrison had kept a couple of cases of fine bourbon in his office at city hall. The city's stern Protestant upper class saw him as a civic satyr whose tolerance of prostitution, gambling and alcohol had allowed the city's vice districts, most notably the Levee— home of the infamous bartender and robber Mickey Finn—to swell to new heights of depravity. Root was a notorious bon vivant, whom Louis Sullivan once described as "a man of the world, of the flesh, and considerably of the devil." And Burnham, in addition to monitoring the global passage of his Madeira, each year bottled four hundred quarts of lesser stuff sent to him by a friend and personally selected the wines for the cellar of the Union League Club.

With great ceremony Burnham handed a silver-plated trowel to Mrs. T. B. Carse, president of the Temple Building Association, whose smile suggested she knew nothing of these monstrous habits or at least was willing for the moment to ignore them. She scooped up a mound of mortar previously laid for purposes of the ceremony, then reapplied it and tapped it back into place, prompting a witness to observe, "she patted the mortar as a man sometimes pats the head of a curly-haired boy." She passed the trowel to the fearsome Mrs. Willard, "who stopped the mortar more heartily, and got some of it on her gown."

Root, according to a witness, leaned toward friends and suggested sotto voce that they all cut away for cocktails.

Nearby, at the distribution warehouse of the *Chicago Inter Ocean,* a widely read and respected newspaper, a young Irish immigrant—and staunch supporter of Carter Harrison—completed his workday. His name was Patrick Eugene Joseph Prendergast. He ran a squad of obstreperous newsboys, whom he loathed, and who loathed him in return, as was clear by their taunts and practical jokes. That Prendergast might one day shape the destiny of the World's Columbian Exposition would have seemed ridiculous to these boys, for Prendergast to them was about as hapless and sorry a human being as they could imagine.

He was twenty-two years old, born in Ireland in 1868; his family emigrated to the United States in 1871 and in August that year moved to Chicago, just in time to experience the Great Fire. He was always, as his mother said, "a shy and retiring kind of a boy." He got his grade-school education at Chicago's De La Salle Institute. Brother Adjutor, one of his teachers, said, "While in school he was a remarkable boy in this way, that he was very quiet and took no part in the play of the other students at noon time. He would generally stand around. From the appearance of the boy I would be led to think that he was not well; that he was sick." Prendergast's father got him a job delivering telegrams for Western Union, which the boy held for a year and a half. When Prendergast was thirteen, his father died, and he lost his only friend. For a time his withdrawal from the world seemed complete. He awakened slowly. He began reading books about law and politics and attending meetings of the Single-Tax Club, which embraced Henry George's belief that private landowners should pay a tax, essentially rent, to reflect the underlying truth that land belonged to everyone. At these meetings Prendergast insisted on taking part in every conversation and once had to be carried from the room. To his mother, he seemed to be a different man: well read, animated, involved. She said: "He got smart all of a sudden."

In fact, his madness had become more profound. When he was not working, he wrote postcards, scores of them, perhaps hundreds, to the most powerful men in the city, in a voice that presumed he was their equal in social stature. He wrote to his beloved Harrison and to assorted other politicians, including the governor of Illinois. It's possible even that Burnham received a card, given his new prominence.

That Prendergast was a troubled young man was clear; that he might be dangerous seemed impossible. To anyone who met him, he appeared to be just another poor soul crushed by the din and filth of Chicago. But Prendergast had grand hopes for the future, all of which rested on one man: Carter Henry Harrison.

He threw himself eagerly into Harrison's mayoral campaign, albeit without Harrison's knowledge, sending postcards by the dozens and telling anyone who would listen that Harrison, staunch friend of the Irish and the working man, was the best candidate for the job.

He believed that when Harrison at last won his fifth two-year term—ideally in the upcoming April 1891 election, but perhaps not until the next, in 1893—he would reward Prendergast with a job. That was how Chicago politics worked. He had no doubt that Harrison would come through and rescue him from the frozen mornings and venomous newsboys that for the moment defined his life.

Among the most progressive alienists, this kind of unfounded belief was known as a delusion, associated with a newly identified disorder called paranoia. Happily, most delusions were harmless.

◦━━━◦

On October 25, 1890, the site for the fair still unchosen, worrisome news arrived from Europe, the first hint of forces gathering that could do infinitely more damage to the fair than the directors' stalemate. The *Chicago Tribune* reported that increasing turbulence in global markets had raised concerns in London that a recession, even a full-blown "panic," could be in the offing. Immediately these concerns began buffeting Wall Street. Railroad stocks tumbled. The value of Western Union's shares fell by five percent.

The next Saturday news of a truly stunning failure stuttered through the submarine cable that linked Britain and America.

In Chicago, before the news arrived, brokers spent a good deal of time discussing the morning's strange weather. An unusually "murky pall" hung over the city. Brokers joked how the gloom might be the signal that a "day of judgment" was at hand.

The chuckling faded with the first telegrams from London: Baring Brothers & Co., the powerful London investment house, was on the verge of closure. "The news," a *Tribune* writer observed, "was almost incredible." The Bank of England and a syndicate of financiers were racing to raise a fund to guarantee Baring's financial obligations. "The wild rush that followed to sell stocks was something terrible. It was a veritable panic for an hour."

For Burnham and the exposition directors, this wave of financial damage was troubling. If it indeed marked the start of a true and deep financial panic, the timing was abysmal. In order for Chicago to live up to its boasts about surpassing the Paris exposition in both size and attendance, the city would have to spend far more heavily than the French and capture a lot more visitors—yet the Paris show had drawn more people than any other peaceful event in history. In the best of times winning an audience of that scale would be a challenge; in the worst, impossible, especially since Chicago's interior location guaranteed that most visitors would have to buy an overnight train ticket. The railroads had made it known early and forcefully that they had no plans to discount their Chicago fares for the exposition.

Other corporate failures occurred both in Europe and in the United States, but their true meaning remained for the moment unclear—in retrospect, a good thing.

In the midst of this intensifying financial turbulence, on October 30 the exposition board appointed Burnham chief of construction, with a salary equivalent to $360,000; Burnham in turn made Root the fair's supervising architect and Olmsted its supervising landscape architect.

Burnham now possessed formal authority to begin building a fair, but he still had no place to put it.

"Don't Be Afraid"

As Englewood gained population, Holmes's sales of tonics and lotions increased. By the end of 1886 the pharmacy was running smoothly and profitably. His thoughts turned now to a woman he had met earlier in the year during his brief stay in Minneapolis, Myrta Z. Belknap. She was young and blond, with blue eyes and a lush figure, but what elevated her above mere beauty was the aura of vulnerability and need that surrounded her. She became an immediate obsession, her image and need locked in his brain. He traveled to Minneapolis, ostensibly on business. He had no doubt he would succeed. It amused him that women as a class were so wonderfully vulnerable, as if they believed that the codes of conduct that applied in their safe little hometowns, like Alva, Clinton, and Percy, might actually still apply once they had left behind their dusty, kerosene-scented parlors and set out on their own.

The city toughened them quickly, however. Best to catch them at the start of their ascent toward freedom, in transit from small places, when they were anonymous, lost, their presence recorded nowhere. Every day he saw them stepping from trains and grip-cars and hansom cabs, inevitably frowning at some piece of paper that was supposed to tell them where they belonged. The city's madams understood this and were known to meet inbound trains with promises of warmth and friendship, saving the important news for later. Holmes adored Chicago, adored in particular how the smoke and din could envelop a woman and leave no hint that she ever had existed, save perhaps a blade-thin track of perfume amid the stench of dung, anthracite, and putrefaction.

To Myrta, Holmes seemed to have stepped from a world far more exciting than her own. She lived with her parents and clerked in a music

62

store. Minneapolis was small, somnolent, and full of Swedish and Norwegian farmers as charming as cornstalks. Holmes was handsome, warm, and obviously wealthy, and he lived in Chicago, the most feared and magnetic of cities. Even during their first meeting he touched her; his eyes deposited a bright blue hope. When he left the store that first day, as motes of dust filled the space he left behind, her own life seemed drab beyond endurance. A clock ticked. Something had to change.

When his first letter arrived, asking sweetly if he might court her, she felt as if a coarse blanket had been lifted from her life. Every few weeks he returned to Minneapolis. He told her about Chicago. He described its skyscrapers and explained how each year the buildings grew taller and taller. He told her pleasantly shocking stories of the stockyards, how the hogs climbed the Bridge of Sighs to an elevated platform where chains were attached to their hind legs and they were swept away, shrieking, along an overhead track down into the bloody core of the slaughter-house. And romantic stories: how Potter Palmer had been so in love with his wife, Bertha, that he had given her a luxurious hotel, the Palmer House, as a wedding present.

There were rules about courtship. Although no one set them down on paper, every young woman knew them and knew instantly when they were being broken. Holmes broke them all—and with such forthright lack of shame that it became clear to Myrta that the rules must be different in Chicago. At first it frightened her, but she found quickly that she liked the heat and risk. When Holmes asked her to be his wife, she accepted immediately. They married on January 28, 1887.

Holmes neglected to tell Myrta that he already had a wife, Clara Lovering, the original Mrs. Herman Webster Mudgett. Two weeks after marrying Myrta, he filed a petition in the Supreme Court of Cook County, Illinois, to divorce Lovering. This was no fine-spirited gesture to clear the record: He charged Lovering with infidelity, a ruinous accusation. He allowed the petition to lapse, however, and eventually the court dismissed it for "failure to prosecute."

In Chicago Myrta saw at once that the stories Holmes had told of the city had only barely captured its glamour and dangerous energy. It was like a cauldron of steaming iron, trains everywhere—jarring, but also a reminder that life had opened to her at last. In Minneapolis there had been only silence and the inevitable clumsy petitions of potato-fingered men looking for someone, anyone, to share the agony of their days. That Holmes lived in Englewood, not the heart of Chicago, was at first a disappointment, but here too there was a vibrancy far beyond what she had experienced at home. She and Holmes settled into the second-floor apartment previously occupied by Mrs. Holton. By the spring of 1888 Myrta was pregnant.

At first she helped run the drugstore. She liked working with her husband and often watched him when he was engaged with a customer. She savored his looks and blue calm and craved the moments when, in the course of routine tasks, their bodies would touch. She admired, too, the charm with which he managed each transaction and how he won the business even of elderly customers loyal to the absent Mrs. Holton. And she smiled, at least initially, as a seemingly endless train of young women entered the store, each insisting that only direct consultation with Dr. Holmes himself would suffice.

Myrta came to see that underneath her husband's warm and charming exterior there flowed a deep current of ambition. He seemed a druggist in name only; he more closely fit the prevailing ideal of the self-made man who through hard work and invention pulled himself rung by rung into the upper strata of society. "Ambition has been the curse of my husband's life," Myrta said later. "He wanted to attain a position where he would be honored and respected. He wanted wealth."

She insisted, however, that his ambition never impaired his character and never distracted him from his role as husband and eventually father. Holmes, she swore, had a gentle heart. He adored children and animals. "He was a lover of pets and always had a dog or cat and usually a horse, and he would play with them by the hour, teaching them little tricks or romping with them." He neither drank nor smoked and did not gamble. He was affectionate and impossible to ruffle. "In his home life I do not think there was ever a better man than my husband," Myrta said. "He never spoke an unkind word to me or our little girl, or my mother. He was never vexed or irritable but was always happy and free from care."

Yet from the start tension suffused their marriage. Holmes expressed no hostility; the heat came from Myrta, who quickly tired of all those young female customers and the way Holmes would smile at them and touch them and channel his blue gaze into their eyes. At first she had found it appealing; then it made her uneasy; finally it made her jealous and watchful.

Her increasing possessiveness did not anger Holmes. Rather he came to see her as an obstacle, just as a sea captain might view an iceberg— something to monitor and avoid. Business was so good, he told Myrta, that he needed her help managing the store's books. She found herself spending more and more time in an office upstairs, writing correspondence and preparing invoices for the drugstore. She wrote to her parents of her sorrow. In the summer of 1888 her parents moved to Wilmette, Illinois, where they occupied a pretty two-story house on John Street, opposite a church. Lonely, sad, and pregnant, Myrta joined them at the house and there bore a daughter, Lucy.

Suddenly Holmes began acting like a dutiful husband. Myrta's parents were cool at first, but he courted their approval with moist-eyed declarations of regret and displays of adoration for his wife and child. He succeeded. "His presence," Myrta said, "was like oil on troubled waters, as mother often said to him. He was so kind, so gentle and thoughtful that we forgot our cares and worries."

He begged their forbearance for his lengthy absences from the Wilmette house. There was so much to do in Chicago. From the way he dressed and the money he gave Myrta, he certainly seemed like a man on the rise, and this perception went a long way to ease the concerns of Myrta's parents. They and Myrta settled into a life marked by increasingly sparse visits from Dr. Holmes, but when he did appear, he brought warmth and gifts and entombed little Lucy in his arms.

"It is said that babies are better judges of people than grown-up persons," Myrta said, "and I never saw a baby that would not go to Mr.

Holmes and stay with him contentedly. They would go to him when they wouldn't come to me. He was remarkably fond of children. Often when we were traveling and there happened to be a baby in the car he would say, 'Go and see if they won't lend you that baby a little while,' and when I brought it to him he would play with it, forgetting everything else, until its mother called for it or I could see that she wanted it. He has often taken babies that were crying from their mothers, and it would hardly be any time until he had them sound asleep or playing as happily as little ones can."

With Englewood booming, Holmes saw an opportunity. Ever since acquiring Holton's drugstore, he had been interested in the undeveloped land across the street. After a few inquiries he learned that it was owned by a woman in New York. In the summer of 1888 he bought the land and, thinking ahead, registered the deed under a false name, H. S. Campbell. Soon afterward he began jotting notes and sketching features for a building he planned to erect on the lot. He did not consult an architect, although a fine one, a Scotsman named A. A. Frazier, had an office in the building that housed Holton's store. To hire an architect would have meant revealing the true character of the structure that suddenly had lodged itself in his imagination.

The building's broad design and its function had come to him all at once, like a blueprint pulled from a drawer. He wanted retail shops on the first floor, to generate income and allow him to employ as many women as possible; apartments would fill the second and third. His personal flat and a large office would occupy the second-floor corner overlooking the intersection of Sixty-third and Wallace. These were the basics. It was the details of the building that gave him the most pleasure. He sketched a wooden chute that would descend from a secret location on the second floor all the way to the basement. He planned to coat the chute with axle grease. He envisioned a room next to his office fitted with a large walk-in vault, with airtight seams and asbestos-coated iron walls. A gas jet embedded in one wall would be controlled from his closet, as would other gas jets installed in apartments throughout the building. There would be a large basement with hidden chambers and a sub-basement for the permanent storage of sensitive material.

As Holmes dreamed and sketched, the features of his building became more elaborate and satisfying. But this was only the dream phase. He could hardly imagine the pleasure that would fill his days when the building was finished and flesh-and-blood women moved among its features. As always, the thought aroused him.

Constructing the building, he knew, would be no small challenge. He devised a strategy that he believed would not only allay suspicions but also reduce the costs of construction.

He placed newspaper advertisements for carpenters and laborers, and soon workers with teams of horses began excavating the land. The resulting hole evoked a giant grave and exuded the same musty chill, but this was not unwelcome for it provided workers with relief from the intensifying summer heat. The men had difficulty with the soil. The top few feet were easy to manage, but lower down the earth became sandy and wet. The sides of the pit had to be shored with timber. The walls bled water. A later report by a Chicago building inspector noted, "There is an uneven settlement of foundations, in some places as much as four inches in a span of 20 feet." Bricklayers set the foundation and laid the exterior walls, while carpenters erected the interior frame. The street resonated with the wheeze of handsaws.

Holmes cast himself as a demanding contractor. As workers came to him for their wages, he berated them for doing shoddy work and refused to pay them, even if the work was perfect. They quit, or he fired them. He recruited others to replace them and treated these workers the same way. Construction proceeded slowly, but at a fraction of the proper cost. The high rate of turnover had the corollary benefit of keeping to a minimum the number of individuals who understood the building's secrets. A worker might be ordered to perform a certain task—for example, to install the gas nozzle inside the big walk-in vault—but in the narrow context within which the worker functioned, the assignment could seem reasonable or at worst merely eccentric.

Even so, a bricklayer named George Bowman found the experience of working for Holmes somewhat chilling. "I don't know what to make of Holmes," Bowman said. "I hadn't been working for him but two days before he came around and asked me if I didn't think it pretty hard work, this bricklaying. He asked me if I wouldn't like to make money easier than that, and of course I told him yes. A few days after, he came over to me and, pointing down to the basement, said, 'You see that man down there? Well, that's my brother-in-law, and he has got no love for me, neither have I for him. Now, it would be the easiest matter for you to drop a stone on that fellow's head while you're at work and I'll give you fifty dollars if you do.' "

What made the incident particularly frightening was Holmes's manner as he made the offer—"about the same manner one would expect from a friend who was asking you the most trivial question," Bowman said.

Whether Holmes truly meant for Bowman to kill the man cannot be known. It would have been wholly within character for Holmes to have first persuaded the "brother-in-law" to take out a life insurance policy with Holmes as beneficiary. It was possible, too, that Holmes was merely testing Bowman to determine how useful he might be in the future. If so, it was a test that Bowman failed. "I was so badly scared I didn't know what to say or do," Bowman said, "but I didn't drop the stone and got out of the place soon after."

Three men did meet Holmes's standard of trustworthiness. Each worked for him throughout the period of construction and continued to associate with him after the building was completed. One was Charles Chappell, a machinist who lived near Cook County Hospital. He first worked for Holmes as a common laborer but soon proved to possess a talent that Holmes found particularly valuable. Another was Patrick Quinlan, who lived at Forty-seventh and Morgan in Englewood until he moved into Holmes's building as its caretaker. He was a small, twitchy man in his late thirties, with light curly hair and a sandy mustache.

The third and most important was Benjamin Pitezel, a carpenter, who joined Holmes in November 1889. He replaced a worker named Robert Latimer, who had quit to take over as gatekeeper at the rail intersection in front of Holmes's drugstore. At first, Latimer said, Pitezel took care of the horses involved in the construction of Holmes's building, but later he became his all-round assistant. Holmes and Pitezel seemed to have a close relationship, close enough at least for Holmes to do Pitezel a costly favor. Pitezel was arrested in Indiana for attempting to pass forged checks. Holmes posted bail and forfeited the amount when Pitezel, as planned, failed to return for trial.

Pitezel had smooth features and a sharp well-defined chin. He might have been handsome if not for a certain hungry gauntness and the way the lids of his eyes cloaked the top of each iris. "In a general way," Holmes said, "I should describe him as a man nearly six feet high (at least five feet ten inches), always thin in flesh and weighing from one hundred and forty-five to one hundred and fifty-five lbs., having very black and somewhat coarse hair, very thick, with no tendency to baldness; his mustache was a much lighter color and I think of a red tinge, though I have seen him have it colored black at times, which gave him quite a different appearance."

Pitezel was plagued with various maladies: sore knees from the installation of one too many floors, a wart on his neck that kept him from wearing a stiff collar, and teeth so painful that at one point he had to suspend his work for Holmes. Despite being a chronic alcoholic, he was, in the appraisal of one doctor, a man of "fine physique."

Pitezel was married to Carrie Canning of Galva, Illinois, and the father of a fast-increasing number of children. Photographs of the children show a sweet if sober bunch who seem ready at a moment's notice to swing into action with brooms and dishcloths. The couple's first daughter, Dessie, had been born out of wedlock, an event entirely within the realm of what Pitezel's parents had come to expect of their son. In a last plea for Pitezel to take a more righteous path, his father wrote: "Come with me and I will do the good is the Savior's command. Will you go? I will take that wicked nature out of you, and I will wash from you all stains, and I will be a father to you and you shall be a son and an heir." The pain in his father's words was palpable. "I love you," he wrote, "although you have gone far astray."

Alice, the second child, was born soon after the marriage. Another daughter and three sons followed, although one boy died of diphtheria shortly after birth. Three of the children—Alice, Nellie, and Howard—would become so well known throughout America that headline writers would refer to them by their first names alone, confident that even the most remote reader understood exactly who they were.

Pitezel too would achieve a certain fame because of Holmes. "Pitezel was his tool," a district attorney said, "his creature."

Construction of Holmes's building occurred in ragged stages and more or less halted each winter at the close of what workers called the "building season," although Holmes had read how architects in the Loop were using techniques that allowed construction year-round. Eventually, much would be made of the fact that Holmes had erected his building during the same period in which Jack the Ripper, thousands of miles away, began his killings.

The first of Jack's murders occurred on August 31, 1888, the last on the night of November 9, 1888 when he met a prostitute named Mary Kelly and accompanied her back to her rooms. He slashed her throat in a Van Gogh stroke that nearly removed her head from her spine. Over the next few hours, secure within walls, he carved off her breasts and placed these on a table along with her nose. He slashed her from throat to pubis, skinned her thighs, removed her internal organs, and arranged them in a pile between her feet. He cut off a hand, which he then thrust into her bisected abdomen. Kelly had been three months' pregnant at the time.

Abruptly the murders stopped, as if that tryst with Mary Kelly had sated the killer's need at last. Five confirmed victims, only five, and Jack the Ripper became the embodiment, forever, of pure evil.

Every Chicago resident who could read devoured these reports from abroad, but none with quite so much intensity as Dr. H. H. Holmes.

On June 29, 1889, when Holmes's building was half completed, Chicago annexed Englewood and soon afterward established a new police precinct, the Tenth, Second Division, at Sixty-third and Wentworth, seven blocks from Holmes's pharmacy. Soon patrolmen under the command of Captain Horace Elliott began making regular walks past the store, where in accord with custom they stopped to chat with the young and personable owner. Periodically the officers ambled across the street to watch construction of the new building. Englewood already had a number of substantial structures, including the YMCA, the Cook County Normal School, which trained teachers, and the lavish Timmerman Opera House, now nearing completion at Sixty-third and Stewart, but the village still had a lot of open terrain, and any building destined to occupy an entire block was a topic of conversation.

Construction took another year, with the usual hiatus for winter. By May 1890 the building was largely finished. The second floor had six corridors, thirty-five rooms, and fifty-one doors, the third another three dozen rooms. The building's first floor had space for five retail stores, the best of which was a large and inviting corner shop on the intersection of Sixty-third and Wallace.

One month after moving into his building, Holmes sold the former Holton drugstore and assured the buyer that he would face little competition.

To the buyer's chagrin, Holmes promptly opened a new drugstore just across the street, in his own corner shop.

Holmes installed a variety of other businesses in his remaining first-floor stores, including a barbershop and restaurant. City directories also listed at Holmes's address the office of a doctor named Henry D. Mann, possibly a Holmes alias, and the headquarters of the Warner Glass Bending Company, which Holmes formed ostensibly to enter the booming new business of making and shaping the large sheets of plate glass suddenly in so much demand.

Holmes equipped his shops with furniture and fixtures that he bought on credit. He had no intention of paying his debts and was confident he could evade prosecution through guile and charm. When creditors came by demanding to see the owner of the building, Holmes referred them happily to the fictive H. S. Campbell.

"He was the smoothest man I ever saw," said C. E. Davis, whom Holmes had hired to manage the drugstore's jewelry counter. Creditors, Davis said, would "come here raging and calling him all the names imaginable, and he would smile and talk to them and set up the cigars and drinks and send them away seemingly his friends for life. I never saw him angry. You couldn't have trouble with him if you tried."

Davis gestured toward the store. "If all the writs of mechanic's lien that have been levied on this structure were pasted on these three walls, the block would look like a mammoth circus billboard. But I never heard of a lien being collected. Holmes used to tell me he had a lawyer paid to keep him out of trouble, but it always seemed to me that it was the courteous, audacious rascality of the fellow that pulled him through. One day he bought some furniture for his restaurant and moved it in, and that very evening the dealer came around to collect his bill or remove his goods. Holmes set up the drinks, took him to supper, bought him a cigar and sent the man off laughing at a joke, with a promise to call the next week for his money. In thirty minutes after he took his car Holmes had wagons in front loading up that furniture and the dealer never got a cent. Holmes didn't go to jail, either. He was the only man in the United States that could do what he did."

Holmes had the money to pay his debts. Davis estimated that Holmes made $200,000 through his drugstore and other business ventures, most of which were fraudulent. Holmes attempted, for example, to sell investors a machine that turned water into natural gas. He secretly connected his prototype to city gas lines.

He was always charming and cordial, but there were times when even these traits failed to put his business associates at ease. A druggist named Erickson recalled how Holmes used to come into his store to buy chloroform, a potent but unpredictable anesthetic in use since the Civil War. "I sometimes sold him the drug nine or ten times a week and each time it was in large quantities. I asked him what he used it for on several occasions, but he gave me very unsatisfactory answers. At last I refused to let him have any more unless he told me, as I pretended that I was afraid that he was not using it for any proper purpose."

Holmes told Erickson he was using the chloroform for scientific experiments. Later, when Holmes returned for more chloroform, Erickson asked him how his experiments were coming.

Holmes gave him a blank look and said he was not conducting any experiments.

"I could never make him out," Erickson said.

A woman named Strowers occasionally did Holmes's laundry. One day he offered to pay her $6,000 if she would acquire a $10,000 life insurance policy and name him beneficiary. When she asked why he would do such a thing, he explained that upon her death he'd make a profit of $4,000, but in the meantime she'd be able to spend her $6,000 in whatever manner she chose.

To Mrs. Strowers, this was a fortune, and all she had to do was sign a few documents. Holmes assured her it was all perfectly legal.

She was healthy and expected to live a good long while. She was on the verge of accepting the offer when Holmes said to her, softly, "Don't be afraid of me."

Which terrified her.

In November 1890 Holmes learned along with the rest of Chicago that the directors of the World's Columbian Exposition had at last reached a decision as to where to build the fair. To his delight, he read that the main site was to be Jackson Park, due east of his building at the lake end of Sixty-third, with exhibits also in downtown Chicago and Washington Park and along the full length of Midway Boulevard.

Holmes knew the parks from his bicycle journeys. Like most Americans, he had become caught up in the bicycle craze that was ignited by the advent of the "safety" bicycle, with its same-sized wheels and chain-and-sprocket drive. Unlike most Americans, however, Holmes sought also to capitalize on the craze by buying bicycles on credit, then reselling them without ever paying off the initial purchase. He himself rode a Pope.

The Exposition Company's decision raised a groundswell of greed throughout Chicago's South Side. An advertisement in the *Tribune* offered a six-room house for sale at Forty-first and Ellis, a mile or so north of Jackson Park, and boasted that during the fair the new owner could expect to let four of the six rooms for nearly a thousand dollars a month (about $30,000 in twenty-first-century currency). Holmes's building and land were valuable to begin with, given Englewood's continued growth, but now his property seemed the equivalent of a seam of gold ore.

An idea came to him for a way to mine that ore and also satisfy his other needs. He placed a new advertisement seeking more construction workers and once again called for the help of his loyal associates, Chappell, Quinlan, and Pitezel.

Pilgrimage

On Monday evening, December 15, 1890, a day noteworthy in Chicago for its extraordinary warmth and elsewhere for the gunshot death of Sitting Bull, Daniel Burnham stepped aboard a train bound for New York and what he knew would be the most crucial encounter of the exposition odyssey.

He entered a bright green coach, one of George Pullman's Palace cars, where the air hung with the stillness of a heavy tapestry. A bell clanged and continued clanging in a swinging rhythm as the train surged at grade level into the heart of the city at twenty miles an hour, despite the presence at arm's reach of grip-cars, carriages, and pedestrians. Everyone on the street paused to watch as the train leaped past crossing gates waving a raccoon's tail of white and black smoke. The train clicked by the Union Stock Yards, doubly pungent in the day's strange warmth, and skirted sierras of black coal capped with grimy melting snow. Burnham treasured beauty but saw none for miles and miles and miles, just coal, rust, and smoke in endless repetition until the train entered the prairie and everything seemed to go quiet. Darkness fell, leaving a false twilight of old snow.

The exposition directors' decision on where to locate the fair had caused a rapid acceleration of events that was encouraging but also unsettling, because suddenly the whole thing had become more real, its true magnitude more daunting. Immediately the directors had ordered a rough plan of the fair, to be delivered to them within twenty-four hours. John Root, guided by Burnham and Olmsted, had produced a drawing on a sheet of brown paper measuring forty square feet, which the men delivered to the committee with a barbed aside to the effect that the designers of the Paris exposition had been able to spend a whole year thinking, planning, and sketching before reaching the same point. The drawing envisioned a mile-square plain on the lakeshore sculpted by dredges into a wonderland of lagoons and canals. Ultimately, the designers knew, the exposition would have hundreds of buildings, including one for each state of the union and for many countries and industries, but on the drawing they sketched only the most important, among them five immense palaces sited around a central Grand Court. They also made room for a tower to be built at one end of the court, although no one knew exactly who would build this tower or what it would look like, only that it would have to surpass Eiffel's tower in every way. The directors and their federal overseers, the National Commission, approved the plan with uncharacteristic speed.

For outsiders, it was the sheer size of the exposition that made it seem such an impossible challenge. That the fair's grounds would be vast and its buildings colossal was something every Chicago resident took for granted; what mystified them was how anyone could expect to build the biggest thing ever constructed on American soil, far bigger than Roebling's Brooklyn Bridge, in so little time. Burnham knew, however, that the fair's size was just one element of the challenge. The gross features of the fair envisioned in the plan concealed a billion smaller obstacles that the public and most of the exposition's own directors had no idea existed. Burnham would have to build a railroad within the fairgrounds to transport steel, stone, and lumber to each construction site. He would have to manage the delivery of supplies, goods, mail, and all exhibit articles sent to the grounds by transcontinental shipping companies, foremost among them the Adams Express Company. He would need a police force and a fire department, a hospital and an ambulance service. And there would be horses, thousands of them—something would have to be done about the tons of manure generated each day.

Immediately after the brown-paper plan received approval, Burnham requested authority to build "at once cheap wooden quarters in Jackson Park for myself and force," quarters in which he would live almost continuously for the next three years. This lodging quickly became known as "the shanty," though it had a large fireplace and an excellent wine cellar stocked by Burnham himself. With a power of perception that far outpaced his era, Burnham recognized that the tiniest details would shape the way people judged the exposition. His vigilance extended even to the design of the fair's official seal. "It may not occur to you how very important a matter this Seal is," he wrote in a December 8, 1890, letter to George R. Davis, the fair's director-general, its chief political officer. "It will be very largely distributed throughout foreign countries, and is one of those trivial things by which these people will judge the artistic standard of the Fair."

All these, however, were mere distractions compared to the single most important task on Burnham's roster: the selection of architects to design the fair's major buildings.

He and John Root had considered designing the whole exposition themselves, and indeed their peers jealously expected they would do so. Harriet Monroe, Root's sister-in-law, recalled how one evening Root came home "cut to the quick" because an architect whom he had considered a friend "had apparently refused to recognize Mr. Burnham when they met at a club." Root grumbled, "I suppose he thinks we are going to hog it all!" He resolved that to preserve his credibility as supervising architect, a role in which he would be compelled to oversee the work of other exposition architects, he would not himself design any of the buildings.

Burnham knew exactly whom he wanted to hire but was less aware of how incendiary his selections would prove. He wanted the best architects America had to offer, not just for their talent but also for how their affiliation instantly would shatter the persistent eastern belief that Chicago would produce only a country fair.

In December, though he lacked an official mandate to do so, Burnham secretly mailed inquiries to five men, "feeling confident that I would carry my point." And indeed soon afterward the fair's Grounds and Buildings Committee authorized him to invite the men to join the exposition. Unquestionably they were five of the greatest architects America had produced, but of the five, three were from the land of "unclean beasts" itself:

George B. Post, Charles McKim, and Richard M. Hunt, the nation's most venerable architect. The others were Robert Peabody of Boston and Henry Van Brunt, Kansas City.

None was from Chicago, even though the city took great pride in its architectural pioneers, in Sullivan, Adler, Jenney, Beman, Cobb, and the others. Somehow, despite his powers of anticipation, Burnham failed to realize that Chicago might see his choices as betrayal.

⌐────⌐

What troubled Burnham at the moment, as he rode in his Pullman compartment, was the fact that only one of his candidates, Van Brunt of Kansas City, had replied with any enthusiasm. The others had expressed only a tepid willingness to meet once Burnham arrived in New York.

Burnham had asked Olmsted to join him for the meeting, aware that in New York the landscape architect's reputation exerted a force like gravity, but Olmsted could not get away. Now Burnham faced the prospect of having to go alone to meet these legendary architects—one of them, Hunt, a man also of legendary irascibility.

Why were they so unenthusiastic? How would they react to his attempts at persuasion? And if they declined and word of their refusal became public, what then?

The landscape outside his windows gave him little solace. As his train roared across Indiana, it overtook a cold front. Temperatures plunged. Strong gusts of wind buffeted the train, and ghostly virga of ice followed it through the night.

⌐────⌐

There was something Burnham did not know. Soon after receiving his letter the eastern architects, Hunt, Post, Peabody, and McKim, had held a meeting of their own in the offices of McKim, Mead and White in New York to discuss whether the fair would be anything more than a display of overfed cattle. During the meeting Hunt—the architect Burnham most hoped to recruit—announced that he would not participate. George Post persuaded him at least to hear what Burnham had to say, arguing that if Hunt stood down, the others would feel pressed to do likewise, for such was Hunt's influence.

McKim had opened this meeting with a wandering talk about the fair and its prospects. Hunt cut him off: "McKim, damn your preambles. Get down to facts!"

⁃⸺⸺⸺⸺⸺⸺⸺⸺

In New York the wind blew hard and harsh all week. On the Hudson ice produced the earliest halt to navigation since 1880. Over breakfast at his hotel on Thursday morning, Burnham read with uneasiness about the failure of S. A. Kean & Co., a private bank in Chicago. It was one more sign of a gathering panic.

⁃⸺⸺⸺⸺⸺⸺⸺⸺

Burnham met the eastern architects Monday evening, December 22, at the Players Club, for dinner. Their cheeks were red from the cold. They shook hands: Hunt, McKim, Post, and Peabody—Peabody, down from Boston for the meeting. Here they were, gathered at one table, the nation's foremost practitioners of what Goethe and Schelling called "frozen music." All were wealthy and at the peaks of their careers, but all also bore the scars of nineteenth-century life, their pasts full of wrecked rail cars, fevers, and the premature deaths of loved ones. They wore dark suits and crisp white collars. All had mustaches, some dark, some gray. Post was huge, the largest man in the room. Hunt was fierce, a frown in a suit, with a client list that included most of America's richest families. Every other mansion in Newport, Rhode Island, and along Fifth Avenue in New York seemed to have been designed by him, but he also had built the base for the Statue of Liberty and was a founder of the American Institute of Architects. All the men had one or more elements of shared background. Hunt, McKim, and Peabody had all studied at L'Ecole des Beaux Arts in Paris; Van Brunt and Post had studied under Hunt; Van Brunt had been Peabody's mentor. For Burnham, with his failed attempts at getting into Harvard and Yale and his lack of formal architectural training, sitting down to dinner with these men was like being a stranger at someone else's Thanksgiving.

The men were cordial. Burnham described his vision of a fair larger and grander than the Paris exposition. He played up the fact of Olmsted's participation. Both Olmsted and Hunt were hard at work on George Washington Vanderbilt's manor, Biltmore, near Asheville, North Carolina, and together had built the Vanderbilt family's mausoleum. But Hunt was skeptical and not shy about expressing his doubts. Why should he and the others interrupt their already full schedules to build temporary structures in a far-off city where they would have little control over the final product?

Their skepticism shook Burnham. He was accustomed to the headlong civic energy of Chicago. He wished Olmsted and Root were beside him: Olmsted, to counter Hunt; Root because of his wit, and because the other architects all knew him from his role as secretary of the American Institute of Architects. Ordinarily it was in situations like this that Burnham could be most effective. "To himself, and indeed to most of the world in general, he was always right," wrote Harriet Monroe, "and by knowing this so securely he built up the sheer power of personality which accomplished big things." But this night he felt ill at ease, a choirboy among cardinals.

He argued that Chicago's fair, unlike any other before it, would be primarily a monument to architecture. It would awaken the nation to the power of architecture to conjure beauty from stone and steel. Olmsted's plans alone would make the exposition unique, with lagoons, canals, and great lawns all set against the cobalt-blue steppe of Lake Michigan. In exhibit space, he told them, the fair would be at least one-third larger than what the French had allotted in Paris. This was no mere dream, he said. Chicago had the resolve to make this exposition a reality, the same resolve that had made the city the second largest in America. And, he added, Chicago had the money.

The architects' questions became slightly less challenging, more practical. What kind of structures did he envision, and in what style? The issue of the Eiffel Tower arose: What could Chicago do to equal that? On this score Burnham had no plan other than somehow to surpass Eiffel. Secretly, he was disappointed that the engineers of America had not yet stepped forward with some novel but feasible scheme to eclipse Eiffel's achievement.

The architects worried that anyone who joined the fair would find himself in the grip of innumerable committees. Burnham guaranteed complete artistic independence. They wanted to know in detail how Olmsted felt about the sites selected for the fair, in particular about a central feature called the Wooded Island. Their insistence prompted Burnham to telegraph Olmsted immediately and urge him once again to come. Again Olmsted demurred.

One question came up repeatedly throughout the evening: Was there enough time?

Burnham assured them that ample time remained but that he had no illusions. The work had to start at once.

He believed he had won them. As the evening ended, he asked, would they join?

There was a pause.

Burnham left New York the next morning on the North Shore Limited. Throughout the day his train pushed through a landscape scoured by snow as a blizzard whitened the nation in a swath from the Atlantic to Minnesota. The storm destroyed buildings, broke trees, and killed a man in Barberton, Ohio, but it did not stop the Limited.

While aboard the train, Burnham wrote a letter to Olmsted that contained a less-than-candid description of the meeting with the architects. "They all approved the proposition to have them take hold of the artistic part of the main buildings. . . . The general layout seemed to meet the hearty approval, first of Mr. Hunt then of the others, but they were desirous of knowing your views of the landscape on and about the island. Therefore I telegraphed you urgently to come. They were very much disappointed, as was I, when it was found impossible to get you. The gentlemen are all to be here on the 10th of next month and at that time they urgently request, as do I, that you will be here personally. I find that Mr. Hunt especially lays large stress upon your opinions in the entire matter."

In fact, the evening had ended rather differently. At the Player's Club, sips of cognac and exhalations of smoke had filled that last difficult pause. The dream was an appealing one, the architects agreed, and no one doubted Chicago's sincerity in imagining this fantasy precinct of lagoons and palaces, but the reality was something else entirely. The only real certainty was the disruption that would be caused by long-distance travel and the myriad other difficulties inherent in building a complex structure far from home. Peabody did commit to the fair, but Hunt and the others did not: "they said," as Burnham later revealed, "they would think it over."

They did, however, agree to come to the January 10 meeting in Chicago to confer again and examine the chosen ground.

None of the architects had been to Jackson Park. In its raw state, Burnham knew, it was not a setting likely to win anyone's heart. This time Olmsted had to be present. In the meantime Root too would have to become involved in the courtship. The architects respected him but were leery of his powers as supervising architect. It was critical that he go to New York.

Outside the sky was blank, the light pewter. Despite Pullman's vestibules ice as fine as dust settled between coaches and filled Burnham's train with the tang of deep winter. Wind-felled trees appeared beside the railbed.

———

Daniel Burnham arrived in Chicago to find the city's architects and members of the exposition board outraged that he had gone outside the city—to New York, of all godforsaken places—to court architects for the fair; that he had snubbed the likes of Adler, Sullivan, and Jenney. Sullivan saw it as a sign that Burnham did not truly believe Chicago had the talent to carry the fair by itself. "Burnham had believed that he might best serve

his country by placing all of the work exclusively with Eastern architects," Sullivan wrote; "solely, he averred, on account of their surpassing
culture." The chairman of the Grounds and Buildings Committee was
Edward T. Jefferey. "With exquisite delicacy and tact," Sullivan said, "Jefferey, at a meeting of the Committee, persuaded Daniel, come to Judgment, to add the Western men to the list of his nominations."

Hastily, Root and Burnham conferred and chose five Chicago firms to
join the effort, among them Adler & Sullivan. Burnham visited each the
next day. Four of the five put aside their hurt feelings and accepted immediately. Only Adler & Sullivan resisted. Adler was sulking. "I think he,
Adler, had hoped to be in the position I was in," Burnham said. "He was
rather disgruntled and did 'not know.' "

Ultimately, Adler did accept Burnham's invitation.

Now it was Root's turn to go to New York. He had to go anyway to
attend a meeting of the directors of the American Institute of Architects
and planned afterward to take a train to Atlanta to inspect one of the
firm's buildings. Root was in his office at the Rookery on the afternoon
of New Year's Day 1891, shortly before his departure, when an employee
stopped by to see him. "He said he was tired," the man recalled, "and
felt inclined to resign the secretaryship of the Institute. This was alarming, as he had never been heard to complain of too much work, and while
it only indicated extreme physical exhaustion and before he went home
he became cheerful and hopeful again, it has its significance in the light
of subsequent events."

In New York, Root assured the architects again and again that he
would do nothing to interfere with their designs. Despite his charm—the
Chicago Inter Ocean once called him "another Chauncey M. Depew in
postprandial wit and humor"—he failed to arouse their enthusiasm and
left New York for Atlanta feeling the same degree of disappointment
Burnham had felt two weeks earlier. His journey south did little to cheer

him up. Harriet Monroe saw him upon his return to Chicago. He was depressed, she said, "by the attitude of the Eastern men, whom he found singularly apathetic, utterly incredulous that any association of Western businessmen would give art a free hand in the manner he set forth. The dream was too extravagant ever to be realized, and they were extremely reluctant to undertake its realization against the hampering and tampering, the interferences petty and great, which they felt were certain to ensue."

Root was tired and discouraged. He told Monroe he just could not get the men interested. "He felt that this was the greatest opportunity ever offered to his profession in this country, and he could not make them appreciate it," she said. The architects did plan to come to Chicago for the January meeting, he told her, "but reluctantly; their hearts were not in it."

———

On January 5, 1891, the Committee on Grounds and Buildings authorized Burnham to offer formal commissions to all ten architects and pay each $10,000 (equivalent today to about $300,000). It was a rich fee, considering that all Burnham wanted them to do was provide working drawings and make a few visits to Chicago. Burnham and Root would see to the construction of the buildings and manage the niggling details that typically haunted an architect's life. There would be no artistic interference.

The eastern men gave their tentative acceptance, but their concerns had not diminished.

And they still had not seen Jackson Park.

A Hotel for the Fair

HOLMES'S NEW IDEA WAS TO turn his building into a hotel for visitors to the World's Columbian Exposition—no Palmer House or Richelieu, certainly, but just comfortable enough and cheap enough to lure a certain kind of clientele and convincing enough to justify a large fire insurance policy. After the fair he intended to burn the building to collect the insurance and, as a happy dividend, destroy whatever surplus "material" might remain in its hidden storage chambers, although ideally, given other disposal measures available to him, the building by then would contain nothing of an incriminating nature. The thing was, one never knew. In the most transcendent moment, it was easy to make a mistake and forget some little thing that a clever detective might eventually use to propel him to the gallows. Whether the Chicago police even possessed that kind of talent was open to question. The Pinkerton National Detective Agency was the more dangerous entity, but its operatives of late seemed to be spending most of their energy battling strikers at coalfields and steel mills around the country.

Again acting as his own architect, Holmes early in 1891 began planning the necessary modifications, and soon carpenters were at work on the second and third floors. Once again Holmes's method of segregating tasks and firing workers was proving successful. Clearly none of the workers had gone to the police. Patrolmen from the new Chicago police precinct house on Wentworth walked past Holmes's building each day. Far from being suspicious, the officers had become friendly, even protective. Holmes knew each man by name. A cup of coffee, a free meal in his restaurant, a fine black cigar—policemen valued these gestures of affinity and grace.

Holmes was, however, beginning to feel mounting pressure from creditors, in particular from several furniture and bicycle dealers. He could still charm them and commiserate over their inability to locate the elusive deedholder, H. S. Campbell, but Holmes knew they soon would lose patience and in fact was a bit surprised they had not pursued him more forcefully than had been the case thus far. His techniques were too new, his skills too great, the men around him too naïve, as if they had never before experienced a falsehood. For every business that now refused to sell him goods, there were a dozen more that fawned over him and accepted his notes endorsed by H. S. Campbell or secured by the assets of the Warner Glass Bending Company. When pressed, sensing that a particular creditor was on the verge of legal action, even violence, Holmes paid his bills in cash using money harvested from his own ventures, such as lease income from his apartments and stores, sales from his pharmacy, and the proceeds from his newest venture, a mail-order medicine company. In a parody of Aaron Montgomery Ward's fast-growing empire in central Chicago, Holmes had begun selling sham drugs that he guaranteed would cure alcoholism and baldness.

He was always open to new financial opportunities but was especially so now, since he knew that no matter how deftly he kept labor costs down, he still would have to pay for at least some of the transformation of his building. When Myrta's great-uncle, Jonathan Belknap of Big Foot Prairie, Illinois, came to Wilmette for a visit, that challenge suddenly seemed likely to resolve itself. Belknap was not a rich man, but he was well off.

Holmes began appearing more frequently at the Wilmette house. He brought toys for Lucy, jewelry for Myrta and her mother. He filled the house with love.

Belknap had never met Holmes but knew all about his troubled marriage to Myrta and was prepared to dislike the young doctor. On first meeting he found Holmes far too smooth and self-assured for a man of so few years. He was struck, however, by how enthralled Myrta seemed to be whenever Holmes was around and by how even Myrta's mother—Belknap's niece by marriage—appeared to glow in Holmes's presence. After several more encounters Belknap began to appreciate why Myrta had fallen so thoroughly for the man. He was handsome and clean and dressed well and spoke in fine sentences. His gaze was blue and forthright. In conversation he listened with an intensity that was almost alarming, as if Belknap were the most fascinating man in the world, not just an elderly uncle visiting from Big Foot Prairie.

Belknap still did not like Holmes, but he found his candor sufficiently disarming that when Holmes asked him to endorse a note for $2,500 to help cover the cost of a new house in Wilmette for himself and Myrta, Belknap agreed. Holmes thanked him warmly. A new house, away from Myrta's parents, might be all the couple needed to end their growing estrangement. Holmes promised to pay the money back as soon as his business affairs allowed.

Holmes returned to Englewood and promptly forged Belknap's signature to a second note for the same amount, intending to use the proceeds for his hotel.

On Holmes's next visit to Wilmette, he invited Belknap to visit Englewood for a tour of his building and of the newly chosen site for the World's Columbian Exposition.

Although Belknap had read much about the world's fair and did want to see its future home, he did not relish the idea of spending a full day with Holmes. Holmes was charming and gracious, but something about him made Belknap uneasy. He could not have defined it. Indeed, for the next several decades alienists and their successors would find themselves hardpressed to describe with any precision what it was about men like Holmes that could cause them to seem warm and ingratiating but also telegraph the vague sense that some important element of humanness was missing. At first alienists described this condition as "moral insanity" and those who exhibited the disorder as "moral imbeciles." They later adopted the term "psychopath," used in the lay press as early as 1885 in William Stead's *Pall Mall Gazette,* which described it as a "new malady" and stated, "Beside his own person and his own interests, nothing is sacred to the psychopath." Half a century later, in his path-breaking book *The Mask of Sanity*, Dr. Hervey Cleckley described the prototypical psychopath as "a subtly constructed reflex machine which can mimic the human personality perfectly. . . . So perfect is his reproduction of a whole and normal man that no one who examines him in a clinical setting can point out in scientific or objective terms why, or how, he is not real." People exhibiting this purest form of the disorder would become known, in the jargon of psychiatry, as "Cleckley" psychopaths.

When Belknap refused Holmes's offer, Holmes seemed to crumble with hurt and disappointment. A tour was necessary, Holmes pleaded, if only to bolster his own sense of honor and to demonstrate to Belknap that he really was a man of means and that Belknap's note was as secure an investment as any man could make. Myrta too looked crestfallen.

Belknap gave in. During the train journey to Englewood, Holmes pointed out landmarks: the skyscrapers of the city, the Chicago River, the stockyards. Belknap found the stench overpowering, but Holmes seemed not to notice it. The men exited the train at Englewood station.

The town was alive with movement. Trains rumbled past every few minutes. Horse-drawn streetcars moved east and west along Sixty-third, amid a dense traffic of carriages and drays. Everywhere Belknap looked some building was under construction. Soon the level of construction would increase even more, as entrepreneurs prepared to cash in on the expected crush of exposition visitors. Holmes described his own plans. He took Belknap on a tour of his pharmacy, with its marble countertops and glass containers filled with wildly colored solutions, then took him up to the second floor, where he introduced him to the building's caretaker, Patrick Quinlan. Holmes walked Belknap through the building's many corridors and described how the place would look as a hotel. Belknap found it bleak and strange, with passages that struck off in unexpected directions.

Holmes asked Belknap if he would like to see the roof and the construction already under way. Belknap declined, claiming falsely that he was too old a man to climb that many steps.

Holmes promised stirring views of Englewood, perhaps even a glimpse of Jackson Park off to the east, where the buildings of the fair soon would begin to rise. Again Belknap resisted, this time with more force.

Holmes tried a different approach. He invited Belknap to spend the night in his building. At first Belknap declined this offer as well, but feeling perhaps that he had been overly rude in avoiding the roof, he relented.

After nightfall Holmes led Belknap to a room on the second floor. Gas lamps had been installed at haphazard intervals along the corridor, leaving pockets of gloom whose borders shivered as Belknap and Holmes moved past. The room was furnished and comfortable enough and overlooked the street, which was still reassuringly busy. As far as Belknap could tell, he and Holmes were by now the only occupants of the building. "When I went to bed," Belknap said, "I carefully locked the door."

Soon the street sounds receded, leaving only the rumble of trains and the hollow clip-clop of an occasional horse. Belknap had difficulty sleeping. He stared at the ceiling, which was bathed in the shifting light of the streetlamps below his window. Hours passed. "Presently," Belknap said, "I heard my door tried and then a key was slipped into the lock."

Belknap called out, asking who was at the door. The noise stopped. He held his breath and listened and heard the sound of feet moving down the hall. He was certain that initially two men had been outside his door, but now one of them had left. He called again. This time a voice answered. Belknap recognized it as belonging to Patrick Quinlan, the caretaker.

Quinlan wanted to come in.

"I refused to open the door," Belknap said. "He insisted for a time and then went away."

Belknap lay awake the rest of the night.

Soon afterward he discovered Holmes's forgery. Holmes apologized, claiming a dire need for money, and was so persuasive and abject that even Belknap felt mollified, although his distrust of Holmes persisted. Much later Belknap realized why Holmes had wanted so badly to show him the building's roof. "If I'd gone," Belknap said, "the forgery probably wouldn't have been discovered, because I wouldn't have been around to discover it.

"But I didn't go," he said. "I'm afraid of heights."

<hr>

As carpenters and plasterers worked on his building, Holmes turned his attention to the creation of an important accessory. He sketched a number of possible designs, relying perhaps on past observations of similar equipment, then settled on a configuration that seemed likely to work: a large rectangular box of fireproof brick about eight feet deep, three feet high, and three feet wide, encased within a second box of the same material, with the space between them heated by flames from an oil burner. The inner box would serve as an elongated kiln. Although he had never built a kiln before, he believed his design would generate temperatures extreme enough to incinerate anything within. That the kiln would also be able to destroy any odors emanating from the interior box was singularly important.

He planned to install the kiln in the basement and hired a bricklayer named Joseph E. Berkler to do the job. He told him he intended to use the kiln to produce and bend plate glass for his Warner Glass Bending Company. At Holmes's instructions Berkler added a number of components made of iron. He worked quickly, and soon the kiln was ready for its first test.

Holmes ignited the burner. There was a satisfying whoosh. A wave of warmth rolled from the chamber to the far walls of the basement. The scent of partially combusted oil suffused the air.

But the test was disappointing. The box did not generate as much heat as Holmes had hoped. He adjusted the burner and tried again but achieved little improvement.

He used the city directory to locate a furnace company and requested an appointment with an experienced man. He identified himself as the founder of Warner Glass. If for some reason officials of the furnace company felt moved to verify that Warner Glass existed, all they had to do was check the 1890 Englewood directory to find the company's listing, with Holmes named as proprietor.

The manager of the furnace company—his name was never made public—decided to attend to the matter personally and met Holmes at his building. He found a young good-looking man, almost delicate, who conveyed an air of confidence and prosperity. He had striking blue eyes. His building was on the gloomy side, the construction obviously below the standards of structures rising elsewhere on Sixty-third, but it was well located in a community that clearly was booming. For so young a man to own most of a city block was itself an accomplishment.

The manager followed Holmes to his second-floor office and there in the pleasant cross breeze from the corner windows studied Holmes's drawings of his kiln. Holmes explained that he could not obtain "the necessary amount of heat." The manager asked to see the apparatus.

That wasn't necessary, Holmes said. He did not wish to trouble the manager, only to seek his advice, for which he would pay an appropriate fee.

The furnace man insisted he could do nothing without actually examining the kiln.

Holmes smiled. Of course. If the manager did not mind spending the extra time, he would be glad to show it to him.

Holmes led his visitor down the stairs to the first floor and from there down another, darker flight to the basement.

They entered a large rectangular cavern that ran the entire length of the block, interrupted only by beams and posts. In the shadows stood vats and barrels and mounds of dark matter, possibly soil. A long narrow table with a steel top stood under a series of unlit lamps and two worn leather cases rested nearby. The cellar had the look of a mine, the smell of a surgeon's suite.

The furnace man examined the kiln. He saw that it contained an inner chamber of firebrick constructed in a manner that kept flames from reaching the interior, and he noted the clever addition of two openings in the top of the inner box that would allow gases from the box to flow into the surrounding flames, where they would then be consumed. It was an interesting design and seemed likely to work, although he did observe to himself that the shape of the kiln seemed unsuited to the task of bending glass. The inner box was too small to admit the broad panes now appearing in storefronts throughout the city. Otherwise, he noticed nothing unusual and foresaw no difficulty in improving the kiln's operation.

He returned with a work crew. The men installed a more powerful burner that, once ignited, heated the kiln to three thousand degrees Fahrenheit. Holmes seemed pleased.

Only later did the furnace man recognize that the kiln's peculiar shape and extreme heat made it ideal for another, very different application. "In fact," he said, "the general plan of the furnace was not unlike that of a crematory for dead bodies, and with the provision already described there would be absolutely no odor from the furnace."

But again, that was later.

◦───────◦

Holmes's absences from Wilmette lengthened once again, although at regular intervals he sent Myrta and his daughter enough money to keep them comfortable. He even insured the girl's life, since children after all were such fragile things and could be taken from the world in a heartbeat.

His businesses were doing well. His mail-order company brought in a surprising amount of cash, and he began trying to find a way to capitalize on the latest medical rage, a cure for alcoholism invented by a physician named Keeley in Dwight, Illinois. The corner drugstore ran smoothly and profitably, although one woman in the neighborhood observed that he seemed to have difficulty retaining the young and typically attractive women he often hired as clerks. These clerks, as far as she could tell, had an unfortunate habit of departing without warning, sometimes even leaving their personal belongings in their rooms on the second floor. She saw such behavior as a troubling sign of the rising shiftlessness of the age.

The work of turning Holmes's building into a hotel proceeded slowly, with the usual bouts of rancor and delay. Holmes left the task of finding replacement workers to his three helpers, Quinlan, Chappell, and Pitezel.

They seemed to have little difficulty finding new men for each new opening. Thousands of workers laid off elsewhere had come to Chicago hoping for jobs building the fair, only to find that too many workers had gotten the same idea, thus leaving a large pool of men available for work—any work, at any price.

Holmes turned his attention to other, more pleasant distractions. Sheer fate had brought two new women into his life, one of them nearly six feet tall and possessed of a rapturous body, the other, her sister-in-law, a lovely young woman with black hair and exquisite dark eyes.

That the tall one came equipped with a husband and daughter made the situation infinitely more appealing.

The Landscape of Regret

THE EASTERN ARCHITECTS LEFT New Jersey at 4:50 P.M., January 8, 1891, in car 5, section 6, of the North Shore Limited, which Hunt had reserved so that they all could travel together. Olmsted had come down from Boston the night before in order to join them.

It was a bewitching moment: a gorgeous train rocketing through the winter landscape carrying five of history's greatest architects, all in the same car, gossiping, joking, drinking, smoking. Olmsted used the opportunity to describe in detail Jackson Park and the trials of dealing with the exposition's many layers of committees that for the moment seemed to have so much power. He respected Burnham for his candor, his directness, and the air of leadership he exuded, and no doubt he told the architects as much. That he spent a good deal of time asserting his own vision of the exposition's landscape is also beyond doubt, especially his belief that the Wooded Island should remain entirely free of conspicuous man-made structures.

Two hours before the train reached Chicago, during a brief stop, McKim received a cable notifying him that his mother, Sarah McKim, had died unexpectedly in her home, at seventy-eight. The two had been very close. He left the group and caught a return train.

The architects arrived in Chicago late Friday night, January 9, and took carriages to the Wellington Hotel, where Burnham had arranged rooms for all. Van Brunt, arriving from Kansas City, joined them there. The next morning they boarded carriages for the journey south to Jackson Park. Root, absent, was to return that day from Atlanta.

The ride to the park took about an hour. "It was one of those cold winter days," Burnham recalled. "The sky was overcast with clouds and the lake covered with foam."

At the park the architects eased from the carriages puffing blasts of steam into the frigid air. The wind picked up motes of sand that stung their cheeks and forced them to shield their eyes. They stumbled over the frozen ground, Hunt wincing from gout, cursing, disbelieving; Olmsted, his teeth inflamed, his night an ordeal of wakefulness, limping from his long-ago carriage accident.

The lake was gray, darkening to a band of black at the horizon. The only color in the vicinity was the frost rouge on the men's cheeks and the blue of Burnham's and Olmsted's eyes.

Olmsted watched for the architects' reactions. Now and then he and Burnham caught each other's glances.

The architects were stunned: "they gazed," Burnham said, "with a feeling almost of despair."

Jackson Park was one square mile of desolation, mostly treeless, save for pockets of various kinds of oak—burr, pin, black, and scarlet—rising from a tangled undergrowth of elder, wild plum, and willow. In the most exposed portions there was only sand tufted with marine and prairie grasses. One writer called the park "remote and repulsive"; another, a "sandy waste of unredeemed and desert land." It was ugly, a landscape of last resort. Olmsted himself had said of Jackson Park: "If a search had been made for the least parklike ground within miles of the city, nothing better meeting the requirement could have been found."

In fact, the site was even worse than it appeared. Many of the oaks were dead. Given the season, the dead were hard to distinguish from the living. The root systems of others were badly damaged. Test borings showed that the earth within the park consisted of a top layer of black soil about one foot thick, followed by two feet of sand, then eleven feet of sand so saturated with water, Burnham wrote, "it became almost like quicksand and was often given this name." The Chicago men understood the challenge that this soil presented; the New York men, accustomed to bedrock, did not.

The park's gravest flaw, at least from Olmsted's perspective, was that its shoreline was subject to dramatic annual changes in the level of the lake, sometimes as much as four feet. Such fluctuations, Olmsted recognized, would greatly increase the difficulty of planting the banks and shores. If the water level fell, visitors to the fair would be treated to an offensive band of bare earth at the waterline. If it rose too high, the water would submerge and kill shore plantings.

The architects climbed back into their carriages. They drove toward the lake over the park's rough roads at the pace of a funeral cortege and with equal gloom. Burnham wrote: "a feeling of discouragement allied to hopelessness came over those who then first realized the extent and magnitude of the proposed undertaking, and appreciated the inexorable conditions of a time-limitation to the work. . . . Twenty-one months later was the day fixed by Act of Congress for the dedication of the buildings, and in the short space of twenty-seven and one-half months, or on May 1, 1893, the entire work of construction must be finished, the landscape perfected, and the exhibits installed."

At the lake they again left their carriages. Peabody of Boston climbed atop a pier. He turned to Burnham. "Do you mean to say that you really propose opening a Fair here by Ninety-three?"

"Yes," Burnham said. "We intend to."

Peabody said, "It can't be done."

Burnham looked at him. "That point is settled," he said.

But even he did not, and could not, grasp what truly lay ahead.

Root returned to Chicago while the architects were in Jackson Park. It was his forty-first birthday. He went directly from the train station to the Rookery. "He went down to the office in a gay humor," Harriet Monroe said, "and that very day received a commission for a large commercial building."

But that afternoon draftsman Paul Starrett encountered Root in one of the Rookery's elevators "looking ill." His good spirits had fled. He complained again of being tired.

The architects returned from their tour discouraged and full of regret. They gathered again in the firm's library, where Root, suddenly revitalized, now joined them. He was gracious, funny, warm. If anyone could sway these men and ignite their passion, Burnham knew, Root was the one. Root invited the outside men to come to his house on Astor Place the next day, Sunday, for high tea, then went home at last to greet his children and his wife, Dora, who according to Harriet Monroe was in bed "ill almost unto death" from a recent miscarriage.

Root told Dora of his weariness and suggested that in the coming summer they should escape somewhere for a long rest. The last months had been full of frustration and long nights of work and travel. He was exhausted. The trip south had done nothing to ease his stress. He looked forward to the end of the week, January 15, when the architects would conclude their conference and go home.

"After the 15th," he told his wife, "I shall not be so busy."

The eastern and Chicago architects reconvened that night at the University Club for a dinner in their honor hosted by the fair's Grounds and Buildings Committee. Root was too tired to attend. Clearly the dinner was a weapon meant to ignite enthusiasm and show the easterners that Chicago fully intended to follow through on its grand boasts about the exposition. It was the first in a sequence of impossibly rich and voluminous banquets whose menus raised the question of whether any of the city's leading men could possibly have a functional artery.

As the men arrived, reporters intercepted them. The architects were gracious but closemouthed.

They were to sit at a large T-shaped table, with Lyman Gage, president of the exposition, at the center of the topmost table, Hunt on his right, Olmsted on his left. Bundles of carnations and pink and red roses transformed the tables into cutting beds. A boutonniere rested beside each plate. Everyone wore tuxedos. There was not a woman in sight.

At precisely eight P.M. Gage took Hunt and Olmsted by the arm and led the way from the Club's reception room to the banquet hall.

⟨———⟩

Oysters.
A glass or two of *Montrachet.*
Consommé of Green Turtle.
Amontillado.
Broiled Shad à la Maréchel.
Cucumbers. Potatoes à la Duchesse.
Filet Mignon à la Rossini.
Chateau Lafite and *Rinnart Brut.*
Fonds d'Artichaut Farcis.
Pommery Sec.
Sorbet au Kirsch.
Cigarettes.
Woodcock on Toast.
Asparagus Sala.
Ices: Canton Ginger.
Cheeses: Pont l'Eveque; Rocquefort. Coffee. Liquers.
Madeira, 1815.
Cigars.

⟨———⟩

Gage spoke first. He offered a rousing oration on the brilliance of the future exposition and the need now for the great men in the banquet hall to think first of the fair, last of themselves, affirming that only through the subordination of self would the exposition succeed. The applause was warm and enthusiastic.

Burnham spoke next. He described his own vision of the fair and Chicago's resolve to make that vision real. He too urged teamwork and self-sacrifice. "Gentlemen," he said, "1893 will be the third great date in our country's history. On the two others, 1776 and 1861, all true Americans served, and so now I ask you to serve again!"

This time the room erupted. "The men left the banquet hall that night united like soldiers in a campaign," Burnham said.

It was the Chicagoans, however, who did all the marching. At Root's house the next day Harriet Monroe met the eastern architects and came away shaken. "In talking with them I was amazed at their listless and hopeless attitude," she said. "Beautiful effects were scarcely to be expected in buildings so enormous and so cheaply constructed; the level of monotony of ground surfaces in Chicago made effective grouping practically impossible; the time for preparation and construction was too short: these and other criticisms indicated a general feeling of disparagement."

At tea's end Root escorted the visitors to their carriages. It was dark and bitterly cold. A sharp wind scythed along Astor Place. Much was made, in retrospect, of the fact that Root, in evening dress, charged into the rock-cold night without first putting on a coat.

Vanishing Point

AFTER YEARS SPENT DRIFTING from town to town and job to job, a young jeweler named Icilius Conner—he preferred the nickname "Ned"—moved to Chicago with his wife Julia and their eight-year-old daughter Pearl and quickly found that Chicago was indeed a city of opportunity. At the start of 1891 Ned found himself managing a jewelry counter that occupied one wall of a thriving drugstore on the city's South Side, at Sixty-third and Wallace. For once in Ned's adult life, the future gleamed.

The owner of the drugstore, though very young, was prosperous and dynamic, truly a man of the age, and seemed destined for even greater success given that the World's Columbian Exposition was to be built just a short streetcar ride east, at the end of Sixty-third. There was talk too that a new elevated rail line, nicknamed the Alley L for the way its trestles roofed city alleys, would be extended eastward along Sixty-third directly to Jackson Park, thus providing visitors with another means of reaching the future fair. Already traffic on the street had increased sharply, as each day hundreds of citizens drove their carriages to the park to see the chosen site. Not that there was much to see. Ned and Julia had found the park an ugly, desolate place of sandy ridges and half-dead oaks, although Pearl had enjoyed trying to catch tadpoles in its pools of stagnant water. That anything wonderful could rise on that ground seemed beyond possibility, although Ned, like most new visitors to Chicago, was willing to concede that the city was a place unlike any he had encountered. If any city could make good on the elaborate boasts circulated thus far, Chicago was the one. Ned's new employer, Dr. H. H.

Holmes, seemed a perfect example of what everyone called the "Chicago spirit." To be so young, yet own a block-long building, would be incredible in any other place of Ned's experience. Here it seemed an ordinary accomplishment.

The Conners lived in a flat on the second floor of the building, near Dr. Holmes's own suite of rooms. It was not the brightest, most cheerful apartment, but it was warm and close to work. Moreover, Holmes offered to employ Julia as a clerk in the drugstore and to train her to keep his books. Later, when Ned's eighteen-year-old sister, Gertrude, moved to Chicago, Holmes asked to hire her as well, to manage his new mail-order medicine company. With three incomes, the family might soon be able to afford a house of their own, perhaps on one of the wide macadam streets of Englewood. Certainly they'd be able to afford bicycles and trips to Timmerman's theater down the street.

One thing did make Ned uneasy, however. Holmes seemed inordinately attentive to Gertie and Julia. On one level this was natural and something to which Ned had become accustomed, for both women were great beauties, Gertie slim and dark, Julia tall and felicitously proportioned. It was clear to Ned, clear in fact from the first moment, that Holmes was a man who liked women and whom women liked in return. Lovely young women seemed drawn to the drugstore. When Ned tried to help them, they were remote and uninterested. Their manner changed markedly if Holmes happened then to enter the store.

Always a plain man, Ned now seemed to become part of the background, a bystander to his own life. Only his daughter Pearl was as attentive to him as always. Ned watched with alarm as Holmes flattered Gertie and Julia with smiles and gifts and treacly praise—especially Gertie—and how the women glowed in response. When Holmes left them, they appeared crestfallen, their demeanor suddenly brittle and snappish.

Even more disconcerting was the change in how customers responded to Ned himself. It was not what they said but what they carried in their eyes, something like sympathy, even pity.

—————

One night during this period Holmes asked Ned a favor. He led him to the big vault and stepped inside, then told Ned to close the door and listen for the sound of his shouting. "I shut the door and put my ear to the crack," Ned recalled, "but could hear only a faint sound." Ned opened the door, and Holmes stepped out. Now Holmes asked Ned if he would go inside and try shouting, so that Holmes could hear for himself how little sound escaped. Ned did so but got back out the instant Holmes reopened the door. "I didn't like that kind of business," he said.

Why anyone would even want a soundproof vault was a question that apparently did not occur to him.

—————

For the police there were warnings of a different sort—letters from parents, visits from detectives hired by parents—but these were lost in the chaos. Vanishment seemed a Chicago pastime. There were too many disappearances, in all parts of the city, to investigate properly, and too many forces impeding the detection of patterns. Patrolmen, many of them, were barely competent, appointed solely at the direction of ward bosses. Detectives were few, their resources and skills minimal. Class obscured their vision. Ordinary vanishings—Polish girls, stockyard boys, Italian laborers, Negro women—merited little effort. Only the disappearance of moneyed souls drew a forceful response, and even then there was little that detectives could do other than send telegrams to other cities and periodically check the morgue for each day's collection of unidentified men, women, and children. At one point half the city's detective force was involved in investigating disappearances, prompting the chief of the city's central detective unit to announce he was considering the formation of a separate bureau, "a mysterious disappearances department."

Women and men vanished in equal proportion. Fannie Moore, a young visitor from Memphis, failed to return to the home where she was boarding and was never seen again. J. W. Highleyman left work one day, caught a suburban train, and vanished, the *Tribune* said, "as completely as though swallowed by the earth." The women were presumed to have been ravished, the men robbed, their corpses plunged into the turgid waters of the Chicago River or the alleys of Halsted and the Levee and that hard stretch of Clark between Polk and Taylor known to veteran officers as Cheyenne. Found bodies went to the morgue; if unclaimed, they traveled next to the dissection amphitheater at Rush Medical College or perhaps Cook County Hospital and from there to the articulation laboratory for the delicate task of picking flesh and connective tissue from the bones and skull, washing all with bleach, and remounting same for the subsequent use of doctors, anatomy museums, and the occasional private collector of scientific novelties. The hair was sold for wigs, the clothing given to settlement houses.

Like the Union Stock Yards, Chicago wasted nothing.

Alone

THE EASTERN AND CHICAGO ARCHITECTS met again on Monday morning, January 12, in Burnham & Root's library on the top floor of the Rookery. Root was absent. William R. Mead had come from New York to stand in for his grieving partner, McKim. As the men waited for everyone to arrive, the visitors from time to time would drift to the library's east-facing windows and stare out at the vastness of Lake Michigan. The light entering the room was preternaturally intense, carrying with it the surplus radiance of the lake and its frozen shore.

Burnham rose to offer the men a formal welcome, but he did not seem at ease. He was aware of the lingering reticence of the eastern men and seemed hell-bent on winning them with flattery that verged on unction—a tactic that Louis Sullivan had known Burnham to deploy with great effect. "Himself not especially susceptible to flattery except in a sentimental way, he soon learned its efficacy when plastered thick on big business men," Sullivan wrote. "Louis saw it done repeatedly, and at first was amazed at Burnham's effrontery, only to be more amazingly amazed at the drooling of the recipient. The method was crude but it worked."

Said Sullivan, "It soon became noticeable that he was progressively and grossly apologizing to the Eastern men for the presence of their benighted brethren of the West."

Hunt noticed it too. *"Hell,"* he snapped, "we haven't come here on a missionary expedition. Let's get to work."

Murmurs of agreement rose through the room. Adler was cheered; Sullivan smirked. Olmsted watched, deadpan, as he listened to a roaring in his ears that would not subside. Hunt grimaced; the trip from New York and the excursion to Jackson Park had worsened his gout.

Hunt's interjection startled Burnham. It brought back in a rush the hurt of the great dual snub by the East, his rejection by Harvard and Yale; but the remark and the obvious support it garnered in the room also caused Burnham to shift focus to the work at hand. As Sullivan saw it, "Burnham came out of his somnambulistic vagary and joined in. He was keen enough to understand that 'Uncle Dick' "—meaning Hunt— "had done him a needed favor."

Burnham told the men that henceforth they would serve as the fair's Board of Architects. He invited them to choose a chairman. They elected Hunt. "The natural dominance of the master again asserted itself without pretension," wrote Van Brunt, "and we once more became his willing and happy pupils."

For secretary they elected Sullivan, who most decidedly was *not* a happy pupil of Hunt's. To him, Hunt was the janissary of a dead vernacular. Burnham, too. Both men symbolized all that stood in the way of Sullivan's own emerging ethos that a building's function should express itself in its design—not merely that form should follow function but that "the function *created* or organized its form."

To Sullivan, Hunt was merely a relic, Burnham something far more dangerous. In him Sullivan saw a kindred capacity for obsession. Sullivan had come to see Chicago architecture as dominated by only two firms: Burnham & Root and Adler & Sullivan. "In each firm was a man with a fixed irrevocable purpose in life, for the sake of which he would bend or sacrifice all else," Sullivan wrote. "Daniel Burnham was obsessed by the feudal idea of power. Louis Sullivan was equally obsessed by the beneficent idea of Democratic power." Sullivan admired both Root and Adler but believed they functioned on a lesser plane. "John Root was so self-indulgent that there was a risk he might never draw upon his underlying power; Adler was essentially a technician, an engineer, a conscientious administrator. . . . Unquestionably, Adler lacked sufficient imagination; so in a way did John Root—that is to say, the imagination of the dreamer. In the dream-imagination lay Burnham's strength and Louis's passion."

Shortly before noon Burnham left the room to take a telephone call from Dora Root. She told him her husband had awakened with a bad cold and would not be able to attend the meeting. Several hours later she called again: A doctor had come and diagnosed pneumonia.

Root's spirits were good. He joked and sketched. "I haven't escaped sickness all my life to get off easily now," he told Harriet Monroe. "I knew when my turn came, it would be a Tartar."

The architects continued to meet but without Burnham, who stayed beside his partner's bed except for occasional departures to help resolve issues back in the library or to visit Hunt, whose gout had grown so painful he was confined to his room in the Wellington Hotel. Root joked with his nurses. At its regular Wednesday meeting the Grounds and Buildings Committee passed a resolution wishing Root a speedy recovery. That day Burnham wrote to a Chicago architect named W. W. Boyington: "Mr. Root is quite low, and there is uncertainty about his recovery, but still a chance for him."

On Thursday Root seemed to rally. Burnham again wrote to Boyington: "am able this morning to give you a little better report. He has passed a pretty good night and is easier. While the danger is not over, we are hopeful."

Enthusiasm among the architects rose. With Hunt still confined to his room, Post stood in as chairman. He and Van Brunt shuttled to and from Hunt's hotel. The architects approved the original brown-paper plan fashioned by Burnham, Olmsted, and Root with few changes. They decided how big the main buildings should be and how they should be situated on the site. They chose a uniform style, neoclassical, meaning the buildings would have columns and pediments and evoke the glories of ancient Rome. This choice was anathema to Sullivan, who abhorred derivative architecture, but during the meeting he made no objection. The architects also made what would prove to be one of the most important decisions of the fair: They set a uniform height, sixty feet, for the cornice of each of the palaces of the Grand Court. A cornice was merely a horizontal decorative projection. Walls, roofs, domes, and arches could rise far higher, but by establishing this one point of commonality the architects ensured a fundamental harmony among the fair's most imposing structures.

At about four o'clock Thursday afternoon Codman and Burnham drove to Root's house. Codman waited in the carriage as Burnham went inside.

Burnham found Root struggling for breath. Throughout the day Root had experienced strange dreams, including one that had come to him many times in the past of flying through the air. When Root saw Burnham, he said, "You won't leave me again, will you?"

Burnham said no, but he did leave, to check on Root's wife, who was in a neighboring room. As Burnham talked with her, a relative also entered the room. She told them Root was dead. In his last moments, she said, he had run his fingers over his bedding as if playing the piano. "Do you hear that?" he whispered. "Isn't it wonderful? That's what I call music."

The house settled into an eerie postmortem quiet broken only by the hiss of gas lamps and the weary tick of clocks. Burnham paced the floor below. He did not know it, but he was being watched. Harriet Monroe's Aunt Nettie sat on a step high on the dark upper curve of the stairway that rose from Root's living room to the second floor. The woman listened as Burnham paced. A fire burned in the hearth behind him and cast large shadows on the opposing wall. "I have worked," Burnham said, "I have schemed and dreamed to make us the greatest architects in the world—I have made him see it and kept him at it—and now he dies—*damn!—damn!—damn!*"

Root's death stunned Burnham, stunned Chicago. Burnham and Root had been partners and friends for eighteen years. Each knew the other's thoughts. Each had come to rely on the other for his skills. Now Root was gone. Outsiders wondered if Root's death might mean the death of the exposition. The newspapers were full of interviews in which the city's leading men described Root as the guiding force behind the fair, that without him the city could not hope to realize its dreams. The *Tribune* said Root was "easily" Chicago's "most distinguished architect, if indeed he had his superior in the whole country." Edward Jefferey, chairman of the Grounds and Buildings Committee, said, "There is no man in the profession of architects who has the genius and ability to take up the Exposition work where Mr. Root left off."

Burnham kept silent. He considered quitting the fair. Two forces warred within him: grief, and a desire to cry out that *he,* Burnham, had been the engine driving the design of the fair; that *he* was the partner who had propelled the firm of Burnham & Root to greater and greater achievement.

The eastern architects departed on Saturday, January 17. On Sunday Burnham attended a memorial service for Root at Root's Astor Place house and his burial in Graceland Cemetery, a charming haven for the well-heeled dead a few miles north of the Loop.

On Monday he was back at his desk. He wrote twelve letters. Root's office next to his was silent, draped in bunting. Hothouse flowers perfumed the air.

The challenge ahead looked more daunting than ever.

◦═══◦

On Tuesday a large bank failed in Kansas City. The following Saturday Lyman Gage announced that he would quit as president of the fair, effective April 1, to tend to his own bank. The fair's director-general, George Davis, at first refused to believe it. "It's all nonsense," he snapped. "Gage has got to stay with us. We can't do without him."

There was labor unrest. Just as Burnham had feared, union leaders began using the future fair as a vehicle for asserting such goals as the adoption of a minimum wage and an eight-hour day. There was the threat of fire and weather and disease: Already foreign editors were asking who would dare attend the exposition given Chicago's notorious problems with sewage. No one had forgotten how in 1885 fouled water had ignited an outbreak of cholera and typhoid that killed ten percent of the city's population.

Darker forces marshaled in the smoke. Somewhere in the heart of the city a young Irish immigrant sank still more deeply into madness, the preamble to an act that would shock the nation and destroy what Burnham dreamed would be the single greatest moment of his life.

Closer at hand a far stranger creature raised his head in equally intent anticipation. "I was born with the devil in me," he wrote. "I could not help the fact that I was a murderer, no more than the poet can help the inspiration to sing."

PART II

An Awful Fight

Chicago, 1891–93

Manufactures and Liberal Arts Building, after the storm of June 13, 1892.

Convocation

On Tuesday, February 24, 1891, Burnham, Olmsted, Hunt, and the other architects gathered in the library on the top floor of the Rookery to present drawings of the fair's main structures to the Grounds and Buildings Committee. The architects met by themselves throughout the morning, with Hunt serving as chairman. His gout forced him to keep one leg on the table. Olmsted looked worn and gray, except for his eyes, which gleamed beneath his bald skull like marbles of lapis. A new man had joined the group, Augustus St. Gaudens, one of America's best-known sculptors, whom Charles McKim had invited to help evaluate the designs. The members of the Grounds and Buildings Committee arrived at two o'clock and filled the library with the scent of cigars and frosted wool.

The light in the room was sallow, the sun already well into its descent. Wind thumped the windows. In the hearth at the north wall a large fire cracked and lisped, flushing the room with a dry sirocco that caused frozen skin to tingle.

At Hunt's brusque prodding the architects got to work.

One by one they walked to the front of the room, unrolled their drawings, and displayed them upon the wall. Something had happened among the architects, and it became evident immediately, as though a new force had entered the room. They spoke, Burnham said, "almost in whispers."

Each building was more lovely, more elaborate than the last, and all were immense—fantastic things on a scale never before attempted.

Hunt hobbled to the front and displayed his Administration Building, intended to be the most important at the fair and the portal through which most visitors would enter. Its center was an octagon topped by a dome that rose 275 feet from floor to peak, higher than the dome of the U.S. Capitol.

The next structure presented was even bigger. If successfully erected, George B. Post's Manufactures and Liberal Arts Building would be the largest building ever constructed and consume enough steel to build two Brooklyn Bridges. All that space, moreover, was to be lit inside and out with electric lamps. Twelve electric elevators would carry visitors to the building's upper reaches. Four would rise through a central tower to an interior bridge 220 feet above the floor, which in turn would lead to an exterior promenade offering foot-tingling views of the distant Michigan shore, "a panorama," as one guidebook later put it, "such as never before has been accorded to mortals."

Post proposed to top his building with a dome 450 feet high, which would have made the building not only the biggest in the world but also the tallest. As Post looked around the room, he saw in the eyes of his peers great admiration but also something else. A murmur passed among them. Such was this new level of cohesion among the architects that Post understood at once. The dome was too much—not too tall to be built, simply too proud for its context. It would diminish Hunt's building and in so doing diminish Hunt and disrupt the harmony of the other structures on the Grand Court. Without prodding, Post said quietly, "I don't think I shall advocate that dome; probably I shall modify the building." There was unspoken but unanimous approval.

Sullivan had already modified his own building, at Burnham's suggestion. Originally Burnham wanted Adler & Sullivan to design the fair's Music Hall, but partly out of a continued sense of having been wronged by Burnham, the partners had turned the project down. Burnham later offered them the Transportation Building, which they accepted. Two weeks before the meeting Burnham wrote to Sullivan and urged him to modify his design to create "one grand entrance toward the east and make this much richer than either of the others you had proposed. . . . Am sure that the effect of your building will be much finer than by the old method of two entrances on this side, neither of which could be so fine and effective as the one central feature." Sullivan took the suggestion but never acknowledged its provenance, even though that one great entrance eventually became the talk of the fair.

All the architects, including Sullivan, seemed to have been captured by the same spell, although Sullivan later would disavow the moment. As each architect unrolled his drawings, "the tension of feeling was almost painful," Burnham said. St. Gaudens, tall and lean and wearing a goatee, sat in a corner very still, like a figure sculpted from wax. On every face Burnham saw a "quiet intentness." It was clear to him that now, finally, the architects understood that Chicago had been serious about its elaborate plans for the fair. "Drawing after drawing was unrolled," Burnham said, "and as the day passed it was apparent that a picture had been forming in the minds of those present—a vision far more grand and beautiful than hitherto presented by the richest imagination."

As the light began to fade, the architects lit the library's gas jets, which hissed like mildly perturbed cats. From the street below, the top floor of the Rookery seemed aflame with the shifting light of the jets and the fire in the great hearth. "The room was still as death," Burnham said, "save for the low voice of the speaker commenting on his design. It seemed as if a great magnet held everyone in its grasp."

The last drawing went up. For a few moments afterward the silence continued.

Lyman Gage, still president of the exposition, was first to move. He was a banker, tall, straight-backed, conservative in demeanor and dress, but he rose suddenly and walked to a window, trembling with emotion. "You are dreaming, gentlemen, dreaming," he whispered. "I only hope that half the vision may be realized."

Now St. Gaudens rose. He had been quiet all day. He rushed to Burnham and took his hands in his own. "I never expected to see such a moment," he said. "Look here, old fellow, do you realize this has been the greatest meeting of artists since the fifteenth century?"

Olmsted too sensed that something extraordinary had occurred, but the meeting also troubled him. First, it confirmed his growing concern that the architects were losing sight of the nature of the thing they were proposing to build. The shared vision expressed in their drawings struck him as being too sober and monumental. After all, this was a world's fair, and fairs should be fun. Aware of the architects' increasing emphasis on size, Olmsted shortly before the meeting had written to Burnham suggesting ways to enliven the grounds. He wanted the lagoons and canals strewn with waterfowl of all kinds and colors and traversed continually by small boats. Not just any boats, however: *becoming* boats. The subject became an obsession for him. His broad view of what constituted landscape architecture included anything that grew, flew, floated, or otherwise entered the scenery he created. Roses produced dabs of red; boats added intricacy and life. But it was crucial to choose the right kind of boat. He dreaded what would happen if the decision were left to one of the fair's many committees. He wanted Burnham to know his views from the start.

"We should try to make the boating feature of the exposition a gay and lively one," he wrote. He loathed the clatter and smoke of steam launches; he wanted electric boats designed specifically for the park, with emphasis on graceful lines and silent operation. It was most important that these boats be constantly but quietly in motion, to provide diversion for the eye, peace for the ear. "What we shall want is a regular service of boats like that of an omnibus line in a city street," he wrote. He also envisioned a fleet of large birchbark canoes paddled by Indians in deerskin and feathers and recommended that various foreign watercraft be moored in the fair's harbor. "I mean such as Malay proas, catamarans, Arab dhows, Chinese sanpans, Japanese pilot boats, Turkish caiques, Esquimaux kiacks, Alaskan war canoes, the hooded boats of the Swiss Lakes, and so on."

A far more important outcome of the Rookery meeting, however, was Olmsted's recognition that the architects' noble dreams magnified and complicated the already-daunting challenge that faced him in Jackson Park. When he and Calvert Vaux had designed Central Park in New York, they had planned for visual effects that would not be achieved for decades; here he would have just twenty-six months to reshape the desolation of the park into a prairie Venice and plant its shores, islands, terraces, and walks with whatever it took to produce a landscape rich enough to satisfy his vision. What the architects' drawings had shown him, however, was that in reality he would have far fewer than twenty-six months. The portion of his work that would most shape how visitors appraised his landscape—the planting and grooming of the grounds immediately surrounding each building—could only be done *after* the major structures were completed and the grounds cleared of construction equipment, temporary tracks and roads, and other aesthetic impedimenta. Yet the palaces unveiled in the Rookery were so immense, so detailed, that their construction was likely to consume nearly all the remaining time, leaving little for him.

Soon after the meeting Olmsted composed a strategy for the transformation of Jackson Park. His ten-page memorandum captured the essence of all he had come to believe about the art of landscape architecture and how it should strive to conjure effects greater than the mere sum of petals and leaves.

He concentrated on the fair's central lagoon, which his dredges soon would begin carving from the Jackson Park shore. The dredges would leave an island at the center of the lagoon, to be called, simply, the Wooded Island. The fair's main buildings would rise along the lagoon's outer banks. Olmsted saw this lagoon district as the most challenging portion of the fair. Just as the Grand Court was to be the architectural heart of the fair, so the central lagoon and Wooded Island were to constitute its landscape centerpiece.

Above all he wanted the exposition landscape to produce an aura of "mysterious poetic effect." Flowers were not to be used as an ordinary gardener would use them. Rather, every flower, shrub, and tree was to be deployed with an eye to how each would act upon the imagination. This was to be accomplished, Olmsted wrote, "through the mingling intricately together of many forms of foliage, the alternation and complicated crossing of salient leaves and stalks of varying green tints in high lights with other leaves and stalks, behind and under them, and therefore less defined and more shaded, yet partly illumined by light reflected from the water."

He hoped to provide visitors with a banquet of glimpses—the undersides of leaves sparkling with reflected light; flashes of brilliant color between fronds of tall grass waving in the breeze. Nowhere, he wrote, should there be "a display of flowers demanding attention as such. Rather, the flowers to be used for the purpose should have the effect of flecks and glimmers of bright color imperfectly breaking through the general greenery. Anything approaching a gorgeous, garish or gaudy display of flowers is to be avoided."

Sedges and ferns and graceful bulrush would be planted on the banks of the Wooded Island to conjure density and intricacy and "to slightly screen, without hiding, flowers otherwise likely to be too obtrusive." He envisioned large patches of cattails broken by bulrush, iris, and flag and pocketed with blooming plants, such as flame-red cardinal flower and yellow creeping buttercup—planted, if necessary, on slightly raised mounds so as to be just visible among the swaying green spires in the foreground.

On the far shore, below the formal terraces of the buildings, he planned to position fragrant plants such as honeysuckle and summersweet, so that their perfume would rise into the nostrils of visitors pausing on the terraces to view the island and the lagoon.

The overall effect, he wrote, "is thus to be in some degree of the character of a theatrical scene, to occupy the Exposition stage for a single summer."

It was one thing to visualize all this on paper, another to execute it. Olmsted was nearly seventy, his mouth aflame, his head roaring, each night a desert of wakefulness. Even without the fair he faced an intimidating portfolio of works in progress, chief among them the grounds of Biltmore, the Vanderbilt estate in North Carolina. If everything went perfectly—*if* his health did not degrade any further, *if* the weather held, *if* Burnham completed the other buildings on time, *if* strikes did not destroy the fair, *if* the many committees and directors, which Olmsted called "that army our hundreds of masters," learned to leave Burnham alone—Olmsted *might* be able to complete his task on time.

A writer for *Engineering Magazine* asked the question no one had raised at the Rookery: "How is it possible that this vast amount of construction, greatly exceeding that of the Paris Exhibition of 1889, will be ready in two years?"

For Burnham, too, the meeting in the Rookery had produced a heightened awareness of how little time remained. Everything seemed to take longer than it should, and nothing went smoothly. The first real work in Jackson Park began on February 11, when fifty Italian immigrants employed by McArthur Brothers, a Chicago company, began digging a drainage ditch. It was nothing, routine. But word of the work spread, and five hundred union men stormed the park and drove the workers off. Two days later, Friday the thirteenth, six hundred men gathered at the park to protest McArthur's use of what they alleged were "imported" workers. The next day two thousand men, many armed with sharpened sticks, advanced on McArthur's workers, seized two, and began beating them. Police arrived. The crowd backed off. McArthur asked Mayor Cregier for protection; Cregier assigned the city's corporation counsel, a young lawyer named Clarence Darrow, to look into it. Two nights later the city's unions met with officers of the fair to demand that they limit the workday to eight hours, pay union-scale wages, and hire union workers before all others. After two weeks of deliberation the fair's directors accepted the eight-hour day but said they'd think about the rest.

There was conflict, too, among the fair's overseers. The National Commission, made up of politicians and headed by Director-General George Davis, wanted financial control; the Exposition Company, run by Chicago's leading businessmen and headed by President Lyman Gage, refused: The company had raised the money, and by God the company would spend it, in whatever way it chose.

Committees ruled everything. In his private practice Burnham was accustomed to having complete control over expenditures needed to build his skyscrapers. Now he needed to seek approval from the Exposition Company's executive committee at every step, even to buy drafting boards. It was all immensely frustrating. "We must push this now," Burnham said. "The delays have seemed interminable."

But he did make progress. For example, he directed a contest to choose a female architect to design the Woman's Building for the fair. Sophia Hayden of Boston won. She was twenty-one years old. Her fee was the prize money: a thousand dollars. The male architects each got ten thousand. There had been skepticism that a mere woman would be able to conceive such an important building on her own. "Examination of the facts show[s] that this woman had no help whatever in working up the designs," Burnham wrote. "It was done by herself in her home."

In March, however, all the architects acknowledged that things were proceeding far too slowly—that if they built their structures as originally planned out of stone, steel, and brick, the buildings could not possibly be finished by Opening Day. They voted instead to clad their buildings in "staff," a resilient mixture of plaster and jute that could be molded into columns and statuary and spread over wood frames to provide the illusion of stone. "There will not be a brick on the grounds," Burnham said.

In the midst of all this, as the workload increased, Burnham realized he could put off no longer the hiring of a designer to replace his beloved John Root. He needed someone to manage his firm's ongoing work while he tended to the exposition. A friend recommended Charles B. Atwood of New York. McKim shook his head. There were stories about Atwood, and questions of dependability. Nonetheless, Burnham arranged to meet Atwood in New York, at the Brunswick Hotel.

Atwood stood him up. Burnham waited an hour, then left to catch his train. As he was crossing the street, a handsome man in a black bowler and cape with black gun-muzzle eyes approached him and asked if he was Mr. Burnham.

"I am," Burnham said.

"I'm Charles Atwood. Did you want to see me?"

Burnham glared. "I am going back to Chicago; I'll think it over and let you know." Burnham caught his train. Once back in Chicago he went directly to his office. A few hours later Atwood walked in. He had followed Burnham from New York.

Burnham gave him the job.

Atwood had a secret, as it happens. He was an opium addict. It explained those eyes and his erratic behavior. But Burnham thought him a genius.

＊＊＊

As a reminder to himself and anyone who visited his office in the shanty, Burnham posted a sign over his desk bearing a single word: RUSH.

＊＊＊

Time was so short, the Executive Committee began planning exhibits and appointing world's fair commissioners to secure them. In February the committee voted to dispatch a young army officer, Lieutenant Mason A. Schufeldt, to Zanzibar to begin a journey to locate a tribe of Pygmies only recently revealed to exist by explorer Henry Stanley, and to bring to the fair "a family of twelve or fourteen of the fierce little midgets."

The committee gave Lieutenant Schufeldt two and a half years to complete his mission.

＊＊＊

Beyond the fairgrounds' new fence, turmoil and grief engulfed Chicago. Union leaders threatened to organize unions worldwide to oppose the fair. *The Inland Architect,* a prominent Chicago journal, reported: "That un-American institution, the trades union, has developed its un-American principle of curtailing or abolishing the personal freedom of the individual in a new direction, that of seeking, as far as possible, to cripple the World's Fair." Such behavior, the journal said, "would be called treason in countries less enlightened and more arbitrary than ours." The nation's financial condition worsened. Offices in the newest of Chicago's skyscrapers remained vacant. Just blocks from the Rookery, Burnham & Root's Temperance Building stood huge and black and largely empty. Twenty-five thousand unemployed workers roamed the city. At night they slept in police stations and in the basement of City Hall. The unions grew stronger.

The old world was passing. P. T. Barnum died; grave-robbers attempted to steal his corpse. William Tecumseh Sherman died, too. Atlanta cheered. Reports from abroad asserted, erroneously, that Jack the Ripper had returned. Closer at hand, a gory killing in New York suggested he might have migrated to America.

In Chicago the former warden of the Illinois State Penitentiary at Joliet, Major R. W. McClaughry, began readying the city for the surge in crime that everyone expected the fair to produce, establishing an office in the Auditorium to receive and distribute Bertillon identifications of known criminals. Devised by French criminologist Alphonse Bertillon, the system required police to make a precise survey of the dimensions and physical peculiarities of suspects. Bertillon believed that each man's measurements were unique and thus could be used to penetrate the aliases that criminals deployed in moving from city to city. In theory, a detective in Cincinnati could telegraph a few distinctive numbers to investigators in New York with the expectation that if a match existed, New York would find it.

A reporter asked Major McClaughry whether the fair really would attract the criminal element. He paused a moment, then said, "I think it quite necessary that the authorities here should be prepared to meet and deal with the greatest congregation of criminals that ever yet met in this country."

Cuckoldry

AT THE HOLMES BUILDING at Sixty-third and Wallace, now known widely in the neighborhood as "the castle," the Conner family was in turmoil. Lovely, dark Gertrude—Ned's sister—one day came to Ned in tears and told him she could not stay in the house another moment. She vowed to catch the first train back to Muscatine, Iowa. Ned begged her to tell him what had occurred, but she refused.

Ned knew that she and a young man had begun courting, and he believed her tears must have resulted from something he had said or done. Possibly the two had been "indiscreet," although he did not think Gertrude capable of so drastic a moral lapse. The more he pressed her for an explanation, the more troubled and adamant she became. She wished she had never come to Chicago. It was a blighted, hellish place full of noise and dust and smoke and inhuman towers that blocked the sun, and she hated it—hated especially this gloomy building and the ceaseless clamor of construction.

When Holmes came by, she would not look at him. Her color rose. Ned did not notice.

Ned hired an express company to collect her trunk and saw her to the station. Still she would not explain. Through tears, she said good-bye. The train huffed from the station.

In Iowa—in safe, bland Muscatine—Gertrude fell ill, an accident of nature. The disease proved fatal. Holmes told Ned how sorry he was to hear of her passing, but in his eyes there was only a flat blue calm, like the lake on a still August morning.

With Gertrude gone, the tension between Ned and Julia increased. Their marriage never had been tranquil. Back in Iowa they had come close to separating. Now, again, their relationship was crumbling. Their daughter, Pearl, became commensurately more difficult to manage, her behavior marked by periods of sullen withdrawal and eruptions of anger. Ned understood none of it. He was "of an easy-going innocent nature," a reporter later observed, "he mistrusted nothing." He did not see what even his friends and regular customers saw. "Some of my friends told me there was something between Holmes and my wife," he said later. "At first I did not believe it."

Despite the warnings and his own mounting uneasiness, Ned admired Holmes. While he, Ned, was but a jeweler in someone else's store, Holmes controlled a small empire—and had yet to turn thirty years old. Holmes's energy and success made Ned feel even smaller than he already was inclined to feel, especially now that Julia had begun looking at him as if he had just emerged from a rendering vat at the stockyards.

Thus Ned was particularly susceptible to an offer from Holmes that seemed likely to increase his own stature in Julia's eyes. Holmes proposed to sell Ned the entire pharmacy, under terms that Ned—naïve Ned—found generous beyond all expectation. Holmes would increase his salary from twelve to eighteen dollars a week, so that Ned could pay Holmes six dollars a week to cover the purchase. Ned wouldn't even have to worry about handling the six dollars—Holmes would deduct it from the new eighteen-dollar salary each week, automatically. Holmes promised also to take care of all the legal details and to record the transfer with city officials. Ned would get his twelve dollars a week just as always, but now he would be the owner of a fine store in a prosperous neighborhood destined to become even wealthier once the world's fair began operation.

Ned accepted, giving no thought to why Holmes would wish to shed such a healthy business. The offer eased his concerns about Holmes and Julia. If Holmes and she were involved in an indiscreet liaison, would he offer Ned the jewel of his Englewood empire?

To Ned's sorrow, he soon found that his new status did nothing to ease the tension between himself and Julia. The ferocity of their arguments only increased, as did the length of the cold silences that filled whatever other time they spent together. Holmes was sympathetic. He bought Ned lunch at the first-floor restaurant and told Ned how certain he was that the marriage would be salvaged. Julia was an ambitious woman and clearly a very beautiful one, but she would come to her senses in short order.

Holmes's sympathy was disarming. The idea that Holmes might be the cause of Julia's discontent seemed more and more improbable. Holmes even wanted Ned to buy life insurance, for surely once his marital strife subsided, he would want to protect Julia and Pearl from destitution in the event of his death. He recommended that Ned also consider insuring Pearl's life and offered to pay the initial premiums. He brought an insurance man, C. W. Arnold, to meet with Ned.

Arnold explained that he was building a new agency and wanted to sell as many policies as possible in order to attract the attention of the biggest insurance companies. To secure a policy, all Ned had to pay was a dollar, Arnold said—just one dollar to begin protecting his family forever.

But Ned did not want a policy. Arnold tried to change his mind. Ned refused and refused and finally told Arnold that if he really needed a dollar, Ned would simply give him one.

Arnold and Holmes looked at each other, their eyes empty of all expression.

Soon creditors began appearing at the pharmacy demanding repayment of mortgages secured by the store's furnishings and its stock of salves and ointments and other goods. Ned was unaware of the existence of these debts and believed the creditors were trying to defraud him— until they presented documents signed by the previous owner, H. H. Holmes. Convinced now that these were bona-fide debts, Ned promised to pay them as soon as he was able.

Here too Holmes was sympathetic, but there was nothing he could do. Any thriving venture accumulated debts. He had assumed that Ned understood at least that much about business. At any rate it was something to which Ned would now have to become accustomed. The sale, he reminded Ned, was final.

———

This latest disappointment rekindled Ned's uneasiness about Holmes and Julia. He began to suspect that his friends might indeed be correct in believing that Holmes and Julia were engaged in an illicit affair. It would explain the change in Julia, certainly, and might even explain Holmes's sale of the pharmacy—an unstated trade: the store in exchange for Julia.

Ned did not yet confront Julia with his suspicions. He told her simply that if her behavior toward him did not change, if her coldness and hostility continued, he and she would have to separate.

She snapped, "Separation couldn't come too soon to suit me."

But they remained together a short while longer. Their battles became more frequent. Finally Ned shouted that he was done, the marriage was over. He spent the night in the barbershop on the first floor, directly below their apartment. He heard her footsteps as she moved about on the floor above.

The next morning he told Holmes he was leaving and would abandon his interest in the store. When Holmes urged him to reconsider, Ned merely laughed. He moved out and took a new job with a jewelry store in downtown Chicago, H. Purdy & Co. Pearl remained with Julia and Holmes.

Ned made one more attempt to win back his wife. "I told her after I left the building that if she would return to me and stop her quarreling we would live together again, but she refused to come back."

Ned vowed that one day he would return for Pearl. Soon he left Chicago and moved to Gilman, Illinois, where he met a young woman and began a formal courtship, which compelled him to visit Holmes's building one more time, to seek a divorce decree. He got it but failed to gain custody of Pearl.

———

With Ned gone and the divorce final, Holmes's interest in Julia began to dissipate. He had promised her repeatedly that he would marry her once the decree was confirmed, but now he found the prospect repulsive. Pearl's sullen, accusing presence had become especially unappealing.

At night, after the first-floor stores had closed and Julia and Pearl and the building's other tenants were asleep, he sometimes would descend to the basement, careful to lock the door behind him, and there ignite the flames of his kiln and marvel at its extraordinary heat.

Vexed

BURNHAM SAW HIS FAMILY RARELY now. By the spring of 1891 he was living full time in the shanty at Jackson Park; Margaret stayed in Evanston with a few servants who helped her care for their five children. Only a modest train ride separated the Burnhams, but the mounting demands of the fair made that distance as difficult to span as the Isthmus of Panama. Burnham could send telegrams, but they forced a cold and clumsy brevity and afforded little privacy. So Burnham wrote letters, and wrote them often. "You must not think this hurry of my life will last forever," he wrote in one letter. "I shall stop after the World's Fair. I have made up my mind to this." The exposition had become a "hurricane," he said. "To be done with this flurry is my strongest wish."

Every dawn he left his quarters and inspected the grounds. Six steam-powered dredges the size of floating barns gnawed at the lakeshore, as five thousand men with shovels and wheelbarrows and horse-drawn graders slowly scraped the landscape raw, many of the men wearing bowlers and suitcoats as if they just happened to be passing by and on impulse chose to pitch in. Despite the presence of so many workers, there was a maddening lack of noise and bustle. The park was too big, the men too spread out, to deliver any immediate sense of work being done. The only reliable signs were the black plumes of smoke from the dredges and the ever-present scent of burning leaves from slash piles set aflame by workers. The brilliant white stakes that marked the perimeters of buildings imparted to the land the look of a Civil War burial ground. Burnham did find beauty in the rawness—"Among the trees of the Wooded Island the long white tents of the contractor's camp gleamed in the sun, a soft, white note in the dun-colored landscape, and the pure blue line of the lake horizon made a cheerful contrast to the rugged and barren fore-ground"—but he also found deep frustration.

The work advanced slowly, impeded by the worsening relationship between the fair's two ruling bodies, the National Commission and the Exposition Company, and by the architects' failure to get their drawings to Chicago on time. All the drawings were late. Equally aggravating was the fact that there still was no Eiffel challenger. Moreover, the exposition had entered that precarious early phase common to every great construc-tion project when unexpected obstacles suddenly emerge.

Burnham knew how to deal with Chicago's notoriously flimsy soil, but Jackson Park surprised even him.

Initially the bearing capacity of its ground was "practically an unknown quality," as one engineer put it. In March 1891 Burnham ordered tests to gauge how well the soil would support the grand palaces then on the architects' drafting tables. Of special concern was the fact that the buildings would be sited adjacent to newly dug canals and lagoons. As any engineer knew, soil under pressure tended to shift to fill adjacent excavations. The fair's engineers conducted the first test twelve feet from the lagoon on ground intended to support the northeast corner of the Electricity Building. They laid a platform four feet square and loaded it with iron to a pressure of 2,750 pounds per square foot, twenty-two tons in all. They left it in place for fifteen days and found that it settled only one-quarter of an inch. Next they dug a deep trench four feet from the platform. Over the next two days the platform sank another eighth of an inch but no farther. This was good news. It meant that Burnham could use Root's floating *grillage* for foundations without hav-ing to worry about catastrophic settlement.

To make sure these properties were constant throughout the park, Burnham had his chief engineer, Abraham Gottlieb, test locations ear-marked for other buildings. The tests yielded similar results—until Gottlieb's men came to the site intended for George Post's gigantic Man-ufactures and Liberal Arts Building. The soil destined to support the northern half of the building showed total settlement of less than one inch, consistent with the rest of the park. At the southern end of the site, however, the men made a disheartening discovery. Even as workers loaded the platform, it sank eight inches. Over the next four days it settled thirty inches more, and would have continued sinking if the engineers had not simply called off the test.

Of course: Nearly all the soil of Jackson Park was competent to support floating foundations *except* the one portion destined to bear the fair's biggest and heaviest building. Here, Burnham realized, contractors would have to drive piles at least down to hard-pan, an expensive complication and a source of additional delay.

The problems with this building, however, had only just begun.

In April 1891 Chicago learned the results of the latest mayoral election. In the city's richest clubs, industrialists gathered to toast the fact that Carter Henry Harrison, whom they viewed as overly sympathetic to organized labor, had lost to Hempstead Washburne, a Republican. Burnham, too, allowed himself a moment of celebration. To him, Harrison represented the old Chicago of filth, smoke, and vice, everything the fair was designed to repudiate.

The celebrations were tempered, however, by the fact that Harrison had lost by the narrowest of margins, fewer than four thousand votes. What's more, he had achieved this near-victory without the support of a major party. Shunned by the Democrats, he had run as an independent.

Elsewhere in the city, Patrick Prendergast grieved. Harrison was his hero, his hope. The margin was so narrow, however, that he believed that if Harrison ran again, he would win. Prendergast resolved to double his own efforts to help Harrison succeed.

In Jackson Park Burnham faced repeated interruptions stemming from his de facto role as ambassador to the outside world, charged with cultivating goodwill and future attendance. Mostly these banquets, talks, and tours were time-squandering annoyances, as in June 1891 when, at the request of Director-General Davis, Burnham hosted a visit to Jackson Park by a battalion of foreign dignitaries that consumed two full days. Others were purely a pleasure. A few weeks earlier Thomas Edison, known widely as "the Wizard of Menlo Park," had paid a visit to Burnham's shanty. Burnham showed him around. Edison suggested the exposition use incandescent bulbs rather than arc lights, because the incandescent variety produced a softer light. Where arc lights could not be avoided, he said, they should be covered with white globes. And of course Edison urged the fair to use direct current, DC, the prevailing standard.

The civility of this encounter belied a caustic battle being waged outside Jackson Park for the rights to illuminate the exposition. On one side was General Electric Company, which had been created when J. P. Morgan took over Edison's company and merged it with several others and which now proposed to install a direct current system to light the fair. On the other side was Westinghouse Electric Company, with a bid to wire Jackson Park for alternating current, using patents that its founder, George Westinghouse, had acquired a few years earlier from Nikola Tesla.

General Electric offered to do the job for $1.8 million, insisting the deal would not earn a penny's profit. A number of exposition directors held General Electric stock and urged William Baker, president of the fair since Lyman Gage's April retirement, to accept the bid. Baker refused, calling it "extortionate." General Electric rather miraculously came back with a bid of $554,000. But Westinghouse, whose AC system was inherently cheaper and more efficient, bid $399,000. The exposition went with Westinghouse, and helped change the history of electricity.

———

The source of Burnham's greatest dismay was the failure of the architects to finish their drawings on schedule.

If he had once been obsequious to Richard Hunt and the eastern men, he was not now. In a June 2, 1891, letter to Hunt, he wrote, "We are at a dead standstill waiting for your scale drawings. Can't we have them as they are, and finish here?"

Four days later he again prodded Hunt: "The delay you are causing us by not forwarding scale drawings is embarrassing in the extreme."

That same month a serious if unavoidable interruption hobbled the Landscape Department. Olmsted became ill—severely so. He attributed his condition to poisoning from an arsenic-based pigment called Turkey Red in the wallpaper of his Brookline home. It may, however, simply have been another bout of deep blue melancholia, the kind that had assailed him off and on for years.

During his recuperation Olmsted ordered bulbs and plants for cultivation in two large nurseries established on the fairgrounds. He ordered Dusty Miller, Carpet Bugle, President Garfield heliotrope, Speedwell, Pennyroyal, English and Algerian ivies, verbena, vinca, and a rich palette of geraniums, among them Black Prince, Christopher Columbus, Mrs. Turner, Crystal Palace, Happy Thought, and Jeanne d'Arc. He dispatched an army of collectors to the shores of Lake Calumet, where they gathered twenty-seven traincar loads of iris, sedge, bulrush, and other semiaquatic plants and grasses. They collected an additional four thousand crates of pond lily roots, which Olmsted's men quickly planted, only to watch most of the roots succumb to the ever-changing levels of the lake.

In contrast to the lush growth within the nurseries, the grounds of the park had been scraped free of all vegetation. Workers enriched the soil with one thousand carloads of manure shipped from the Union Stock Yards and another two thousand collected from the horses working in Jackson Park. The presence of so much exposed earth and manure became a problem. "It was bad enough during the hot weather, when a south wind could blind the eyes of man and beast," wrote Rudolf Ulrich, Olmsted's landscape superintendent at the park, "but still worse during wet weather, the newly filled ground, which was still undrained, becoming soaked with water."

Horses sank to their bellies.

It was midsummer 1891 by the time the last of the architects' drawings were completed. As each set came in, Burnham advertised for bids. Recognizing that the architects' delays had put everything behind schedule, he inserted into the construction contracts clauses that made him a "czar," as the *Chicago Tribune* put it. Each contract contained a tight deadline for completion, with a financial penalty for every day beyond. Burnham had advertised the first contract on May 14, this for the Mines Building. He wanted it finished by the end of the year. That left at best about seven months for construction (roughly the amount of time a twenty-first-century homeowner would need to build a new garage). "He is the arbiter of all disputes and no provision is made for an appeal from his decision," the *Tribune* reported. "If in the opinion of Mr. Burnham the builder is not employing a sufficient force of men to complete the work on time, Mr. Burnham is authorized to engage men himself and charge the cost to the builder." The Mines Building was the first of the main exposition buildings to begin construction, but the work did not start until July 3, 1891, with less than sixteen months remaining until Dedication Day.

As construction of the buildings at last got under way, anticipation outside the park began to increase. Colonel William Cody—Buffalo Bill—sought a concession for his Wild West show, newly returned from a hugely successful tour of Europe, but the fair's Committee on Ways and Means turned him down on grounds of "incongruity." Undeterred, Cody secured rights to a large parcel of land adjacent to the park. In San Francisco a twenty-one-year-old entrepreneur named Sol Bloom realized that the Chicago fair would let him at last take advantage of an asset he had acquired in Paris two years earlier. Entranced by the Algerian Village at the Paris exposition, he had bought the rights to display the village and its inhabitants at future events. The Ways and Means Committee rejected him, too. He returned to San Francisco intent on trying a different, more oblique means of winning a concession—one that ultimately would get him a lot more than he had bargained for. Meanwhile young Lieutenant Schufeldt had reached Zanzibar. On July 20 he telegraphed Exposition President William Baker that he was confident he could acquire as many

Pygmies from the Congo as he wished, provided the king of Belgium consented. "President Baker wants these pygmies," the *Tribune* said, "and so does everybody else around headquarters."

On the drafting board the fair did look spectacular. The centerpiece was the Grand Court, which everyone had begun calling the Court of Honor. With its immense palaces by Hunt, Post, Peabody, and the rest, the court by itself would be a marvel, but now nearly every state in the nation was planning a building, as were some two hundred companies and foreign governments. The exposition promised to surpass the Paris exposition on every level—every level that is, except one, and that persistent deficit troubled Burnham: The fair still had nothing planned that would equal, let alone eclipse, the Eiffel Tower. At nearly one thousand feet in height, the tower remained the tallest structure in the world and an insufferable reminder of the triumph of the Paris exposition. "To out-Eiffel Eiffel" had become a battle cry among the directors.

A competition held by the *Tribune* brought a wave of implausible proposals. C. F. Ritchel of Bridgeport, Connecticut, suggested a tower with a base one hundred feet high by five hundred feet wide, within which Ritchel proposed to nest a second tower and, in this one, a third. At intervals a complicated system of hydraulic tubes and pumps would cause the towers to telescope slowly upward, a journey of several hours, then allow them to sink slowly back to their original configuration. The top of the tower would house a restaurant, although possibly a bordello would have been more apt.

Another inventor, J. B. McComber, representing the Chicago-Tower Spiral-Spring Ascension and Toboggan Transportation Company, proposed a tower with a height of 8,947 feet, nearly nine times the height of the Eiffel Tower, with a base one thousand feet in diameter sunk two thousand feet into the earth. Elevated rails would lead from the top of the tower all the way to New York, Boston, Baltimore, and other cities. Visitors ready to conclude their visit to the fair and daring enough to ride elevators to the top would then toboggan all the way back home. "As the cost of the tower and its slides is of secondary importance," McComber noted, "I do not mention it here, but will furnish figures upon application."

A third proposal demanded even more courage from visitors. This inventor, who gave his initials as R. T. E., envisioned a tower four thousand feet tall from which he proposed to hang a two-thousand-foot cable of "best rubber." Attached at the bottom end of this cable would be a car seating two hundred people. The car and its passengers would be shoved off a platform and fall without restraint to the end of the cable, where the car would snap back upward and continue bouncing until it came to a stop. The engineer urged that as a precaution the ground "be covered with eight feet of feather bedding."

Everyone was thinking in terms of towers, but Burnham, for one, did not think a tower was the best approach. Eiffel had done it first and best. More than merely tall, his tower was grace frozen in iron, as much an evocation of the spirit of the age as Chartres had been in its time. To build a tower would be to follow Eiffel into territory he already had conquered for France.

In August 1891 Eiffel himself telegraphed the directors to ask if he might submit a proposal for a tower. This was a surprise and at first a welcome one. Exposition President Baker immediately cabled Eiffel that the directors would be delighted to see whatever he proposed. If the fair was to have a tower, Baker said in an interview, "M. Eiffel is the man to build it. It would not be so much of an experiment if he should be in charge of its construction. He might be able to improve on his design for the Eiffel Tower in Paris, and I think it fair to assume that he would not construct one in any way inferior to that famous structure." To the engineers of America, however, this embrace of Eiffel was a slap in the face. Over the next week and a half telegrams shot from city to city, engineer to engineer, until the story became somewhat distorted. Suddenly it seemed as if an Eiffel Tower in Chicago was a certainty—that Eiffel himself was to do the out-Eiffeling. The engineers were outraged. A long letter of protest arrived at Burnham's office, signed by some of the nation's leading engineers.

Acceptance of "the distinguished gentleman's offer," they wrote, would be "equivalent to a statement that the great body of civil engineers in this country, whose noble works attest their skill abroad as well as throughout the length and breadth of the land, lack the ability to cope with such a problem, and such action could have a tendency to rob them of their just claim to professional excellence."

Burnham read this letter with approval. It pleased him to see America's civil engineers at last expressing passion for the fair, although in fact the directors had promised nothing to Eiffel. His formal proposal arrived a week later, envisioning a tower that was essentially a taller version of what he had built in Paris. The directors sent his proposal out for translation, reviewed it, then graciously turned it down. If there was to be a tower at the fair, it would be an American tower.

But the drafting boards of America's engineers remained dishearteningly barren.

Sol Bloom, back in California, took his quest for a concession for his Algerian Village to an influential San Franciscan, Mike De Young, publisher of the *San Francisco Chronicle* and one of the exposition's national commissioners. Bloom told him about the rights he had acquired in Paris and how the exposition had rebuffed his petition.

De Young knew Bloom. As a teenager Bloom had worked in De Young's Alcazar Theater and worked his way up to become its treasurer at age nineteen. In his spare time Bloom had organized the ushers, checkers, and refreshment sellers into a more efficient, cohesive structure that greatly increased the theater's profits and his own salary. Next he organized these functions at other theaters and received regular commissions from each. At the Alcazar he inserted into scripts the names of popular products, bars, and restaurants, including the Cliff House, and for this received another stream of income. He also organized a cadre of professional applauders, known as a "claque," to provide enthusiastic ovations, demand encores, and cry *"Brava!"* for any performer willing to pay. Most performers did pay, even the most famous diva of the time, Adelina Patti.

One day Bloom saw an item in a theatrical publication about a novel Mexican band that he believed Americans would adore, and he convinced the band's manager to let him bring the musicians north for a tour. Bloom's profit was $40,000. At the time he was only eighteen.

De Young told Bloom he would investigate the situation. One week later he summoned Bloom back to his office.

"How soon could you be ready to go to Chicago?" he asked.

Bloom, startled, said, "In a couple of days, I guess." He assumed De Young had arranged a second opportunity for him to petition the fair's Ways and Means Committee. He was hesitant and told De Young he saw no value in making the journey until the exposition's directors had a better idea of the kinds of attractions they wanted.

"The situation has advanced since our talk," De Young said. "All we need now is somebody to take charge." He gave Bloom a cable from the Exposition Company that empowered De Young to hire someone to select the concessions for the Midway Plaisance and guide their construction and promotion. "You've been elected," he said.

"I can't do it," Bloom said. He did not want to leave San Francisco. "Even if I did, I've got too much at stake here to consider it."

De Young watched him. "I don't want to hear another word from you till tomorrow," he said.

In the meantime De Young wanted Bloom to think about how much money he would have to be paid to overcome his reluctance. "When you come back you can name your salary," he said. "I will either accept or reject it. There will be no argument. Is that agreeable?"

Bloom did agree, but only because De Young's request gave him a graceful way of refusing the job. All he had to do, he figured, was name such an outrageous sum that De Young could not possibly accept it, "and as I walked down the street I decided what it would be."

⸺

Burnham tried to anticipate every conceivable threat to the fair. Aware of Chicago's reputation for vice and violence, Burnham insisted on the creation of a large police force, the Columbian Guard, and placed it

under the command of Colonel Edmund Rice, a man of great valor who
had faced Pickett's Charge at Gettysburg. Unlike conventional police
departments, the Guard's mandate explicitly emphasized the novel idea
of preventing crime rather than merely arresting wrongdoers after
the fact.

Disease, too, posed dangers to the fair, Burnham knew. An outbreak
of smallpox or cholera or any of the other lethal infections that roamed
the city could irreparably taint the exposition and destroy any hopes the
directors had of achieving the record attendance necessary to generate
a profit.

By now the new science of bacteriology, pioneered by Robert Koch
and Louis Pasteur, had convinced most public health officials that contaminated drinking water caused the spread of cholera and other bacter-
ial diseases. Chicago's water teemed with bacteria, thanks mainly to the
Chicago River. In a monumental spasm of civic engineering the city in
1871 reversed the river's direction so that it no longer flowed into Lake
Michigan, but ran instead into the Des Plaines River and ultimately into
the Mississippi, the theory being that the immense flows of both rivers
would dilute the sewage to harmless levels—a concept downriver towns
like Joliet did not wholeheartedly embrace. To the engineers' surprise,
however, prolonged rains routinely caused the Chicago River to regress
and again pour dead cats and fecal matter into the lake, and in such volume that tendrils of black water reached all the way to the intake cribs
of the city water system.

Most Chicago residents had no choice but to drink the water.
Burnham, however, believed from the start that the fair's workers and
visitors needed a better, safer supply. In this too he was ahead of the age.
On his orders his sanitary engineer, William S. MacHarg, built a water-
sterilization plant on the fairgrounds that pumped lake water through a
succession of large tanks in which the water was aerated and boiled.
MacHarg's men set big casks of this sterilized water throughout the park
and replenished them every day.

Burnham planned to close the purification plant by Opening Day and
give visitors a choice between two other supplies of safe water: lake water

purified with Pasteur filters and offered free of charge, or naturally pure water for a penny a cup, piped one hundred miles from the coveted springs of Waukesha, Wisconsin. In November 1891 Burnham ordered MacHarg to investigate five of Waukesha's springs to gauge their capacity and purity, but to do so "quietly," suggesting he was aware that running a pipeline through the village's comely landscape might prove a sensitive issue. No one, however, could have imagined that in a few months MacHarg's efforts to secure a supply of Waukesha's best would lead to an armed encounter in the middle of a fine Wisconsin night.

What most worried Burnham was fire. The loss of the Grannis Block, with his and Root's headquarters, remained a vivid, humiliating memory. A catastrophic fire in Jackson Park could destroy the fair. Yet within the park fire was central to the construction process. Plasterers used small furnaces called salamanders to speed drying and curing. Tinners and electricians used fire pots for melting, bending, and fusing. Even the fire department used fire: Steam engines powered the pumps on the department's horse-drawn fire trucks.

Burnham established defenses that by prevailing standards seemed elaborate, even excessive. He formed an exposition fire department and ordered the installation of hundreds of fire hydrants and telegraphic alarm boxes. He commissioned the construction of a fire boat, the *Fire Queen,* built specifically to negotiate the park's shallow canals and to pass under its many low bridges. Design specifications required that every building be surrounded by an underwater main and be plumbed with interior standpipes. He also banned all smoking on the grounds, although here he made at least two exceptions: one for a contractor who pleaded that his crew of European artisans would quit if denied their cigars, the other for the big hearth in his own shanty, around which he and his engineers, draftsmen, and visiting architects gathered each night for wine, talk, and cigars.

With the onset of winter Burnham ordered all hydrants packed in horse manure to prevent freezing.

On the coldest days the manure steamed, as if the hydrants themselves were on fire.

When Sol Bloom returned to the office of Mike De Young, he was confident De Young could not possibly accept his salary request, for he had decided to ask for the same salary as the president of the United States: $50,000. "The more I thought about it," Bloom recalled, "the more I enjoyed the prospect of telling Mike De Young that no less a sum could compensate me for my sacrifice in leaving San Francisco."

De Young offered Bloom a seat. His expression was sober and expectant.

Bloom said: "Much as I appreciate the compliment, I find that my interests lie right here in this city. As I look ahead I can see myself—"

De Young cut him off. Softly he said, "Now, Sol, I thought you were going to tell me how much you wanted us to pay you."

"I didn't want you to think I didn't appreciate—"

"You said that a minute ago," De Young said. "Now tell me how much money you want."

This was not going quite the way Bloom had expected. With some trepidation, Bloom told him the number: "A thousand dollars a week."

De Young smiled. "Well, that's pretty good pay for a fellow of twenty-one, but I have no doubt you'll earn it."

In August, Burnham's chief structural engineer, Abraham Gottlieb, made a startling disclosure: He had failed to calculate wind loads for the fair's main buildings. Burnham ordered his key contractors—including Agnew & Co., erecting the Manufactures and Liberal Arts Building—to stop work immediately. For months Burnham had been combating rumors that he had forced his men to work at too fast a pace and that as a result some buildings were unsafe; in Europe, press reports held that certain structures had been "condemned." Now here was Gottlieb, conceding a potentially catastrophic error.

Gottlieb protested that even without an explicit calculation of wind loads, the buildings were strong enough.

"I could not, however, take this view," Burnham wrote in a letter to James Dredge, editor of the influential British magazine *Engineering*. Burnham ordered all designs strengthened to withstand the highest winds recorded over the previous ten years. "This may be going to extremes," he told Dredge, "but to me it seems wise and prudent, in view of the great interests involved."

Gottlieb resigned. Burnham replaced him with Edward Shankland, an engineer from his own firm who possessed a national reputation as a designer of bridges.

On November 24, 1891, Burnham wrote to James Dredge to report that once again he was under fire over the issue of structural integrity. "The criticism now," he wrote, "is that the structures are unnecessarily strong."

Bloom arrived in Chicago and quickly discovered why so little had been accomplished at the Midway Plaisance, known officially as Department M. Until now it had been under the control of Frederick Putnam, a Harvard professor of ethnology. He was a distinguished anthropologist, but putting him in charge of the Midway, Bloom said years later, "was about as intelligent a decision as it would be today to make Albert Einstein manager of the Ringling Brothers and Barnum & Bailey Circus." Putnam would not have disagreed. He told a Harvard colleague he was "anxious to get this whole Indian circus off my hands."

Bloom took his concerns to Exposition President Baker, who turned him over to Burnham.

"You are a very young man, a very young man indeed, to be in charge of the work entrusted to you," Burnham said.

But Burnham himself had been young when John B. Sherman walked into his office and changed his life.

"I want you to know that you have my full confidence," he said. "You are in complete charge of the Midway. Go ahead with the work. You are responsible only to me. I will write orders to that effect. Good luck."

By December 1891 the two buildings farthest along were the Mines Building and the Woman's Building. Construction of the Mines Building had gone smoothly, thanks to a winter that by Chicago standards had been mercifully benign. Construction of the Woman's Building, however, had become an ordeal, both for Burnham and its young architect, Sophia Hayden, mainly because of modifications demanded by Bertha Honore Palmer, head of the fair's Board of Lady Managers, which governed all things at the fair having to do with women. As the wife of Potter Palmer, she was accustomed by wealth and absolute social dominance to having her own way, as she had made clear earlier in the year when she suppressed a revolt led by the board's executive secretary that had caused open warfare between factions of elegantly coiffed and dressed women. In the thick of it one horrified lady manager had written to Mrs. Palmer, "I *do* hope that Congress will not become disgusted with our sex."

Hayden came to Chicago to produce final drawings, then returned home, leaving their execution to Burnham. Construction began July 9; workers began applying the final coat of staff in October. Hayden returned in December to direct the decoration of the building's exterior, believing this to be her responsibility. She discovered that Bertha Palmer had other ideas.

In September, without Hayden's knowledge, Palmer had invited women everywhere to donate architectural ornaments for the building and in response had received a museum's worth of columns, panels, sculpted figures, window grills, doors, and other objects. Palmer believed the building could accommodate all the contributions, especially those sent by prominent women. Hayden, on the other hand, knew that such a hodgepodge of materials would result in an aesthetic abomination. When an influential Wisconsin woman named Flora Ginty sent an elaborately carved wooden door, Hayden turned it down. Ginty was hurt and angry. "When I think of the days I worked and the miles I traveled to achieve these things for the Woman's building, my ire rises a little yet." Mrs. Palmer was in Europe at the time, but her private secretary, Laura Hayes, a gossip of virtuosic scope, made sure her employer learned all the details. Hayes also relayed to Palmer a few words of advice that she herself had given the architect: " 'I think it would be better to have the build-ing look like a patchwork quilt, than to refuse these things which the Lady Managers have been to such pains in soliciting.' "

A patchwork quilt was not what Hayden had in mind. Despite Mrs. Palmer's blinding social glare, Hayden continued to decline donations. A battle followed, fought in true Gilded Age fashion with oblique snubs and poisonous courtesy. Mrs. Palmer pecked and pestered and catapulted icy smiles into Hayden's deepening gloom. Finally Palmer assigned the decoration of the Woman's Building to someone else, a designer named Candace Wheeler.

Hayden fought the arrangement in her quiet, stubborn way until she could take it no longer. She walked into Burnham's office, began to tell him her story, and promptly, literally, went mad: tears, heaving sobs, cries of anguish, all of it. "A severe breakdown," an acquaintance called it, "with a violent attack of high nervous excitement of the brain."

Burnham, stunned, summoned one of the exposition surgeons. Hayden was discreetly driven from the park in one of the fair's innova-tive English ambulances with quiet rubber tires and placed in a sanitar-ium for a period of enforced rest. She lapsed into "melancholia," a sweet name for depression.

◦━━━━◦

At Jackson Park aggravation was endemic. Simple matters, Burnham found, often became imbroglios. Even Olmsted had become an irritant. He was brilliant and charming, but once fixed on a thing, he was as unyielding as a slab of Joliet limestone. By the end of 1891 the question of what kind of boats to allow on the fair's waterways had come to obsess him, as if boats alone would determine the success of his quest for "poetic mystery."

In December 1891 Burnham received a proposal from a tugboat man-ufacturer arguing the case for steam launches at the exposition. Olmsted got wind of it from Harry Codman, who in addition to being his chief operating man in Chicago served as a kind of spy, keeping Olmsted abreast of all threats to Olmsted's vision. Codman sent Olmsted a copy of the letter, adding his own note that the tugboat maker seemed to enjoy Burnham's confidence.

On December 23 Olmsted wrote to Burnham: "I suspect that even Codman is inclined to think that I make too much of a hobby of this boat question and give an amount of worry, if not thought, to it that would be better expended on other and more critical matters, and I fear that you may think me a crank upon it."

He proceeded, however, to vent his obsession yet again. The tugmaker's letter, he complained, framed the boat question solely in terms of moving the greatest number of passengers between different points at the exposition as cheaply and quickly as possible. "You perfectly well know that the main object to be accomplished was nothing of this sort. I need not try to make a statement of what it was. You are as alive to it as I am. You know that it was a poetic object, and you know that if boats are to be introduced on these waters, it would be perfect nonsense to have them of a kind that would antagonize this poetic object."

Mere transportation was never the goal, he fumed. The whole point of having boats was to enhance the landscape. "Put in the waters unbecoming boats and the effect would be utterly disgusting, destroying the value of what would otherwise be the most valuable original feature of this Exposition. I say destroy deliberately. A thousand times better [to] have no boats."

◦━━━◦

Despite increasing committee interference and intensified conflict between Burnham and Director-General Davis, and with the threat of labor strikes ever present, the main buildings rose. Workers laid foundations of immense timbers in crisscrossed layers in accord with Root's *grillage* principle, then used steam-powered derricks to raise the tall posts of iron and steel that formed each building's frame. They cocooned the frames in scaffolds of wood and faced each frame with hundreds of thousands of wooden planks to create walls capable of accepting two thick layers of staff. As workers piled mountains of fresh lumber beside each building, jagged foothills of sawdust and scrap rose nearby. The air smelled of cut wood and Christmas.

In December the exposition experienced its first death: a man named Mueller at the Mines Building, dead of a fractured skull. Three other deaths followed in short order:

Jansen, fractured skull, Electricity Building;

Allard, fractured skull, Electricity Building;

Algeer, stunned to oblivion by a new phenomenon, electric shock, at the Mines Building.

Dozens of lesser accidents occurred as well. Publicly Burnham struck a pose of confidence and optimism. In a December 28, 1891, letter to the editor of the *Chicago Herald,* he wrote, "A few questions of design and plan are still undetermined, but there is nothing which is not well in hand, and I see no reason why we will not be able to complete our work in time for the ceremonies in October, 1892"—Dedication Day—"and for the opening of the Exposition, May 1st, 1893."

In reality, the fair was far behind schedule, with worse delay forestalled only by the winter's mildness. The October dedication was to take place inside the Manufactures and Liberal Arts Building, yet as of January only the foundation of the building had been laid. For the fair to be even barely presentable in time for the ceremony, everything would have to go perfectly. The weather especially would have to cooperate.

Meanwhile, banks and companies were failing across America, strikes threatened everywhere, and cholera had begun a slow white trek across Europe, raising fears that the first plague ships would soon arrive in New York Harbor.

As if anyone needed extra pressure, the *New York Times* warned: "the failure of the fair or anything short of a positive and pronounced success would be a discredit to the whole country, and not to Chicago alone."

Remains of the Day

In November 1891 Julia Conner announced to Holmes she was pregnant; now, she told him, he had no choice but to marry her. Holmes reacted to her news with calm and warmth. He held her, stroked her hair, and with moist eyes assured her that she had nothing to worry about, certainly he would marry her, as he long had promised. There was, however, a condition that he now felt obligated to impose. A child was out of the question. He would marry her only if she agreed to allow him to execute a simple abortion. He was a physician, he had done it before. He would use chloroform, and she would feel nothing and awaken to the prospect of a new life as Mrs. H. H. Holmes. Children would come later. Right now there was far too much to do, especially given all the work that lay ahead to complete the hotel and furnish each of its rooms in time for the world's fair.

Holmes knew he possessed great power over Julia. First there was the power that accrued to him naturally through his ability to bewitch men and women alike with false candor and warmth; second, the power of social approbation that he now focused upon her. Though sexual liaisons were common, society tolerated them only as long as their details remained secret. Packinghouse princes ran off with parlormaids and bank presidents seduced typewriters; when necessary, their attorneys arranged quiet solo voyages to Europe to the surgical suites of discreet but capable doctors. A public pregnancy without marriage meant disgrace and destitution. Holmes possessed Julia now as fully as if she were an antebellum slave, and he reveled in his possession. The operation, he told Julia, would take place on Christmas Eve.

Snow fell. Carolers moved among the mansions on Prairie Avenue, pausing now and then to enter the fine houses for hot mulled cider and cocoa. The air was scented with woodsmoke and roasting duck. In Graceland Cemetery, to the north, young couples raced their sleighs over the snow-heaped undulations, pulling their blankets especially tight as they passed the tall, gloomy guardian at the tomb of Dexter Graves, *Eternal Silence,* a hooded figure that from a distance seems to have only darkness where the face should have been. To look into this emptiness, legend held, was to receive a glimpse into the underworld.

At 701 Sixty-third Street in Englewood Julia Conner put her daughter to bed and did her best to smile and indulge the child's delighted anticipation of Christmas. Yes, Saint Nicholas would come, and he would bring wonderful things. Holmes had promised a bounty of toys and sweets for Pearl, and for Julia something truly grand, beyond anything she could have received from her poor bland Ned.

Outside the snow muffled the concussion of passing horses. Trains bearing fangs of ice tore through the crossing at Wallace.

Julia walked down the hall to an apartment occupied by Mr. and Mrs. John Crowe. Julia and Mrs. Crowe had become friends, and now Julia helped Mrs. Crowe decorate a Christmas tree in the Crowes' apartment, meant for Pearl as a Christmas-morning surprise. Julia talked of all that she and Pearl would do the next day, and told Mrs. Crowe that soon she would be going to Davenport, Iowa, to attend the wedding of an older sister, "an old maid," Mrs. Crowe said, who to everyone's surprise was about to marry a railroad man. Julia was awaiting the rail pass that the groom was supposed to have put in the mail.

Julia left the apartment late that night, in good spirits, Mrs. Crowe later recalled: "there was nothing about her conversation that would lead any of us to think she intended going away that night."

⁘━━━⁘

Holmes offered Julia a cheerful "Merry Christmas" and gave her a hug, then took her hand and led her to a room on the second floor that he had readied for the operation. A table lay draped in white linen. His surgical kits stood open and gleaming, his instruments laid out in a sun-flower of polished steel. Fearful things: bonesaws, abdomen retractor, trocar and trepan. More instruments, certainly, than he really needed and all positioned so that Julia could not help but see them and be sickened by their hard, eager gleam.

He wore a white apron and had rolled back his cuffs. Possibly he wore his hat, a bowler. He had not washed his hands, nor did he wear a mask. There was no need.

She reached for his hand. There would be no pain, he assured her. She would awaken as healthy as she was now but without the encumbrance she bore within. He pulled the stopper from a dark amber bottle of liq-uid and immediately felt its silvery exhalation in his own nostrils. He poured the chloroform into a bunched cloth. She gripped his hand more tightly, which he found singularly arousing. He held the cloth over her nose and mouth. Her eyes fluttered and rolled upward. Then came the inevitable, reflexive disturbance of muscles, like a dream of running. She released his hand and cast it away with splayed fingers. Her feet trembled as if tapping to a wildly beating drum. His own excitement rose. She tried to pull his hand away, but he was prepared for this sudden surge of muscle stimulation that always preceded stupor, and with great force clamped the cloth to her face. She beat at his arms. Slowly the energy left her, and her hands began to move in slow arcs, soothing and sensuous, the wild drums silent. Ballet now, a pastoral exit.

He kept one hand on the cloth and with the other dribbled more of the liquid between his fingers into its folds, delighting in the sensation of frost where the chloroform coated his fingers. One of her wrists sagged to the table, followed shortly by the other. Her eyelids stuttered, then closed. Holmes did not think her so clever as to feign coma, but he held tight just the same. After a few moments he reached for her wrist and felt her pulse fade to nothing, like the rumble of a receding train.

He removed the apron and rolled down his sleeves. The chloroform and his own intense arousal made him feel light-headed. The sensation, as always, was pleasant and induced in him a warm languor, like the feeling he got after sitting too long in front of a hot stove. He stoppered the chloroform, found a fresh cloth, and walked down the hall to Pearl's room.

It took only a moment to bunch the fresh cloth and douse it with chloroform. In the hall, afterward, he examined his watch and saw that it was Christmas.

—

The day meant nothing to Holmes. The Christmas mornings of his youth had been suffocated under an excess of piety, prayer, and silence, as if a giant wool blanket had settled over the house.

—

On Christmas morning the Crowes waited for Julia and Pearl in glad anticipation of watching the girl's eyes ignite upon spotting the lovely tree and the presents arrayed under its boughs. The apartment was warm, the air rouged with cinnamon and fir. An hour passed. The Crowes waited as long as they could, but at ten o'clock they set out to catch a train for central Chicago, where they planned to visit friends. They left the apartment unlocked, with a cheerful note of welcome.

The Crowes returned at eleven o'clock that night and found everything as they had left it, with no evidence that Julia and her daughter had come. The next morning they tried Julia's apartment, but no one answered. They asked neighbors inside and outside the building if any had seen Julia or Pearl, but none had.

When Holmes next appeared, Mrs. Crowe asked him where Julia might be. He explained that she and Pearl had gone to Davenport earlier than expected.

Mrs. Crowe heard nothing more from Julia. She and her neighbors thought the whole thing very odd. They all agreed that the last time anyone had seen Julia or Pearl was Christmas Eve.

This was not precisely accurate. Others did see Julia again, although by then no one, not even her own family back in Davenport, Iowa, could have been expected to recognize her.

Just after Christmas Holmes asked one of his associates, Charles Chappell, to come to his building. Holmes had learned that Chappell was an "articulator," meaning he had mastered the art of stripping the flesh from human bodies and reassembling, or articulating, the bones to form complete skeletons for display in doctors' offices and laboratories. He had acquired the necessary techniques while articulating cadavers for medical students at Cook County Hospital.

During his own medical education Holmes had seen firsthand how desperate schools were to acquire corpses, whether freshly dead or skeletonized. The serious, systematic study of medicine was intensifying, and to scientists the human body was like the polar icecap, something to be studied and explored. Skeletons hung in doctors' offices where they served as visual encyclopedias. With demand outpacing supply, doctors established a custom of graciously and discreetly accepting any offered cadaver. They frowned on murder as a means of harvest; on the other hand, they made little effort to explore the provenance of any one body. Grave-robbing became an industry, albeit a small one requiring an exceptional degree of sang-froid. In periods of acute shortage doctors themselves helped mine the newly departed.

It was obvious to Holmes that even now, in the 1890s, demand remained high. Chicago's newspapers reported ghoulish tales of doctors raiding graveyards. After a foiled raid on a graveyard in New Albany, Indiana, on February 24, 1890, Dr. W. H. Wathen, head of the Kentucky Medical College, told a *Tribune* reporter, "The gentlemen were acting not for the Kentucky School of Medicine nor for themselves individually, but for the medical schools of Louisville to which the human subject is as necessary as breath to life." Just three weeks later the physicians of Louisville were at it again. They attempted to rob a grave at the State Asylum for the Insane in Anchorage, Kentucky, this time on behalf of the University of Louisville. "Yes, the party was sent out by us," a senior school official said. "We must have bodies, and if the State won't give them to us we must steal them. The winter classes were large and used up so many subjects that there are none for the spring classes." He saw no need to apologize. "The Asylum Cemetery has been robbed for years," he said, "and I doubt if there is a corpse in it. I tell you we must have bodies. You cannot make doctors without them, and the public must understand it. If we can't get them any other way we will arm the students with Winchester rifles and send them to protect the body-snatchers on their raids."

Holmes had an eye for opportunity, and with demand for corpses so robust, opportunity now beckoned.

He showed Charles Chappell into a second-floor room that contained a table, medical instruments, and bottles of solvents. These did not trouble Chappell, nor did the corpse on the table, for Chappell knew that Holmes was a physician. The body was clearly that of a woman, although of unusual height. He saw nothing to indicate her identity. "The body," he said, "looked like that of a jack rabbit which had been skinned by splitting the skin down the face and rolling it back off the entire body. In some places considerable of the flesh had been taken off with it."

Holmes explained that he had been doing some dissection but now had completed his research. He offered Chappell thirty-six dollars to cleanse the bones and skull and return to him a fully articulated skeleton. Chappell agreed. Holmes and Chappell placed the body in a trunk lined with duckcloth. An express company delivered it to Chappell's house.

Soon afterward Chappell returned with the skeleton. Holmes thanked him, paid him, and promptly sold the skeleton to Hahneman Medical College—the Chicago school, not the Philadelphia school of the same name—for many times the amount he had paid Chappell.

◦━━━━◦

In the second week of January 1892 new tenants, the Doyle family, moved into Julia's quarters in Holmes's building. They found dishes on the table and Pearl's clothes hung over a chair. The place looked and felt as if the former occupants planned to return within minutes.

The Doyles asked Holmes what had happened.

With his voice striking the perfect sober note, Holmes apologized for the disarray and explained that Julia's sister had fallen gravely ill and Julia and her daughter had left at once for the train station. There was no need to pack up their belongings, as Julia and Pearl were well provided for and would not be coming back.

Later Holmes offered a different story about Julia: "I last saw her about January 1, 1892, when a settlement of her rent was made. At this time she had announced not only to me, but to her neighbors and friends, that she was going away." Although she had told everyone her destination was Iowa, in fact, Holmes said, "she was going elsewhere to avoid the chance of her daughter being taken from her, giving the Iowa destination to mislead her husband." Holmes denied that he and Julia had ever engaged each other physically, or that she had undergone "a criminal operation," a then-current euphemism for abortion. "That she is a woman of quick temper and perhaps not always of a good disposition may be true, but that any of her friends and relatives will believe her to be an amoral woman, or one who would be a party to a criminal act I do not think."

A Gauntlet Dropped

EIGHTEEN NINETY-TWO BROKE COLD, with six inches of snow on the ground and temperatures falling to ten degrees below zero, certainly not the coldest weather Chicago had ever experienced but cold enough to clot the valves of all three of the city water system's intake valves and temporarily halt the flow of Chicago's drinking water. Despite the weather, work at Jackson Park progressed. Workers erected a heated movable shelter that allowed them to apply staff to the exterior of the Mines Building no matter what the temperature. The Woman's Building was nearly finished, all its scaffolding gone; the giant Manufactures and Liberal Arts Building had begun rising above its foundation. In all, the workforce in the park numbered four thousand. The ranks included a carpenter and furniture-maker named Elias Disney, who in coming years would tell many stories about the construction of this magical realm beside the lake. His son Walt would take note.

Beyond the exposition's eight-foot fence and its two tiers of barbed wire, there was tumult. Wage reductions and layoffs stoked unrest among workers nationwide. Unions gained strength; the Pinkerton National Detective Agency gained revenue. A rising union man named Samuel Gompers stopped by Burnham's office to discuss allegations that the exposition discriminated against union workers. Burnham ordered his construction superintendent, Dion Geraldine, to investigate. As labor strife increased and the economy faltered, the general level of violence rose. In taking stock of 1891, the *Chicago Tribune* reported that 5,906 people had been murdered in America, nearly 40 percent more than in 1890. The increase included Mr. and Mrs. Borden of Fall River, Massachusetts.

The constant threat of strike and the onset of deep cold shaded the new year for Burnham, but what most concerned him was the fast-shrinking treasury of the Exposition Company. In advancing the work so quickly and on such a grand scale, Burnham's department had consumed far more money than anyone had anticipated. There was talk now among the directors of seeking a $10 million appropriation from Congress, but the only immediate solution was to reduce expenditures. On January 6 Burnham commanded his department chiefs to take immediate, in some cases draconian, measures to cut costs. He ordered his chief draftsman, in charge of exposition work under way in the attic of the Rookery, to fire at once any man who did "inaccurate or 'slouchy' work" or who failed to do more than his full duty. He wrote to Olmsted's landscape superintendent, Rudolf Ulrich, "it seems to me you can now cut your force down one-half, and at the same time let very many expensive men go." Henceforth, Burnham ordered, all carpentry work was to be done only by men employed by the fair's contractors. To Dion Geraldine, he wrote, "You will please dismiss every carpenter on your force. . . ."

Until this point Burnham had shown a level of compassion for his workers that was extraordinary for the time. He had paid them even when illness or injury kept them out of work and established an exposition hospital that provided free medical care. He built quarters within the park where they received three large meals a day and slept in clean beds and well-heated rooms. A Princeton professor of political economy named Walter Wyckoff disguised himself as an unskilled laborer and spent a year traveling and working among the nation's growing army of unemployed men, including a stint at Jackson Park. "Guarded by sentries and high barriers from unsought contact with all beyond, great gangs of us, healthy, robust men, live and labor in a marvelous artificial world," he wrote. "No sight of misery disturbs us, nor of despairing poverty out in vain search for employment. . . . We work our eight hours a day in peaceful security and in absolute confidence of our pay."

But now even the fair was laying off men, and the timing was awful. With the advent of winter the traditional building season had come to an end. Competition for the few jobs available had intensified as thousands of unemployed men from around the country—unhappily bearing the label "hobo," derived possibly from the railroad cry "ho, boy"— converged on Chicago in hopes of getting exposition work. The dismissed men, Burnham knew, faced homelessness and poverty; their families confronted the real prospect of starvation.

But the fair came first.

The absence of an Eiffel challenger continued to frustrate Burnham. Proposals got more and more bizarre. One visionary put forth a tower five hundred feet taller than the Eiffel Tower but made entirely of logs, with a cabin at the top for shelter and refreshment. The cabin was to be a log cabin.

If an engineer capable of besting Eiffel did not step forward soon, Burnham knew, there simply would not be enough time left to build anything worthy of the fair. Somehow he needed to rouse the engineers of America. The opportunity came with an invitation to give a talk to the Saturday Afternoon Club, a group of engineers who had begun meeting on Saturdays at a downtown restaurant to discuss the construction challenges of the fair.

There was the usual meal in multiple courses, with wine, cigars, coffee, and cognac. At one table sat a thirty-three-year-old engineer from Pittsburgh who ran a steel-inspection company that had branch offices in New York and Chicago and that already possessed the exposition contract to inspect the steel used in the fair's buildings. He had an angular face, black hair, a black mustache, and dark eyes, the kind of looks soon to be coveted by an industry that Thomas Edison was just then bringing to life. He "was eminently engaging and social and he had a keen sense of humor," his partners wrote. "In all gatherings he at once became the center of attraction, having a ready command of language and a constant fund of amusing anecdotes and experiences."

Like the other members of the Saturday Afternoon Club, he expected to hear Burnham discuss the challenges of building an entire city on such a short schedule, but Burnham surprised him. After asserting that "the architects of America had covered themselves with glory" through their exposition designs, Burnham rebuked the nation's civil engineers for failing to rise to the same level of brilliance. The engineers, Burnham charged, "had contributed little or nothing either in the way of originating novel features or of showing the possibilities of modern engineering practice in America."

A tremor of displeasure rolled through the room.

"Some distinctive feature is needed," Burnham continued, "something to take the relative position in the World's Columbian Exposition that was filled by the Eiffel Tower at the Paris Exposition."

But not a tower, he said. Towers were not original. Eiffel had built a tower already. "Mere bigness" wasn't enough either. "Something novel, original, daring and unique must be designed and built if American engineers are to retain their prestige and standing."

Some of the engineers took offense; others acknowledged that Burnham had a point. The engineer from Pittsburgh felt himself "cut to the quick by the truth of these remarks."

As he sat there among his peers, an idea came to him "like an inspiration." It arrived not as some half-formed impulse, he said, but rich in detail. He could see it and touch it, hear it as it moved through the sky.

There was not much time left, but if he acted quickly to produce drawings and managed to convince the fair's Ways and Means Committee of the idea's feasibility, he believed the exposition could indeed out-Eiffel Eiffel. And if what happened to Eiffel happened to him, his fortune would be assured.

* * *

It must have been refreshing for Burnham to stand before the Saturday Afternoon Club and openly chide its members for their failure, because most of his other encounters over exposition business invariably became exercises in self-restraint, especially when he went before the fair's many and still-multiplying committees. This constant Victorian minuet of false grace consumed time. He needed more power—not for his own ego but for the sake of the exposition. Unless the pace of decision-making accelerated, he knew, the fair would fall irreparably behind schedule, yet if anything the barriers to efficiency were increasing in size and number. The Exposition Company's shrinking war chest had driven its relationship with the National Commission to a new low, with Director-General Davis arguing that any new federal money should be controlled by his commission. The commission seemed to form new departments every day, each with a paid chief—Davis named a superintendent of sheep, for a salary that today would total about $60,000 a year—and each claiming some piece of jurisdiction that Burnham thought belonged to him.

Soon the struggle for control distilled to a personal conflict between Burnham and Davis, its primary battlefield a disagreement over who should control the artistic design of exhibits and interiors. Burnham thought it obvious that the territory belonged to him. Davis believed otherwise.

At first Burnham tried the oblique approach. "We are now organizing a special interior decorative and architectural force to handle this part," he wrote to Davis, "and I have the honor to offer the services of my department to yours in such matters. I feel a delicacy in having my men suggest to yours artistic arrangements, forms and decorations of exhibits, without your full approval, which I hereby respectfully ask."

But Davis told a reporter, "I think it is pretty well understood by this time that no one but the Director-General and his agents have anything to do with exhibits."

The conflict simmered. On March 14 Burnham joined Davis for dinner with Japan's delegate to the fair, at the Chicago Club. Afterward Davis and Burnham remained at the club arguing quietly until five o'clock the next morning. "The time was well spent," he wrote to Margaret, who was then out of town, "and we have come to a better feeling so that the path will be much smoother from this time forward."

An uncharacteristic weariness crept into his letter. He told Margaret he planned to end work early that night and go to Evanston, "and sleep in your dear bed, my love, and I shall dream of you. What a rush this life is! Where do the years go to?"

There were moments of grace. Burnham looked forward to evenings on the grounds when his lieutenants and visiting architects would gather for dinner at the shanty and converse into the night in front of Burnham's immense fireplace. Burnham treasured the camaraderie and the stories. Olmsted recounted the endless trials of protecting Central Park from ill-thought modifications. Colonel Edmund Rice, chief of the exposition's Columbian Guard, described what it was like to stand in a shaded wood at Gettysburg as Pickett launched his men across the intervening field.

Late in March 1892 Burnham invited his sons to join him at the shanty for one of their periodic overnight stays. They failed to arrive at the scheduled time. At first everyone attributed their absence to a routine railroad delay, but as the hours passed, Burnham's anxiety grew. He knew as well as anyone that train wrecks in Chicago were nearly a daily occurrence.

Darkness began to fall, but at last the boys arrived. Their train had been held up by a broken bridge on the Milwaukee & St. Paul line. They reached the shanty, Burnham wrote to Margaret, "just in time to hear Col. Rice tell some yarns about the war and life in the plains among the scouts and Indians."

As Burnham wrote this letter, his sons were near at hand. "They are very happy to be here and are now looking at the large photographic album with Mr. Geraldine." The album was a collection of construction photographs taken by Charles Dudley Arnold, a photographer from Buffalo, New York, whom Burnham had hired as the fair's official photographer. Arnold also was present, and soon the children were to join him in a sketching session.

Burnham closed, "We are all well and satisfied with the amount and variety of work our good fortune has given us to do."

Such peaceful intervals never lasted long.

The conflict between Burnham and Davis again flared to life. The directors of the Exposition Company did decide to seek a direct appropriation from Congress, but their request triggered a congressional investigation of the fair's expenditures. Burnham and President Baker expected a general review but instead found themselves grilled about the most mundane expenses. For example, when Baker listed the total spent on carriage rental, the subcommittee demanded the names of the people who rode in the carriages. At one session in Chicago the committee asked Davis to estimate the final cost of the exposition. Without consulting Burnham, Davis gave an estimate ten percent below the amount Burnham had calculated for President Baker, which Baker had then included in his own statement to investigators. Davis's testimony carried with it the unstated accusation that Burnham and Baker had inflated the amount of money needed to complete the fair.

Burnham leaped to his feet. The subcommittee chairman ordered him to sit. Burnham remained standing. He was angry, barely able to keep himself composed. "Mr. Davis has not been to see me or any of my people," he said, "and any figures he has given he has jumped at. He knows nothing about the matter."

His outburst offended the subcommittee chairman. "I object to any such remarks addressed to a witness before this committee," the chairman said, "and I will ask that Mr. Burnham withdraw his remark."

At first Burnham refused. Then, reluctantly, he agreed to withdraw the part about Davis knowing nothing. But only that part. He did not apologize.

The committee left for Washington to study the evidence and report on whether an appropriation was warranted. The congressmen, Burnham wrote, "are dazed with the size and scope of this enterprise. We gave them each a huge pile of data to digest, and I think their report will be funny, because I know that months would not be enough time for me to work out a report, even with my knowledge."

⌁

On paper at least, the fair's Midway Plaisance began to take shape. Professor Putnam had believed the Midway ought first and foremost to provide an education about alien cultures. Sol Bloom felt no such duty.

The Midway was to be fun, a great pleasure garden stretching for more than a mile from Jackson Park all the way to the border of Washington Park. It would thrill, titillate, and if all went well perhaps even shock. He considered his great strength to be "spectacular advertising." He placed notices in publications around the world to make it known that the Midway was to be an exotic realm of unusual sights, sounds, and scents. There would be authentic villages from far-off lands inhabited by authentic villagers—even Pygmies, if Lieutenant Schufeldt succeeded. Bloom recognized also that as czar of the Midway he no longer had to worry about seeking a concession for his Algerian Village. He could approve the village himself. He produced a contract and sent it off to Paris.

Bloom's knack for promotion caught the attention of other fair officials, who came to him for help in raising the exposition's overall profile. At one point he was called upon to help make reporters understand how truly immense the Manufactures and Liberal Arts Building would be. So far the exposition's publicity office had given the press a detailed list of monumental but dreary statistics. "I could tell they weren't in the least interested in the number of acres or tons of steel," Bloom wrote, "so I said, 'Look at it this way—it's going to be big enough to hold the entire standing army of Russia.' "

Bloom had no idea whether Russia even had a standing army, let alone how many soldiers it might include and how many square feet they would cover. Nonetheless, the fact became gospel throughout America. Readers of Rand, McNally's exposition guidebooks eventually found themselves thrilling to the vision of millions of fur-hatted men squeezed onto the building's thirty-two-acre floor.

Bloom felt no remorse.

The Angel from Dwight

IN THE SPRING OF 1892 Holmes's assistant Benjamin Pitezel found himself in the city of Dwight, Illinois, about seventy-five miles southwest of Chicago, taking the famous Keeley cure for alcoholism. Patients stayed in the three-story Livingston Hotel, a red-brick building of simple appealing design, with arched windows and a veranda along the full length of its façade, a fine place to rest between injections of Dr. Leslie Enraught Keeley's "gold cure." Gold was the most famous ingredient in a red, white, and blue solution nicknamed the "barber pole" that employees of the Keeley Institute injected into patients' arms three times a day. The needle, one of large nineteenth-century bore—like having a garden hose shoved into a bicep—invariably deposited a yellow aureole on the skin surrounding the injection site, a badge for some, an unsightly blemish for others. The rest of the formula was kept secret, but as best doctors and chemists could tell, the solution included substances that imparted a pleasant state of euphoria and sedation trimmed with amnesia—an effect the Chicago post office found problematic, for each year it wound up holding hundreds of letters sent from Dwight that lacked important elements of their destination addresses. The senders simply forgot that things like names and street numbers were necessary for the successful delivery of mail.

Pitezel had long been a heavy drinker, but his drinking must have become debilitating, for it was Holmes who sent him to Keeley and paid for his treatment. He explained it to Pitezel as a gesture born of kindness, a return for Pitezel's loyalty. As always, he had other motives. He recognized that Pitezel's drinking impaired his usefulness and threatened to disrupt schemes already in play. Holmes later said of Pitezel, "he was too valuable a man, even with his failings taken into consideration, for me to dispense with." It's likely Holmes also wanted Pitezel to gather whatever intelligence he could about the cure and its labeling, so that he could mimic the product and sell it through his own mail-order drug company. Later, indeed, Holmes would establish his own curative spa on the second floor of his Englewood building and call it the Silver Ash Institute. The Keeley cure was amazingly popular. Thousands of people came to Dwight to shed their intemperate ways; many thousands more bought Dr. Keeley's oral version of the cure, which he marketed in bottles so distinctive that he urged purchasers to destroy the empties, to keep unscrupulous companies from filling them with their own concoctions.

Every day Pitezel joined three dozen other men in the daily ritual of "passing through the line" to receive his injections. Women received theirs in their own rooms and were kept separated from the men to protect their reputations. In Chicago hostesses always knew when guests had taken the cure, because upon being offered a drink, those guests invariably answered, "No, thank you. I've been to Dwight."

Pitezel returned to Englewood in April. The psychotropic powers of Keeley's injections may account for the story Pitezel now told Holmes, of how at Keeley he had met a young woman of great beauty—to hear him tell it, preternatural beauty—named Emeline Cigrand. She was blond, twenty-four years old, and since 1891 had worked as a stenographer in Dr. Keeley's office. Pitezel's almost hallucinatory description must have tantalized Holmes, for he wrote to Cigrand and offered her a job as his personal secretary, at twice the salary she was making in Keeley. "A flattering offer," as a member of the Cigrand family later described it.

Emeline accepted without hesitation. The institute had a certain cachet, but the village of Dwight was no Chicago. To be able to earn twice her salary and live in that city of legendary glamour and excitement, with the world's fair set to open in a year, made the offer irresistible. She left Keeley in May, bringing along her $800 in savings. Upon arriving in Englewood, she rented rooms in a boardinghouse near Holmes's building.

Pitezel had exaggerated Emeline's beauty, Holmes saw, but not by much. She was indeed lovely, with luminous blond hair. Immediately Holmes deployed his tools of seduction, his soothing voice and touch and frank blue gaze.

He bought her flowers and took her to the Timmerman Opera House down the block. He gave her a bicycle. They spent evenings riding together on the smooth macadam of Yale and Harvard streets, the picture of a happy young couple blessed with looks and money. ("White pique hats with black watered-ribbon bands and a couple of knife feathers set at the side are the latest novelty for women cyclists," the *Tribune*'s society column observed.) As Emeline became more accustomed to her "wheel," a term everyone still used even though the old and deadly hugewheeled bicycles of the past had become thoroughly obsolete, she and Holmes took longer and longer rides and often rode along the willowed Midway to Jackson Park to watch the construction of the world's fair, where inevitably they found themselves among thousands of other people, many of them also bicyclists.

On a few Sundays Emeline and Holmes rode into the park itself, where they saw that construction was still in its early phase—a surprise, given the rapid onset of the fair's two most important deadlines, Dedication Day and Opening Day. Much of the park was still barren land, and the biggest building, Manufactures and Liberal Arts, was barely under way. A few buildings had advanced at a far greater pace and appeared to be more or less complete, in particular the Mines Building and the Woman's Building. There were so many distinguished-looking men in the park these days—statesmen, princes, architects, and the city's industrial barons. Society matrons came as well, to attend meetings of the Board of Lady Managers. Mrs. Palmer's great black carriage often came roaring through the fair's gate, as did the carriage of her social opposite, Carrie Watson, the madam, her coach distinctive for its gleaming white enamel body and yellow wheels and its black driver in scarlet silk.

Emeline found that riding her bicycle was best in the days after a good downpour. Otherwise the dust billowed like sand over Khartoum and sifted deep into her scalp, where even a good brushing failed to dislodge it.

One afternoon as Emeline sat before her typewriter in Holmes's office, a man entered looking for Holmes. He was tall, with a clean jaw and modest mustache, and wore a cheap suit; in his thirties; good looking, in a way, but at the same time self-effacing and plain—though at the moment he appeared to be angry. He introduced himself as Ned Conner and said he had once run the jewelry counter in the pharmacy downstairs. He had come to discuss a problem with a mortgage.

She knew the name—had heard it somewhere, or seen it in Holmes's papers. She smiled and told Ned that Holmes was out of the building. She had no idea when he would return. Could she help?

Ned's anger cooled. He and Emeline "got to talking about Holmes," as Ned later recalled.

Ned watched her. She was young and pretty—a "handsome blonde," as he later described her. She wore a white shirtwaist and black skirt that accentuated her trim figure, and she was seated beside a window, her hair candescent with sunlight. She sat before a black Remington, new and doubtless never paid for. From his own hard experience and from the look of adoration that entered Emeline's eyes when she spoke of Holmes, Ned guessed her relationship involved a good deal more than typewriting. Later he recalled, "I told her I thought he was a bad lot and that she had better have little to do with him and get away from him as soon as possible."

For the time being, at least, she ignored his advice.

On May 1, 1892, a doctor named M. B. Lawrence and his wife moved into a five-room apartment in Holmes's building, where they often encountered Emeline, although Emeline herself did not yet live in the building. She still occupied rooms in a nearby boardinghouse.

"She was one of the prettiest and most pleasant young women I ever met," said Dr. Lawrence, "and my wife and I learned to think a great deal of her. We saw her every day and she often came in for a few minutes' chat with Mrs. Lawrence." The Lawrences often saw Emeline in Holmes's company. "It was not long," Dr. Lawrence said, "before I became aware that the relations between Miss Cigrand and Mr. Holmes were not strictly those of an employer and employee, but we felt that she was to be more pitied than blamed."

Emeline was infatuated with Holmes. She loved him for his warmth, his caresses, his imperturbable calm, and his glamour. Never had she met a man quite like him. He was even the son of an English lord, a fact he had confided in strictest secrecy. She was to tell no one, which dampened the fun quite a bit but added to the mystery. She did reveal the secret to friends, of course, but only after first securing their oaths that they absolutely would tell no one else. To Emeline, Holmes's claim of lordly heritage had credibility. The name Holmes clearly was English—to know that, all one had to do was read the immensely popular stories of Sir Arthur Conan Doyle. And an English heritage would explain his extraordinary charm and smooth manner, so unusual in brutish, clangorous Chicago.

⁕

Emeline was a warm and outgoing woman. She wrote often to her family in Lafayette, Indiana, and to the friends she had made in Dwight. She acquired friends easily. She still dined at regular intervals with the woman who ran the first boardinghouse in which she had stayed after her arrival in Chicago and considered the woman an intimate friend.

In October two of her second cousins, Dr. and Mrs. B. J. Cigrand, paid her a visit. Dr. Cigrand, a dentist with an office at North and Milwaukee Avenues on Chicago's North Side, had contacted Emeline because he was working on a history of the Cigrand family. They had not previously met. "I was charmed by her pleasing manners and keen wit," Dr. Cigrand said. "She was a splendid woman physically, being tall, well formed, and with a wealth of flaxen hair." Dr. Cigrand and his wife did not encounter Holmes on this visit and in fact never did meet him face to face, but they heard glowing stories from Emeline about his charm, generosity, and business prowess. Emeline took her cousins on a tour of Holmes's building and told them of his effort to transform it into a hotel for exposition guests. She explained, too, how the elevated railroad being erected over Sixty-third Street would carry guests directly to Jackson Park. No one doubted that by the summer of 1893 armies of visitors would be advancing on Englewood. To Emeline, success seemed inevitable.

Emeline's enthusiasm was part of her charm. She was headlong in love with her young physician and thus in love with all that he did. But Dr. Cigrand did not share her glowing assessment of the building and its prospects. To him, the building was gloomy and imposing, out of spirit with its surrounding structures. Every other building of substance in Englewood seemed to be charged with the energy of anticipation, not just of the world's fair but of a grand future expanding far beyond the fair's end. Within just a couple of blocks of Sixty-third rose huge, elaborate houses of many colors and textures, and down the street stood the Timmerman Opera House and the adjacent New Julien Hotel, whose owners had spent heavily on fine materials and expert craftsmen. In contrast, Holmes's building was dead space, like the corner of a room where the gaslight could not reach. Clearly Holmes had not consulted an architect, at least not a competent one. The building's corridors were dark and pocked with too many doors. The lumber was low grade, the carpentry slipshod. Passages veered at odd angles.

Still, Emeline seemed entranced. Dr. Cigrand would have been a cold man indeed to have dashed that sweet, naïve adoration. Later, no doubt, he wished he had been more candid and had listened more closely to the whisper in his head about the wrongness of that building and the discontinuity between its true appearance and Emeline's perception of it. But again, Emeline was in love. It was not his place to wound her. She was young and enraptured, her joy infectious, especially to Dr. Cigrand, the dentist, who saw so little joy from day to day as he reduced grown men of proven courage to tears.

Soon after the Cigrands' visit, Holmes asked Emeline to marry him, and she accepted. He promised her a honeymoon in Europe during which, of course, they would pay a visit to his father, the lord.

Dedication Day

OLMSTED'S TEETH HURT, HIS EARS roared, and he could not sleep, yet throughout the first months of 1892 he kept up a pace that would have been punishing for a man one-third his age. He traveled to Chicago, Asheville, Knoxville, Louisville, and Rochester, each overnight leg compounding his distress. In Chicago, despite the tireless efforts of his young lieutenant Harry Codman, the work was far behind schedule, the task ahead growing more enormous by the day. The first major deadline, the dedication set for October 21, 1892, seemed impossibly near—and would have seemed even more so had not fair officials changed the original date, October 12, to allow New York City to hold its own Columbus celebration. Given the calumny New York previously had shoveled on Chicago, the postponement was an act of surprising grace.

Construction delays elsewhere on the grounds were especially frustrating for Olmsted. When contractors fell behind, his own work fell behind. His completed work also suffered. Workmen trampled his plantings and destroyed his roads. The U.S. Government Building was a case in point. "All over its surroundings," reported Rudolf Ulrich, his landscape superintendent, "material of any kind and all descriptions was piled up and scattered in such profusion that only repeated and persistent pressure brought to bear upon the officials in charge could gain any headway in beginning the work; and, even then, improvements being well under way, no regard was paid to them. What had been accomplished one day would be spoiled the next."

The delays and damage angered Olmsted, but other matters distressed him even more. Unbelievably, despite Olmsted's hectoring, Burnham still seemed to consider steam-powered launches an acceptable choice for the exposition's boat service. And no one seemed to share his conviction that the Wooded Island must remain free of all structures.

The island had come under repeated assault, prompting a resurfacing of Olmsted's old anger about the compulsion of clients to tinker with his landscapes. Everyone wanted space on the island. First it was Theodore Thomas, conductor of Chicago's symphony, who saw the island as the ideal site, the *only* site, for a music hall worthy of the fair. Olmsted would not allow it. Next came Theodore Roosevelt, head of the U.S. Civil Service Commission and a human gunboat. The island, he insisted, was perfect for the hunting camp exhibit of his Boone and Crockett Club. Not surprisingly, given Roosevelt's power in Washington, the politicians of the fair's National Commission strongly endorsed his plan. Burnham, partly to keep the peace, also urged Olmsted to accept it. "Would you object to its being placed on the north end of the Island, snuggled in among the trees, purely as an exhibit, provided it shall be so concealed as to only be noticed casually by those on the Island and not at all from the shore?"

Olmsted did object. He agreed to let Roosevelt place his camp on a lesser island but would not allow any buildings, only "a few tents, some horses, camp-fire, etc." Later he permitted the installation of a small hunter's cabin.

Next came the U.S. government, seeking to place an Indian exhibit on the island, and then Professor Putnam, the fair's chief of ethnology, who saw the island as the ideal site for several exotic villages. The government of Japan also wanted the island. "They propose an outdoor exhibit of their temples and, as has been usual, they desire space on the wooded island," Burnham wrote in February 1892. To Burnham it now seemed inevitable that something would occupy the island. The setting was just too appealing. Burnham urged Olmsted to accept Japan's proposal. "It seems beyond any question to be the thing fitting to the locality and I cannot see that it will in any manner detract essentially from the features which you care for. They propose to do the most exquisitely beautiful things and desire to leave the buildings as a gift to the City of Chicago after the close of the Fair."

Fearing much worse, Olmsted agreed.

It did not help his mood any that as he battled to protect the island, he learned of another attack on his beloved Central Park. At the instigation of a small group of wealthy New Yorkers, the state legislature had quietly passed a law authorizing the construction of a "speedway" on the west side of the park so that the rich could race their carriages. The public responded with outrage. Olmsted weighed in with a letter describing the proposed road as "unreasonable, unjust and immoral." The legislature backed off.

His insomnia and pain, the crushing workload, and his mounting frustration all tore at his spirit until by the end of March he felt himself on the verge of physical and emotional collapse. The intermittent depression that had shadowed him throughout his adult life was about to envelop him once again. "When Olmsted is blue," a friend once wrote, "the logic of his despondency is crushing and terrible."

Olmsted, however, believed that all he needed was a good rest. In keeping with the therapeutic mores of the age, he decided to do his convalescing in Europe, where the scenery also would provide an opportunity for him to enrich his visual vocabulary. He planned forays to public gardens and parks and the grounds of the old Paris exposition.

He put his eldest son, John, in charge of the Brookline office and left Harry Codman in Chicago to guide the work on the world's fair. At the last minute he decided to bring along two of his children, Marion and Rick, and another young man, Phil Codman, who was Harry's younger brother. For Marion and the boys, it promised to be a dream journey; for Olmsted it became something rather more dark.

They sailed on Saturday, April 2, 1892, and arrived in Liverpool under a barrage of hail and snow.

In Chicago Sol Bloom received a cable from France that startled him. He read it a couple of times to make sure it said what he thought it said. His Algerians, scores of them along with all their animals and material possessions, were already at sea, sailing for America and the fair—one year early.

"They had picked the right month," Bloom said, "but the wrong year."

———

Olmsted found the English countryside charming, the weather bleak and morbid. After a brief stay at the home of relatives in Chislehurt, he and the boys left for Paris. Daughter Marion stayed behind.

In Paris Olmsted went to the old exposition grounds. The gardens were sparse, suppressed by a long winter, and the buildings had not weathered well, but enough of the fair remained to give him "a tolerable idea" of what the exposition once had been. Clearly the site was still popular. During one Sunday visit Olmsted and the boys found four bands playing, refreshment stands open, and a few thousand people roaming the paths. A long line had formed at the base of the Eiffel Tower.

With the Chicago fair always in mind, Olmsted examined every detail. The lawns were "rather poor," the gravel walks "not pleasant to the eye nor to the foot." He found the Paris fair's extensive use of formal flower beds objectionable. "It seemed to me," he wrote, in a letter to John in Brookline, "that at the least it must have been extremely disquieting, gaudy & childish, if not savage and an injury to the Exposition, through its disturbance of dignity, and injury to breadth, unity & composure." He reiterated his insistence that in Chicago "simplicity and reserve will be practiced and petty effects and frippery avoided."

The visit rekindled his concern that in the quest to surpass the Paris exposition Burnham and his architects had lost sight of what a world's fair ought to be. The Paris buildings, Olmsted wrote, "have much more color and much more ornament in color, but much less in moulding and sculpture than I had supposed. They show I think more fitness for their purposes, seem more designed for the occasion and to be less like grand permanent architectural monuments than ours are to be. I question if ours are not at fault in this respect and if they are not going to look too assuming of architectural stateliness and to be overbonded with sculptural and other efforts for grandeur and grandiloquent pomp."

Olmsted liked traveling with his youthful entourage. In a letter to his wife in Brookline he wrote, "I am having a great deal of enjoyment, and I hope laying in a good stock of better health." Soon after the party returned to Chislehurst, however, Olmsted's health degraded and insomnia again shattered his nights. He wrote to Harry Codman, who was himself ill with a strange abdominal illness, "I can only conclude now that I am older and more used up than I had supposed."

A doctor, Henry Rayner, paid a social visit to Chislehurst to meet Olmsted. He happened to be a specialist in treating nervous disorders and was so appalled by Olmsted's appearance that he offered to take him to his own house in Hampstead Heath, outside London, and care for him personally. Olmsted accepted.

Despite Rayner's close attention, Olmsted's condition did not improve; his stay at Hampstead Heath became wearisome. "You know that I am practically in prison here," he wrote to Harry Codman on June 16, 1892. "Every day I look for decided improvement and thus far everyday, I am disappointed." Dr. Rayner too was perplexed, according to Olmsted. "He says, with confidence, after repeated examinations, of all my anatomy, that I have no organic trouble and that I may reasonably expect under favorable circumstances to keep at work for several years to come. He regards my present trouble as a variation in form of the troubles which led me to come abroad."

Most days Olmsted was driven by carriage through the countryside, "every day more or less on a different road," to view gardens, churchyards, private parks, and the natural landscape. Nearly every ornamental flowerbed offended him. He dismissed them as "childish, vulgar, flaunting, or impertinent, out of place and discordant." The countryside itself, however, charmed him: "there is nothing in America to be compared with the pastoral or with the picturesque beauty that is common property in England. I cannot go out without being delighted. The view before me as I write, veiled by the rain, is just enchanting." The loveliest scenes, he found, were comprised of the simplest, most natural juxtapositions of native plants. "The finest combination is one of gorse, sweet briar, brambles, hawthorn, and ivy. Even when there is no bloom this is charming. And these things can be had by the hundred thousand at very low prices."

At times the scenes he saw challenged his vision of Jackson Park, at other times they affirmed it. "Everywhere the best ornamental grounds that we see are those in which vines and creepers are outwitting the gardener. We can't have little vines and weeds enough." He knew there was too little time to let nature alone produce such effects. "Let us as much as possible, train out creepers, and branches of trees, upon bridges, pulling down and nailing the branches, aiming to obtain shade and reflection of foliage and broken obscuration of water."

Above all, his sorties reinforced his belief that the Wooded Island, despite the Japanese temple, should be made as wild as possible. "I think more than ever of the value of the island," he wrote to Harry Codman, "and of the importance of using all possible, original means of securing impervious screening, dense massive piles of foliage on its borders; with abundant variety of small detail in abject subordination to general effect. . . . There cannot be enough of bulrush, adlumia, Madeira vine, catbriar, virgin's bower, brambles, sweet peas, Jimson weed, milkweed, the smaller western sunflowers and morning glories."

But he also recognized that the wildness he sought would have to be tempered with excellent groundskeeping. He worried that Chicago would not be up to the task. "The standard of an English laborer, hack driver or cad in respect to neatness, smugness and elegance of gardens and grounds and paths and ways is infinitely higher than that of a Chicago merchant prince or virtuoso," he wrote to Codman, "and we shall be disgraced if we fail to work up to a far higher level than our masters will be prepared to think suitable."

Overall Olmsted remained confident that his exposition landscape would succeed. A new worry troubled him, however. "The only cloud I see over the Exposition now is the Cholera," he wrote in a letter to his Brookline office. "The accounts from Russia and from Paris this morning are alarming."

As Sol Bloom's Algerians neared New York Harbor, workers assigned to the Midway erected temporary buildings to house them. Bloom went to New York to meet the ship and reserved two traincars to bring the villagers and their cargo back to Chicago.

As the Algerians left the ship, they began moving in all directions at once. "I could see them getting lost, being run over, and landing in jail," Bloom said. No one seemed to be in charge. Bloom raced up to them, shouting commands in French and English. A giant black-complected man walked up to Bloom and in perfect House of Lords English said, "I suggest you be more civil. Otherwise I may lose my temper and throw you into the water."

The man identified himself as Archie, and as the two settled into a more peaceful conversation, he revealed to Bloom that he had spent a decade in London serving as a rich man's bodyguard. "At present," he said, "I am responsible for conveying my associates to a place called Chicago. I understand it is somewhere in the hinterland."

Bloom handed him a cigar and proposed that he become his bodyguard and assistant.

"Your offer," Archie said, "is quite satisfactory."

Both men lit up and puffed smoke into the fragrant murk above New York Harbor.

Burnham fought to boost the rate of construction, especially of the Manufactures and Liberal Arts Building, which had to be completed by Dedication Day. In March, with just half a year remaining until the dedication, he invoked the "czar" clause of his construction contracts. He ordered the builder of the Electricity Building to double his workforce and to put the men to work at night under electric lights. He threatened the Manufactures contractor with the same fate if he did not increase the pace of his work.

Burnham had all but given up hope of surpassing the Eiffel Tower. Most recently he had turned down another outlandish idea, this from an earnest young Pittsburgh engineer who had attended his lecture to the

Saturday Afternoon Club. The man was credible enough—his company held the contract for inspecting all the steel used in the fair's structures— but the thing he proposed to build just did not seem feasible. "Too fragile," Burnham told him. The public, he said, would be afraid.

A hostile spring further hampered the fair's progress. On Tuesday, April 5, 1892, at 6:50 A.M., a sudden windstorm demolished the fair's just-finished pumping station and tore down sixty-five feet of the Illinois State Building. Three weeks later another storm destroyed eight hundred feet of the south wall of the Manufactures and Liberal Arts Building. "The wind," the *Tribune* observed, "seems to have a grudge against the World's Fair grounds."

To find ways to accelerate the work, Burnham called the eastern architects to Chicago. One looming problem was how to color the exteriors of the main buildings, especially the staff-coated palisades of the Manufactures and Liberal Arts Building. During the meeting an idea arose that in the short run promised a dramatic acceleration of the work, but that eventually served to fix the fair in the world's imagination as a thing of otherworldly beauty.

⁌————⁍

By all rights, the arena of exterior decoration belonged to William Pretyman, the fair's official director of color. Burnham admitted later that he had hired Pretyman for the job "largely on account of his great friendship for John Root." Pretyman was ill suited to the job. Harriet Monroe, who knew him and his wife, wrote, "His genius was betrayed by lofty and indomitable traits of character which could not yield or compromise. And so his life was a tragedy of inconsequence."

The day of the meeting Pretyman was on the East Coast. The architects proceeded without him. "I was urging everyone on, knowing I had an awful fight against time," Burnham said. "We talked about the colors, and finally the thought came, 'let us make it all perfectly white.' I do not remember who made that suggestion. It might have been one of those things that reached all minds at once. At any rate, I decided it."

The Mines Building, designed by Chicago's Solon S. Beman, was nearly finished. It became the test building. Burnham ordered it painted a creamy white. Pretyman returned and "was outraged," Burnham recalled.

Pretyman insisted that any decision on color was his alone.

"I don't see it that way," Burnham told him. "The decision is mine."

"All right," Pretyman said. "I will get out."

Burnham did not miss him. "He was a brooding sort of man and very cranky," Burnham said. "I let him go, then told Charles McKim that I would have to have a man who could actually take charge of it, and that I would not decide from the point of friendship."

McKim recommended the New York painter Francis Millet, who had sat in on the color meeting. Burnham hired him.

Millet quickly proved his worth. After some experimentation he settled on "ordinary white lead and oil" as the best paint for staff, then developed a means of applying the paint not by brush but through a hose with a special nozzle fashioned from a length of gas pipe—the first spray paint. Burnham nicknamed Millet and his paint crews "the Whitewash Gang."

In the first week of May a powerful storm dropped an ocean of rain on Chicago and again caused the Chicago River to reverse flow. Again the sewage threatened the city's water supply. The decaying carcass of a horse was spotted bobbing near one of the intake cribs.

This new surge underscored for Burnham the urgency of completing his plan to pipe Waukesha spring water to the fair by Opening Day. Earlier, in July 1891, the exposition had granted a contract for the work to the Hygeia Mineral Springs Company, headed by an entrepreneur named J. E. McElroy, but the company had accomplished little. In March Burnham ordered Dion Geraldine, his chief construction superintendent, to press the matter "with the utmost vigor and see that no delay occurs."

Hygeia secured rights to lay its pipe from its springhouse in Waukesha through the village itself but failed to anticipate the intensity of opposition from citizens who feared the pipeline would disfigure their landscape and drain their famous springs. Hygeia's McElroy, under mounting pressure from Burnham, turned to desperate measures.

On Saturday evening, May 7, 1892, McElroy loaded a special train with pipes, picks, shovels, and three hundred men and set off for Waukesha to dig his pipeline under cover of darkness.

Word of the expedition beat the train to Waukesha. As it pulled into the station, someone rang the village firebell, and soon a large force of men armed with clubs, pistols, and shotguns converged on the train. Two fire engines arrived hissing steam, their crews ready to blast the pipelayers with water. One village leader told McElroy that if he went ahead with his plan, he would not leave town alive.

Soon another thousand or so townspeople joined the small army at the station. One group of men dragged a cannon from the town hall and trained it on Hygeia's bottling plant.

After a brief standoff, McElroy and the pipelayers went back to Chicago.

Burnham still wanted that water. Workers had already laid pipes in Jackson Park for two hundred springwater booths.

McElroy gave up trying to run pipes directly into the village of Waukesha. Instead he bought a spring in the town of Big Bend, twelve miles south of Waukesha, just inside the Waukesha County line. Fair visitors would be able to drink Waukesha springwater after all.

That the water came from the county and not the famous village was a subtlety upon which Burnham and McElroy did not dwell.

⁓———

In Jackson Park everyone became caught up in the accelerating pace of construction. As the buildings rose, the architects spotted flaws in their designs but found the forward crush of work so overwhelming, it threatened to leave the flaws locked in stone, or at least staff. Frank Millet unofficially kept watch over the buildings of the eastern architects during their lengthy absences from the park, lest some ad hoc decision cause irreparable aesthetic damage. On June 6, 1892, he wrote to Charles McKim, designer of the Agriculture Building, "You had better write a letter embodying all the ideas of changes you have, because before you know it they'll have you by the umbilicus. I staved them off from a cement floor in the Rotunda to-day and insisted that you must have brick. . . . It takes no end of time and worry to get a thing settled right but only a second to have orders given out for a wrong thing to be done. All these remarks are in strict confidence, and I write in this way to urge you to be explicit and flat-footed in your wishes."

At the Manufactures and Liberal Arts Building workers employed by contractor Francis Agnew began the dangerous process of raising the giant iron trusses that would support the building's roof and create the widest span of unobstructed interior space ever attempted.

The workers installed three sets of parallel railroad tracks along the length of the building. Atop these, on railcar wheels or "trucks," they erected a "traveler," a giant derrick consisting of three tall towers spanned at the top by a platform. Workers using the traveler could lift and position two trusses at a time. George Post's design called for twenty-two trusses, each weighing two hundred tons. Just getting the components to the park had required six hundred railcars.

On Wednesday, June 1, exposition photographer Charles Arnold took a photograph of the building to record its progress. Anyone looking at that photograph would have had to conclude that the building could not possibly be finished in the four and a half months that remained until Dedication Day. The trusses were in place but no roof. The walls were just beginning to rise. When Arnold took the photograph, hundreds of men were at work on the building, but its scale was so great that none of the men was immediately visible. The ladders that rose from one level of scaffold to the next had all the substance of matchsticks and imparted to the structure an aura of fragility. In the foreground stood mountains of debris.

Two weeks later Arnold returned for another photograph and captured a very different scene—one of devastation.

On the night of June 13, just after nine o'clock, another abrupt storm had struck the fairgrounds, and this one also seemed to single out the Manufactures and Liberal Arts Building. A large portion of the building's north end collapsed, which in turn caused the failure of an elevated gallery designed to ring the interior of the building. One hundred thousand feet of lumber crashed to the floor. Arnold's photograph of the aftermath showed a Lilliputian man, possibly Burnham, standing before a great mound of shattered wood and tangled steel.

This, of all buildings.

The contractor, Francis Agnew, acknowledged the wall had been inadequately braced but blamed this condition on Burnham for pushing the men to build too quickly.

Now Burnham pushed them even harder. He made good on his threat and doubled the number of men working on the building. They worked at night, in rain, in stifling heat. In August alone the building took three lives. Elsewhere on the grounds four other men died and dozens more suffered all manner of fractures, burns, and lacerations. The fair, according to one later appraisal, was a more dangerous place to work than a coal mine.

Burnham intensified his drive for more power. The constant clash between the Exposition Company and the National Commission had become nearly unbearable. Even the congressional investigators had recognized that the overlapping jurisdiction was a source of discord and needless expense. Their report recommended that Davis's salary be cut in half, a clear sign that the balance of power had shifted. The company and commission worked out a truce. On August 24 the executive committee named Burnham director of works. Chief of everything.

Soon afterward Burnham dispatched letters to all his department heads, including Olmsted. "I have assumed personal control of the active work within the grounds of the World's Columbian Exposition," he wrote. "Henceforward, and until further notice, you will report to and receive orders from me exclusively."

In Pittsburgh the young steel engineer became more convinced than ever that his challenge to the Eiffel Tower could succeed. He asked a partner in his inspection firm, W. F. Gronau, to calculate the novel forces that would play among the components of his structure. In engineering parlance, it embodied little "dead load," the static weight of immobile masses of brick and steel. Nearly all of it was "live load," meaning weight that changes over time, as when a train passes over a bridge. "I had no precedent," Gronau said. After three weeks of intense work, however, he came up with detailed specifications. The numbers were persuasive, even to Burnham. In June the Ways and Means Committee agreed that the thing should be built. They granted a concession.

The next day the committee revoked it—second thoughts, after a night spent dreaming of freak winds and shrieking steel and two thousand lives gone in a wink. One member of the committee now called it a "monstrosity." A chorus of engineers chanted that the thing could not be built, at least not with any margin of safety.

Its young designer still did not concede defeat, however. He spent $25,000 on drawings and additional specifications and used them to recruit a cadre of investors that included two prominent engineers, Robert Hunt, head of a major Chicago firm, and Andrew Onderdonk, famous for helping construct the Canadian Pacific Railway.

Soon he sensed a change. The new man in charge of the Midway, Sol Bloom, had struck like a bolt of lightning and seemed amenable to just about anything—the more novel and startling the better. And Burnham had gained almost limitless power over the construction and operation of the fair.

The engineer readied himself for a third try.

⌁

In the first week of September 1892 Olmsted and his young party left England for home, departing Liverpool aboard the *City of New York*. The seas were high, the crossing difficult. Seasickness felled Marion and left Rick perpetually queasy. Olmsted's own health again declined. His insomnia came back. He wrote, "I was more disabled when I returned than when I left." Now, however, he had no time to recuperate. Dedication Day was only a month away, and Harry Codman was again ill, incapacitated by the same stomach problem that had struck him during the summer. Olmsted left for Chicago to take over direct supervision of the work while Codman recovered. "I am still tortured a good deal with neuralgia and toothache," Olmsted wrote, "and I am tired and have a growing dread of worry & anxiety."

In Chicago he found a changed park. The Mines Building was finished, as was the Fisheries Building. Most of the other buildings were well under way, including, incredibly, the giant Manufactures and Liberal Arts Building, where hundreds of workers swarmed its scaffolds and roof. The building's floor alone had consumed five traincar loads of nails.

Amid all this work, however, the landscape had suffered. Temporary tracks latticed the grounds. Wagons had gouged chasms across paths, roads, and would-be lawns. Litter lay everywhere. A first-time visitor might wonder if Olmsted's men had done any work at all.

Olmsted, of course, knew that tremendous progress had been made, but it was the sort that escaped casual notice. Lagoons existed now where once there had been barren land. The elevated sites upon which the buildings stood had not existed until his grading teams created them. The previous spring his men had planted nearly everything raised in the exposition's nurseries, plus an additional 200,000 trees, aquatic plants, and ferns, and 30,000 more willow cuttings, all this under the direction of his aptly named head gardener, E. Dehn.

In the time left before Dedication Day Burnham wanted Olmsted's men to concentrate on cleaning the grounds and dressing them with flowers and temporary lawns of sod, actions that Olmsted understood were necessary but that clashed with his career-long emphasis on designing for scenic effects that might not be achieved for decades. "Of course the main work suffers," he wrote.

One indisputably positive development had occurred during his absence, however. Burnham had awarded the boat concession to a company called the Electric Launch and Navigation Company, which had produced a lovely electric vessel of exactly the character Olmsted wanted.

On Dedication Day even the press was polite enough to overlook the stark appearance of the grounds and the unfinished feel of the Manufactures and Liberal Arts Building. To have done otherwise would have been an act of disloyalty to Chicago and the nation.

The dedication had been anticipated nationwide. Francis J. Bellamy, an editor of *Youth's Companion,* thought it would be a fine thing if on that day all the schoolchildren of America, in unison, offered something to their nation. He composed a pledge that the Bureau of Education mailed to virtually every school. As originally worded, it began, "I pledge allegiance to my Flag and to the Republic for which it stands . . ."

A great parade brought Burnham and other dignitaries to the Manufactures and Liberal Arts Building, where a standing army of 140,000 Chicagoans filled the thirty-two-acre floor. Shafts of sunlight struck through the rising mist of human breath. Five thousand yellow chairs stood on the red-carpeted speaker's platform, and in these chairs sat businessmen dressed in black, and foreign commissioners and clerics in scarlet, purple, green, and gold. Ex-mayor Carter Harrison, again running for a fifth term, strode about shaking hands, his black slouch hat raising cheers from supporters in the crowd. At the opposite end of the building a five-thousand-voice choir sang Handel's "Hallelujah" chorus to the accompaniment of five hundred musicians. At one point a spectator recalled, "Ninety thousand people suddenly rose and stood upon their feet and simultaneously waved and fluttered ninety thousand snowy pocket-handkerchiefs; the air was cut into dusty spirals, which vibrated to the great iron-ribbed ceiling. . . . One had a sense of dizziness, as if the entire building rocked."

The chamber was so immense that visual signals had to be used to let the chorus know when a speaker had stopped talking and a new song could begin. Microphones did not yet exist, so only a small portion of the audience actually heard any speeches. The rest, with faces contorted from the strain of trying to listen, saw distant men gesturing wildly into the sound-killing miasma of whispers, coughs and creaking shoe leather. Harriet Monroe, the poet who had been John Root's sister-in-law, was there and watched as two of the nation's greatest speakers, Colonel

Henry Watterson of Kentucky and Chauncey M. Depew of New York, took turns at the podium, "both orators waving their windy words toward a vast, whispering, rustling audience which could not hear."

This was a big day for Miss Monroe. She had composed a lengthy poem for the event, her "Columbian Ode," and pestered her many powerful friends into having it placed on the day's program. She watched with pride as an actress read it to the few thousand people close enough to hear it. Unlike the majority of the audience, Monroe believed the poem to be rather a brilliant work, so much so that she had hired a printer to produce five thousand copies for sale to the public. She sold few and attributed the debacle to America's fading love of poetry.

That winter she burned the excess copies for fuel.

Prendergast

On November 28, 1892, Patrick Eugene Joseph Prendergast, the mad Irish immigrant and Harrison supporter, selected one of his postal cards. He was twenty-four years old now and despite his accelerating mental decline was still employed by the *Inter Ocean* as a delivery contractor. The card, like all the others, was four inches wide by five inches long, blank on one face, with postal insignia and a printed one-cent stamp on the other. In this time when writing long letters was everyday practice, men of normal sensibility saw these cards as the most crabbed of media, little better than telegrams, but to Prendergast this square of stiff paper was a vehicle that gave him a voice in the skyscrapers and mansions of the city.

He addressed this particular card to "A. S. Trude, Lawyer." He sketched the letters of the name in large floral script, as if seeking to dispatch the cumbersome duty of addressing the card as quickly as possible, before advancing to the message itself.

That Prendergast had selected Trude to be one of his correspondents was not surprising. Prendergast read widely and possessed a good grasp of the grip-car wrecks, murders, and City Hall machinations covered so fervently by the city's newspapers. He knew that Alfred S. Trude was one of Chicago's best criminal defense attorneys and that from time to time he was hired by the state to serve as prosecutor, a practice customary in particularly important cases.

Prendergast filled the postcard from top margin to bottom, from edge to edge, with little regard for whether the sentences formed level lines or not. He gripped the pen so tightly it impressed channels into the tips of his thumb and forefinger. "My Dear Mr. Trude," he began. "Were you much hurt?" An accident, reported in the press, had caused Trude minor injuries. "Your humble servant hereby begs leave to tender you his sincere sympathy and trusts that while he does not appear before you in person, you nonetheless will not have any doubts as to his real sympathy for you in your misfortunes—you are wished by him a speedy recovery from the results of the accident which you had the misfortune to meet with."

He wrote with a tone of familiarity that presumed Trude would consider him a peer. As the note progressed, his handwriting shrank, until it seemed like something extruded rather than written. "I suppose Mr. Trude that you do understand that the greatest authority on the subject of law is Jesus Christ—and that you also know that the fulfillment of the whole law depends upon the observance of these two commands thou shalt Love God most of all & your neighbor as your self—these are the greatest commands if you please sir."

The note clicked from theme to theme like the wheels of a train crossing a freightyard. "Have you ever saw the picture of the fat man who looked for his dog while his dog was at his feet and still did not have the wit to see what was the matter—have you observed the cat?"

He did not add a closing and did not sign the note. He simply ran out of room, then posted the card.

Trude read the note and at first dismissed it as the work of a crank. The number of troubled men and women seemed to be increasing with each passing year. The jails were full of them, a warden later would testify. Inevitably some became dangerous, like Charles Guiteau, the man who had assassinated President Garfield in Washington.

For no clear reason, Trude kept the card.

"I Want You at Once"

IN LATE NOVEMBER THE young Pittsburgh engineer once again put his proposal for out-Eiffeling Eiffel before the Ways and Means Committee. This time in addition to drawings and specifications he included a list of investors, the names of the prominent men on his board, and proof that he had raised enough money to finance the project to completion. On December 16, 1892, the committee granted him a concession to build his structure in the Midway Plaisance. This time the decision held.

He needed an engineer willing to go to Chicago and supervise the construction effort and thought he knew just the man: Luther V. Rice, assistant engineer of the Union Depot & Tunnel Company, St. Louis. His letter to Rice began, "I have on hand a great project for the World's Fair in Chicago. I am going to build a vertically revolving wheel 250' in dia."

Nowhere in this letter, however, did he reveal the true dimension of his vision: that this wheel would carry thirty-six cars, each about the size of a Pullman, each holding sixty people and equipped with its own lunch counter, and how when filled to capacity the wheel would propel 2,160 people at a time three hundred feet into the sky over Jackson Park, a bit higher than the crown of the now six-year-old Statue of Liberty.

He told Rice, "I want you at once if you can come." He signed the letter: George Washington Gale Ferris.

Chappell Redux

ONE DAY IN THE FIRST week of December 1892 Emeline Cigrand set out for Holmes's building in Englewood bearing a small neatly wrapped parcel. Initially her mood was bright, for the parcel contained an early Christmas present she planned to give to her friends the Lawrences, but as she neared the corner of Sixty-third and Wallace, her spirits dimmed. Where once the building had seemed almost a palace—not for its architectural nobility but for what it promised—now it looked drab and worn. She climbed the stairs to the second floor and went directly to the Lawrences' apartment. The warmth and welcome resurrected her good spirits. She handed the parcel to Mrs. Lawrence, who opened it immediately and pulled from the wrapping a tin plate upon which Emeline had painted a lovely forest.

The gift delighted Mrs. Lawrence but also perplexed her. Christmas was only three weeks off, she said kindly: Why hadn't Emeline simply waited and given the plate then, when Mrs. Lawrence could have offered a gift in return?

Her face brightening, Emeline explained that she was going home to Indiana to spend Christmas with her family.

"She seemed delighted with the anticipation of a visit to them," Mrs. Lawrence said. "She spoke in most affectionate terms of them and seemed as happy as a child." But Mrs. Lawrence also sensed a note of finality in Emeline's voice that suggested Emeline's journey might have another purpose. She said, "You are not going away from us?"

"Well," Emeline said. "I don't know. Maybe."

Mrs. Lawrence laughed. "Why, Mr. Holmes could never get along without you."

Emeline's expression changed. "He could if he had to."

The remark confirmed something for the Lawrences. "It had seemed to me for some time that Miss Cigrand was changing in her feelings toward Holmes," said Dr. Lawrence. "In the light of what has happened since, I believe now that she had found out to a certain extent the real character of Holmes and determined to leave him."

She may have begun to believe the stories she heard in the neighborhood of Holmes's penchant for acquiring things on credit and then not paying for them—stories she had heard all along, for they were rife, but that she at first had dismissed as the gossip of envious hearts. Later there was speculation that Emeline herself had trusted Holmes with her $800 savings, only to have it disappear in a fog of promises of lavish future returns. Ned Conner's warning echoed in her mind. Lately she had begun talking of returning one day to Dwight to resume her work for Dr. Keeley.

Emeline never told the Lawrences good-bye. Her visits simply stopped. That she would leave without a parting word struck Mrs. Lawrence as being very much out of character. She wasn't sure whether to feel wounded or worried. She asked Holmes what he knew about Emeline's absence.

Ordinarily Holmes looked at Mrs. Lawrence with a directness that was unsettling, but now he avoided her gaze. "Oh, she's gone away to get married," Holmes said, as if nothing could have interested him less.

The news shocked Mrs. Lawrence. "I don't see why she didn't mention something to me about getting married."

It was a secret, Holmes explained: Emeline and her betrothed had revealed their wedding plans only to him.

But for Mrs. Lawrence this explanation only raised more questions. Why would the couple want such privacy? Why had Emeline said nothing to Mrs. Lawrence, when together they had shared so many other confidences?

Mrs. Lawrence missed Emeline and the way her effervescence and physical brightness—her prettiness and sunflower hair—lit the sullen halls of Holmes's building. She remained perplexed and a few days later again asked Holmes about Emeline.

He pulled a square envelope from his pocket. "This will tell you," he said.

The envelope contained a wedding announcement. Not engraved, as was customary, merely typeset. This too surprised Mrs. Lawrence. Emeline never would have accepted so mundane a means of communicating news of such magnitude.

The announcement read:

Mr. Robert E. Phelps.
Miss Emeline G. Cigrand.
Married
Wednesday, December 7th
1892
CHICAGO

Holmes told Mrs. Lawrence he had received his copy from Emeline herself. "Some days after going away she returned for her mail," he explained in his memoir, "and at this time gave me one of her wedding cards, and also two or three others for tenants in the building who were not then in their rooms; and in response to inquiries lately made I have learned that at least five persons in and about Lafayette, Ind., received such cards, the post mark and her handwriting upon the envelope in which they were enclosed showing that she must have sent them herself after leaving my employ."

Emeline's family and friends did receive copies of the announcement through the mail, and indeed these appeared to have been addressed by Emeline herself. Most likely Holmes forged the envelopes or else duped Emeline into preparing them by persuading her they would be used for a legitimate purpose, perhaps for Christmas cards.

For Mrs. Lawrence the announcement explained nothing. Emeline had never mentioned a Robert Phelps. And if Emeline had come to the building bearing marriage announcements, she surely would have presented one in person.

The next day Mrs. Lawrence stopped Holmes yet again, and this time asked what he knew about Phelps. In the same dismissive manner Holmes said, "Oh, he is a fellow Miss Cigrand met somewhere. I do not know anything about him except that he is a traveling man."

News of Emeline's marriage reached her hometown newspaper, which reported it on December 8, 1892, in a small chatty bulletin. The item called Emeline a "lady of refinement" who "possesses a character that is strong and pure. Her many friends feel that she has exercised good judgment in selecting a husband and will heartily congratulate her." The item offered a few biographical details, among them the fact that Emeline once had been employed as a stenographer in the county recorder's office. "From there," the item continued, "she went to Dwight, and from there to Chicago, where she met her fate."

"Fate" being the writer's coy allusion to marriage.

In the days that followed Mrs. Lawrence asked Holmes additional questions about Emeline, but he responded only in monosyllables. She began to think of Emeline's departure as a disappearance and recalled that soon after Emeline's last visit a curious change in routine had occurred within Holmes's building.

"The day after Miss Cigrand disappeared, or the day we last saw her, the door of Holmes' office was kept locked and nobody went into it except Holmes and Patrick Quinlan," Mrs. Lawrence said. "About 7 o'clock in the evening Holmes came out of his office and asked two men who were living in the building if they would not help him carry a trunk downstairs." The trunk was new and large, about four feet long. Its contents clearly were heavy and made the big trunk difficult to manage. Holmes repeatedly cautioned his helpers to be careful with it. An express wagon arrived and took it away.

Mrs. Lawrence later claimed that at this point she became convinced Holmes had killed Emeline. Yet she and her husband made no effort to move from the building, nor did they go to the police. No one did. Not Mrs. Lawrence, not Mr. and Mrs. Peter Cigrand, not Ned Conner, and not Julia's parents, Mr. and Mrs. Andrew Smythe. It was as if no one expected the police would be interested in yet another disappearance or, if they were, that they would be competent enough to conduct an effective investigation.

⁘

Soon afterward Emeline's own trunk, filled with her belongings and all the clothing she had brought with her when she left home in 1891 to work for Keeley, arrived at a freight depot near her hometown. Her parents at first believed—hoped—she had sent the trunk home because now that she was marrying a wealthy man, she no longer needed such old and worn things. The Cigrands received no further mail from Emeline, not even at Christmas. "This," said Dr. B. J. Cigrand, Emeline's second cousin, the North Side dentist, "in spite of the fact that she was in the habit of writing to her parents two or three times a week."

Emeline's parents still did not imagine murder, however. Peter Cigrand said, "I had at last come to the belief she must have died in Europe and her husband either did not know our address or neglected to notify us."

The Cigrands and Lawrences would have found their anxiety intensified manyfold had they known a few other facts:

That the name Phelps was an alias that Holmes's assistant, Benjamin Pitezel, had used when he first met Emeline at the Keeley Institute;

That on January 2, 1893, Holmes again had enlisted the help of Charles Chappell, the articulator, and sent him a trunk containing the corpse of a woman, her upper body stripped nearly bare of flesh;

That a few weeks later the LaSalle Medical College of Chicago had taken delivery of a nicely articulated skeleton;

And that something peculiar had occurred in the room-sized vault in Holmes's building, a phenomenon that when finally discovered by police three years later would defy scientific explanation.

Somehow a footprint had become etched into the smooth enameled finish on the inside of the vault door at a point roughly two feet above the floor. The toes, the ball, and the heel were so clearly outlined as to leave no doubt that a woman had left the print. The degree of detail mystified the police, as did the print's resilience. They tried rubbing it off by hand, then with a cloth and soap and water, but it remained as clear as ever.

No one could explain it with any certainty. The best guess posited that Holmes had lured a woman into the vault; that the woman was shoeless at the time, perhaps nude; and that Holmes then had closed the airtight door to lock her inside. She had left the print in a last hopeless effort to force the door open. To explain the print's permanence, detectives theorized that Holmes, known to have an avid interest in chemistry, had first poured a sheen of acid onto the floor to hasten by chemical reaction the consumption of oxygen in the vault. The theory held that Emeline had stepped in the acid, then placed her feet against the door, thus literally etching the print into the enamel.

But again, this revelation came much later. As of the start of 1893, the year of the fair, no one, including Holmes, had noticed the footprint on the door.

"The Cold-Blooded Fact"

AT THE START OF JANUARY 1893 the weather turned cold and stayed cold, the temperature falling to twenty degrees below zero. In his dawn tours, Burnham faced a hard pale world. Cairns of frozen horse manure punctuated the landscape. Along the banks of the Wooded Island ice two feet thick locked Olmsted's bulrush and sedge in cruel contortions. Burnham saw that Olmsted's work was far behind. And now Olmsted's man in Chicago, Harry Codman, upon whom everyone had come to depend, was in the hospital recovering from surgery. His recurring illness had turned out to be appendicitis. The operation, under ether, had gone well and Codman was recuperating, but his recovery would be slow. Only four months remained until Opening Day.

The extreme cold increased the threat of fire. The necessary fires alone—the salamanders and tinner's pots—had caused dozens of small blazes, easily put out, but the cold increased the likelihood of far worse. It froze water lines and hydrants and drove workers to break Burnham's ban on smoking and open flame. The men of the Columbian Guard stepped up their vigilance. It was they who suffered most from the cold, standing watch around the clock in far-flung reaches of the park where no shelter existed. "The winter of 1892–3 will always be remembered by those who served on the guard during that period," wrote Colonel Rice, their commander. Its members most dreaded being assigned to an especially bleak sector at the extreme south end of the park below the Agriculture Building. They called it Siberia. Colonel Rice used their dread to his advantage: "any Guard ordered to the post along the South fence would realize that he had been guilty of some minor breach of discipline, or that his personal appearance rendered him too unsightly for the more public parts of the grounds."

George Ferris fought the cold with dynamite, the only efficient way to penetrate the three-foot crust of frozen earth that now covered Jackson Park. Once opened, the ground still posed problems. Just beneath the crust lay a twenty-foot stratum of the same quicksand Chicago builders always confronted, only now it was ice cold and a torment to workers. The men used jets of live steam to thaw dirt and prevent newly poured cement from freezing. They drove timber piles to hard-pan thirty-two feet underground. On top of these they laid a *grillage* of steel, then filled it with cement. To keep the excavated chambers as dry as possible, they ran pumps twenty-four hours a day. They repeated the process for each of the eight 140-foot towers that would support the Ferris Wheel's giant axle.

At first, Ferris's main worry was whether he could acquire enough steel to build his machine. He realized, however, that he had an advantage over anyone else trying to place a new order. Through his steel-inspection company he knew most of the nation's steel executives and the products they made. He was able to pull in favors and spread his orders among many different companies. "No one shop could begin to do all the work, therefore contracts were let to a dozen different firms, each being chosen because of some peculiar fitness for the work entrusted to it," according to an account by Ferris's company. Ferris also commanded a legion of inspectors who evaluated the quality of each component as it emerged from each mill. This proved to be a vital benefit since the wheel was a complex assemblage of 100,000 parts that ranged in size from small bolts to the giant axle, which at the time of its manufacture by Bethlehem Steel was the largest one-piece casting ever made. "Absolute precision was necessary, as few of the parts could be put together until they were upon the ground and an error of the smallest fraction of an inch might be fatal."

The wheel Ferris envisioned actually consisted of two wheels spaced thirty feet apart on the axle. What had frightened Burnham, at first, was the apparent insubstantiality of the design. Each wheel was essentially a gigantic bicycle wheel. Slender iron rods just two and a half inches thick and eighty feet long linked the rim, or felloe, of each wheel to a "spider" affixed to the axle. Struts and diagonal rods ran between the two wheels to stiffen the assembly and give it the strength of a railroad bridge. A chain weighing twenty thousand pounds connected a sprocket on the axle to sprockets driven by twin thousand-horsepower steam engines. For aesthetic reasons the boilers were to be located seven hundred feet outside the Midway, the steam shunted to the engines through ten-inch underground pipes.

This, at least, is how it looked on paper. Just digging and installing the foundation, however, had proven more difficult than Ferris and Rice had expected, and they knew that far greater hurdles lay ahead, foremost among them the challenge of raising that huge axle to its mount atop the eight towers. Together with its fittings, the axle weighed 142,031 pounds. Nothing that heavy had ever been lifted before, let alone to such a height.

Olmsted, in Brookline, got the news by telegram: Harry Codman was dead. Codman, his protégé, whom he loved like a son. He was twenty-nine. "You will have heard of our great calamity," Olmsted wrote to his friend Gifford Pinchot. "As yet, I am as one standing on a wreck and can hardly see when we shall be afloat again."

Olmsted recognized that now he himself would have to take over direct supervision of the exposition work, but he felt less up to the duty than ever. He and Phil, Harry's brother, arrived in Chicago at the beginning of February to find the city locked in brutal cold, the temperature eight degrees below zero. On February 4 he sat down at Codman's desk for the first time and found it awash with stacks of invoices and memoranda. Olmsted's head raged with noise and pain. He had a sore throat. He was deeply sad. The task of sorting through Codman's accumulated papers and of taking over the exposition work now seemed beyond him. He asked a former assistant, Charles Eliot, now one of Boston's best landscape architects, if he would come to help. After some hesitation Eliot agreed. On arrival Eliot saw immediately that Olmsted was ill. By the evening of February 17, 1893, as a blizzard bore down on Chicago, Olmsted was under a doctor's care, confined to his hotel.

The same night Olmsted wrote to John in Brookline. Weariness and sorrow freighted each page of his letter. "It looks as if the time has come when it is necessary for you to count me out," he wrote. The work in Chicago had begun to look hopeless. "It is very plain that as things are, we are not going to be able to do our duty here."

⁕━━━⁕

By early March Olmsted and Eliot were back in Brookline, Eliot now a full-fledged partner, the firm newly renamed Olmsted, Olmsted & Eliot. The exposition work was still far behind schedule and a major source of worry, but Olmsted's health and the pressure of other work had forced him from Chicago. With deep misgivings Olmsted had left the work in the care of his superintendent, Rudolf Ulrich, whom he had come to distrust. On March 11 Olmsted dispatched a long letter to Ulrich full of instructions.

"I have never before, in all the numerous works for which I have been broadly responsible, trusted as much to the discretion of an assistant or co-operator," Olmsted wrote. "And the results have been such that in the straights in which we are placed by the death of Mr. Codman and my ill health, and the consequent excessive pressure of other duties, I am more than ever disposed to pursue this policy, and to carry it further. But I must confess that I can not do so without much anxiety."

He made it clear that this anxiety was due to Ulrich, specifically, Ulrich's "constitutional propensity" to lose sight of the broad scheme and throw himself into minute tasks better handled by subordinates, a trait that Olmsted feared had left Ulrich vulnerable to demands by other officials, in particular Burnham. "Never lose sight of the fact that our special responsibility as *landscape* artists applies primarily to the broad, comprehensive *scenery* of the Exposition," Olmsted wrote. (The emphases were his.) "This duty is not to make a garden, or to produce garden effects, but relates to the scenery of the Exposition as a whole; first of all and most essentially the scenery, in a broad and comprehensive way. . . . If, for lack of time and means, or of good weather, we come short in matters of detailed decoration, our failure will be excusable. If we fall short in matters affecting broad landscape effects we shall fail in our primary and essential duty."

He went on to identify for Ulrich the things that most worried him about the fair, among them the color scheme chosen by Burnham and the architects. "Let me remind you that the whole field of the Exposition has already come to be popularly called 'THE WHITE CITY'. . . . I fear that against the clear blue sky and the blue lake, great towering masses of white, glistening in the clear, hot, Summer sunlight of Chicago, with the glare of the water that we are to have both within and without the Exposition grounds, will be overpowering." This, he wrote, made it more important than ever to provide a counterbalance of "dense, broad, luxuriant green bodies of foliage."

Clearly the possibility of failure at the exposition had occurred to Olmsted and troubled him. Time was short, the weather terrible. The spring planting season would be brief. Olmsted had begun to think in terms of fallback arrangements. He warned Ulrich, "Do not lay out to do anything in the way of decorative planting that you shall not be quite certain that you will have ample time and means to perfect of its kind. There can be little fault found with simple, neat turf. Do not be afraid of plain, undecorated, smooth surfaces."

It was far better, Olmsted lectured, to underdecorate than to overdecorate. "Let us be thought over-much plain and simple, even bare, rather than gaudy, flashy, cheap and meretricious. Let us manifest the taste of gentlemen."

⌇————⌇

Snow fell, bales of it. It fell day after day until hundreds of tons of it lay upon the rooftops at Jackson Park. The exposition was to be a warm-weather affair, set to run from May through October. No one had thought to design the roofs to resist such extreme loading from snow.

Men working at the Manufactures and Liberal Arts Building heard the shriek of failed steel and ran for cover. In a great blur of snow and silvery glass the building's roof—that marvel of late nineteenth-century hubris, enclosing the greatest volume of unobstructed space in history—collapsed to the floor below.

⌒‌‌‌‌‌‌‌‌⟶

Soon afterward, a reporter from San Francisco made his way to Jackson Park. He had come prepared to admire the grand achievement of Burnham's army of workers but instead found himself troubled by what he saw in the stark frozen landscape.

"This seems to be an impossibility," he wrote. "To be sure, those in charge claim that they will be ready on time. Still the cold-blooded fact stares one in the face that only the Woman's Building is anywhere near completion inside and out."

Yet the fair was to open in little more than two months.

Acquiring Minnie

FOR HOLMES, DESPITE THE PERSISTENT deep cold of the first two months of 1893, things never looked better. With Emeline gone and neatly disposed of, he now was able to concentrate on his growing web of enterprises. He savored its scope: He owned a portion of a legitimate company that produced a machine for duplicating documents; he sold mail-order ointments and elixirs and by now had established his own alcohol-treatment company, the Silver Ash Institute, his answer to Keeley's gold cure; he collected rents from the Lawrences and his other tenants and owned two houses, one on Honoré Street, the other the new house in Wilmette now occupied by his wife Myrta and daughter Lucy, which he himself had designed and then built with the help of as many as seventy-five largely unpaid workers. And soon he would begin receiving his first world's fair guests.

He spent much of his time outfitting his hotel. He acquired high-grade furnishings from the Tobey Furniture Company, and crystal and ceramics from the French, Potter Crockery Company, and did so without paying a dime, though he recognized that soon the companies would attempt to collect on the promissory notes he had given them. This did not worry him. He had learned through experience that delay and heartfelt remorse were powerful tools with which he could fend off creditors for months and years, sometimes forever. Such prolonged standoffs would not be necessary, however, for he sensed that his time in Chicago was nearing an end. Mrs. Lawrence's questioning had become more pointed, almost accusing. And lately some of his creditors had begun exhibiting an extraordinary hardening of resolve. One firm, Merchant & Co., which had supplied the iron for his kiln and vault, had gone so far as to secure a writ of replevin to take the iron back. In an inspection of the building, however, its agents had been unable to find anything they could identify conclusively as a Merchant product.

Far more annoying were the letters from parents of missing daughters and the private detectives who had begun showing up at his door. Independently of each other, the Cigrand and Conner families had hired "eyes" to search for their missing daughters. Although at first these inquiries troubled Holmes, he realized quickly that neither family believed he had anything to do with the disappearances. The detectives made no mention of suspecting foul play. They wanted information—the names of friends, forwarding addresses, suggestions on where to look next.

He was, of course, happy to oblige. Holmes told his visitors how much it grieved him, truly deeply grieved him, that he was unable to provide any new information to ease the worry of the parents. If he heard from the women, he of course would notify the detectives at once. Upon parting, he shook each detective's hand and told him that if his work should happen to bring him back to Englewood anytime in the future, by all means stop in. Holmes and the detectives parted as cheerily as if they had known each other all their lives.

At the moment—March 1893—the greatest inconvenience confronting Holmes was his lack of help. He needed a new secretary. There was no shortage of women seeking work, for the fair had drawn legions of them to Chicago. At the nearby Normal School, for example, the number of women applying to become teacher trainees was said to be many times the usual. Rather, the trick lay in choosing a woman of the correct sensibility. Candidates would need a degree of stenographic and typewriting skill, but what he most looked for and was so very adept at sensing was that alluring amalgam of isolation, weakness, and need. Jack the Ripper had found it in the impoverished whores of Whitechapel; Holmes saw it in transitional women, fresh clean young things free for the first time in history but unsure of what that freedom meant and of the risks it entailed. What he craved was possession and the power it gave him; what he adored was anticipation—the slow acquisition of love, then life, and finally the secrets within. The ultimate disposition of the material was irrelevant, a recreation. That he happened to have found a way to make disposal both efficient and profitable was simply a testament to his power.

In March fortune brought him the perfect acquisition. Her name was Minnie R. Williams. He had met her several years earlier during a stay in Boston and had considered acquiring her even then, but the distance was too great, the timing awkward. Now she had moved to Chicago. Holmes guessed that he himself might be part of the reason.

She would be twenty-five years old by now. Unlike his usual selections, she was plain, short, and plump, her weight somewhere between 140 and 150. She had a masculine nose, thick dark eyebrows, and virtually no neck. Her expression was bland, her cheeks full—"a baby face," as one witness put it. "She didn't seem to know a great deal."

In Boston, however, Holmes had discovered that she possessed other winning attributes.

Born in Mississippi, Minnie Williams and her younger sister, Anna, were orphaned at an early age and sent to live with different uncles. Anna's new guardian was the Reverend Dr. W. C. Black, of Jackson, Mississippi, editor of the Methodist *Christian Advocate*. Minnie went to Texas, where her guardian-uncle was a successful businessman. He treated her well and in 1886 enrolled her at the Boston Academy of Elocution. He died in the midst of her three-year program and bequeathed to her an estate valued at between $50,000 and $100,000, (about $1.5 to $3 million in twenty-first-century dollars).

Anna, meanwhile, became a schoolteacher. She taught in Midlothian, Texas, at the Midlothian Academy.

When Holmes met Minnie, he was traveling on business under the alias Henry Gordon and found himself invited to a gathering at the home of one of Boston's leading families. Through various inquiries Holmes learned of Minnie's inheritance and of the fact that it consisted largely of a parcel of property in the heart of Fort Worth, Texas.

Holmes extended his Boston stay. Minnie called him Harry. He took her to plays and concerts and bought her flowers and books and sweets. Wooing her was pathetically easy. Each time he told her he had to return to Chicago, she seemed crushed, delightfully so. Throughout 1889 he traveled regularly to Boston and always swept Minnie into a whirl of shows and dinners, although what he looked forward to most were the days before his departure when her need flared like fire in a dry forest.

After a time, however, he tired of the game. The distance was too great, Minnie's reticence too profound. His visits to Boston became fewer, though he still responded to her letters with the ardor of a lover.

Holmes's absence broke Minnie's heart. She had fallen in love. His visits had thrilled her, his departures destroyed her. She was perplexed—he had seemed to be conducting a courtship and even urged her to abandon her studies and run with him to Chicago, but now he was gone and his letters came only rarely. She gladly would have left Boston under the flag of marriage, but not under the reckless terms he proposed. He would have made an excellent husband. He was affectionate in ways she rarely encountered in men, and he was adept at business. She missed his warmth and touch.

Soon there were no letters at all.

Upon graduation from the Academy of Elocution, Minnie moved to Denver, where she tried to establish her own theatrical company, and in the process lost $15,000. She still dreamed about Harry Gordon. As her theater company collapsed, she thought of him more and more. She dreamed also of Chicago, a city everyone seemed to be talking about and to which everyone seemed to be moving. Between Harry and the soon-to-begin World's Columbian Exposition, the city became irresistible to her.

She moved to Chicago in February 1893 and took a job as a stenographer for a law firm. She wrote to Harry to tell him of her arrival.

Harry Gordon called on her almost immediately and greeted her with tears in his eyes. He was so warm and affectionate. It was as if they had never parted. He suggested she come work for him as his personal stenographer. They could see each other every day, without having to worry about the interventions of Minnie's landlady, who watched them as if she were Minnie's own mother.

The prospect thrilled her. He still said nothing about marriage, but she could tell he loved her. And this was Chicago. Things were different here, less rigid and formal. Everywhere she went she found women her own age, unescorted, holding jobs, living their own lives. She accepted Harry's offer. He seemed delighted.

But he imposed a curious stipulation. Minnie was to refer to him in public as Henry Howard Holmes, an alias, he explained, that he had adopted for business reasons. She was never to call him Gordon, nor act surprised when people referred to him as Dr. Holmes. She could call him "Harry" at any time, however.

She managed his correspondence and kept his books, while he concentrated on getting his building ready for the world's fair. They dined together in his office, on meals brought in from the restaurant below. Minnie showed "a remarkable aptitude for the work," Holmes wrote in his memoir. "During the first weeks she boarded at a distance, but later, from about the 1st of March until the 15th of May, 1893, she occupied rooms in the same building and adjoining my offices."

Harry touched her and caressed her and let his eyes fill with tears of adoration. At last he asked her to marry him. She felt very lucky. Her Harry was so handsome and dynamic, she knew that once married they would share a wonderful life full of travel and fine possessions. She wrote of her hopes to her sister Anna.

In recent years the sisters had become very close, overcoming an earlier estrangement. They wrote to each other often. Minnie filled her letters with news of her fast-intensifying romance and expressed wonder that such a handsome man had chosen her to be his wife.

Anna was skeptical. The romance was advancing too quickly and with a degree of intimacy that violated all the intricate rules of courtship. Minnie was sweet, Anna knew, but certainly no beauty.

If Harry Gordon was such a paragon of looks and enterprise, why had he selected her?

In mid-March Holmes received a letter from Peter Cigrand, Emeline's father, asking yet again for help in finding his daughter. The letter was dated March 16. Holmes responded promptly, on March 18, with a typed letter in which he told Cigrand that Emeline had left his employ on December 1, 1892. It is possible that Minnie in her role as Holmes's personal secretary did the typing.

"I received her wedding cards about Dec. 10," he wrote. She had come to see him twice since her marriage, the last time being January 1, 1893, "at which point she was disappointed at not finding any mail here for her, and my impression is that she spoke of having written to you previous to that time. Before going away in December she told me personally that the intention was that she and her husband should go to England on business with which he was connected, but when she called here the last time she spoke as though the trip had been given up. Please let me know within a few days if you did not hear from her and give me her uncle's address here in the city and I will see him personally and ask if she has been there, as I know she was in the habit of calling upon him quite often."

He added a postscript in ink: "Have you written her Lafayette friends asking them if they have heard from her? If not I should think it well to do so. Let me hear from you at all events."

Holmes promised Minnie a voyage to Europe, art lessons, a fine home, and of course children—he adored children—but first there were certain financial matters that required their mutual attention. Assuring her that he had come up with a plan from which only great profit would result,

Holmes persuaded her to transfer the deed to her Fort Worth land to a man named Alexander Bond. She did so on April 18, 1893, with Holmes himself serving as notary. Bond in turn signed the deed over to another man, Benton T. Lyman. Holmes notarized this transfer as well.

Minnie loved her husband-to-be and trusted him, but she did not know that Alexander Bond was an alias for Holmes himself, or that Benton Lyman actually was Holmes's assistant Benjamin Pitezel—and that with a few strokes of his pen her beloved Harry had taken possession of the bulk of her dead uncle's bequest. Nor did she know that on paper Harry was still married to two other women, Clara Lovering and Myrta Belknap, and that in each marriage he had fathered a child.

As Minnie's adoration deepened, Holmes executed a second financial maneuver. He established the Campbell-Yates Manufacturing Company, which he billed as a firm that bought and sold everything. When he filed its papers of incorporation, he listed five officers: H. H. Holmes, M. R. Williams, A. S. Yates, Hiram S. Campbell, and Henry Owens. Owens was a porter employed by Holmes. Hiram S. Campbell was the fictive owner of Holmes's Englewood building. Yates was supposed to be a businessman living in New York City but in reality was as much a fiction as Campbell. And M. R. Williams was Minnie. The company made nothing and sold nothing: It existed to hold assets and provide a reference for anyone who became skeptical of Holmes's promissory notes.

Later, when questions arose as to the accuracy of the corporation papers, Holmes persuaded Henry Owens, the porter, to sign an affidavit swearing not only that he was secretary of the company but that he had met both Yates and Campbell and that Yates personally had handed him the stock certificates representing his share of the company. Owens later said of Holmes: "He induced me to make these statements by promising me my back wages and by his hypnotizing ways, and I candidly believe that he had a certain amount of influence over me. While I was with him I was always under his control."

He added, "I never received my back wages."

Holmes—Harry—wanted the wedding done quickly and quietly, just him, Minnie, and a preacher. He arranged everything. To Minnie the little ceremony appeared to be legal and in its quiet way very romantic, but in fact no record of their union was entered into the marriage registry of Cook County, Illinois.

Dreadful Things
Done by Girls

THROUGHOUT THE SPRING OF 1893 the streets of Chicago filled with unemployed men from elsewhere, but otherwise the city seemed immune to the nation's financial troubles. Preparations for the fair kept its economy robust, if artificially so. Construction of the Alley L extension to Jackson Park still provided work for hundreds of men. In the company town of Pullman, just south of Chicago, workers labored around the clock to fill backlogged orders for more cars to carry visitors to the fair, though the rate of new orders had fallen off sharply. The Union Stock Yards commissioned Burnham's firm to build a new passenger depot at its entrance, to manage the expected crush of fairgoers seeking a crimson break from the White City. Downtown, Montgomery Ward installed a new Customer's Parlor, where excursive fair visitors could loiter on soft couches while browsing the company's five-hundred-page catalog. New hotels rose everywhere. One entrepreneur, Charles Kiler, believed that once his hotel opened, "money would be so plentiful it would come a runnin' up hill to get into our coffers."

At Jackson Park exhibits arrived daily, in ever-mounting volume. There was smoke, clatter, mud, and confusion, as if an army were massing for an assault on Chicago. Caravans of Wells-Fargo and Adams Express wagons moved slowly through the park, drawn by gigantic horses. Throughout the night freight trains huffed into the park. Switching locomotives nudged individual boxcars over the skein of temporary tracks to their destinations. Lake freighters disgorged pale wooden crates emblazoned with phrases in strange alphabets. George Ferris's steel arrived, on five trains of thirty cars each. The Inman steamship line delivered a full-sized section of one of its ocean liners. Bethlehem Steel brought giant ingots and great slabs of military armor, including a curved plate seventeen inches thick meant for the gun turret of the dreadnought *Indiana*. Great Britain delivered locomotives and ship models, including an exquisite thirty-foot replica of Britain's latest warship, *Victoria*, so detailed that even the links of chain in its handrails were to scale.

From Baltimore came a long dark train that chilled the hearts of the men and women who monitored its passage across the prairie but delighted the innumerable small boys who raced open-jawed to the railbed. The train carried weapons made by the Essen Works of Fritz Krupp, the German arms baron, including the largest artillery piece until then constructed, capable of firing a one-ton shell with enough force to penetrate three feet of wrought-iron plate. The barrel had to be carried on a specially made car consisting of a steel cradle straddling two extra-long flatcars. An ordinary car had eight wheels; this combination had thirty-two. To ensure that the Pennsylvania Railroad's bridges could support the gun's 250,000-pound weight, two Krupp engineers had traveled to America the previous July to inspect the entire route. The gun quickly acquired the nickname "Krupp's Baby," although one writer preferred to think of it as Krupp's "pet monster."

A train with a more lighthearted cargo also headed for Chicago, this one leased by Buffalo Bill for his Wild West show. It carried a small army: one hundred former U.S. Cavalry soldiers, ninety-seven Cheyenne, Kiowa, Pawnee, and Sioux Indians, another fifty Cossacks and Hussars, 180 horses, eighteen buffalo, ten elk, ten mules, and a dozen other animals. It also carried Phoebe Anne Moses of Tiffin, Ohio, a young woman with a penchant for guns and an excellent sense of distance. Bill called her Annie, the press called her Miss Oakley.

At night the Indians and soldiers played cards.

Ships began converging on U.S. ports from all over the world bearing exposition cargoes of the most exotic kind. Sphinxes. Mummies. Coffee trees and ostriches. By far the most exotic cargo, however, was human. Alleged cannibals from Dahomey. Lapps from Lapland. Syrian horsemen. On March 9 a steamer named *Guildhall* set sail for New York from Alexandria, Egypt, carrying 175 bona-fide residents of Cairo recruited by an entrepreneur named George Pangalos to inhabit his Street in Cairo in the Midway Plaisance. In the *Guildhall*'s holds he stashed twenty donkeys, seven camels, and an assortment of monkeys and deadly snakes. His passenger list included one of Egypt's foremost practitioners of the *danse du ventre*, the young and lushly feminine Farida Mazhar, destined to become a legend in America. Pangalos had secured choice ground at the middle of the Midway, adjacent to the Ferris Wheel, in a Muslim diaspora that included a Persian concession, a Moorish palace, and Sol Bloom's Algerian Village, where Bloom had converted the Algerians' premature arrival into a financial windfall.

Bloom had been able to open his village as early as August 1892, well before Dedication Day, and within a month had covered his costs and begun reaping a generous profit. The Algerian version of the *danse du ventre* had proven a particularly powerful draw, once people realized the phrase meant "belly dance." Rumors spread of half-clad women jiggling away, when in fact the dance was elegant, stylized, and rather chaste. "The crowds poured in," Bloom said. "I had a gold mine."

With his usual flare for improvisation, Bloom contributed something else that would forever color America's perception of the Middle East. The Press Club of Chicago invited him to present a preview of the *danse du ventre* to its members. Never one to shun free publicity, Bloom accepted instantly and traveled to the club with a dozen of his dancers. On arrival, however, he learned that all the club had provided for music was a lone pianist who had no idea what kind of piece might accompany such an exotic dance.

Bloom thought a moment, hummed a tune, then plinked it out on the keyboard one note at a time:

Over the next century this tune and its variations would be deployed in a succession of mostly cheesy movies, typically as an accompaniment to the sinuous emergence of a cobra from a basket. It would also drive the schoolyard lyric, "And they wear no pants in the southern part of France."

Bloom regretted his failure to copyright the tune. The royalties would have run into the millions.

———

Sad news arrived from Zanzibar: There would be no Pygmies. Lieutenant Schufeldt was dead, of unclear causes.

———

There was advice, much of it of course from New York. The advice that rankled most came from Ward McAllister, factotum and chief slipperlick to Mrs. William Astor, empress of New York society. Appalled by the vision conjured by Chicago's Dedication Day, of crème and rabble mixing in such volume and with such indecorous propinquity, McCallister in a column in the *New York World* advised "it is not quantity but quality that the society people here want. Hospitality which includes the whole human race is not desirable."

He urged Chicago hostesses to hire some French chefs to improve their culinary diction. "In these modern days, society cannot get along without French chefs," he wrote. "The man who has been accustomed to delicate fillets of beef, terrapin pâté de foie gras, truffled turkey and things of that sort would not care to sit down to a boiled leg of mutton dinner with turnips." The thing is, McAllister was serious.

And there was more. "I should also advise that they do not frappé their wine too much. Let them put the bottle in the tub and be careful to keep the neck free from ice. For, the quantity of wine in the neck of the bottle being small, it will be acted upon by the ice first. In twenty-five minutes from the time of being placed in the tub it will be in a perfect condition to be served immediately. What I mean by a perfect condition is that when the wine is poured from the bottle it should contain little flakes of ice. That is a real frappé."

To which the *Chicago Journal* replied, "The mayor will not frappé his wine too much. He will frappé it just enough so the guests can blow the foam off the tops of the glasses without a vulgar exhibition of lung and lip power. His ham sandwiches, sinkers and Irish quail, better known in the Bridgeport vernacular as pigs' feet, will be triumphs of the gastronomic art." One Chicago newspaper called McAllister "A Mouse Colored Ass."

Chicago delighted in such repartee—for the most part. On some level, however, McAllister's remarks stung. McAllister was one particularly snooty voice, but it was clear to everyone that he spoke with the sanction of New York's blue bloods. Among Chicago's leading citizens there was always a deep fear of being second class. No one topped Chicago in terms of business drive and acumen, but within the city's upper echelons there was a veiled anxiety that the city in its commercial advance may indeed have failed to cultivate the finer traits of man and woman. The exposition was to be a giant white banner waved in Mrs. Astor's face. With its gorgeous classical buildings packed with art, its clean water and electric lights, and its overstaffed police department, the exposition was Chicago's conscience, the city it wanted to become.

Burnham in particular embodied this insecurity. Denied admission to Harvard and Yale and the "right" beginning, he had become a self-conscious connoisseur of fine things. He arranged recitals at his home and office and joined the best clubs and collected the best wines and was now leading the greatest nonmilitary campaign in the nation's history. Even so, the social columnists still did not write about his wife's dresses when he and she attended the opera, the way they described the nightly couture of *mesdames* Palmer, Pullman, and Armour. The fair was to be Burnham's redemption, and Chicago's. "Outside peoples already concede our material greatness and that we are well nigh supreme in manufactures and commerce," he wrote. "They do, however, claim that we are not cultivated and refined to the same extent. To remove this impression, the thought and work of this bureau has been mostly bent from the start."

Advice arrived also by the bookful. An author named Adelaide Hollingsworth chose to honor the fair with more than seven hundred pages of it, which she published early in the year under the title *The Columbia Cook Book*. Although her book did include compelling recipes for scrapple, ox cheek, and baked calf's head and tips for the preparation of raccoon, possum, snipe, plovers, and blackbirds (for blackbird pie) and "how to broil, fricassee, stew or fry a squirrel," it was much more than just a cookbook. Hollingsworth billed it as an overall guide to helping modern young housewives create a peaceful, optimistic, and sanitary household. The wife was to set the tenor of the day. "The breakfast table should not be a bulletin-board for the curing of horrible dreams and depressing symptoms, but the place where a bright key-note of the day is struck." In places Hollingsworth's advice revealed, by refraction, a certain Victorian raciness. In a segment on how best to wash silk underwear, she advised, "If the article is black, add a little ammonia, instead of acid to the rinsing water."

One of the most persistent problems of the day was "offensive feet," caused by the prevailing habit of washing feet only once a week. To combat this, Hollingsworth wrote, "Take one part muriatic acid to ten parts of water; rub the feet every night with this mixture before retiring to bed." To rid your mouth of the odor of onions, drink strong coffee. Oysters made the best rat-bait. To induce cream to whip, add a grain of salt. To keep milk sweet longer, add horseradish.

Hollingsworth offered sage medical advice—"Don't sit between a fever patient and a fire"—and provided various techniques for dealing with medical emergencies, such as accidental poisoning. Among a list of measures effective for inducing vomiting, she included: "Injections of tobacco into the anus through a pipe stem."

Jacob Riis, the New York journalist who had devoted himself to revealing the squalid housing of America's poor, came to Chicago bearing counsel of a graver sort. In March he gave a talk at Hull House, a reform settlement founded by Jane Addams, "Saint Jane." Hull House had become a bastion of progressive thought inhabited by strong-willed young women, "interspersed," as one visitor put it, "with earnest-faced, self-subordinating and mild-mannered men who slide from room to room apologetically." Clarence Darrow regularly walked the short distance from his office in the Rookery to Hull House, where he was admired for his intellect and social empathy but disparaged, privately, for his slovenly dress and less-than-exemplary hygiene.

At the time of Riis's talk, Riis and Addams were two of the best known people in America. Riis had toured Chicago's foulest districts and pronounced them worse than anything he had seen in New York. In his talk he noted the fast approach of the exposition and warned his audience, "You ought to begin house cleaning, so to speak, and get your alleys and streets in better condition; never in our worst season have we had so much filth in New York City."

In fact, Chicago had been trying to tidy itself for some time and had found the challenge monumental. The city stepped up its efforts to remove garbage and began repaving alleys and streets. It deployed smoke inspectors to enforce a new antismoke ordinance. Newspapers launched crusades against pestilent alleys and excess smoke and identified the worst offenders in print—among them Burnham's newly opened Masonic Temple, which the *Chicago Tribune* likened to Mount Vesuvius.

Carrie Watson, Chicago's foremost madam, decided her own operation merited a little sprucing up. Her place already was luxurious, with a bowling alley where the pins were bottles of chilled champagne, but now she resolved to increase the number of bedrooms and double her staff. She and other brothel owners anticipated a big spike in demand. They would not be disappointed. Nor, apparently, would their clients. Later, a madam named Chicago May recalled the boisterous year of the fair with a cringe: "What dreadful things were done by some of the girls! It always made me sick even to think of them. The mere mention of the details of some of the 'circuses' is unprintable. I think Rome at its worst had nothing on Chicago during those lurid days."

The man who helped make Chicago so hospitable to Carrie Watson and Chicago May, as well as to Mickey Finn and Bathhouse John Coughlin and a few thousand other operators of saloons and gambling dens, was Carter Henry Harrison, whose four terms as mayor had gone a long way to establish Chicago as a place that tolerated human frailty even as it nurtured grand ambition. After his failed run for the office in 1891, Harrison had acquired a newspaper, the *Chicago Times,* and settled into the job of editor. By the end of 1892, however, he had made it clear that he would love to be the "Fair Mayor" and lead the city through its most glorious time, but insisted that only a clear signal of popular demand could make him actually enter the campaign. He got it. Carter H. Harrison Associations sprang up all over town, and now, at the start of 1893, Carter was one of two candidates for the Democratic nomination, the other being Washington Hesing, editor of the powerful German daily *Staats-Zeitung.*

Every newspaper in the city, other than his own *Times,* opposed Harrison, as did Burnham and most of Chicago's leading citizens. To Burnham and the others the new Chicago, as symbolized by the White City rising in Jackson Park, required new leadership—certainly not Harrison.

The city's legions of working men disagreed. They always had counted Harrison as one of their own, "Our Carter," even though he was a plantation-reared Kentucky man who had gone to Yale, spoke fluent French and German, and recited lengthy passages from Shakespeare. He had served four terms; that he should serve a fifth in the year of the fair seemed fitting, and a wave of nostalgia swept the city's wards.

Even his opponents recognized that Harrison, despite his privileged roots, made an intensely appealing candidate for the city's lesser tier. He was magnetic. He was able and willing to talk to anyone about anything and had a way of making himself the center of any conversation. "His friends all noticed it," said Joseph Medill, once an ally but later Harrison's most ardent opponent, "they would laugh or smile about it, and called it 'Carter Harrisonia.' " Even at sixty-eight Harrison exuded strength and energy, and women generally agreed that he was more handsome now than he had been in his fifties. Widowed twice, he was rumored to be involved with a much younger woman. He had deep blue eyes with large pupils and an unwrinkled face. He attributed his youthful aspect to a heavy dose of morning coffee. His quirks made him endearing. He loved watermelon; when it was in season, he ate it at all three meals. He had a passion for shoes—a different pair each day of the week—and for silk underwear. Almost everyone had seen Harrison riding the streets on his white Kentucky mare, in his black slouch hat, trailing a plume of cigar smoke. At his campaign talks he often addressed his remarks to a stuffed eagle that he carried with him as a prop. Medill accused him of nurturing the city's basest instincts but also called him "the most remarkable man that our city has ever produced."

To the astonishment of the city's ruling class, 78 percent of the 681 delegates to the Democratic convention voted for Harrison on the first ballot. The Democratic elite implored the Republicans to come up with a candidate whom they too could support, anything to keep Harrison from returning to office. The Republicans chose Samuel W. Allerton, a rich packer from Prairie Avenue. The biggest and most powerful newspapers formed an explicit combine to back Allerton and undermine Harrison.

The ex-mayor countered their attacks with humor. During a talk before a large group of supporters at the Auditorium, Harrison called Allerton "a most admirable pig sticker and pig slaughterer. I admit it, and I don't arraign him because he slaughters the queen's English; he can't help it."

Harrison rapidly gained ground.

Patrick Prendergast, the young mad Irish immigrant, took pride in Harrison's renewed popularity and believed his own efforts at promoting the ex-mayor for reelection had had a lot do with the campaign's new momentum. An idea came to Prendergast. Just when it entered his brain he could not say, but it was there, and it gave him satisfaction. He had read extensively into law and politics and understood that political machines operated on a first principle of power: If you worked to advance the interests of the machine, the machine paid you back. Harrison was in his debt.

This notion came to Prendergast initially as a glimmer, like the first sunlight to strike the Masonic tower each morning, but now he thought of it a thousand times a day. It was his treasure and made him square his shoulders and raise his chin. When Harrison won, things would change. And Harrison *would* win. The great upwelling of enthusiasm in the wards seemed to assure Harrison's victory. Once elected, Prendergast believed, Harrison would offer him an appointment. He would have to. It was the law of the machine, as immutable as the forces that propelled the Chicago Limited across the prairie. Prendergast wanted to be corporation counsel. No more dealing with newsboys who did not know their place; no more walking in the yellow stew that bubbled between pavers; no more having to breathe the awful perfume of mortified horses left in the middle of the street. When Harrison took office, salvation would come to Patrick Prendergast.

The idea caused moments of exultation. Prendergast bought more postcards and sent exuberant notes to the men who soon would be his associates and clubmates—the judges, lawyers, and merchant princes of Chicago. He of course sent another card to his good friend Alfred S. Trude, the defense attorney.

"My Dear Mr. Trude," he began. He intended the next word to be "Hallelujah!" but certain words gave him trouble. In his fever to write, he plunged ahead.

"Allielliuia!" he wrote. "The attempt of the Herald gang to prevent the manifestation of the popular will has been checked—& Carter H. Harrison the popular choice will be our next mayor. The newspaper trust has been ingloriously sat down upon. What do I know about the candidacy of a Washington Hesing poor fellow—he has the 'tail end' of my sympathy. In his present trouble I hope it will not overcome him—& the noble newspaper trust. Glory to The Father Son & Holy Ghost!" He rambled on for a few more lines, then closed, "Friendship is the true test of character after all Sincerely,

"P. E. J. Prendergast."

Again something in the card drew Trude's attention. Many other recipients of Prendergast's cards also took note, despite the crush of mail each received from his true peers, this being a time when everyone who knew how to write did so and at length. In that glacier of words grinding toward the twentieth century, Prendergast's card was a single fragment of mica glinting with lunacy, pleading to be picked up and pocketed.

Once again Trude kept the letter.

In April 1893 the citizens of Chicago elected Carter Henry Harrison to his fifth term. In preparation for the fair, he ordered two hundred barrels of whiskey, to be used by his office in the entertainment of dignitaries.

He gave no thought whatsoever to Patrick Eugene Joseph Prendergast.

The Invitation

For the moment Holmes held off on doing anything more with Minnie's property. Minnie had told her sister, Anna, of the transfer of the Fort Worth land, and now Holmes sensed that Anna was becoming suspicious of his true intentions. This did not trouble him, however. The solution was really quite simple.

One bright and fragrant spring day—as if on a wild equinoctial whim—Holmes suggested that Minnie invite her sister to Chicago to see the world's fair, at his expense.

Minnie was delighted and sent the good news to Anna, who immediately accepted. Holmes knew she would, for how could she have done otherwise? The chance to see Minnie was compelling in itself. Add Chicago and the great fair, and the combination became too alluring to turn down, no matter what Anna suspected about his and Minnie's relationship.

Minnie could hardly wait for the end of the school year, when her sister at last would be able to extricate herself from her duties at the Midlothian Academy. Minnie planned to show Anna all the wonders of Chicago—the skyscrapers, Marshall Field's store, the Auditorium, and of course the world's fair—but above all she looked forward to introducing Anna to her own personal wonder, Mr. Henry Gordon. Her Harry.

At last Anna would see that she could put her suspicions to rest.

Final Preparations

In the first two weeks of April 1893 the weather was gorgeous, but other cruelties abounded. Four exposition workers lost their lives, two from fractured skulls, two electrocuted. The deaths brought the year's total to seven. The exposition's union carpenters, aware of their great value in this final phase of construction, seized the moment and walked off the job, demanding a minimum union wage and other long-sought concessions. Only one of the eight towers of the Ferris Wheel was in place and workers had not yet completed repairs to the Manufactures and Liberal Arts Building. Each morning hundreds of men climbed to its roof; each evening they picked their way gingerly back down in a long dense line that from a distance resembled a column of ants. Frank Millet's "Whitewash Gang" worked furiously to paint the buildings of the Court of Honor. In places the staff coating already had begun to crack and chip. Patch crews patrolled the grounds. The air of "anxious effort" that suffused the park reminded Candace Wheeler, the designer hired to decorate the Woman's Building, "of an insufficiently equipped household preparing for visitors."

Despite the carpenters' strike and all the work yet to be done, Burnham felt optimistic, his mood bolstered by the fine weather. The winter had been deep and long, but now the air was scented with first blossoms and thawed earth. And he felt loved. In late March he had been feted at a grand banquet arranged largely by Charles McKim and held in New York at Madison Square Garden—the *old* Garden, an elegant Moorish structure designed by McKim's partner, Stanford White. McKim assigned Frank Millet to secure the attendance of the nation's finest painters, and these took their seats beside the most prominent writers and architects and the patrons who supported them all, men like Marshall Field and Henry Villard, and together they spent the night lauding Burnham—prematurely—for achieving the impossible. Of course, they ate like gods.

The menu:

Blue Points à l'Alaska.

Sauternes.

POTAGES.

Consommé printanier. Crème de Celeri.

Amontillado.

HORS D'OEUVRES.

Rissoles Chateaubriand. Amandes salées. Olives, etc.

POISSON.

Bass rayée, sauce hollandaise. Pommes parisiennes.

Miersfeiner. Moet et Chandon. Perrier Jouet, Extra Dry Special.

REFEVE.

Filet de Boeuf aux champignons. Haricots verts. Pommes duchesse.

ENTRÉE.

Ris de Veau en cotelette. Petits Pois.

SORBET.

Romaine fantaisie. Cigarettes.

ROTI.

Canard de Tête Rouge. Salade de Laitue.

Pontet Canet.

DESSERT.

Petits Moules fantaisies. Gateaux assortis. Bonbons. Petits-fours.

Fruits assortis.

FROMAGES.

Roquefort et Camembert.

Café.

Apollinaris.

Cognac. Cordials. Cigars.

Newspapers reported that Olmsted also was present, but in fact he was in Asheville, North Carolina, continuing his work on Vanderbilt's estate. His absence prompted speculation that he had stayed away out of pique at not being invited to share the podium and because the invitation had identified the major arts only as painting, architecture, and sculpture, with no reference to landscape architecture. While it is true that Olmsted had struggled throughout his career to build respect for landscape architecture as a distinct branch of the fine arts, for him to shun the banquet because of hurt feelings would have been out of character. The simplest explanation seems best: Olmsted was ill, his work everywhere was behind schedule, he disliked ceremonies, and above all he loathed long-distance train travel, especially in transitional months when railcars, even the finest Pullman Palaces, were likely to be too hot or too cold. Had he attended, he would have heard Burnham tell the guests, "Each of you knows the name and genius of him who stands first in the heart and confidence of American artists, the creator of your own and many other city parks. He it is who has been our best advisor and our constant mentor. In the highest sense he is the planner of the Exposition, Frederick Law Olmsted. . . . An artist, he paints with lakes and wooded slopes; with lawns and banks and forest-covered hills; with mountain sides and ocean views. He should stand where I do tonight. . . ."

Which is not to say that Burnham wanted to sit down. He reveled in the attention and adored the engraved silver "loving cup" that was filled with wine and held to the lips of every man at the table—despite the prevalence in the city outside of typhoid, diphtheria, tuberculosis, and pneumonia. He knew the praise was premature, but the banquet hinted at the greater glory that would accrue to him at fair's end, provided of course the exposition met the world's elaborate expectations.

Without doubt huge progress had been made. The six grandest buildings of the exposition towered over the central court with an effect more dramatic and imposing than even he had imagined. Daniel Chester French's "Statue of the Republic"—nicknamed "Big Mary"—stood in the basin complete and gleaming, its entire surface gilded. Including plinth, the Republic was 111 feet tall. More than two hundred other buildings erected by states, corporations, and foreign governments stippled the surrounding acreage. The White Star Line had built a charming little temple at the northwest bank of the lagoon opposite the Wooded Island, with steps to the water. The monstrous guns of Krupp were in place in their pavilion on the lake south of the Court of Honor.

"The scale of the whole thing is more and more tremendous as the work proceeds," McKim wrote to Richard Hunt. A bit too tremendous, he noted cattily, at least in the case of the Manufactures and Liberal Arts Building. His own Agriculture Building, he wrote, "must suffer by comparison with its huge neighbor opposite, whose volume—215 feet high—off the main axis, is bound to swamp us and everything else around it." He told Hunt he had just spent two days with Burnham, including two nights at the shanty. "He is keeping up under his responsibilities and looking well, and we all owe him a great debt for his constant watchfulness and attention to our slightest wishes."

Even the carpenters' strike did not trouble Burnham. There seemed to be plenty of unemployed nonunion carpenters willing to step in for the absent strikers. "I fear nothing at all from this source," he wrote on April 6 in a letter to Margaret. The day was cold "but clear, bright and beautiful, a splendid day to live and work in." Workers were putting in "the embellishments," he wrote. "A lot of ducks were put in the lagoons yesterday, and they are floating around contentedly and quite like life this morning." Olmsted had ordered more than eight hundred ducks and geese, seven thousand pigeons, and for the sake of accent a number of exotic birds, including four snowy egrets, four storks, two brown pelicans, and two flamingoes. So far only the common white ducks had been introduced into the waters. "In two or three days," Burnham wrote, "all the birds will be in the water, which already commences to be still more beautiful than last year." The weather remained lovely: crisp, clear, and dry. On Monday, April 10, he told Margaret, "I am very happy."

Over the next few days his mood changed. There was talk that other unions might join the carpenters' strike and bring all work in Jackson Park to a halt. Suddenly the exposition seemed dangerously far from ready. Construction of the sheds for the stock exhibits at the south end of the grounds had yet to begin. Everywhere Burnham looked he saw rail tracks and temporary roads, empty boxcars and packing crates. Tumbleweeds of excelsior roved the grounds. He was disappointed with the unfinished appearance of the park, and he was peeved at his wife.

"Why do you not write me every day?" he asked on Thursday. "I look in vain for your letters."

He kept a photograph of Margaret in his office. Every time he walked by it, he picked it up and stared at it with longing. So far that day, he told her, he had looked at it ten times. He had counted on a rest after May 1 but realized now that the intensity would persist until long afterward. "The public will regard the work as entirely done, and I wish it were, so far as I am concerned. I presume anyone running a race has moments of half despair, along toward the end; but they must never be yielded to."

Margaret sent him a four-leafed clover.

There was disarray in the fairgrounds, but not next door on the fifteen acres of ground leased by Buffalo Bill for his show, which now bore the official title "Buffalo Bill's Wild West and Congress of Rough Riders of the World." He was able to open his show on April 3 and immediately filled his eighteen-thousand-seat arena. Visitors entered through a gate that featured Columbus on one side, under the banner "PILOT OF THE OCEAN, THE FIRST PIONEER," and Buffalo Bill on the other, identified as "PILOT OF THE PRAIRIE, THE LAST PIONEER."

His show and camp covered fifteen acres. Its hundreds of Indians, soldiers, and workers slept in tents. Annie Oakley always made hers very homey, with a garden outside of primrose, geranium, and hollyhock. Inside she placed her couch, cougar skins, an Axminister carpet, rocking chairs, and assorted other artifacts of domestic life. And of course a diverse collection of guns.

Buffalo Bill always began his show with his Cowboy Band playing "The Star-Spangled Banner." Next came the "Grand Review," during which soldiers from America, England, France, Germany, and Russia paraded on horseback around his arena. Annie Oakley came next, blasting away at an array of impossible targets. She hit them. Another of the show's staples was an Indian attack on an old stagecoach, the Deadwood Mail Coach, with Buffalo Bill and his men coming to the rescue. (During the show's earlier engagement in London, the Indians attacked the coach as it raced across the grounds of Windsor Castle carrying four kings and the prince of Wales. Buffalo Bill drove.) Late in the program Cody himself demonstrated some fancy marksmanship, dashing around the arena on horseback while firing his Winchester at glass balls hurled into the air by his assistants. The climax of the show was the "Attack on a Settler's Cabin," during which Indians who once had slaughtered soldiers and civilians alike staged a mock attack on a cabin full of white settlers, only to be vanquished yet again by Buffalo Bill and a company of cowboys firing blanks. As the season advanced, Cody replaced the attack with the even more dramatic "Battle of the Little Big Horn . . . showing with historical accuracy the scene of Custer's Last Charge."

The fair was hard on Colonel Cody's marriage. The show always kept him away from his home in North Platte, Nebraska, but his absence wasn't the main problem. Bill liked women, and women liked Bill. One day his wife, Louisa—"Lulu"—traveled to Chicago for a surprise conjugal visit. She found that Bill's wife already had arrived. At the hotel's front desk a clerk told her she would now be escorted up to "Mr. and Mrs. Cody's suite."

Fearful that a wider strike could hobble the fair, even destroy it, Burnham began negotiations with the carpenters and ironworkers and agreed at last to establish a minimum wage and to pay time and a half for extra hours and double time for Sundays and key holidays, including, significantly, Labor Day. The union men, in turn, signed a contract to work until the end of the fair. Burnham's clear relief suggests that his earlier bravado might have been just for show. "You can imagine though tired I go to bed happy," he wrote to his wife. One measure of his exhaustion was the fact that the contorted syntax he usually worked so hard to suppress had now resurfaced. "We sat from early in the afternoon to nine o'clock. Till the fair is over this trial will not recur I believe, so your picture before me is unusually lovely as it looks up from the desk."

Burnham claimed the agreement was a victory for the exposition, but in fact the fair's concessions were a breakthrough for organized labor, and the resulting contracts became models for other unions to emulate. The fair's capitulation pumped steam into America's—and Chicago's—already-boiling labor movement.

Olmsted returned to Chicago accompanied by his usual troika of affliction and found the place galvanized, Burnham everywhere at once. On Thursday, April 13, Olmsted wrote to his son John, "Every body here in a keen rush, the greatest in imaginable outward confusion." Winds raced over the park's barren stretches and raised blizzards of dust. Train after train arrived bearing exhibits that should have been installed long before. The delayed installations meant that temporary tracks and roads had to remain in place. Two days later Olmsted wrote: "We shall have to bear the blame of everyone else's tardiness, as their operations are now everywhere in our way. At best the most important part of all our work will have to be done at night after the opening of the Exposition. I cannot see any way through the confusion but there are thousands of men at work under various chiefs & I suppose by & by the great labor will begin to tell together."

He assigned some of the blame for the incomplete landscape to himself, for failing to install a trustworthy overseer in Chicago after the death of Harry Codman. On April 15, 1893, he wrote to John, "I am afraid that we were wrong in leaving the business so much to Ulrich & Phil. Ulrich is not I hope intentionally dishonest but he is perverse to the point of deceiving & misleading us & cannot be depended on. His energy is largely exhausted on matters that he sh'd not be concerned with. . . . I cannot trust him from day to day."

His frustration with Ulrich grew, his distrust deepened. Later, in another note to John, he said, "Ulrich is unwittingly faithless to us. The difficulty is that he is ambitious of honors out of his proper line; cares more to be more extraordinarily active, industrious, zealous & generally useful, than to achieve fine results in L.A. [Landscape Architecture]." Olmsted grew especially leery of Ulrich's slavish attentiveness to Burnham. "He is all over the grounds, about all sorts of business, and Mr. Burnham & every head of Department is constantly calling for 'Ulrich!' In going over the works with Burnham I find him constantly repeating to his Secretary: 'Tell Ulrich to'—do this & that. I remonstrate, but it does little good. I can never find him at the work except by special appointment and then he is impatient to get away."

At heart what Olmsted feared was that Burnham had transferred his loyalty to Ulrich. "I suppose that our time is out—our engagement ended, and I fear that Burnham is disposed to let us go and depend on Ulrich—for Burnham is not competent to see the incompetency of Ulrich & the need of deliberate thought. I have to be cautious not to bore Burnham, who is, of course, enormously overloaded."

Other obstacles quickly appeared. An important shipment of plants from California failed to arrive, worsening an already critical shortage of all plants. Even the fine weather that prevailed in the first couple of weeks of April caused delays. The lack of rain and the fact that the park's water-works were not yet completed meant Olmsted could not plant exposed portions of the grounds. The wind-blown dust—"frightful dust," he said, "regular sandstorms of the desert"—continued and stung his eyes and propelled grit into his inflamed mouth. "I am trying to suggest why I seem to be accomplishing so little. . . ." he wrote. "I think the public for a time will be awfully disappointed with our work—dissatisfied & a strong hand will be required here for weeks to come to prevent Ulrich's energies from being wrongly directed."

By April 21 Olmsted was again confined to bed "with sore throat, an ulcerating tooth, and much pain preventing sleep."

Despite all this his spirits began slowly to improve. When he looked past the immediate delays and Ulrich's duplicity, he saw progress. The shore of the Wooded Island was just now beginning to burst forth in a dense profusion of new leaves and blossoms, and the Japanese temple, the Hoo-den, crafted in Japan and assembled by Japanese artisans, detracted little from the sylvan effect. The electric boats had arrived and were lovely, exactly what Olmsted had hoped for, and the waterfowl on the lagoons provided enchanting sparks of energy in counterpoint to the static white immensity of the Court of Honor. Olmsted recognized that Burnham's forces could not possibly finish patching and painting by May 1 and that his own work would be far from complete, but he saw clear improvement. "A larger force is employed," he wrote, "and every day's work tells."

Even this flicker of optimism was about to disappear, however, for a powerful weather front was moving across the prairie, toward Chicago.

During this period, the exact date unclear, a milk peddler named Joseph McCarthy stopped his cart near Chicago's Humboldt Park. It was morning, about eleven o'clock. A man in the park had caught his attention. He realized he knew the man: Patrick Prendergast, a newspaper distributor employed by the *Inter Ocean*.

The odd thing was, Prendergast was walking in circles. Odder still, he walked with his head tipped back and his hat pulled so low it covered his eyes.

As McCarthy watched, Prendergast walked face-first into a tree.

Rain began to fall. At first it did not trouble Burnham. It suppressed the dust that rose from the unplanted portions of the grounds—of which, he was disappointed to see, there were far too many—and by now all the roofs were finished, even the roof of the Manufactures and Liberal Arts Building.

"It rains," Burnham wrote to Margaret, on Tuesday, April 18, "and for the first time I say, let it. My roofs are in such good order at last, as to leaks we care little."

But the rain continued and grew heavier. At night it fell past the electric lights in sheets so thick they were nearly opaque. It turned the dust to mud, which caused horses to stagger and wagons to stall. And it found leaks. On Wednesday night a particularly heavy rain came pounding through Jackson Park, and soon a series of two-hundred-foot cataracts began tumbling from the glass ceiling of the Manufactures and Liberal Arts Building onto the exhibits below. Burnham and an army of workers and guards converged on the building and together spent the night fighting the leaks.

"Last night turned out the most terrible storm we have had in Jackson Park," Burnham wrote Margaret on Thursday. "No damage was done to the buildings on grounds except that the roofs of the Manufactures Building leaked on the east side, and we stayed there until midnight covering up goods. One of the papers says that Genl Davis was on hand and attending to things & that he never left the building till all was safe. Of course Mr. D had nothing whatever to do with it."

The rain seemed to bring into focus just how much work remained. That same Thursday Burnham wrote another letter to Margaret. "The weather is very bad here and has so continued since last Tuesday, but I keep right along although the most gigantic work lies before us. . . . The intensity of this last month is very great indeed. You can little imagine it. I am surprised at my own calmness under it all." But the challenge, he said, had tested his lieutenants. "The strain on them shows who is made of good metal and who is not. I can tell you that very few come right up to the mark under these conditions, but there are some who can be depended on. The rest have to be pounded every hour of the day, and they are the ones who make me tired."

As always, he longed for Margaret. She was out of the city but due back for the opening. "I will be on the look out for you, my dear girl," he wrote. "You must expect to give yourself up when you come."

For this buttoned-up age, for Burnham, it was a letter that could have steamed itself open.

⌕══╸

Day after day the same thing: fogged windows, paper curled from ambient moisture, the demonic applause of rain on rooftops, and everywhere the stench of sweat and moist wool, especially in the workers'

mess at lunch hour. Rain filled electrical conduits and shorted circuits. At
the Ferris Wheel the pumps meant to drain the tower excavations ran
twenty-four hours but could not conquer the volume of water. Rain
poured through the ceiling of the Woman's Building and halted the installation of exhibits. In the Midway the Egyptians and Algerians and
half-clothed Dahomans suffered. Only the Irish, in Mrs. Hart's Irish Village, seemed to take it in stride.

For Olmsted the rain was particularly disheartening. It fell on ground
already saturated, and it filled every dip in every path. Puddles became
lakes. The wheels of heavily loaded wagons sank deep into the mud and
left gaping lacerations, adding to the list of wounds to be filled,
smoothed, and sodded.

Despite the rain the pace of work increased. Olmsted was awed by the
sheer numbers of workers involved. On April 27, three days before the
opening, he reported to his firm, "I wrote you that there were 2,000 men
employed—*foolishly*. There have been 2,000 men employed *directly* by
Mr. Burnham. This week there are more than twice that number, *exclusive* of contractors forces. Including contractors and concessionaires'
forces, there are now 10,000 men at work on the ground, and would be
more if more of certain classes could be obtained. Our work is badly
delayed because teams cannot be hired in sufficient numbers." (His estimate was low: In these closing weeks the total number of workers in the
park was almost twenty thousand.) He was still desperately short of
plants, he complained. "All resources for these seem to have failed and
the want of them will be serious in its result."

His ulcerated tooth, at least, had improved, and he was no longer confined to bed. "My ulcer has shrunk," he wrote. "I still have to live on
bread & milk but am going about in the rain today and getting better."

That same day, however, he wrote John a private and far bleaker letter. "We are having bad luck. Heavy rain again today." Burnham was
pressuring him to take all manner of shortcuts to get the Court of Honor
into presentable shape, such as having his men fill pots with rhododen-

drons and palms to decorate terraces, precisely the kind of showy transient measures that Olmsted disdained. "I don't like it at all," he wrote.
He resented having "to resort to temporary expedients merely to make a
poor show for the opening." He knew that immediately after the opening all such work would have to be redone. His ailments, his frustration,
and the mounting intensity of the work taxed his spirits and caused him
to feel older than his age. "The diet of the provisional mess table, the
noise & scurry and the puddles and rain do not leave a dilapidated old
man much comfort & my throat & mouth are still in such condition that
I have to keep slopping victuals."

He did not give up, however. Despite the rain he jolted around the
grounds to direct planting and sodding and every morning at dawn
attended Burnham's mandatory muster of key men. The exertion and
weather reversed the improvement in his health. "I took cold & was up
all night with bone trouble and am living on toast & tea," he wrote on
Friday, April 28. "Nearly constant heavy rain all the day, checking our
work sadly." Yet the frenzy of preparations for Monday's opening continued unabated. "It is queer to see the painters at work on ladders &
scaffolds in this heavy rain," Olmsted wrote. "Many are completely
drenched and I should think their painting must be streaky." He noticed
that the big Columbia Fountain at the western end of the central basin
still was not finished, even though it was to be a key feature of the opening ceremony. A test was scheduled for the following day, Saturday. "It
does not look ready by any means," Olmsted wrote, "but it is expected
that it will play before the President next Monday."

As for the work under his own department, Olmsted was disappointed. He had hoped to accomplish far more by now. He knew, also,
that others shared his disappointment. "I get wind of much misplaced
criticism, by men as clever even as Burnham, because of impressions from
incomplete work and undeveloped compositions," he wrote. He knew
that in many places the grounds did look sparse and unkempt and that
much work remained—anyone could see the gaps—but to hear about it
from others, especially from a man whom he admired and respected, was
profoundly depressing.

The deadline was immutable. Too much had been set in motion for anyone even to consider postponement. The opening ceremony was scheduled to begin, *would* begin, on Monday morning with a parade from the Loop to Jackson Park, led by the new president of the United States, Grover Cleveland. Train after train now entered Chicago bringing statesmen, princes, and tycoons from all over the world. President Cleveland arrived with his vice president and a retinue of cabinet officials, senators, and military leaders and their wives, children, and friends. The rain steamed off black locomotives. Porters hauled great trunks from the baggage cars. Caravans of water-slicked black carriages lined the streets outside the city's train stations, their red waiting lights haloed by the rain. The hours slipped past.

On the evening of April 30, the night before Opening Day, a British reporter named F. Herbert Stead visited the fairgrounds. The name Stead was well known in America because of Herbert's more famous brother, William, the former editor of London's *Pall Mall Gazette* and recent founder of *The Review of Reviews*. Assigned to cover the opening ceremony, Herbert decided to scout the grounds ahead of time to get a more detailed sense of the fair's topography.

It was raining hard when he exited his carriage and entered Jackson Park. Lights blazed everywhere as shawls of rain unfurled around them. The ponds that had replaced Olmsted's elegant paths shuddered under the impact of a billion falling droplets. Hundreds of empty freight cars stood black against the lights. Lumber and empty crates and the remains of workers' lunches lay everywhere.

The whole scene was heartbreaking but also perplexing: The fair's Opening Day celebration was set to begin the next morning, yet the grounds were clotted with litter and debris—in a state, Stead wrote, of "gross incompleteness."

The rain continued through the night.

Later that Sunday night, as rain thumped their windowsills, editors of Chicago's morning dailies laid out bold and elaborate headlines for Monday's historic editions. Not since the Chicago Fire of 1871 had the city's newspapers been so galvanized by a single event. But there was more quotidian work to be done as well. The more junior typesetters leaded and shimmed the classifieds and personals and all the other advertisements that filled the inside pages. Some that night worked on a small notice announcing the opening of a new hotel, clearly another hastily built affair meant to capitalize on the expected crush of exposition visitors. This hotel at least seemed to be well located—at Sixty-third and Wallace in Englewood, a short ride on the new Alley L from the fair's Sixty-third Street gate.

The owner called it the World's Fair Hotel.

PART III

In the White City

(May–October 1893)

The Court of Honor.

Opening Day

TWENTY-THREE GLEAMING BLACK CARRIAGES stood in the yellow mud of Michigan Avenue in front of the Lexington Hotel. President Cleveland boarded the seventh carriage, a landau. Burnham and Davis shared the sixth. Both men behaved, although they still had not shed their mutual distrust nor resolved their struggle for supreme control of the fair. The duke of Veragua, a direct descendent of Columbus, sat in the fourteenth carriage; the duchess occupied the fifteenth with Bertha Palmer, whose diamonds radiated an almost palpable heat. Mayor Harrison took the very last carriage and drew the loudest cheers. Assorted other dignitaries filled the remaining carriages. As the procession rumbled south along Michigan Avenue toward Jackson Park, the street behind became a following sea of 200,000 Chicagoans on foot and horseback, in phaetons, victorias, and stanhopes, and packed into omnibuses and streetcars. Many thousands of others boarded trains and jammed the bright yellow cars, dubbed "cattle cars," built by the Illinois Central to haul as many people as possible to the fair. Anyone with a white handkerchief waved it, and white flags hung from every lamppost. Damp bunting swelled from building façades. Fifteen hundred members of the Columbian Guard in their new uniforms of light blue sackcloth, white gloves, and yellow-lined black capes met the throng and cordially directed everyone to the Administration Building, recognizable by its lofty gold dome.

The procession approached the fair from the west, through the Midway Plaisance. Just as the president's carriage turned into the Avenue of Nations, which ran the thirteen-block length of the Midway, the sun emerged, igniting a roar of approval from spectators as it lit the forty concessions that lined the avenue, some the size of small towns. The carriages rolled past Sitting Bull's Cabin, the Lapland Village, the compound of the allegedly cannibalistic Dahomans, and, directly opposite, the California Ostrich Farm, redolent of simmering butter and eggs. The farm offered omelets made from ostrich eggs, though in fact the eggs came from domestic chickens. The procession passed the Austrian Village and Captive Balloon Park, where a hydrogen balloon tethered to the ground took visitors aloft. At the center of the Midway, the procession veered around the woefully incomplete Ferris Wheel, which Burnham eyed with displeasure. It was a half-moon of steel encased in a skyscraper of wooden falsework.

When President Cleveland's carriage came to Sol Bloom's Algerian Village, at the Muslim core of the Midway, Bloom gave a nod, and the women of the village dropped their veils. Bloom swore it was a customary gesture of respect, but of course with Bloom one could never be sure. The carriages skirted the Street in Cairo—not yet open, another disappointment—and passed the Turkish Village and the Java Lunch Room. Outside Hagenback's Animal Show, the most famous traveling zoo of the day, handlers prodded four trained lions into full roar. To the right, in the smoky distance, the president saw the banners of Buffalo Bill's Wild West flying over the arena Colonel Cody had built at Sixty-second Street.

At last the carriages entered Jackson Park.

There would be miracles at the fair—the chocolate Venus de Milo would not melt, the 22,000-pound cheese in the Wisconsin Pavilion would not mold—but the greatest miracle was the transformation of the grounds during the long soggy night that had preceded Cleveland's arrival. When Herbert Stead returned the next morning, a plain of wind-rippled water still covered portions of the park, but the empty boxcars and packing debris were gone. Ten thousand men working through the night had touched up the paint and staff and planted pansies and laid sod as a thousand scrubwomen washed, waxed, and polished the floors of the great buildings. As the morning advanced, the sun emerged more fully. In the bright rain-scrubbed air those portions of the landscape not still submerged looked cheerful, trim, and neat. "When the Fair opened," said Paul Starrett, one of Burnham's men, "Olmsted's lawns were the first amazement."

At eleven o'clock President Cleveland ascended the stairs to the speakers' platform, erected outside at the east end of the Administration Building, and took his seat, the signal for the ceremony to begin. The crowd surged forward. Twenty women fainted. Reporters lucky enough to be in the front rows rescued one elderly woman by hauling her over a railing and laying her out on a press table. Members of the Guard waded in with swords drawn. Mayhem reigned until Director-General Davis signaled the orchestra to begin playing the introductory "Columbian March."

Chastened by criticism of the stupefying length of October's Dedication Day ceremony, the fair's officers had kept the Opening Day program short and pledged to honor the timetable at all costs. First came a blessing, given by a blind chaplain to an audience made deaf by size and distance. Next came a poetic ode to Columbus that was as long and difficult to endure as the admiral's voyage itself: "Then from the *Pinta*'s foretop fell a cry, a trumpet song, 'Light ho! Light ho! Light!' "

That kind of thing.

Director-General Davis spoke next and offered a meaty helping of distorted reality, praising the way the National Commission, the Exposition Company, and the Board of Lady Managers had worked together without strife to produce such a brilliant exposition. Those privy to the warfare within and between these agencies watched Burnham closely but saw no change in his expression. Davis offered the podium to the president.

Cleveland, immense in black, paused a moment in sober examination of the crowd before him. Nearby stood a table draped in an American flag, on top of which lay a blue and red velvet pillow supporting a telegraph key made of gold.

Every bit of terrace, lawn, and railing in the Court of Honor was occupied, the men in black and gray, many of the women in gowns of extravagant hues—violet, scarlet, emerald—and wearing hats with ribbons, sprigs, and feathers. A tall man in a huge white hat and a white buckskin coat heavily trimmed in silver stood a full head above the men around him: Buffalo Bill. Women watched him. Sunlight fell between tufts of fast-shredding cloud and lit the white Panamas that flecked the audience. From the president's vantage point the scene was festive and crisp, but at ground level there was water and mud and the mucid sucking that accompanied any shift in position. The only human form with dry feet was that of Daniel Chester French's Statue of the Republic—Big Mary—which stood hidden under a silo of canvas.

Cleveland's speech was the shortest of all. As he concluded, he moved to the flag-draped table. "As by a touch the machinery that gives light to this vast Exposition is set in motion," he said, "so at the same instant let our hopes and aspirations awaken forces which in all time to come shall influence the welfare, the dignity, and the freedom of mankind."

At precisely 12:08 he touched the gold key. A roar radiated outward as successive strata of the crowd learned that the key had been pressed. Workmen on rooftops immediately signaled to peers stationed throughout the park and to sailors aboard the warship *Michigan* anchored in the lake. The key closed an electric circuit that activated the Electro-Automatic Engine Stop and Starter attached to the giant three-thousand-horsepower Allis steam engine at the Machinery Building. The starter's silver-plated gong rang, a sprocket turned, a valve opened, and the engine whooshed to life on exquisitely machined shafts and bearings. Immediately thirty other engines in the building began to thrum. At the fair's waterworks three huge Worthington pumps began stretching their shafts and pistons, like praying mantises shaking off the cold. Millions of gallons of water began surging through the fair's mains. Engines everywhere took steam until the ground trembled. An American flag the size of a mainsail unfurled from the tallest flagpole in the Court of Honor, and immediately two more like-sized flags tumbled from flanking poles, one representing Spain, the other Columbus. Water pressurized by the Worthington pumps exploded from the MacMonnies Fountain and soared a hundred feet into the sky, casting a sheet rainbow across the sun and driving visitors to raise their umbrellas against the spray. Banners and flags and gonfalons suddenly bellied from every cornice, a huge red banner unscrolled along the full length of the Machinery Building, and the canvas slipped from Big Mary's gold-leaf shoulders. Sunlight clattering from her skin caused men and women to shield their eyes. Two hundred white doves leaped for the sky. The guns of the *Michigan* fired. Steam whistles shrieked. Spontaneously the throng began to sing "My Country 'Tis of Thee," which many thought of as the national anthem although no song had yet received that designation. As the crowd thundered, a man eased up beside a thin, pale woman with a bent neck. In the next instant Jane Addams realized her purse was gone.

The great fair had begun.

Although Burnham recognized that much work lay ahead—that Olmsted had to redouble his efforts and Ferris needed to finish that damned wheel—the success of the exposition now seemed assured. Congratulations arrived by telegraph and post. A friend told Burnham, "The scene burst on me with the beauty of a full blown rose." The official history of the fair estimated that a quarter of a million people packed Jackson Park on Opening Day. Two other estimates put the total at 500,000 and 620,000. By day's end there was every indication that Chicago's fair would become the most heavily attended entertainment in the history of the world.

This optimism lasted all of twenty-four hours.

On Tuesday, May 2, only ten thousand people came to Jackson Park, a rate of attendance that, if continued, would guarantee the fair a place in history as one of the greatest failures of all time. The yellow cattle cars were mostly empty, as were the cars of the Alley L that ran along Sixty-third Street. All hope that this was merely an anomaly disappeared the next day, when the forces that had been battering the nation's economy erupted in a panic on Wall Street that caused stock prices to plummet. Over the next week the news grew steadily more disturbing.

On the night of Thursday, May 5, officials of the National Cordage Company, a trust that controlled 80 percent of America's rope production, placed itself in receivership. Next Chicago's Chemical National Bank ceased operation, a closure that seemed particularly ominous to fair officials because Chemical alone had won congressional approval to open a branch at the world's fair, in no less central a location than the Administration Building. Three days later another large Chicago bank failed, and soon after that a third, the Evanston National Bank, in Burnham's town. Dozens of other failures occurred around the country. In Brunswick, Georgia, the presidents of two national banks held a meeting. One president calmly excused himself, entered his private office, and shot himself through the head. Both banks failed. In Lincoln, Nebraska, the Nebraska Savings Bank had become the favorite bank of school-children. The town's teachers served as agents of the bank and every week collected money from the children for deposit in each child's pass-book account. Word that the bank was near failure caused the street out front to fill with children pleading for their money. Other banks came to Nebraska Savings' rescue, and the so-called "children's run" was quelled.

People who otherwise might have traveled to Chicago to see the fair now stayed home. The terrifying economy was discouraging enough, but so too were reports of the unfinished character of the fair. If people had only one chance to go, they wanted to do it when all the exhibits were in place and every attraction was in operation, especially the Ferris Wheel, said to be a marvel of engineering that would make the Eiffel Tower seem like a child's sculpture—provided it ever actually worked and did not collapse in the first brisk wind.

Too many features of the fair remained unfinished, Burnham acknowledged. He and his brigade of architects, draftsmen, engineers, and contractors had accomplished so much in an impossibly short time, but apparently not enough to overcome the damping effect of the fast-degrading economy. The elevators in the Manufactures and Liberal Arts Building, touted as one of the wonders of the fair, still had not begun operation. The Ferris Wheel looked only half finished. Olmsted had yet to complete grading and planting the grounds around the Krupp Pavilion, the Leather

Building, and the Cold Storage Building; he had not yet laid the brick pavement at the fair's train station or sodded the New York Central exhibit, the Pennsylvania Railroad exhibit, Choral Hall, and the Illinois State Building, which to many Chicagoans was the single most important building at the fair. The installation of exhibits and company pavilions within the Electricity Building was woefully behind schedule. Westinghouse only began building its pavilion on Tuesday, May 2.

Burnham issued stern directives to Olmsted and Ferris and to every contractor still at work. Olmsted in particular felt the pressure but also felt hobbled by the persistent delays in installation of exhibits and the damage done by the repeated comings and goings of drays and freight cars. General Electric alone had fifteen carloads of exhibit materials stored on the grounds. Preparations for the Opening Day ceremony had cost Olmsted's department valuable time, as did the planting and grading required to repair the damage the day's crowd had inflicted throughout the park. Many of the fair's fifty-seven miles of roadway were still either submerged or coated with mud, and others had been gouged and trenched by vehicles that had used the roads while they were still sodden. Olmsted's road contractor deployed a force of eight hundred men and one hundred teams of horses to begin regrading the roads and laying new gravel. "I remain fairly well," Olmsted wrote to his son, on May 15, "but get horribly tired every day. It is hard to get things done; my body is so overworked, and I constantly fail to accomplish what I expect to do."

First and foremost, Burnham knew, the fair had to be *finished,* but in the meantime lures had to be cast to encourage people to shed their fears of financial ruin and come to Chicago. He created the new post of director of functions and assigned Frank Millet to the job, giving him wide latitude to do what he could to boost attendance. Millet orchestrated fireworks shows and parades. He set aside special days to honor individual states and nations and to fete distinct groups of workers, including cobblers, millers, confectioners, and stenographers. The Knights of Pythias got their own day, as did the Catholic Knights of America. Millet set August 25 as Colored People Fete Day, and October 9 as Chicago Day. Attendance began to increase, but not by much. By the end of May the daily average of paying visitors was only thirty-three thousand, still far below what Burnham and everyone else had expected and, more to the point, far below the level required to make the fair profitable. Worse yet, Congress and the National Commission, bowing to pressure from the Sabbatarian movement, had ordered the fair closed on Sundays, thus withdrawing its wonders from a few million wage-earners for whom Sunday was the only day off.

Burnham hoped for an early cure to the nation's financial malaise, but the economy did not oblige. More banks failed, layoffs increased, industrial production sagged, and strikes grew more violent. On June 5 worried depositors staged runs on eight Chicago banks. Burnham's own firm saw the flow of new commissions come to a halt.

The World's Fair Hotel

THE FIRST GUESTS BEGAN ARRIVING at Holmes's World's Fair Hotel, though not in the volume he and every other South Side hotelier had expected. The guests were drawn mainly by the hotel's location, with Jackson Park a short trip east on the Sixty-third Street leg of the Alley L. Even though the rooms on Holmes's second and third floors were largely empty, when male visitors asked about accommodations Holmes told them with a look of sincere regret that he had no vacancies and kindly referred them to other hotels nearby. His guest rooms began to fill with women, most quite young and apparently unused to living alone. Holmes found them intoxicating.

Minnie Williams's continual presence became increasingly awkward. With the arrival of each dewy new guest, she became more jealous, more inclined to stay close to him. Her jealousy did not particularly annoy him. It simply became inconvenient. Minnie was an asset now, an acquisition to be warehoused until needed, like cocooned prey.

Holmes checked newspaper advertisements for a rental flat far enough from his building to make impromptu visits unlikely. He found a place on the North Side at 1220 Wrightwood Avenue, a dozen or so blocks west of Lincoln Park, near Halsted. It was a pretty, shaded portion of the city, though its prettiness was to Holmes merely an element to be entered into his calculations. The flat occupied the top floor of a large private house owned by a man named John Oker, whose daughters managed its rental. They first advertised the flat in April 1893.

Holmes went alone to examine the apartment and met John Oker. He introduced himself as Henry Gordon and told Oker he was in the real estate business.

Oker was impressed with this prospective tenant. He was neat—maybe fastidious was the better word—and his clothing and behavior suggested financial well-being. Oker was delighted when Henry Gordon said he would take the apartment; even more delighted when Gordon paid him forty dollars, cash, in advance. Gordon told Oker he and his wife would arrive in a few weeks.

Holmes explained the move to Minnie as a long-overdue necessity. Now that they were married, they needed a bigger, nicer place than what they currently occupied in the castle. Soon the building would be bustling with visitors to the fair. Even without the guests, however, it was no place to raise a family.

The idea of a large, sunny flat did appeal to Minnie. Truth was, the castle could be gloomy. Was always gloomy. And Minnie wanted everything as perfect as possible for Anna's visit. She was a bit perplexed, however, as to why Harry would choose a place so far away, on the North Side, when there were so many lovely homes in Englewood. She reasoned, perhaps, that he did not want to pay the exorbitant rents that everyone was charging now that the world's fair was under way.

Holmes and Minnie moved into the new flat on June 1, 1893. Lora Oker, the owner's daughter, said Gordon "seemed to be very attentive to his wife." The couple went on bicycle rides and for a time kept a hired girl. "I can only say that his behavior was all that could be wished during his sojourn with us," Miss Oker said. "Minnie Williams he introduced as his wife and we always addressed her as 'Mrs. Gordon.' She called him 'Henry.' "

With Minnie housed on Wrightwood Avenue, Holmes found himself free to enjoy his World's Fair Hotel.

His guests spent most of their time at Jackson Park or on the Midway and often did not return until after midnight. While present in the hotel they tended to stay in their rooms, since Holmes provided none of the common areas—the libraries, game parlors, and writing rooms—that the big hotels like the Richelieu and Metropole and the nearby New Julien offered as a matter of routine. Nor did he supply the darkroom facilities that hotels closest to Jackson Park had begun installing to serve the growing number of amateur photographers, so-called "Kodak fiends," who carried the newest portable cameras.

The women found the hotel rather dreary, especially at night, but the presence of its handsome and clearly wealthy owner helped dispel some of its bleakness. Unlike the men they knew back in Minneapolis or Des Moines or Sioux Falls, Holmes was warm and charming and talkative and touched them with a familiarity that, while perhaps offensive back home, somehow seemed all right in this new world of Chicago—just another aspect of the great adventure on which these women had embarked. And what good was an adventure if it did not feel a little dangerous?

As best anyone could tell, the owner also was a forgiving soul. He did not seem at all concerned when now and then a guest checked out without advance notice, leaving her bills unpaid. That he often smelled vaguely of chemicals—that in fact the building as a whole often had a medicinal odor—bothered no one. He was, after all, a physician, and his building had a pharmacy on the ground floor.

Prendergast

PATRICK PRENDERGAST BELIEVED HIS APPOINTMENT as corporation counsel was about to occur. He wanted to be ready and began making plans for how to staff his office once the appointment came through. On May 9, 1893, he got out another of his postcards and addressed it to a man named W. F. Cooling, in the *Staats-Zeitung* Building. Prendergast lectured Cooling on the fact that Jesus was the ultimate legal authority, then gave him the good news.

"I am candidate for corporation counsel," he wrote. "If I become corporation counsel you shall be my assistant."

Night Is the Magician

DESPITE ITS INCOMPLETE EXHIBITS, rutted paths, and stretches of unplanted ground, the exposition revealed to its early visitors a vision of what a city could be and ought to be. The Black City to the north lay steeped in smoke and garbage, but here in the White City of the fair visitors found clean public bathrooms, pure water, an ambulance service, electric streetlights, and a sewage-processing system that yielded acres of manure for farmers. There was daycare for the children of visitors, and much fun was made of the fact that when you left your child at the Children's Building, you received a claim check in return. Chicago's small but vocal censorians feared that impoverished parents would turn the building into a depository for unwanted children. Only one child, poor Charlie Johnson, was ever thus abandoned, and not a single child was lost, although anxiety invested the closing moments of each day.

Within the fair's buildings visitors encountered devices and concepts new to them and to the world. They heard live music played by an orchestra in New York and transmitted to the fair by long-distance telephone. They saw the first moving pictures on Edison's Kinetoscope, and they watched, stunned, as lightning chattered from Nikola Tesla's body. They saw even more ungodly things—the first zipper; the first-ever all-electric kitchen, which included an automatic dishwasher; and a box purporting to contain everything a cook would need to make pancakes, under the brand name Aunt Jemima's. They sampled a new, oddly flavored gum called Juicy Fruit, and caramel-coated popcorn called Cracker Jack. A new cereal, Shredded Wheat, seemed unlikely to succeed—"shredded doormat," some called it—but a new beer did well, winning the exposition's top beer award. Forever afterward, its brewer called it

Pabst Blue Ribbon. Visitors also encountered the latest and arguably most important organizational invention of the century, the vertical file, created by Melvil Dewey, inventor of the Dewey Decimal System. Sprinkled among these exhibits were novelties of all kinds. A locomotive made of spooled silk. A suspension bridge built out of Kirk's Soap. A giant map of the United States made of pickles. Prune makers sent along a full-scale knight on horseback sculpted out of prunes, and the Avery Salt Mines of Louisiana displayed a copy of the Statue of Liberty carved from a block of salt. Visitors dubbed it "Lot's Wife."

One of the most compelling, and chilling, exhibits was the Krupp Pavilion, where Fritz Krupp's "pet monster" stood at the center of an array of heavy guns. A popular guide to the fair, called the Time-Saver, rated every exhibit on a scale of one to three, with one being merely "interesting" and three being "remarkably interesting," and gave the Krupp Pavilion a three. For many visitors, however, the weapons were a disturbing presence. Mrs. D. C. Taylor, a frequent visitor to the fair, called Krupp's biggest gun "a fearful hideous thing, breathing of blood and carnage, a triumph of barbarism crouching amid the world's triumphs of civilization."

Mrs. Taylor adored the Court of Honor and was struck by the oddly sober manner people adopted as they walked among its palaces. "Every one about us moved softly and spoke gently. No one seemed hurried or impatient, all were under a spell, a spell that held us from the opening of the fair until its close."

In the Midway she found a very different atmosphere. Here Mrs. Taylor ventured into the Street in Cairo, open at last, and witnessed her first belly dance. She watched the dancer carefully. "She takes a few light steps to one side, pauses, strikes the castanets, then the same to the other side; advances a few steps, pauses, and causes her abdomen to rise and fall several times in exact time to the music, without moving a muscle in any other part of her body, with incredible rapidity, at the same time holding her head and feet perfectly rigid."

As Mrs. Taylor and her companions left the Street, she sang quietly to herself, "My Country 'Tis of Thee," like a frightened child easing past a graveyard.

The fair was so big, so beyond grasp, that the Columbian Guards found themselves hammered with questions. It was a disease, rhetorical smallpox, and every visitor exhibited it in some degree. The Guards answered the same questions over and over, and the questions came fast, often with an accusatory edge. Some questions were just odd.

"In which building is the pope?" one woman asked. She was overheard by writer Teresa Dean, who wrote a daily column from the fair.

"The pope is not here, madame," the guard said.

"Where is he?"

"In Italy, Europe, madame."

The woman frowned. "Which way is that?"

Convinced now that the woman was joking, the guard cheerfully quipped, "Three blocks under the lagoon."

She said, "How do I get there?"

Another visitor, hunting for an exhibit of wax figures, asked a guard, "Can you tell me where the building is that has the artificial human beings?"

He began telling her he did not know, when another visitor jumped in. "I have heard of them," he said. "They are over in the Woman's Building. Just ask for the Lady Managers."

One male visitor, who had lost both his legs and made his way around the fair on false limbs and crutches, must have looked particularly knowledgeable, because another visitor peppered him incessantly with questions, until finally the amputee complained that the strain of answering so many questions was wearing him out.

"There's just one more thing I'd like to know," his questioner said, "and I'll not trouble ye anymore."

"Well, what is it?"

"I'd like to know how you lost your legs."

The amputee said he would answer only on strict condition that this was indeed the last question. He would allow no others. Was that clear?

His persecutor agreed.

The amputee, fully aware that his answer would raise an immediate corollary question, said, "They were bit off."

"*Bit off.* How—"

But a deal was a deal. Chuckling, the amputee hobbled away.

—⌁—

As the fair fought for attendance, Buffalo Bill's Wild West drew crowds by the tens of thousands. If Cody had gotten the fair concession he had asked for, these crowds first would have had to pay admission to Jackson Park and would have boosted the fair's attendance and revenue to a welcome degree. Cody also was able to hold performances on Sundays and, being outside the fairgrounds, did not have to contribute half his revenue to the Exposition Company. Over the six months of the fair an average of twelve thousand people would attend each of Cody's 318 performances, for a total attendance of nearly four million.

Often Cody upstaged the fair. His main entrance was so close to one of the busiest exposition gates that some visitors thought his show *was* the world's fair, and were said to have gone home happy. In June a group of cowboys organized a thousand-mile race from Chadron, Nebraska, to Chicago, in honor of the fair and planned to end it in Jackson Park. The prize was a rich one, $1,000. Cody contributed another $500 and a fancy saddle on condition the race end in his own arena. The organizers accepted.

Ten riders, including "Rattlesnake" Pete and a presumably reformed Nebraska bandit named Doc Middleton, set out from the Baline Hotel in Chadron on the morning of June 14, 1893. The rules of the race allowed each rider to start with two horses and required that he stop at various checkpoints along the way. The most important rule held that when he crossed the finish line, he had to be riding one of the original horses.

The race was wild, replete with broken rules and injured animals. Middleton dropped out soon after reaching Illinois. Four others likewise failed to finish. The first rider across the line was a railroad man named John Berry, riding Poison, who galloped into the Wild West arena on

June 27 at nine-thirty in the morning. Buffalo Bill, resplendent in white buckskin and silver, was there to greet him, along with the rest of the Wild West company and ten thousand or so residents of Chicago. John Berry had to settle for the saddle alone, however, for subsequent investigation revealed that shortly after the start of the race he had loaded his horses on an eastbound train and climbed aboard himself to take the first hundred miles in comfort.

Cody upstaged the fair again in July, when exposition officials rejected a request from Mayor Carter Harrison that the fair dedicate one day to the poor children of Chicago and admit them at no charge. The directors thought this was too much to ask, given their struggle to boost the rate of paid admission. Every ticket, even half-price children's tickets, mattered. Buffalo Bill promptly declared Waif's Day at the Wild West and offered any kid in Chicago a free train ticket, free admission to the show, and free access to the whole Wild West encampment, plus all the candy and ice cream the children could eat.

Fifteen thousand showed up.

Buffalo Bill's Wild West may indeed have been an "incongruity," as the directors had declared in rejecting his request for a concession within Jackson Park, but the citizens of Chicago had fallen in love.

⸻

The skies cleared and stayed clear. Roadways dried, and newly opened flowers perfumed the air. Exhibitors gradually completed their installations, and electricians removed the last misconnects from the elaborate circuits that linked the fair's nearly 200,000 incandescent bulbs. Throughout the fairgrounds, on Burnham's orders, clean-up efforts intensified. On June 1, 1893, workers removed temporary railroad tracks that had scarred the lawns near the lagoon and just south of the Electricity and Mines buildings. "A strikingly noticeable change in the general condition of things is the absence of large piles of boxes stacked up in the exterior courts around Manufactures, Agriculture, Machinery, and other large buildings," the *Tribune* reported on June 2. Unopened crates and rubbish that just one week earlier had cluttered the interior of the

Manufactures and Liberal Arts Building, particularly at the pavilions erected by Russia, Norway, Denmark, and Canada, likewise had been removed, and now these spaces presented "an entirely different and vastly improved appearance."

Although such interior exhibits were compelling, the earliest visitors to Jackson Park saw immediately that the fair's greatest power lay in the strange gravity of the buildings themselves. The Court of Honor produced an effect of majesty and beauty that was far greater than even the dream conjured in the Rookery library. Some visitors found themselves so moved by the Court of Honor that immediately upon entering they began to weep.

No single element accounted for this phenomenon. Each building was huge to begin with, but the impression of mass was amplified by the fact that all the buildings were neoclassical in design, all had cornices set at the same height, all had been painted the same soft white, and all were so shockingly, beautifully unlike anything the majority of visitors ever had seen in their own dusty hometowns. "No other scene of man's creation seemed to me so perfect as this Court of Honor," wrote James Fullerton Muirhead, an author and guidebook editor. The court, he wrote, "was practically blameless; the aesthetic sense of the beholder was as fully and unreservedly satisfied as in looking at a masterpiece of painting or sculpture, and at the same time was soothed and elevated by a sense of amplitude and grandeur such as no single work of art could produce." Edgar Lee Masters, Chicago attorney and emerging poet, called the Court "an inexhaustible dream of beauty."

The shared color, or more accurately the shared absence of color, produced an especially alluring range of effects as the sun traveled the sky. In the early morning, when Burnham conducted his inspections, the buildings were a pale blue and seemed to float on a ghostly cushion of ground mist. Each evening the sun colored the buildings ochre and lit the motes of dust raised by the breeze until the air itself became a soft orange veil.

One such evening Burnham led a tour of the fair aboard an electric launch for a group that included John Root's widow, Dora, and a number of foreign emissaries. Burnham loved escorting friends and dignitaries through the grounds but sought always to orchestrate the journeys so that his friends saw the fair the way he believed it should be seen, with the buildings presented from a certain perspective, in a particular order, as if he were still back in his library showing drawings instead of real structures. He had tried to impose his aesthetic will on all the fair's visitors by insisting during the first year of planning that the number of entrances to Jackson Park be limited to a few and that these be situated so that people had to enter first through the Court of Honor, either through a large portal at the rail station on the west side of the park or an entry on the east from the exposition wharf. His quest to create a powerful first impression was good showmanship, but it also exposed the aesthetic despot residing within. He did not get his way. The directors insisted on many gates, and the railroads refused to channel their exposition traffic through a single depot. Burnham never quite surrendered. Throughout the fair, he said, "we insisted on sending our *own* guests whose opinions we specially valued into the Grand Court first."

The electric launch carrying Burnham, Dora Root, and the foreign dignitaries cut silently through the lagoon, scattering the white city reflected upon its surface. The setting sun gilded the terraces on the east bank but cast the west bank into dark blue shadow. Women in dresses of crimson and aquamarine walked slowly along the embankments. Voices drifted across the water, laced now and then with laughter that rang like crystal touched in a toast.

The next day, after what surely had been a difficult night, Dora Root wrote to Burnham to thank him for the tour and to attempt to convey the complexity of her feelings.

"Our hour on the lagoon last evening proved the crown of a charming day," she wrote. "Indeed I fear we would have lingered on indefinitely had not our foreign friends prepared a more highly spiced entertainment. I think I should never willingly cease drifting in that dreamland." The scenes elicited conflicting emotions. "I find it all infinitely sad," she wrote, "but at the same time so entrancing, that I often feel as if it would be the part of wisdom to fly at once to the woods or mountains where one can always find peace. There is much I long to say to you about your work of the past two years—which has brought about this superb realization of John's vision of beauty—but I cannot trust myself. It means too much to me and I think, I hope, you understand. For years his hopes and ambitions were mine, and in spite of my efforts the old interests still go on. It is a relief to me to write this. I trust you will not mind."

If evenings at the fair were seductive, the nights were ravishing. The lamps that laced every building and walkway produced the most elaborate demonstration of electric illumination ever attempted and the first large-scale test of alternating current. The fair alone consumed three times as much electricity as the entire city of Chicago. These were important engineering milestones, but what visitors adored was the sheer beauty of seeing so many lights ignited in one place, at one time. Every building, including the Manufactures and Liberal Arts Building, was outlined in white bulbs. Giant searchlights—the largest ever made and said to be visible sixty miles away—had been mounted on the Manufactures' roof and swept the grounds and surrounding neighborhoods. Large colored bulbs lit the hundred-foot plumes of water that burst from the MacMonnies Fountain.

For many visitors these nightly illuminations were their first encounter with electricity. Hilda Satt, a girl newly arrived from Poland, went to the fair with her father. "As the light was fading in the sky, millions of lights were suddenly flashed on, all at one time," she recalled, years later. "Having seen nothing but kerosene lamps for illumination, this was like getting a sudden vision of Heaven."

Her father told her the lights were activated by electric switches.

"Without matches?" she asked.

Between the lights and the ever-present blue ghosts of the Columbian Guard, the fair achieved another milestone: For the first time Chicagoans could stroll at night in perfect safety. This alone began to draw an increased number of visitors, especially young couples locked in the rictus of Victorian courtship and needful of quiet dark places.

At night the lights and the infilling darkness served to mask the exposition's many flaws—among them, wrote John Ingalls in *Cosmopolitan*, the "unspeakable debris of innumerable luncheons"—and to create for a few hours the perfect city of Daniel Burnham's dreams.

"Night," Ingalls wrote, "is the magician of the fair."

The early visitors returned to their homes and reported to friends and family that the fair, though incomplete, was far grander and more powerful than they had been led to expect. Montgomery Schuyler, the leading architectural critic of Burnham's day, wrote, "It was a common remark among visitors who saw the Fair for the first time that nothing they had read or seen pictured had given them an idea of it, or prepared them for what they saw." Reporters from far-flung cities wired the same observation back to their editors, and stories of delight and awe began to percolate through the most remote towns. In fields, dells, and hollows, families terrified by what they read in the papers each day about the collapsing national economy nonetheless now began to think about Chicago. The trip would be expensive, but it was starting to look more and more worthwhile. Even necessary.

If only Mr. Ferris would get busy and finish that big wheel.

Modus Operandi

AND SO IT BEGAN. A waitress disappeared from Holmes's restaurant, where his guests ate their meals. One day she was at work, the next gone, with no clear explanation for her abrupt departure. Holmes seemed as stumped as anyone. A stenographer named Jennie Thompson disappeared, as did a woman named Evelyn Stewart, who either worked for Holmes or merely stayed in his hotel as a guest. A male physician who for a time had rented an office in the castle and who had befriended Holmes—they were seen together often—also had decamped, with no word to anyone.

Within the hotel chemical odors ebbed and flowed like an atmospheric tide. Some days the halls were suffused with a caustic scent, as of a cleanser applied too liberally, other days with a silvery medicinal odor, as if a dentist were at work somewhere in the building easing a customer into a deep sleep. There seemed to be a problem with the gas lines that fed the building, for periodically the scent of uncombusted gas permeated the halls.

There were inquiries from family and friends. As always Holmes was sympathetic and helpful. The police still did not become involved. Apparently there was too much else for them to do, as wealthy visitors and foreign dignitaries began arriving in ever-greater numbers, shadowed by a swarm of pickpockets, thugs, and petty swindlers.

◦━━━━◦

Holmes did not kill face to face, as Jack the Ripper had done, gorging himself on warmth and viscera, but he did like proximity. He liked being near enough to hear the approach of death in the rising panic of his victims. This was when his quest for possession entered its most satisfying phase. The vault deadened most of the cries and pounding but not all. When the hotel was full of guests, he settled for more silent means. He filled a room with gas and let the guest expire in her sleep, or he crept in with his passkey and pressed a chloroform-soaked rag to her face. The choice was his, a measure of his power.

No matter what the approach, the act always left him in possession of a fresh supply of material, which he could then explore at will.

The subsequent articulation by his very talented friend Chappell constituted the final phase of acquisition, the triumphal phase, though he used Chappell's services only sparingly. He disposed of other spent material in his kiln or in pits filled with quicklime. He dared not keep Chappell's frames for too long a time. Early on he had made it a rule not to retain trophies. The possession he craved was a transient thing, like the scent of a fresh-cut hyacinth. Once it was gone, only another acquisition could restore it.

One Good Turn

IN THE FIRST WEEK of June 1893 Ferris's men began prying the last timbers and planks from the falsework that had encased and supported the big wheel during its assembly. The rim arced through the sky at a height of 264 feet, as high as the topmost occupied floor in Burnham's Masonic Temple, the city's tallest skyscraper. None of the thirty-six cars had been hung—they stood on the ground like the coaches of a derailed train—but the wheel itself was ready for its first rotation. Standing by itself, unbraced, Ferris's wheel looked dangerously fragile. "It is impossible for the non-mechanical mind to understand how such a Brobdingnag continues to keep itself erect," wrote Julian Hawthorne, son of Nathaniel; "it has no visible means of support—none that appear adequate. The spokes look like cobwebs; they are after the fashion of those on the newest make of bicycles."

On Thursday, June 8, Luther Rice signaled the firemen at the big steam boilers seven hundred feet away on Lexington Avenue, outside the Midway, to build steam and fill the ten-inch underground mains. Once the boilers reached suitable pressure, Rice nodded to an engineer in the pit under the wheel, and steam whooshed into the pistons of its twin thousand-horsepower engines. The drive sprockets turned smoothly and quietly. Rice ordered the engine stopped. Next workers attached the ten-ton chain to the sprockets and to a receiving sprocket at the wheel. Rice sent a telegram to Ferris at his office in the Hamilton Building in Pittsburgh: "Engines have steam on and are working satisfactorily. Sprocket chain connected up and are ready to turn wheel."

Ferris was unable to go to Chicago himself but sent his partner W. F. Gronau to supervise the first turn. In the early morning of Friday, June 9, as his train passed through the South Side, Gronau saw how the great wheel towered over everything in its vicinity, just as Eiffel's creation did in Paris. The exclamations of fellow passengers as to the wheel's size and apparent fragility filled him with a mixture of pride and anxiety. Ferris, himself fed up with construction delays and Burnham's pestering, had told Gronau to turn the wheel or tear it off the tower.

Last-minute adjustments and inspections took up most of Friday, but just before dusk Rice told Gronau that everything appeared to be ready.

"I did not trust myself to speak," Gronau said, "so merely nodded to start." He was anxious to see if the wheel worked, but at the same time "would gladly have assented to postpone the trial."

Nothing remained but to admit steam and see what happened. Never had anyone built such a gigantic wheel. That it would turn without crushing its bearings and rotate smoothly and true were engineering hopes supported only by calculations that reflected known qualities of iron and steel. No structure ever had been subjected to the unique stresses that would come to bear upon and within the wheel once in motion.

Ferris's pretty wife, Margaret, stood nearby, flushed with excitement. Gronau believed she was experiencing the same magnitude of mental strain as he.

"Suddenly I was aroused from these thoughts by a most horrible noise," he said. A growl tore through the sky and caused everyone in the vicinity—the Algerians of Bloom's village, the Egyptians and Persians and every visitor within one hundred yards—to halt and stare at the wheel.

"Looking up," Gronau said, "I saw the wheel move slowly. What can be the matter! What is this horrible noise!"

Gronau ran to Rice, who stood in the engine pit monitoring pressures and the play of shafts and shunts. Gronau expected to see Rice hurriedly trying to shut down the engine, but Rice looked unconcerned.

Rice explained that he had merely tested the wheel's braking system, which consisted of a band of steel wrapped around the axle. The test alone had caused the wheel to move one eighth of its circumference. The noise, Rice said, was only the sound of rust being scraped off the band.

The engineer in the pit released the brake and engaged the drive gears. The sprockets began to turn, the chain to advance.

By now many of the Algerians, Egyptians, and Persians—possibly even a few belly dancers—had gathered on the wheel's loading platforms, which were staged like steps so that once the wheel opened six cars could be loaded at a time. Everyone was silent.

As the wheel began to turn, loose nuts and bolts and a couple of wrenches rained from its hub and spokes. The wheel had consumed 28,416 pounds of bolts in its assembly; someone was bound to forget something.

Unmindful of this steel downpour, the villagers cheered and began dancing on the platforms. Some played instruments. The workmen who had risked their lives building the wheel now risked them again and climbed aboard the moving frame. "No carriages were as yet placed in position," Gronau said, "but this did not deter the men, for they clambered among the spokes and sat upon the crown of the wheel as easy as I am sitting in this chair."

The wheel needed twenty minutes for a single revolution. Only when it had completed its first full turn did Gronau feel the test had been successful, at which point he said, "I could have yelled out loud for joy."

Mrs. Ferris shook his hand. The crowd cheered. Rice telegraphed Ferris, who had been waiting all day for word of the test, his anxiety rising with each hour. The Pittsburgh office of Western Union received the cable at 9:10 P.M., and a blue-suited messenger raced through the cool spring night to bring it to Ferris. Rice had written: "The last coupling and final adjustment was made and steam turned on at six o'clock this evening one complete revolution of the big wheel was made everything working satisfactory twenty minutes time was taken for the revolution—I congratulate you upon it complete success midway is wildly enthusiastic."

The next day, Saturday, June 10, Ferris cabled Rice, "Your telegram stating that first revolution of wheel had been made last night at six o'clock and that same was successful in every way has caused great joy in this entire camp. I wish to congratulate you in all respects in this matter and ask that you rush the putting in of cars working day and night—

if you can't put the cars in at night, babbitt the car bearings at night so as to keep ahead." By "babbitt" he no doubt meant that Rice should install the metal casings in which the bearings were to sit.

The wheel had worked, but Ferris, Gronau, and Rice all knew that far more important tests lay ahead. Beginning that Saturday workers would begin hanging cars, thus placing upon the wheel its first serious stresses. Each of the thirty-six cars weighed thirteen tons, for a total of just under one million pounds. And that did not include the 200,000 pounds of additional live load that would be added as passengers filled the cars.

On Saturday, soon after receiving Ferris's congratulatory telegram, Rice cabled back that in fact the first car already had been hung.

Beyond Jackson Park the first turn of Ferris's wheel drew surprisingly little attention. The city, especially its *frappé* set, had focused its interest on another event unfolding in Jackson Park—the first visit by Spain's official emissary to the fair, the Infanta Eulalia, the youngest sister of Spain's dead King Alfonso XII and daughter of exiled Queen Isabel II.

The visit wasn't going very well.

The infanta was twenty-nine and, in the words of a State Department official, "rather handsome, graceful and bright." She had arrived two days earlier by train from New York, been transported immediately to the Palmer House, and lodged there in its most lavish suite. Chicago's boosters saw her visit as the first real opportunity to demonstrate the city's new refinement and to prove to the world, or at least to New York, that Chicago was as adept at receiving royalty as it was at turning pig bristles into paintbrushes. The first warning that things might not go as planned should perhaps have been evident in a wire-service report cabled from New York alerting the nation to the scandalous news that the young woman smoked cigarettes.

In the afternoon of her first day in Chicago, Tuesday, June 6, the infanta had slipped out of her hotel incognito, accompanied by her lady-in-waiting and an aide appointed by President Cleveland. She delighted in moving about the city unrecognized by Chicago's residents. "Nothing could be more entertaining, in fact, than to walk among the moving crowds of people who were engaged in reading about me in the newspapers, looking at a picture which looked more or less like me," she wrote.

She visited Jackson Park for the first time on Thursday, June 8, the day Ferris's wheel turned. Mayor Harrison was her escort. Crowds of strangers applauded her as she passed, for no other reason than her royal heritage. Newspapers called her the Queen of the Fair and put her visit on the front page. To her, however, it was all very tiresome. She envied the freedom she saw exhibited by Chicago's women. "I realize with some bitterness," she wrote to her mother, "that if this progress ever reaches Spain it will be too late for me to enjoy it."

By the next morning, Friday, she felt she had completed her official duties and was ready to begin enjoying herself. For example, she rejected an invitation from the Committee on Ceremonies and instead, on a whim, went to lunch at the German Village.

Chicago society, however, was just getting warmed up. The infanta was royalty, and by God she would get the royal treatment. That night the infanta was scheduled to attend a reception hosted by Bertha Palmer at the Palmer mansion on Lake Shore Drive. In preparation, Mrs. Palmer had ordered a throne built on a raised platform.

Struck by the similarity between her hostess's name and the name of the hotel in which she was staying, the infanta made inquiries. Upon discovering that Bertha Palmer was the wife of the hotel's owner, she inflicted a social laceration that Chicago would never forget or forgive. She declared that under no circumstances would she be received by an "innkeeper's wife."

Diplomacy prevailed, however, and she agreed to attend. Her mood only worsened. With nightfall the day's heat had given way to heavy rain. By the time Eulalia made it to Mrs. Palmer's front door, her white satin slippers were soaked and her patience for ceremony had been extinguished. She stayed at the function for all of one hour, then bolted.

The next day she skipped an official lunch at the Administration Building and again dined unannounced at the German Village. That night she arrived one hour late for a concert at the fair's Festival Hall that had been arranged solely in her honor. The hall was filled to capacity with members of Chicago's leading families. She stayed five minutes.

Resentment began to stain the continuing news coverage of her visit. On Saturday, June 10, the *Tribune* sniffed, "Her Highness . . . has a way of discarding programs and following independently the bent of her inclination." The city's papers made repeated reference to her penchant for acting in accord with "her own sweet will."

In fact, the infanta was coming to like Chicago. She had loved her time at the fair and seemed especially to like Carter Harrison. She gave him a gold cigarette case inlaid with diamonds. Shortly before her departure, set for Wednesday, June 14, she wrote to her mother, "I am going to leave Chicago with real regret."

Chicago did not regret her leaving. If she had happened to pick up a copy of the *Chicago Tribune* that Wednesday morning, she would have found an embittered editorial that stated, in part, "Royalty at best is a troublesome customer for republicans to deal with and royalty of the Spanish sort is the most troublesome of all. . . . It was their custom to come late and go away early, leaving behind them the general regret that they had not come still later and gone away still earlier, or, better still perhaps, that they had not come at all."

Such prose, however, bore the unmistakable whiff of hurt feelings. Chicago had set its table with the finest linen and crystal—not out of any great respect for royalty but to show the world how fine a table it could set—only to have the guest of honor shun the feast for a lunch of sausage, sauerkraut, and beer.

Nannie

ANNA WILLIAMS — "NANNIE" — ARRIVED from Midlothian, Texas, in mid-June 1893. While Texas had been hot and dusty, Chicago was cool and smoky, full of trains and noise. The sisters hugged tearfully and congratulated each other on how fine they looked, and Minnie introduced her husband, Henry Gordon. Harry. He was shorter than Minnie's letters had led Anna to expect, and not as handsome, but there was something about him that even Minnie's glowing letters had not captured. He exuded warmth and charm. He spoke softly. He touched her in ways that made her glance apologetically at Minnie. Harry listened to the story of her journey from Texas with an attentiveness that made her feel as if she were alone with him in the carriage. Anna kept looking at his eyes.

His warmth and smile and obvious affection for Minnie caused Anna's suspicions quickly to recede. He did seem to be in love with her. He was cordial and tireless in his efforts to please her and, indeed, to please Anna as well. He brought gifts of jewelry. He gave Minnie a gold watch and chain specially made by the jeweler in the pharmacy downstairs. Without even thinking about it, Anna began calling him "Brother Harry."

First Minnie and Harry took her on a tour of Chicago. The city's great buildings and lavish homes awed her, but its smoke and darkness and the ever-present scent of rotting garbage repulsed her. Holmes took the sisters to the Union Stock Yards, where a tour guide led them into the heart of the slaughter. The guide cautioned that they should watch their feet lest they slip in blood. They watched as hog after hog was upended and whisked screaming down the cable into the butchering chambers below, where men with blood-caked knifes expertly cut their throats. The hogs, some still alive, were dipped next in a vat of boiling water, then scrapèd clean of bristle—the bristle saved in bins below the scraping tables. Each steaming hog then passed from station to station, where knifemen drenched in blood made the same few incisions time after time until, as the hog advanced, slabs of meat began thudding wetly onto the tables. Holmes was unmoved; Minnie and Anna were horrified but also strangely thrilled by the efficiency of the carnage. The yards embodied everything Anna had heard about Chicago and its irresistible, even savage drive toward wealth and power.

The great fair came next. They rode the Alley L along Sixty-third Street. Just before the train entered the fairgrounds, it passed the arena of Buffalo Bill's Wild West. From the elevated trestle they saw the earthen floor of the arena and the amphitheater seating that surrounded it. They saw his horses and buffalo and an authentic stagecoach. The train passed over the fair's fence, then descended to the terminal at the rear of the Transportation Building. Brother Harry paid the fifty-cent admission for each of them. At the fair's turnstiles even Holmes could not escape paying cash.

Naturally they first toured the Transportation Building. They saw the Pullman Company's "Ideal of Industry" exhibit, with its detailed model of Pullman's company town, which the company extolled as a workers' paradise. In the building's annex, packed with trains and locomotives, they walked the full length of an exact duplicate of the all-Pullman New York & Chicago Limited, with its plush chairs and carpeting, crystal glassware, and polished wood walls. At the pavilion of the Inman line a full-sized slice of an ocean liner towered above them. They exited the building through the great Golden Door, which arced across the light-red face of the building like a gilt rainbow.

Now, for the first time, Anna got a sense of the true, vast scale of the fair. Ahead lay a broad boulevard that skirted on the left the lagoon and the Wooded Island, on the right the tall facades of the Mines and Electricity buildings. In the distance she saw a train whooshing over the fair's all-electric elevated railway along the park's perimeter. Closer at hand, silent electric launches glided through the lagoon. At the far end of the boulevard, looming like an escarpment in the Rockies, stood the

Manufactures and Liberal Arts Building. White gulls slid across its face. The building was irresistibly huge. Holmes and Minnie took her there next. Once inside she saw that the building was even more vast than its exterior had led her to believe.

A blue haze of human breath and dust blurred the intricate bracing of the ceiling 246 feet above. Halfway to the ceiling, seemingly in midair, were five gigantic electric chandeliers, the largest ever built, each seventy-five feet in diameter and generating 828,000 candlepower. Below the chandeliers spread an indoor city of "gilded domes and glittering minarets, mosques, palaces, kiosks, and brilliant pavilions," according to the popular Rand, McNally & Co. *Handbook to the World's Columbian Exposition*. At the center stood a clock tower, the tallest of the interior structures, rising to a height of 120 feet. Its self-winding clock told the time in days, hours, minutes, and seconds, from a face seven feet in diameter. As tall as the tower was, the ceiling was yet another 126 feet above.

Minnie stood beaming and proud as Anna's gaze moved over the interior city and upward to its steel sky. There had to be thousands of exhibits. The prospect of seeing even a fraction of them was daunting. They saw Gobelin tapestries at the French Pavilion and the life-mask of Abraham Lincoln among the exhibits of the American Bronze Company. Other U.S. companies exhibited toys, weapons, canes, trunks, every conceivable manufactured product—and a large display of burial hardware, including marble and stone monuments, mausoleums, mantels, caskets, coffins, and miscellaneous other tools and furnishings of the undertaker's trade.

Minnie and Anna rapidly grew tired. They exited, with relief, onto the terrace over the North Canal and walked into the Court of Honor. Here once again Anna found herself nearly overwhelmed. It was noon by now, the sun directly overhead. The gold form of the Statue of the Republic, Big Mary, stood like a torch aflame. The basin in which the statue's plinth was set glittered with ripples of diamond. At the far end stood thirteen tall white columns, the Peristyle, with slashes of the blue lake visible between them. The light suffusing the Court was so plentiful and intense, it hurt their eyes. Many of the people around them donned spectacles with blue lenses.

They retreated for lunch. They had innumerable choices. There were lunch counters in most of the main buildings. The Manufactures and Liberal Arts Building alone had ten, plus two large restaurants, one German, the other French. The café in the Transportation Building, on a terrace over the Golden Door, was always popular and offered a spectacular view of the lagoon district. As the day wore on, Holmes bought them chocolate and lemonade and root beer at one of the Hires Root Beer Oases that dotted the grounds.

They returned to the fair almost daily, two weeks being widely considered the minimum needed to cover it adequately. One of the most compelling buildings, given the nature of the age, was the Electricity Building. In its "theatorium" they listened to an orchestra playing at that very moment in New York. They watched the moving pictures in Edison's Kinetoscope. Edison also displayed a strange metal cylinder that could store voices. "A man in Europe talks to his wife in America by boxing up a cylinder full of conversation and sending it by express," the Rand, McNally guidebook said; "a lover talks by the hour into a cylinder, and his sweetheart hears as though the thousand leagues were but a yard."

And they saw the first electric chair.

They reserved a separate day for the Midway. Nothing in Mississippi or Texas had prepared Anna for what she now experienced. Belly dancers. Camels. A balloon full of hydrogen that carried visitors more than a thousand feet into the sky. "Persuaders" called to her from raised platforms, seeking to entice her into the Moorish Palace with its room of mirrors, its optical illusions, and its eclectic wax museum, where visitors saw figures as diverse as Little Red Riding Hood and Marie Antoinette about to be guillotined. There was color everywhere. The Street in Cairo glowed with soft yellows, pinks, and purples. Even the concession tickets provided a splash of color—brilliant blue for the Turkish Theater, pink for the Lapland Village, and mauve for the Venetian gondolas.

Sadly, the Ferris Wheel was not quite ready.

They exited the Midway and strolled slowly south back to Sixty-third Street and the Alley L. They were tired, happy, and sated, but Harry promised to bring them back one more time—on July 4, for a fireworks display that everyone expected would be the greatest the city had ever witnessed.

Brother Harry seemed delighted with Anna and invited her to stay for the summer. Flattered, she wrote home to request that her big trunk be shipped to the Wrightwood address.

Clearly she had hoped something like this would happen, for she had packed the trunk already.

Holmes's assistant Benjamin Pitezel also went to the fair. He bought a souvenir for his son Howard—a tin man mounted on a spinning top. It quickly became the boy's favorite possession.

Vertigo

As Ferris's men became accustomed to handling the big cars, the process of attaching them to the wheel accelerated. By Sunday evening, June 11, six cars had been hung—an average of two a day since the first turn of the wheel. Now it was time for the first test with passengers, and the weather could not have been better. The sun was gold, the sky a darkling blue in the east.

Mrs. Ferris insisted on being aboard for the first ride, despite Gronau's attempts to dissuade her. Gronau inspected the wheel to make sure the car would swing without obstruction. The engineer in the pit started the engines and rotated the wheel to bring the test car to one of the platforms. "I did not enter the carriage with the easiest feeling at heart," Gronau said. "I felt squeamish; yet I could not refuse to take the trip. So I put on a bold face and walked into the car."

Luther Rice joined them, as did two draftsmen and the city of Chicago's former bridge engineer, W. C. Hughes. His wife and daughter also stepped aboard.

The car swung gently as the passengers took positions within the car. Glass had not yet been installed in its generous windows, nor the iron grill that would cover the glass. As soon as the last passenger had entered, Rice casually nodded to the engineer, and the wheel began to move. Instinctively everyone reached for posts and sills to keep themselves steady.

As the wheel turned, the car pivoted on the trunnions that both connected it to the frame and kept it level. "Owing to our car not having made a trip," Gronau said, "the trunnions stuck slightly in their bearings

269

and a crunching noise resulted, which in the condition of our nerves was not pleasant to hear."

The car traveled a bit higher, then unexpectedly stopped, raising the question of how everyone aboard would get down if the wheel could not be restarted. Rice and Gronau stepped to the unglazed windows to investigate. They looked down over the sill and discovered the problem: The fast-growing crowd of spectators, emboldened by seeing passengers in the first car, had leaped into the next car, ignoring shouts to stay back. Fearful that someone would be hurt or killed, the engineer had stopped the wheel and allowed the passengers to board.

Gronau estimated that one hundred people now occupied the car below. No one sought to kick them out. The wheel again began to move.

Ferris had created more than simply an engineering novelty. Like the inventors of the elevator, he had conjured an entirely new physical sensation. Gronau's first reaction—soon to change—was disappointment. He had expected to feel something like what he felt when riding a fast elevator, but here he found that if he looked straight ahead he felt almost nothing.

Gronau stationed himself at one end of the car to better observe its behavior and the movement of the wheel. When he looked out the side of the car into the passing web of spokes, the car's rapid ascent became apparent: ". . . it seemed as if every thing was dropping away from us, and the car was still. Standing at the side of the car and looking into the network of iron rods multiplied the peculiar sensation. . . ." He advised the others that if they had weak stomachs, they should not do likewise.

When the car reached its highest point, 264 feet above the ground, Mrs. Ferris climbed onto a chair and cheered, raising a roar in the following car and on the ground.

Soon, however, the passengers became silent. The novelty of the sensation wore off, and the true power of the experience became apparent.

"It was a most beautiful sight one obtains in the descent of the car, for then the whole fair grounds is laid before you," Gronau said. "The view is so grand that all timidity left me and my watch on the movement of the car was abandoned." The sun had begun its own descent and now cast an orange light over the shorescape. "The harbor was dotted with vessels of every description, which appeared mere specks from our exalted position, and the reflected rays of the beautiful sunset cast a gleam upon the surrounding scenery, making a picture lovely to behold." The entire park came into view as an intricate landscape of color, texture, and motion. Lapis lagoons. Electric launches trailing veils of diamond. Carmine blossoms winking from bulrush and flag. "The sight is so inspiring that all conversation stopped, and all were lost in admiration of this grand sight. The equal of it I have never seen, and I doubt very much if I shall again."

This reverie was broken as more bolts and nuts bounded down the superstructure onto the car's roof.

Spectators still managed to get past the guards and into the following cars, but now Gronau and Rice shrugged it off. The engineer in the pit kept the wheel running until the failing light made continued operation a danger, but even then thrill-seekers clamored for a chance. Finally Rice informed those who had shoved their way into the cars that if they remained he would run them to the top of the wheel and leave them there overnight. "This," Gronau said, "had the desired effect."

Immediately after leaving the car, Mrs. Ferris telegraphed her husband details of the success. He cabled back, "God bless you my dear."

The next day, Monday, June 12, Rice cabled Ferris, "Six more cars hung today. People are wild to ride on wheel & extra force of guards is required to keep them out." On Tuesday the total of cars hung reached twenty-one, with only fifteen more to add.

Burnham, obsessing as always over details, sought to decree the style and location of a fence for the wheel. He wanted an open, perforated fence, Ferris wanted it closed.

Ferris was fed up with Burnham's pressure and aesthetic interference. He cabled Luther Rice, ". . . Burnham nor anyone else has any right to dictate whether we shall have a closed or open fence, any more than from an artistic standpoint."

Ferris prevailed. The eventual fence was a closed one.

At last all the cars were hung and the wheel was ready for its first paying passengers. Rice wanted to begin accepting riders on Sunday, June 18, two days earlier than planned, but now with the wheel about to experience its greatest test—a full load of paying passengers, including entire families—Ferris's board of directors urged him to hold off one more day. They cabled Ferris, "Unwise to open wheel to public until opening day because of incompleteness and danger of accidents."

Ferris accepted their directive but with reluctance. Shortly before he left for Chicago, he cabled Rice, "If the board of directors have decided not to run until Wednesday you may carry out their wishes."

It's likely the board had been influenced by an accident that had occurred the previous Wednesday, June 14, at the Midway's Ice Railway, a descending elliptical track of ice over which two coupled bobsleds full of passengers could reach speeds of forty miles an hour. The owners had just completed the attraction and begun conducting their first tests with passengers, employees only, when a group of spectators pushed their way into the sleds, eight in the first, six in the second. The interlopers included three of Bloom's Algerians, who had come to the railway, one explained, because "none of us had ever seen ice," a doubtful story given that the Algerians had just endured one of Chicago's coldest winters.

At about six forty-five P.M. the operator released the sleds, and soon they were rocketing along the ice at maximum speed. "It was about sundown when I heard the sleds coming around the curve," said a Columbian Guard who witnessed the run. "They seemed to be flying. The first went around the curve. It struck the angle near the west end of the road, but went along all right. The second struck the same point, but it jumped the track. The top of the car, with the people holding tightly to the seats, broke the railing and fell to the ground. As it fell, the sled turned over and the people fell under it."

The sled plummeted fifteen feet to the ground. One passenger was killed; another, a woman, suffered fractures of her jaw and both wrists. Four other men, including two of the Algerians, sustained contusions.

The accident had been tragic and was a black mark for the fair, but everyone understood that the Ferris Wheel, with thirty-six cars carrying more than two thousand passengers, embodied the potential for a catastrophe of almost unimaginable scale.

Heathen Wanted

DESPITE HIS MISGIVINGS OLMSTED LEFT the completion of the exposition landscape in the hands of Ulrich and adopted a punishing schedule of work and travel that took him through sixteen states. By mid-June he was back at Vanderbilt's North Carolina estate. Along the way, in railcars, stations, and hotels, he solicited the views of strangers about the fair while keeping his own identity a secret. The fair's lackluster attendance troubled and perplexed him. He asked travelers if they had visited the fair yet, and if so what they had thought of it, but he was especially interested in the opinions of people who had not yet gone—what had they heard, did they plan to go, what was holding them back?

"Everywhere there is growing interest in the Exposition," he told Burnham in a June 20 letter from Biltmore. "Everywhere I have found indications that people are planning to go to it." Firsthand accounts of the fair were sparking heightened interest. Clergymen who had seen it were working the fair into sermons and lectures. He was delighted to find that what visitors liked best were not the exhibits but the buildings, waterways, and scenery and that the fair had surprised them. "People who have gone to the Fair have, in the main, found more than the newspapers . . . had led them to expect." He concluded, "There is a rising tidal wave of enthusiasm over the land."

But he saw that other factors were exerting a countervailing force. While personal accounts of the fair were enthusiastic, Olmsted wrote, "nearly always incompletenesses are referred to, favoring the idea that much remains to be done, and that the show will be better later." Farmers planned to wait until after harvest. Many people had put off their visits in the expectation that the nation's worsening economic crisis and pressure from Congress eventually would compel the railroads to reduce their Chicago fares. Weather was also an issue. Convinced that Chicago was too hot in July and August, people were postponing their visits until the fall.

One of the most pernicious factors, Olmsted found, was the widespread fear that anyone who ventured to Chicago would be "fleeced unmercifully," especially in the fair's many restaurants, with their "extortionate" prices. "This complaint is universal, and stronger than you in Chicago are aware of, I am sure," he told Burnham. "It comes from rich and poor alike. . . . I think that I have myself paid ten times as much for lunch at the Exposition as I did a few days ago, for an equally good one in Knoxville, Tenn. The frugal farming class yet to come to the Fair will feel this greatly."

Olmsted had another reason to worry about high meal prices. "The effect," he wrote, "will be to induce people more and more to bring their food with them, and more and more to scatter papers and offal on the ground."

It was critical now, Olmsted argued, to concentrate on making improvements of a kind most likely to increase the gleam in the stories people took back to their hometowns. "This is the advertising now most important to be developed; that of high-strung, contagious enthusiasm, growing from actual excellence: the question being not whether people shall be satisfied, but how much they shall be carried away with admiration, and infect others by their unexpected enjoyment of what they found."

Toward this end, he wrote, certain obvious flaws needed immediate attention. The exposition's gravel paths, for example. "There is not a square rod of admirable, hardly one of passable, gravel-walk in all of the Exposition Ground," he wrote. "It appears probable to me that neither the contractor, nor the inspector, whose business it is to keep the contractor up to his duty, can ever have seen a decently good gravel walk, or that they have any idea of what good gravel walks are. What are the defects of your walks?"—*Your* walks, he says here, not *mine* or *ours,* even though the walks were the responsibility of his own landscape department—"In some places there are cobbles or small boulders protruding from the surface, upon which no lady, with Summer shoes, can step without pain. In other places, the surface material is such that when damp enough to make it coherent it becomes slimy, and thus unpleasant to walk upon; also, without care, the slime is apt to smear shoes and dresses, which materially lessens the comfort of ladies." His voyage to Europe had shown him that a really good gravel path "should be as even and clean as a drawing room floor."

The cleanliness of the grounds also fell short of European standards, as he had feared it would. Litter was everywhere, with too few men assigned to clean it up. The fair needed twice as many, he said, and greater scrutiny of their work. "I have seen papers that had been apparently swept off the terraces upon the shrubbery between them and the lagoons," Olmsted wrote. "Such a shirking trick in a workman employed to keep the terraces clean should be a criminal offence."

He was bothered, too, by the noise of the few steam vessels that Burnham, over his repeated objections, had authorized to travel the exposition's waters alongside the electric launches. "The boats are cheap, graceless, clumsy affairs, as much out of place in what people are calling the 'Court of Honor' of the Exposition as a cow in a flower garden."

Olmsted's greatest concern, however, was that the main, Jackson Park portion of the exposition simply was not fun. "There is too much appearance of an impatient and tired doing of sight-seeing duty. A stint to be got through before it is time to go home. The crowd has a melancholy air in this respect, and strenuous measures should be taken to overcome it."

Just as Olmsted sought to conjure an aura of mystery in his landscape, so here he urged the engineering of seemingly accidental moments of charm. The concerts and parades were helpful but were of too "stated or programmed" a nature. What Olmsted wanted were "minor incidents . . . of a less evidently prepared character; less formal, more apparently spontaneous and incidental." He envisioned French horn players on the Wooded Island, their music drifting across the waters. He wanted Chinese lanterns strung from boats and bridges alike. "Why not skipping and dancing masqueraders with tambourines, such as one sees in Italy? Even lemonade peddlers would help if moving about in picturesque dresses; or cake-sellers, appearing as cooks, with flat cap, and in spotless white from top to toe?" On nights when big events in Jackson Park drew visitors away from the Midway, "could not several of the many varieties of 'heathen,' black, white and yellow, be cheaply hired to mingle, unobtrusively, but in full native costume, with the crowd on the Main Court?"

◦——◦

When Burnham read Olmsted's letter, he must have thought Olmsted had lost his mind. Burnham had devoted the last two years of his life to creating an impression of monumental beauty, and now Olmsted wanted to make visitors laugh. Burnham wanted them struck dumb with awe. There would be no skipping and dancing. No heathen.

The exposition was a dream city, but it was Burnham's dream. Everywhere it reflected the authoritarian spandrels of his character, from its surfeit of policemen to its strict rules against picking flowers. Nowhere was this as clearly evident as in the fair's restrictions on unauthorized photography.

Burnham had given a single photographer, Charles Dudley Arnold, a monopoly over the sale of official photographs of the fair, which arrangement also had the effect of giving Burnham control over the kinds of images that got distributed throughout the country and explains why neat, well-dressed, upper-class people tended to populate each frame. A second contractor received the exclusive right to rent Kodaks to fair visitors, the Kodak being a new kind of portable camera that eliminated the need for lens and shutter adjustments. In honor of the fair Kodak called the folding version of its popular model No. 4 box camera the Columbus. The photographs these new cameras created were fast becoming known as "snap-shots," a term originally used by English hunters to describe a quick shot with a gun. Anyone wishing to bring his own Kodak to the fair had to buy a permit for two dollars, an amount beyond the reach of most visitors; the Midway's Street in Cairo imposed an additional one-dollar fee. An amateur photographer bringing a conventional large camera and the necessary tripod had to pay ten dollars, about what many out-of-town visitors paid for a full day at the fair, including lodging, meals, and admission.

For all Burnham's obsession with detail and control, one event at the fair escaped his attention. On June 17 a small fire occurred in the Cold Storage Building, a castlelike structure at the southwest corner of the grounds built by Hercules Iron Works. Its function was to produce ice, store the perishable goods of exhibitors and restaurants, and operate an ice rink for visitors wishing to experience the novelty of skating in July. The building was a private venture: Burnham had nothing to do with its construction beyond approving its design. Oddly enough, its architect was named Frank P. Burnham, no relation.

The fire broke out in the cupola at the top of the central tower but was controlled quickly and caused only a hundred dollars in damage. Even so, the fire prompted insurance underwriters to take a closer look at the building, and what they saw frightened them. A key element of the design had never been installed. Seven insurers canceled their policies. Fire Marshal Edward W. Murphy, acting chief of the World's Fair Fire Department, told a committee of underwriters, "That building gives us more trouble than any structure on the grounds. It is a miserable firetrap and will go up in smoke before long."

No one told Burnham about the fire, no one told him of the cancellations, and no one told him of Murphy's forecast.

At Last

AT THREE-THIRTY P.M. on Wednesday, June 21, 1893, fifty-one days late, George Washington Gale Ferris took a seat on the speakers' platform built at the base of his wheel. The forty-piece Iowa State Marching Band already had boarded one of the cars and now played "My Country 'Tis of Thee." Mayor Harrison joined Ferris on the platform, as did Bertha Palmer, the entire Chicago city council, and an assortment of fair officials. Burnham apparently was not present.

The cars were fully glazed, and wire grills had been placed over all the windows so that, as one reporter put it, "No crank will have an opportunity to commit suicide from this wheel, no hysterical woman shall jump from a window." Conductors trained to soothe riders who were afraid of heights stood in handsome uniforms at each car's door.

The band quieted, the wheel stopped. Speeches followed. Ferris was last to take the podium and happily assured the audience that the man condemned for having "wheels in his head" had gotten them out of his head and into the heart of the Midway Plaisance. He attributed the success of the enterprise to his wife, Margaret, who stood behind him on the platform. He dedicated the wheel to the engineers of America.

Mrs. Ferris gave him a gold whistle, then she and Ferris and the other dignitaries climbed into the first car. Harrison wore his black slouch hat.

When Ferris blew the whistle, the Iowa State band launched into "America," and the wheel again began to turn. The group made several circuits, sipping champagne and smoking cigars, then exited the wheel to the cheers of the crowd that now thronged its base. The first paying passengers stepped aboard.

The wheel continued rolling with stops only for loading and unloading until eleven o'clock that night. Even with every car full, the wheel never faltered, its bearings never groaned.

The Ferris Company was not shy about promoting its founder's accomplishment. In an illustrated pamphlet called the "Ferris Wheel Souvenir" the company wrote: "Built in the face of every obstacle, it is an achievement which reflects so much credit upon the inventor, that were Mr. Ferris the subject of a Monarchy, instead of a citizen of a great Republic, his honest heart would throb beneath a breast laden with the decorations of royalty." Ferris could not resist tweaking the Exposition Company for not granting him a concession sooner than it did. "Its failure to appreciate its importance," the souvenir said, "has cost the Exposition Company many thousands of dollars."

This was an understatement. Had the Exposition Company stood by its original June 1892 concession rather than waiting until nearly six months later, the wheel would have been ready for the fair's May 1 opening. Not only did the exposition lose its 50 percent share of the wheel's revenue for those fifty-one days—it lost the boost in overall admission that the wheel likely would have generated and that Burnham so desperately wanted. Instead it had stood for that month and a half as a vivid advertisement of the fair's incomplete condition.

Safety fears lingered, and Ferris did what he could to ease them. The souvenir pamphlet noted that even a full load of passengers had "no more effect on the movements or the speed than if they were so many flies"—an oddly ungracious allusion. The pamphlet added, "In the construction of this great wheel, every conceivable danger has been calculated and provided for."

But Ferris and Gronau had done their jobs too well. The design was so elegant, so adept at exploiting the strength of thin strands of steel, that the wheel appeared incapable of withstanding the stresses placed upon it. The wheel may not have been unsafe, but it looked unsafe.

"In truth, it seems too light," a reporter observed. "One fears the slender rods which must support the whole enormous weight are too puny to fulfill their office. One cannot avoid the thought of what would happen if a high wind should come sweeping across the prairie and attack the structure broadside. Would the thin rods be sufficient to sustain not only the enormous weight of the structure and that of the 2,000 passengers who might chance to be in the cars, but the pressure of the wind as well?"

In three weeks that question would find an answer.

Rising Wave

AND SUDDENLY THEY BEGAN to come. The enthusiasm Olmsted had identified during his travels, though still far from constituting a tidal wave, at last seemed to begin propelling visitors to Jackson Park. By the end of June, even though the railroads still had not dropped their fares, paid attendance at the exposition had more than doubled, the average for the month rising to 89,170 from May's dismal 37,501. It was still far below the 200,000 daily visitors the fair's planners originally had dreamed of, but the trend was encouraging. From Englewood to the Loop, hotels at last began to fill. The Roof Garden Café of the Woman's Building now served two thousand people a day, ten times the number it had served on Opening Day. The resulting volume of garbage overwhelmed its disposal system, which consisted of janitors bumping large barrels of fetid garbage down the same three flights of stairs used by customers. The janitors could not use the elevators because Burnham had ordered them turned off after dark to conserve power for the fair's nightly illuminations. As stains and stench accumulated, the restaurant's manager built a chute on the roof and threatened to jettison the garbage directly onto Olmsted's precious lawns.

Burnham retracted his order.

The fair had become so intensely compelling that one woman, Mrs. Lucille Rodney of Galveston, Texas, walked thirteen hundred miles along railroad tracks to reach it. "Call it no more the White City on the Lake," wrote Sir Walter Besant, the English historian and novelist, in *Cosmopolitan,* "it is Dreamland."

Even Olmsted now seemed happy with it, although of course he had his criticisms. He too had wanted to manage the first impressions of visitors by having a central entry point. The failure of this idea, he wrote in a formal critique for *The Inland Architect,* "deducted much" from the fair's value, although he hastened to add that he was making this criticism "not in the least in a complaining way" but as a professional offering guidance to others who might confront a similar problem. He still wished the Wooded Island had been left alone, and he decried the unplanned proliferation of concession buildings that "intercepted vistas and disturbed spaces intended to serve for the relief of the eye from the too nearly constant demands upon attention of the Exposition Buildings." The effect, he wrote, "has been bad."

Overall, however, he was pleased, especially with the process of construction. "Really," he wrote, "I think that it is a most satisfactory and encouraging circumstance that it could be found feasible for so many men of technical education and ability to be recruited and suitably organized so quickly and made to work together so well in so short a time. I think it a notable circumstance that there should have been so little friction, so little display of jealousy, envy and combativeness, as has appeared in the progress of this enterprise."

He attributed this circumstance to Burnham: "too high an estimate cannot be placed on the industry, skill and tact with which this result was secured by the master of us all."

Visitors wore their best clothes, as if going to church, and were surprisingly well behaved. In the six months of the fair the Columbian Guard made only 2,929 arrests, about sixteen per day, typically for disorderly conduct, petty theft, and pickpocketing, with pickpockets most favoring the fair's always-crowded aquarium. The guard identified 135 ex-convicts and removed them from the grounds. It issued thirty fines for carrying Kodaks without a permit, thirty-seven for taking unauthorized photographs. It investigated the discovery on the grounds of three fetuses; a Pinkerton detective "assaulting visitors" at the Tiffany Pavilion; and a "Zulu acting improperly." In his official report to Burnham Colonel Rice, commander of the Guard, wrote, "With the tens of thousands of employees and the millions of visitors, it must be admitted that our success was phenomenal."

With so many people packed among steam engines, giant rotating wheels, horse-drawn fire trucks, and rocketing bobsleds, the fair's ambulances superintended by a doctor named Gentles were constantly delivering bruised, bloody, and overheated visitors to the exposition hospital. Over the life of the fair the hospital treated 11,602 patients, sixty-four a day, for injuries and ailments that suggest that the mundane sufferings of people have not changed very much over the ages. The list included:

820 cases of diarrhea;
154, constipation;
21, hemorrhoids;
434, indigestion;
365, foreign bodies in the eyes;
364, severe headaches;
594 episodes of fainting, syncope, and exhaustion;
1 case of extreme flatulence;
and 169 involving teeth that hurt like hell.

One of the delights of the fair was never knowing who might turn up beside you at the chocolate Venus de Milo or at the hearse exhibit or under the barrel of Krupp's monster, or who might sit at the table next to yours at the Big Tree Restaurant or the Philadelphia Café or the Great White Horse Inn, a reproduction of the public house described by Dickens in *The Pickwick Papers*; or who might suddenly clutch your arm aboard the Ferris Wheel as your car began its ascent. Archduke Francis Ferdinand, described by an escort as being "half-boor, half-tightwad," roamed the grounds incognito—but much preferred the vice districts of Chicago. Indians who had once used hatchets to bare the skulls of white men drifted over from Buffalo Bill's compound, as did Annie Oakley and assorted Cossacks, Hussars, Lancers, and members of the U.S. Sixth Cavalry on temporary furlough to become actors in Colonel Cody's show. Chief Standing Bear rode the Ferris Wheel in full ceremonial headdress, his two hundred feathers unruffled. Other Indians rode the enameled wooden horses of the Midway carousel.

There were Paderewski, Houdini, Tesla, Edison, Joplin, Darrow, a Princeton professor named Woodrow Wilson, and a sweet old lady in black summer silk flowered with forget-me-not-blue named Susan B. Anthony. Burnham met Teddy Roosevelt for lunch. For years after the fair Burnham used the exclamation, "Bully!" Diamond Jim Brady dined with Lillian Russell and indulged his passion for sweet corn.

No one saw Twain. He came to Chicago to see the fair but got sick and spent eleven days in his hotel room, then left without ever seeing the White City.

Of all people.

⟁

Chance encounters led to magic.

Frank Haven Hall, superintendent of the Illinois Institution for the Education of the Blind, unveiled a new device that made plates for printing books in Braille. Previously Hall had invented a machine capable of typing in Braille, the Hall Braille Writer, which he never patented because he felt profit should not sully the cause of serving the blind. As he stood by his newest machine, a blind girl and her escort approached him. Upon learning that Hall was the man who had invented the typewriter she used so often, the girl put her arms around his neck and gave him a huge hug and kiss.

Forever afterward, whenever Hall told this story of how he met Helen Keller, tears would fill his eyes.

⟁

One day as the Board of Lady Managers debated whether to support or oppose opening the fair on Sunday, an angry male Sabbatarian confronted Susan B. Anthony in the hall of the Woman's Building to challenge her contention that the fair should remain open. (Anthony was not a lady manager and therefore despite her national stature could not participate in the board's meeting.) Deploying the most shocking analogy he could muster, the clergyman asked Anthony if she'd prefer having a son of hers attend Buffalo Bill's show on Sunday instead of church.

Yes, she replied, "he would learn far more. . . ."

To the pious this exchange confirmed the fundamental wickedness of Anthony's suffragist movement. When Cody learned of it, he was tickled, so much so that he immediately sent Anthony a thank-you note and invited her to attend his show. He offered her a box at any performance she chose.

At the start of the performance Cody entered the ring on horseback, his long gray hair streaming from under his white hat, the silver trim of his white jacket glinting in the sun. He kicked his horse into a gallop and raced toward Anthony's box. The audience went quiet.

He halted his horse in a burst of dirt and dust, removed his hat, and with a great sweeping gesture bowed until his head nearly touched the horn of his saddle.

Anthony stood and returned the bow and—"as enthusiastic as a girl," a friend said—waved her handkerchief at Cody.

The significance of the moment escaped no one. Here was one of the greatest heroes of America's past saluting one of the foremost heroes of its future. The encounter brought the audience to its feet in a thunder of applause and cheers.

The frontier may indeed have closed at last, as Frederick Jackson Turner proclaimed in his history-making speech at the fair, but for that moment it stood there glittering in the sun like the track of a spent tear.

———

There was tragedy. The British draped their elaborate ship model of the H.M.S. *Victoria* in black bunting. On June 22, 1893, during maneuvers off Tripoli, this marvel of naval technology had been struck by the H.M.S. *Camperdown*. The *Victoria*'s commander ordered the ship to proceed full speed toward shore, intending to ground her there in accord with standing fleet orders meant to make it easier to raise a sunken ship. Ten minutes later, her engines still at full steam, the cruiser heeled and sank with many of her crew still trapped belowdecks. Others lucky enough to have jumped free now found themselves mauled by her whirling propellers or burned to death when her boilers exploded. "Screams and shrieks arose, and in the white foam appeared reddened arms and legs and wrenched and torn bodies," a reporter said. "Headless trunks were tossed out of the vortex to linger a moment on the surface and sink out of sight."

The accident cost four hundred lives.

———

The Ferris Wheel quickly became the most popular attraction of the exposition. Thousands rode it every day. In the week beginning July 3 Ferris sold 61,395 tickets for a gross return of $30,697.50. The Exposition Company took about half, leaving Ferris an operating profit for that one week of $13,948 (equivalent today to about $400,000).

There were still questions about the wheel's safety, and unfounded stories circulated about suicides and accidents, including one that alleged that a frightened pug had leaped to its death from one of the car's windows. Not true, the Ferris Company said; the story was the concoction of a reporter "short on news and long on invention." If not for the wheel's windows and iron grates, however, its record might have been different. On one ride a latent terror of heights suddenly overwhelmed an otherwise peaceful man named Wherritt. He was fine until the car began to move. As it rose, he began to feel ill and nearly fainted. There was no way to signal the engineer below to stop the wheel.

Wherritt staggered in panic from one end of the car to the other, driving passengers before him "like scared sheep," according to one account. He began throwing himself at the walls of the car with such power that he managed to bend some of the protective iron. The conductor and several male passengers tried to subdue him, but he shook them off and raced for the door. In accord with the wheel's operating procedures, the conductor had locked the door at the start of the ride. Wherritt shook it and broke its glass but could not get it open.

As the car entered its descent, Wherritt became calmer and laughed and sobbed with relief—until he realized the wheel was not going to stop.

It always made two full revolutions. Wherritt again went wild, and again the conductor and his allies subdued him, but they were growing tired. They feared what might happen if Wherritt escaped them. Structurally the car was sound, but its walls, windows, and doors had been designed merely to discourage attempts at self-destruction, not to resist a human pile driver. Already Wherritt had broken glass and bent iron.

A woman stepped up and unfastened her skirt. To the astonishment of all aboard, she slipped the skirt off and threw it over Wherritt's head, then held it in place while murmuring gentle assurances. The effect was immediate. Wherritt became "as quiet as an ostrich."

A woman disrobing in public, a man with a skirt over his head—the marvels of the fair seemed endless.

⚬────⚬

The exposition was Chicago's great pride. Thanks mainly to Daniel Burnham the city had proved it could accomplish something marvelous against obstacles that by any measure should have humbled the builders. The sense of ownership was everywhere, not just among the tens of thousands of citizens who had bought exposition stock. Hilda Satt noticed it in the change that came over her father as he showed her the grounds. "He seemed to take a personal pride in the fair, as if he had helped in the planning," she said. "As I look back on those days, most people in Chicago felt that way. Chicago was host to the world at that time and we were part of it all."

But the fair did more than simply stoke pride. It gave Chicago a light to hold against the gathering dark of economic calamity. The Erie Railroad wobbled, then collapsed. Next went the Northern Pacific. In Denver three national banks failed in one day and pulled down an array of other businesses. Fearing a bread riot, city authorities called out the militia. In Chicago the editors of *The Inland Architect* tried to be reassuring: "Existing conditions are only an accident. Capital is only hidden. Enterprise is only frightened, not beaten." The editors were wrong.

In June two businessmen committed suicide on the same day in the same Chicago hotel, the Metropole. One slit his throat with a razor at ten-thirty in the morning. The other learned of the suicide from the hotel barber. That night in his own room he tied one end of the silk sash of his smoking jacket around his neck, then stretched out on the bed and tied the other end to the bedstead. He rolled off.

"Everyone is in a blue fit of terror," wrote Henry Adams, "and each individual thinks himself more ruined than his neighbor."

Long before the fair's end, people began mourning its inevitable passage. Mary Hartwell Catherwood wrote, "What shall we do when this Wonderland is closed?—when it disappears—when the enchantment comes to an end?" One lady manager, Sallie Cotton of North Carolina, a mother of six children staying in Chicago for the summer, captured in her diary a common worry: that after seeing the fair, "everything will seem small and insignificant."

The fair was so perfect, its grace and beauty like an assurance that for as long as it lasted nothing truly bad could happen to anyone, anywhere.

Independence Day

THE MORNING OF JULY 4, 1893, broke gray and squally. The weather threatened to dull the elaborate fireworks display that Frank Millet had planned as a further boost for the exposition's attendance, which despite steady week-to-week increases still lagged behind expectations. The sun emerged late in the morning, though squalls continued to sweep Jackson Park through much of the day. By late afternoon a soft gold light bathed the Court of Honor and storm clouds walled the northern sky. The storms came no closer. The crowds built quickly. Holmes, Minnie, and Anna found themselves locked within an immense throng of humid men and women. Many people carried blankets and hampers of food but quickly found that no room remained to spread a picnic. There were few children. The entire Columbian Guard seemed to be present, their pale blue uniforms standing out like crocuses against black loam. Gradually the gold light cooled to lavender. Everyone began walking toward the lake. "For half a mile along the splendid sweep of the Lake-Front men were massed a hundred deep," the *Tribune* reported. This "black sea" of people was restless. "For hours they sat and waited, filling the air with a strange, uneasy uproar." One man began singing "Nearer My God to Thee," and immediately a few thousand people joined in.

As darkness fell, everyone watched the sky for the first rockets of the night's display. Thousands of Chinese lanterns hung from trees and railings. Red lights glowed from each car of the Ferris Wheel. On the lake a hundred or more ships, yachts, and launches lay at anchor with colored lights on their bows and booms and strung along their rigging.

The crowd was ready to cheer for anything. It cheered when the exposition orchestra played "Home Sweet Home," a song that never failed to reduce grown men and women to tears, especially the newest arrivals to the city. It cheered when the lights came on within the Court of Honor and all the palaces became outlined in gold. It cheered when the big searchlights atop the Manufactures and Liberal Arts Building began sweeping the crowd, and when colorful plumes of water—"peacock feathers," the *Tribune* called them—began erupting from the MacMonnies Fountain.

At nine o'clock, however, the crowd hushed. A small bright light had arisen in the sky to the north and appeared to be drifting along the lakeshore toward the wharf. One of the searchlights found it and revealed it to be a large manned balloon. A light flared well below its basket. In the next instant bursts of sparks in red, white, and blue formed a huge American flag against the black sky. The balloon and flag drifted overhead. The searchlight followed, its beam clearly outlined in the sulphur cloud that trailed the balloon. Seconds later rockets began arcing over the lakeshore. Men with flares raced along the beach lighting mortars, as other men aboard barges set off large rotating flares and hurled bombs into the lake, causing the water to explode in extravagant geysers of red, white, and blue. Bombs and rockets followed in intensifying numbers until the climax of the show, when an elaborate wire network erected at Festival Hall, on the lakeshore, abruptly flared into a giant explosive portrait of George Washington.

The crowd cheered.

Everyone began moving at the same time, and soon a great black tide was moving toward the exits and the stations of the Alley L and Illinois Central. Holmes and the Williams sisters waited hours for their turn to board one of the northbound trains, but the wait did nothing to dampen their spirits. That night the Oker family heard joking and laughter coming from the upstairs flat at 1220 Wrightwood.

There was good reason for the merriment within. Holmes had further sweetened the night with an astonishingly generous offer to Minnie and Anna.

Before bed Anna wrote home to her aunt in Texas to tell her the excellent news.

"Sister, brother Harry, and myself will go to Milwaukee tomorrow, and will go to Old Orchard Beach, Maine, by way of the St. Lawrence River. We'll visit two weeks in Maine, then on to New York. Brother Harry thinks I am talented; he wants me to look around about studying art. Then we will sail for Germany, by way of London and Paris. If I like it, I will stay and study art. Brother Harry says you need never trouble any more about me, financially or otherwise; he and sister will see to me."

"Write me right away," she added, "and address to Chicago, and the letter will be forwarded to me."

She said nothing about her trunk, which was still in Midlothian awaiting shipment to Chicago. She would have to get along without it for now. Once it arrived, she could arrange by telegraph to have it forwarded as well, perhaps to Maine or New York, so that she could have all her things in hand for the voyage to Europe.

Anna went to bed that night with her heart still racing from the excitement of the fair and Holmes's surprise. Later William Capp, an attorney with the Texas firm of Capp & Canty, said, "Anna had no property of her own, and such a change as described in her letter meant everything for her."

The next morning promised to be pleasant as well, for Holmes had announced he would take Anna—just her—to Englewood for a brief tour of his World's Fair Hotel. He had to attend to a few last-minute business matters before the departure for Milwaukee. In the meantime Minnie would ready the Wrightwood flat for whatever tenant happened to rent it next.

Holmes was such a charming man. And now that Anna knew him, she saw that he really was quite handsome. When his marvelous blue eyes caught hers, they seemed to warm her entire body. Minnie had done well indeed.

Worry

AT THE FAIRGROUNDS LATER that night the ticketmen counted their sales and found that for that single day, July 4, paid attendance had totaled 283,273—far greater than the entire first week of the fair.

It was the first clear evidence that Chicago might have created something extraordinary after all, and it renewed Burnham's hopes that the fair at last would achieve the level of attendance he had hoped for.

But the next day, only 79,034 paying visitors came to see the fair. Three days later the number sagged to 44,537. The bankers carrying the fair's debt grew anxious. The fair's auditor already had discovered that Burnham's department had spent over $22 million to build the fair (roughly $660 million in twenty-first-century dollars), more than twice the amount originally planned. The bankers were pressuring the exposition's directors to appoint a Retrenchment Committee empowered not just to seek out ways of reducing the fair's expenses but to execute whatever cost-saving measures it deemed necessary, including layoffs and the elimination of departments and committees.

Burnham knew that placing the future of the fair in the hands of bankers would mean its certain failure. The only way to ease the pressure was to boost the total of paid admissions to far higher levels. Estimates held that to avoid financial failure—a humiliation for Chicago's prideful leading men who counted themselves lords of the dollar—the fair would have to sell a minimum of 100,000 tickets a day for the rest of its run.

To have even a hope of achieving this, the railroads would have to reduce their fares, and Frank Millet would have to intensify his efforts to attract people from all corners of the country.

With the nation's economic depression growing ever more profound—banks failing, suicides multiplying—it seemed an impossibility.

Claustrophobia

HOLMES KNEW THAT MOST if not all of his hotel guests would be at the fair. He showed Anna the drugstore, restaurant, and barbershop and took her up to the roof to give her a broader view of Englewood and the pretty, tree-shaded neighborhood that surrounded his corner. He ended the tour at his office, where he offered Anna a seat and excused himself. He picked up a sheaf of papers and began reading.

Distractedly, he asked Anna if she would mind going into the adjacent room, the walk-in vault, to retrieve for him a document he had left inside.

Cheerfully, she complied.

Holmes followed quietly.

———

At first it seemed as though the door had closed by accident. The room was utterly without light. Anna pounded on the door and called for Harry. She listened, then pounded again. She was not frightened, just embarrassed. She did not like the darkness, which was more complete than anything she had ever experienced—far darker, certainly, than any moonless night in Texas. She rapped the door with her knuckles and listened again.

The air grew stale.

———

Holmes listened. He sat peacefully in a chair by the wall that separated his office and the vault. Time passed. It was really very peaceful. A soft breeze drifted through the room, cross-ventilation being one of the benefits of a corner office. The breeze, still cool, carried the morning scent of prairie grasses and moist soil.

———

Anna removed her shoe and beat the heel against the door. The room was growing warmer. Sweat filmed her face and arms. She guessed that Harry, unaware of her plight, had gone elsewhere in the building. That would explain why he still had not come despite her pounding. Perhaps he had gone to check on something in the shops below. As she considered this, she became a bit frightened. The room had grown substantially warmer. Catching a clean breath was difficult. And she needed a bathroom.

He would be so apologetic. She could not show him how afraid she was. She tried shifting her thoughts to the journey they would begin that afternoon. That she, a Texas schoolmarm, soon would be walking the streets of London and Paris still seemed an impossibility, yet Harry had promised it and made all the arrangements. In just a few hours she would board a train for the short trip to Milwaukee, and soon afterward she, Minnie, and Harry would be on their way to the lovely, cool valley of the St. Lawrence River, between New York and Canada. She saw herself sitting on the spacious porch of some fine riverside hotel, sipping tea and watching the sun descend.

She hammered the door again and now also the wall between the vault and Harry's breeze-filled office.

———

The panic came, as it always did. Holmes imagined Anna crumpled in a corner. If he chose, he could rush to the door, throw it open, hold her in his arms, and weep with her at the tragedy just barely averted. He could do it at the last minute, in the last few seconds. He could do that.

Or he could open the door and look in on Anna and give her a big smile—just to let her know that this was no accident—then close the door again, slam it, and return to his chair to see what might happen next. Or he could flood the vault, right now, with gas. The hiss and repulsive odor would tell her just as clearly as a smile that something extraordinary was under way.

He could do any of these things.

He had to concentrate to hear the sobs from within. The airtight fittings, the iron walls, and the mineral-wool insulation deadened most of the sound, but he had found with experience that if he listened at the gas pipe, he heard everything much more clearly.

This was the time he most craved. It brought him a period of sexual release that seemed to last for hours, even though in fact the screams and pleading faded rather quickly.

He filled the vault with gas, just to be sure.

Holmes returned to the Wrightwood apartment and told Minnie to get ready—Anna was waiting for them at the castle. He held Minnie and kissed her and told her how lucky he was and how much he liked her sister.

During the train ride to Englewood, he seemed well rested and at peace, as if he had just ridden his bicycle for miles and miles.

Two days later, on July 7, the Oker family received a letter from Henry Gordon stating that he no longer needed the apartment. The letter came as a surprise. The Okers believed Gordon and the two sisters still occupied the flat. Lora Oker went upstairs to check. She knocked, heard nothing, then entered.

"I do not know how they got out of the house," she said, "but there were evidences of hasty packing, a few books and odds and ends being left lying about. If there had been any writing in the books all traces were removed, for the fly leaves had been torn out."

Also on July 7 the Wells-Fargo agent in Midlothian, Texas, loaded a large trunk into the baggage car of a northbound train. The trunk—Anna's trunk—was addressed to "Miss Nannie Williams, c/o H. Gordon, 1220 Wrightwood Ave., Chicago."

The trunk reached the city several days later. A Wells-Fargo drayman tried to deliver it to the Wrightwood address but could not locate anyone named Williams or Gordon. He returned the trunk to the Wells-Fargo office. No one came to claim it.

Holmes called upon an Englewood resident named Cephas Humphrey, who owned his own team and dray and made a living transporting furniture, crates, and other large objects from place to place. Holmes asked him to pick up a box and a trunk. "I want you to come after the stuff about dark," Holmes said, "as I do not care to have the neighbors see it go away."

Humphrey showed up as requested. Holmes led him into the castle and upstairs to a windowless room with a heavy door.

"It was an awful looking place," Humphrey said. "There were no windows in it at all and only a heavy door opening into it. It made my flesh creep to go in there. I felt as if something was wrong, but Mr. Holmes did not give me much time to think about that."

The box was a long rectangle made of wood, roughly the dimensions of a coffin. Humphrey carried it down first. Out on the sidewalk, he stood it on end. Holmes, watching from above, rapped hard on the window and called down, "Don't do that. Lay it down flat."

Humphrey did so, then walked back upstairs to retrieve the trunk. It was heavy, but its weight gave him no trouble.

Holmes instructed him to take the long box to the Union Depot and told him where on the platform to place it. Apparently Holmes had made prior arrangements with an express agent to pick up the box and load it on a train. He did not disclose its destination.

As for the trunk, Humphrey could not recall where he took it, but later evidence suggests he drove it to the home of Charles Chappell, near Cook County Hospital.

Soon afterward Holmes brought an unexpected but welcome gift to the family of his assistant, Benjamin Pitezel. He gave Pitezel's wife,

Carrie, a collection of dresses, several pairs of shoes, and some hats that had belonged to his cousin, a Miss Minnie Williams, who had gotten married and moved east and no longer needed her old things. He recommended that Carrie cut up the dresses and use the material to make clothing for her three daughters. Carrie was very grateful.

Holmes also surprised his caretaker, Pat Quinlan, with a gift: two sturdy trunks, each bearing the initials MRW.

Storm and Fire

BURNHAM'S WORK DID NOT CEASE, the pace at his office did not slow. The fair buildings were complete and all exhibits were in place, but just as surely as silver tarnishes, the fair became subject to the inevitable forces of degradation and decline—and tragedy.

On Sunday, July 9, a day of heat and stillness, the Ferris Wheel became one of the most sought-after places to be, as did the basket of the Midway's captive balloon. The balloon, named *Chicago*, was filled with 100,000 cubic feet of hydrogen and controlled by a tether connected to a winch. By three o'clock that afternoon it had made thirty-five trips aloft, to an altitude of one thousand feet. As far as the concession's German aerialist was concerned, the day had been a perfect one for ascensions, so still, he estimated, that a plumb line dropped from the basket would have touched the winch directly below.

At three o'clock, however, the manager of the concession, G. F. Morgan, checked his instruments and noted a sudden decline in barometric pressure, evidence that a storm was forming. He halted the sale of new tickets and ordered his men to reel in the balloon. The operators of the Ferris Wheel, he saw, did not take equivalent precautions. The wheel continued to turn.

Clouds gathered, the sky purpled, and a breeze rose from the northwest. The sky sagged toward the ground and a small funnel cloud appeared, which began wobbling south along the lakeshore, toward the fair.

The Ferris Wheel was full of passengers, who watched with mounting concern as the funnel did its own *danse du ventre* across Jackson Park directly toward the Midway.

At the base of the captive balloon, Manager Morgan ordered his men to grab mooring ropes and hang on tight.

———

Within Jackson Park the sudden shift from sunlight to darkness drew Burnham outside. A powerful wind reared from all directions. Lunch wraps took flight and wheeled in the air like gulls. The sky seemed to reach into the exposition, and somewhere glass shattered, not the gentle tinkling of a window extinguished by a stone but the hurt-dog yelp of large sheets falling to the ground.

In the Agriculture Building a giant pane of glass fell from the roof and shattered the table at which, just a few seconds earlier, a young woman had been selling candy. Six roof panes blew from the Manufactures and Liberal Arts Building. Exhibitors raced to cover their displays with duckcloth.

The wind tore a forty-square-foot segment from the dome of the Machinery Building and lifted the roof off the fair's Hungarian Café. The crew of one of Olmsted's electric launches made a hasty landing to evacuate all passengers and had just begun motoring toward shelter when a burst of wind caught the boat's awning and whipped the five-ton craft onto its side. The pilot and conductor swam to safety.

Giant feathers rocked in the air. The twenty-eight ostriches of the Midway ostrich farm bore the loss with their usual aplomb.

———

In the wheel, riders braced themselves. One woman fainted. A passenger later wrote to *Engineering News,* "It took the combined effort of two of us to close the doors tight. The wind blew so hard the rain drops appeared to be flowing almost horizontal instead of vertical." The wheel continued to turn, however, as if no wind were blowing. Passengers felt only a slight vibration. The letter-writer, apparently an engineer, estimated the wind deflected the wheel to one side by only an inch and a half.

The riders watched as the wind gripped the adjacent captive balloon and tore it from the men holding it down and briefly yanked Manager

Morgan into the sky. The wind pummeled the balloon as if it were an inverted punching bag, then tore it to pieces and cast shreds of its nine thousand yards of silk as far as half a mile away.

Morgan took the disaster calmly. "I got some pleasure out of watching the storm come up," he said, "and it was a sight of a lifetime to see the balloon go to pieces, even if it was a costly bit of sightseeing for the people who own stock in the company."

Whether the storm had anything to do with the events of the next day, Monday, July 10, can't be known, but the timing was suspicious.

On Monday, shortly after one o'clock, as Burnham supervised repairs and crews removed storm debris from the grounds, smoke began to rise from the cupola of the Cold Storage tower, where the fire of June 17 also had taken light.

The tower was made of wood and housed a large iron smokestack, which vented three boilers located in the main building below. Paradoxically, heat was required to produce cold. The stack rose to a point thirty inches short of the top of the tower, where an additional iron assembly, called a thimble, was to have been placed to extend the stack so that it cleared the top completely. The thimble was a crucial part of architect Frank Burnham's design, meant to shield the surrounding wooden walls from the superheated gases exiting the stack. For some reason, however, the contractor had not installed it. The building was like a house whose chimney ended not above the roof but inside the attic.

The first alarm reached the fire department at 1:32 P.M. Engines thundered to the building. Twenty firemen led by Captain James Fitzpatrick entered the main structure and climbed to its roof. From there they made their way to the tower and climbed stairs another seventy feet to the tower's exterior balcony. Using ropes they hauled up a line of hose and a twenty-five-foot ladder. They secured the hose firmly to the tower.

Fitzpatrick and his men didn't realize it, but the fire at the top of the tower had set a lethal trap. Fragments of burning debris had fallen into the space between the iron stack and the inner walls of the tower, made of smooth white pine. These flaming brands ignited a fire that, in those narrow confines, soon depleted the available air and extinguished its own flames, leaving in their place a superheated plasma that needed only a fresh supply of oxygen to become explosive.

As the firemen on the tower balcony concentrated on the fire above them, a small plume of white smoke appeared at their feet.

The Fire Department rang a second alarm at 1:41 P.M. and activated the big siren at the exposition's Machinery Building. Thousands of visitors now moved toward the smoke and packed the lawns and paths surrounding the building. Some brought lunch. Burnham came, as did Davis. The Columbian Guard arrived in force to clear the way for additional engines and ladder wagons. Riders on the Ferris Wheel got the clearest, most horrific view of what happened next.

"Never," the Fire Department reported, "was so terrible a tragedy witnessed by such a sea of agonized faces."

Suddenly flames erupted from the tower at a point about fifty feet *below* Fitzpatrick and his men. Fresh air rushed into the tower. An explosion followed. To the firemen, according to the department's official report, it appeared "as though the gaseous contents of the air-shaft surrounding the smokestack had become ignited, and the entire interior of the tower at once became a seething furnace."

Fireman John Davis was standing on the balcony with Captain Fitzpatrick and the other men. "I saw there was only one chance, and I made up my mind to take it," Davis said. "I made a leap for the hose and had the good luck to catch it. The rest of the boys seemed transfixed with horror and unable to move."

Davis and one other man rode the hose to the ground. The firemen still on the balcony knew their situation was deadly and began to tell each other good-bye. Witnesses watched them hug and shake hands. Captain Fitzpatrick grabbed a rope and swung down through the fire to the main roof below, where he lay with a fractured leg and internal injuries, half his huge mustache burned away. Other men jumped to their deaths, in some cases penetrating the main roof.

Fire Marshal Murphy and two other firemen on the ground climbed a ladder to retrieve Fitzpatrick. They lowered him by rope to colleagues waiting below. He was alive but fading.

In all, the blaze killed twelve firemen and three workers. Fitzpatrick died at nine o'clock that night.

The next day attendance exceeded 100,000. The still-smoking rubble of the Cold Storage Building had proved irresistible.

———

The coroner immediately convened an inquest, during which a jury heard testimony from Daniel Burnham; Frank Burnham; officials of Hercules Iron Works; and various firemen. Daniel Burnham testified he had not known of the previous fire or the omitted thimble and claimed that since the building was a private concession he had no authority over its construction beyond approving its design. On Tuesday, July 18, the jury charged him, Fire Marshal Murphy, and two Hercules officers with criminal negligence and referred the charges to a grand jury.

Burnham was stunned but kept his silence. "The attempt to hold you in any degree responsible or censurable for the loss of life is an outrage," wrote Dion Geraldine, his construction superintendent at the fair. "The men who gave this verdict must have been very stupid, or sadly misinformed."

Under customary procedures, Burnham and the others would have been placed under arrest pending bail, but in this instance even the coroner's office seemed taken aback. The sheriff made no move to arrest the director of works. Burnham posted bond the next morning.

With the stink of charred wood still heavy in the air, Burnham closed the roof walks of the Transportation and Manufactures and Liberal Arts buildings and the balconies and upper galleries of the Administration Building, fearing that a fire in the buildings or among their exhibits could start a panic and cause a tragedy of even greater magnitude. Hundreds of people had crowded the roof walk of the Manufactures Building each day, but their only way down was by elevator. Burnham imagined terrified men, women, and children trying to slide down the glass flanks of the roof and breaking through, then falling two hundred feet to the exhibit floor.

———

As if things could not get any blacker, on the same day that the coroner's jury ordered Burnham's arrest, July 18, the directors of the exposition bowed to bank pressure and voted to establish a Retrenchment Committee with nearly unrestricted powers to cut costs throughout the fair, and appointed three cold-eyed men to staff it. A subsequent resolution approved by the Exposition Company's directors stated that as of August 1, "no expenditures whatever connected with the construction, maintenance or conduct of the Exposition shall be incurred unless authorized by said committee." It was clear from the start that the committee's primary target was Burnham's Department of Works.

Equally clear, at least to Burnham, was that the last thing the fair needed right now, as he and Millet continued their fight to boost the rate of paid admissions—a campaign with its own necessary costs—was a troika of penny-pinchers sitting in judgment on every new expense. Millet had some extraordinary ideas for events in August, including an elaborate Midway ball during which fair officials, including Burnham, would dance with Dahoman women and Algerian belly dancers. That the committee would view the expense of this ball and other Millet events as frivolous seemed certain. Yet Burnham knew that such expenditures, as well as continued spending on police, garbage removal, and maintenance of roads and lawns, was vital.

He feared that the Retrenchment Committee would cripple the fair for once and for all.

Love

THE REMAINS OF THE Cold Storage fire were still visible as a party of schoolteachers arrived from St. Louis, accompanied by a young reporter. The twenty-four teachers had won a contest held by the *St. Louis Republic* that entitled them to a free stay at the fair at the newspaper's expense. Along with assorted friends and family members—for a total of forty travelers—they had piled into a luxurious sleeper car, named *Benares,* provided by the Chicago & Alton Railroad. They arrived at Chicago's Union Depot on Monday, July 17, at eight o'clock in the morning and went immediately by carriage to their hotel, the Varsity, located close enough to the fair that from its second-floor balcony the teachers could see the Ferris Wheel, the top of the Manufactures and Liberal Arts Building, and Big Mary's gilded head.

The reporter—Theodore Dreiser—was young and suffused with a garish self-confidence that drew the attention of the young women. He flirted with all but of course was drawn most to the one woman who seemed least interested, a small, pretty, and reserved woman named Sara Osborne White, whom a past suitor had nicknamed "Jug" for her tendency to wear brown. She was hardly Dreiser's type: By now he was sexually experienced and in the middle of an entirely physical affair with his landlady. To him Sara White exuded "an intense something concealed by an air of supreme innocence and maidenly reserve."

Dreiser joined the teachers on the Ferris Wheel and accompanied them on a visit to Buffalo Bill's show, where Colonel Cody himself greeted the women and shook hands with each. Dreiser followed the ladies through the Manufactures and Liberal Arts Building where, he said, a man "could trail round from place to place for a year and not get tired." In the

Midway Dreiser persuaded James J. Corbett to meet the women. Corbett was the boxer who had downed John L. Sullivan in the great fight of September 1892, a battle that had consumed the entire front page of the next morning's *Chicago Tribune*. Corbett too shook the women's hands, although one teacher declined the opportunity. Her name was Sullivan.

Every chance he got, Dreiser tried to separate Sara White from the *Republic*'s entourage, which Dreiser called the "Forty Odd," but Sara had brought along her sister Rose, which complicated things. On at least one occasion Dreiser tried to kiss Sara. She told him not to be "sentimental."

He failed at seduction, but was himself successfully seduced—by the fair. It had swept him, he said, "into a dream from which I did not recover for months." Most captivating were the nights, "when the long shadows have all merged into one and the stars begin to gleam out over the lake and the domes of the palaces of the White City."

Sara White remained on his mind long after he and the Forty Odd departed the fair. In St. Louis he wrote to her and courted her and in the process resolved to make more of himself as a writer. He left St. Louis for a job editing a rural Michigan newspaper but found that the realities of being a small-town editor did not live up to the fantasy. After a few other stops he reached Pittsburgh. He wrote to Sara White and visited her whenever he returned to St. Louis. He asked her to sit in his lap. She refused.

She did, however, accept his proposal of marriage. Dreiser showed a friend, John Maxwell of the *St. Louis Globe-Democrat,* her photograph. Where Dreiser saw an enticing woman of mystery, Maxwell saw a schoolmarm of drab demeanor. He tried to warn Dreiser: "If you marry now—and a conventional and narrow woman at that, one older than you, you're gone."

It was good advice for a man like Dreiser. But Dreiser did not take it.

The Ferris Wheel became a vector for love. Couples asked permission to be married at the highest point on the wheel. Luther Rice never allowed it, but in two cases where the couples already had mailed invitations, he did permit weddings in his office.

Despite the wheel's inherent romantic potential, however, rides at night never became popular. The favorite hour was the golding time between five and six in the evening.

Holmes, newly free and land rich, brought a new woman to the fair, Georgiana Yoke, whom he had met earlier in the year at a department store, Schlesinger & Meyer, where she worked as a saleswoman. She had grown up in Franklin, Indiana, and lived there with her parents until 1891, when she set out for a bigger, more glamorous life in Chicago. She was only twenty-three when she met Holmes, but her small size and sun-blond hair made her look much younger, almost like a child—save for the sharp features of her face and the intelligence that inhabited her very large blue eyes.

She had never met anyone like him. He was handsome, articulate, and clearly well off. He even possessed property in Europe. She felt a certain sadness for him, however. He was so alone—all his family was dead, save one aunt living in Africa. His last uncle had just died and left him a large fortune consisting of property in the South and in Fort Worth, Texas.

Holmes gave her many presents, among them a Bible, diamond earrings, and a locket—"a little heart," she said, "with pearls."

At the fair he took her on the Ferris Wheel and hired a gondola and walked with her on the dark fragrant paths of the Wooded Island, in the soft glow of Chinese lanterns.

He asked her to be his wife. She agreed.

He cautioned, however, that for the marriage he would have to use a different name, Henry Mansfield Howard. It was his dead uncle's name, he said. The uncle was blood proud and had bequeathed Holmes his estate on condition he first adopt the uncle's name in full. Holmes had obliged, out of respect for his uncle's memory.

Mayor Harrison too believed he was in love, with a New Orleans woman named Annie Howard. He was sixty-eight and a widower twice over; she was in her twenties—no one knew exactly where in her twenties, but estimates put her between twenty-one and twenty-seven years old. She was "very plump," by one account, and "full of life." She had come to Chicago for the duration of the fair and was renting a mansion near the mayor's. She spent her days at the fair buying art.

Harrison and Miss Howard had some news for the city, but the mayor had no plans to reveal it until October 28, when the exposition would host American Cities Day. *His* day, really—two days before the official close, but the day when he would get to stand before several thousand mayors from around the country and revel in his stature as mayor of Chicago, the city that built the greatest fair of all time.

Freaks

On July 31, 1893, after two investigative hearings, the Retrenchment Committee gave its report to the exposition's Board of Directors. The report stated that the financial management of the fair "can only be characterized as shamefully extravagant." Drastic cuts in spending and staff were necessary, immediately. "As to the Construction Department, we hardly know what to say," the report continued. "We had no time to go into details, but have formed the decided impression that this is being run now, as in the past, upon the general theory that money is no object."

The Retrenchment Committee made it clear that, at least for its three members, the financial success of the fair was as important as its obvious aesthetic success. The honor of Chicago's leading men, who prided themselves on their unsentimental—some might say ruthless—pursuit of maximum profit, was in peril. The report closed, "If we are not to be disgraced before the public as business-men, this matter must be followed up sharply and decisively."

In separate statements, the Retrenchment Committee urged the directors to make the committee permanent and invest it with the power to approve or deny every expenditure at the exposition, no matter how small.

This was too much, even for the equally hardened businessmen of the exposition board. President Higinbotham said he would resign before he would cede such power to anyone. Other directors felt likewise. Stung by this rejection, the three men of the Retrenchment Committee themselves resigned. One told a reporter, "If the directory had seen fit to continue the committee with power as originally intended, it would have dropped heads enough to fill the grand court basin. . . ."

The retrenchers' report had been too harsh, too much a rebuke, at a time when the mood throughout Chicago was one of sustained exultation at the fact that the fair had gotten built at all and that it had proven more beautiful than anyone had imagined. Even New York had apologized—well, at least one editor from New York had done so. Charles T. Root, editor of the *New York Dry Goods Reporter* and no relation to Burnham's dead partner, published an editorial on Thursday, August 10, 1893, in which he cited the ridicule and hostility that New York editors had expressed ever since Chicago won the right to build the exposition. "Hundreds of newspapers, among them scores of the strongest Eastern dailies, held their sides with merriment over the exquisite humor of the idea of this crude, upstart, pork-packing city undertaking to conceive and carry out a true World's Fair. . . ." The carping had subsided, he wrote, but few of the carpers had as yet made the *"amende honorable"* that now clearly was due Chicago. He compounded his heresy by adding that if New York had won the fair, it would not have done as fine a job. "So far as I have been able to observe New York never gets behind any enterprise as Chicago got behind this, and without that splendid pulling together, prestige, financial supremacy, and all that sort of thing would not go far toward paralleling the White City." It was time, he said, to acknowledge the truth: "Chicago has disappointed her enemies and astonished the world."

None of the exposition directors or officers had any illusions, however. The rate of paid admissions, though rising steadily, had to be increased still more, and soon. Only three months remained until the closing ceremony on October 30. (The closure was supposed to happen at the end of October, meaning October 31, but some unidentified crafter of the federal legislation erred in thinking October only had thirty days.)

The directors pressured the railroads to lower fares. The *Chicago Tribune* made fare reductions a crusade and openly attacked the railroads. "They are unpatriotic, for this is a national not a local fair," an editorial charged on August 11, 1893. "They are also desperately and utterly selfish." The next day the newspaper singled out Chauncey Depew, president of the New York Central, for a particularly caustic appraisal. "Mr.

Depew all along has posed as the special friend of the World's Fair and has been lavish in his declarations that his roads would do the fair thing and would enable tens of thousands to come here beyond Niagara Falls. . . ." Yet Depew had failed to do what he promised, the *Tribune* said. "It is in order for Chauncey M. Depew to hand in his resignation as Chicago's adopted son. Chicago wants no more of him."

Frank Millet, director of functions, meanwhile stepped up his own efforts to promote the fair and arranged an increasingly exotic series of events. He organized boat races in the basin of the Court of Honor that pitted inhabitants of the Midway villages against one another. They did battle every Tuesday evening in vessels native to their homelands. "We want to do something to liven up the lagoons and basin," Millet told an interviewer. "People are getting tired of looking at the electric launches. If we can get the Turks, the South Sea Islanders, the Singalese, the Esquimos, and the American Indians to float about the grand basin in their native barks, it will certainly add some novelty as well as interest to the scene."

Millet also organized swim meets between the Midway "types," as the press called them. He scheduled these for Fridays. The first race took place August 11 in the lagoon, with Zulus swimming against South American Indians. The Dahomans also competed, as did the Turks, "some of them as hairy as gorillas," the *Tribune* said, with the anthropological abandon common to the age. "The races were notable for the lack of clothing worn by the contestants and the serious way in which they went at the task of winning five-dollar gold pieces."

Millet's big coup was the great Midway ball, held on the night of Wednesday, August 16. The *Tribune* called it "The Ball of the Midway Freaks" and sought to whet the nation's appetite with an editorial that first noted a rising furor within the Board of Lady Managers over the belly dancers of the Midway. "Whether the apprehensions of the good ladies . . . were due to infringements of morality or to the anticipation that the performers may bring on an attack of peritonitis if they persist in their contortions is not clear, but all the same they have taken the position that what is not considered very much out of the way on the banks of the Nile or in the market places of Syria is entirely improper on the Midway between Jackson and Washington Parks."

But now, the *Tribune* continued, the belly dancers and every other depraved jiggling half-dressed woman of the Midway had been invited to the great ball, where they were expected to dance with the senior officers of the fair, including Burnham and Davis. "The situation therefore, as will be seen, is full of horrifying possibilities," the *Tribune* said. "It should cause a shiver in the composite breast of the Board of Lady Managers when they consider what may happen if Director-General Davis should lead out some fascinating Fatima at the head of the grand procession and she should be taken with peritonitis in the midst of the dance; or if [Potter] Palmer should escort a votary of the Temple of Luxor only to find her with the same ailment; or if Mayor Harrison, who belongs to all nations, should dance with the whole lot. Will they suppress their partners' contortions by protest or by force, or, following the fashion of the country, will they, too, attempt Oriental contortions? Suppose that President Higinbotham finds as his vis-à-vis an anointed, bare-backed Fiji beauty or a Dahomeyite amazon bent upon the extraordinary antics of the cannibal dance, is he to join in and imitate her or risk his head in an effort to restrain her?"

Further enriching the affair was the presence at Jackson Park of George Francis Train—known universally as "Citizen Train"—in his white suit, red belt, and red Turkish fez, invited by Millet to host the ball and the boat and swim races and anything else that Millet could devise. Train was one of the most famous men of the day, though no one knew quite why. He was said to have been the model for Phileas Fogg, the globe-trotter in *Around the World in Eighty Days*. Train claimed the real reason he was invited to the exposition was to save it by using his psychic powers to increase attendance. These powers resided in his body in the form of electrical energy. He walked about the fairgrounds rubbing his palms to husband that energy and refused to shake hands with anyone lest the act discharge his potency. "Chicago built the fair," he said.

"Everybody else tried to kill it. Chicago built it. I am here to save it and I'll be hanged if I haven't."

The ball took place in the fair's Natatorium, a large building on the Midway devoted to swimming and bathing and equipped with a ballroom and banquet rooms. Bunting of yellow and red hung from the ceiling. The galleries that overlooked the ballroom were outfitted with opera boxes for fair officials and socially prominent families. Burnham had a box, as did Davis and Higinbotham and of course the Palmers. The galleries also had seats and standing room for other paying guests. From railings in front of the boxes hung triangles of silk embroidered with gold arabesques, all glowing with the light of adjacent incandescent bulbs. The effect was one of indescribable opulence. The Retrenchment Committee would not have approved.

At nine-fifteen that night Citizen Train—dressed in his usual white, but now for some reason carrying an armful of blooming sweet pea—led the procession of exotics, many barefoot, down the stairway of the Natatorium to the ballroom below. He held the hand of a ten-year-old Mexican ballerina and was followed by scores of men and women in the customary clothing of their native cultures. Sol Bloom kept order on the ballroom floor.

The official program dedicated dances to particular officials and guests. Director-General Davis was to lead a quadrille, Burnham a "Berlin," Mayor Harrison a polka. Once the dances were completed, the crowd was to sing "Home Sweet Home."

It was hot. Chief Rain-in-the-Face, the Sioux chief who had killed Custer's brother and now occupied Sitting Bull's cabin in the Midway, wore green paint that streamed down his face. A Laplander wore a fur shirt; Eskimo women wore blouses of walrus skin. The maharajah of Kapurthala, visiting that week from India, sat in a makeshift throne on the ballroom stage fanned by three servants.

The ballroom burst with color and energy: Japanese in red silk, Bedouins in red and black, Romanians in red, blue, and yellow. Women who ordinarily would have come wearing almost nothing—like Aheze, an Amazon, and Zahtoobe, a Dahoman—were given short skirts constructed of small American flags. The *Tribune,* in an unintended parody of its own penchant for describing the gowns of the rich, noted that Lola, a South Sea Islander, wore her "native costume of bark cloth covering about half the body, with low cut and sleeveless bodice." As the night wore on and the wine flowed, the line to dance with Lola grew long. Sadly, the belly dancers came in robes and turbans. Men in black dress suits circled the floor, "swinging black Amazons with bushy hair and teeth necklaces." Chicago—and perhaps the world—had never seen anything like it. The *Tribune* called the ball "the strangest gathering since the destruction of the Tower of Babel."

There was food, of course. The official menu:

RELISHES.
Hard boiled potatoes, à la Irish Village.
International hash, à la Midway Plaisance

COLD DISHES.
Roast Missionary, à la Dahomey, west coast of Africa.
Jerked buffalo, à la Indian Village.
Stuffed ostrich, à la Ostrich Farm.
Boiled camel humps, à la Cairo street.
Monkey stew, à la Hagenbeck.

ENTREES.
Fricassee of reindeer, à la Lapland.
Fried snowballs, à la Ice Railway.
Crystallized frappé, from Libby glass exhibit.

PASTRY.
Wind doughnuts, à la Captive Balloon.
Sandwiches (assorted), especially prepared by the
Leather Exhibit.

And for dessert, the program said, "Twenty-five percent of gross receipts."

The ball ended at four-thirty A.M. The exotics walked slowly back to the Midway. The guests climbed into their carriages and slept or softly sang "After the Ball"—the hit song of the day—as their liverymen drove them home over empty streets that echoed with the plosive rhythm of hooves on granite.

⸻

The ball and Frank Millet's other inventions imparted to the exposition a wilder, happier air. The exposition by day might wear a chaste gown of white staff, but at night it danced barefoot and guzzled champagne.

Attendance rose. The daily average of paid admissions for August was 113,403—at last topping the vital 100,000 threshold. The margin was slim, however. And the nation's economic depression was growing steadily worse, its labor situation more volatile.

On August 3 a big Chicago bank, Lazarus Silverman, failed. Burnham's firm had long been a client. On the night of August 10 Charles J. Eddy, a former top official of the bankrupt Reading Railroad, one of the first casualties of the panic, walked into Washington Park just north of the Midway and shot himself. Of course he had been staying at the Metropole. He was the hotel's third suicide that summer. Mayor Harrison warned that the ranks of the unemployed had swollen to an alarming degree. "If Congress does not give us money we will have riots that will shake this country," he said. Two weeks later workers scuffled with police outside City Hall. It was a minor confrontation, but the *Tribune* called it a riot. A few days after that, 25,000 unemployed workers converged on the downtown lakefront and heard Samuel Gompers, standing at the back of speaker's wagon No. 5, ask, "Why should the wealth of the country be stored in banks and elevators while the idle workman wanders homeless about the streets and the idle loafers who hoard the gold only to spend it in riotous living are rolling about in fine carriages from which they look out on peaceful meetings and call them riots?"

For the city's industrialists and merchant princes who learned of

Gompers's speech in their Sunday morning newspapers, this was a particularly unsettling question, for it seemed to embody a demand for much more than simply work. Gompers was calling for fundamental change in the relationship between workers and their overseers.

This was dangerous talk, to be suppressed at all costs.

Prendergast

IT WAS EXCITING, THIS PROSPECT of becoming one of the city's most important officials. At last Prendergast could leave behind the cold mornings and filthy streets and the angry newsboys who disobeyed and taunted him. He was growing impatient, however. His appointment as corporation counsel should have occurred by now.

One afternoon in the first week of October Prendergast took a grip-car to City Hall to see his future office. He found a clerk and introduced himself.

Incredibly, the clerk did not recognize his name. When Prendergast explained that Mayor Harrison planned to make him the city's new corporation counsel, the clerk laughed.

Prendergast insisted on seeing the current counsel, a man named Kraus. Certainly Kraus would recognize his name.

The clerk went to get him.

Kraus emerged from his office and extended his hand. He introduced Prendergast to the other men on his staff as his "successor." Suddenly everyone was smiling.

At first Prendergast thought the smiling was an acknowledgment that soon he would be in charge, but now he saw it as something else.

Kraus asked if he'd like the position immediately.

"No," Prendergast said. "I am in no hurry about it."

Which was not true, but the question had thrown Prendergast. He did not like the way Kraus asked it. Not at all.

Toward Triumph

By TEN O'CLOCK IN THE MORNING on Monday, October 9, 1893, the day Frank Millet had designated as Chicago Day, ticket-takers at the fair's Sixty-fourth Street gate made an informal count of the morning's sales thus far and found that this one gate had recorded 60,000 paid admissions. The men knew from experience that on any ordinary day sales at this gate accounted for about one-fifth of the total admissions to the fair for any given time, and so came up with an estimate that some 300,000 paid visitors already had entered Jackson Park—more than any other full day's total and close to the world's record of 397,000 held by the Paris exposition. Yet the morning had barely begun. The ticket-takers sensed that something odd was happening. The pace of admissions seemed to be multiplying by the hour. In some ticket booths the volume grew so great, so quickly, that silver coins began piling on the floors and burying the ticket-takers' shoes.

Millet and other fair officials had expected high attendance. Chicago was proud of its fair, and everyone knew that only three weeks remained before it would close forever. To assure maximum attendance, Mayor Harrison had signed an official proclamation that urged every business to suspend operation for the day. The courts closed, as did the Board of Trade. The weather helped, too. Monday was an apple-crisp day with temperatures that never exceeded sixty-two degrees, under vivid cerulean skies. Every hotel had filled to capacity, even beyond capacity, with some managers finding themselves compelled to install cots in lobbies and halls. The Wellington Catering Company, which operated eight restaurants and forty lunch counters in Jackson Park, had braced for the day by shipping in two traincar loads of potatoes, 4,000 half-barrels of beer,

15,000 gallons of ice cream, and 40,000 pounds of meat. Its cooks built 200,000 ham sandwiches and brewed 400,000 cups of coffee.

No one, however, expected the sheer crush of visitors that actually did arrive. By noon the chief of admissions, Horace Tucker, wired a message to fair headquarters, "The Paris record is broken to smithereens, and the people are still coming." A single ticket-seller, L. E. Decker, a nephew of Buffalo Bill who had sold tickets for Bill's Wild West for eight years, sold 17,843 tickets during his shift, the most by any one man, and won Horace Tucker's prize of a box of cigars. Lost children filled every chair at the headquarters of the Columbian Guard; nineteen spent the night and were claimed by their parents the next day. Five people were killed in or near the fair, including a worker obliterated while helping prepare the night's fireworks and a visitor who stepped from one grip-car into the path of another. A woman lost her foot when a surging crowd knocked her from a train platform. George Ferris, riding his wheel that day, looked down and gasped, "There must be a million people down there."

The fireworks began at eight o'clock sharp. Millet had planned an elaborate series of explosive "set pieces," fireworks affixed to large metal frames shaped to depict various portraits and tableaus. The first featured the Great Fire of 1871, including an image of Mrs. O'Leary's cow kicking over a lantern. The night boomed and hissed. For the finale the fair's pyrotechnicians launched five thousand rockets all at once into the black sky over the lake.

The true climax occurred after the grounds closed, however. In the silence, with the air still scented with exploded powder, collectors accompanied by armed guards went to each ticket booth and collected the accumulated silver, three tons of it. They counted the money under heavy guard. By one forty-five A.M., they had an exact total.

Ferris had nearly gotten it right. In that single day 713,646 people had paid to enter Jackson Park. (Only 31,059—four percent—were children.) Another 37,380 visitors had entered using passes, bringing the total admission for the day to 751,026, more people than had attended any single day of any peaceable event in history. The *Tribune* argued that the only greater gathering was the massing of Xerxes' army of over five million souls in the fifth century B.C. The Paris record of 397,000 had indeed been shattered.

When the news reached Burnham's shanty, there were cheers and champagne and stories through the night. But the best news came the next day, when officials of the World's Columbian Exposition Company, whose boasts had been ridiculed far and wide, presented a check for $1.5 million to the Illinois Trust and Savings Company and thereby extinguished the last of the exposition's debts.

The Windy City had prevailed.

—⌖—

Now Burnham and Millet made final arrangements for Burnham's own great day, the grand closing ceremony of October 30 that would recognize once and for all that Burnham really had done it and that his work was now complete—that for once there was nothing left to do. At this point, Burnham believed, nothing could tarnish the fair's triumph or his own place in architectural history.

Departures

FRANK MILLET HOPED THE closing ceremony would attract even more people than the fair's Chicago Day. While Millet did his planning, many of the other men who had helped Burnham construct the fair began the return to ordinary life.

Charles McKim disengaged reluctantly. For him the fair had been a brilliant light that for a time dispelled the shadows that had accumulated around his life. He left Jackson Park abruptly on the morning of October 23 and later that day wrote to Burnham, "You know my dislike for saying 'Good-bye' and were prepared to find that I had skipped this morning. To say that I was sorry to leave you all is to put it only one half as strongly as I feel.

"You gave me a beautiful time and the last days of the Fair will always remain in my mind, as were the first, especially identified with yourself. It will be pleasant for the rest of our natural lives to be able to look back to it and talk it over and over and over again, and it goes without saying that you can depend upon me in every way as often hereafter as you may have need of me."

The next day McKim wrote to a friend in Paris of the deepening consensus among himself, Burnham, and most of Chicago that the fair was too wonderful a thing to be allowed simply to fall into disrepair after its official closure on October 30, just six days thence: "indeed it is the ambition of all concerned to have it swept away in the same magical manner in which it appeared, and with the utmost despatch. For economy, as well as for obvious reasons, it has been proposed that the most glorious way would be to blow up the buildings with dynamite. Another scheme is to destroy them with fire. This last would be the easiest and grandest spectacle except for the danger of flying embers in the event of a change of wind from the lake."

Neither McKim nor Burnham truly believed the fair should be set aflame. The buildings, in fact, had been designed to maximize the salvage value of their components. Rather, this talk of conflagration was a way of easing the despair of watching the dream come to an end. No one could bear the idea of the White City lying empty and desolate. A *Cosmopolitan* writer said, "Better to have it vanish suddenly, in a blaze of glory, than fall into gradual disrepair and dilapidation. There is no more melancholy spectacle than a festal hall, the morning after the banquet, when the guests have departed and the lights are extinguished."

Later, these musings about fire would come to seem like prophecy.

Olmsted too severed his connection. Toward the end of summer his busy schedule and the stifling heat caused his health to fail once again and reactivated his insomnia. He had many projects under way, chief among them Biltmore, but he felt himself nearing the end of his career. He was seventy-one years old. On September 6, 1893, he wrote to a friend, Fred Kingsbury, "I can't come to you and often dream of a ride through our old haunts and meeting you and others but have pretty well surrendered to Fate. I must flounder along my way to the end." Olmsted did, however, allow himself a rare expression of satisfaction. "I enjoy my children," he told Kingsbury. "They are one of the centers of my life, the other being the improvement of scenery and making the enjoyment of it available. Spite of my infirmities which do drag me cruelly, I am not to be thought of as an unhappy old man."

Louis Sullivan, engorged with praise and awards for his Transportation Building—especially its Golden Door—again took up his work with Dankmar Adler but under changed circumstances. The deepening depression and missteps by the two partners had left the firm with few projects. For all of 1893 they would complete only two buildings. Sullivan, never easy on his peers, became furious with one of the firm's junior architects when he discovered the man had been using his free time to design houses for clients of his own. Sullivan fired him.

The junior man was Frank Lloyd Wright.

———

Ten thousand construction workers also left the fair's employ and returned to a world without jobs, already crowded with unemployed men. Once the fair closed, many thousands more would join them on Chicago's streets. The threat of violence was as palpable as the deepening cold of autumn. Mayor Harrison was sympathetic and did what he could. He hired thousands of men to clean streets and ordered police stations opened at night for men seeking a place to sleep. Chicago's *Commercial and Financial Chronicle* reported, "Never before has there been such a sudden and striking cessation of industrial activity." Pig iron production fell by half, and new rail construction shrank almost to nothing. Demand for railcars to carry visitors to the exposition had spared the Pullman Works, but by the end of the fair George Pullman too began cutting wages and workers. He did not, however, reduce the rents in his company town.

The White City had drawn men and protected them; the Black City now welcomed them back, on the eve of winter, with filth, starvation, and violence.

———

Holmes too sensed it was time to leave Chicago. The pressure from creditors and families was growing too great.

First he set fire to the top floor of his castle. The blaze did minimal damage, but he filed a claim for $6,000 on a policy acquired by his fictional alter ego, Hiram S. Campbell. An investigator for one of the insurance companies, F. G. Cowie, became suspicious and began a detailed investigation. Though he found no concrete evidence of arson, Cowie believed Holmes or an accomplice had started the fire. He advised the insurers to pay the claim, but only to Hiram S. Campbell and only if Campbell presented himself in person.

Holmes could not claim the money himself, for by now Cowie knew him. Ordinarily he simply would have recruited someone else to masquerade as Campbell and claim the money, but of late he had become increasingly wary. The guardians of Minnie Williams had dispatched an attorney, William Capp, to look for Minnie and to protect the assets of her estate. Anna's guardian, the Reverend Dr. Black, had hired a private detective who had come to Holmes's building. And letters continued to arrive from the Cigrands and Smythes and other parents. No one yet had accused Holmes of foul play, but the intensity of this new wave of inquiry was greater, more obliquely accusatory, than anything he previously had experienced. Hiram S. Campbell never claimed the money.

But Holmes found that Cowie's investigation had a secondary, more damaging effect. In the course of digging up information about Holmes, he had succeeded in stirring up and uniting Holmes's creditors, the furniture dealers and iron suppliers and bicycle manufacturers and contractors whom Holmes had cheated over the previous five years. The creditors now hired an attorney named George B. Chamberlin, counsel for Chicago's Lafayette Collection Agency, who had been pestering Holmes ever since he failed to pay the furnace company for improving his kiln. Later Chamberlin would claim to be the first man in Chicago to suspect Holmes of being a criminal.

In the fall of 1893 Chamberlin contacted Holmes and requested he come to a meeting at his office. Holmes believed he and Chamberlin would be meeting alone, one on one, but when Holmes arrived at the office, he found it occupied by two dozen creditors and their attorneys and one police detective.

This surprised Holmes but did not faze him. He shook hands and met the angry gazes of his creditors head on. Tempers immediately cooled a few degrees. He had that effect.

Chamberlin had planned the meeting as a trap to try to shatter Holmes's imperturbable façade, and was impressed with Holmes's ability to maintain his insouciance despite the rancor in the room. Chamberlin told Holmes that all together he owed the creditors at least $50,000.

Holmes adopted his most sober expression. He understood their concerns. He explained his lapses. His ambition had gotten ahead of his ability to pay his debts. Things would have been fine, all the debts resolved, if not for the Panic of 1893, which had ruined him and destroyed his hopes, just as it had for countless others in Chicago and the nation at large.

Incredibly, Chamberlin saw, some of the creditors nodded in sympathy.

Tears filled Holmes's eyes. He offered his deepest, most heartfelt apologies. And he suggested a solution. He proposed to settle his debts by giving the group a mortgage secured by his various properties.

This nearly made Chamberlin laugh, yet one of the attorneys present in the room actually advised the group to accept Holmes's offer. Chamberlin was startled to see that Holmes's false warmth seemed to be mollifying the creditors. A few moments earlier the group had wanted the detective to arrest Holmes the moment he entered the room. Now they wanted to talk about what to do next.

Chamberlin told Holmes to wait in an adjacent room.

Holmes did so. He waited peacefully.

As the meeting progressed—and grew heated—the attorney who previously had wanted to accept Holmes's mortgage stepped out of Chamberlin's office and entered the room where Holmes waited, ostensibly for a drink of water. He and Holmes talked. Exactly what happened next is unclear. Chamberlin claimed later that this attorney had been so angry at having his recommendation rebuffed that he tipped Holmes to the fact the creditors were again leaning toward arrest. It is possible, too, that Holmes simply offered the attorney cash for the information, or deployed his false warmth and teary regret to seduce the attorney into revealing the group's mounting consensus.

The attorney returned to the meeting.

Holmes fled.

Soon afterward Holmes set out for Fort Worth, Texas, to take better advantage of Minnie Williams's land. He had plans for the property. He would sell some of it and on the rest build a three-story structure exactly like the one in Englewood. Meanwhile he would use the land to secure loans and to float notes. He expected to lead a very prosperous and satisfying life, at least until the time came to move on to the next city. He brought along his assistant, Benjamin Pitezel, and his new fiancée, the small and pretty Miss Georgiana Yoke. Just before leaving Chicago Holmes acquired a life insurance policy, from the Fidelity Mutual Life Association of Philadelphia, to insure Pitezel's life for $10,000.

Nightfall

THROUGHOUT OCTOBER ATTENDANCE AT the fair rose sharply as more and more people realized that the time left to see the White City was running short. On October 22 paid attendance totaled 138,011. Just two days later it reached 244,127. Twenty thousand people a day now rode the Ferris Wheel, 80 percent more than at the start of the month. Everyone hoped attendance would continue rising and that the number of people drawn to the closing ceremony of October 30 would break the record set on Chicago Day.

To attract visitors for the close, Frank Millet planned a day-long celebration with music, speeches, fireworks, and a landing by "Columbus" himself from the exposition's full-sized replicas of the *Niña, Pinta,* and *Santa María,* built in Spain for the fair. Millet hired actors to play Columbus and his captains; the crew would consist of the men who had sailed the ships to Chicago. Millet arranged to borrow tropical plants and trees from the Horticulture Building and have them moved to the lakeshore. He planned also to coat the beach with fallen oak and maple leaves to signify the fact that Columbus landed in autumn, even though live palms and dead deciduous leaves were not precisely compatible. Upon landing, Columbus was to thrust his sword into the ground and claim the New World for Spain, while his men assumed positions that mimicked those depicted on a two-cent postage stamp commemorating Columbus's discovery. Meanwhile, according to the *Tribune,* Indians recruited from Buffalo Bill's show and from various fair exhibits would "peer cautiously" at the landing party while shouting incoherently and running "to and fro." With this enactment Millet hoped to carry visitors "back 400 years"—despite the steam tugboats that would nudge the Spanish ships toward shore.

First, however, came Mayor Harrison's big day, American Cities Day, on Saturday, October 28. Five thousand mayors and city councilmen had accepted Harrison's invitation to the fair, among them the mayors of San Francisco, New Orleans and Philadelphia. The record is silent as to whether New York's mayor attended or not.

That morning Harrison delighted reporters by announcing that yes, the rumors about him and the very young Miss Annie Howard were true, and not only that, the two planned to marry on November 16.

The glory time came in the afternoon, when he rose to speak to the assembled mayors. Friends said he had never looked so handsome, so full of life.

He praised the remarkable transformation of Jackson Park. "Look at it now!" he said. "These buildings, this hall, this dream of poets of centuries is the wild aspiration of crazy architects alone." He told his audience, "I myself have taken a new lease of life"—an allusion perhaps to Miss Howard—"and I believe I shall see the day when Chicago will be the biggest city in America, and the third city on the face of the globe." He was sixty-eight years old but announced, "I intend to live for more than half a century, and at the end of that half-century London will be trembling lest Chicago shall surpass it. . . ."

With a glance at the mayor of Omaha, he graciously offered to accept Omaha as a suburb.

He changed course. "It sickens me when I look at this great Exposition to think that it will be allowed to crumble to dust," he said. He hoped the demolition would be quick, and he quoted a recent remark by Burnham: " 'Let it go; it has to go, so let it go. Let us put the torch to it and burn it down.' I believe with him. If we cannot preserve it for another year I would be in favor of putting a torch to it and burning it down and let it go up into the bright sky to eternal heaven."

Prendergast could stand it no longer. His visit to the corporation counsel's office—by rights *his* office—had been humiliating. They had humored him. Smirked. Yet Harrison had promised him the job. What did he have to do to get the mayor's attention? All his postcards had achieved nothing. No one wrote to him, no one took him seriously.

At two o'clock on American Cities Day Prendergast left his mother's house and walked to a shoe dealer on Milwaukee Avenue. He paid the dealer four dollars for a used six-chamber revolver. He knew that revolvers of this particular model had a penchant for accidental discharge when bumped or dropped, so he loaded it with only five cartridges and kept the empty chamber under the hammer.

Later, much would be made of this precaution.

———

At three o'clock, about the time Harrison was giving his speech, Prendergast walked into the Unity Building in central Chicago where Governor John P. Altgeld had an office.

Prendergast looked pale and strangely excited. An official of the building found his demeanor troubling and told him he could not enter.

Prendergast returned to the street.

———

It was nearly dark when Harrison left Jackson Park and drove north through the cold smoky evening toward his mansion on Ashland Avenue. Temperatures had fallen sharply over the week, down to the thirties at night, and the sky seemed perpetually overcast. Harrison reached his home by seven o'clock. He tinkered with a first-floor window, then sat down to supper with two of his children, Sophie and Preston. He had other children, but they were grown and gone. The meal, of course, included watermelon.

In the midst of supper, at approximately seven-thirty, someone rang the bell at the front door. Mary Hanson, the parlor maid, answered and found a gaunt young man with a smooth-shaven face and close-cut black hair. He looked ill. He asked to see the mayor.

By itself, there was nothing peculiar about the request. Evening visits by strangers were a regular occurrence at the Ashland house, for Harrison prided himself on being available to any citizen of Chicago, regardless of social stature. Tonight's visitor seemed seedier than most, however, and behaved oddly. Nonetheless, Mary Hanson told him to come back in half an hour.

The day had been an exciting one for the mayor but also exhausting. He fell asleep at the table. Shortly before eight o'clock his son left the dining room to go up to his room and dress for an engagement in the city later that night. Sophie also went upstairs, to write a letter. The house was cozy and well lit. Mary Hanson and the other servants gathered in the kitchen for their own supper.

At precisely eight o'clock the front bell again rang, and again Hanson answered it.

The same young man stood at the threshold. Hanson asked him to wait in the hall and went to get the mayor.

"It must have been about eight o'clock when I heard a noise," Harrison's son Preston said. "I was startled; it sounded like a picture falling." Sophie heard it, too, and heard her father cry out. "I thought nothing of it," she said, "because I thought it was some screens falling on the floor near the back hall. Father's voice I took to be a yawn. He had a way of yawning very loud."

Preston left his room and saw smoke drifting up from the entry hall. As he came down the steps, he heard two more reports. "The last shot was clear and penetrating," he said. "I knew it to be a revolver shot." It sounded "like a manhole explosion."

He ran to the hall and found Harrison lying on his back surrounded by servants, the air silvered with gunsmoke. There was very little blood. Preston shouted, "Father is not hurt, is he?"

The mayor himself answered. "Yes," he said. "I am shot. I will die."

Three more shots sounded from the street. The coachman had fired his own revolver once in the air to alert police, once at Prendergast, and Prendergast had returned the shot.

The commotion brought a neighbor, William J. Chalmers, who folded his coat under Harrison's head. Harrison told him he had been shot over the heart, but Chalmers did not believe it. There was too little blood.

They argued.

Chalmers told Harrison he had *not* been shot over the heart.

Harrison snapped, "I tell you I am; this is death."

A few moments later his heart stopped.

"He died angry," Chalmers said, "because I didn't believe him. Even in death he is emphatic and imperious."

⸺

Prendergast walked to the nearby Desplaines Street police station and calmly told desk sergeant O. Z. Barber, "Lock me up; I am the man who shot the mayor." The sergeant was incredulous, until Prendergast gave him the revolver, which smelled strongly of blown powder. Barber found that its cylinder contained four spent cartridges and a single live one. The sixth chamber was empty.

Barber asked Prendergast why he had shot the mayor.

"Because he betrayed my confidence. I supported him through his campaign and he promised to appoint me corporation counsel. He didn't live up to his word."

⸺

The Exposition Company canceled the closing ceremony. There would be no Jubilee March, no landing by Columbus, no address by Harlow Higinbotham, George Davis, or Bertha Palmer; no presentation of awards, no praise for Burnham and Olmsted; no "Hail Columbia"; no mass rendition of "Auld Lang Syne." The closing became instead a memorial assembly in the fair's Festival Hall. As the audience entered, an organist played Chopin's "Funeral March" on the hall's giant pipe organ. The hall was so cold, the presiding officer announced that men could keep their hats on.

Reverend Dr. J. H. Barrows read a blessing and benediction and then, at the request of exposition officials, read a speech that Higinbotham had prepared for the originally planned ceremony. The remarks still seemed appropriate, especially one passage. "We are turning our backs upon the fairest dream of civilization and are about to consign it to the dust," Barrows read. "It is like the death of a dear friend."

The audience exited slowly into the cold gray afternoon.

At exactly four forty-five, sunset, the warship *Michigan* fired one of its cannon and continued to fire twenty times more as one thousand men quietly took up positions at each of the exposition's flags. With the last boom of the *Michigan*'s gun, the great flag at the Administration Building fell to the ground. Simultaneously, the thousand other flags also fell, as massed trumpeters and bassoonists in the Court of Honor played "The Star-Spangled Banner" and "America." Two hundred thousand visitors, many in tears, joined in.

The fair was over.

———

The six hundred carriages in Carter Harrison's cortege stretched for miles. The procession moved slowly and quietly through a black sea of men and women dressed for mourning. A catafalque carrying Harrison's black casket led the cortege and was followed immediately by Harrison's beloved Kentucky mare, stirrups crossed on its empty saddle. Everywhere the white flags that had symbolized the White City hung at half mast. Thousands of men and women wore buttons that said "Our Carter" and watched in silence as, carriage by carriage, the city's greatest men drove past. Armour, Pullman, Schwab, Field, McCormick, Ward.

And Burnham.

It was a difficult ride for him. He had passed this way before, to bury John Root. The fair had begun with death, and now it had ended with death.

So grand was the procession, it needed two hours to pass any one point. By the time it reached Graceland Cemetery, north of the city, darkness had fallen and a soft mist hugged the ground. Long lines of policemen flanked the path to the cemetery's brownstone chapel. Off to the side stood fifty members of the United German Singing Societies.

Harrison had heard them sing at a picnic and, joking, had asked them to sing at his funeral.

———

Harrison's murder fell upon the city like a heavy curtain. There was the time before, there was the time after. Where once the city's newspapers would have run an endless series of stories about the aftereffects of the fair, now there was mostly silence. The fair remained open, informally, on October 31, and many men and women came to the grounds for one last visit, as if paying their respects to a lost relative. A tearful woman told columnist Teresa Dean, "The good-by is as sad as any I have known in all the years that I have lived." William Stead, the British editor whose brother Herbert had covered the fair's opening, arrived in Chicago from New York on the night of its official close but made his first visit to the grounds the next day. He claimed that nothing he had seen in Paris, Rome, or London was as perfect as the Court of Honor.

That night the exposition illuminated the fairgrounds one last time. "Beneath the stars the lake lay dark and sombre," Stead wrote, "but on its shores gleamed and glowed in golden radiance the ivory city, beautiful as a poet's dream, silent as a city of the dead."

The Black City

THE EXPOSITION PROVED UNABLE to hold the Black City at bay for very long. With its formal closure thousands more workers joined the swelling army of the unemployed, and homeless men took up residence among the great abandoned palaces of the fair. "The poor had come lean and hungry out of the terrible winter that followed the World's Fair," wrote novelist Robert Herrick in *The Web of Life.* "In that beautiful enterprise the prodigal city had put forth her utmost strength and, having shown the world the supreme flower of her energy, had collapsed. . . . The city's huge garment was too large for it; miles of empty stores, hotels, flat-buildings, showed its shrunken state. Tens of thousands of human beings, lured to the festive city by abnormal wages, had been left stranded, without food or a right to shelter in its tenant-less buildings." It was the contrast that was so wrenching. "What a spectacle!" wrote Ray Stannard Baker in his *American Chronicle.* "What a human downfall after the magnificence and prodigality of the World's Fair which had so recently closed its doors! Heights of splendor, pride, exaltation in one month: depths of wretchedness, suffering, hunger, cold, in the next."

In that first, brutal winter Burnham's photographer, Charles Arnold, took a very different series of photographs. One shows the Machinery Building soiled by smoke and litter. A dark liquid had been thrown against one wall. At the base of a column was a large box, apparently the home of an out-of-work squatter. "It is desolation," wrote Teresa Dean, the columnist, about a visit she made to Jackson Park on January 2, 1894. "You wish you had not come. If there were not so many around, you would reach out your arms, with the prayer on your lips for it all to come back to you. It seems cruel, cruel, to give us such a vision; to let us dream and drift through heaven for six months, and then to take it out of our lives."

Six days after her visit the first fires occurred and destroyed several structures, among them the famous Peristyle. The following morning Big Mary, chipped and soiled, stood over a landscape of twisted and blackened steel.

The winter became a crucible for American labor. To workers, Eugene Debs and Samuel Gompers came increasingly to seem like saviors, Chicago's merchant princes like devils. George Pullman continued to cut jobs and wages without reducing rents, even though his company's treasury was flush with over $60 million in cash. Pullman's friends cautioned that he was being pigheaded and had underestimated the anger of his workers. He moved his family out of Chicago and hid his best china. On May 11, 1894, two thousand Pullman workers went on strike with the support of Debs's American Railway Union. Other strikes broke out around the country, and Debs began planning a nationwide general strike to begin in July. President Cleveland ordered federal troops to Chicago and placed them under the command of General Nelson A. Miles, previously the grand marshal of the exposition. Miles was uneasy about his new command. He sensed in the spreading unrest something unprecedented, "more threatening and far-reaching than anything that had occurred before." He followed orders, however, and the former grand marshal of the fair wound up fighting the men who had built it.

Strikers blocked trains and burned railcars. On July 5, 1894, arsonists set fire to the seven greatest palaces of the exposition—Post's immense Manufactures and Liberal Arts Building, Hunt's dome, Sullivan's Golden Door, all of them. In the Loop men and women gathered on rooftops and in the highest offices of the Rookery, the Masonic Temple, the Temperance Building, and every other high place to watch the distant conflagration. Flames rose a hundred feet into the night sky and cast their gleam far out onto the lake.

Belatedly, Burnham had gotten his wish. "There was no regret," observed the *Chicago Tribune,* "rather a feeling of pleasure that the elements and not the wrecker should wipe out the spectacle of the Columbian season."

Later, in the next year, came the wonder:

"There are hundreds of people who went to Chicago to see the Fair and were never heard from again," said the *New York World.* "The list of the 'missing' when the Fair closed was a long one, and in the greater number foul play suspected. Did these visitors to the Fair, strangers to Chicago, find their way to Holmes' Castle in answer to delusive advertisements sent out by him, never to return again? Did he erect his Castle close to the Fair grounds so as to gather in these victims by the wholesale . . . ?"

Initially the Chicago police had no answers, other than the obvious: That in Chicago in the time of the fair, it was so very easy to disappear.

The secrets of Holmes's castle eventually did come to light, but only because of the persistence of a lone detective from a far-off city, grieving his own terrible loss.

PART IV

Cruelty Revealed

1895

Dr. H. H. Holmes.

"Property of H. H. Holmes"

DETECTIVE FRANK GEYER WAS A big man with a pleasant, earnest face, a large walrus mustache, and a new gravity in his gaze and demeanor. He was one of Philadelphia's top detectives and had been a member of the force for twenty years, during which time he had investigated some two hundred killings. He knew murder and its unchanging templates. Husbands killed wives, wives killed husbands, and the poor killed one another, always for the usual motives of money, jealousy, passion, and love. Rarely did a murder involve the mysterious elements of dime novels or the stories of Sir Arthur Conan Doyle. From the start, however, Geyer's current assignment—it was now June 1895—had veered from the ordinary. One unusual aspect was that the suspect already was in custody, arrested seven months earlier for insurance fraud and now incarcerated in Philadelphia's Moyamensing Prison.

The suspect was a physician whose given name was Mudgett but was known more commonly by the alias H. H. Holmes. He once had lived in Chicago where he and an associate, Benjamin Pitezel, had run a hotel during the World's Columbian Exposition of 1893. They had moved next to Fort Worth, Texas, then to St. Louis, and on to Philadelphia, committing frauds along the way. In Philadelphia Holmes had swindled the Fidelity Mutual Life Association of nearly $10,000 by apparently faking the death of a policyholder, Ben Pitezel. Holmes had bought the insurance in 1893 from Fidelity's Chicago office, just before the close of the exposition. As evidence of fraud accumulated, Fidelity had hired the Pinkerton National Detective Agency—"The Eye That Never Sleeps"— to search for Holmes. The agency's operatives picked up his trail in Burlington, Vermont, and followed him to Boston, where they arranged to have him arrested by police. Holmes confessed to the fraud and agreed to be extradited to Philadelphia for trial. At that point the case appeared to be closed. But now in June 1895 it was becoming increasingly apparent that Holmes had not *faked* the death of Ben Pitezel, he had killed him and then arranged the scene to make the death seem accidental. Now three of Pitezel's five children—Alice, Nellie, and Howard—were missing, last seen in Holmes's company.

Geyer's assignment was to find the children. He was invited to join the case by Philadelphia district attorney George S. Graham, who over the years had come to rely on Geyer for the city's most sensitive investigations. Graham had thought twice this time, however, for he knew that just a few months earlier Geyer had lost his wife, Martha, and his twelve-year-old daughter, Esther, in a house fire.

Geyer interviewed Holmes in his cell but learned nothing new. Holmes insisted that when he had last seen the Pitezel children, they were alive and traveling with a woman named Minnie Williams, en route to the place where their father was hiding out.

Geyer found Holmes to be smooth and glib, a social chameleon. "Holmes is greatly given to lying with a sort of florid ornamentation," Geyer wrote, "and all of his stories are decorated with flamboyant draperies, intended by him to strengthen the plausibility of his statements. In talking, he has the appearance of candor, becomes pathetic at times when pathos will serve him best, uttering his words with a quaver in his voice, often accompanied by a moistened eye, then turning quickly with a determined and forceful method of speech, as if indignation or resolution had sprung out of tender memories that had touched his heart."

Holmes claimed to have secured a cadaver that resembled Ben Pitezel and to have placed it on the second floor of a house rented especially for the fraud. By coincidence or out of some malignant expression of humor, the house was located right behind the city morgue, a few blocks north of City Hall. Holmes admitted arranging the cadaver to suggest that Pitezel had died in an accidental explosion. He poured a solvent on the cadaver's upper body and set it on fire, then positioned the body on the floor in direct sunlight. By the time the body was discovered, its features had been distorted well beyond recognition. Holmes volunteered to assist the coroner in making an identification. At the morgue he not only helped locate a distinctive wart on the dead man's neck, he pulled out his own lancet and removed the wart himself, then matter-of-factly handed it to the coroner.

The coroner had wanted a member of the Pitezel family also to be present at the identification. Pitezel's wife, Carrie, was ill and could not come. Instead she sent her second-eldest daughter, Alice, fifteen years old. The coroner's men draped the body so as to allow Alice to see only Pitezel's teeth. She seemed confident that the corpse was her father. Fidelity paid the death benefit. Next Holmes traveled to St. Louis, where the Pitezel family now lived. Still in possession of Alice, he persuaded Carrie to let him pick up two more of her children, explaining that their father, in hiding, was desperate to see them. He took Nellie, eleven, and Howard, eight, and embarked with all three children on a strange and sad journey.

Geyer knew from Alice's letters that initially she found the trip to be something of an adventure. In a letter to her mother, dated September 20, 1894, Alice wrote, "I wish you could see what I have seen." In the same letter she expressed her distaste for Holmes's treacly manner. "I don't like him to call me babe and child and dear and all such trash." The next day she wrote again, "Mamma have you ever seen or tasted a red banana? I have had three. They are so big that I can just reach around it and have my thumb and next finger just tutch." Since leaving St. Louis, Alice had heard nothing from home and feared her mother's illness might have gotten much worse. "Have you gotten 4 letters from me besides this?" Alice wrote. "Are you sick in bed yet or are you up? I wish that I could hear from you."

One of the few things that Detective Geyer knew with certainty was that neither of these letters ever reached Carrie Pitezel. Alice and Nellie had written to their mother repeatedly while in Holmes's custody and had given the letters to Holmes with the expectation that he would mail them. He never did. Shortly after his arrest police discovered a tin box, marked "Property of H. H. Holmes," containing various documents and a dozen letters from the girls. He had stored them in the box as if they were seashells collected from a beach.

Now Mrs. Pitezel was nearly crushed with anxiety and grief, despite Holmes's latest assurances that Alice, Nellie, and Howard were in London, England, under the able care of Minnie Williams. A search by Scotland Yard had found no trace of any of them. Geyer had little hope that his own search would fare any better. With more than half a year having elapsed since anyone had heard from the children, Geyer wrote, "it did not look like a very encouraging task to undertake, and it was the general belief of all interested, that the children would never be found. The District Attorney believed, however, that another final effort to find the children should be made, for the sake of the stricken mother, if for nothing else. I was not placed under any restrictions, but was told to go and exercise my own judgment in the matter, and to follow wherever the clues led me."

Geyer set out on his search on the evening of June 26, 1895, a hot night in a hot summer. Earlier in June a zone of high pressure, the "permanent high," had settled over the middle Atlantic states and driven temperatures in Philadelphia well into the nineties. A humid stillness held the countryside. Even at night the air inside Geyer's train was stagnant and moist. Leftover cigar smoke drifted from men's suits, and at each stop the roar of frogs and crickets filled the car. Geyer slept in jagged stretches.

The next day, as the train sped west through the heat-steamed hollows of Pennsylvania and Ohio, Geyer reread his copies of the children's letters to look for anything he might have missed that could help direct his search. The letters not only provided irrefutable proof that the children had been with Holmes but contained geographic references that allowed Geyer to plot the broad contours of the route Holmes and the children had followed. Their first stop appeared to have been Cincinnati.

Detective Geyer reached Cincinnati at seven-thirty P.M. on Thursday,

June 27. He checked into the Palace Hotel. The next morning he went to police headquarters to brief the city's police superintendent on his mission. The superintendent assigned a detective to assist him, Detective John Schnooks, an old friend of Geyer's.

Geyer hoped to reconstruct the children's travels from Cincinnati onward. There was no easy way to achieve his goal. He had few tools other than his wits, his notebook, a handful of photographs, and the children's letters. He and Detective Schnooks made a list of all the hotels in Cincinnati located near railroad stations, then set out on foot to visit each one and check its registrations for some sign of the children and Holmes. That Holmes would use an alias seemed beyond doubt, so Geyer brought along his photographs, even a depiction of the children's distinctive "flat-top" trunk. Many months had passed since the children had written their letters, however. Geyer had little hope that anyone would remember one man and three children.

On that point, as it happens, he was wrong.

———

The detectives trudged from one hotel to the next. The day got hotter and hotter. The detectives were courteous and never showed impatience, despite having to make the same introductions and tell the same story over and over again.

On Central Avenue they came to a small inexpensive hotel, the Atlantic House. As they had done at all the other hotels, they asked the clerk if they could see his registration book. They turned first to Friday, September 28, 1894, the day that Holmes, while already in possession of Alice, had picked up Nellie and Howard from their St. Louis home. Geyer guessed Holmes and the children had reached Cincinnati later that same day. Geyer ran his finger down the page and stopped at an entry for "Alex E. Cook," a guest who according to the register was traveling with three children.

The entry jogged Geyer's memory. Holmes had used the name before, to rent a house in Burlington, Vermont. Also, Geyer by now had seen a lot of Holmes's handwriting. The writing in the ledger looked familiar.

The "Cook" party stayed only one night, the register showed. But Geyer knew from the girls' letters that they had remained in Cincinnati an additional night. It seemed odd that Holmes would go to the trouble of moving to a second hotel, but Geyer knew from experience that making assumptions about the behavior of criminals was always a dangerous thing. He and Schnooks thanked the clerk for his kind attention, then set out to canvass more hotels.

The sun was high, the streets steamed. Cicadas scratched off messages from every tree. At Sixth and Vine the detectives came to a hotel called the Bristol and discovered that on Saturday, September 29, 1894, a party identified as "A. E. Cook" had checked in, with three children. When the clerk saw Geyer's photographs, he confirmed that the guests were Holmes, Alice, Nellie, and Howard. They checked out the next morning, Sunday, September 30. The date fit the likely chronology of events: Geyer knew from the children's letters that on that Sunday morning they had left Cincinnati and by evening had arrived in Indianapolis.

Geyer was not yet ready to leave Cincinnati, however. Now he played a hunch. The Pinkertons had found that Holmes sometimes rented houses in the cities through which he traveled, as he had done in Burlington. Geyer and Schnooks turned their attention to Cincinnati's real estate agents.

Their search eventually took them to the realty office of J. C. Thomas, on East Third Street.

Something about Holmes must have caused people to take notice, because both Thomas and his clerk remembered him. Holmes had rented a house at 305 Poplar Street, under the name "A. C. Hayes," and had made a substantial advance payment.

The date of the agreement, Thomas said, was September 28, 1894, the Friday when Holmes and the children had arrived in Cincinnati. Holmes held the house only two days.

Thomas could offer no further details but referred the detectives to a woman named Henrietta Hill, who lived next door to the house.

Geyer and Schnooks immediately set out for Miss Hill's residence and found her to be an acute observer and a willing gossip. "There is really very little to tell," she said—then told them a lot.

⁕⸺⸺⸺,

She first had noticed the new tenant on Saturday, September 29, when a furniture wagon stopped in front of the rental house. A man and a boy descended. What most caught Miss Hill's attention was the fact that the furniture wagon was empty save for an iron stove that seemed much too large for a private residence.

Miss Hill found the stove sufficiently strange that she mentioned it to her neighbors. The next morning Holmes came to her front door and told her he was not going to stay in the house after all. If she wanted the stove, he said, she could have it.

Detective Geyer theorized that Holmes must have sensed an excess of neighborly scrutiny and changed his plans. But what were those plans? At the time, Geyer wrote, "I was not able to appreciate the intense significance of the renting of the Poplar Street house and the delivery of a stove of such immense size." He was certain, however, that he had "taken firm hold of the end of the string" that would lead to the children.

Based on the girls' letters, Geyer's next stop was obvious. He thanked Detective Schnooks for his companionship and caught a train to Indianapolis.

⁕⸺⸺⸺,

It was even hotter in Indianapolis. Leaves hung in the stillness like hands of the newly dead.

Early Sunday morning Geyer went to the police station and picked up a new local partner, Detective David Richards.

One part of the trail was easy to find. In Nellie Pitezel's letter from Indianapolis, she had written "we are at the English H." Detective Richards knew the place: The Hotel English.

In the hotel's register Geyer found an entry on September 30 for "three Canning children." Canning, he knew, was Carrie Pitezel's maiden name.

Nothing was simple, however. According to the register, the Canning children had checked out the next day, Monday, October 1. Yet Geyer knew, again from their letters, that the children had remained in Indianapolis for at least another week. Holmes seemed to be repeating the pattern he had established in Cincinnati.

Geyer began the same methodical canvass he had conducted in Cincinnati. He and Detective Richards checked hotel after hotel but found no further reference to the children.

They did, however, find something else.

At a hotel called the Circle Park they discovered an entry for a "Mrs. Georgia Howard." Howard was one of Holmes's more common aliases, Geyer now knew. He believed this woman could be Holmes's latest wife, Georgiana Yoke. The register showed that "Mrs. Howard" had checked in on Sunday, September 30, 1894, and stayed four nights.

Geyer showed his photographs to the hotel's proprietor, a Mrs. Rodius, who recognized Holmes and Yoke but not the children. Mrs. Rodius explained that she and Yoke had become friends. In one conversation Yoke had told her that her husband was "a very wealthy man, and that he owned real estate and cattle ranches in Texas; also had considerable real estate in Berlin, Germany, where they intended to go as soon as her husband could get his business affairs into shape to leave."

The timing of all these hotel stays was perplexing. As best Geyer could tell, on that one Sunday, September 30, Holmes somehow had managed to maneuver the three children and his own wife into different hotels in the same city, without revealing their existence to one another.

But where had the children gone next?

Geyer and Richards examined the registers of every hotel and boardinghouse in Indianapolis but found no further trace of the children.

The Indianapolis leg of Geyer's search seemed to have reached a dead end, when Richards remembered that a hotel called the Circle House had been open during the fall of 1894 but had since closed. He and Geyer checked with other hotels to find out who had run the Circle House, and learned from its former clerk that the registration records were in the possession of a downtown attorney.

The records had been poorly kept, but among the guests who had arrived on Monday, October 1, Geyer found a familiar entry: "Three Canning children." The register showed the children were from Galva, Illinois—the town where Mrs. Pitezel had grown up. Geyer now felt a pressing need to talk to the hotel's past manager and found him running a saloon in West Indianapolis. His name was Herman Ackelow.

Geyer explained his mission and immediately showed Ackelow his photographs of Holmes and the Pitezel children. Ackelow was silent a moment. Yes, he said, he was sure of it: The man in the photograph had come to his hotel.

It was the children, however, that he remembered most clearly, and now he told the detectives why.

Until this point all Geyer knew about the children's stay in Indianapolis was what he had read in the letters from the tin box. Between October 6 and 8 Alice and Nellie had written at least three letters that Holmes had intercepted. The letters were brief and poorly written, but they offered small bright glimpses into the daily lives of the children and the state of near-captivity in which Holmes held them. "We are all well here," Nellie wrote on Saturday, October 6. "It is a little warmer to-day. There is so many buggies go by that you can't hear yourself think. I first wrote you a letter with a crystal pen. . . . It is all glass so I hafto be careful or else it will break, it was only five cents."

Alice wrote a letter the same day. She had been away from her mother the longest, and for her the trip had become wearisome and sad. It was Saturday, raining hard. She had a cold and was reading *Uncle Tom's Cabin* so much that her eyes had begun to hurt. "And I expect this Sunday will pass away slower than I don't know what. . . . Why don't you write to me. I have not got a letter from you since I have been away and it will be three weeks day after tomorrow."

On Monday Holmes allowed a letter from Mrs. Pitezel to reach the children, which prompted Alice to write an immediate reply, observing, "It seems as though you are awful homesick." In this letter, which

Holmes never mailed, Alice reported that little Howard was being difficult. "One morning Mr. H. told me to tell him to stay in the next morning that he wanted him and he would come and get him and take him
out." But Howard had not obeyed, and when Holmes came for him, the
boy was nowhere to be found. Holmes had gotten angry.

Despite her sorrow and boredom, Alice found a few cheery moments
worth celebrating. "Yesterday we had mashed potatoes, grapes, chicken
glass of milk each ice cream each a big sauce dish full awful good too
lemon pie cake don't you think that is pretty good."

The fact that the children were so well fed might have comforted Mrs.
Pitezel, had she ever received the letter. Not so, however, the story the
former hotel manager now told Geyer.

Each day Ackelow would send his eldest son up to the children's room
to call them for their meals. Often the boy reported back that the children were crying, "evidently heartbroken and homesick to see their
mother, or hear from her," Geyer wrote. A German chambermaid named
Caroline Klausmann had tended the children's room and observed the
same wrenching scenes. She had moved to Chicago, Ackelow said. Geyer
wrote her name in his notebook.

"Holmes said that Howard was a very bad boy," Ackelow recalled,
"and that he was trying to place him in some institution, or bind him out
to some farmer, as he wanted to get rid of the responsibility of looking
after him."

Geyer still nurtured a small hope that the children really were alive, as
Holmes insisted. Despite his twenty years on the police force, Geyer found
it difficult to believe that anyone could kill three children for absolutely
no reason. Why had Holmes gone to the trouble and expense of moving
the children from city to city, hotel to hotel, if only to kill them? Why had
he bought each of them a crystal pen and taken them to the zoo in Cincinnati and made sure they received lemon pie and ice cream?

⁕

Geyer set out for Chicago but felt deep reluctance about leaving
Indianapolis—"something seemed to tell me that Howard had never left

there alive." In Chicago he found, to his surprise, that the city's police department knew nothing about Holmes. He tracked down Caroline Klausmann, who was now working at the Swiss Hotel on Clark Street. When he showed her his photographs of the children, tears welled in her eyes.

Geyer caught a train to Detroit, the city where Alice had written the last of the letters in the tin box.

°———9

Geyer was getting a feel for his quarry. There was nothing rational about Holmes, but his behavior seemed to follow a pattern. Geyer knew what to look for in Detroit and, with the assistance of another police detective, once again began a patient canvass of hotels and boarding-houses. Though he told his story and showed his photographs a hundred times, he never tired and was always patient and polite. These were his strengths. His weakness was his belief that evil had boundaries.

Once again he picked up the children's trail and the parallel registrations of Holmes and Yoke, but now he discovered something even stranger—that during this same period Carrie Pitezel and her two other children, Dessie and baby Wharton, had also checked into a Detroit hotel, this one called Geis's Hotel. Geyer realized to his astonishment that Holmes now was moving *three* different parties of travelers from place to place, shoving them across the landscape as if they were toys.

And he discovered something else.

In walking from lodging to lodging, he saw that Holmes had not only kept Carrie away from Alice, Nellie, and Howard: He had placed them in establishments only three blocks apart. Suddenly the true implication of what Holmes had done became clear to him.

He reread Alice's final letter. She had written it to her grandparents on Sunday, October 14, the same day her mother, along with Dessie and the baby, had checked into Geis's Hotel. This was the saddest letter of them all. Alice and Nellie both had colds, and the weather had turned wintry. "Tell Mama that I have to have a coat," Alice wrote. "I nearly freeze in that thin jacket." The children's lack of warm clothing forced them to stay in their room day after day. "All that Nell and I can do is to draw and I get so tired sitting that I could get up and fly almost. I wish I could see you all. I am getting so homesick that I don't know what to do. I suppose Wharton walks by this time don't he I would like to have him here he would pass away the time a goodeal."

Geyer was appalled. "So when this poor child Alice was writing to her grandparents in Galva, Illinois, complaining of the cold, sending a message to her mother, asking for heavier and more comfortable clothing, wishing for little Wharton, the baby who would help them pass away the time—while this wearied, lonely, homesick child was writing this letter, her mother and her sister and the much wished for Wharton, were within ten minutes walk of her, and continued there for the next five days."

It was a game for Holmes, Geyer realized. He possessed them all and reveled in his possession.

One additional phrase of Alice's letter kept running through Geyer's brain.

"Howard," she had written, "is not with us now."

Moyamensing Prison

Holmes sat in his cell at Moyamensing Prison, a large turreted and crenellated building at Tenth and Reed streets, in south Philadelphia. He did not seem terribly troubled by his incarceration, although he complained of its injustice. "The great humiliation of feeling that I am a prisoner is killing me far more than any other discomforts I have to endure," he wrote—though in fact he felt no humiliation whatsoever. If he felt anything, it was a smug satisfaction that so far no one had been able to produce any concrete evidence that he had killed Ben Pitezel or the missing children.

He occupied a cell that measured nine by fourteen feet, with a narrow barred window high in its outer wall and a single electric lamp, which guards extinguished at nine o'clock each night. The walls were whitewashed. The stone construction of the prison helped blunt the extreme heat that had settled on the city and much of the country, but nothing could keep out the humidity for which Philadelphia was notorious. It clung to Holmes and his fellow prisoners like a cloak of moist wool, yet this too he seemed not to mind. Holmes became a model prisoner— became in fact the *model* of a model prisoner. He made a game of using his charm to gain concessions from his keepers. He was allowed to wear his own clothes "and to keep my watch and other small belongings." He discovered also that he could pay to have food, newspapers, and magazines brought in from outside. He read of his increasing national notoriety. He read too that Frank Geyer, a Philadelphia police detective who had interviewed him in June, was now in the Midwest searching for Pitezel's children. The search delighted Holmes. It satisfied his profound need for attention and gave him a sense of power over the detective. He knew that Geyer's search would be in vain.

Holmes's cell was furnished with a bed, a stool, and a writing table, upon which he composed his memoir. He had begun it, he said, the preceding winter—to be exact, on December 3, 1894.

He opened the memoir as if it were a fable: "Come with me, if you will, to a tiny quiet New England village, nestling among the picturesquely rugged hills of New Hampshire. . . . Here, in the year 1861, I, Herman W. Mudgett, the author of these pages, was born. That the first years of my life were different from those of any other ordinary country-bred boy, I have no reason to think." The dates and places were correct; his description of his boyhood as a typical country idyll was most certainly a fabrication. It is one of the defining characteristics of psychopaths that as children they lied at will, exhibited unusual cruelty to animals and other children, and often engaged in acts of vandalism, with arson an especially favored act.

Holmes inserted into his memoir a "prison diary" that he claimed to have kept since the day he arrived at Moyamensing. It is more likely that he invented the diary expressly for the memoir, intending it as a vehicle for reinforcing his claims of innocence by fostering the impression that he was a man of warmth and piety. He claimed in the diary to have established a daily schedule aimed at personal betterment. He would wake at six-thirty each day and take his "usual sponge bath," then clean his cell. He would breakfast at seven. "I shall eat no more meat of any kind while I am so closely confined." He planned to exercise and read the morning newspapers until ten o'clock. "From 10 to 12 and 2 to 4 six days in the week, I shall confine myself to my old medical works and other college studies including stenography, French and German." The rest of the day he would devote to reading various periodicals and library books.

At one point in his diary he notes that he was reading *Trilby*, the 1894 best seller by George Du Maurier about a young singer, Trilby O'Farrell, and her possession by the mesmerist Svengali. Holmes wrote that he "was much pleased with parts of it."

Elsewhere in the diary Holmes went for the heart.

One entry, for May 16, 1895: "My birthday. Am 34 years old. I wonder if, as in former years, mother will write me. . . ."

In another entry he described a visit from his latest wife, Georgiana Yoke. "She has suffered, and though she tried heroically to keep me from seeing it, it was of no avail: and in a few minutes to again bid her good-bye and know she was going out into the world with so heavy a load to bear, caused me more suffering than any death struggles can ever do. Each day until I know she is safe from harm and annoyance will be a living death to me."

From his cell Holmes also wrote a long letter to Carrie Pitezel, which he composed in a manner that shows he was aware the police were reading his mail. He insisted that Alice, Nellie, and Howard were with "Miss W." in London, and that if the police would only check his story in detail, the mystery of the children would be solved. "I was as careful of the children as if they were my own, and you know me well enough to judge me better than strangers here can do. Ben would not have done anything against me, or I against him, any quicker than brothers. We *never* quarrelled. Again, he was worth too much to me for me to have killed him, if I had no other reason not to. As to the children, I never will believe, until you tell me so yourself, that you think they are dead or that I did anything to put them out of the way. Knowing me as you do, can you imagine me killing little and innocent children, especially without any motive?"

He explained the lack of mail from the children. "They have no doubt written letters which Miss W., for her own safety, has withheld."

Holmes read the daily papers closely. Clearly the detective's search had borne little fruit. Holmes had no doubt that Geyer soon would be forced to end his hunt and return to Philadelphia.

The prospect of this was pleasing in the extreme.

The Tenant

ON SUNDAY, JULY 7, 1895, Detective Geyer took his search to Toronto, where the city's police department assigned Detective Alf Cuddy to assist him. Together Geyer and Cuddy scoured the hotels and boardinghouses of Toronto and after days of searching found that here, too, Holmes had been moving three parties of travelers simultaneously.

Holmes and Yoke had stayed at the Walker House: "G. Howe and wife, Columbus."

Mrs. Pitezel at the Union House: "Mrs. C. A. Adams and daughter, Columbus."

The girls at the Albion: "Alice and Nellie Canning, Detroit."

No one remembered seeing Howard.

Now Geyer and Cuddy began searching the records of real estate agencies and contacting the owners of rental homes, but Toronto was far larger than any other city Geyer had searched. The task seemed impossible. On Monday morning, July 15, he awoke facing the prospect of yet another day of mind-numbing routine, but when he arrived at headquarters, he found Detective Cuddy in an unusually good mood. A tip had come in that Cuddy found promising. A resident named Thomas Ryves had read a description of Holmes in one of the city's newspapers and thought it sounded like a man who in October 1894 had rented the house next door to his, at 16 St. Vincent Street.

Geyer was leery. The intensive press coverage of his mission and his arrival in Toronto had generated thousands of tips, all useless.

Cuddy agreed that the latest tip was probably another wild goose chase, but at least it offered a change of pace.

By now Geyer was a national fascination, America's Sherlock Holmes. Reports of his travels appeared in newspapers throughout the country. In that day the possibility that a man had killed three young children was still considered a horror well beyond the norm. There was something about Detective Geyer's lone search through the sweltering heat of that summer that captured everyone's imagination. He had become the living representation of how men liked to think of themselves: one man doing an awful duty and doing it well, against the odds. Millions of people woke each morning hoping to read in their newspapers that this staunch detective at last had found the missing children.

Geyer paid little attention to his new celebrity. Nearly a month had passed since the start of his search, but what had he accomplished? Each new phase seemed only to raise new questions: Why had Holmes taken the children? Why had he engineered that contorted journey from city to city? What power did Holmes possess that gave him such control?

There was something about Holmes that Geyer just did not understand. Every crime had a motive. But the force that propelled Holmes seemed to exist outside the world of Geyer's experience.

He kept coming back to the same conclusion: Holmes was enjoying himself. He had arranged the insurance fraud for the money, but the rest of it was for fun. Holmes was testing his power to bend the lives of people.

What irked Geyer most was that the central question was still unanswered: Where were the children now?

The detectives found Thomas Ryves to be a charming Scotsman of considerable age, who welcomed them with enthusiasm. Ryves explained why the renter next door had caught his attention. For one thing, he had arrived with little furniture—a mattress, an old bed, and an unusually large trunk. One afternoon the tenant came to Ryves's house to borrow a shovel, explaining that he wanted to dig a hole in the cellar for the storage of potatoes. He returned the shovel the next morning and the following day removed the trunk from the house. Ryves never saw him again.

Detective Geyer, now galvanized, told Ryves to meet him in front of the neighboring house in exactly one hour; then he and Cuddy sped to the home of the realtor who had arranged the rental. With little preamble Geyer showed her a photograph of Holmes. She recognized him instantly. He had been very handsome, with amazing blue eyes.

"This seemed too good to be true," Geyer wrote. He and Cuddy offered quick thanks and rushed back to St. Vincent Street. Ryves was waiting outside.

Now Geyer asked to borrow a shovel, and Ryves returned with the same one he had lent the tenant.

The house was charming, with a steeply pitched central gable and scalloped trim like the gingerbread house in a fairy tale, except this house sat not alone in a deep wood, but in the heart of Toronto on a fine street closely lined with elegant homes and yards fenced with fleur-de-lis pickets. Clematis in full bloom climbed one post of the veranda.

The current tenant, a Mrs. J. Armbrust, answered the door. Ryves introduced the detectives. Mrs. Armbrust led them inside. They entered a central hall that divided the house into halves of three rooms each. A stairwell led to the second floor. Geyer asked to see the cellar.

Mrs. Armbrust led the detectives into the kitchen, where she lifted a sheet of oilcloth from the floor. A square trap door lay underneath. As the detectives opened it, the scent of moist earth drifted upward into the kitchen. The cellar was shallow but very dark. Mrs. Armbrust brought lamps.

Geyer and Cuddy descended a steep set of steps, more ladder than stairway, into a small chamber about ten feet long by ten feet wide and only four feet high. The lamps shed a shifting orange light that exaggerated the detectives' shadows. Hunched over, wary of the overhead beams,

Geyer and Cuddy tested the ground with the spade. In the southwest corner Geyer found a soft spot. The spade entered with disconcerting ease.

"Only a slight hole had been made," Geyer said, "when the gases burst forth and the stench was frightful."

At three feet they uncovered human bone.

———

They summoned an undertaker named B. D. Humphrey to help recover the remains. Geyer and Cuddy gingerly climbed back down into the cellar. Humphrey leaped down.

The stench now suffused the entire house. Mrs. Armbrust looked stricken.

Then the coffins arrived.

The undertaker's men put them in the kitchen.

———

The children had been buried nude. Alice lay on her side, her head at the west end of the grave. Nellie lay face-down, partially covering Alice. Her rich black hair, nicely plaited, lay along her back as neatly as if she had just combed it. The men spread a sheet on the cellar floor.

They began with Nellie.

"We lifted her as gently as possible," Geyer said, "but owing to the decomposed state of the body, the weight of her plaited hair hanging down her back pulled the scalp from her head."

They discovered something else: Nellie's feet had been amputated. During the search of the residence that followed, police found no trace of them. At first this seemed a mystery, until Geyer recalled that Nellie was clubfooted. Holmes had disposed of her feet to remove this distinctive clue to her identity.

———

Mrs. Pitezel learned of the discovery of her girls by reading a morning newspaper. She had been visiting friends back in Chicago and thus Geyer had been unable to telegraph the news to her directly. She caught a train to Toronto. Geyer met her at the station and took her to his hotel, the Rossin House. She was exhausted and sad and seemed perpetually near fainting. Geyer roused her with smelling salts.

Geyer and Cuddy came for her the next afternoon to bring her to the morgue. They carried brandy and smelling salts. Geyer wrote, "I told her that it would be absolutely impossible for her to see anything but Alice's teeth and hair, and only the hair belonging to Nellie. This had a paralyzing effect upon her and she almost fainted."

The coroner's men did what they could to make the viewing as endurable as possible. They cleaned the flesh from Alice's skull and carefully polished her teeth, then covered her body with canvas. They laid paper over her face, and cut a hole in the paper to expose only her teeth, just as the Philadelphia coroner had done for her father.

They washed Nellie's hair and laid it carefully on the canvas that covered Alice's body.

Cuddy and Geyer took positions on opposite sides of Mrs. Pitezel and led her into the dead house. She recognized Alice's teeth immediately. She turned to Geyer and asked, "Where is Nellie?" Only then did she notice Nellie's long black hair.

<hr>

The coroner, unable to find any marks of violence, theorized that Holmes had locked the girls in the big trunk, then filled it with gas from a lamp valve. Indeed, when police found the trunk they discovered a hole drilled through one side, covered with a makeshift patch.

"Nothing could be more surprising," Geyer wrote, "than the apparent ease with which Holmes murdered the two little girls in the very center of the city of Toronto, without arousing the least suspicion of a single person there." If not for Graham's decision to send him on his search, he believed, "these murders would never have been discovered, and Mrs. Pitezel would have gone to her grave without knowing whether her children were alive or dead."

For Geyer, finding the girls was "one of the most satisfactory events of my life," but his satisfaction was tempered by the fact that Howard remained missing. Mrs. Pitezel refused to believe Howard was dead; she "clung fondly to the hope that he would ultimately be found alive."

Even Geyer found himself hoping that in this one case Holmes had not lied and had done exactly what he had told the clerk in Indianapolis. "Had [Howard] been placed in some institution, as Holmes had intimated his intention of doing, or was he hidden in some obscure place beyond reach or discovery? Was he alive or dead? I was puzzled, nonplussed, and groping in the dark."

A Lively Corpse

In Philadelphia, on the morning of Tuesday, July 16, 1895—the day Geyer's Toronto discoveries were reported in the nation's newspapers—the district attorney's office telephoned an urgent message to the warden at Moyamensing Prison, instructing him to keep all the morning's newspapers away from Holmes. The order came from Assistant District Attorney Thomas W. Barlow. He wanted to surprise Holmes with the news, hoping it would rattle him so thoroughly that he would confess.

Barlow's order came too late. The guard sent to intercept the morning papers found Holmes sitting at his table reading the news as calmly as if reading about the weather.

In his memoir Holmes contended that the news did shock him. His newspaper came that morning at eight-thirty as it always did, he wrote, "and I had hardly opened it before I saw in large headlines the announcement of the finding of the children in Toronto. For the moment it seemed so impossible, that I was inclined to think it one of the frequent newspaper excitements that had attended the earlier part of the case. . . ." But suddenly, he wrote, he realized what must have happened. Minnie Williams had killed them or had ordered them killed. Holmes knew she had an unsavory associate named "Hatch." He guessed that Williams had suggested the killings and Hatch had carried them out. It was all too horrible to comprehend: "I gave up trying to read the article, and saw instead the two little faces as they had looked when I hurriedly left them—felt the innocent child's kiss so timidly given and heard again their earnest words of farewell, and I realized that I had received another burden to carry to my grave. . . . I think at this time I should have lost my senses utterly had I not been hurriedly called to prepare to be taken to the District Attorney's office."

The morning was hot. Holmes was driven north on Broad Street to City Hall through air as sticky as taffy. In the DA's office he was questioned by Barlow. The *Philadelphia Public Ledger* reported that Holmes's "genius for explanation had deserted him. For two hours he sat under a shower of questions and refused to talk. He was not cowed by any means, but he would give absolutely no satisfaction."

Holmes wrote, "I was in no condition to bear his accusations, nor disposed to answer many of his questions." He told Barlow that Miss Williams and Hatch apparently had killed Howard as well.

Holmes was driven back to Moyamensing. He began earnestly trying to find a publisher for his memoir, hoping to get it quickly into print to help turn public opinion to his favor. If he could not exert his great powers of persuasion directly, he could at least attempt to do so indirectly. He struck a deal with a journalist named John King to arrange publication and market the book.

He wrote to King, "My ideas are that you should get from the New York *Herald* and the Philadelphia *Press* all the cuts they have and turn those we want over to the printer, to have them electroplated at his expense." In particular he wanted a *Herald* picture of himself in a full beard. He also wanted to have "the autographs of my two names (Holmes and Mudgett) engraved and electroplated at the same time to go under the picture." He wanted this done quickly so that as soon as the manuscript was set in type, all components of the book would be in hand, ready for the presses.

He offered King some marketing advice: "As soon as the book is published, get it onto the Philadelphia and New York newsstands. Then get reliable canvassers who will work *afternoons* here in Philadelphia. Take one good street at a time, leave the book, then return about a half hour later for the money. No use to do this in the forenoon when people are busy. I canvassed when a student in this way and found the method successful.

"Then, if you have any liking for the road, go over the ground covered by the book, spending a few days in Chicago, Detroit, and Indianapolis. Give copies to the newspapers in these cities to comment upon, it will assist the sale. . . ."

Aware that this letter, too, would be read by the authorities, Holmes used it to reinforce, obliquely, his claims of innocence. He urged King that when his sales effort took him to Chicago, he should to go a particular hotel and look for evidence in the register, and collect affidavits from clerks, proving that Minnie Williams had stayed there with Holmes long after she was supposed to have been murdered.

"If she was a corpse then," Holmes wrote to King, "she was a very lively corpse indeed."

"All the Weary Days"

IT WAS A STRANGE MOMENT for Geyer. He had examined every lead, checked every hotel, visited every boardinghouse and real estate agent, and yet now he had to begin his search anew. Where? What path was left? The weather remained stifling, as if taunting him.

His instincts kept telling him that Holmes had killed Howard in Indianapolis. He returned there on July 24 and again received the assistance of Detective David Richards, but now Geyer also called in the press. The next day every newspaper in the city reported his arrival. Dozens of people visited him at his hotel to make suggestions about where he ought to look for Howard. "The number of mysterious persons who had rented houses in and about Indianapolis multiplied from day to day," Geyer wrote. He and Richards trudged through the heat from office to office, house to house, and found nothing. "Days came and passed, but I continued to be as much in the dark as ever, and it began to look as though the bold but clever criminal had outwitted the detectives . . . and that the disappearance of Howard Pitezel would pass into history as an unsolved mystery."

Meanwhile the mystery of Holmes himself grew deeper and darker.

Geyer's discovery of the girls prompted Chicago police to enter Holmes's building in Englewood. Each day they delved more deeply into the secrets of the "castle," and each day turned up additional evidence that Holmes was something far worse than even Geyer's macabre discoveries indicated. There was speculation that during the world's fair he might have killed dozens of people, most of them young women. One estimate, certainly an exaggeration, put the toll at two hundred. To most people, it seemed impossible that Holmes could have done so much killing without detection. Geyer would have agreed, except that his own search had revealed again and again Holmes's talent for deflecting scrutiny.

Chicago detectives began their exploration of the castle on the night of Friday, July 19. First they made a broad survey of the building. The third floor contained small hotel rooms. The second floor had thirty-five rooms that were harder to classify. Some were ordinary bedrooms; others had no windows and were fitted with doors that made the rooms airtight. One room contained a walk-in vault, with iron walls. Police found a gas jet with no apparent function other than to admit gas into the vault. Its cut-off valve was located in Holmes's personal apartment. In Holmes's office they found a bank book belonging to a woman named Lucy Burbank. It listed a balance of $23,000. The woman could not be located.

The eeriest phase of the investigation began when the police, holding their flickering lanterns high, entered the hotel basement, a cavern of brick and timber measuring 50 by 165 feet. The discoveries came quickly: a vat of acid with eight ribs and part of a skull settled at the bottom; mounds of quicklime; a large kiln; a dissection table stained with what seemed to be blood. They found surgical tools and charred high-heeled shoes.

And more bones:

Eighteen ribs from the torso of a child.

Several vertebrae.

A bone from a foot.

One shoulder blade.

One hip socket.

Articles of clothing emerged from walls and from pits of ash and quicklime, including a girl's dress and bloodstained overalls. Human hair clotted a stovepipe. The searchers unearthed two buried vaults full of quicklime and human remains. They theorized the remains might be the last traces of two Texas women, Minnie and Anna Williams, whom Chicago police had only recently learned were missing. In the ash of a large stove they found a length of chain that the jeweler in Holmes's pharmacy recognized as part of a watch chain Holmes had given Minnie as a gift. They also found a letter Holmes had written to the pharmacist in his drugstore. "Do you ever see anything of the ghost of the Williams sisters," Holmes wrote, "and do they trouble you much now?"

The next day the police discovered another hidden chamber, this one at the cellar's southwest corner. They were led to it by a man named Charles Chappell, alleged to have helped Holmes reduce corpses to bone. He was very cooperative, and soon the police recovered three fully articulated skeletons from their owners. A fourth was expected from Chicago's Hahneman Medical College.

One of the most striking discoveries came on the second floor, in the walk-in vault. The inside of the door showed the unmistakable imprint of a woman's bare foot. Police theorized the print had been made by a woman suffocating within. Her name, they believed, was Emeline Cigrand.

———

Chicago police telegraphed District Attorney Graham that their search of the Holmes building had uncovered the skeleton of a child. Graham ordered Geyer to Chicago to see if the remains might be those of Howard Pitezel.

Geyer found the city transfixed by the revelations emerging from the castle. Press coverage had been exhaustive, taking up most of the front page of the daily newspapers. One *Tribune* headline had cried VICTIMS OF A FIEND, and reported that the remains of Howard Pitezel had been found in the building. The story took up six of the seven columns of the front page.

Geyer met with the lead police inspector and learned that a physician who had just examined the child's skeleton had ruled it to be that of a little girl. The inspector thought he knew the girl's identity and mentioned a name, Pearl Conner. The name meant nothing to Geyer.

Geyer telegraphed his disappointment to Graham, who ordered him back to Philadelphia for consultation and rest.

⌐━━━⌐

On Wednesday evening, August 7, with temperatures in the nineties and traincars like ovens, Geyer set out again, this time accompanied by Fidelity Mutual's top insurance investigator, Inspector W. E. Gary. Geyer was glad for the company.

They went to Chicago, then to Indiana, where they stopped in Logansport and Peru, then to Montpelier Junction, Ohio, and Adrian, Michigan. They spent days searching the records of every hotel, boardinghouse, and real estate office they could find, "all," Geyer said, "to no purpose."

Although Geyer's brief rest in Philadelphia had recharged his hopes, he now found them "fast dwindling away." He still believed his original instinct was correct, that Howard was in Indianapolis or somewhere nearby. He went there next, his third visit of the summer.

"I must confess I returned to Indianapolis in no cheerful frame of mind," Geyer wrote. He and Inspector Gary checked into Geyer's old hotel, the Spencer House. The failure to find Howard after so much effort was frustrating and puzzling. "The mystery," Geyer wrote, "seemed to be impenetrable."

⌐━━━⌐

On Thursday, August 19, Geyer learned that during the preceding night Holmes's castle in Englewood, his own dark dreamland, had burned to the ground. Front-page headlines in the *Chicago Tribune* shouted, "Holmes' Den Burned; Fire Demolishes the Place of Murder and Mystery." The fire department suspected arson; police theorized that whoever set the fire had wanted to destroy the secrets still embedded within. They arrested no one.

⌐━━━⌐

Together Detective Geyer and Inspector Gary investigated nine hundred leads. They expanded their search to include small towns outside Indianapolis. "By Monday," Geyer wrote in a report to headquarters, "we will have searched every outlying town, except Irvington, and another day will conclude that. After Irvington, I scarcely know where we shall go."

They went to Irvington on Tuesday morning, August 27, 1895, aboard an electric trolley, a new kind of streetcar that drew its power through a wheeled conducting apparatus on the roof called a troller. Just before the trolley reached its final stop, Geyer spotted a sign for a real estate office. He and Gary resolved to begin their search there.

The proprietor was a Mr. Brown. He offered the detectives each a chair, but they remained standing. They did not think the visit would last long, and there were many other offices to touch before nightfall. Geyer opened his now-soiled parcel of photographs.

Brown adjusted his glasses and examined the picture of Holmes. After a long pause he said, "I did not have the renting of the house, but I had the keys, and one day last fall, this man came into my office and in a very abrupt way said I want the keys for that house." Geyer and Gary stood very still. Brown continued: "I remember the man very well, because I did not like his manner, and I felt that he should have had more respect for my gray hairs."

The detectives looked at each other. Both sat down at the same time. "All the toil," Geyer said, "all the weary days and weeks of travel—toil and travel in the hottest months of the year, alternating between faith and hope, and discouragement and despair, all were recompensed in that one moment, when I saw the veil about to lift."

———

At the inquest that followed a young man named Elvet Moorman testified he had helped Holmes set up a large woodstove in the house. He recalled asking Holmes why he didn't install a gas stove instead. Holmes answered "that he did not think gas was healthy for children."

The owner of an Indianapolis repair shop testified that Holmes had come into his shop on October 3, 1894, with two cases of surgical instruments and asked to have them sharpened. Holmes picked them up three days later.

Detective Geyer testified how during his search of the house he had opened the base of a chimney flue that extended from roof to cellar. While sifting the accumulated ash through a fly screen, he found human teeth and a fragment of jaw. He also retrieved "a large charred mass, which upon being cut, disclosed a portion of the stomach, liver and spleen, baked quite hard." The organs had been packed too tightly into the chimney and thus never had burned.

And of course Mrs. Pitezel was summoned. She identified Howard's overcoat and his scarf pin, and a crochet needle that belonged to Alice.

Finally the coroner showed her a toy that Geyer himself had found in the house. It consisted of a tin man mounted on a spinning top. She recognized it. How could she not? It was Howard's most important possession. Mrs. Pitezel herself had put it in the children's trunk just before she sent them off with Holmes. His father had bought it for him at the Chicago world's fair.

Malice Aforethought

On September 12, 1895, a Philadelphia grand jury voted to indict Holmes for the murder of Benjamin Pitezel. Only two witnesses presented evidence, L. G. Fouse, president of Fidelity Mutual Life, and Detective Frank Geyer. Holmes stuck to his claim that Minnie Williams and the mysterious Hatch had killed the children. Grand juries in Indianapolis and Toronto found this unconvincing. Indianapolis indicted Holmes for the murder of Howard Pitezel, Toronto for the murders of Alice and Nellie. If Philadelphia failed to convict him, there would be two more chances; if the city succeeded, the other indictments would be moot, for given the nature of the Pitezel murder, a conviction in Philadelphia would bring a death sentence.

Holmes's memoir reached newsstands. In its final pages he stated, "In conclusion, I wish to say that I am but a very ordinary man, even below average in physical strength and mental ability, and to have planned and executed the stupendous amount of wrong-doing that has been attributed to me would have been wholly beyond my power. . . ."

He asked the public to suspend judgment while he worked to disprove the charges against him, "a task which I feel able to satisfactorily and expeditiously accomplish. And here I cannot say finis—it is not the end—for besides doing this there is also the work of bringing to justice those for whose wrong-doings I am to-day suffering, and this not to prolong or save my own life, for since the day I heard of the Toronto horror I have not cared to live; but that to those who have looked up to and honored me in the past it shall not in the future be said that I suffered the ignominious death of a murderer."

The thing editors could not understand was how Holmes had been able to escape serious investigation by the Chicago police. The *Chicago Inter Ocean* said, "It is humiliating to think that had it not been for the exertions of the insurance companies which Holmes swindled, or attempted to swindle, he might yet be at large, preying upon society, so well did he cover up the traces of his crime." Chicago's "feeling of humiliation" was not surprising, the *New York Times* said; anyone familiar with the saga "must be amazed at the failure of the municipal police department and the local prosecuting officers not only to prevent those awful crimes, but even to procure any knowledge of them."

One of the most surprising and perhaps dismaying revelations was that Chicago's chief of police, in his prior legal career, had represented Holmes in a dozen routine commercial lawsuits.

The *Chicago Times-Herald* took the broad view and said of Holmes: "He is a prodigy of wickedness, a human demon, a being so unthinkable that no novelist would dare to invent such a character. The story, too, tends to illustrate the end of the century."

EPILOGUE

The Last Crossing

Statue of the Republic, after the Peristyle fire, 1894.

The Fair

THE FAIR HAD A POWERFUL and lasting impact on the nation's psyche, in ways both large and small. Walt Disney's father, Elias, helped build the White City; Walt's Magic Kingdom may well be a descendant. Certainly the fair made a powerful impression on the Disney family. It proved such a financial boon that when the family's third son was born that year, Elias in gratitude wanted to name him Columbus. His wife, Flora, intervened; the baby became Roy. Walt came next, on December 5, 1901. The writer L. Frank Baum and his artist-partner William Wallace Denslow visited the fair; its grandeur informed their creation of Oz. The Japanese temple on the Wooded Island charmed Frank Lloyd Wright, and may have influenced the evolution of his "Prairie" residential designs. The fair prompted President Harrison to designate October 12 a national holiday, Columbus Day, which today serves to anchor a few thousand parades and a three-day weekend. Every carnival since 1893 has included a Midway and a Ferris Wheel, and every grocery store contains products born at the exposition. Shredded Wheat did survive. Every house has scores of incandescent bulbs powered by alternating current, both of which first proved themselves worthy of large-scale use at the fair; and nearly every town of any size has its little bit of ancient Rome, some beloved and becolumned bank, library or post office. Covered with graffiti, perhaps, or even an ill-conceived coat of paint, but underneath it all the glow of the White City persists. Even the Lincoln Memorial in Washington can trace its heritage to the fair.

The fair's greatest impact lay in how it changed the way Americans perceived their cities and their architects. It primed the whole of America—not just a few rich architectural patrons—to think of cities in a way they never had before. Elihu Root said the fair led "our people out of the wilderness of the commonplace to new ideas of architectural beauty and nobility." Henry Demarest Lloyd saw it as revealing to the great mass of Americans "possibilities of social beauty, utility, and harmony of which they had not been able even to dream. No such vision could otherwise have entered into the prosaic drudgery of their lives, and it will be felt in their development into the third and fourth generation." The fair taught men and women steeped only in the necessary to see that cities did not have to be dark, soiled, and unsafe bastions of the strictly pragmatic. They could also be beautiful.

William Stead recognized the power of the fair immediately. The vision of the White City and its profound contrast to the Black City drove him to write *If Christ Came to Chicago,* a book often credited with launching the City Beautiful movement, which sought to elevate American cities to the level of the great cities of Europe. Like Stead, civic authorities throughout the world saw the fair as a model of what to strive for. They asked Burnham to apply the same citywide thinking that had gone into the White City to their own cities. He became a pioneer in modern urban planning. He created citywide plans for Cleveland, San Francisco, and Manila and led the turn-of-the-century effort to resuscitate and expand L'Enfant's vision of Washington, D.C. In each case he worked without a fee.

While helping design the new Washington plan, Burnham persuaded the head of the Pennsylvania Railroad, Alexander Cassatt, to remove his freight tracks and depot from the center of the federal mall, thus creating the unobstructed green that extends today from the Capitol to the Lincoln Memorial. Other cities came to Daniel Burnham for citywide plans, among them Fort Worth, Atlantic City, and St. Louis, but he turned them down to concentrate on his last plan, for the city of Chicago. Over the years many aspects of his Chicago plan were adopted, among them the creation of the city's lovely ribbon of lakefront parks and Michigan Avenue's "Miracle Mile." One portion of the lakefront, named Burnham Park in his honor, contains Soldier Field and the Field Museum, which he designed. The park runs south in a narrow green border along the lakeshore all the way to Jackson Park, where the fair's Palace of Fine Arts, transformed into a permanent structure, now houses the Museum of Science and Industry. It looks out over the lagoons and the Wooded Island, now a wild and tangled place that perhaps would make Olmsted smile—though no doubt he would find features to criticize.

Early in the twentieth century the fair became a source of heated debate among architects. Critics claimed the fair extinguished the Chicago School of architecture, an indigenous vernacular, and replaced it with a renewed devotion to obsolete classical styles. Parroted from thesis to thesis, this view first gained prominence through a curiously personal dynamic that made it difficult and—as is often the case in the cramped and stuffy rooms of academic debate—even dangerous to resist.

It was Louis Sullivan who first and most loudly condemned the fair's influence on architecture, but only late in his life and long after Burnham's death.

Things had not gone well for Sullivan after the fair. During the first year of the postfair depression the firm of Adler & Sullivan received only two commissions; in 1895, none. In July 1895 Adler quit the firm. Sullivan was thirty-eight and incapable of cultivating the relationships that might have generated enough new commissions to keep him solvent. He was a loner and intellectually intolerant. When a fellow architect asked Sullivan for suggestions on how to improve one of his designs, Sullivan replied, "If I told you, you wouldn't know what I was talking about."

As his practice faltered, Sullivan found himself forced to leave his office in the Auditorium and to sell his personal belongings. He drank heavily and took mood-altering drugs called bromides. Between 1895 and 1922 Sullivan built only twenty-five new structures, roughly one a year. From time to time he came to Burnham for money, although whether he sought outright loans or sold Burnham artwork from his personal collection is unclear. An entry in Burnham's diary for 1911 states, "Louis Sullivan called to get more money of DHB." That same year Sullivan inscribed a set of drawings, "To Daniel H. Burnham, with the best wishes of his friend Louis H. Sullivan."

But Sullivan laced his 1924 autobiography with hyperbolic attacks on

Burnham and the fair's impact on the masses who came through its gates. The classical architecture of the White City made such a profound impression, Sullivan claimed, that it doomed America to another half-century of imitation. The fair was a "contagion," a "virus," a form of "progressive cerebral meningitis." In his view it had fatal consequences. "Thus Architecture died in the land of the free and the home of the brave—in a land declaring its fervid democracy, its inventiveness, its resourcefulness, its unique daring, enterprise and progress."

Sullivan's low opinion of Burnham and the fair was counterbalanced only by his own exalted view of himself and what he saw as his role in attempting to bring to architecture something fresh and distinctly American. Frank Lloyd Wright took up Sullivan's banner. Sullivan had fired him in 1893, but later Wright and Sullivan became friends. As Wright's academic star rose, so too did Sullivan's. Burnham's fell from the sky. It became de rigueur among architecture critics and historians to argue that Burnham in his insecurity and slavish devotion to the classical yearnings of the eastern architects had indeed killed American architecture.

But that view was too simplistic, as some architecture historians and critics have more recently acknowledged. The fair awakened America to beauty and as such was a necessary passage that laid the foundation for men like Frank Lloyd Wright and Ludwig Mies van der Rohe.

For Burnham personally the fair had been an unqualified triumph. It allowed him to fulfill his pledge to his parents to become the greatest architect in America, for certainly in his day he had become so. During the fair an event occurred whose significance to Burnham was missed by all but his closest friends: Both Harvard and Yale granted him honorary master's degrees in recognition of his achievement in building the fair. The ceremonies occurred on the same day. He attended Harvard's. For him the awards were a form of redemption. His past failure to gain admission to both universities—the denial of his "right beginning"—had haunted him throughout his life. Even years after receiving the awards, as he lobbied Harvard to grant provisional admission to his son Daniel, whose own performance on the entry exams was far from stellar, Burnham wrote, "He needs to know that he is a winner, and, as soon as he does, he will show his real quality, as I have been able to do. It is the keenest regret of my life that someone did not follow me up at Cambridge . . . and let the authorities know what I could do."

Burnham had shown them himself, in Chicago, through the hardest sort of work. He bristled at the persistent belief that John Root deserved most of the credit for the beauty of the fair. "What was done up to the time of his death was the faintest suggestion of a plan," he said. "The impression concerning his part has been gradually built up by a few people, close friends of his and mostly women, who naturally after the Fair proved beautiful desired to more broadly identify his memory with it."

Root's death had crushed Burnham, but it also freed him to become a broader, better architect. "It was questioned by many if the loss of Mr. Root was not irreparable," wrote James Ellsworth in a letter to Burnham's biographer, Charles Moore. Ellsworth concluded that Root's death "brought out qualities in Mr. Burnham which might not have developed, as early anyway, had Mr. Root lived." The common perception had always been that Burnham managed the business side of the firm, while Root did all the designs. Burnham did seem to "lean more or less" on Root's artistic abilities, Ellsworth said, but added that after Root's death "one would never realize anything of this kind . . . or ever know from his actions that he ever possessed a partner or did not always command in *both* directions."

In 1901 Burnham built the Fuller Building at the triangular intersection of Twenty-third and Broadway in New York, but neighborhood residents found an uncanny resemblance to a common domestic tool and called it the Flatiron Building. Burnham and his firm went on to build scores of other structures, among them the Gimbel's department store in New York, Filene's in Boston, and the Mount Wilson Observatory in Pasadena, California. Of the twenty-seven buildings he and John Root built in Chicago's Loop, only three remain today, among them the Rookery, its top-floor library much as it was during that magical meeting in

February 1891, and the Reliance Building, beautifully transformed into the Hotel Burnham. Its restaurant is called the Atwood, after Charles Atwood, who replaced Root as Burnham's chief designer.

Burnham became an early environmentalist. "Up to our time," he said, "strict economy in the use of natural resources has not been practiced, but it must be henceforth unless we are immoral enough to impair conditions in which our children are to live." He had great, if misplaced, faith in the automobile. The passing of the horse would "end a plague of barbarism," he said. "When this change comes, a real step in civilization will have been taken. With no smoke, no gases, no litter of horses, your air and streets will be clean and pure. This means, does it not, that the health and spirits of men will be better?"

On winter nights in Evanston he and his wife went sleigh-riding with Mr. and Mrs. Frank Lloyd Wright. Burnham became an avid player of bridge, though he was known widely for being utterly inept at the game. He had promised his wife that after the exposition the pace of his work would ease. But this did not happen. He told Margaret, "I thought the fair was an intense life, but I find the pressing forward of all these important interests gives me quite as full a day, week or year."

Burnham's health began to decline early in the twentieth century, when he was in his fifties. He developed colitis and in 1909 learned he had diabetes. Both conditions forced him to adopt a more healthful diet. His diabetes damaged his circulatory system and fostered a foot infection that bedeviled him for the rest of his life. As the years passed, he revealed an interest in the supernatural. One night in San Francisco, in a bungalow he had built at the fog-licked summit of Twin Peaks, his planning shanty, he told a friend, "If I were able to take the time, I believe that I could prove the continuation of life beyond the grave, reasoning from the necessity, philosophically speaking, of a belief in an absolute and universal power."

He knew that his day was coming to an end. On July 4, 1909, as he stood with friends on the roof of the Reliance Building, looking out over the city he adored, he said, "You'll see it lovely. I never will. But it *will* be lovely."

Recessional

THE ROARING IN OLMSTED'S EARS, the pain in his mouth, and the sleeplessness never eased, and soon an emptiness began to appear in his gaze. He became forgetful. On May 10, 1895, two weeks after his seventy-third birthday, he wrote to his son John, "It has today, for the first time, become evident to me that my memory for recent occurrences is no longer to be trusted." He was seventy-three years old. That summer, on his last day in the Brookline office, he wrote three letters to George Vanderbilt, each saying pretty much the same thing.

During a period in September 1895 that he described as "the bitterest week of my life," he confessed to his friend Charles Eliot his terror that his condition soon would require that he be placed in an asylum. "You cannot think how I have been dreading that it would be thought expedient that I should be sent to an 'institution,'" he wrote on September 26. "Anything but that. My father was a director of an Insane Retreat, and first and last, having been professionally employed and behind the scenes in several, my dread of such places is intense."

His loss of memory accelerated. He became depressed and paranoid and accused son John of orchestrating a "coup" to remove him from the firm. Olmsted's wife, Mary, took Olmsted to the family's island home in Maine, where his depression deepened and he at times became violent. He beat the family horse.

Mary and her sons realized there was little they could do for Olmsted. He had become unmanageable, his dementia profound. With deep sorrow and perhaps a good deal of relief, Rick lodged his father in the McLean Asylum in Waverly, Massachusetts. Olmsted's memory was not so destroyed that he did not realize he himself had designed McLean's grounds. This fact gave him no solace, for he saw immediately that the same phenomenon that had diminished nearly every one of his works—Central Park, Biltmore, the world's fair, and so many others—had occurred yet again. "They didn't carry out my plan," he wrote, "confound them!"

Olmsted died at two in the morning on August 28, 1903. His funeral was spare, family only. His wife, who had seen this great man disappear before her eyes, did not attend.

The Ferris Wheel cleared $200,000 at the fair and remained in place until the spring of 1894, when George Ferris dismantled it and reassembled it on Chicago's North Side. By then, however, it had lost both its novelty and the volume of ridership that the Midway had guaranteed. The wheel began losing money. These losses, added to the $150,000 cost of moving it and the financial damage done to Ferris's steel-inspection company by the continuing depression, caused Ferris to sell most of his ownership of the wheel.

In the autumn of 1896 Ferris and his wife separated. She went home to her parents; he moved into the Duquesne Hotel in downtown Pittsburgh. On November 17, 1896, he was taken to Mercy Hospital, where he died five days later, apparently of typhoid fever. He was thirty-seven years old. One year later his ashes were still in the possession of the undertaker who had received his body. "The request of Mrs. Ferris for the ashes was refused," the undertaker said, "because the dead man left closer relatives." In a eulogy two friends said Ferris had "miscalculated his powers of endurance, and he died a martyr to his ambition for fame and prominence."

In 1903 the Chicago House Wrecking Company bought the wheel at auction for $8,150, then reassembled it at the Louisiana Purchase Exposition of 1904. There the wheel again became profitable and earned its new owners $215,000. On May 11, 1906, the wrecking company dynamited the wheel, for scrap. The first hundred-pound charge was supposed to cut the wheel loose from its supports and topple it onto its side.

Instead the wheel began a slow turn, as if seeking one last roll through the sky. It crumpled under its own weight into a mountain of bent steel.

Sol Bloom, chief of the Midway, emerged from the fair a rich young man. He invested heavily in a company that bought perishable foods and shipped them in the latest refrigerated cars to far-off cities. It was a fine, forward-looking business. But the Pullman strike halted all train traffic through Chicago, and the perishable foods rotted in their train-cars. He was ruined. He was still young, however, and still Bloom. He used his remaining funds to buy two expensive suits, on the theory that whatever he did next, he had to look convincing. "But one thing was quite clear. . . ." he wrote. "[B]eing broke didn't disturb me in the least. I had started with nothing, and if I now found myself with nothing, I was at least even. Actually, I was much better than even: I had had a wonderful time."

Bloom went on to become a congressman and one of the crafters of the charter that founded the United Nations.

The fair made Buffalo Bill a million dollars (about $30 million today), which he used to found the town of Cody, Wyoming, build a cemetery and fairground for North Platte, Nebraska, pay the debts of five North Platte churches, acquire a Wisconsin newspaper, and further the theatri-cal fortunes of a lovely young actress named Katherine Clemmons, thereby deepening the already pronounced alienation of his wife. At one point he accused his wife of trying to poison him.

The Panic of 1907 destroyed his Wild West and forced him to hire himself out to circuses. He was over seventy years old but still rode the ring under his big white hat trimmed in silver. He died in Denver at his sister's house on January 10, 1917, without the money even to pay for his burial.

Theodore Dreiser married Sara Osborne White. In 1898, two years before publishing *Sister Carrie,* he wrote to Sara, "I went to Jackson Park and saw what is left of the dear old World's Fair where I learned to love you."

He cheated on her repeatedly.

⚬────⚬

For Dora Root life with John had been like living upon a comet. Their marriage had brought her into a world of art and money where every-thing seemed energized and alive. Her husband's wit, his musical talent, those exquisite long fingers so evident in any photograph imparted a gleam to her days that she was never able to recapture after his death. Toward the end of the first decade of the twentieth century, she wrote a long letter to Burnham. "It means so much to me that you think I have done well all these years," she wrote. "I have such grave doubts about myself whenever I stop to think about the subject, that a word of encour-agement from one who has so wonderfully sounded out his life, gives me a new impetus. If absorbing myself before the coming generation, and humbly passing on the torch, is the whole duty of women, I believe I have earned a word of praise."

But she knew that with John's death the doors to a brighter kingdom had softly but firmly closed. "If John had lived," she told Burnham, "all would have been different. Under the stimulus of his exhilarating life, I would have been his wife as well as the mother of his children. And it would have been interesting!"

⚬────⚬

Patrick Eugene Joseph Prendergast stood trial in December 1893. The prosecutor was a criminal attorney hired by the state just for this case.

His name was Alfred S. Trude.

Prendergast's lawyers tried to prove Prendergast was insane, but a jury of angry, grieving Chicagoans believed otherwise. One important piece of evidence tending to support the prosecution's case for sanity was the care Prendergast had taken to keep an empty chamber under the hammer of his revolver as he carried it in his pocket. At 2:28 P.M. on December 29, after conferring for an hour and three minutes, the jury found him guilty. The judge sentenced him to death. Throughout his trial and subsequent appeal, he continued to send Trude postcards. He wrote on February 21, 1894, "No one should be put to death no matter who it is, if it can be avoided, it is demoralizing to society to be barbarous."

Clarence Darrow entered the case and in a novel maneuver won for Prendergast a sanity inquest. This too failed, however, and Prendergast was executed. Darrow called him "a poor demented imbecile." The execution intensified Darrow's already deep hatred of the death penalty. "I am sorry for all fathers and all mothers," he said, years later, during his defense of Nathan Leopold and Richard Loeb, accused of killing a Chicago boy for the thrill of it. "The mother who looks into the blue eyes of her little babe cannot help musing over the end of the child, whether it will be crowned with the greatest promises which her mind can image or whether he may meet death upon the scaffold."

Leopold and Loeb, as they became known worldwide, had stripped their victim to mask his identity. They dumped some of his clothes in Olmsted's lagoons at Jackson Park.

In New York at the Waldorf-Astoria a few years into the new century, several dozen young men in evening clothes gathered around a gigantic pie. The whipped-cream topping began to move. A woman emerged. She was stunning, with olive skin and long black hair. Her name was Farida Mazhar. The men were too young to remember, but once, a long while before, she had done the *danse du ventre* at the greatest fair in history.

What the men noticed now was that she wore nothing at all.

Holmes

In the fall of 1895 Holmes stood trial in Philadelphia for the murder of Benjamin F. Pitezel. District Attorney George Graham brought thirty-five witnesses to Philadelphia from Cincinnati, Indianapolis, Irvington, Detroit, Toronto, Boston, Burlington, and Fort Worth, but they never were called. The judge ruled that Graham could present only evidence tied directly to the Pitezel murder and thus eliminated from the historical record a rich seam of detail on the murders of Dr. Herman W. Mudgett, alias Holmes.

Graham also brought to the courtroom the wart Holmes had removed from Benjamin Pitezel's corpse and a wooden box containing Pitezel's skull. There was a good deal of macabre testimony about decomposition and body fluids and the effects of chloroform. "There was a red fluid issuing from his mouth," testified Dr. William Scott, a pharmacist who had accompanied police to the house where Pitezel's body had been discovered, "and any little pressure on the stomach or over the chest here would cause this fluid to flow more rapidly. . . ."

After one particularly grisly stretch of Dr. Scott's testimony, Holmes stood and said, "I would ask that the Court be adjourned for sufficient time for lunch."

There were sorrowful moments, especially when Mrs. Pitezel took the stand. She wore a black dress, black hat, and black cape and looked pale and sad. Often she paused in midsentence and rested her head on her hands. Graham showed her the letters from Alice and Nellie and asked her to identify the handwriting. These were a surprise to her. She broke down. Holmes showed no emotion. "It was an expression of utmost indifference," a reporter for the *Philadelphia Public Ledger* said. "He made his notes with a manner as unconcerned as if he were sitting in his own office writing a business letter."

Graham asked Mrs. Pitezel whether she had seen the children since the time in 1894 when Holmes took them away. She answered in a voice almost too soft to hear, "I saw them at Toronto in the morgue, side by side."

So many handkerchiefs appeared among the men and women in the gallery that the courtroom looked as if it had just experienced a sudden snowfall.

Graham called Holmes "the most dangerous man in the world." The jury found him guilty; the judge sentenced him to death by hanging. Holmes's attorneys appealed the conviction and lost.

As Holmes awaited execution, he prepared a long confession, his third, in which he admitted killing twenty-seven people. As with two previous confessions, this one was a mixture of truth and falsehood. A few of the people he claimed to have murdered turned out to be alive. Exactly how many people he killed will never be known. At the very least he killed nine: Julia and Pearl Conner, Emeline Cigrand, the Williams sisters, and Pitezel and his children. No one doubted that he had killed many others. Estimates ranged as high as two hundred, though such extravagance seems implausible even for a man of his appetite. Detective Geyer believed that if the Pinkertons had not caught up with Holmes and arranged his arrest in Boston, he would have killed the rest of the Pitezel family. "That he fully intended to murder Mrs. Pitezel and Dessie and the baby, Wharton, is too evident for contradiction."

Holmes, in his confession, also clearly lied, or at least was deeply deluded, when he wrote, "I am convinced that since my imprisonment I have changed woefully and gruesomely from what I was formerly in feature and figure. . . . My head and face are gradually assuming an elongated shape. I believe fully that I am growing to resemble the devil—that the similitude is almost completed."

His description of killing Alice and Nellie rang true, however. He said he placed the girls in a large trunk and made an opening in its top. "Here I left them until I could return and at my leisure kill them. At 5 P.M. I borrowed a spade of a neighbor and at the same time called on Mrs. Pitezel at her hotel. I then returned to my hotel and ate my dinner, and at 7:00 P.M. I again returned to the house where the children were imprisoned, and ended their lives by connecting the gas with the trunk, then came the opening of the trunk and the viewing of their little blackened and distorted faces, then the digging of their shallow graves in the basement of the house."

He said of Pitezel, "It will be understood that from the first hour of our acquaintance, even before I knew he had a family who would later afford me additional victims for the gratification of my blood-thirstiness, I intended to kill him."

Afraid that someone would steal his own body after his execution, Holmes left instructions with his lawyers for how he was to be buried. He refused to allow an autopsy. His lawyers turned down an offer of $5,000 for his body. The Wistar Institute in Philadelphia wanted his brain. This request, too, the lawyers refused, much to the regret of Milton Greeman, curator of Wistar's renowned collection of medical specimens. "The man was something more than a mere criminal who acted on impulse," Greeman said. "He was a man who studied crime and planned his career. His brain might have given science valuable aid."

Shortly before ten A.M. on May 7, 1896, after a breakfast of boiled eggs, dry toast, and coffee, Holmes was escorted to the gallows at Moyamensing Prison. This was a difficult moment for his guards. They liked Holmes. They knew he was a killer, but he was a charming killer. The assistant superintendent, a man named Richardson, seemed nervous as he readied the noose. Holmes turned to him and smiled, and said, "Take your time, old man." At 10:13 Richardson released the trap and hanged him.

Using Holmes's instructions, workmen in the employ of undertaker John J. O'Rourke filled a coffin with cement, then placed Holmes's body inside and covered it with more cement. They hauled him south through the countryside to Holy Cross Cemetery, a Catholic burial ground in Delaware County, just south of Philadelphia. With great effort they transferred the heavy coffin to the cemetery's central vault, where two Pinkerton detectives guarded the body overnight. They took turns sleeping in a white pine coffin. The next day workers opened a double grave and filled this too with cement, then inserted Holmes's coffin. They placed more cement on top and closed the grave. "Holmes' idea was evidently to guard his remains in every way from scientific enterprise, from the pickling vat and the knife," the *Public Ledger* reported.

Strange things began to happen that made Holmes's claims about being the devil seem almost plausible. Detective Geyer became seriously ill. The warden of Moyamensing prison committed suicide. The jury foreman was electrocuted in a freak accident. The priest who delivered Holmes's last rites was found dead on the grounds of his church of mysterious causes. The father of Emeline Cigrand was grotesquely burned in a boiler explosion. And a fire destroyed the office of District Attorney George Graham, leaving only a photograph of Holmes unscathed.

No stone or tomb marks the grave of Herman Webster Mudgett, alias H. H. Holmes. His presence in Holy Cross Cemetery is something of a secret, recorded only in an ancient registry volume that lists his location as section 15, range 10, lot 41, at the center of graves 3 and 4, just off a lane that the cemetery calls Lazarus Avenue, after the biblical character who died and was restored to life. The entry also notes "ten feet of cement." At the gravesite there is only an open lawn in the midst of other old graves. There are children and a World War I pilot.

No one ever left flowers here for Holmes, but as it happens, he was not entirely forgotten.

In 1997 police in Chicago arrested a physician named Michael Swango at O'Hare Airport. The initial charge was fraud, but Swango was suspected of being a serial killer who murdered hospital patients through the administration of lethal doses of drugs. Eventually Dr. Swango pled guilty to four murders, but investigators believed he had committed many more. During the airport arrest police found in Swango's possession a notebook in which he had copied passages from certain books, either for the inspiration they provided or because of some affirming resonance. One passage was from a book about H. H. Holmes called *The Torture Doctor* by David Franke. The copied passage sought to put the reader into Holmes's mind.

" 'He could look at himself in a mirror and tell himself that he was one of the most powerful and dangerous men in the world,' " Swango's notebook read. " 'He could feel that he was a god in disguise.' "

Aboard the *Olympic*

ABOARD THE *OLYMPIC* BURNHAM waited for more news of Frank Millet and his ship. Just before sailing he had written, in longhand, a nineteen-page letter to Millet urging him to attend the next meeting of the Lincoln Commission, which was then on the verge of picking a designer for the Lincoln Memorial. Burnham and Millet had lobbied strongly for Henry Bacon of New York, and Burnham believed that his earlier talk to the Lincoln Commission had been persuasive. "But—I know and you know, dear Frank, that . . . the rats swarm back and begin to gnaw at the same old spot, the moment the dog's back is turned." He stressed how important it was for Millet to attend. "Be there and reiterate the real argument, which is that they should select a man in whom we have confidence. I leave this thing confidently in your hands." He addressed the envelope himself, certain that the United States Post Office would know exactly what to do:

Hon. F. D. Millet
To arrive on
Steamship Titanic.
New York

Burnham hoped that once the *Olympic* reached the site of the *Titanic*'s sinking, he would find Millet alive and hear him tell some outrageous story about the voyage, but during the night the *Olympic* returned to its original course for England. Another vessel already had reached the *Titanic*.

But there was a second reason for the *Olympic*'s return to course. The builder of both ships, J. Bruce Ismay, himself a *Titanic* passenger but one of the few male passengers to survive, was adamant that none of the other survivors see this duplicate of their own lost liner coming to their aid. The shock, he feared, would be too great, and too humiliating to the White Star Line.

The magnitude of the *Titanic* disaster quickly became apparent. Burnham lost his friend. The steward lost his son. William Stead had also been aboard and was drowned. In 1886 in the *Pall Mall Gazette* Stead had warned of the disasters likely to occur if shipping companies continued operating liners with too few lifeboats. A *Titanic* survivor reported hearing him say, "I think it is nothing serious so I shall turn in again."

That night, in the silence of Burnham's stateroom, as somewhere to the north the body of his last good friend drifted frozen in the strangely peaceful seas of the North Atlantic, Burnham opened his diary and began to write. He felt an acute loneliness. He wrote, "Frank Millet, whom I loved, was aboard her . . . thus cutting off my connection with one of the best fellows of the Fair."

Burnham lived only forty-seven more days. As he and his family traveled through Heidelberg, he slipped into a coma, the result apparently of a combined assault of diabetes, colitis, and his foot infection, all worsened by a bout of food poisoning. He died June 1, 1912. Margaret eventually moved to Pasadena, California, where she lived through time of war and epidemic and crushing financial depression, and then war again. She died December 23, 1945. Both are buried in Chicago, in Graceland, on a tiny island in the cemetery's only pond. John Root lies nearby, as do the Palmers, Louis Sullivan, Mayor Harrison, Marshall Field, Philip Armour, and so many others, in vaults and tombs that vary from the simple to the grand. Potter and Bertha still dominate things, as if stature mattered even in death. They occupy a massive acropolis with fifteen giant columns atop the only high ground, overlooking the pond. The others cluster around. On a crystalline fall day you can almost hear the tinkle of fine crystal, the rustle of silk and wool, almost smell the expensive cigars.

NOTES AND SOURCES

The White City, viewed from Lake Michigan.

THE THING THAT ENTRANCED ME about Chicago in the Gilded Age was the city's willingness to take on the impossible in the name of civic honor, a concept so removed from the modern psyche that two wise readers of early drafts of this book wondered why Chicago was so avid to win the world's fair in the first place. The juxtaposition of pride and unfathomed evil struck me as offering powerful insights into the nature of men and their ambitions. The more I read about the fair, the more entranced I became. That George Ferris would attempt to build something so big and novel—and that he would succeed on his first try—seems, in this day of liability lawsuits, almost beyond comprehension.

A rich seam of information exists about the fair and about Daniel Burnham in the beautifully run archives of the Chicago Historical Society and the Ryerson and Burnham libraries of the Art Institute of Chicago. I acquired a nice base of information from the University of Washington's Suzallo Library, one of the finest and most efficient libraries I have encountered. I also visited the Library of Congress in Washington, where I spent a good many happy hours immersed in the papers of Frederick Law Olmsted, though my happiness was at times strained by trying to decipher Olmsted's execrable handwriting.

I read—and mined—dozens of books about Burnham, Chicago, the exposition, and the late Victorian era. Several proved consistently valuable: Thomas Hines's *Burnham of Chicago* (1974); Laura Wood Roper's *FLO: A Biography of Frederick Law Olmsted* (1973); and Witold Rybczynski's *A Clearing in the Distance* (1999). One book in particular, *City of the Century* by Donald L. Miller (1996), became an invaluable companion in my journey through old Chicago. I found four guidebooks to be especially useful: Alice Sinkevitch's *AIA Guide to Chicago* (1993); Matt Hucke and Ursula Bielski's *Graveyards of Chicago* (1999); John Flinn's *Official Guide to the World's Columbian Exposition* (1893); and *Rand, McNally & Co.'s Handbook to the World's Columbian Exposition* (1893). Hucke and Bielski's guide led me to pay a visit to Graceland Cemetery, an utterly charming haven where, paradoxically, history comes alive.

Holmes proved an elusive character, owing in large part to the Philadelphia judge's unfortunate decision to bar District Attorney Graham's three dozen witnesses from giving testimony. Several books have been written about Holmes, but none tells quite the same story. Two of them, Harold Schechter's *Depraved* and David Franke's *The Torture Doctor* (the work quoted by the modern serial killer Dr. Swango), seem the most trustworthy. Two other works exist that provide a concrete foundation of facts. One is Detective Frank Geyer's memoir, *The Holmes-Pitezel Case*, a detailed account of events from the time of Holmes's arrest onward, in which Geyer presents excerpts of primary documents that no longer exist. I was lucky enough to acquire a copy from an online seller of antique books. The second is *The Trial of Herman W. Mudgett, Alias, H. H. Holmes*, published in 1897, a complete transcript of the trial. I found a copy in the law library of the University of Washington.

Holmes left a memoir, *Holmes' Own Story*, which I found in the Library of Congress's rare book collection. He also made at least three confessions. The first two appear in Geyer's book. The third and most sensational appeared in the *Philadelphia Inquirer*, which paid him a rich fee to write it. Though mostly untrue, his memoir and confessions were nuggeted with details that jibed with facts established in court or unearthed by Geyer and by the legions of reporters who covered Holmes's story after his arrest in Boston. I relied heavily on newspaper articles published in the *Chicago Tribune* and in two Philadelphia newspapers, the *Inquirer* and the *Public Ledger*. Many of these articles were full of inaccuracies and, I suspect, embellishments. I mined them for bits

of apparent fact and for reproductions of original documents, such as letters, telegrams, interviews, and other primary materials uncovered by
police or produced by witnesses who stepped forward once the nature of
Holmes's "Castle of Horrors" became front-page news. One of the most
striking, and rather charming, aspects of criminal investigation in the
1890s is the extent to which the police gave reporters direct access to
crime scenes, even while investigations were in progress. At one point
during the Holmes investigation Chicago's chief of police told a *Tribune*
reporter he'd just as soon have a squad of reporters under his command
as detectives.

Exactly what motivated Holmes may never be known. In focusing on
his quest for possession and dominance, I present only one possibility,
though I recognize that any number of other motives might well be
posited. I base my account on known details of his history and behavior
and on what forensic psychiatrists have come to understand about psychopathic serial killers and the forces that drive them. Dr. James O.
Raney, a Seattle psychiatrist who now and then provides forensic evalu-
ations, read the manuscript and gave me his observations about the
nature of psychopaths, known more tediously in today's psychiatric
handbooks as people afflicted with "antisocial personality disorder." It is
a good thing Alfred Hitchcock died before the change was made.

Clearly no one other than Holmes was present during his murders—
no one, that is, who survived—yet in my book I re-create two of his
killings. I agonized over exactly how to do this and spent a good deal of
time rereading Truman Capote's *In Cold Blood* for insights into how
Capote achieved his dark and still deeply troubling account. Sadly,
Capote left no footnotes. To build my murder scenes, I used threads of
known detail to weave a plausible account, as would a prosecutor in his
closing arguments to a jury. My description of Julia Conner's death by
chloroform is based on expert testimony presented at Holmes's trial
about the character of chloroform and what was known at the time
about its effect on the human body.

I do not employ researchers, nor did I conduct any primary research
using the Internet. I need physical contact with my sources, and there's

only one way to get it. To me every trip to a library or archive is like a small detective story. There are always little moments on such trips when the past flares to life, like a match in the darkness. On one visit to the Chicago Historical Society, I found the actual notes that Prendergast sent to Alfred Trude. I saw how deeply the pencil dug into the paper.

I have tried to keep my citations as concise as possible. I cite all quoted or controversial material but omit citations for facts that are widely known and accepted. For the two murder scenes I document my reasoning and my approach and cite the facts upon which I relied. The citations that follow constitute a map. Anyone retracing my steps ought to reach the same conclusions as I.

PROLOGUE

Aboard the *Olympic*

3. *The date was*: Burnham identified the suite numbers in a diary entry dated April 3, 1912; Burnham Archives, Diary, Roll 2. For information about the *Olympic* and *Titanic* see Brinnin; Lynch; Eaton and Haas; and *White Star*. The last, which reprints articles published in 1911 from *Shipping World and Shipbuilder*, includes detailed specifications of both ships as well as maps and schematics of the *Olympic's* decks and accommodations.
3. *"This prolonging*: Moore, *Burnham, Architect*, 2:172.
5. *"the greatest event*: Miller, 488.

PART I: FROZEN MUSIC

The Black City

11. *"Never before*: Miller, 511.
11. *"The parlors and bedrooms*: Ibid., 516.
11. *"a human being*: Ibid., 193.

"The Trouble Is Just Begun"

14. *It was this big talk*: Dedmon, 221.
16. *"the hawks, buzzards*: *Chicago Tribune*, July 24, 1889.
16. *"The men who have helped*: *Chicago Tribune*, August 2, 1889.
17. *"The gloom*: *Chicago Tribune*, February 24, 1890.
17. *"Gentlemen. I am prepared*: Ibid.
19. *"the records of the Old Central*: Hines, 402.
19. *"I went to Harvard*: Ibid., 11.
19. *"greatest architect*: Ibid., 12.
19. *"There is a family tendency*: Miller, 315.
21. *"My idea*: Sullivan, Louis, 285.
21. *"There is a black sheep*: Letter, Daniel Hudson Burnham, Jr., to Charles Moore, February 21, 1918, Burnham Archives, Charles Moore Correspondence, Box 27, File 3.

22. "*A long wait frightened us*: Monroe, *Poet's Life*, 59.

22. "*so completely happy*: Ibid., 60.

23. "*probably not equaled*: Miller, 321.

24. "*our originality*: Moore, *Burnham, Architect*, 1:24.

24. "*if,*" *he said, "the earth*: Ibid., 1:321.

24. "*The building throughout*: Ibid.

25. "*What Chartres was*: Hines, 53.

26. "*who will not have an office*: Miller, 326.

26. "*Daniel Burnham Hudson was*: Starrett, 29.

26. "*Make no little plans*: Ibid., 311.

26. "*I've never seen*: Miller, 319.

27. "*His conversational powers*: Ibid., 316.

27. "*I used always to think*: Ibid., 317

27. "*The office was full*: Starrett, 32.

27. "*The work of each man*: Miller, 318.

28. "*that Gordian city*: Lewis, 19.

28. "*a gigantic peepshow*: Ibid., 136.

28. "*I did it*: Burnham to mother, undated, Burnham Archives, Burnham Family Correspondence, Box 25, File 2.

29. "*You must not worry*: Burnham to Margaret, February 29, 1888, Burnham Archives, Burnham Family Correspondence, Box 25, File 3.

29. "*The coroner*: Burnham to Margaret, March 3, 1888, ibid.

30. "*Burnham was not pleased*: Sullivan, Louis, 294.

30. "*smear another façade*: Morrison, 64.

30. "*an innocent*: Sullivan, Louis, 291.

30. "*He was elephantine*: Ibid., 288.

32. "*When may we see you*: ChicagoTribune, February 25, 1890.

32. "*The most marvelous exhibit*: Ibid.

34. "*Chicago is like*: Chicago Tribune, February 27, 1890.

The Necessary Supply

35. *His height was*: Franke, 24. Franke reproduces an image of a "Rogue's Gallery" file card with details of Holmes's weight, height, and so forth as entered by Boston police upon his arrest.

35. "*The eyes are very big*: Schechter, 282.

36. *A telegraph pole*: Englewood Directory, 37.

36. "*While at times*: Sullivan, Gerald, 49.

36. *Holmes entered the store*: Mudgett, 22–23; Schechter, 13–17; Boswell and Thompson, 81. See also *Town of Lake Directory*, 217.

37. "*an elemental odor*: Sinclair, 25.

37. "*river of death*: Ibid., 34.

37. "*I had daily*: Mudgett, 6.

38. "*Nor did they desist*: Ibid., 6

39. "*mother's boy*: Ibid., 199

39. "*twelve-year-old sweetheart*: Ibid., 200.

39. *Mudgett's only close friend*: Schechter, 12.

40. *"itinerant photographer*: Mudgett, 7.

40. *"Had he next proceeded*: Ibid., 8.

40. *"I kept it for many years*: Ibid., 8.

41. *He enrolled*: Ibid., 14.

41. *"the first really dishonest*: Ibid.,15.

41. *"I could hardly count*: Ibid.,16.

42. *Eventually he came to Mooers Forks*: Ibid., 16; *Chicago Tribune*, July 31, 1895; *New York Times*, July 31, 1895.

42. *"Some of the professors*: Franke, 118.

42. *"In the fall of 1885*: Mudgett, 17.

43. *"This scheme called for*: Ibid.,19.

43. *"the necessary supply*: Ibid.

43. *"This," he said, "necessitated*: Ibid., 20.

43. *"and for the first time*: Ibid.

44. *The owner of the house*: *Chicago Tribune*, July 31, 1895.

44. *"This," he wrote, "was my first*: Mudgett, 21.

45. *"The city had laid*: Dreiser, *Sister Carrie*, 16.

45. *"there was such a rush*: Sullivan, Gerald, 14.

45. *In 1868 a Mrs. H. B. Lewis*: Ibid.

46. *"To the business men*: Catalogue, 3.

46. *"My trade was good*: Mudgett, 23.

46. *He put up a new sign*: Franke, 210.

"Becomingness"

48. *A friend of Burnham's*: Ellsworth to Olmsted, July 26, 1890, Burnham Archives, Box 58, File 13.

49. *"I have all my life*: Rybczynski, *Clearing*, 385–86.

50. *"flecks of white or red*: Olmsted, "Landscape Architecture," 18.

50. *"I design with a view*: Rybczynski, *Clearing*, 396.

50. *"Suppose," he wrote*: Olmsted to Van Brunt, January 22, 1891, Olmsted Papers, Reel 22.

51. *"we are always personally*: Roper, 421.

51. *He was prone*: Rybczynski, *Clearing*, 247–48, 341

51. *"My position is this*: Ellsworth to Olmsted, July 26, 1890.

52. *Certainly that seemed*: Articles of Agreement, 1890, Olmsted Papers, Reel 41; Rybczynski, *Clearing*, 387.

52. *"When can you be here?*: Telegram quoted in Olmsted to Butterworth, August 6, 1890, Burnham Archives, Box 58, File 13.

52. *"Having seen it*: *Chicago Tribune*, July 7, 1890.

53. *a man they could work with*: Codman to Olmsted, October 25, 1890, Olmsted Papers, Reel 57.

54. *"It is to be desired*: Olmsted, *Report*, 51.

57. *"a man of the world*: Sullivan, Louis, 287.

57. *"she patted the mortar*: *Chicago Tribune*, November 2, 1890.

58. *Root, according to a witness*: Miller, 316.

58. *"While in school*: Chicago Record, December 16, 1893, McGoorty Papers.

59. *"He got smart*: Chicago Record, December 15, 1893, Ibid.

60. *"murky pall*: Chicago Tribune, November 16, 1890.

"Don't Be Afraid"

64. *"Ambition has been the curse*: Schechter, 238.

65. *"His presence*: Franke, 112.

65. *"It is said that babies*: Ibid., 112.

66. *The building's broad design*: Philadelphia Public Ledger, July 22, 25, 26, 27, 29, 30, 1895; Chicago Tribune, July 17, 21, 23, 25, 27, 28, 29, August 18, 1895; New York Times, July 25, 26, 29, 31, 1895.

67. *"There is an uneven settlement*: Chicago Tribune, July 25, 1895.

67. *The high rate of turnover*: Ibid.; Schechter, 28–29.

68. *"I don't know*: Franke, 95–96.

69. *At first, Latimer said*: Ibid., 43.

69. *"In a general way*: Geyer, 26–27.

69. *"fine physique*: Trial, 145.

69. *"Come with me*: Schechter, 25.

70. *"Pitezel was his tool*: Trial, 449.

71. *Captain Horace Elliot*: Englewood Directory, 36.

71. *To the buyer's chagrin*: Schechter, 36.

71. *City directories*: Englewood Directory, 179, 399; Franke, 40.

72. *"He was the smoothest man*: Franke, 42–43.

72. *"I sometimes sold him*: Ibid., 111.

73. *"Don't be afraid*: Chicago Tribune, July 31, 1895; New York Times, July 31, 1895; Franke, 110.

73. *Unlike most Americans*: Chicago Tribune, July 26, 1895.

74. *An advertisement*: Hoyt, 177.

Pilgrimage

75. *Immediately the directors*: Burnham and Millet, 14–17; Burnham, *Design*, 7–9; Monroe, Root, 222–23.

76. *"at once cheap wooden quarters*: Burnham to Committee on Buildings and Grounds, December 1, 1890, Burnham Archives, Box 58, File 3.

77. *"It may not occur to you*: Burnham to Davis, December 8, 1890, Burnham Archives, Business Correspondence, vol. 1.

77. *"cut to the quick*: Monroe, Root, 235.

77. *"feeling confident*: Moore, Burnham interview, 3.

79. *"McKim, damn your preambles*: Moore, *McKim*, 113.

80. *"To himself*: Monroe, Poet's Life, 115.

81. *"They all approved*: Burnham to Olmsted, December 23, 1890, Olmsted Papers, Reel 57.

82. *"they said*: Moore, Burnham interview, 3.

82. *"Burnham had believed*: Sullivan, Louis, 319.

83. *"I think he, Adler*: Moore, Burnham interview, 4.

83. *"He said he was tired:* Inland Architect and News Record, vol. 16, no. 8 (January 1891), 88.

84. *He was depressed:* Monroe, *Root,* 249.

84. *"He felt that this:* Ibid., 249.

A Hotel for the Fair

86. *In a parody:* Boswell and Thompson, 81.

86. *When Myrta's great-uncle:* Ibid., 80; Schechter, 235; *Chicago Tribune,* July 27, 1895; *New York Times,* July 29, 1895; *Philadelphia Public Ledger,* July 29, 1895.

87. *Holmes returned to Englewood:* Boswell and Thompson, 80.

87. *"Beside his own person:* See *Oxford English Dictionary,* 2nd ed.

88. *Half a century later:* Cleckley, 369.

88. *People exhibiting:* Millon et al., 124.

89. *"When I went to bed:* Schechter, 235.

89. *"Presently," Belknap said:* Ibid.

89. *"I refused to open:* Ibid.

89. *"If I'd gone:* Boswell and Thompson, 80.

90. *He planned to install:* Chicago Tribune, July 30, 1895.

91. *The manager of the furnace company:* Franke, 94–95

91. *"the necessary amount of heat:* Ibid., 94.

92. *"In fact," he said:* Ibid.

92. *These clerks:* Philadelphia Public Ledger, July 27, 1895.

The Landscape of Regret

94. *The eastern architects left:* Hunt to Olmsted, January 6, 1891, Olmsted Papers, Reel 58.

94. *Two hours before:* Moore, *McKim,* 113; *Chicago Tribune,* January 11, 1891.

94. *"It was one:* Moore, Burnham Interview, 3.

95. *"they gazed:* Burnham, *Design,* 24.

95. *"remote and repulsive:* Ingalls, 142.

95. *"sandy waste:* Bancroft, 46.

95. *"If a search had been made:* "A Report Upon the Landscape," 8, Olmsted Papers, Reel 41.

95. *"it became almost:* Burnham and Millet, 45.

96. *The park's gravest flaw:* "A Report Upon the Landscape," 7, Olmsted Papers, Reel 41.

96. *"a feeling of discouragement:* Burnham and Millet, 5.

96. *"Do you mean to say:* Hines, 82; Moore, Burnham interview, 4;

96. *"He went down to the office:* Monroe, *Root,* 259.

96. *"looking ill:* Starrett, 47.

97. *"ill almost unto death:* Monroe, *Poet's Life,* 113.

97. *"After the 15th:* Ibid., 260.

98. *"Oysters:* Chicago Tribune, January 11, 1891.

98. *"Gentlemen," he said:* Poole, 184; Moore, *Burnham, Architect,* 43.

99. *"The men left:* Burnham, *Design,* 26.

99. *"In talking with them:* Monroe, *Root,* 249; Monroe, *Poet's Life,* 113.

Vanishing Point

100. *After years spent*: Chicago Tribune, July 21, 23, 24, 26, 28, 29, 1895; *Philadelphia Public Ledger*, July 22, 23, 27, 1895; Boswell and Thompson, 83–84; Franke, 98–101; Schechter, 39–44.

102. *"I shut the door*: Chicago Tribune, July 28, 1895.

102. *"a mysterious disappearances*: Chicago Tribune, November 1, 1892.

102. *Fannie Moore*: Ibid.

102. *J. W. Highleyman left*: Ibid.

103. *Cheyenne*: Ibid.

Alone

104. *"Himself not especially*: Sullivan, Louis, 288.

104. *"It soon became noticeable*: Ibid., 320.

104. *"Hell," he snapped*: Ibid.

105. *"Burnham came out*: Ibid.

105. *"The natural dominance*: Baker, *Hunt*, 398.

105. *"the function created*: Sullivan, Louis, 290.

105. *"In each firm*: Ibid., 288.

105. *"John Root was*: Ibid.

106. *"I haven't escaped sickness*: Monroe, *Root*, 261.

106. *"Mr. Root is quite low*: Burnham to Boyington, January 14, 1891, Burnham Archives, Business Correspondence, Vol. 1.

106. *"am able this morning*: Burnham to Boyington, January 15, 1891, ibid.

107. *"You won't leave me*: Moore, Burnham interview, 5.

107. *"Do you hear that?*: Ibid.

107. *"I have worked*: Monroe, *Poet's Life*, 114.

108. *"most distinguished architect*: Chicago Tribune, January 16, 1891.

108. *"There is no man*: Chicago Tribune, January 17, 1891.

108. *"It's all nonsense*: Chicago Tribune, January 25, 1891.

108. *"I was born*: Philadelphia Inquirer, April 12, 1896.

PART II: AN AWFUL FIGHT

Convocation

113. *His gout*: Moore, Burnham interview, 6.

113. *"almost in whispers*: "The Organization, Design and Construction of the Fair," January 7, 1895, 56, Moore Papers.

113. *Its center was an octagon*: Rand, McNally, 49–57.

114. *"a panorama*: Ibid., 126.

114. *"I don't think I shall advocate*: Moore, *Burnham, Architect*, 47 (In Moore, Burnham interview, 4, the phrasing is slightly different: "I do not think I will advocate that dome, I will probably modify the building.")

114. *"one grand entrance*: Burnham to Sullivan, February 11, 1891, Burnham Archives, Business Correspondence, Vol. 1.

115. *"the tension of feeling*: Burnham and Millet, 29.

115. *"quiet intentness*: "The Organization, Design and Construction of the Fair," January 7, 1895, 56, Moore Papers.

115. *"Drawing after drawing*: Burnham and Millet, 29.

115. *"The room was still as death*: Moore, *Burnham, Architect*, 47.

115. *"You are dreaming*: "The Organization, Design and Construction of the Fair," January 7, 1895, 58, Moore Papers.

115. *"I never expected*: Different versions of St. Gaudens's remark appear in the literature. I've combined elements of two. See Burnham, *Design*, 39, and Hines, 90.

116. *"We should try to make*: Olmsted to Burnham, January 26, 1891, Olmsted Papers, Reel 41.

116. *"What we shall want*: Ibid.

116. *"I mean such as Malay proas*: Ibid.

117. *"mysterious poetic effect*: "Memorandum as to What is to be Aimed at in the Planting of the Lagoon District of the Chicago Exposition," Olmsted Papers, Reel 59.

117. *"through the mingling intricately together*: Ibid.

118. *"a display of flowers*: Ibid.

118. *"to slightly screen*: Ibid.

118. *The overall effect*: Ibid.

119. *"that army our hundreds*: Olmsted to "Fred" (most likely Federick J. Kingsbury, a friend), January 20, 1891, Olmsted Papers, Reel 22.

119. *"How is it possible*: Lewis, 172.

120. *"We must push this now*: *Chicago Tribune*, February 20, 1891.

120. *"Examination of the facts*: Director of Works Report, October 24, 1892, Burnham Archives, Box 58, File 12.

120. *"There will not be a brick*: *Chicago Tribune*, March 20, 1891.

120. *Atwood stood him up*: Moore, Burnham interview, 7.

121. *He was an opium addict*: Ibid.

121. RUSH: *Chicago Tribune*, May 16, 1891.

121. *"a family of twelve*: *Chicago Tribune*, February 20, 1891.

121. *"That un-American institution*: *Inland Architect and News Record*, vol. 17, no. 5 (June 1891), 54.

122. *P. T. Barnum died*: *Chicago Tribune*, May 30, 1891.

122. *"I think it quite necessary*: *Chicago Tribune*, February 14, 1891.

Cuckoldry

123. *Lovely, dark Gertrude*: *Chicago Tribune*, July 26, 1895.

124. *"of an easy-going innocent*: *Chicago Tribune*, July 21, 1895.

124. *"Some of my friends*: *Chicago Tribune*, July 26, 1895.

124. *Holmes proposed to sell*: *Chicago Tribune*, July 21, 1895.

125. *Holmes even wanted Ned*: *Chicago Tribune*, July 26, 28, 1895.

126. *"Separation couldn't come*: *Chicago Tribune*, July 26, 1895.

126. *He heard her footsteps*: Ibid.

126. *"I told her after I left*: Ibid.

126. *At night, after the first-floor stores*: This is speculation, but I base it on the following: In

Mooers Holmes was known to pace at midnight, suggesting he was not a restful sleeper. Psychopaths need stimulation. The kiln would have been an irresistible attraction. Admiring it and igniting its flames would have reinforced his sense of power and control over the occupants above.

Vexed

128. *"You must not think*: Burnham to Margaret, March 15, 1892, Burnham Archives, Family Correspondence, File 4.

128. *"Among the trees*: Burnham and Millet, 36.

129. *"practically an unknown*: Inland Architect and News Record, vol. 22, no. 1 (August 1893), 8.

129. *They laid a platform*: Ibid.

131. *Edison suggested*: Chicago Tribune, May 12, 13, 1891.

131. *General Electric offered*: Baker, Life, 158–59.

131. *"We are at a dead standstill*: Burnham to Hunt, June 2, 1891, Burnham Archives, Business Correspondence, Vol. 2.

132. *"The delay you are causing us*: Burnham to Hunt, June 6, 1891, ibid.

132. *He ordered*: "List of bedding plants to be ordered either in this country, or from Europe," July 13, 1891, Olmsted Papers, Reel 59.

132. *"It was bad enough*: Ulrich, 11.

133. *"He is the arbiter*: Chicago Tribune, May 14, 1891.

133. *"incongruity*: World's Fair, 851.

134. *"President Baker wants*: Chicago Tribune, July 21, 1891.

134. *C. F. Ritchel of Bridgeport*: Chicago Tribune, October 12, 1889.

134. *"As the cost: McComber's tower idea*: Chicago Tribune, November 2, 1889.

135. *The engineer urged*: Chicago Tribune, November 9, 1889.

135. *In August 1891*: Chicago Tribune, August 5, 1891.

135. *The engineers were outraged*: Chicago Tribune, August 16, 1891.

137. *"How soon*: Bloom, 117.

140. *"The more I thought*: Ibid.

141. *"I could not*: Burnham to Dredge, November 18, 1891, Burnham Archives, Business Correspondence, vol. 4.

141. *"The criticism now*: Burnham to Dredge, November 24, 1891, ibid.

141. *"was about as intelligent*: Bloom, 119.

141. *"anxious to get*: Sandweiss, 14.

141. *"You are a very young man*: Bloom, 120.

142. *"I do hope*: Allen to Palmer, October 21, 1891, Chicago Historical Society, World's Columbian Exhibition–Board of Lady Managers Archive, Folder 3.

142. *"When I think of the days*: Weimann, 176.

143. *" 'I think it would be better*: Ibid.

143. *"A severe breakdown*: Ibid.,177.

144. *"I suspect that even Codman*: Olmsted to Burnham, December 23, 1891, Olmsted Papers, Reel 22.

145. *In December*: Burnham, Final Official Report, 78.

145. *"A few questions of design*: Interim Report on Construction, "To the Editor of the Chicago *Herald*," December 28, 1891, Burnham Archives, Box 58, File 9.

145. *"the failure of the fair*: Lewis, 175.

Remains of the Day

Holmes left no firsthand account of the method he used to kill Julia and Pearl Conner; nor did he describe how he managed to subdue both victims, although he did at one point state that Julia had died of a "criminal operation," meaning an abortion. I constructed the murder scenes in this chapter using a combination of sources: fragments of known evidence (for example, the fact that he possessed two cases of surgical instruments, equipped his building with dissection tables, and favored chloroform as a weapon and bought large quantities of it); the detective work of other investigators of the Holmes saga (Schechter, Franke, and Boswell and Thompson); statements made by Holmes after the murders; psychiatric research into the character, motives, and needs of criminal psychopaths; and testimony at Holmes's trial as to how a person would react to an overdose of chloroform. The Conner case and the anatomical moonlighting of Charles Chappell received extensive news coverage. In addition to the specific sources cited below, see *Chicago Tribune*, July 21, 23, 24, 25, 26, 28, 29, 30, 1895; *New York Times*, July 29, 1895; *Philadelphia Public Ledger*, July 23, 27, 29, 30, 1895; Boswell and Thompson, 81–86; Franke, 98–101; Schechter, 39–44.

146. *In November 1891*: Schechter, 43–44.

147. *Julia and Mrs. Crowe*: *Chicago Tribune*, July 29, 1895.

148. *dark amber bottle*: *Merck's Manual*, 28.

148. *She gripped his hand*: Trial, 166, 420–422.

149. *On Christmas morning*: *Chicago Tribune*, July 29, 1895.

150. *"The gentlemen were acting*: *Chicago Tribune*, February 27, 1890. See also March 2, 1890, for a tantalizing but likely apocryphal story of a St. Louis man buried alive— allegedly in a deep coma—only to have his body stolen by medical students. The students discovered his true condition with the first incision and quickly deposited him on the steps of the St. Louis courthouse, where he awoke with a painful and inexplicable cut across his abdomen. Or so the story went.

150. *"Yes, the party*: *Chicago Tribune*, March 24, 1890.

151. *"The body," he said*: *Philadelphia Public Ledger*, July 29, 1895. The article also cites the $36 price.

151. *They found dishes*: Franke, 101.

152. *"I last saw her*: Mudgett, 33.

A Gauntlet Dropped

153. *The ranks included*: Hines, 74–75.

153. *A rising union man*: Burnham to Geraldine, February 24, 1892, Burnham Archives, Business Correspondence, vol. 6.

154. *"inaccurate or 'slouchy' work*: Burnham to Cloyes, January 6, 1892, ibid., vol. 5.

154. *"it seems to me*: Burnham to Ulrich, January 6, 1892, ibid.

154. *"You will please dismiss*: Burnham to Geraldine, January 6, 1892, ibid.

154. *"Guarded by sentries*: Wyckoff, 248.

155. *"ho, boy*: *Oxford English Dictionary*, 2nd ed., 278; Wyckoff, 11.

155. *He "was eminently engaging*: Anderson, 53.

155. *"the architects of America*: Untitled typescript, Ferris Papers, 1.

156. *"cut to the quick*: Ibid.

157. *superintendent of sheep*: Chicago Tribune, July 14, 1892.

157. *"We are now organizing*: Burnham to Davis, November 12, 1891, Burnham Archives, Business Correspondence, vol. 4.

157. *"I think it is pretty well understood*: Chicago Tribune, January 5, 1892.

157. *"The time was well spent*: Burnham to Margaret, March 15, 1892, Burnham Archives, Family Correspondence, Box 25, File 4.

158. *Late in March*: Burnham to Margaret, March 31, 1892, ibid.

159. *"Mr. Davis has not been to see me*: Chicago Tribune, April 9, 1892.

159. *The congressmen, Burnham wrote*: Burnham to Margaret, March 31, 1892.

160. *"spectacular advertising*: Bloom, 120.

160. *"I could tell*: Ibid.

The Angel from Dwight

In addition to the specific citations below, for this chapter I relied on detailed coverage of the Cigrand case in the *Chicago Tribune* and *Philadelphia Public Ledger,* as well as broader accounts of the case in Boswell and Thompson, Franke, and Schechter.

H. Wayne Morgan's detailed historical essay on Leslie Enraught Keeley's alcohol-treatment empire, "'No, Thank You, I've Been to Dwight,'" in the *Illinois Historical Journal,* offers a charming look at a bygone rage.

See *Chicago Tribune,* July 26, 27, 29, 30, 31, 1895; *Philadelphia Public Ledger,* July 27, 29, 31, 1895; Boswell and Thompson, 86–87; Franke, 102–105; Schechter, 48–51.

161. *In the spring of 1892*: Schechter, 48.

161. *Gold was the most famous*: Morgan, 149.

161. *the Chicago post office*: Ibid., 159–160.

161. *"he was too valuable*: Mudgett, 122.

162. *Thousands of people*: Morgan, 157.

162. *"passing through the line*: Ibid., 154.

162. *"No, thank you*: Ibid., 158.

162. *the story Pitezel now told*: Schechter, 48, 49.

162. *"a flattering offer*: Chicago Tribune, July 30, 1895.

162. *Emeline accepted*: Ibid.

163 *"White pique hats*: Chicago Tribune, August 7, 1895.

164. *"got to talking*: Chicago Tribune, July 28, 1895.

164. *"a handsome blonde*: Ibid.

164. *"I told her*: Ibid.

164. *"She was one*: Franke, 102.

165. *"It was not long*: Ibid.

165. *son of an English lord*: Schechter, 49.

165. *"I was charmed*: Chicago Tribune, July 30, 1895.

Dedication Day

167. *"All over its surroundings*: Ulrich, 19.

168. *"Would you object*: Burnham to Olmsted, November 20, 1891, Burnham Archives, Business Correspondence, vol. 4.

168. *"a few tents, some horses*: Burnham to Buchanan, December 19, 1891, ibid.

168. *"They propose*: Burnham to Olmsted, February 5, 1892, ibid.

169. *"unreasonable, unjust*: Roper, 434.

169. *"When Olmsted is blue*: Rybczynski, *Clearing*, 247–48.

170. *"They had picked*: Bloom, 122.

170. *"a tolerable idea*: Olmsted, "Report by F.L.O.," April 1892, Olmsted Papers, Reel 41.

170. *"It seemed to me*: Olmsted to John, May 15, 1892, Olmsted Papers, Reel 22.

170. *The Paris buildings*: Olmsted, "Report by F.L.O."

171. *"I am having*: Rybczynski, *Clearing*, 391.

171. *"I can only conclude*: Olmsted to Codman, May 25, 1892, Olmsted Papers, Reel 22.

171. *A doctor, Henry Rayner*: Roper, 439.

171. *"You know that I am*: Olmsted to Codman, June 16, 1892, Olmsted Papers, Reel 22.

171. *"every day more or less*: Olmsted to "Partners," July 21, 1892, ibid.

171. *"childish, vulgar, flaunting*: Ibid.

171. *"there is nothing in America*: Olmsted to Codman, July 30, 1892, ibid.

171. *"The finest combination*: Olmsted to John, May 15, 1892, ibid.

172. *"Everywhere the best ornamental grounds*: Olmsted to John Olmsted, May 19, 1892, ibid., Reel 41.

172. *"Let us as much as possible*: Olmsted to "Partners," July 17, 1892, ibid.

172. *"I think more than ever*: Olmsted to Codman, April 20, 1892, ibid.

172. *"The standard of an English laborer*: Olmsted to Codman, April 21, 1892, ibid., Reel 22.

172. *"The only cloud*: Olmsted to "Partners," July 21, 1892, ibid.

173. *"I could see them*: Bloom, 122.

173. *"I suggest you be more civil*: Ibid.

173. *"At present," he said*: Ibid.

174. *"Too fragile*: Barnes, 177.

174. *"The wind*: *Chicago Tribune*, April 28, 1892.

174. *"largely on account*: Moore, Burnham interview, 8.

174. *"His genius was betrayed*: Monroe, *Poet's Life*, 103.

174. *"I was urging*: Hines, 101.

175. *"I don't see it that way*: Moore, Burnham interview, 8.

175. *"ordinary white lead*: Millet, 708.

175. *"the Whitewash Gang*: Hall, 213.

175. *"with the utmost vigor*: Burnham to Geraldine, March (illegible) 1892, Burnham Archives, Business Correspondence, vol. 6.

176. *On Saturday evening*: McCarthy, "Should We Drink," 8–12; *Chicago Tribune*, March 1, May 8, 9, 13, 20, 1892; Burnham, *Final Official Report*, 69–70.

176. *"You had better write a letter*: Moore, *McKim*, 120.

177. *On Wednesday, June 1*: Photograph, Manufactures and Liberal Arts Building, June 1, 1892, Burnham Archives, Box 64, File 34.

177. *Two weeks later*: Photograph, Manufactures and Liberal Arts Building, June 13, 1892, Burnham Archives, Oversize Portfolio 13.

178. *The contractor*: *Chicago Tribune*, June 15, 1892.

178. "*I have assumed personal control*: Burnham to Olmsted, September 14, 1892, Olmsted Papers, Reel 59.

179. "*I had no precedent*: Anderson, 53.

179. "*monstrosity*: Barnes, 177.

179. "*I was more disabled*: Rybczynski, *Clearing*, 391.

179. "*I am still tortured*: Olmsted to John, October 11, 1892, Olmsted Papers, Reel 22.

180. "*Of course the main work suffers*: Olmsted to John, undated but received in Brookline, Mass., October 10, 1892, ibid.

181. *The dedication had been anticipated*: Schlereth, 174.

181. "*Ninety thousand people*: Wheeler, 846.

182. "*both orators waving*: Monroe, *Poet's Life*, 130.

182. *That winter she burned*: Ibid., 131.

Prendergast

183. *On November 28, 1892*: Prendergast to Alfred Trude, Trude Papers; *Chicago Record*, December 15 and 16, 1893, in McGoorty Papers; *Chicago Tribune*, December 15, 16, 17, 21, 22, 1893.

183. "*My Dear Mr. Trude*: Prendergast to Alfred Trude, Trude Papers.

"I Want You at Once"

185. "*I have on hand*: Ferris to Rice, December 12, 1892, Ferris Correspondence, Miscellaneous, Ferris Papers.

185. *that this wheel*: Anderson, 55; Miller, 497.

Chappell Redux

186. *The gift delighted*: Franke, 102.

186. "*She seemed delighted*: Ibid.

187. "*It had seemed to me*: Ibid., 103.

187. *Later there was speculation*: *Chicago Tribune*, July 30, 1895.

187. "*Oh, she's gone away*: Franke, 104.

188. "*This will tell you*: Ibid.

188. *The announcement read*: Ibid., 105.

189. "*Some days after going*: Mudgett, 247; see also Mudgett, 246–249.

189. "*Oh, he is a fellow*: Franke, 105.

189. "*lady of refinement*: *Chicago Tribune*, July 28, 1895.

189. "*The day after*: Franke, 104.

190. *Soon afterward*: *Chicago Tribune*, July 31, 1895; *Philadelphia Public Ledger*, July 31, 1895.

190. "*This," said Dr. B. J. Cigrand*: *Philadelphia Public Ledger*, July 27, 1895.

190. "*I had at last*: *Chicago Tribune*, July 31, 1895.

190. *That the name Phelps*: *Chicago Tribune*, August 7, 1895.

190. *That on January 2, 1893*: *Chicago Tribune*, July 28, 1895.

190. *That a few weeks later*: Schechter, 51.

190. *Somehow a footprint*: *Chicago Tribune*, July 28, August 1, 1895.

191. *To explain the print's permanence*: *Chicago Tribune*, August 1, 1895.

"The Cold-Blooded Fact"

192. *"The winter of 1892–3*: Rice, 10, 12.

193. *George Ferris fought the cold*: Anderson, 58; Untitled typescript, Ferris Papers, 4; regarding use of dynamite, see Ulrich, 24.

193. *"No one shop*: Untitled typescript, Ferris Papers, 3; Anderson, 55, 57; Meehan, 30.

194. *Together with its fittings*: "Report of Classified and Comparative Weights of Material Furnished by Detroit Bridge & Iron Works for the 'Ferris Wheel,' " Ferris Papers.

194. *"You will have heard*: Stevenson, 416.

195. *"It looks as if*: Olmsted to John, February 17, 1893, Olmsted Papers, Reel 22.

195. *"I have never before*: Olmsted to Ulrich, March 3, 1893, ibid., Reel 41.

197. *"This seems to be an impossibility*: Bancroft, 67.

Acquiring Minnie

I base my conclusions about Holmes's motivation on studies of psychopaths conducted throughout the twentieth century. Holmes's behavior—his swindles, his multiple marriages, his extraordinary charm, his lack of regard for the difference between right and wrong, and his almost eerie ability to detect weakness and vulnerability in others—fits with uncanny precision descriptions of the most extreme sorts of psychopaths. (In the late twentieth century psychiatrists officially abandoned the term *psychopath* and its immediate successor term *sociopath* in favor of *antisocial personality disorder*, though the term *psychopath* remains the favored everyday description.)

For an especially lucid discussion of psychopaths see Dr. Hervey Cleckley's pioneering *The Mask of Sanity*, published in 1976. On page 198 he cites "the astonishing power that nearly all psychopaths and part-psychopaths have to win and to bind forever the devotion of woman." See also *Diagnostic and Statistical Manual of Mental Disorders*, 4th ed., 645–60; Wolman, 362–68; Millon et al., throughout but especially 155, which quotes Philippe Pinel's appraisal of psychopathic serial killers: "Though their crimes may be sickening, they are not sick in either a medical or a legal sense. Instead, the serial killer is typically a sociopathic personality who lacks internal control—guilt or conscience—to guide his own behavior, but has an excessive need to control and dominate others. He definitely knows right from wrong, definitely realizes he has committed a sinful act, but simply doesn't care about his human prey. The sociopath has never internalized a moral code that prohibits murder. Having fun is all that counts."

Also in Millon et al., at page 353, a contributing author describes a particular patient named Paul as having "an uncanny ability to identify naïve, passive and vulnerable women—women who were ripe for being manipulated and exploited."

For details of the Williams case I relied, once again, on an array of newspaper articles, and on Boswell and Thompson, Franke, and Schechter. See *Chicago Tribune*, July 20, 21, 27, 31, August 4, 7, 1895; *New York Times*, July 31, 1895; *Philadelphia Public Ledger*, November 21, 23, 26, 1894, December 22, 1894, July 22, 24, 27, 29, 1895: Boswell and Thompson, 86–90; Franke, 106–109; Schechter, 58–63.

198. *Silver Ash Institute*: *Chicago Tribune*, July 27, 1895.

198. *as many as seventy-five*: *Chicago Tribune*, July 25, 1895.

198. *Tobey Furniture Company*: *Chicago Tribune*, July 27, 1895.

198. *French, Potter Crockery Company*: Ibid.

198. *Merchant & Co.*: *Chicago Tribune*, July 30, 1895.

199. *At the nearby Normal School*: *Chicago Tribune*, June 26, 1892.

200. *"a baby face*: Boswell and Thompson, 87.

200. *Born in Mississippi*: For various details about Minnie and Anna Williams's backgrounds, I relied heavily on the *Chicago Tribune* of July 31, 1895.

201. *Throughout 1889*: Exactly how and when Holmes courted Minnie is unclear, but it's certain he traveled to Boston to see her and that he did so often enough to have won her adoration. The *Chicago Tribune* of July 29, 1895, describes Minnie's first meeting with Holmes. See the *Tribune* of July 20, for other details, such as the date Minnie went to Boston for her education in elocution and a sketch of her subsequent travels, including her loss of $15,000 in an ill-starred attempt to establish a theatrical group. See also *Philadelphia Public Ledger*, November 22, 1894, July 27, 29, 1895.

202. *"a remarkable aptitude*: Mudgett, 45.

203. *Anna was skeptical*: Schechter, 61.

203. *"I received her wedding cards*: *Chicago Tribune*, July 28, 1895.

204. *She did so on*: *Chicago Tribune*, July 27, 31, 1895.

204. *He established'*: *Philadelphia Public Ledger*, November 21, 23, 1894.

204. *"He induced me*: *Philadelphia Public Ledger*, July 25, 1895.

205. *no record of their union*: *Philadelphia Public Ledger*, November 26, 1894.

Dreadful Things Done by Girls

206. *"money would be so plentiful*: Kiler, 61.

208. *"The crowds poured in*: Bloom, 135.

208. *Bloom thought a moment*: Ibid., 135–36.

209. *Bloom regretted*: Ibid., 135.

209. *"it is not quantity*: Dedmon, 223–24.

209. *"the mayor will not frappé*: Ibid., 224.

210. *"A Mouse Colored Ass*: Ibid.

210. *"Outside peoples already concede*: Hines, 108.

211. *"how to broil*: Hollingsworth, 155.

211. *"The breakfast table*: Ibid., 12.

211. *"If the article is black*: Ibid., 581.

211. *"Take one part muriatic acid*: Ibid., 612.

211. *"Don't sit between*: Ibid., 701.

211. *"Injections of tobacco*: Ibid., 749.

211. *"interspersed," as one visitor put it*: Miller, 420.

212. *Clarence Darrow regularly*: Tierney, 140.

212. *"You ought to begin*: Lewis, 36.

212. *"What dreadful things*: Tierney, 84.

213. *"His friends all noticed it*: Miller, 440.

214 *His quirks*: Johnson, 81–88; Poole, 158, 160, 163, 169.

214. *"the most remarkable man*: Miller, 438.

214. *"a most admirable pig*: Abbot, 212.

215. *"My Dear Mr. Trude*: Prendergast to Trude, Daniel P. Trude Papers.

The Invitation

217. *Holmes suggested*: Schechter, 61.

217. *Minnie planned to show*: I've inserted here a few of the attractions that Gilded Age visitors to Chicago found especially compelling. That Minnie planned to take her sister on such a tour is likely but not certain, as unfortunately she left no journal detailing the minutiae of her days.

Final Preparations

218. *"anxious effort*: Wheeler, 832.

219. *The menu*: Program, "Banquet to Daniel Hudson Burnham," Burnham Archives, Box 59.

220. *"Each of you knows*: Moore, *Burnham, Architect*, 74.

221. *"The scale of the whole thing*: Moore, *McKim*, 122.

221. *"I fear nothing*: Burnham to Margaret, April 6, 1893, Burnham Archives, Family Correspondence, Box 25.

221. *"I am very happy*: Burnham to Margaret, April 10, 1893, ibid.

222. *"Why do you not write*: Burnham to Margaret, April 13, 1893, ibid.

222. *"The public will regard*: Ibid.

222. *Margaret sent him*: Burnham to Margaret, April 18, 1893, ibid.

222. PILOT OF THE OCEAN: Carter, 368.

223. *At the hotel's front desk*: Ibid., 374.

223. *"You can imagine*: Burnham to Margaret, April 10, 1893, Burnham Archives, Family Correspondence, Box 25.

224. *"Every body here*: Olmsted to John, April 13, 1893, Olmsted Papers, Reel 22.

224. *"We shall have to bear*: Olmsted to John, April 15, 1893, ibid.

224. *"I am afraid*: Ibid.

224. *"Ulrich is unwittingly faithless*: Olmsted to John, May 3, 1893, ibid.

225. *"I suppose that our time is out*: Ibid.

225. *"frightful dust*: Olmsted to John, April 13, 1893, Olmsted Papers, Reel 22.

225. *"with sore throat*: Olmsted to John, April 23, 1893, ibid.

226. *"A larger force is employed*: Ibid.

226. *The odd thing was*: *Chicago Record*, December 16, 1893, in McGoorty Papers.

226. *"It rains*: Burnham to Margaret, April 18, 1893, Burnham Archives, Family Correspondence, Box 25.

227. *"Last night turned out*: Burnham to Margaret, April 20, 1893, ibid.

227. *"The weather is very bad*: Ibid.

228. *"I wrote you*: Olmsted to unidentified recipient (stamped as received and read by his firm), April 27, 1893, Olmsted Papers, Reel 22.

228. *"My ulcer has shrunk*: Ibid.

228. *"We are having bad luck*: Olmsted to John, April 27, 1893, ibid.

229. *"I don't like it at all*: Ibid.

229. *"The diet of the provisional mess*: Ibid.

229. *"I took cold*: Olmsted to unidentified recipient, April 28, 1893, ibid.

229. *"It is queer*: Ibid.

229. *"It does not look ready*: Ibid.

229. *"I get wind*: Ibid.

230. *"gross incompleteness*: Miller, 489.

231. *the World's Fair Hotel*: Schechter, 56.

PART III: IN THE WHITE CITY

Opening Day

235. *Twenty-three gleaming*: For details of the Opening Day procession: Badger, xi, xii; Burg, 111; *Chicago Tribune*, May 2, 1893; Miller, 490; Muccigrosso, 78–80; Weimann, 141–46; *The World's Fair*, 13–16, 253–63.

235. *Burnham and Davis*: The World's Fair, 254.

235. *the sun emerged*: Ibid.

236. *The farm offered omelets*: Bloom, 137.

236. *Bloom gave a nod*: The World's Fair, 255.

237. *"When the fair opened*: Starrett, 50.

237. *Twenty women fainted*: Burg, 111.

237. *Reporters lucky enough*: Ibid., 23.

237. *"Then from the* Pinta's *foretop*: The World's Fair, 257–58.

237. *Director-General Davis spoke*: Ibid., 259.

237. *Nearby stood a table*: Weimann, 241.

238. *A tall man*: Miller, 490.

238. *"As by a touch*: Badger, xii.

238. *At precisely 12:08*: Chicago Tribune, May 2, 1893.

239. *Jane Addams realized*: Badger, xi; Miller, 490.

239. *"The scene burst on me*: Frank Collier to Burnham, May 1, 1893, Burnham Archives, Box 1, File 13.

239. *The official history*: For crowd estimates, see Badger, xii; Dedmon, 226; Weimann, 242.

239. *On Tuesday, May 2*: Weimann, 556.

240. *On the night of Thursday*: Chicago Tribune, May 5, 1893.

240. *Next Chicago's Chemical National Bank*: Chicago Tribune, May 9, 1893.

240. *Three days later*: Chicago Tribune, May 19, 1893.

240. *In Brunswick, Georgia*: Ibid.

240. *In Lincoln, Nebraska*: Ibid.

240. *Olmsted had yet to complete*: Ulrich, 46–48.

241. *General Electric alone*: Chicago Tribune, May 3, 1893.

241. *"I remain fairly well*: Olmsted to John, May 15, 1893, Olmsted Papers, Reel 22.

242. *On June 5 worried depositors*: Bogart and Mathews, 395.

The World's Fair Hotel

243. *The first guests began arriving*: Boswell and Thompson write, "Every night the rooms on the two upper floors of the Castle were filled to overflowing. Holmes reluctantly accommodated a few men as paying guests, but catered primarily to women—preferably young and pretty ones of apparent means, whose homes were distant from Chicago and who had no one close to them who might make inquiry if they did not soon return. Many never went home. Many, indeed, never emerged from the castle, having once entered it" (87). Franke writes, "We do know that Holmes advertised his 'hotel' as a suitable lodging for visitors to the world's fair; that no fewer than fifty persons, reported to the police as

missing, were traced to the Castle; and that there their trail ended" (109). Schechter: "No one can say exactly how many fairgoers Holmes lured to the Castle between May and October 1893, though he appears to have filled the place to capacity on most nights" (56).

243. *He found a place*: *Chicago Tribune*, July 21, 1895.

243. *They first advertised*: Ibid.

243. *Holmes went alone*: Ibid.

244. *Holmes explained the move*: That Holmes wanted Minnie as far from the hotel as reasonably possible seems certain, given his choice of an apartment on the North Side, though exactly what he told her about the move can't be known. I propose one likely possibility.

244. *Holmes and Minnie moved*: *Chicago Tribune*, July 21, 1895.

244. *"seemed to be very attentive*: Ibid.

245. *That he often smelled*: A barber who worked in Holmes's building reported the many "queer" smells generated within. *Chicago Tribune*, July 30, 1895. In *Tribune*, July 28, 1895, a police detective states, "We have always heard of Holmes' castle as being the abode of bad odors."

Prendergast

246. *"I am a candidate*: *Chicago Record*, December 16, 1893, McGoorty Papers.

"Night Is the Magician"

247. *Only one child*: Weimann, 352. For broader discussion of daycare at the fair, see Weimann, 254–333, 349–52.

247. *Within the fair's buildings*: Burg, 206; Gladwell, 95; Miller, 494; Muccigrosso, 93, 163; Schlereth, 174, 220; Shaw, 28, 42, 49.

248. *A popular guide*: Burg, 199.

248. *"a fearful hideous thing*: Taylor, 9.

248. *"Every one about us*: Ibid., 7.

248. *"She takes a few*: Ibid., 22–23.

249. *"My Country 'Tis of Thee*: Ibid., 23.

249. *"In which building*: Dean, 335.

249. *One male visitor*: Ibid., 378.

250. *Over the six months*: Muccigrosso, 150; *The World's Fair*, 851.

250. *Often Cody upstaged*: Carter, 372–73; Downey, 168–69

251. *"A strikingly noticeable change*: *Chicago Tribune*, June 2, 1893.

252. *"No other scene*: Pierce, *As Others See Chicago*, 352.

252. *"an inexhaustible dream*: Masters, 7.

253. *"we insisted on sending*: Untitled manuscript beginning: "To him who has taken part," Burnham Archives, Box 59, File 37.

253. *"Our hour on the lagoon*: Dora Root to Burnham, undated, Burnham Archives, Box 3, File 63.

254. *The fair alone*: Hines, 117.

254. *"As the light was fading*: Polacheck, 40.

255. *"unspeakable debris*: Ingalls, 141.

255. *"Night," Ingalls wrote*: Ibid.

255. *"It was a common remark*: Schuyler, 574.

Modus Operandi

256. *And so it began*: Chicago Tribune, July 30, 1895, August 1, 1895. In the *Tribune*, July 26, 1895, Chicago's police chief states, "There is no telling how many people this man Holmes has made away with." See also *Philadelphia Inquirer*, April 12, 1896.

256. *chemical odors*: Chicago Tribune, July 30, 1895.

256. *There were inquiries*: Philadelphia Public Ledger, November 21, 1894, July 22, 1895; Franke, 106; Schechter, 233. Also see Eckert, 209–10: Eckert quotes a letter from Julia Conner's mother, dated December 22, 1892. Eckert's book, *The Scarlet Mansion*, is a novel; the letter, Eckert told me in e-mail correspondence, is real.

256. *Holmes did not kill face to face*: Chicago Tribune, July 28, 1895, where a Chicago police inspector states, "While I believe that Holmes would not dispatch a victim with an ax or other deadly weapon, I fully believe him capable of sneaking into a dark room where his victim was asleep and turning on the gas."

257. *The subsequent articulation*: Regarding the work of the "articulator," Charles Chappell, see *Chicago Tribune*, July 21, 23, 24, 25, 26, 28, 29, 30, 1895; *New York Times*, July 29, 1895; *Philadelphia Public Ledger*, July 23, 27, 29, 30, 1895; Boswell and Thompson, 81–86; Franke, 98–101; and Schechter, 39–44.

257. *He disposed of other*: Chicago Tribune, July 20, 23, 24, 25, 26, August 18, 1895; *Philadelphia Public Ledger*, July 22, 24, 25, 26, 27, 29, 30, 1895.

One Good Turn

258. *The rim arced*: The Ferris Wheel had a diameter of 250 feet but a maximum height of 264 feet because of the necessary gap between the bottom of the wheel and the ground. The Masonic Temple was 302 feet tall, but that height included a cavernous roof that rose high above the building's last rentable floor.

258. *"It is impossible*: Hawthorne, 569.

258. *"Engines have steam*: Rice to Ferris, June 8, 1893, Ferris Papers, Ferris Correspondence: Miscellaneous.

259. *"I did not trust myself to speak*: Anderson, 58.

259. *"Suddenly I was aroused*: Ibid.

260. *As the wheel began to turn*: Ibid., 60.

260. *"No carriages were as yet placed*: Ibid.

260. *"I could have yelled out*: Ibid.

260. *"The last coupling*: Rice to Ferris, June 9, 1893, Ferris Papers, Ferris Correspondence: Miscellaneous.

260. *"Your telegram stating*: Ferris to Rice, June 10, 1893, Ferris Papers, Ferris Correspondence: Miscellaneous.

261. *"rather handsome*: Weimann, 560.

262. *"Nothing could be more entertaining*: Ibid.

262. *"I realize with some bitterness*: Ibid., 262.

262. *In preparation*: Weimann, 560.

262. *She declared*: Ibid.

263. *"Her Highness*: Quoted in Wilson, 264.

263. *"I am going to leave*: Ibid., 267.

263. *"Royalty at best*: Ibid., 269.

Nannie

264. *Without even thinking*: Chicago Tribune, July 20, 1895.

264. *First Minnie and Harry*: Despite the stench and pools of blood, the Union Stock Yards were Chicago's single most compelling attraction for visitors, and tour guides did indeed lead men and women into the heart of the operation. It seems likely that Holmes would have brought Minnie and Nannie there, partly because of the yards' status, partly because he would have derived a certain satisfaction from subjecting the women to its horrors. In *The Jungle* Upton Sinclair wrote, "It was too much for some of the visitors—the men would look at each other, laughing nervously, and the women would stand with hands clenched and the blood rushing to their faces, and the tears starting in their eyes" (35). For details on the stockyards and the operation of the overhead hog-butchering line, see Sinclair, especially 34–38; all of Jablonsky; and all of Wade. Wade notes that in the year of the fair more than one million people visited the stockyards (xiv). Rudyard Kipling, in his essay "Chicago," writes, "Turning a corner, and not noting an overhead arrangement of greased rail, wheel and pulley, I ran into the arms of four eviscerated carcasses, all pure white and of a human aspect, pushed by a man clad in vehement red" (341–44, especially 342).

265. *The great fair*: I've presented one likely path, based on guidebooks from the era, maps of the fairgrounds, and reports that described the features that exposition visitors found most attractive. For details of fair exhibits, see Flinn, 96–99, 104, 113–14; *Rand McNally*, 34–36, 71, 119–20, 126.

266. *Below the chandeliers*: Rand, McNally, 119–20.

266. *Minnie and Nannie rapidly grew tired*: Tours of the Manufactures and Liberal Arts Building were said to be exhausting. One common maxim of the day held that a boy entering the building at one end would emerge from the other as an old man. *Rand, McNally & Co's. Handbook to the World's Columbian Exposition* observes, "The standing army of Russia could be mobilized under its roof" (116).

267. *"A man in Europe talks*: Flinn, 71.

267. *the Moorish Palace*: Flinn, 25; Gilbert, 114.

267. *Even the concession tickets*: For a collection of the actual tickets see Burnham Archives, Oversize Portfolio 4, Sheets 16 and 17.

268. *He bought a souvenir*: Geyer, 300.

Vertigo

269. *By Sunday evening*: Anderson, 60.

269. *"I did not enter*: Ibid.

269. *"Owing to our car*: Ibid.

270. *The car traveled*: Ibid.

270. *Gronau's first reaction*: Ibid.

270. "*. . . it seemed as if*: Ibid., 62.

270. "*It was a most beautiful sight*: Ibid.

271. "*This,*" *Gronau said*: Ibid.

271. "*God bless you*: Untitled typescript, Ferris Papers, 6.

271. "*Six more cars*: Rice to Ferris, June 12, 1893, Ferris Papers, Ferris Correspondence: Miscellaneous.

272. "*Burnham nor anyone*: Ferris to Rice, June 14, 1893, ibid.

272. "*Unwise to open*: Robert W. Hunt to Ferris, June 17, 1893, ibid.

272. "*If the directors*: Ferris to Rice, June 17, 1893, ibid.

272. "*It was about sundown*: *Chicago Tribune*, June 15, 1893.

Heathen Wanted

274. *He traveled through*: Olmsted to Burnham, June 20, 1893, Olmsted Papers, Reel 41.

274. "*Everywhere there is*: Ibid.

278. *On June 17*: *Chicago Tribune*, July 11,19, 1893.

278. "*That building gives us*: *Chicago Tribune*, July 11, 1893.

At Last

279. *At three-thirty* P.M.: Anderson, 62; Barnes, 180.

279. "*No crank will have*: *Alleghenian*, July 1, 1893.

279. "*wheels in his head*: Untitled typescript, Ferris Papers, 6.

280. "*Built in the face*: "The Ferris Wheel Souvenir," Ferris Papers, 1.

280. "*In truth, it seems too light*: *Alleghenian*, July 1, 1893.

Rising Wave

282. *By the end of June*: *Chicago Tribune*, August 1, 1893.

282. *The Roof Garden Café*: Weimann, 267.

282. *Mrs. Lucille Rodney*: Badger, 162.

282. "*Call it no more*: Besant, 533.

283. *The failure of this*: Olmsted, "Landscape Architecture."

283. *In the six months*: Rice, 85.

283. *In his official report*: Ibid., Appendix I, 2.

284. *Over the life of the fair*: Burnham, *Final Official Report*, 77–80.

284. "*half-boor, half-tightwad*: Dedmon, 232; May, 334–35, 340–41.

285. *Frank Haven Hall*: Hendrickson, 282.

286. "*he would learn far more*: Weimann, 566.

286. *When Cody learned of it*: Badger, 163–64; Weimann, 565–66.

286. "*as enthusiastic as a girl*: Weimann, 566.

286. *There was tragedy*: *Chicago Tribune*, June 27, 1893.

287. *In the week beginning*: "Ferris Wheel, Statement of Business by the Week," Ferris Papers.

287. "*short on news*: Untitled typescript, Ferris Papers, 7.

287. *Wherritt staggered*: Anderson, 66.

288. "*He seemed to take*: Polacheck, 40.

288. "*Existing conditions*: *Inland Architect and News Record*, vol. 22, no. 2 (September 1893), 24.

288. *In June two businessmen*: Chicago Tribune, June 4, 1893.
289. *"Everyone is in a blue fit*: Steeples and Whitten, 1.
289. *"What shall we do*: Muccigrosso, 183.
289. *"everything will seem small*: Weimann, 577.

Independence Day
290. *"For half a mile*: Chicago Tribune, July 5, 1895.
290. *One man began singing*: Ibid.
290. *Red lights glowed*: Ibid.
290. *"Home Sweet Home*: Ibid.
291. *At nine o'clock*: For details about the night's fireworks displays see Chicago Tribune, July 5, 1895; Burg, 43; Gilbert, 40.
291. *That night the Oker family*: Franke, 108.
292. *"Sister, brother Harry and myself*: Boswell and Thompson, 88. This letter is quoted also in Franke, 106, and Schechter, 62.
292. *"Anna had no property*: Chicago Tribune, July 30, 1895.
292. *Holmes had announced*: Schechter proposes the scenario wherein Holmes invites Anna, alone, to accompany him on a tour of the hotel. It seems likely. Another possibility is that Holmes asked for Anna's help with some last-minute clerical work at his office and recommended that Minnie stay behind in the apartment to handle final preparations for their mutual journey. Certainly Holmes would have wanted to separate the women, for he was not physically strong. His power lay in persuasion and cunning. Schechter, 62.

Worry
293. *At the fairgrounds*: See daily attendance statistics in Chicago Tribune, August 1, 1893.
293. *But the next day*: Ibid.
293. *The fair's auditor*: Chicago Tribune, August 16, 1893.
293. *The bankers were pressuring*: Chicago Tribune, August 2, 3, 1893.
293. *Estimates held*: Chicago Tribune, August 1, 1893.

Claustrophobia
Police speculated that Holmes killed Nannie and Minnie Williams in his vault. Schechter proposes this scenario: "As they got ready to leave, Holmes paused abruptly, as though struck by a sudden realization. He needed to fetch something from his vault, he explained—an important business document that he kept stored inside a safe-deposit box. It would only take a moment.

"Grasping Nannie by the hand, he led her toward the vault" (62).

Something like this must have occurred, although I think my proposal that Holmes sent her into the vault on a false errand, then followed her and shut the door, would have suited more closely his temperament. He was a killer but a cowardly one. See note above from p. 292.

That Holmes killed the women on July 5 is supported by a March 14, 1895, letter from an attorney, E. T. Johnson, who had been dispatched to hunt for the missing women. He states they left the Wrightwood house "about July 5, 1893, and none of us have ever heard from them any more" (Chicago Tribune, July 21, 1895). Taken together, this letter and Anna's happy letter to her aunt written on the evening of July 4, cited above from page 292, provide evidence that the murders did indeed occur on July 5.

296. *Two days later*: Franke, 108.

296. *"I do not know how*: *Chicago Tribune*, July 21, 1895.

296. *Also on July 7*: The *Chicago Tribune* of July 20, 1895, identifies the express company as Wells-Fargo. The *Philadelphia Public Ledger* of November 23, 1894, states that the trunk was shipped from Midlothian, Texas, on July 7, 1893.

296. *The trunk was addressed*: *Chicago Tribune*, July 20, 1895; *Philadelphia Public Ledger*, November 23, 1894.

296. *A Wells-Fargo drayman tried*: Ibid.

297. *"I want you to come*: *Chicago Tribune*, July 28, 1895; *Philadelphia Public Ledger*, July 29, 1895.

297. *"It was an awful looking place*: *Chicago Tribune*, July 28, 1895; *Philadelphia Public Ledger*, July 29, 1895.

297. *"Don't do that*: *Chicago Tribune*, July 28, 1895; *Philadelphia Public Ledger*, July 29, 1895.

297. *He gave Pitezel's wife*: *Chicago Tribune*, August 1, 1895.

298. *Holmes also surprised*: Ibid.

Storm and Fire

299. *The balloon*: *Chicago Tribune*, July 10, 1893.

300. *The sky seemed to reach*: Ibid.

300. *In the Agriculture Building*: Ibid.

300. *"It took the combined effort*: Anderson, 66.

301. *"I got some pleasure*: *Chicago Tribune*, July 10, 1893.

301. *The tower*: *Chicago Tribune*, July 11, 12, 1893.

301. *The first alarm*: Burnham, *Final Official Report*, 61, 74; *Chicago Tribune*, July 11, 1893; *Graphic*, July 15, 1893, Chicago Historical Society; *Synoptical History*, 74–77.

302. *"Never," the Fire Department reported*: *Synoptical History*, 75.

302. *"as though the gaseous*: Burnham, *Final Official Report*, 61.

302. *"I saw there was*: *Chicago Tribune*, July 11, 1893.

303. *Daniel Burnham testified*: *Chicago Tribune*, July 12, 1893

303. *On Tuesday, July 18*: *Chicago Tribune*, July 19, 1893.

303. *"The attempt to hold you*: Geraldine to Burnham, July 19, 1893, Burnham Archives, Business Correspondence, Box 1, File 32.

303. *With the stink*: *Chicago Tribune*, July 14, 1893.

304. *As if things*: *Chicago Tribune*, August 3, 1893.

304. *"no expenditures whatever*: Ibid.

Love

305. *The twenty-four teachers*: Dreiser, *Journalism*, 121.

305. *"an intense something*: Lingeman, 118.

305. *Dreiser followed the ladies*: For details about the teachers' visit to the fair, see Dreiser, *Journalism*, 121–38.

306. *"sentimental*: Lingeman, 121.

306. *"into a dream*: Ibid., 119.

306. *"If you marry now*: Ibid., 122.

306. *Couples asked permission*: Untitled typescript, Ferris Papers, 9.

307. *Georgiana Yoke*: Trial, 364.

307. *He was so alone*: Ibid., 436.
307. *"a little heart*: Ibid., 364.
307. *He cautioned, however*: Ibid., 436.
308. *Mayor Harrison too*: Abbot, 233; *Chicago Tribune*, August 24, 1893; Muccigrosso, 181.

Freaks

309. *"can only be characterized*: *Chicago Tribune*, August 3, 1893.
309. *"If the directory had seen fit*: *Chicago Tribune*, August 2, 1893.
310. *"Hundreds of newspapers*: *Chicago Tribune*, August 13, 1893.
311. *"We want to do something*: *Chicago Tribune*, August 9, 1893.
311. *Millet also organized*: *Chicago Tribune*, August 12, 1893.
311. *"Whether the apprehensions*: *Chicago Tribune*, August 11, 1893.
312. *Further enriching the affair*: *Chicago Tribune*, August 17, 1893; Downey, 168.
312. *"Chicago built the fair*: *Chicago Tribune*, August 16, 1893.
313. *At nine-fifteen that night*: *Chicago Tribune*, August 17, 1893.
313. *It was hot*: Ibid.
314. *"native costume of bark*: Ibid.
314. *The official menu*: Ibid.
315. *Attendance rose*: *Chicago Tribune*, October 10, 1893.
315. *"If Congress does not give*: *Chicago Tribune*, August 9, 1893.
315. *"Why should the wealth*: *Chicago Tribune*, August 31, 1893.

Prendergast

316. *One afternoon*: *Chicago Record*, December 16, 1893, McGoorty Papers.
316. *"No," Prendergast said*: Ibid.

Toward Triumph

317. *By ten o'clock*: Dybwad and Bliss, 38–40.
318. *"The Paris record*: Ibid., 38.
318. *"There must be a million*: Ibid., 39.
318. *The fireworks*: Ibid., 64–68.
318. *In that single day*: *Chicago Tribune*, October 10, 1893.
318. *The* Tribune *argued*: Ibid.
319. *But the best news*: Badger, 109.

Departures

320. *"You know my dislike*: Moore, *McKim*, 127.
321 *"indeed it is the ambition*: Ibid., 126.
322 *"better to have it vanish*: Boyesen, 186.
322. *"I can't come to you*: Stevenson, 415.
322. *For all of 1893*: Crook, 102.
323. *"Never before*: Bogart and Mathews, 398.
323. *The pressure*: *Philadelphia Public Ledger*, November 21, 1894.
323. *First he set fire*: *Philadelphia Public Ledger*, November 23, 1894; Boswell and Thompson, 89; Franke, 41; Schechter, 64–65.
323. *He advised the insurers*: Ibid.

324. *The guardians of Minnie*: *Philadelphia Public Ledger,* November 21, 1894; July 27, 1895; Franke, 106.

324. *In the fall of 1893*: *Philadelphia Inquirer,* May 8, 1896.

325. *Holmes fled*: Ibid.

325. *Soon afterward Holmes set out*: Geyer, 346; *Trial,* 302, 608; Franke, 213.

326. *Just before leaving*: Geyer, 346; *Trial,* 210.

Nightfall

327. *Throughout October*: *Chicago Tribune,* October 29, 1893.

327. *Twenty thousand people*: "Ferris Wheel, Statement of Business by the Week," Ferris Papers.

327. *"peer cautiously*: *Chicago Tribune,* October 25, 1893.

328. *"Look at it now*: Abbot, 228.

329. *At two o'clock*: *Chicago Tribune,* October 29, 1893.

329. *At three o'clock*: *Chicago Tribute,* December 20, 1893.

329. *In the midst of supper*: *Chicago Times,* December 14, 1893, McGoorty Papers.

330. *"It must have been*: Ibid.

331. *They argued*: *Chicago Record,* December 15, 1893, and *Chicago Daily News,* October 23, 1943, McGoorty Papers.

331. *"Lock me up*: *Chicago Record,* December 15, 1893, McGoorty Papers.

332. *"We are turning our backs*: *Chicago Tribune,* October 31, 1893.

332. *At exactly four-forty-five*: Ibid.

332. *The six hundred carriages*: *Chicago Tribune,* November 2, 1893; Miller, 101.

333. *Harrison had heard them*: *Chicago Tribune,* November 2, 1893.

333. *"The good-by*: Dean, 418.

333. *"Beneath the stars*: Pierce, *As Others See Chicago,* 357.

The Black City

334. *"The poor had come*: Herrick, 135.

334. *"What a spectacle!*: Gilbert, 211.

334. *One shows*: Hales, 47.

334. *"It is desolation*: Dean, 424.

335. *George Pullman continued*: Wish, 290.

335. *"more threatening*: Papke, 29.

335. *On July 5, 1894*: Gilbert, 210; Miller, 550.

335. *"There was no regret*: Miller, 550.

336. *"There are hundreds*: Quoted in *Chicago Tribune,* August 18, 1895.

PART IV: CRUELTY REVEALED

"Property of H. H. Holmes"

339. *Detective Frank Geyer*: For details about Geyer, I relied heavily on his book, *The Holmes-Pitezel Case,* a detailed, dispassionate, and above all accurate account of the murder of Benjamin Pitezel, and Geyer's search for Benjamin Pitezel's children. Salted throughout are copies of letters written by the children and excerpts of other valuable documents, such as interrogations and confessions. I found additional material about Geyer at the Free

Library of Philadelphia in annual reports from the city's superintendent of police included in the "Annual Message" of the city's mayor. (See City of Philadelphia, below.) These reports contain valuable bits of information, for example, the fact that for routine detective work Geyer was paired with another top detective, Thomas G. Crawford, the man who escorted Holmes to Philadelphia from Boston. On that trip Holmes asked permission to hypnotize Crawford. The detective refused. Holmes asked again, this time offering to pay $500 for the privilege—a thinly veiled bribe. Geyer and Crawford consistently ranked first or second among the city's two-man teams of detectives for the dollar value of stolen goods they recovered.

I also mined details from *The Trial of Herman W. Mudgett, Alias, H. H. Holmes,* a word-for-word transcript of the trial, with closing arguments and the appellate court's opinion. See also Franke, 61–81 and Schechter, 195–205.

340. *Geyer's assignment:* Geyer, 158–61, 171–74.

340. *Graham had thought twice:* Schechter states, "In March 1895 a fire had consumed Geyer's home, killing his beloved wife, Martha, and their only child, a blossoming twelve-year-old girl name Esther" (202).

340. *"Holmes is greatly given:* Geyer, 54.

340. *Holmes claimed:* Ibid., 53–57. The first half of Geyer's book (13–172) provides a richly detailed portrait of the insurance fraud and the murder of Benjamin Pitezel. For still more detail, see *The Trial.*

341. *The coroner:* Geyer, 33–40.

341. *"I wish you could see:* Ibid., 353–54.

341. *"Mamma have you:* Ibid., 355.

342. *"Property of H. H. Holmes:* Ibid., 158.

342. *"it did not look like:* Ibid., 173.

342. *Geyer reached Cincinnati:* Ibid., 174. Geyer devotes pages 173–298 to a nearly day-by-day account of his search.

345. *"There is really:* Ibid., 174.

345. *"I was not able:* Ibid., 180.

346. *"a very wealthy man:* Ibid., 188.

347. *"We are all well here:* Ibid., 269–70.

347. *"And I expect:* Ibid., 271.

347. *"It seems as though:* Ibid., 272.

348. *"evidently heartbroken:* Ibid., 190.

348. *"Holmes said that Howard:* Ibid., 189.

348. *"something seemed to tell me:* Ibid., 190.

349. *Geyer realized:* Ibid., 213–14.

349. *"Tell mama:* Reprinted in Franke, 223–24.

350. *"So when this poor child:* Geyer, 258.

350. *"Howard," she had written:* Franke, 224.

Moyamensing Prison

351. *"The great humiliation:* Mudgett, 215.

351. *"and to keep my watch:* Ibid., 216.

352. "*Come with me*: Ibid., 5.

352. *It is one of the defining*: Diagnostic, 646; Karpman, 499; Silverman, 21, 28, 32–33.

352. "*prison diary*: Mudgett, 210. His supposed diary appears on 211–21.

353. "*I was as careful*: Letter reprinted in Geyer, 163–71.

The Tenant

354. *On Sunday, July 7, 1895*: Geyer, 214.

356. "*This seemed too good*: Ibid., 230.

357. "*Only a slight hole*: Philadelphia Public Ledger, August 5, 1895.

357. "*We lifted her*: Geyer, 233.

357. *Nellie's feet*: Schechter, 224.

358. "*I told her*: Geyer, 244.

358. "*Where is Nellie?*: Ibid., 245.

358. "*Nothing could be more*: Ibid., 250.

358. "*one of the most satisfactory*: Philadelphia Public Ledger, August 5, 1895.

359. "*Had he been placed*: Geyer, 251–52.

A Lively Corpse

360. *In Philadelphia*: Barlow's attempt to catch Holmes by surprise is detailed in *Philadelphia Public Ledger*, July 17, 1895.

360. "*and I hardly opened it*: Mudgett, 226.

361. "*genius for explanation*: Philadelphia Public Ledger, July 17, 1895.

361. "*I was in no condition*: Mudgett, 227.

361. "*My ideas are*: Boswell and Thompson, 112–13.

"All the Weary Days"

363. "*The number of mysterious persons*: Geyer, 268.

363. "*Days came and passed*: Ibid., 269.

364. *at two hundred*: Boswell and Thompson, 87; Franke, 109.

364. *Chicago detectives*: The search of Holmes's castle conducted by Chicago police was heavily reported in the nation's newspapers. See *Philadelphia Public Ledger*, July 22, 25, 26, 27, 29, 30, 1895; *Chicago Tribune*, July 17, 21, 23, 25, 27, 28, 29, August 18, 1895; and *New York Times*, July 25, 26, 29, 31, 1895.

365. "*Do you ever see*: Chicago Tribune, July 26, 1895.

365. *One* Tribune *headline*: Chicago Tribune, July 20, 1895.

366. "*all,*" *Geyer said*: Geyer, 283.

366. "*I must confess*: Ibid., 283–84.

366. "*The mystery*: Ibid., 284.

366. "*Holmes' Den Burned*: Chicago Tribune, August 19, 1895.

366. "*By Monday*: Geyer, 285.

367. "*I did not have the renting*: Ibid., 286.

367. "*All the toil*: Ibid., 287.

367. "*that he did not think*: Ibid., 301.

368. "*a large charred mass*: Ibid., 297.

368. *It was Howard's*: Ibid., 300.

Malice Aforethought

369. *On September 12, 1895*: For news reports on the Philadelphia, Indianapolis, and Toronto indictments, see *Philadelphia Public Ledger,* September 13, 1895.

369. *"In conclusion*: Mudgett, 255–56.

370. *"It is humiliating*: Quoted in *Literary Digest,* vol. 11, no. 15 (1896) 429.

370. *Chicago's "feeling of humiliation*: Ibid.

370. *One of the most surprising*: *Chicago Tribune,* July 30, 1895.

370. *"He is a prodigy*: Schechter, 228.

EPILOGUE: THE LAST CROSSING

The Fair

373. *Walt Disney's father*: Mosley, 25–26; Schickel, 46.

373. *The writer L. Frank Baum*: Adams, 115; Updike, 84–85.

373. *The Japanese temple*: Miller, 549.

373. *The fair prompted*: Jahn, 22.

373. *Even the Lincoln Memorial*: The fair's success boosted Burnham's prestige and helped get him appointed to the federal commission charged with building the monument. His own devotion to classical styles then held sway. See page 389 and corresponding note below. Also see Hines, 154–57.

374. *"our people out*: Moore, *McKim,* 245.

374. *"possibilities of social beauty*: Hines, 120.

374. *William Stead recognized*: Whyte, 53.

374. *They asked Burnham*: Hines, 140, 180–83, 188–89, 190–91. See also Burnham and Bennett, *Plan*; Burnham and Bennett, *Report*; McCarthy, "Chicago Businessmen."

374. *While helping design*: Hines, 148–49.

374. *Other cities came to Daniel Burnham*: Hines, 347.

375. *"If I told you*: Crook, 112. See Crook throughout for an excellent if dry account of Sullivan's decline after the world's fair—dry because the work is a doctoral thesis.

375. *"Louis Sullivan called*: Hines, 232.

375. *"To Daniel H. Burnham*: Ibid.

376. *"contagion*: Sullivan, Louis, 321, 324.

376. *"virus*: Ibid., 324

376. *"progressive cerebral meningitis*: Ibid.

376. *"Thus Architecture died*: Ibid., 325.

376. *Both Harvard and Yale*: Hines, 125.

377. *"He needs to know*: Ibid., 254, 263.

377. *"What was done*: Daniel Burnham, "Biography of Daniel Hudson Burnham of Chicago," Moore Papers, Speech, Article and Book File, Burnham 1921, Proofs and Biographical Sketches.

377. *"It was questioned by many*: Ellsworth to Moore, February 8, 1918, Moore Papers, Speech, Article and Book File, Burnham Correspondence, 1848–1927, Box 13, File 2.

377. *In 1901 Burnham built*: Hines, 288.

377. *Of the twenty-seven buildings*: Lowe, 122.

378. *"Up to our time*: Hines, 351.

378. *"I thought the fair*: Burnham to Margaret, April 7, 1894, Burnham Archives, Family Correspondence, Box 25, File 5.

378. *"If I were able*: Edward H. Bennett, "Opening of New Room for the Burnham Library of Architecture," October 8, 1929, Burnham Archives, Box 76.

378. *"You'll see it lovely*: Undated biography, Burnham Archives, Box 28, File 2.

Recessional

379. *"It has today*: Olmsted, May 10, 1895, memory no longer to be trusted.

379. *That summer*: Stevenson, 424.

379. *"the bitterest week*: Rybczynski, *Clearing*, 407.

379. *"You cannot think*: Ibid.

379. *He beat the family horse*: Roper, 474.

379. *"They didn't carry out*: Ibid.

379. *His wife*: Rybczynski, *Clearing*, 411.

380. *In the autumn of 1896*: Anderson, 75.

380. *On November 17*: Ibid., 75.

380. *"The request of Mrs. Ferris*: Ibid., 77.

380. *"miscalculated his powers*: Ibid., 75.

380. *In 1903*: For details on the fate of Ferris's wheel, see Anderson, 77–81.

381. *"But one thing*: Bloom, 143.

381. *The fair made Buffalo Bill*: Carter, 376; Monaghan, 422.

381. *He died in Denver*: Monaghan, 423.

382. *"I went to Jackson Park*: Lingeman, 114.

382. *"It means so much*: Hines, 266–67.

383. *"No one should be*: Prendergast to Alfred Trude (the letter is dated February 21, 1893, but the date is clearly incorrect, as the letter was written after his conviction; the return address is the Cook County Jail), Trude Papers.

383. *"a poor demented imbecile*: Darrow, 425.

383. *"I am sorry for all fathers*: Weinberg, 38.

383. *They dumped*: Darrow, 228.

383. *In New York*: Legend holds that a notorious belly dancer named Little Egypt made her debut at the world's fair. Sol Bloom says she was never there (Bloom, 137). Donna Carlton, in *Looking for Little Egypt*, says it's possible a dancer named Little Egypt was indeed at the fair but that many dancers adopted the name. Some sources also claim that Little Egypt's name was Farida Mazhar. (Half a dozen spellings exist; I've chosen this one.) About all that can be said with certainty is that a dancer named Farida Mazhar likely did appear at the fair. Carlton says she "probably performed" (74) on the Midway and cites a source who contends that Farida believed "'the title of Little Egypt belonged to her.'" George Pangalos, the impresario who brought the Street in Cairo to the Midway, stated publicly that he hired Mazhar to dance at his concession in the Midway and that she was considered one of the finest dancers in Cairo. And columnist Teresa Dean describes a visit to the theater in the Street in Cairo where she saw "Farida, the pretty girl who goes through her contortions" (157). In any event a young woman using the name Little Egypt apparently did pop out of a whipped-cream pie in New York several years after the fair, at a stag party that became so notorious it was called the Awful Seeley Dinner. Its host was

Herbert Barnum Seeley, a nephew of the late P. T. Barnum, who threw the party on behalf of his brother, Clinton Barnum Seeley, who was about to be married (Carlton, 65).

Holmes

384. *"There was a red fluid*: Trial, 117.

384. *"I would ask*: Ibid., 124.

384. *"It was an expression*: Philadelphia Public Ledger, October 31, 1895.

385. *"I saw them at Toronto*: Trial, 297.

385. *"the most dangerous man*: Schechter, 315.

385. *"That he fully intended*: Geyer, 317.

385. *"I am convinced*: Philadelphia Inquirer, April 12, 1896.

385. *"Here I left them*: Ibid.

386. *"It will be understood*: Ibid.

386. *His lawyers turned down*: Franke, 189.

386. *The Wistar Institute*: Philadelphia Inquirer, May 10, 1896.

386. *"The man was something*: Ibid.

386. *"Take your time, old man*: Philadelphia Inquirer, May 8, 1896. The *Philadelphia Public Ledger* of the same date offers a slightly different version: "Don't be in a hurry, Aleck. Take your time."

387. *"Holmes' idea*: Philadelphia Inquirer, May 8, 1896.

387. *Strange things*: I derived this account mainly from news clippings gathered as an appendix in Holmes's memoir. See Mudgett, after page 256. Schechter offers a nice distillation of these strange events on 333–37.

387. *No stone*: My observations.

387. *In 1997*: Stewart, 70.

Aboard the *Olympic*

389. *"But—I know*: Burnham to Millet, April 12, 1912, Moore Papers, Speech, Article and Book File, Burnham Correspondence, 1848–1927. Box 13, File 1.

389. *Hon. F. D. Millet*: Envelope, April 11, 1912, ibid.

390. *The builder of both ships*: Lynch, 159.

390. *"I think it is nothing serious*: Whyte, 314.

390. *"Frank Millet, whom I loved*: Hines, 359.

390. *As he and his family traveled*: Hines, 360, 433.

390. *Both are buried*: My observations. See also Hucke and Bielski, 13–30.

BIBLIOGRAPHY

Abbot, Willis John. *Carter Henry Harrison: A Memoir.* Dodd, Mead, 1895.

Adams, Henry. *The Education of Henry Adams.* Modern Library, 1999 (1918).

Adams, Rosemary. *What George Wore and Sally Didn't.* Chicago Historical Society, 1998.

Anderson, Norman D. *Ferris Wheels: An Illustrated History.* Bowling Green State University Popular Press, 1992. Chicago Historical Society.

Badger, Reid. *The Great American Fair.* Nelson Hall, 1979.

Baker, Charles. *Life and Character of William Taylor Baker, President of the World's Columbian Exposition and of the Chicago Board of Trade.* Premier Press, 1908.

Baker, Paul R. *Richard Morris Hunt.* MIT Press, 1980.

Bancroft, Hubert Howe. *The Book of the Fair.* Bancroft Co., 1893.

Barnes, Sisley. "George Ferris' Wheel, The Great Attraction of the Midway Plaisance," *Chicago History,* vol. 6, no. 3 (Fall 1977). Chicago Historical Society.

Besant, Walter. "A First Impression." *Cosmopolitan,* vol. 15, no. 5 (September 1893).

Bloom, Sol. *The Autobiography of Sol Bloom.* G. P. Putnam's Sons, 1948.

Bogart, Ernest Ludlow, and John Mabry Mathews. *The Modern Commonwealth, 1893–1918.* Illinois Centennial Commission, 1920.

Boswell, Charles, and Lewis Thompson. *The Girls in Nightmare House.* Fawcett, 1955.

Boyesen, Hjalmar Hjorth. "A New World Fable." *Cosmopolitan,* vol. 16, no. 2 (December 1893).

Brinnin, John Malcolm. *The Sway of the Grand Saloon.* Delacorte Press, 1971.

Burg, David F. *Chicago's White City of 1893.* University of Kentucky Press, 1976.

Burnham, Daniel H. Archives, 1943.1, Series I–IX, Art Institute of Chicago.

———. *The Design of the Fair.* Report. Burnham Archives, Box 58.

———. *The Final Official Report of the Director of Works of the World's Columbian Exposition.* Garland, 1989.

Burnham, Daniel H., and Edward H. Bennett. *Plan of Chicago.* Da Capo Press, 1970 (1909).

———. *Report on a Plan for San Francisco.* Urban Books, 1971 (1906).

Burnham, Daniel H., and Francis Davis Millet. *The Book of the Builders.* Columbian Memorial Publication Society, 1894.

Carlton, Donna. *Looking for Little Egypt.* IDD Books, undated.

Carter, Robert A. *Buffalo Bill Cody: The Man Behind the Legend.* John Wiley & Sons, 2000.

Catalogue of 200 Residence Lots. Chicago Real Estate Exchange, 1881. Chicago Historical Society.

City of Philadelphia. "Report of the Superintendent of Police," in *First Annual Message of Charles F. Warwick, Mayor of the City of Philadelphia.* (For the year ended December 31, 1895.) Free Library of Philadelphia.

———."Report of the Superintendent of Police," in *Fourth Annual Message of Edwin S. Stuart, Mayor of the City of Philadelphia.* (For the year ended December 31, 1894.) Free Library of Philadelphia.

Cleckley, Hervey. *The Mask of Sanity.* C. V. Mosby, 1976.

Commager, Henry Steele. *The American Mind.* Yale University Press, 1950.

Crook, David Heathcote. *Louis Sullivan, The World's Columbian Exposition and American Life.* Unpublished thesis, Harvard University, 1963.

Darrow, Clarence. *The Story of My Life.* Charles Scribner's Sons, 1934.

Dean, Teresa. *White City Chips.* Warren Publishing Co., 1895. Chicago Historical Society.

Dedmon, Emmett. *Fabulous Chicago.* Atheneum, 1981.

Diagnostic and Statistical Manual of Mental Disorders, 4th ed. American Psychiatric Association.

Douglas, John, and Mark Olshaker. *The Anatomy of Motive.* Pocket Books, 1999.

———. *The Cases That Haunt Us.* Scribner, 2000.

Downey, Dennis B. *A Season of Renewal: The Columbian Exposition and Victorian America.* Praeger, 2002.

Dreiser, Theodore. *Journalism.* Edited by T. D. Nostwich. Vol. 1. University of Pennsylvania Press, 1988.

———. *Sister Carrie.* Penguin, 1994 (1900).

Dybwad, G. L., and Joy V. Bliss. *Chicago Day at the World's Columbian Exposition.* The Book Stops Here (Albuquerque), 1997.

Eaton, John P., and Charles A. Haas. *Falling Star.* W. W. Norton, 1990.

Eckert, Alan W. *The Scarlet Mansion.* Little, Brown, 1985.

The Englewood Directory. George Amberg & Co, 1890. Chicago Historical Society.

Ferris, George Washington Gale. Papers. Chicago Historical Society.

Flinn, John. *Official Guide to the World's Columbian Exposition.* Columbian Guide Co., 1893.

Franke, David. *The Torture Doctor.* Hawthorn Books, 1975.

Geyer, Frank P. *The Holmes-Pitezel Case.* Frank P. Geyer, 1896.

Gilbert, James. *Perfect Cities: Chicago's Utopias of 1893.* University of Chicago Press, 1991.

Gladwell, Malcolm. "The Social Life of Paper." *New Yorker.* March 25, 2002.

Hales, Peter. *Constructing the Fair. Platinum Photographs by C. D. Arnold.* Art Institute of Chicago, 1993.

Hall, Lee. *Olmsted's America.* Little, Brown, 1995.

Hawthorne, Julian. "Foreign Folk at the Fair." *Cosmopolitan,* vol. 15, no. 5 (September 1893).

Hendrickson, Walter B. "The Three Lives of Frank H. Hall." *Journal of the Illinois State Historical Society,* vol. 49, no. 3 (Autumn 1956).

Herrick, Robert. *The Web of Life.* Grosset & Dunlap, 1900.

Hines, Thomas S. *Burnham of Chicago.* Oxford University Press, 1974.

Hollingsworth, Adelaide. *The Columbia Cook Book.* Columbia Publishing Co., c.1893.

Hoyt, Homer. *One Hundred Years of Land Values in Chicago.* University of Chicago Press, 1933.

Hucke, Matt, and Ursula Bielski. *Graveyards of Chicago.* Lake Claremont Press, 1999.

Ingalls, John J. "Lessons of the Fair." *Cosmopolitan*, vol. 16, no. 2 (December 1893).

Jablonsky, Thomas J. *Pride in the Jungle: Community and Everyday Life in Back of the Yards Chicago*. Johns Hopkins University Press, 1993.

Jahn, Raymond. *Concise Dictionary of Holidays*. Philosophical Library, 1958.

Johnson, Claudius O. *Carter Henry Harrison I: Political Leader*. University of Chicago Press, 1928.

Karpman, Ben. "The Problem of Psychopathies." *Psychiatric Quarterly*, vol. 3 (1929).

Kiler, Charles Albert. *On the Banks of the Boneyard*. Illinois Industrial University, 1942.

Kipling, Rudyard. "Chicago." *Kipling's Works*. "Sahib Edition." Vol. 6 (undated). Author's collection.

Lewis, Arnold. *An Early Encounter with Tomorrow*. University of Illinois, 1997.

Lingeman, Richard. *Theodore Dreiser*. G. P. Putnam's Sons, 1986.

Lowe, David. *Lost Chicago*. Houghton Mifflin, 1975.

Lynch, Don. *Titanic: An Illustrated History*. Hyperion, 1992.

Masters, Edgar Lee. *The Tale of Chicago*. G. P. Putnam's Sons, 1933.

May, Arthur J. "The Archduke Francis Ferdinand in the United States." *Journal of the Illinois State Historical Society*, vol. 39, no. 3 (September 1946).

McCarthy, Michael P. "Chicago Businessmen and the Burnham Plan." *Journal of the Illinois State Historical Society*, vol. 63, no. 3 (Autumn 1970).

——. "Should We Drink the Water? Typhoid Fever Worries at the Columbian Exposition." *Illinois Historical Journal*, vol. 86, no. 1 (Spring 1993).

McGoorty, John P. Papers. Chicago Historical Society.

Meehan, Pat. "The Big Wheel." *University of British Columbia Engineer*, vol. 5 (1965).

Merck's Manual of the Materia Medica. Merck & Co., 1899.

Miller, Donald L. *City of the Century*. Simon & Schuster, 1996.

Millet, F. D. "The Decoration of the Exposition." *Harper's*, vol. 12, no. 6 (December 1892).

Millon, Theodore, et al. *Psychopathy: Antisocial, Criminal, and Violent Behavior*. Guilford Press, 1998.

Monaghan, James. "The Stage Career of Buffalo Bill." *Journal of the Illinois State Historical Society*, vol. 31, no. 4 (December 1938).

Monroe, Harriet. *A Poet's Life*. Macmillan, 1938.

——. *John Wellborn Root: A Study of His Life and Work*. Prairie School Press, 1896.

Moore, Charles. Burnham interview, Burnham Archives, 1943.1, World's Columbian Exposition, Box 59.

——. *Daniel H. Burnham, Architect, Planner of Cities*. Vols. 1 and 2. Houghton Mifflin, 1921.

——. *The Life and Times of Charles Follen McKim*. Da Capo, 1970 (1929).

——. Papers. Library of Congress.

Morgan, H. Wayne. " 'No, Thank You, I've Been to Dwight': Reflections on the Keeley Cure for Alcoholism." *Illinois Historical Journal*, vol. 82, no. 3 (Autumn 1989).

Morrison, Hugh. *Louis Sullivan: Prophet of Modern Architecture*. W.W. Norton, 1998.

Mosley, Leonard. *Disney's World*. Scarborough House, 1990.

Muccigrosso, Robert. *Celebrating the New World: Chicago's Columbian Exposition of 1893*. Ivan R. Dee, 1993.

Mudgett, Herman W. *Holmes' Own Story*. Burk & McFetridge, 1895. Library of Congress.

Olmsted, Frederick Law. "The Landscape Architecture of the World's Columbian Exposition." *Inland Architect and News Record,* vol. 22, no. 2 (September 1893).

———. Papers. Library of Congress.

———. *Report on Choice of Site of the World's Columbian Exposition.* Reprinted in Jack Tager and Park Dixon Goist, *The Urban Vision.* Dorsey Press, 1970.

Papke, David Ray. *The Pullman Case.* University Press of Kansas, 1999.

Pierce, Bessie Louise. *A History of Chicago,* vol. 3. Alfred A. Knopf, 1957.

Pierce, Bessie Louise, ed. *As Others See Chicago: Impressions of Visitors, 1673–1933.* University of Chicago Press, 1933.

Polacheck, Hilda Satt. *I Came a Stranger: The Story of a Hull-House Girl.* Edited by Dena J. Polacheck Epstein. University of Illinois Press, 1991.

Poole, Ernest. *Giants Gone: Men Who Made Chicago.* Whittlesey/McGraw-Hill, 1943.

Rand, McNally & Co.'s Handbook to the World's Columbian Exposition. Rand, McNally, 1893.

Rice, Edmund. *Report of the Columbian Guard.* World's Columbian Exposition, Chicago. 1894. Chicago Historical Society.

Roper, Laura Wood. *FLO: A Biography of Frederick Law Olmsted.* Johns Hopkins, 1973.

Rybczynski, Witold. *A Clearing in the Distance: Frederick Law Olmsted and America in the 19th Century.* Touchstone/Simon & Schuster, 1999.

———. *The Look of Architecture.* New York Public Library/Oxford University Press, 2001.

Sandweiss, Eric. "Around the World in a Day." *Illinois Historical Journal,* vol. 84, no. 1 (Spring 1991).

Schechter, Harold. *Depraved.* Pocket Books, 1994.

Schickel, Richard. *The Disney Version.* Simon & Schuster, 1968.

Schlereth, Thomas J. *Victorian America: Transformations in Everyday Life, 1876–1915.* HarperCollins, 1991.

Schuyler, Montgomery. *American Architecture and Other Writings,* vol. 2. Belknap Press/Harvard University Press, 1961.

Shaw, Marian. *World's Fair Notes: A Woman Journalist Views Chicago's 1893 Columbian Exposition.* Pogo Press, 1992. Chicago Historical Society.

Silverman, Daniel. "Clinical and Electroencephalographic Studies on Criminal Psychopaths." *Archives of Neurology and Psychiatry.* vol. 30, no. 1 (July 1943).

Sinclair, Upton. *The Jungle.* University of Illinois, 1988 (1906).

Sinkevitch, Alice, ed. *AIA Guide to Chicago.* Harvest/Harcourt Brace, 1993.

Smith, F. Hopkinson. "A White Umbrella at the Fair." *Cosmopolitan,* vol. 16, no. 2 (December 1893).

Starrett, Paul. *Changing the Skyline.* Whittlesey House, 1938.

Steeples, Douglas, and David O. Whitten. *Democracy in Desperation: The Depression of 1893.* Greenwood Press, 1998.

Stevenson, Elizabeth. *Park Maker: A Life of Frederick Law Olmsted.* Macmillan, 1977.

Stewart, James. "The Bench: A Murderer's Plea." *New Yorker.* September 18, 2000.

Sullivan, Gerald E., ed. *The Story of Englewood, 1835–1923.* Englewood Business Men's Association, 1924.

Sullivan, Louis H. *The Autobiography of an Idea.* Dover Publications, 1956 (1924).

A Synoptical History of the Chicago Fire Department. Benevolent Association of the Paid Fire Department, Chicago, 1908. Chicago Historical Society.

Taylor, D. C. *Halcyon Days in the Dream City,* 1894. Chicago Historical Society.

Tierney, Kevin. *Darrow: A Biography.* Thomas Y. Crowell, 1979.

Town of Lake Directory. George Amberg and Co., 1886. Chicago Historical Society.

The Trial of Herman W. Mudgett, Alias, H. H. Holmes. George T. Bisel, 1897.

Trude, Daniel P. Papers. Chicago Historical Society.

Ulrich, Rudolf. *Report of Superintendent. Landscape, Road and Miscellaneous Departments.* Burnham Archives, 1943.1, Box 58.

Updike, John. "Oz Is Us." *New Yorker.* September 25, 2000.

Wade, Louise Carroll. *Chicago's Pride: The Stockyards, Packingtown, and the Environs in the Nineteenth Century.* University of Illinois Press, 1987.

Weimann, Jeanne Madeline. *The Fair Women.* Academy Chicago, 1981.

Weinberg, Arthur, ed. *Attorney for the Damned.* Simon & Schuster, 1957.

Wheeler, Candace. "A Dream City." *Harper's,* vol. 86, no. 516 (May 1893).

The White Star Triple Screw Atlantic Liners, Olympic and Titanic. Ocean Liners of the Past. Patrick Stephens, Cambridge, 1983.

Whyte, Frederic. *The Life of W. T. Stead,* vol. 2. Houghton Mifflin, 1925.

Wilson, Robert E. "The Infanta at the Fair." *Journal of the Illinois State Historical Society,* vol. 59, no. 3 (Autumn 1966).

Wish, Harvey. "The Pullman Strike: A Study in Industrial Warfare." *Journal of the Illinois State Historical Society,* vol. 32, no. 3 (September 1939).

Wolman, Benjamin B., ed. *International Encyclopedia of Psychiatry, Psychology, Psycho-analysis, and Neurology,* vol. 10. Aesculapius Publishers/Van Nostrand, 1977.

The World's Fair, Being a Pictorial History of the Columbian Exposition. Chicago Publication and Lithograph, 1893. Chicago Historical Society.

Wyckoff, Walter A. *The Workers: An Experiment in Reality.* Charles Scribner's Sons, 1899.

ACKNOWLEDGMENTS

THIS IS MY THIRD BOOK with Crown Publishers and with my editor, Betty Prashker, who once again proved herself to be one of New York's supreme editors—confident, obliquely forceful, always reassuring. Every writer needs support, and she gave it unstintingly. Every book also needs support, and once again Crown marshaled a team of committed men and women to help the book find its way to as many readers as possible. Thanks, here, to Steve Ross, publisher; Andrew Martin, Joan DeMayo, and Tina Constable, marketing wizards; and Penny Simon, the kind of veteran publicist most writers wish they had but seldom get.

I have been blessed as well with one hell of an agent, David Black, a man whose instinct for narrative drive—and excellent wine—is unparalleled. He also happens to be an excellent human being.

On the homefront my family kept me sane. I could not have written this book without the help of my wife, Christine Gleason, a doctor by profession but also one of the best natural editors I've encountered. Her confidence was a beacon. My three daughters showed me what really matters. My dog showed me that nothing matters but dinner.

Two friends, both writers, generously agreed to read the entire manuscript and offered their wise critiques. Robin Marantz Henig sent me a dozen pages of pinpoint suggestions, most of which I adopted. Carrie Dolan, one of the best and funniest writers I know, offered her criticisms in a way that made them seem like compliments. Hers is a knack that few editors possess.

Thanks also to Dr. James Raney, Seattle psychiatrist and forensic consultant, who read the manuscript and offered his diagnosis of the psychic malaise that likely drove Holmes's behavior. Gunny Harboe, the Chicago architect who led the restoration of two of Burnham & Root's remaining buildings—the Reliance and the Rookery—gave me a tour of both and showed me Burnham's library, restored to its original warmth.

Finally, a word about Chicago: I knew little about the city until I began work on this book. Place has always been important to me, and one thing today's Chicago exudes, as it did in 1893, is a sense of place. I fell in love with the city, the people I encountered, and above all the lake and its moods, which shift so readily from season to season, day to day, even hour to hour.

I must confess a shameful secret: I love Chicago best in the cold.

ILLUSTRATION CREDITS

INDEX

Note: Page numbers in *italic* type refer to illustrations.

ABOUT THE AUTHOR

Erik Larson, author of the international best-seller *Isaac's Storm,* has written for *Harper's, The New Yorker, The Atlantic Monthly,* and *Time Magazine,* where he is a contributing writer. He is a former staff writer for *The Wall Street Journal.* He lives in Seattle with his wife, three daughters, and assorted pets, including a dog named Molly.

OXFORD WORLD'S CLASSICS

AN ENEMY OF THE PEOPLE
THE WILD DUCK
ROSMERSHOLM

HENRIK IBSEN was born in 1828, the son of a Norwegian merchant, who suffered financial setbacks during the boy's childhood, causing him to be apprenticed to an apothecary at the age of 15. In 1850 Ibsen came to Christiania (Oslo) with the intention of studying at the university there, but soon abandoned this idea in order to devote himself to writing. His first play, *Catiline*, aroused little interest, but his second, *The Burial Mound*, was staged, and not unsuccessfully. He held posts as producer and resident dramatist in theatres in Bergen and Christiania successively, but his policies in the latter post were severely criticized, and in 1864 he embarked on a long period of self-imposed exile abroad with his wife and their only child, Sigurd. Recognition of Ibsen's true genius came after the publication in 1866 of the dramatic poem *Brand*, and he was at last awarded an annual grant by the Norwegian Parliament to devote himself to writing. From 1868 to 1891 he lived mainly in Dresden, Munich, and Rome, and during this period wrote most of the prose plays which established his European reputation. He returned to live in Norway in 1891, and his seventieth birthday was the occasion of national celebrations. His literary career was terminated by a stroke in 1900, and he died on 23 May 1906.

JAMES MCFARLANE, editor of the Oxford Ibsen, is Emeritus Professor of European Literature at the University of East Anglia. His publications include several critical studies of modern European and Scandinavian Literature. He is a Fellow of both the Norwegian and the Danish Academies of Science and Letters, and in 1975 was created Knight Commander of the Royal Norwegian Order of St Olav for services to Scandinavian culture.

OXFORD WORLD'S CLASSICS

For over 100 years Oxford World's Classics have brought readers closer to the world's great literature. Now with over 700 titles—from the 4,000-year-old myths of Mesopotamia to the twentieth century's greatest novels—the series makes available lesser-known as well as celebrated writing.

The pocket-sized hardbacks of the early years contained introductions by Virginia Woolf, T. S. Eliot, Graham Greene, and other literary figures which enriched the experience of reading. Today the series is recognized for its fine scholarship and reliability in texts that span world literature, drama and poetry, religion, philosophy and politics. Each edition includes perceptive commentary and essential background information to meet the changing needs of readers.

OXFORD WORLD'S CLASSICS

HENRIK IBSEN

An Enemy of the People
The Wild Duck
Rosmersholm

Translated with an Introduction by
JAMES McFARLANE

OXFORD
UNIVERSITY PRESS

OXFORD

UNIVERSITY PRESS

Great Clarendon Street, Oxford OX2 6DP

Oxford University Press is a department of the University of Oxford.
It furthers the University's objective of excellence in research, scholarship,
and education by publishing worldwide in

Oxford New York

Athens Auckland Bangkok Bogotá Buenos Aires Calcutta
Cape Town Chennai Dar es Salaam Delhi Florence Hong Kong Istanbul
Karachi Kuala Lumpur Madrid Melbourne Mexico City Mumbai
Nairobi Paris São Paulo Singapore Taipei Tokyo Toronto Warsaw

with associated companies in Berlin Ibadan

Oxford is a registered trade mark of Oxford University Press
in the UK and in certain other countries

Published in the United States
by Oxford University Press Inc., New York

First published as a World's Classics paperback 1988
Reissued as an Oxford World's Classics paperback 1999
Reissued 2009

British Library Cataloguing in Publication Data

Data available

Library of Congress Cataloging in Publication Data

Data available

ISBN 978–0–19–953913–0

3

Printed in Great Britain by
Clays Ltd, St Ives plc

CONTENTS

PREFACE

The translations in this volume are based on the Norwegian text as printed in the Centenary Edition (*Hundreårsutgave*, 1928–57), edited by Francis Bull, Halvdan Koht, and Didrik Arup Seip.

All three plays represented here have been translated a number of times before, and I have not left these earlier versions unregarded—in addition to the Archer versions, I might mention in particular those of R. Farquharson Sharp, Una Ellis-Fermor, and Eva Le Gallienne—but neither have I paid them any importunate attention, preferring to approach them more as a possible contributor to their fascinating conversation than as a potential borrower; and it is as such that I feel I owe them a general debt of gratitude for their company rather than specific debts in respect of particular items. Nevertheless, there are of course frequent coincidences, not a few of which are there as a result of a decision I early made not to alter a phrase merely because (as naturally quite often happened) it turned out to have been used in one or another of the earlier versions.

The best translation, says the man with no knowledge of the original, is one that does not read like a translation; for anybody familiar with the original, on the other hand, it is imperative that he should be reminded of it at every stage, and in every possible particular. If I have had any definable policy at all in shaping the present versions, it was to reconcile as far as I was able these two factors—making something that to the knowledgeable was recognizably a 'translation' and not a 'free-rendering' or 'adaptation' or something equally undisciplined, and yet at the same time making the lines 'sayable'. One other point may be referred to here: in deciding whether characters should address each other by first name or surname, I have chosen what seemed appropriate to the equivalent English context of situation, rather than follow the Norwegian conventions mechanically; titles, such as 'Rektor', 'Frøken', and so on, have been similarly treated; and I have also tried to exploit this device to the point where it would, I hoped, deal relatively unobtrusively with the perennial problem of 'De' and 'du', the formal and familiar modes of address.

In connection with the staging of Ibsen's plays, there is one point of some interest: 'left' and 'right' in the stage directions mean 'as seen from the point of view of the audience'. In a letter of 22 November 1884 to the Swedish actor-manager, August Lindberg, Ibsen wrote: 'In answer to your question, I hasten to inform you that *The Wild Duck* is disposed from the auditorium and not from the stage, as indeed all my plays are. I position everything as I see it in my mind's eye as I am writing it down.'

UNIVERSITY OF EAST ANGLIA   J. McF.
NORWICH.
October 1987

INTRODUCTION

It was Georg Brandes who suggested that much of *An Enemy of the People* (1882), *The Wild Duck* (1884), and *Rosmersholm* (1886) might be traced to a point of common origin: the hurt, the distress and disgust Ibsen felt at the hostile reception given in 1881 by the Norwegian public and critics to *Ghosts*. Within a year of this bitterly resented publication, Ibsen had given his answer to those who had abused him: a play (actually begun before *Ghosts* but now splendidly appropriate to the new situation) which traces the bewilderment and incredulity and ultimate exasperation of one who, for publishing unpalatable truths about the polluted sources of the community's economy, is subjected to insult and slander and even physical violence from his fellows. After thus venting his immediate anger, Ibsen in his next play allowed himself a second and more searching look at this phenomenon of a man who makes it his mission to proclaim truth; and *The Wild Duck*, in asking whether it really does add to the sum total of human happiness to put the average person in possession of the truth, redresses a balance. The tertiary stage of exasperation was reached with *Rosmersholm*, a further exploration of the theme of one whose dementia was truth, who like his earlier counterparts had improving designs on his fellows, but whose ultimate achievement is equally unavailing, though not in the same way and not for the same reasons.

Comparable though the three plays may be in this particular respect, they nevertheless vary greatly in quality. *An Enemy of the People* generally ranks as one of the thinnest of Ibsen's maturer works, one which, to use William Archer's phrase, is 'not so richly woven, not as it were, so deep in pile'. Archer goes on: 'Written in half the time Ibsen usually devoted to a play, it is an outburst of humorous indignation, a *jeu d'esprit*, one might almost say, though the *jeu* of a giant *esprit*.... *An Enemy of the People* is a straightforward spirited melody; *The Wild Duck* and *Rosmersholm* are subtly and intricately harmonized.'[1] The two latter plays are often to be observed in the critics' estimates vying with each other as rivals for the top place among Ibsen's works: Nils Kjær's characterization of *The Wild Duck* as 'the master's masterpiece' has been echoed many times in the critical studies of recent decades; and

[1] *Play-Making* (London 1912), p. 79.

it is repeatedly claimed on behalf of *Rosmersholm* that never was Ibsen's constructional skill more confidently or more successfully exploited.

To plot these three dramas against the co-ordinates of technique and ultimate meaning provides evidence, however, of something more than the mere amplification, or even enrichment, of things already there in essence at the beginning; it is to testify also, and more importantly, to a distinct turning-point in Ibsen's authorship, a change of direction arguably no less profound and no less significant than his earlier abandonment of verse as the medium of his dramas in favour of prose. As a rule it was only with the greatest reluctance that Ibsen was ever drawn to comment on his own work; his letters to his publisher and to his friends tended to harden into a drily formal, almost communiqué-like phraseology whenever it was a question of reporting progress on his own work: a bare admission that he *was* busy, a hint of whether or not the thing had a contemporary theme, a forecast of the number of acts it would be in, and (for his publisher) perhaps an estimated time for completion, or some indication of the number of printed pages it would fill. Rarely was there anything else of much significance. It is precisely this habitual uncommunicativeness that makes his unsolicited comment on *The Wild Duck* the rather startling thing it is: writing to his publisher on 2 September 1884, he was moved to admit that he thought of this new work of his as something rather special, adding that his methods were new, and that some of the country's younger dramatists might possibly be encouraged by them to launch out along new tracks. It is therefore not without a certain measure of approval from Ibsen himself that one is tempted to consider *An Enemy of the People* as the culmination of a distinct 'period' in the dramatist's career, as something that set a terminus to the line of the development that had begun with *Pillars of Society* in 1877, and had continued by way of *A Doll's House* (1879) and *Ghosts* (1881). There is encouragement also to see *Rosmersholm* as the inauguration of the later mode of composition serving the group of plays that marked the end of his career: *The Lady from the Sea* (1888), *Hedda Gabler* (1890), *The Master Builder* (1892), *Little Eyolf* (1894), *John Gabriel Borkman* (1896), and *When We Dead Awaken* (1899). And—intractable, transitional, between two 'periods'—*The Wild Duck*, composed at a time when its author's dramatic *credo* was profoundly changing.

The pace of *An Enemy of the People* is unusual for Ibsen; elsewhere, at least in the later dramas, the progression is purposefully deliberate, like an exploratory advance over uncertain country which has had careful preliminary study but no close reconnaissance. In this play, by contrast, the advance is conducted with eager exuberance, moving over ground familiar as it might be from regular patrol activity, and not seeming to care greatly if on occasion it happens to put a foot wrong. Part of the terrain had in fact been one of Ibsen's favourite stamping-grounds for over ten years, if not longer: a hatred, carefully nurtured in correspondence and in conversation, of anything in the way of party or association or society or indeed any identifiable grouping that went in for 'majority' practices, that invited majority decisions or accepted majority rule. As early as 1872, he had even talked enthusiastically about undermining the whole concept of state-hood, asserting that 'the state is the curse of the individual'. Such political sympathies as he had at the time were reserved for nihilists and anarchists and the extreme left-wing, from a feeling that they at least cared about the big things in life and honestly strove to realize their ideals, whilst the larger parties with their mass appeal struck him as trafficking in nothing but sham and humbug. Organized Liberalism he considered freedom's worst enemy.

To these convictions, the events of the year 1881—the hostile reception given to *Ghosts*—brought peculiar reinforcement. To his scorn of organized politics was now added a consuming contempt for the press, especially the so-called Liberal press. Ibsen was confirmed in his view that the press as then constituted was no better than a parasite on a grotesque and deformed body politic, for ever talking about freedom, but terrified of the realities of it, for ever proclaiming independence although itself merely the slave of public opinion and organized pressure-groups and its own circulation figures.

Three items, chiefly, 'seeded' his mind, super-saturated as it was by bitterness and contempt for these things; and they provided the nuclei around which the drama eventually crystallized. One was an anecdote, reported to him by a German acquaintance, Alfred Meissner, about a spa doctor who had been persecuted by his fellow-townsmen for reporting, to the great detriment of the tourist trade, a local case of cholera. Another was the incident in February 1881 involving a chemist called Harald Thaulow and the Christiania Steam Kitchens, in which Thaulow was prevented at a public meeting from reading his indictment of the management of the Kitchens and instead delivered an impromptu speech of denunciation. And the third was the person-ality of his great contemporary Bjørnstjerne Bjørnson.

The life-long relationship between these two men was marked by almost every emotion and attitude except indifference. Never was Ibsen, the self-sufficient, introverted exile, able for long to put out of his mind the image of the popular, rhetorical, extroverted Bjørnson. His feelings were always mixed—admiration, contempt, envy, exasperation, gratitude, affection, resentment, with sometimes one thing preponderating, and sometimes another. At the time Ibsen was working on *An Enemy of the People*, he had cause to think of Bjørnson with gratitude, particularly for the latter's spirited defence of *Ghosts*; and the courage, the bluff honesty, and the fundamental decency that he acknowledged in Bjørnson reappear also in his created hero, Dr. Stockmann.

But the piquancy of the situation can surely not have been lost on the author. Ibsen *à la* Bjørnson! The opportunities were too good to be missed. And there, accompanying his quite genuine regard and affection for his hero, one finds a good deal of dry mockery, directed in particular against Dr. Stockmann's simple-minded, self-opinionated interpretation of things. (One must beware, of course, of ascribing *all* Stockmann's traits to Bjørnson or even to what Ibsen might have wanted to pin on Bjørnson—the relevance is to be found rather in the author's implicit attitude to his created character, and not in the details.) Dr. Stockmann does not find it easy to relate the immediate problem to any wider context of things; his strength and his weakness lie in his simple directness, his inability to see more than one side of the question; and his brother's remonstrance that the alleged pollution cannot be regarded in isolation as a merely scientific matter but is also political and economic, is not without justification. He lacks any deeper understanding of the motives of human conduct and is even perhaps too easily misled about his own. It is no coincidence that both Stockmann and Gregers have spent much of their adult lives in remote parts, the former stuck away in Arctic Norway as a doctor, and the latter brooding 'up at the works' in Höidal for fifteen years; their conduct lacks the corrective of the 'reality principle', that which could tell them what may be presumed socially possible, and what may not.

It is precisely these temperamental and very human weaknesses in the main character, however, that prevent the drama from degenerating into a theatrical tract; and Ibsen was able to make his Kierkegaardian points about the need for individual decision, the necessity for individual responsibility, and the value of individual courage—especially the courage of one's convictions—and to enlist the sympathies of the

audience unambiguously on the side of the lone champion without at
the same time making him too offensively virtuous. Against his hero,
Ibsen marshals an alliance of vested interest, political hypocrisy, and
editorial opportunism: the Mayor, the influential representative of
entrenched authority, not without courage of a kind and horribly
experienced in the manipulation of others by veiled threat and the
promise of favour, who masks self-interest and self-preservation as 'the
common good'; Aslaksen, embodying the inherent timidity of public
opinion, and making a virtuous 'moderation' out of his essential
servility; and Hovstad, hawking his influence to the highest bidder.
These are the elements that determine the ultimate shape of the drama,
in which principles are balanced against expediency, integrity weighed
against quick profits, and the 'individual' involved in a fight against
what Hebbel was inclined to call the Idea—the reaction of those who
wish to maintain the *status quo* and the inertia and the intolerance of the
undifferentiated masses who are their dupes.

Among the earliest jottings preliminary to *The Wild Duck* are two
which make special reference to the business of growing up, the
transition from childhood to adulthood: one of them compares the
advance of civilization to a child's growing up, whereby instinct is
weakened, the power of logical thought is developed, and 'the ability
to play with dolls' is lost; the other draws a parallel between the
revisionary changes in man's attitude to his past achievements and the
way in which a child mind is absorbed into the adult spirit. This manifest interest in the phenomenon of childhood and its advance to
maturity was not without its personal side. In 1881 Ibsen had begun a
short autobiographical account which, however, never got beyond a
description of the days of his earliest childhood in Skien. One can nevertheless well imagine how his memories of those days were jogged by
this exercise: of his sister Hedvig; of his father who suffered the shame
of bankruptcy and who reduced a once prosperous family to something near penury; of the attic at Venstøp (a few miles out of Skien)
where the Ibsen family subsequently lived; of the furniture there and
the books and the other old lumber left by a previous occupant; and of
the puppet theatre, with which as a boy he had been in the habit of
devising little entertainments for family and friends. Particular details
like these can easily be picked out as having contributed to *The Wild Duck*
in fairly obvious ways; but the more reflective items in the preliminary
notes about childhood and its problems count perhaps for even more.

One way of looking at *The Wild Duck* is to see it as a dramatic commentary on the shock of growing up. The Ekdal household, seen as an entity, enjoys an innocent and child-like happiness until this is upset by its introduction, through the agency of Gregers, to a new and disturbing awareness; it gives an account of the thoughtless, brutal imposition of a new and demanding consciousness upon a ménage totally unprepared to face it, and of the sad consequences; it presents a history of shattered illusions and the destruction of make-believe, an account of what happens when a family's 'ability to play with dolls'—or as Relling puts it, its 'life-lie'—is destroyed.

Its most literal representative of childhood is, of course, Hedvig. Standing fearfully yet expectantly on the threshold of adulthood, taking a secret delight in playing with fire, she has all the genuine imaginativeness of the child, and a naïve and still active sense of mystery; responding intuitively to language's more magical powers, she is greatly impressionable and pathetically sensitive to the moods of those about her. Her death is the consequence of her being caught up in the emotional entanglements of an adult world, the result of confused loyalties; and the senselessness of her self-sacrifice and the pity of her fate are things that the drama is particularly concerned to communicate. Balancing her in the composition of the piece is Old Ekdal, who also enjoys 'the ability to play with dolls', but in his case it is the ability of one who has reached a second childhood; he enjoys dressing-up, wearing his old uniform for private and family celebrations; his enthusiasm for the surrogate reality of the attic is genuine and unassumed; helped on occasion by the brandy bottle, he can live himself without difficulty into a world of his own imagining; and his sad and —by its rather touching ridiculousness—moving presence is also an important ingredient in the whole. Between them is Hjalmar. Between the representatives of nonage and dotage, between the embodiments of the puerile and the senile is this defining figure of childishness: a child without the innocence or the sensitivity of a child, a big baby, sometimes petulant and querulous, sometimes appealing and charming, happy to let himself be spoilt by the attentions of others, skilled in tantrum but quite ready (as Hedvig knows) to be distracted by some little treat or favourite toy, by a bottle of beer or his flute. He takes refuge from the disappointments and frustrations of life in daydreams of worldly success, of clearing the family name, which provide him with a kind of substitute purposefulness. He too retains something of 'the ability to play with dolls', but it is a self-conscious, a less wholeheartedly spontaneous thing than that of Hedvig or his father; so that when he uneasily shows the loft and its contents to Gregers, he is quick to shelter behind the excuse that it is for the old man's sake.

What the drama emphasizes is that, before the coming of Gregers, this household was a generally happy one, the members of which had succeeded in amalgamating reality and dream, in bringing them both under one roof as they had conjoined their prosaic studio with their fantastic attic. Access from the one to the other was just too easy. What they do not at this stage realize is that the relative stability of their world depends on Werle's unobtrusive manipulations and the cynical adjustments of Relling. These two are the people in ultimate control, secretly supplying both the worldly goods and the stuff of fantasy without which life *chez* Ekdal would be impossible. Hidden subventions provide the material means to bear reality, inspired suggestions sustain their dream-life. That the Ekdals in return help to satisfy some craving or need in the lives of those who thus manipulate them— serving, one imagines, self-interest or conscience or cynicism or a sense of secret power—is a further integral though subsidiary element in the drama. What is important is that a balanced existence is contrived for the whole family unit, permitting all its members to fulfil themselves as completely as ever they are likely to. This existence is brought into a state of violent unbalance by the arrival of Gregers, who, seeing or suspecting something of the conspiracy that thus controls the Ekdals, feels that he has a duty to expose it; applying a moral imperative, he sets out to reveal what he regards as the dishonesty inherent in the whole situation.

Like Hjalmar, Gregers gains extra definition in the play from two flanking characters: his father Haakon Werle and Relling. To the former he stands in contrast by virtue of his lack of practical sense, his alienation from life as it is really lived; fifteen years in the backwoods is set against the father's successful business career at the centre of things; his inability even to light his own stove gives heightened emphasis to the quietly purposeful way his father, with his sure grasp of opportunity and his *savoir faire*, has organized his own life and the lives of so many of those around him. With Relling—the soul of cynicism, a maker of dreams for all but himself, whose only solution for his own problems is a good binge—the contrast is on the plane of idealism. He takes his fellows firmly by the arm, and beguiling them with pleasant fictions, leads them quietly away from their own frustrations and the jagged edges of reality; Gregers, by contrast, rubs their

noses in the truth. Gregers represents what Ibsen had by now rejected—
the principle of making universal demands regardless of person or
situation or circumstance. He is the self-elected agent of his fellows'
betterment, trafficking in truth and liberty without any sense of what is
appropriate, or of what allowances to make: liberty, wrote Ibsen in
one of the preliminary notes, 'consists in giving the individual the right
to liberate himself, each according to his personal needs'. Gregers's
approach is based on an inflexibly abstract view of life, a theorist's;
wanting the best for his fellows, and convinced of their power to
achieve it by heroic methods, he blunders in with his missionary
fervour and upsets what he does not understand. Human kind, he fails
to realize, cannot bear very much reality.

The compositional pattern of *The Wild Duck* thus poses two figures
en face, Hjalmar and Gregers, each with his two supporting figures:
Hedvig and Old Ekdal for the one, and Werle and Relling for the
other. But to resolve what would otherwise be merely a dramatic
encounter into a dramatic situation, there are cross-references and
cross-tensions. Werle is linked to the Ekdal household by former business association and (through Gina) by illicit relations and a suspected
paternity; Relling is attached to the Ekdals by his tenancy and daily
association, to Gregers by earlier acquaintance up at the works; both
are tenuously related to each other through Mrs. Sörby, and so on.
The result is a plexus of intimacies, affinities, bonds, transactions,
intrusions, importunities. It was perhaps to dispose these elements
more eloquently and to control them more effectively that Ibsen seems
to have been particularly concerned during the preliminary stages
with what one might reasonably call 'depth', a certain quality of
perspective. The drafts show how some characters were brought much
nearer the foreground, others were stood back, and some even (like
Old Ekdal's wife, for instance) taken out of the composition altogether.
Then there were others whose actual location seems to have remained
very largely unchanged yet whose focus was altered—like the three
guests at Werle's party who were originally named characters and
then later became anonymously typed; or like Mrs. Sörby who in the
first mention was an unnamed middle-aged woman. Hand in hand with
this went a certain reduction in the definition of what was supplied to
the composition by past event; facts in the final version are not things
to prove or determine or demonstrate, there is no concern to annex
certainty, but instead the design is built up by hint, allusion, suggestion
or obliquity generally: Hedvig's paternity, Ekdal's alleged crime,

Werle's treatment of his former wife, all these things are deliberately blurred in the interests of the design as a whole. Nor must one forget the extra quality of 'depth' that the language is made to sustain, the loading of it with extra and secretly shared significance, as when Gregers talks to Hedvig.

Finally, is it perhaps in some such terms that the Wild Duck itself is best explained; as something arbitrarily interposed, which additionally to its function in the drama as one of the 'Requisiten' serves also to make more explicit the relationship of the other elements in 'depth'. Because it is not difficult in the circumstances to imagine a *human* reaction without it, it gives the impression of being inserted; what really integrates it into the play is the realization that no genuinely *dramatic* reaction is possible without it. Part of its effect on the play is comparable with that produced by the traditional dramatic unities: it concentrates, it holds together a number of otherwise separate things, it permits that density by which art distinguishes itself from the more diffuse nature of life, it helps to compose the drama. To call it a 'symbol', however, is possibly to emphasize unduly the similarity of the many disparate things it is successively made to stand for: Hedvig, in its role as gift from Werle to the Ekdals; Old Ekdal, whom life has winged and who has forgotten what real life is like; Hjalmar, who has dived down deep into the mud; Gregers, who suggests that he too will soon accustom himself to his new surroundings; or the object of Gregers's mission, the thing he will, like some extraordinarily clever dog, save from the depths. It is not so much that there is some kind of identity which all these things share, there is no 'falling together' such as the etymology of 'symbol' might suggest; rather it is that the Wild Duck is at the point of convergence of a series of comparisons, the purpose of which is to enable the onlooker to discriminate among the things it serves, to sort them out rather than heap them together, and ultimately to place them in perspective. What happens is that a number of characters are moved to say, or think, or unconsciously propose: 'This or that or he or she equals the Wild Duck', so that the Wild Duck functions almost like a recurrent element in a series of simultaneous metaphorical equations about life and the living of it, a kind of 'x' quality for which a whole range of variables might be substituted in an effort to find some kind of answer to things. Express your answer (the drama seems to enjoin from those who are tempted to try to solve such problems) in terms of truth and human happiness, and comment on the degree of incompatability indicated.

One of the contributory sources of *Rosmersholm* was undoubtedly Ibsen's disappointment following his first visit to Norway for eleven years. When in the late spring of 1885 he left Italy for Norway, it was not without the hope that he might find life there congenial enough to make him want to settle; but after only four months he was away again to Munich, sickened by too many of the things he had seen and heard to want to stay in the North. 'Never have I felt more alienated by the *Tun und Treiben* of my Norwegian compatriots than after the lessons they read me last year', he wrote to Georg Brandes in November 1886. 'Never more repelled. Never more discomfited.' Many of the less admirable qualities pilloried in *Rosmersholm* have their origin in this sense of repulsion: the cruel fanaticism of Kroll, whom Ibsen created to represent extreme right-wing thought in Norway; the sacrifice of principles to expediency and party advantage that the left-wing Mortensgaard represents—both of these characters reflecting the disgust Ibsen felt for politicians, a disgust that led him in one of his notes to *The Wild Duck* to suggest that politicians and journalists might serve nicely for vivisection experiments. And there was the ineffectualness of Brendel, who with his visionary dreams and his lack of practical sense mirrored Ibsen's scorn of those who claimed to be poets in spirit, enjoying visions of great brilliance and yet nauseated, they said, by the thought of having to write it all down. Equally there is good reason to suppose that some of the more positive elements also grew out of this visit and out of the contacts he made or renewed: Carl Snoilsky, whose company he enjoyed for several days at Molde, seems to have served in some measure as the model for Rosmer; and Snoilsky's second wife provided something of Rebecca.

Above all, however, it was the pettiness and the self-seeking that he could not stomach, the air of narrow provinciality which to him seemed to characterize such a great deal of Norwegian public and private life. The speech that he delivered to a workers' meeting in Trondheim, only about a week after his arrival in the country, expressed both his impatience with democracy as it was then operating and his conviction that what was lacking was nobility of mind: 'Our democracy, as it now is [he said], is hardly in a position to deal with these problems. An element of nobility must find its way into our public life, into our government, among our representatives and into our press. Of course I am not thinking of nobility of birth nor of money, nor a nobility of learning, nor even of ability or talent. What I am thinking of is a nobility of character, of mind and of will.' These are sentiments one finds, in almost identical phrases, not only among his preliminary notes to *The Wild Duck*, but also allotted to Rosmer at that moment when he seeks to define his mission in life. Democracy is no better than the individuals who constitute it; and some form of *individual* regeneration is necessary if the ruthlessness of the party politician and the brutishness of the masses are to be vanquished.

This is one of the things Ibsen stressed when, on one of those rare occasions when he was persuaded to give an opinion about his own work, he offered an explanation of the meaning of *Rosmersholm*; in response to an inquiry from some grammar-school boys in Christiania, he agreed that the play dealt among other things with 'the need to work', but went on to draw attention to the conflict within the individual between principle and expediency, between conscience and acquisitiveness, between the 'progressive' and the 'conservative' in his nature, pointing out at the same time the difference in tempo in the way these things change. *Rosmersholm* considers the dialectics of change, and the consequences for the individuals concerned, that follow an encounter between a predominantly conservative nature and a predominantly progressive one: Rosmer, contemplative by nature, conservative by family, generous by inclination, of the highest personal integrity, and with his roots deep in a landed tradition; and Rebecca, swept along by her passions, of questionable antecedents, 'advanced' in her thinking, and with a ruthless will-power. He is stimulated by her example to act, to take personal decisions, to commit himself; and she is moved by his example to adopt some of the Rosmer scruples. Both of them have a vision of glory as the consummation of their endeavours, a glad cause, stimulating not strife but the friendly rivalry of noble minds, all splendid. But the reality of it is profound disappointment. Rebecca is 'ennobled', but in winning generosity of mind loses her power to act; Rosmer in daring to commit himself to action discovers that he has unwittingly but inevitably involved himself in guilt; and any joy they may separately have had from life is killed.

Between the policies of Rosmer and the earlier Gregers, the difference is fundamental: Gregers seeks to impose a general regulation, Rosmer wants rather to interpose *himself*, to make a personal contribution by mixing with his fellows and helping them to self-help—there is, he says, no other way. One of the reasons for his failure is that he is too fine-grained, too passively receptive, too retiring for the evangelical life. Rosmersholm is a refinery in which all the roughage is extracted from existence—is it not said that Rosmer children have never cried, nor the men ever laughed?—and in which all sense of initiative is filtered away. Rebecca testifies how it kills joy, and some of her remarks show how she suspects it kills sorrow, too; indeed, that it annihilates all the stronger, cruder, and more elemental aspects of life. The innocence of saintliness and the innocence of pathetic gullibility are equally Rosmer's, and he is greatly vulnerable; he has no idea how pitilessly he is manipulated by others, he sees very little of what really goes on. He stands there as one whose authority is largely inherited, taken from the family name; and also whose opinions are 'received', taken from the stronger personalities he yields to: first Brendel who was in the early days his tutor, then Kroll to whom he had turned for advice ever since his student days, and finally Rebecca. When ultimately his faith in Rebecca is destroyed, the ideals she has represented for him also crumble, their validity for him derives only from a faith in their guarantor, and it is characteristic of him that he turns at once to Kroll for a replacement of faith. When Brendel reappears to show himself a broken man, this betokens yet a further assault on what pass for Rosmer's convictions. His ideals, dependent as they are on the borrowed life they take from their sponsors, are not sturdy enough for independent existence, so that when at the end a final claim is made on Rosmer's faith—that Rebecca loves him—he is drawn as by an obsession to demand a living sacrifice, to request that the total personality should underwrite this new proposal.

But whereas Rosmer comes to rely utterly on this 'advanced' woman who has invaded his house, she herself, whose past has been a Nietzschean amoral life 'beyond good and evil' and who has all the instinctive ruthlessness of an animal of prey, falls victim to the insidious power of the Rosmer tradition. She encounters something, a sense of scruple, that turns out to be even stronger than her own pagan will, and she submits to it, numbed, 'ennobled'. The two things—integrity and initiative, innocence and committal, nobility of mind and tenacity of purpose, or however they are termed—seem on this evidence totally incompatible, mutually exclusive; and in this respect the play is profoundly pessimistic. The point where such destinies finally meet and merge is death; when, as Rosmer insists, the two of them become one, one course alone is adequate for *her* to prove her love, for *him* to prove his will, and for both to invite a just retribution for their guilty past.

It is this more than anything that invalidates the traditional question as to whether this play is a Rebecca tragedy or a Rosmer tragedy, for it is both and it is neither. The world that Ibsen constructs in *Rosmersholm* is a world of relationships, a lattice of conjoined characters linked each to each, in which dramatically speaking it is less important to evaluate the constituent elements as discrete phenomena than it is to see how they stand to each other; less important to¹ see how they separately change than it is to see how, in the flux of changing circumstance, the relations between them change; less important to 'place' them by political belief, or psychological type, than it is to note the sightings they separately take on each other, and continue to take (often with unexpected results) in the light of new events; not forgetting that any change in these latticed relationships will be reflected in changes all round, in the sense that Rosmer's relations with Kroll, or Rebecca's, are also functions of their own private relationship, and that any change *there* will have its consequences *here*.

Consider, to take an extreme example, the strangely influential role of Beata, Rosmer's deceased wife, who 'exists' in the play not by reason of her physical presence but solely through the memories and through the assessments of those who remembered her. We know her only through them and what they say: Rosmer, though during her lifetime repelled by her over-passionate nature which he obviously associated with the growing insanity that drove her to suicide in the mill stream, can now think of her with tenderness; Rebecca, who at first speaks sympathetically of her until circumstances make her change her words; Kroll, whose sister she was and who puts first one and then a very different interpretation on some of her last actions; Mortensgaard, to whom she wrote a secret and compromising letter shortly before her death; and Mrs. Helseth, the housekeeper and intermediary between them. Such items constitute bearings, taken from vantage points that can be approximately determined because those who occupy them *appear* and so declare themselves. But of course there is no neat answer. Instead of all converging upon some single point of corroboration, their testimonies are so widely divergent that together they do no more than demarcate an area in which a number of different interpretations of Beata are possible. Allowances have to be made, corrections calculated—for individual bias, for distorted or defective vision, for deceit. How ignorant is Rosmer of the real state of affairs? How unscrupulous is Rebecca? How reliable Mortensgaard? Statements about Beata have not only a demonstrative but also a betrayal value; they are also *admissions*, sometimes involuntary, which provide a two-way link with every other character in the drama, except possibly Brendel. Any change in the relationships among those who make these admissions tends to be reflected there, as well as in their attitude to each other.

Further variables can add to the complexity of the dramatic structure. When, for example, Ulrik Brendel is announced, and before he shows himself, the three people assembled in the living-room line up their minds on this new phenomenon: for Kroll, it is that 'waster' whom he last heard of as being in the workhouse; for Rebecca, it is that 'strange man' of whom she wonders that he is still alive; and for Rosmer—to the astonishment of both Kroll and the housekeeper who cannot think that Brendel is a fit person for the living-room at Rosmersholm—he is, as a former tutor in the house, welcome. Three snap bearings help to locate this as yet unknown quantity. *After* he has made his appearance, and after it has been noted not only what valuation he places on himself but also what by his conduct he involuntarily reveals, the initial bearings can be given some adjustment and thus one's ideas about those who took them refined. The importance of looking to the relations, expressed and implied, *between* the characters and not merely to the characters as independent creations is underlined by the letter Ibsen wrote on 25 March 1887 to Sofie Reimers. Invited to play Rebecca in the first Kristiania production, she had begged Ibsen's advice; his answer was that she would do well to note carefully what the other characters said about Rebecca, and not make the mistake of studying the part in isolation. Expanding this, one might say that the truth about the individual characters lies within an area bounded by: what they assert is the case; what they wantonly or unwittingly conceal; what they betray of themselves; and what they draw by way of comment from others. And when it is remembered that it is quite possible for these characters to mislead, to be misled or misinformed, or to be in the grip of instincts or impulses they cannot wholly comprehend, then the unreliability of the raw, untreated evidence is at once apparent. To fit in the separate parts as coherent items in a shifting pattern of event and belief is very largely a question of allotting appropriate values to the various hints, suggestions, and allusions the play is strewn with. What hidden meanings in the opening conversation between Rebecca and Kroll, for example, are subsequently brought to light by the momentary revelation that he had once been infatuated by her? What modifications must be made to Rosmer's implicit allegation that Beata was over-sexed, when his attitude to Rebecca, and the evidence of the past year of their living alone together in the house, carries the suggestion that he himself was under-sexed? And with such suspicions, should one then begin to wonder where in fact the sterility in his marriage to Beata lay—with her, as she was given to understand, or with him? How much had Kroll suspected about Rebecca before, that his thrust about her one-time relations with Dr. West struck home? And by implanting the idea that she had been guilty of incest, was he merely taking revenge on her with the same weapon she had already employed on his sister Beata: fostering suspicion on a minimum of evidence, knowing just how vulnerable her mind was to such suggestions? All these are things that cause one to look again at remarks that are otherwise deceptively obvious or perversely obscure.

Truth, its establishment and its promotion, is a thing all three plays have something to say about. In *An Enemy of the People* truth is provable and demonstrable; it inhabits a few scribbled lines of an analyst's report, it is expressible as a chemical formula. Stockmann, in becoming its spokesman, provokes a bold pattern of communal response to the revelations which, by the authority of science, he is able to make; and the local community is goaded into disposing itself in attitudes of hostility round the main character. Truth lights up the whole as from a central pendant fitting, a naked lamp lowered into the dark places of society, making a composition in strong light and shade. Each individual is the incarnation of the principles he professes, or lack of them; attitudes are adopted and persisted in, word and deed are concerted, and there is plain speaking. In *Rosmersholm* on the other hand, truth is an equivocal thing, being no more than what anybody at any particular time believes to be the case; it is a matter of partly knowing, or not knowing any better; there is no real laying bare of fact but rather a submission of possibilities, no establishment of what in reality was so, but an appeal to plausibility; any authenticity can be substantiated only by stealthy and oblique methods. Things are as they seem, or as they can be made to seem, and genuine motives are buried beneath layer upon layer of self-deception and duplicity; secret shifts and subsidences are for ever taking place in the minds of those concerned, and lighting is dim and indirect and full of flickering cross-shadows, and the wool is pulled over more than one pair of eyes.

The path leading from the earlier drama to the later runs from the outspoken to the unspoken, from bluff honesty to shifty evasiveness, from the self-evident to the merely ostensible, from proclamation to dissimulation, from the ingenuous to the disingenuous, from open debate and public uproar to secret eavesdropping and private intimation, from events urged on by a live issue to events brought up short by a dead woman. By the polluted baths there is enacted a tableau, a positioning of one to many in a generally radial pattern of static relationships, with Stockmann as the hub and cynosure. Beside the millstream, on the other hand, none of the characters is central in the same way, and instead of the build-up of a linear pattern one finds a sequence of positional changes, a ballet of death in which the manœuvres of the principals trace out a complex pattern of movement. In *An Enemy of the People* the author fashioned a vessel, a parabolic mould, into which he poured his wrath. *Rosmersholm*, however, has no such containing walls; its parts hold together rather on the analogy of particles in a complex magnetic field, they cohere not in obedience to some central solar force but rather because the resultant of all the various and varying attractions and repulsions they exert (or have exerted upon them) moves them the way it does. There is nothing at the centre except Nothing, the great void to which Brendel is finally attracted, and which draws the two anguished principals as though into the eye of a vortex. By comparison with *An Enemy of the People*, *Rosmersholm* seems to dispose over an extra dimension, and to enjoy a dynamic rather than a static existence; it differs from the earlier drama as a mobile differs from a blue-print, the one making a seemingly arbitrary but actually carefully balanced and *necessary* pattern of movement, and the other displaying all the clarity and self-assurance of something that recognizes its own dimensional limitations. By these tokens *The Wild Duck* is photographic, rather, and so ordered as to give an astonishingly successful illusion of perspective depth.

Hand in hand with these changes went an extra care in what Ibsen termed the 'individualization' of chararacter and other 'finesses' attaching to the creation of dramatic dialogue. So, for instance, in conversation with John Paulsen some time in the early 1880s about 'the thousand and one finesses of dramatic art', he is reported to have asked whether his companion had ever considered 'how the dialogue in a play ought to have a different timbre if it was meant to be spoken in the morning from what it would be at night'. In letters written whilst engaged on revising *The Wild Duck*, he stressed that his attention was being given to the 'energetic individualization of character' and the finer formulation of the dialogue; and many years later, when replying to a young Frenchman who wanted permission to translate this play, he returned to this matter and pointed out the great demands the play makes on any translator, since 'one must be extremely familiar with the Norwegian language to be able to understand how thoroughly each separate character in the play has his own individual and idiosyncratic mode of expression'. Ibsen had always been an extremely conscientious artist, painstaking in the care that he gave the successive drafts of his work; now, and especially from *The Wild Duck* onward, he applied his massive revisionary capacity to the problem of the finer delineation of character; the separate figures are now no longer in the first instance the embodiment of general principles or attitudes, but instead personalities whose individuality and uniqueness are emphasized at every point in the drama. They cease to be object lessons, and become instead subjects of study. It is one of the chief fascinations of the draft manuscripts of these plays that they document at a number of points this process of 'individualization'.

Of the *fact* of some fundamental change in Ibsen's writing about the time of these three plays, there is general recognition, although there is not the same unanimity about where precisely to locate the turning point, nor how best to style it. Some critics have seen it as a transition from the 'social' to the 'visionary', from the 'naturalistic' to the 'symbolic', from the 'problematical' to the 'psychological'; there have been arguments in favour of calling the earlier group 'moralist' and for distinguishing *two* later phases, the 'humanist' and the 'visionary'; whilst yet another critic has argued persuasively for regarding the shift as being from a 'demonstrative' to an 'evocative' mood. It may indeed be necessary to relate the change to terms even more fundamental than these, and to see the crux as being a substantial shift in Ibsen's whole scheme of values. Writing to Theodor Caspari on 27 June 1884, Ibsen confessed that he had long since given up making general or universal demands, believing that one could not with any real justification make such blanket claims on people, and added: 'I do not believe any of us can do anything other or anything better than realize ourselves in truth and in spirit.' What seemed to matter to him now were particulars rather than generalities; his attention was addressed to private dilemma rather than public abuse, to what was individual and personal rather than typical or representative. He abandoned collective indictment for singular, distinctive investigation; he became less comprehensive in his scrutiny of things, more selective, more penetrative; and with it all went an increasing impatience with the mass mind and all its works.

SELECT BIBLIOGRAPHY

1. COLLECTED WORKS IN ENGLISH TRANSLATION

There is no lack of editions of Ibsen's plays: these are of greater or lesser comprehensiveness. William Archer (ed.), *The Collected Works of Henrik Ibsen*, 12 vols (London, 1906–12), was the first comprehensive collection in English translation to be published, and the version by which Ibsen became generally known in the English-speaking world. James McFarlane (ed.), The Oxford Ibsen, 8 vols (London, 1960–77), includes the complete plays, together with Ibsen's notes, jottings and earlier draft versions, as well as critical introductions and other editorial commentary.

2. LETTERS

The Correspondence of Henrik Ibsen, ed. Mary Morison (London, 1905)

Speeches and New Letters, tr. Arne Kildal (London, 1911)

Ibsen: Letters and Speeches, ed. Evert Sprinchorn (New York, 1964; London, 1965)

3. BIOGRAPHIES

Henrik Jæger, *The Life of Henrik Ibsen*, tr. Clara Bell (London, 1890)

Edmund Gosse, *Ibsen* (London, 1907)

Halvdan Koht, *The Life of Ibsen* (London, 1931; rev. ed. New York, 1971)

Adolph E. Zucker, *Ibsen the Master Builder* (London, 1929)

Bergliot Ibsen, *The Three Ibsens*, tr. G. Schjelderup (London, 1951)

Michael Meyer, *Henrik Ibsen*, 3 vols (London, 1967–71)

Hans Heiberg, *Ibsen: A Portrait of the Artist*, tr. Joan Tate (London, 1969)

4. CRITICISM (in chronological order)

George Bernard Shaw, *The Quintessence of Ibsenism* (London, 1891; second augmented ed., London, 1913)

George Bernard Shaw, *Our Theatres in the Nineties*. 3 vols (London, 1932)

James Huneker, *Iconoclasts: a book of dramatists* (London, 1905)

Jeanette Lee, *The Ibsen Secret* (London, 1907)

Haldane Macfall, *Ibsen: the man, his art and his significance* (London, 1907)

Hermann J. Weigand, *The Modern Ibsen: a reconsideration* (New York, 1925)

Brian W. Downs, *Ibsen: the intellectual background* (Cambridge, 1946)

M. C. Bradbrook, *Ibsen the Norwegian* (London, 1948)

P. F. D. Tennant, *Ibsen's Dramatic Technique* (Cambridge, 1948)

Brian W. Downs, *A Study of Six Plays by Ibsen* (Cambridge, 1950)

Janko Lavrin, *Ibsen: an approach* (London, 1950)

Raymond Williams, *Drama from Ibsen to Eliot* (London, 1952); 2nd rev. ed. *Drama from Ibsen to Brecht* (London, 1969)

John Northam, *Ibsen's Dramatic Method: a study of the prose dramas* (London, 1953)

James McFarlane, *Ibsen and the Temper of Norwegian Literature* (London, 1960, 2nd ed. New York, 1979)

F. L. Lucas, *The Drama of Ibsen and Strindberg* (London, 1962)

M. J. Valency, *The Flower and the Castle* (New York, 1964)

Rolf Fjelde (ed.), *Twentieth-century Views on Ibsen* (New York, 1965)

Daniel Haakonsen (ed.), *Contemporary Approaches to Ibsen*, no. 1 (Oslo, 1966); no. 2 (Oslo, 1971); no. 3 (Oslo, 1977)

James McFarlane (ed.), *Henrik Ibsen*. Penguin critical anthology (London, 1970)

Orley, J. Holtan, *Mythic Patterns in Ibsen's Last Plays* (Minneapolis, 1970)

Michael Egan (ed.), *Ibsen: the Critical Heritage* (London, 1972)

James Hurt, *Catiline's Dream: an essay on Ibsen's plays* (Illinois, 1972)

Charles R. Lyons, *Henrik Ibsen: the Divided Consciousness* (S. Illinois, 1972)

John Northam, *Ibsen, a Critical Study* (Cambridge, 1973)

Brian Johnston, *The Ibsen Cycle* (Boston, 1975)

Frederick J. and Lise-Lone Marker, *The Scandinavian Theatre: A Short History* (Totowa, N.J., 1975)

Harold Clurman, *Ibsen* (New York, 1977)

Ronald Gray, *Ibsen—a Dissenting View* (Cambridge, 1977)

Einar Haugen, *Ibsen's Drama* (Minneapolis, 1979)

Edvard Beyer, *Henrik Ibsen* (London, 1979)

J. L. Wisenthal, *Shaw and Ibsen* (Toronto, 1979)

Errol Durbach (ed.), *Ibsen and the Theatre* (London, 1980)

Brian Johnston, *To the Third Empire. Ibsen's Early Drama* (Minneapolis, 1980)

Richard Hornby, *Patterns in Ibsen's Middle Plays* (London, 1981)

John S. Chamberlain, *Ibsen: The Open Vision* (London, 1982)

Errol Durbach, *Ibsen the Romantic* (London, 1982)

David Thomas, *Henrik Ibsen* (London, 1982)

Thomas Postlewait (ed.), *William Archer on Ibsen: The Major Essays 1889–1919* (London, 1984)

John Northam (tr. and ed.), *Ibsen's Poems* (Oslo, 1986)

Charles R. Lyons (ed.), *Critical Essays on Henrik Ibsen* (Boston, 1987)

Per Schelde Jacobsen and Barbara Fass Leavy, *Ibsen's Forsaken Merman. Folklore in the Late Plays* (London, 1988)

Robert A. Schanke, *Ibsen in America: A Century of Change* (Metuchen, N.J., 1988)

James McFarlane, *Ibsen and Meaning: Studies, essays and prefaces 1953–87* (Norwich, 1989)

Robin Young, *Time's Disinherited Children: Childhood, Regression and Sacrifice in the plays of Henrik Ibsen* (Norwich, 1989)

Brian Johnston, *Text and Supertext in Ibsen's Drama* (Pennsylvania, 1989)

Frederick J. Marker and Lise-Lone Marker, *Ibsen's Lively Art: A performance study of the major plays* (Cambridge, 1989)

Asbjørn Aarseth, *'Peer Gynt' and 'Ghosts': Text and Performance* (London, 1989)

Naomi Lebowitz, *Ibsen and the great world* (Baton Rouge, 1990)

Charles R. Lyons, *'Hedda Gabler.' Gender, Role and World* (Boston, 1991)

Contemporary Approaches to Ibsen (ed. Daniel Haakonsen, Bjørn Hemmer, Vigdis Ystad et al.), vols. I–VII (Oslo, 1966–91)

John Northam (ed. and trans.), *Ibsen's Peer Gynt* (Oslo, 1993)

The Cambridge Companion to Ibsen (ed. James McFarlane) (Cambridge, 1994)

CHRONOLOGY OF HENRIK IBSEN

1828   20 March Born in Skien, a small timber port about 150 kilometres south-west of Christiania (now Oslo), the second son in a family of six children

1835   June The Ibsen family moves out of town to a smaller house at Venstøp

1843   Leaves Skien for Grimstad to work as an apothecary's apprentice

1846   9 October A servant girl in the household bears him an illegitimate son

1850   12 April His first play, *Catiline*, published, privately and unsuccessfully
        28 April Arrives in Christiania in the hope of studying at the university
        26 September *The Burial Mound* performed at the Christiania Theatre

1851   26 October Takes up an appointment at the theatre in Bergen as producer and 'dramatic author'

1852   Study tour of theatres in Hamburg, Copenhagen and Dresden

1853   2 January *St John's Night* performed at the Bergen theatre

1855   2 January *Lady Inger* performed

1856   2 January *The Feast at Solhoug* performed

1857   2 January *Olaf Liljekrans* performed
        11 August Moves to a post at the Norwegian Theatre in Christiania

1858   25 April *The Vikings at Helgeland* published
        18 June Marries Suzannah Thoresen

1859   His son (and only legitimate child) Sigurd born

1861   Accused of neglect and inefficiency in his post at the Norwegian Theatre

1862   31 December *Love's Comedy* published

1863   October *The Pretenders* published

1864   Leaves Norway and travels via Copenhagen, Lübeck, Berlin and Vienna to Italy, where he remains resident until 1868

1866   15 March *Brand* published. Awarded an annual grant by the Norwegian Parliament

1867   14 November *Peer Gynt* published

1868   October Takes up residence in Dresden

1869   30 September *The League of Youth* published
        October–December Travels to Egypt and the Middle East
        and attends the opening of the Suez Canal, as Norway's
        representative

1871   3 May His collected *Poems* published

1873   16 October *Emperor and Galilean* published

1874   July–September Summer visit to Norway. Invites Edvard
        Grieg to compose incidental music for *Peer Gynt*

1875   April Moves from Dresden to Munich for the sake of his
        son's education

1877   11 October *Pillars of Society* published

1878   Returns to Italy 'for the winter', but remains largely resident
        there (in Rome) until 1885

1879   4 December *A Doll's House* published

1881   12 December *Ghosts* published

1882   28 November *An Enemy of the People* published

1884   11 November *The Wild Duck* published

1885   June–September Summer visit to Norway
        October Takes up residence once again in Munich

1886   23 November *Rosmersholm* published

1887   9 January Berlin performance of *Ghosts* creates a sensation
        July–October Summer visit to Denmark and Sweden

1888   28 November *The Lady from the Sea* published

1889   7 June *A Doll's House* performed in London—the first
        substantial Ibsen production in England

1890   December *Hedda Gabler* published

1891   13 March J. T. Grein's Independent Theatre performs *Ghosts*
        in London to a storm of criticism
        July Leaves Munich for Norway and takes up permanent
        residence there

1892   11 October His son Sigurd marries Bjørnson's daughter
        Bergliot
        December *The Master Builder* published

1894   December *Little Eyolf* published

1896   12 December *John Gabriel Borkman* published

1898   Collected editions of his works in Norwegian and German
        begin publication

1899   19 December *When We Dead Awaken* published

1900   15 March Suffers a stroke, and is unable to do any further literary work

1906   23 May Dies, and is given a public funeral

AN ENEMY OF THE PEOPLE
[*En Folkefiende*]

PLAY IN FIVE ACTS
(1882)

CHARACTERS

DR. THOMAS STOCKMANN, doctor at the Baths

MRS. KATHERINE STOCKMANN, his wife

PETRA, their daughter, a teacher

EJLIF
MORTEN } their sons, 13 and 10 years old

PETER STOCKMANN, the doctor's elder brother, Mayor, Chief of Police, Chairman of the Board of the Baths, &c.

MORTEN KIIL, owner of a tannery, Mrs. Stockmann's foster-father

HOVSTAD, editor of the *People's Herald*

BILLING, a journalist

CAPTAIN HORSTER

ASLAKSEN, a printer

Attending a public meeting are: men of all classes, some women and a group of schoolboys

The action takes place in a coastal town in Southern Norway

ACT ONE

Evening. DR. STOCKMANN'S *living-room, simply but tastefully furnished. In the side-wall, right, are two doors, one of which up-stage leads to the hall, and the other to the doctor's study. On the opposite wall and directly facing the hall door, another door leads to the rest of the house. In the middle of this wall stands a stove; down-stage of it is a sofa; above it hangs a mirror and in front of it is an oval table covered with a cloth. On the table, a shaded lamp is burning. In the back wall, the door to the dining-room stands open. Within, the table is laid for supper; a lighted lamp stands on the table.*

BILLING, a napkin tucked under his chin, is seated within at the supper table. MRS. STOCKMANN stands by the table and hands him a serving dish on which is a large joint of beef. The other places at table are empty, and the table is in disarray as though after a meal.

MRS. STOCKMANN. Well, if you will arrive an hour late, Mr. Billing, you'll have to put up with everything being cold.

BILLING [*eating*]. It's absolutely delicious, really excellent.

MRS. STOCKMANN. You know how strict my husband is about keeping punctually to his mealtimes. . . .

BILLING. It doesn't matter to me in the least. In fact I almost believe it tastes better, sitting down like this to it, alone and undisturbed.

MRS. STOCKMANN. Ah well, as long as you enjoy it. . . . [*Turns to the hall door and listens.*] That's probably Hovstad.

BILLING. Quite likely.

[PETER STOCKMANN, *the Mayor, enters; he is wearing an overcoat and his mayor's hat, and he carries a stick.*]

MAYOR. A very good evening to you, Katherine.

MRS. STOCKMANN [*coming into the living-room*]. Oh. It's you! Good evening. How nice of you to drop in like this.

MAYOR. I happened to be passing, so . . . [*With a glance towards the dining-room.*] Oh, but it seems you have company.

MRS. STOCKMANN [*rather embarrassed*]. No, not really. He just happened to drop in. [*Quickly.*] Wouldn't you like to join him and let me get you something to eat?

MAYOR. Who, me? No thank you. Heavens above! A cooked meal in the evening! Not with my digestion.

MRS. STOCKMANN. Oh, couldn't you just for once. . . ?

MAYOR. Bless you, no. I stick to my tea and bread and butter. It's better for one's health in the long run . . . as well as being more economical.

MRS. STOCKMANN [*smiles*]. Now you mustn't get the idea that Thomas and I are terribly extravagant, either.

MAYOR. Not *you*, Katherine. I'd never think that of you. [*Points to the doctor's study.*] Isn't he at home?

MRS. STOCKMANN. No, he's gone for a little walk after his supper . . . with the boys.

MAYOR. I wonder if that really does one any good? [*Listens.*] That's him now.

MRS. STOCKMANN. No, I don't think it's him. [*There is a knock on the door.*] Come in!

[HOVSTAD *comes in from the hall.*]

MRS. STOCKMANN. Oh, it's Mr. Hovstad.

HOVSTAD. Yes, you must excuse me, but I got held up at the printer's. Good evening, Mr. Mayor.

MAYOR [*bowing rather stiffly*]. Good evening! A business call, no doubt?

HOVSTAD. Partly. It's in connection with something for the paper.

MAYOR. That I can imagine. From all accounts, my brother is a prolific contributor to the *People's Herald*.

HOVSTAD. Yes, whenever he wants to get any particular home-truths off his chest, he writes a piece for the *Herald*.

MRS. STOCKMANN [*to* HOVSTAD]. But won't you . . . ? [*She points to the dining-room.*]

MAYOR. Indeed, and why not? Who am I to blame him if he decides to write for the class of reader he can expect the greatest response from! And in any case, there's no reason for me to feel any personal animosity towards your paper, Mr. Hovstad.

HOVSTAD. No, I don't think there is.

MAYOR. All in all, there is an admirable spirit of tolerance in our little town . . . a sense of civic pride. That's what comes of having a great communal undertaking to unite us . . . an undertaking which concerns all right-thinking citizens in equal measure. . . .

HOVSTAD. The Baths, you mean.

MAYOR. Exactly. We have our splendid new Baths. Mark my words! The prosperity of the town will come to depend more and more on the Baths, Mr. Hovstad. No doubt about it!

MRS. STOCKMANN. Thomas says the same.

MAYOR. Just look at the quite extraordinary way things have improved, even in the last year or two. People have more money! There's more life, more things going on. Land and property are going up in value every day.

HOVSTAD. And unemployment falling.

MAYOR. Yes, that too. The burden of the poor-rate on the propertied classes has, I am happy to say, been considerably reduced—and it will be even less if only we have a really good summer this year . . . with plenty of visitors, and lots of convalescents to help to give the place a reputation.

HOVSTAD. And things are looking pretty promising in that way, they tell me.

MAYOR. The prospects are very encouraging. Every day we receive more inquiries about accommodation and things like that.

HOVSTAD. Well then, I suppose the doctor's article will just come in nicely.

MAYOR. Has he been writing something else?

HOVSTAD. This is something he wrote during the winter, giving an account of the Baths and recommending the place generally as a very healthy spot. But I didn't use the article at the time.

MAYOR. Aha! I expect there was a snag in it somewhere.

HOVSTAD. No, it wasn't that. But I thought it might be better to hold it over till the spring; now's the time when people start thinking about their summer holidays. . . .

MAYOR. Very sensible, very sensible indeed, Mr. Hovstad.

MRS. STOCKMANN. Yes, Thomas is quite indefatigable if it's anything to do with the Baths.

MAYOR. Well, as he's one of its officials it's only natural.

HOVSTAD. Besides, he was the one who started the whole thing.

MAYOR. *He* was! Indeed! Yes, this isn't the first time I've heard of people getting that idea. But I rather imagined *I* too had had a modest part in this enterprise.

MRS. STOCKMANN. Yes, that's what Thomas is always saying.

HOVSTAD. Of course, who would want to deny that, Mr. Mayor. It was you who got things moving, got it going as a practical concern, we all know that, of course. All I meant was that the idea came first from Dr. Stockmann.

MAYOR. Yes, my brother's always had plenty of ideas—more's the pity. But when it's a matter of getting things done, you have to look round for a different type of man, Mr. Hovstad. I should at least have thought that the members of *this* household would . . .

MRS. STOCKMANN. My dear Peter . . .

HOVSTAD. But Mr. Mayor, how can you . . . ?

MRS. STOCKMANN. You go and get yourself something to eat, Mr. Hovstad. My husband is sure to be back by the time you're finished.

HOVSTAD. Thanks. Perhaps just a bite.

[*He goes into the dining-room.*]

MAYOR [*lowering his voice*]. Funny, these people from peasant stock! They never have any tact.

MRS. STOCKMANN. But there's no point in upsetting yourself about it! Can't you and Thomas share the credit like brothers!

MAYOR. Yes, one would have thought so. But apparently it isn't everybody who is content to share.

MRS. STOCKMANN. Oh, nonsense. You and Thomas get on perfectly well together on this point. [*Listens.*] That's him now, I think.

[*She goes over and opens the door into the hall.*]

DR. STOCKMANN [*laughing and talking outside*]. Here we are, another visitor for you, Katherine. Isn't this fun, eh! Come in, Captain Horster. Hang your coat on that peg there. You don't bother with an overcoat, eh? You know, Katherine, I ran into him on the street. . . . Had a terrible job persuading him to come along.

[CAPTAIN HORSTER *enters and bows to* MRS. STOCKMANN.]

DR. STOCKMANN [*in the doorway*]. In you go, lads. They are absolutely ravenous again, my dear. Come along, Captain Horster, what do you say to a bit of roast beef. . . ?

[*He urges* HORSTER *into the dining-room;* EJLIF *and* MORTEN *go in also.*]

MRS. STOCKMANN. But Thomas, don't you see . . . ?

DR. STOCKMANN [*turns in the doorway*]. Oh, it's you, Peter. [*Walks across and shakes hands.*] Well, this is very pleasant.

MAYOR. Unfortunately I can only stay a minute or two. . . .

DR. STOCKMANN. Rubbish! There'll be some hot toddy coming up soon. You haven't forgotten the toddy, Katherine, have you?

MRS. STOCKMANN. Of course not! I've got the kettle on.

[*She goes into the dining-room.*]

MAYOR. Toddy as well!

DR. STOCKMANN. Yes, sit yourself down and we'll make an evening of it.

MAYOR. Thanks, but I don't care for drinking parties.

DR. STOCKMANN. This isn't a drinking party.

MAYOR. It seems to me . . . [*He looks into the dining-room.*] It's incredible the amount of food they manage to put away.

DR. STOCKMANN [*rubbing his hands*]. Yes, isn't it grand to see young people eating well? Such an appetite they've got! That's as it ought to be. They need food . . . need to build up their strength. They'll be the ones to stir things up a bit in the coming years, Peter.

MAYOR. And what, if I may ask, is it that requires 'stirring up', as you put it?

DR. STOCKMANN. Ah, you'll have to ask the younger generation about that—when the time comes. We just can't see it, of course. Stands to reason! A couple of old fogies like you and me . . . !

MAYOR. Well, really! That's a most extraordinary description. . . .

DR. STOCKMANN. Oh, you mustn't take me too seriously, Peter. Thing is, I feel so full of the joy of everything, you see. I can't tell you how happy I feel, surrounded by all this growing, vigorous life. What a glorious age this is to live in! It's as if a whole new world were springing up all around.

MAYOR. Do you really think so?

foreshadowing

DR. STOCKMANN. Well, you can't see it as clearly as I can, of course. All your life you've lived amongst this kind of thing, and it doesn't make the same sharp impression on you. But think of me, living all those years in the North, cut off from everything, hardly ever seeing a new face, never the chance of any decent conversation . . . for me it's like coming to some great throbbing metropolis.

MAYOR. Huh! Metropolis. . . !

Sets him apart

DR. STOCKMANN. Well, I know everything's on a small scale compared with a lot of other places. But there's life here . . . and promise . . . and innumerable things to work and strive for. *That's* what counts. [*Shouts.*] Katherine, has the postman been?

MRS. STOCKMANN [*in the dining-room*]. No, nobody's been.

DR. STOCKMANN. And then what it is to have a decent income, Peter! That's something one learns to appreciate after living on a starvation wage as we did. . . .

MAYOR. Surely now . . .

DR. STOCKMANN. Oh yes we did. Let me tell you, things were often pretty tight up there. But now I can live like a gentleman. Today, for instance, we had a joint of beef for dinner; it did us for supper, too. Wouldn't you like a taste? Or let me show it to you, anyway. Come here. . . .

MAYOR. No, no, it's not necessary. . . .

DR. STOCKMANN. Well, come here then. Look, we've got a new table-cloth.

MAYOR. So I noticed.

DR. STOCKMANN. And we've got a lampshade. See? Katherine managed to save all that. Don't you think it makes the room look cosy? Just stand over here—no, no, not there—here, that's right! See? How it directs the light down like that. . . ? I think it looks really elegant, don't you?

MAYOR. Yes, for those who can afford such luxuries. . . .

DR. STOCKMANN. Oh, yes! Of course I can afford it. Katherine says I earn very nearly as much as we spend.

MAYOR. Nearly . . . yes!

[margin, handwritten: Showing financial inconsistency— honest]

DR. STOCKMANN. But a man of science ought to have a decent standard of living. I bet you there's many a civil servant spends more in a year than I do.

MAYOR. Well, I dare say there is. A civil servant, a senior executive. . . .

DR. STOCKMANN. Well, an ordinary businessman then. I'm sure that sort of person spends very much more. . . .

MAYOR. That depends on circumstances.

DR. STOCKMANN. Anyway, I don't go throwing my money away on any old thing, Peter. But I feel I can't deny myself the pleasure of having people in. I need something like that, you see, after being out of things for so long. For me it's like one of the necessities of life—to enjoy the company of eager young people, with initiative and minds of their own. That's the kind of person you'll find sitting at my table, enjoying their food. I wish you knew Hovstad a bit better. . . .

[margin, handwritten: makes mayor uncomfortable]

[bottom, handwritten: Recurring: youth vs. conventionality]

MAYOR. Ah, Hovstad, that's right. He was telling me he's going to print another one of your articles.

DR. STOCKMANN. One of my articles?

MAYOR. Yes, about the Baths. An article you'd apparently written during the winter.

DR. STOCKMANN. Oh, that one! Well, I don't want that one in just now.

MAYOR. Don't you? This seems to me to be exactly the right time for it.

DR. STOCKMANN. Yes, that's right . . . in ordinary circumstances. . . .

[*He walks about the room.*]

MAYOR [*watching him*]. And what's so extraordinary about the present circumstances?

DR. STOCKMANN [*halts*]. In point of fact, Peter, that's something I can't tell you for the moment. Not this evening, anyway. There might be quite a lot that's unusual about the present state of affairs; on the other hand, it might be nothing at all. It might very well be just my imagination.

MAYOR. I must admit it all sounds very mysterious. What's going on? Why am I being kept out of it? I would remind you that, as Chairman of the Board of the Baths, I . . .

DR. STOCKMANN. And I would remind you that I . . . Oh, let's not jump down each other's throats, Peter.

MAYOR. Heaven forbid! I'm not in the habit of jumping down people's throats, as you put it. But I must insist most emphatically that all matters be considered and dealt with through the proper channels and by the appropriate authorities. I cannot permit any dubious or underhand methods.

DR. STOCKMANN. Since when have *I* used dubious or underhand methods?

MAYOR. You have a chronic disposition to take things into your own hands, at least. And in a well-ordered community, that can be equally reprehensible. The individual must be ready to subordinate himself to the community as a whole; or, more precisely, to the authorities charged with the welfare of that community.

DR. STOCKMANN. That may well be. But what the devil has that got to do with me?

MAYOR. Everything. Because, my dear Thomas, that's just the thing you don't seem to want to learn. But mark my words; one of these days you'll pay for it . . . sooner or later. I'm telling you. Goodbye.

DR. STOCKMANN. Have you gone stark, staring mad? You are barking up the wrong tree altogether. . . .

MAYOR. I'm not in the habit of doing that. And now if I may be excused. . . . [*He calls into the dining-room.*] Goodbye, Katherine. Goodbye, gentlemen.

[*He leaves.*]

MRS. STOCKMANN [*comes into the living-room*]. Has he gone?

DR. STOCKMANN. Yes, he has; and in high dudgeon.

MRS. STOCKMANN. Thomas, my dear, what have you been doing to him this time?

DR. STOCKMANN. Absolutely nothing. He can't expect an account from me before the proper time.

MRS. STOCKMANN. What are you expected to give him an account of?

DR. STOCKMANN. Hm! Don't bother me about that now, Katherine.— Funny the postman doesn't come.

[*HOVSTAD, BILLING and HORSTER have risen from the table and come into the living-room. EJLIF and MORTEN follow them after a while.*]

BILLING [*stretches himself*]. Ah! A supper like that and, damn me, if it doesn't make you feel like a new man!

HOVSTAD. Our Mayor wasn't in the best of moods this evening.

DR. STOCKMANN. It's his stomach. Digestion's none too good.

HOVSTAD. It was mainly us two from the *Herald* he couldn't stomach, I reckon.

MRS. STOCKMANN. I thought you seemed to be getting on quite nicely with him.

HOVSTAD. Oh yes, but it's only a kind of armistice.

BILLING. That's it. That describes it exactly.

DR. STOCKMANN. We mustn't forget that Peter's a lonely person, poor chap. He hasn't any proper home where he can relax. Business, nothing but business! And all that damned weak tea he keeps pouring into himself. Now then, lads, pull your chairs up to the table. Katherine, don't we get any toddy?

MRS. STOCKMANN [*makes for the dining-room*]. I'm just going to get it.

DR. STOCKMANN. Come and sit beside me on the sofa, Captain Horster. It's so rarely we see you. Do sit down, my friends.

[*The men seat themselves round the table.* MRS. STOCKMANN *enters with a tray on which there is a kettle, glasses, decanters and so on.*]

MRS. STOCKMANN. There we are. This is Arrack, and this is rum, and this is cognac. Everybody just help themselves.

DR. STOCKMANN [*takes a glass*]. Ah, we will that! [*Whilst the toddy is being mixed.*] Let's have the cigars out, too. Ejlif, you know where the box is kept. And you, Morten, can bring my pipe. [*The boys go into the room on the right.*] I have a suspicion Ejlif helps himself to a cigar now and then, but I don't let on I know. [*Calls.*] My smoking-cap as well, Morten! Katherine, could you tell him where I've put it. Ah! he's got it. [*The boys bring the various articles.*] Help yourselves, my friends. I'll stick to my pipe. Many's the time this one's done the rounds with me, fair weather and foul, up there in the North. [*They clink glasses.*] Your health! Ah, it's much better to be sitting nice and snug in here.

MRS. STOCKMANN [*sits knitting*]. Will you be sailing soon, Captain Horster?

HORSTER. I reckon we'll be ready by next week.

MRS. STOCKMANN. And then you're off to America?

HORSTER. That's the intention.

BILLING. Then you won't be able to vote in the municipal election.

HORSTER. Is there going to be an election?

BILLING. Didn't you know?

HORSTER. No, I don't bother about things like that.

BILLING. But you take an interest in public affairs, I suppose?

HORSTER. No, I don't know the first thing about them.

BILLING. I think people ought to vote, all the same.

HORSTER. Even those who have no idea what it's all about?

BILLING. No idea? What do you mean? Society's like a ship; everybody must help to steer it. *# Low individualism*

HORSTER. That might be all very well on dry land; but it wouldn't work very well at sea.

HOVSTAD. It's strange how little most seafaring people care about what goes on ashore.

BILLING. Quite remarkable.

DR. STOCKMANN. Sailors are like birds of passage, equally at home in the north or in the south. All the more reason for the rest of us to be even more active, Mr. Hovstad. Is there anything of public interest in the *Herald* tomorrow?

HOVSTAD. Nothing about municipal affairs. But I thought of putting in your article the day after. . . .

DR. STOCKMANN. Oh damn it, yes! That article. Listen, you must hold it over for a while.

HOVSTAD. Really! It just happens we have room for it now, and it seemed to be the right time for it. . . .

DR. STOCKMANN. Yes, yes, maybe you are right; but you'll have to wait all the same. I'll explain later. . . .

[PETRA, *wearing a hat and a cloak, comes in from the hall, a pile of exercise books under her arm.*]

PETRA. Good evening.

DR. STOCKMANN. Is that you, Petra? Good evening!

[*Greetings all round.* PETRA *takes off her things and puts them, along with the exercise books, on a chair beside the door.*]

PETRA. So you've all been sitting here enjoying yourselves while I've been out slaving.

DR. STOCKMANN. Now *you* come and enjoy yourself too, then.

BILLING. Can I get you something to drink?

PETRA [*comes over to the table*]. Thanks. But I'd rather do it myself. You always make it too strong. But I'm forgetting, Father, I have a letter for you.

[*Goes over to the chair where her things are.*]

DR. STOCKMANN. A letter? Who from?

PETRA [*feels in her coat pocket*]. The postman gave me it just as I was going out. . . .

DR. STOCKMANN [*gets up and goes across to her*]. And you haven't brought it out before now!

PETRA. I hadn't time to run back again with it. Here it is.

DR. STOCKMANN [*seizing the letter*]. Let me see it. Let me see it, child. [*Looks at the address.*] Yes, that's it. . . .

MRS. STOCKMANN. Is *that* the one you have been waiting for, Thomas?

DR. STOCKMANN. Yes, that's the one. Excuse me if I take it straight into . . . Where can I find a light, Katherine? Is there still no lamp in my study!

MRS. STOCKMANN. Yes, of course. There's a lamp already lit on your desk.

DR. STOCKMANN. Good, good. Excuse me a minute. . . .

[*He goes into his room, right.*]

PETRA. What can that be, Mother?

MRS. STOCKMANN. I don't know. He's done nothing else these last few days but ask whether the postman's been.

BILLING. Presumably some country patient.

PETRA. Poor Father! All this work, it's getting too much for him. [*She mixes her drink.*] Ah, I'm going to enjoy this!

HOVSTAD. Have you been taking Evening Classes again today?

PETRA [*sipping her glass*]. Two hours.

BILLING. And four hours this morning at the Institute.

PETRA [*sits at the table*]. Five hours.

MRS. STOCKMANN. And tonight I see you have essays to correct.

PETRA. A whole bundle of them.

HORSTER. You've got plenty of work to do yourself, it seems.

PETRA. Yes, but that's all right. It makes you feel so gloriously tired afterwards.

BILLING. Do you like that?

PETRA. Yes, it makes you sleep so well.

MORTEN. You must be a dreadful sinner, Petra!

PETRA. Sinner?

MORTEN. Working as hard as you do. Mr. Rörlund says that work is a punishment for our sins.

EJLIF. Puh! You must be stupid, believing a thing like that!

MRS. STOCKMANN. Now, now, Ejlif!

BILLING [*laughs*]. Oh, that's good, that is!

HOVSTAD. Don't you want to work as hard as that, Morten?

MORTEN. No, I don't.

HOVSTAD. Well, what *do* you want to be when you grow up?

MORTEN. I want to be a Viking.

EJLIF. Well, you'd have to be a heathen.

MORTEN. All right, I'll be a heathen.

BILLING. I'm with you there, Morten. I say exactly the same.

MRS. STOCKMANN [*making signs*]. I'm sure you wouldn't really do anything of the kind.

BILLING. Yes I would, so help me! I *am* a heathen, and proud of it. You watch, we'll all be heathens before long.

MORTEN. And *then* can we do exactly what we like?

BILLING. Well, you see, Morten . . .

MRS. STOCKMANN. Now, boys, off you go now; I'm sure you've got some homework for tomorrow.

EJLIF. Couldn't *I* just stay on a little bit longer... ?

MRS. STOCKMANN. No. Off you go now, both of you.

[*The boys say good night and go into the room, left.*]

HOVSTAD. Do you really think it's bad for the boys to listen to things like that?

MRS. STOCKMANN. Oh, I don't know. But I don't much like it.

PETRA. Oh, Mother! I think you're quite mistaken there.

MRS. STOCKMANN. Yes, that's quite possible. But I *don't* like it, not in my own home.

PETRA. All this hypocrisy, both at home and at school. At home one mustn't say anything; and at school we have to stand there and lie to the children.

HORSTER. Lie to them?

PETRA. Yes. Can't you see we have to teach all sorts of things we don't even believe in ourselves?

BILLING. That's only too true.

PETRA. If only I had the money, I'd start a school myself, where things would be run very differently.

BILLING. Huh! The money!

HORSTER. Well, if you've got anything like that in mind, Miss Stockmann, I'd be glad to offer you the necessary accommodation. My father's big old house is standing there practically empty; there's an enormous dining-room on the ground floor. . . .

PETRA [*laughs*]. Thanks, thanks very much. But nothing's likely to come of it.

HOVSTAD. No, I think Miss Petra's much more likely to join the ranks of the journalists. By the way, have you had any time to look at that English story you promised to translate for us?

PETRA. No, not yet. But you'll have it in good time.

[DOCTOR STOCKMANN *comes out of his room, with the open letter in his hand.*]

DR. STOCKMANN [*waving the letter*]. Well! Here's a bit of news that will set a few tongues wagging about the town!

BILLING. News?

MRS. STOCKMANN. What news?

DR. STOCKMANN. A great discovery, Katherine!

HOVSTAD. Really?

MRS. STOCKMANN. Which you've made?

DR. STOCKMANN. Which I've made, yes. [*Walks up and down.*] Now let them come as they always do, and say it's some madman's crazy idea! Ah, but they'll watch their step this time! They'll watch out this time, I'll bet.   *Not a new experience*

PETRA. But, Father, tell us what this is all about.

DR. STOCKMANN. Yes, yes, just give me time and you'll hear all about it. Ah, if only I had Peter here! Yes, it lets you see how we men go about our affairs as blind as bats. . . .

HOVSTAD. What do you mean, Doctor?

DR. STOCKMANN [*stands by the table*]. Is it not generally believed that our town is a healthy place?

HOVSTAD. Yes, of course.

DR. STOCKMANN. A quite exceptionally healthy place, in fact . . . a place highly commended on this score both for the sick and for the healthy. . . .

MRS. STOCKMANN. Yes, but my dear Thomas . . .

DR. STOCKMANN. And have we not recommended it and acclaimed it? I myself have written repeatedly, both in the *Herald* and in a number of pamphlets. . . .

HOVSTAD. Well, what of it?

DR. STOCKMANN. And then these Baths—the so-called 'artery' of the town, or the 'nerve centre', and the devil only knows what else they've been called. . . .

BILLING. 'The throbbing heart of the town', as I was once, in a festive moment, moved to call it.

DR. STOCKMANN. Quite so. But do you know what they are in reality, these great and splendid and glorious Baths that have cost such a lot of money—do you know what they are?

HOVSTAD. No, what are they?

MRS. STOCKMANN. Yes, what are they?

DR. STOCKMANN. The Baths are nothing but a cesspool.

PETRA. The Baths, Father!

MRS. STOCKMANN [*at the same time*]. Our Baths!

HOVSTAD [*likewise*]. But, Doctor . . . !

BILLING. Absolutely incredible!

DR. STOCKMANN. The whole establishment is a whited poisoned sepulchre, I tell you! A most serious danger to health! All that filth up at Mölledal, where there's such an awful stench—it's all seeping into the pipes that lead to the pump-room! And that same damned, poisonous muck is seeping out on the beach as well!

HORSTER. Where the bathing place is, you mean?

DR. STOCKMANN. Exactly.

HOVSTAD. How are you so certain about all this, Doctor?

DR. STOCKMANN. I have investigated the position with scrupulous thoroughness. Oh, I've had my suspicions long enough. Last year there were a number of curious cases of sickness among the visitors . . . typhoid and gastric fever. . . .

MRS. STOCKMANN. Yes, so there were.

DR. STOCKMANN. It was thought at the time that the visitors had brought their infections with them. But afterwards . . . during the winter . . . I began to have other ideas. So I carried out a few tests on the water, as far as I could.

MRS. STOCKMANN. So *that's* what's been keeping you so busy!

DR. STOCKMANN. Yes, you may well say I've been busy, Katherine. But of course I didn't have all the necessary scientific equipment. So I sent some samples—drinking water as well as sea-water—up to the university to get an exact chemical analysis.

HOVSTAD. Which you have now received?

DR. STOCKMANN [*shows the letter*]. Here it is! It testifies to the presence in the water of putrefied organic matter . . . it's full of bacteria. It is extremely dangerous to health, internally and externally.

MRS. STOCKMANN. What a mercy you found out in time!

DR. STOCKMANN. You may well say so.

HOVSTAD. And what do you intend to do now, Doctor?

DR. STOCKMANN. To see the matter put right, of course.

HOVSTAD. Can that be done?

DR. STOCKMANN. It must be done. Otherwise the whole establishment is useless, ruined. But there's no need for that. It's quite clear to me what must now be done.

MRS. STOCKMANN. But, my dear Thomas, what made you keep all this so secret?

DR. STOCKMANN. Did you expect me to run all round town gossiping about it before I was absolutely certain? No thank you! I'm not such a fool as all that.

PETRA. Still, your own family . . .

DR. STOCKMANN. No, not a living soul. Still, you can run round in the morning to the old 'Badger'. . . .

MRS. STOCKMANN. Please, Thomas!

DR. STOCKMANN. All right, to your grandfather, then. Yes, now we'll give that old boy something that will really open his eyes. He's another one who thinks I'm a bit cracked—oh yes, there are plenty more with the same idea, I can see. But now these good people are going to see something—they're certainly going to see something, this time. [*He walks round rubbing his hands.*] What a commotion this is going to cause in the town, Katherine! You've no idea! All the pipes will have to be re-laid.

HOVSTAD [*rising*]. All the pipes . . . ?

DR. STOCKMANN. Naturally. The intake is sited too low down; it will have to be moved much higher up.

PETRA. So you were right after all.

DR. STOCKMANN. Ah, you remember, Petra? I wrote in opposing it, when they were drawing up the plans. But at that time nobody would listen to me. Well, now I'm going to let them have it. Naturally I've written a report for the Board—it's been lying there all ready for the past week. I was only waiting for this to come. [*He points to the letter.*] But now we'll get this off at once. [*He goes into his room and comes back with a sheaf of papers.*] Look! Four closely written sheets! And the letter attached. A newspaper, Katherine! Something to wrap it in. Good! There we are! Give it to ... to ... [*Stamps his foot.*] ... what the devil's her name again? Anyway, give it to that girl, and tell her to take it straight down to the Mayor.

[MRS. STOCKMANN *takes the packet and goes out through the dining-room.*]

PETRA. What do you think Uncle Peter's going to say, Father?

DR. STOCKMANN. What do you expect him to say? He can't help but be pleased that an important matter like this has been brought to light, surely.

HOVSTAD. Do you mind if we put a little paragraph in the *Herald* about your discovery?

DR. STOCKMANN. I should be extremely grateful if you would.

HOVSTAD. The sooner the public hears about this, the better.

DR. STOCKMANN. Certainly.

MRS. STOCKMANN [*returning*]. She's just gone with it now.

BILLING. You'll be the leading light of the town, Dr. Stockmann, damn me if you won't!

DR. STOCKMANN [*walks happily up and down*]. Oh, don't be silly! I've only done my duty. It just happened to be a lucky strike, that's all. All the same ...

BILLING. Hovstad, don't you think the town ought to organize something to show its appreciation to Dr. Stockmann?

HOVSTAD. I'll certainly put it forward.

BILLING. And I'll talk it over with Aslaksen.

DR. STOCKMANN. Please, please, my dear friends! Let's have no more of this nonsense. I won't hear of it. And if the Board starts getting any ideas about increasing my salary, I shall refuse. Do you hear me, Katherine?—I won't take it.

MRS. STOCKMANN. Quite right, Thomas.

PETRA [*raising her glass*]. Your health, Father!

HOVSTAD.
BILLING. } Your health, Dr. Stockmann!

HORSTER [*clinking glasses with him*]. Here's wishing you joy of it!

DR. STOCKMANN. Thank you, my dear friends, thank you! I am extremely happy. . . . What a wonderful thing it is to feel that one's been of some service to one's home town and fellow citizens. Hurrah, Katherine!

[*He puts his arms round her and whirls her round and round; she screams and tries to resist. Laughter, applause and cheering for the Doctor. The boys poke their heads in at the door.*]

ACT TWO

The DOCTOR'S *living-room; the door to the dining-room is shut. It is morning.* MRS. STOCKMANN *comes out of the dining-room, carrying in her hand a sealed letter; she crosses to the door of the* DOCTOR'S *study, right, and peeps in.*

MRS. STOCKMANN. Are you there, Thomas?

DR. STOCKMANN [*within*]. Yes, I've just got back. [*Comes in.*] What is it?

MRS. STOCKMANN. A letter from your brother.

[*She hands him the letter.*]

DR. STOCKMANN. Aha, let us see. [*He opens the envelope and reads.*] 'Your manuscript is herewith returned. . . .' [*He reads on to himself in a low murmur.*] Hm!

MRS. STOCKMANN. What does he say?

DR. STOCKMANN. Oh, just that he'll look in about midday.

MRS. STOCKMANN. You mustn't forget to be at home this time.

DR. STOCKMANN. I'll manage that all right; I've finished all my morning calls.

MRS. STOCKMANN. I'm awfully curious to know how he's taking it.

DR. STOCKMANN. He'll not be very pleased that I was the one to make the discovery and not he, you'll see.

MRS. STOCKMANN. Doesn't that worry you a little?

DR. STOCKMANN. Oh, he'll be glad enough really, you know. It's just that Peter can't bear to see anybody other than himself doing things for the town.

MRS. STOCKMANN. Well, you know what I think, Thomas? I think you should be a dear and share the credit with him. Couldn't you drop a hint that it was he who first put you on the track. . . ?

DR. STOCKMANN. Certainly, for all it matters to me. I only want to see that something gets done about it. . . .

[*Old* MORTEN KIIL *puts his head round the hall door, looks round inquiringly, and chuckles to himself.*]

MORTEN KIIL [*slyly*]. This thing . . . is it true?

MRS. STOCKMANN [*crosses towards him*]. Father! What are you doing here!

DR. STOCKMANN. Well, well! Good morning, Father-in-law!

MRS. STOCKMANN. Do come in.

KIIL. I will if it's true; if it isn't, I'm off again.

DR. STOCKMANN. If what's true?

KIIL. This queer business about the water-works. Well, is it true?

DR. STOCKMANN. Certainly it's true. But how did you get to know about it?

KIIL [*comes in*]. Petra dashed in on her way to school. . . .

DR. STOCKMANN. Oh, did she?

KIIL. Yes, and from what she says . . . I thought she was just pulling my leg; but it isn't like Petra to do that.

DR. STOCKMANN. No, what made you think a thing like that!

KIIL. Oh, you should never trust anybody. You can be taken in almost before you know where you are. But it really is true, then?

DR. STOCKMANN. Definitely. Just you sit down now. [*Urges him to sit on the sofa.*] Isn't this a real stroke of luck for the town. . . ?

KIIL [*fighting his laughter*]. A stroke of luck for the town?

DR. STOCKMANN. Yes, the fact that I found out in time. . . .

KIIL [*as before*]. Oh, yes, of course! But I never thought you would try any monkey tricks on your own brother.

DR. STOCKMANN. Monkey tricks?

MRS. STOCKMANN. Really, Father!

KIIL [*resting his hands and his chin on the handle of his stick and winking slyly at the* DOCTOR]. Let me see, how was it now? Wasn't it something about some little creatures that had got into the water pipes?

DR. STOCKMANN. That's right. Bacteria.

KIIL. And from what Petra said, a whole lot of these animals had got in. An enormous number.

DR. STOCKMANN. That's right. Hundreds of thousands of them!

KIIL. And yet nobody can see them—isn't that what they say?

DR. STOCKMANN. Of course. Nobody can *see* them.

KIIL [*quietly chuckling*]. Damn me if this isn't the best you've managed yet.

DR. STOCKMANN. I don't know what you mean!

KIIL. But you'll never get the Mayor to believe a thing like this.

DR. STOCKMANN. We'll see about that.

KIIL. You don't think he's such a fool as all that!

DR. STOCKMANN. I hope the whole town's going to be such fools as all that.

KIIL. The whole town. Well, that's not such a bad idea, after all. It'll serve them right . . . do them good. They all think they're so much smarter than us older men. They hounded me off the Council, they did, I tell you. Treated me like a dog, they did. But now they'll get what's coming to them. You just carry on with your little tricks, Stockmann.

DR. STOCKMANN. But really . . .

KIIL. You just keep it up, I say. [*Gets up.*] If you can manage to put a thing like this across on the Mayor and his lot, I'll give a hundred crowns to charity on the spot.

DR. STOCKMANN. That's very good of you.

KIIL. Yes, I haven't all that much money to throw about, I'll have you know, but if you pull this off, I'll give fifty crowns to charity next Christmas.

[HOVSTAD *comes in from the hall.*]

HOVSTAD. Good morning! [*Stops.*] Oh, I beg your pardon. . . .

DR. STOCKMANN. No, come in, come in.

KIIL [*chuckles again*]. Him! Is he in on this as well?

HOVSTAD. What do you mean?

DR. STOCKMANN. Of course he's in on it.

KIIL. I might have known! It has to get into the papers. Ah! You're a right one, Stockmann. I'll leave you to talk it over; and now I'll be off.

DR. STOCKMANN. Oh, can't you stay a bit longer?

KIIL. No, I must be off now. Keep it up and bring out all the tricks you can think of. I'm damned sure you won't lose by it.

[*He goes, accompanied by* MRS. STOCKMANN.]

DR. STOCKMANN [*laughs*]. Fancy—the old man doesn't believe a word about this business of the water-works!

HOVSTAD. Ah, so that was what you . . . !

DR. STOCKMANN. Yes, that was what we were talking about. And you've probably come about the same thing, eh?

HOVSTAD. Yes, I have. Can you spare me a moment or two, Doctor?

DR. STOCKMANN. As long as you like, my dear fellow.

HOVSTAD. Have you heard anything from the Mayor?

DR. STOCKMANN. Not yet. He's coming round here later.

HOVSTAD. I've been thinking a lot about this thing since last night.

DR. STOCKMANN. Well?

HOVSTAD. As a doctor and a man of science, you regard this matter of the water-supply as something quite on its own, no doubt. What I mean is—it probably hasn't struck you that it's tied up with a lot of other things?

DR. STOCKMANN. In what way. . . ? Come and sit down, my dear fellow. No, on the sofa there.

[HOVSTAD *sits down on the sofa, the* DOCTOR *in an armchair on the other side of the table.*]

DR. STOCKMANN. Now, what was it you were saying. . . ?

HOVSTAD. You said yesterday that the water was contaminated by impurities in the soil.

DR. STOCKMANN. Yes, there's no doubt it all comes from that poisonous swamp up at Mölledal.

HOVSTAD. You'll forgive me, Doctor, but I think it comes from a very different swamp.

DR. STOCKMANN. What swamp?

HOVSTAD. The swamp that our whole community is standing rotting in.

DR. STOCKMANN. What kind of damned nonsense is this you're talking, Mr. Hovstad?

HOVSTAD. Everything in this town has gradually found its way into the hands of a certain group of officials. . . .

DR. STOCKMANN. Come now, not every one of them is an official.

HOVSTAD. No, but those that aren't officials are friends and hangers-on of those that are—the wealthy ones of the town, and the well-connected. These are the people in control.

DR. STOCKMANN. Yes, but you mustn't forget these are people of ability and insight.

HOVSTAD. How much ability and insight did they show when they laid the water pipes where they are now?

DR. STOCKMANN. *That*, of course, was a tremendous piece of stupidity. But that's going to be put right now.

HOVSTAD. Do you think it will be as easy as all that?

DR. STOCKMANN. Easy or not, it's going to be done.

HOVSTAD. Yes, as long as the press takes a hand.

DR. STOCKMANN. That won't be necessary, my dear fellow. I am sure my brother . . .

HOVSTAD. Excuse me, Doctor, but what I'm trying to tell you is that I intend taking the matter up.

DR. STOCKMANN. In the paper?

HOVSTAD. Yes. When I took over the *Herald* it was with the express intention of breaking up this ring of obstinate old buffers who'd got hold of all the power. *each has his own goals*

DR. STOCKMANN. But you told me yourself what the outcome of that was; it nearly ruined the paper.

HOVSTAD. Yes, it's true we had to pipe down on that occasion. Only because there was a danger that the whole business about the Baths might have fallen through if those men had been turned out then. But now we've got the Baths, and now these fine gentlemen can be dispensed with.

DR. STOCKMANN. Dispensed with, perhaps. But we have much to thank them for.

HOVSTAD. Full acknowledgement will be given, with all punctiliousness. But no popular journalist, such as I am, can afford to let an opportunity like this go by. This myth of official infallibility must be destroyed. A thing like this has to be rooted out just like any other superstition.

DR. STOCKMANN. I agree with you whole-heartedly, Mr. Hovstad! If there is any superstition, then away with it!

HOVSTAD. I should be most reluctant to implicate the Mayor, seeing that he's your brother. But I'm sure you agree with me that truth must come first.

DR. STOCKMANN. That goes without saying. [*Vehemently.*] Yes, but . . . but . . .

HOVSTAD. You mustn't think so badly of me. I am no more egotistical or ambitious than most.

DR. STOCKMANN. But, my dear fellow, who's suggesting you are?

HOVSTAD. I came from a fairly poor home, as you know. And I've had plenty of opportunity of seeing what's needed most among the working classes. And it's this: to have some say in the control of public affairs, Dr. Stockmann. *That's* the thing for developing people's ability and knowledge and confidence. . . .

DR. STOCKMANN. I can understand that very well. . . .

For someone a driving to get out ones secrets, very B compromising

HOVSTAD. Yes . . . and that's why I think it's a terrible responsibility for a journalist if he neglects any opportunity that might bring some measure of freedom to the humble and the oppressed masses. Oh, I realize all the big noises will just call it 'agitation' and so on. Well, let them say what they like! As long as my conscience is clear . . .

DR. STOCKMANN. Absolutely! Absolutely, my dear Mr. Hovstad. All the same . . . damn it . . . ! [*There is a knock at the door.*] Come in!

[ASLAKSEN, *the printer, appears at the hall door. He is poorly but decently dressed in a black suit, with a slightly crumpled white necktie; he carries in his hand a felt hat and gloves.*]

ASLAKSEN [*bows*]. Excuse me, Doctor, intruding like this . . .

DR. STOCKMANN [*rises*]. Well, well, here's Mr. Aslaksen!

ASLAKSEN. Yes, Doctor.

HOVSTAD [*stands*]. Is it me you're looking for, Aslaksen?

ASLAKSEN. No, it isn't. I didn't know I'd be seeing you here. No, actually it was the Doctor himself. . . .

DR. STOCKMANN. Well, and what can I do for you?

ASLAKSEN. Is it true what Mr. Billing tells me—that you are thinking of trying to get the water-supply improved?

DR. STOCKMANN. Yes, for the Baths.

ASLAKSEN. Well then, I've just called to say that I am ready to give every support to a thing like that.

HOVSTAD [*to the* DOCTOR]. There you are, you see!

DR. STOCKMANN. That's extremely kind of you, thank you very much; but . . .

ASLAKSEN. Because you might easily find you need some middle-class support to back you up. We now form what you might call a compact majority here in town—when we really *want* to, that is. And it's always a good thing to have the majority on your side, Dr. Stockmann.

DR. STOCKMANN. That is undoubtedly true. It's just that I don't quite understand why it should be necessary to take any special measures of that kind here. When it's such an ordinary straightforward thing, it seems to me . . .

ASLAKSEN. Ah, you never know but what it mightn't be a good thing anyway. I know well enough what the local authorities are like. Those in charge are never very keen on any kind of proposal that *other* people put forward. And that's why I think it wouldn't be a bad thing if we made a bit of a demonstration.

HOVSTAD. Yes, exactly.

DR. STOCKMANN. Demonstration, do you say? Well, what way did you think of demonstrating?

ASLAKSEN. Well, with great moderation, of course, Doctor. I try for moderation, in all things. For moderation is the first attribute of a good citizen . . . in my own opinion, that is.

DR. STOCKMANN. That's something that you yourself are well-known for, too, Mr. Aslaksen.

ASLAKSEN. Yes, I think I may say it is. And this matter of the water-supply is an extremely important one for us of the middle classes. The Baths show every sign of becoming a little goldmine for the town, as you might say; it's to them that many of us are looking for a means of livelihood, especially those of us who are house-holders. That's why we want to give the Baths all the support we can. And I happen to be the chairman of the Ratepayers Association . . .

DR. STOCKMANN. Yes?

ASLAKSEN. . . . and as I am moreover the local representative of the Temperance Society—you know, of course, that I take an active part in Temperance affairs?

DR. STOCKMANN. Yes, of course, of course.

ASLAKSEN. Well . . . you can see I meet quite a lot of people one way and another. And as I have the reputation of being a prudent and law-abiding citizen, as the Doctor himself said, it means that I have a certain influence in the town—a kind of little position of power, even though I say it myself.

DR. STOCKMANN. That I know very well, Mr. Aslaksen.

ASLAKSEN. And so, you see, it would be quite a simple matter for me to prepare an address, if such appeared necessary.

DR. STOCKMANN. An address?

ASLAKSEN. Yes, a kind of vote of thanks from the townspeople in appreciation of the way you have dealt with this matter of public interest. It goes without saying that the address would have to be drafted with proper moderation so as not to give offence to the authorities and those in power. And as long as we are careful about *that*, I don't really see that anybody can object, do you?

(handwritten margin note: on to Hovstad)

HOVSTAD. Well, even if they didn't like it very much . . .

ASLAKSEN. No, no, no! Nothing to give offence to the authorities, Mr. Hovstad. Nothing that might antagonize people with so much say in things. I've had quite enough of that sort of thing in my time, and no good ever comes of it, either. But the honest expression of a man's considered opinion surely cannot offend anybody.

DR. STOCKMANN [*shaking his hand*]. I just can't tell you, my dear Mr. Aslaksen, how delighted I am to find this support among my fellow citizens. It gives me great pleasure . . . great pleasure! I tell you what! What about a little glass of sherry, eh?

ASLAKSEN. No, thank you very much. I never touch spirits.

(handwritten margin note: Conservative, prudish)

DR. STOCKMANN. What do you say to a glass of beer, then?

ASLAKSEN. No thank you again, Doctor. I never take anything as early in the day as this. I am going into town now to talk to some of the ratepayers to see if I can prepare public opinion.

DR. STOCKMANN. Well, it really is extremely kind of you, Mr. Aslaksen. But I just cannot see all these arrangements being necessary. I think surely this matter can be managed on its own.

ASLAKSEN. The authorities sometimes take a bit of moving, Dr. Stockmann. Not that I'm trying to blame anybody, of course! Dear me, no!

HOVSTAD. We'll have a go at them in the paper tomorrow, Aslaksen.

ASLAKSEN. Please, Mr. Hovstad, no violence. Proceed with moderation, otherwise you'll get nowhere. You can take my word for it, because my experience was acquired in the school of life.—Well, I'll say goodbye now, Doctor. You now know that we of the middle classes stand solidly behind you. You have the compact majority on your side, Dr. Stockmann.

(handwritten note at bottom: This or Compact sounds so silly / buzzword sounds so silly)

DR. STOCKMANN. Thank you very much, my dear Mr. Aslaksen. [*Holds out his hand.*] Goodbye, goodbye!

ASLAKSEN. Are you coming with me as far as the office, Mr. Hovstad?

HOVSTAD. I'll be along soon. I still have one or two things to see to.

ASLAKSEN. Very good.

[*He bows and goes.* DR. STOCKMANN *accompanies him out into the hall.*]

HOVSTAD [*as the* DOCTOR *returns*]. Well, Doctor, what d'you think of that? Don't you think it's about time we did a bit of shaking up and clearing out of all this weary, cowardly fiddle-faddle?

DR. STOCKMANN. Are you referring to Mr. Aslaksen?

HOVSTAD. Yes, I am. He's one of the ones in the swamp—decent enough sort though he may be in other ways. Most of them are like that round here, teetering along, wobbling one way then the other; they are so damned cautious and scrupulous that they never dare commit themselves to any proper step forward.

DR. STOCKMANN. Yes, but Aslaksen seemed so genuinely anxious to help.

HOVSTAD. There's something I value more than that; and that is to stand firm, like a man with confidence in himself.

DR. STOCKMANN. Yes, I think you are absolutely right there.

HOVSTAD. That's why I'm going to take this opportunity to see if I can't get these well-intentioned people to show a bit of backbone. This worship of authority must be wiped out in this town. The real significance of this tremendous and unforgivable blunder about the water-supply must be brought home to every single person with a vote. *if they were ineligible, it wouldn't matter?*

DR. STOCKMANN. Very well. If you think it is for the public good, so be it. But not till I've had a word with my brother about it.

HOVSTAD. In the meantime I'll be drafting a leading article. And if the Mayor refuses to go on with things . . .

DR. STOCKMANN. Oh, but how could you possibly think that?

HOVSTAD. It's not impossible. And if so . . . ?

DR. STOCKMANN. In that case, I promise you. . . . Listen, in that case you can print my article; every word of it.

HOVSTAD. May I? Is that a promise?

DR. STOCKMANN [*hands him the manuscript*]. Here it is, take it with you. There's no harm in your reading it through; you can give it back to me afterwards.

HOVSTAD. Good! I'll do that. Well then goodbye, Doctor!

DR. STOCKMANN. Goodbye, goodbye! You'll see, Mr. Hovstad, it'll be all plain sailing . . . nothing but plain sailing!

HOVSTAD. Hm! We'll see.

[*He bows and goes out through the door.*]

DR. STOCKMANN [*crosses and looks into the dining-room*]. Katherine . . . ! Ah, are you back, Petra?

PETRA [*comes in*]. Yes, I've just come from school.

MRS. STOCKMANN [*comes in*]. Hasn't he been yet?

DR. STOCKMANN. Peter? No. But I've had a long talk with Hovstad. He's quite worked up about this discovery I've made. It seems there's more in it than I'd first imagined, you know. He's put his paper at my disposal, if it's ever needed.

MRS. STOCKMANN. Do you think it will be needed?

DR. STOCKMANN. No, of course not. But it makes one very proud to think that one has the progressive and independent press on one's side. And what else do you think! I've also had the chairman of the Ratepayers Association here to see me.

MRS. STOCKMANN. Really? What did he want?

DR. STOCKMANN. Also to offer his support. They are all going to support me, if need be. Katherine—do you know what I've got backing me?

MRS. STOCKMANN. Backing you? No. What?

DR. STOCKMANN. The compact majority.

MRS. STOCKMANN. Oh, have you! And is that a good thing, then, Thomas?

DR. STOCKMANN. I should jolly well think it is! [*He walks up and down, rubbing his hands.*] Lord! How wonderful it is to stand, as it were, shoulder to shoulder in the brotherhood of one's fellow citizens!

PETRA. And to be doing such good and useful work, Father!

DR. STOCKMANN. Yes, not to mention that it's for one's own birth-place, too.

MRS. STOCKMANN. There's the bell.

he is moved by smth greater than individual gain

DR. STOCKMANN. That must be him. [*There is a knock on the door.*] Come in!

MAYOR [*comes from the hall*]. Good morning.

DR. STOCKMANN. Glad to see you, Peter!

MRS. STOCKMANN. Good morning, Peter! How are things with you?

MAYOR. Oh, so-so, thank you. [*To the* DOCTOR.] I received from you yesterday, after office hours, a report concerning the state of the water at the Baths.

DR. STOCKMANN. Yes. Have you read it?

MAYOR. Yes, I have.

DR. STOCKMANN. And what have you got to say about it?

MAYOR [*with a sidelong glance*]. Hm . . .

MRS. STOCKMANN. Come along, Petra.

   [MRS. STOCKMANN *and* PETRA *go into the room on the left.*]

MAYOR [*after a pause*]. Was it necessary to make all these investigations behind my back?

DR. STOCKMANN. Yes, because until I knew with absolute certainty . . .

MAYOR. And now you do, you mean?

DR. STOCKMANN. Yes. Surely you are also convinced yourself by now!

MAYOR. Is it your intention to present this document to the Board as an official report?

DR. STOCKMANN. Of course. Something will have to be done about this thing. And quick.

MAYOR. As usual, you use some rather emphatic expressions in your report. Among other things, you say that what we offer our summer visitors is sheer poison.

DR. STOCKMANN. Well, Peter, what else can you call it? Just think! That water's poison whether you drink it or bathe in it! And this is what we offer those poor invalids who come to us in good faith and pay good money hoping to get their health back!

MAYOR. And then you conclude by stating we must build a sewer to deal with these alleged impurities from Mölledal, and that the present water pipes must be re-laid.

DR. STOCKMANN. Well, can you suggest any other solution? I can't.

MAYOR. This morning I made it my business to look in on the town engineer. And—half as a joke, as it might be—I brought up these measures as something we might give consideration to at some future date.

DR. STOCKMANN. Some future date!

MAYOR. He smiled at what he took to be my extravagance—of course. Have you taken the trouble to think what these proposed alterations would cost? According to the information I received, the cost would very probably be several hundred thousand crowns.

DR. STOCKMANN. As much as that?

MAYOR. Yes. But that's not the worst. The work would take at least two years.

DR. STOCKMANN. Two years, eh? Two whole years?

MAYOR. At least. And what's to be done with the Baths in the meantime? Shall we shut them? We'll have to. You don't think people are going to come all the way here if the rumour got about that the water was polluted?

DR. STOCKMANN. But, Peter, that's just what it is.

MAYOR. And all this has to come out just when the Baths were beginning to pay their way. A lot of other places in the district could equally well develop into health resorts. Can't you see they would set to work at once to divert all our tourist traffic to themselves. Of course they would; no doubt whatever. And we'd be left sitting there with all that expensive plant on our hands; we'd probably have to abandon the entire project. The whole town would be <u>ruined</u>, thanks to you!

one bro thinks it will save town
other   ruin

DR. STOCKMANN. Me. . . ? Ruined. . . ?

MAYOR. The whole future prosperity of the town is tied up with the Baths. You can see that as well as I can.

DR. STOCKMANN. Then what should be done, do you think?

MAYOR. I am not entirely convinced by your report that the state of the Baths is as serious as you make out.

DR. STOCKMANN. If anything it is worse. At least, it will be in the summer, when the warm weather comes.

MAYOR. As I said before, I think you exaggerate considerably. Any competent doctor would surely be able to meet this situation . . . take some suitable precautionary measures and treat any noticeable injurious effects, if there actually turned out to be any.

DR. STOCKMANN. Well? And what then?

MAYOR. The existing water-supply for the Baths is now an established fact, and must be treated as such. But it is reasonable to suppose that in time the Directors might not be disinclined to consider how far, in the light of the prevailing financial situation, it would be possible to initiate certain improvements.

DR. STOCKMANN. Do you honestly think I would lend myself to that sort of sharp practice?

MAYOR. Sharp practice?

DR. STOCKMANN. Sharp practice, yes! That's what it would be. A swindle, a fraud, an absolute crime against the public and against society!

MAYOR. As I remarked earlier, I have not been able to persuade myself that there is any actual imminent danger.

DR. STOCKMANN. Oh yes, you have! You couldn't help it. My report is absolutely correct and clear, I know that! And you know it too, Peter, but you won't admit it. You were the one responsible for having the Baths and the water-supply sited where they are now. And it's *this*—this damned blunder of yours—that you won't admit. Puh! Do you think I can't see right through you?

MAYOR. And even if that were so? Even if I may seem to guard my reputation somewhat jealously, it's all for the good of the town. Without some measure of moral authority, I should not be able to guide and direct public affairs in the way I consider best serves the common weal. Therefore—and for various other reasons—I consider it imperative that your report should not be presented to the Board. In the public interest, it must be withheld. Then I shall bring the matter up later, and we'll do all we can privately. But nothing, not a single word, of this disastrous business must be made public.

DR. STOCKMANN. My dear Peter, I doubt if we can prevent that now.

MAYOR. It must and shall be prevented.

DR. STOCKMANN. It's no use, I tell you. Too many people know about it already.

MAYOR. Know about it already! Who? I only hope it's not those people on the *Herald*. . . ?

DR. STOCKMANN. Oh yes, they know already. The progressive and independent press will see to it that you do your duty.

MAYOR [*after a short pause*]. You are an astonishingly indiscreet man, Thomas! Did you never think what consequences this might have for you personally?

DR. STOCKMANN. Consequences? For me?

MAYOR. For you and your family.

DR. STOCKMANN. What the devil do you mean by *that*?

MAYOR. Would you agree I've always been a decent brother to you, always ready to help?

DR. STOCKMANN. Yes, you have. And I'm grateful to you for it.

MAYOR. There's no need to be. In a way I had to be . . . in my own interests. It was always my hope that, by helping to improve your position economically, I might be able to some extent to hold you in check.

DR. STOCKMANN. What's that? It was only in your own interests . . . !

MAYOR. In a way, I said. It is distressing for a public figure to have his nearest relative for ever compromising himself.

DR. STOCKMANN. You mean that's what I do?

MAYOR. Yes, I'm afraid you do, without realizing it. You have a restless, pugnacious, aggressive temperament. And then there's this unfortunate habit of yours of rushing into print about everything under the sun. No sooner do you get some idea or other into your head than you've got to write an article for the papers about it . . . or even a whole pamphlet.

DR. STOCKMANN. But don't you think if a man's got hold of some new idea he has a duty to bring it to the notice of the public?

MAYOR. Oh, the public doesn't need new ideas. The public is best served by the good old, accepted ideas it already has.

DR. STOCKMANN. That's putting it pretty bluntly, anyway!

MAYOR. Yes, for once I'm going to be blunt with you. I've always tried to avoid that hitherto, knowing how irritable you are. But now, Thomas, I'm going to tell you the truth. You have no idea what harm you do yourself by this recklessness of yours. You complain about the authorities . . . about the government, even . . . you are always going on about them. Then you try to insist that you've been passed over, or been badly treated. But what do you expect, when you are so difficult?

DR. STOCKMANN. So I'm difficult too, am I?

MAYOR. Yes, Thomas, you are an extremely difficult man to work with, as I know from experience. You show absolutely no consideration. You seem to forget that it's me you have to thank for your appointment here as medical officer to the Baths. . . .

DR. STOCKMANN. I was the only possible man for the job! I, and nobody else! Wasn't I the first to see that the town could be made into a flourishing health resort? And wasn't I the only one to realize it at the time? Alone and single-handed I fought for the idea, year after year, writing and writing. . . .

MAYOR. Undoubtedly. But the time wasn't ripe for it then. Of course, you couldn't very well be any judge of that, living up there at the back of beyond. But when a more appropriate time came, then I— and some of the others—took the matter in hand. . . .

DR. STOCKMANN. Yes, and messed up the whole issue! My lovely plans! Oh yes, it's clear enough now all right what a brainy lot you turned out to be!

MAYOR. The only thing that's clear in my opinion is that you are simply trying to pick a quarrel again. You must find some outlet, so you go for your superiors—that's an old habit of yours. You just can't bear to submit to authority; you take a jaundiced view of anybody holding a superior appointment, regard him as a personal enemy. And straightway any weapon that happens to come to hand is good enough to attack him with. But now I've made it clear to you what other interests are at stake for the town as a whole—and consequently also for me personally. And that's why I'm telling you, Thomas, that I intend to be quite ruthless in demanding of you certain things.

DR. STOCKMANN. And what is it you demand?

MAYOR. Since you have been so indiscreet as to discuss this delicate matter with certain unauthorized persons—despite the fact that it should have been treated as a matter confidential to the Board— things can of course no longer be hushed up. All sorts of rumours will spread, and the more spiteful ones among us can be relied on to embellish them with all sorts of extras. It will therefore be necessary for you to make a public denial of these rumours.

DR. STOCKMANN. For me! How? I don't understand you.

MAYOR. We shall expect you, after making further investigations, to come to the conclusion that the matter is not by any means as dangerous or as serious as you in the first instance imagined it to be.

DR. STOCKMANN. Aha! So that's what you expect, is it?

MAYOR. Furthermore we shall expect you to make public declaration of your confidence in the Board, in its efficiency and its integrity, and in its readiness to take all necessary steps to remedy such defects as may arise.

DR. STOCKMANN. Yes, but don't you see, you'll never do anything just by fiddling with the problem, hoping to patch things up. I'm telling you straight, Peter, and I'm absolutely and utterly convinced . . .

MAYOR. As an employee you have no right to any private opinion.

DR. STOCKMANN [*falters*]. No right. . . ?

MAYOR. As an employee, I mean. As a private individual—good Lord, yes, that's quite different. But as a subordinate member of the staff of the Baths, you have no right to express any opinion that conflicts with that of your superiors.

DR. STOCKMANN. That's going too far! Are you trying to say that a doctor, a man of science, has no right . . . !

MAYOR. The matter in this instance is by no means a purely scientific one; it is a combination of technical and economic factors.

DR. STOCKMANN. It can be what the hell it likes, as far as I'm concerned. What matters to me is the right to speak my mind about any damn' thing under the sun.

MAYOR. Certainly! Anything at all—except the Baths. That we forbid.

DR. STOCKMANN [*shouts*]. Forbid! You lot!

MAYOR. *I* forbid you. I personally, your superior. And when I give you an order, it's up to you to obey.

DR. STOCKMANN [*controlling himself*]. Peter . . . if it wasn't that you were my brother . . . !

PETRA [*flings the door open*]. Don't stand for it, Father!

MRS. STOCKMANN [*following her*]. Petra! Petra!

MAYOR. Aha! You've been listening!

MRS. STOCKMANN. You were talking so loud, we just couldn't help . . .

PETRA. No! I stood there and listened.

MAYOR. Actually, I'm just as well pleased . . .

DR. STOCKMANN [*approaches him*]. You were saying something to me about ordering and obeying. . . ?

MAYOR. You compelled me to speak to you like that.

DR. STOCKMANN. And you expect me to get up in public and eat my own words?

MAYOR. We consider it absolutely necessary that you issue some sort of statement along the lines I laid down.

DR. STOCKMANN. And supposing I don't . . . obey?

MAYOR. Then we shall ourselves issue a statement to reassure the public.

DR. STOCKMANN. Indeed. Well, then I shall contradict you in the newspapers. I shall stand up for myself. I shall prove that I'm right and you're wrong. And then what will you do?

MAYOR. Then I shall not be able to prevent you from being dismissed.

DR. STOCKMANN. What!

PETRA. Father! Dismissed!

MRS. STOCKMANN. Dismissed!

MAYOR. Dismissed from the Baths. I shall be obliged to arrange for you to be given notice and to see that you sever all connection with the Baths.

DR. STOCKMANN. You wouldn't dare!

MAYOR. Blame your own recklessness.

PETRA. Uncle, this is a disgraceful way to treat a man like Father!

MRS. STOCKMANN. Do be quiet, Petra!

MAYOR [*looks at* PETRA]. Ah! So we can't wait to express our opinions, eh? Naturally. [*To* MRS. STOCKMANN.] Katherine, you are probably the most sensible one in this house. Please use whatever influence you have with your husband. Get him to see what this will mean both for his family . . .

DR. STOCKMANN. My family's got nothing to do with anybody but me!

MAYOR. . . . as I was saying, both for his family, and for the town he lives in.

DR. STOCKMANN. I'm the one with the real welfare of the town at heart. All I want to do is expose certain things that are bound to come out sooner or later anyway. Oh, I'll show them whether I love this town or not.

MAYOR. All you are really doing, by your sheer blind obstinacy, is cutting off the main source of the town's prosperity.

DR. STOCKMANN. That source is poisoned, man! Are you mad! We live by peddling filth and corruption! The whole of the town's prosperity is rooted in a lie! *[handwritten: double meaning: also the mayor]*

MAYOR. Fantastic nonsense—or worse! Any man who can cast such aspersions against his own birthplace is nothing but a public enemy. *[handwritten marginal mark]*

DR. STOCKMANN [*goes up to him*]. You dare . . . !

MRS. STOCKMANN [*throws herself between them*]. Thomas!

PETRA [*seizes her father by the arm*]. Steady, Father!

MAYOR. I am not going to wait to be assaulted. You've had your warning. Try to realize what you owe to yourself and to your family. Goodbye.

[*He goes.*]

DR. STOCKMANN [*walks up and down*]. Have I to stand for this? In my own house, Katherine! What do you think?

MRS. STOCKMANN. I agree it's shameful and disgraceful, Thomas. . . .

PETRA. If only I could get my hands on that uncle of mine. . . !

DR. STOCKMANN. It's my own fault, I should have had it out with them long ago . . . bared my teeth . . . bit back! Calling me a public enemy! Me! By God, I'm not going to stand for that!

MRS. STOCKMANN. But, Thomas my dear, your brother has a lot of power on his side. . . .

DR. STOCKMANN. Yes, but I have *right* on mine!

MRS. STOCKMANN. Right! Yes, of course. But what's the use of right without might?

PETRA. Oh, Mother! How can you say such a thing?

DR. STOCKMANN. So you think having right on your side in a free country doesn't count for anything? You are just being stupid, Katherine. And anyway, haven't I the progressive and independent press to look to, and the compact majority behind me. There's enough might there, surely, isn't there?

[handwritten at bottom: Repetition: he doesn't know them well enough to substitute words. He has faith that that's w/ they are]

MRS. STOCKMANN. But heavens, Thomas! You surely aren't thinking of . . .

DR. STOCKMANN. Not thinking of what?

MRS. STOCKMANN. . . . of setting yourself up against your brother, I mean.

DR. STOCKMANN. What the devil do you expect me to do? What else is there if I'm going to hold to what's right and proper.

PETRA. Yes, that's what I'm wondering too.

MRS. STOCKMANN. But you know very well it won't do a scrap of good. If they won't, they won't.

DR. STOCKMANN. Aha, Katherine, just give me time. I'll fight this thing to a finish, you watch.

MRS. STOCKMANN. Yes, and while you are fighting, you'll lose your job, that's what!

DR. STOCKMANN. Then at least I shall have done my duty by the public . . . and by society. Calling me a public enemy, indeed!

MRS. STOCKMANN. But what about your family, Thomas? What about us at home? Will you be doing your duty by the ones you should provide for first?

PETRA. Oh, stop thinking always about us, Mother!

MRS. STOCKMANN. Yes, it's easy for *you* to talk. You can stand on your own feet, if need be. But don't forget the boys, Thomas. And think a little of yourself too, and of me. . . .

DR. STOCKMANN. You must be absolutely mad, Katherine! If I were to be such a miserable coward as to go grovelling to Peter and his blasted pals, do you think I'd ever be happy again as long as I lived?

MRS. STOCKMANN. I'm sure I don't know. But God preserve us from the kind of happiness we'll have if you insist on carrying on like this. We'll be just where we were before—no job, no regular income. I thought we had enough of that in the old days. Don't forget that, Thomas, and think what all this is going to lead to.

DR. STOCKMANN [*squirming and clenching his fists*]. Oh, the things that a free and decent man has to put up with at the hands of these damned bureaucrats! Isn't it terrible, Katherine?

MRS. STOCKMANN. Yes, they've treated you disgracefully, I will say that. But heavens! Once you start thinking of all the injustices in this world people have to put up with . . . ! There's the boys, Thomas! Look at them! What's going to become of them? Oh no, you'd never have the heart. . . .

[*Meanwhile* EJLIF *and* MORTEN *have come in, carrying their schoolbooks.*]

DR. STOCKMANN. The boys . . . ! [*Suddenly stops with a determined look.*] No! Even if it meant the end of the world, I'm not knuckling under.

[*He walks over to his study.*]

MRS. STOCKMANN [*following him*]. Thomas! What are you going to do?

DR. STOCKMANN [*at the door*]. I want to be able to look my boys in the face when they grow up into free men.

[*He goes in.*]

personal pride is an issue for him as well

MRS. STOCKMANN [*bursts into tears*]. Oh, God help us.

PETRA. Father's grand! He'll never give in.

[*The boys, in amazement, begin to ask what is happening;* PETRA *signs to them to be silent.*]

like Hovstad's "as long as my conscience is clear" Don't they all think they're doing their best?

ACT THREE

The editorial office of the People's Herald. The entrance door is on the back wall, left; on the same wall, right, is a glazed door, through which the printing shop can be seen. On the right wall is another door. A large table stands in the middle of the room covered with papers, newspapers, and books. Downstage, left, is a window, near which is a writing desk with high stool. A couple of armchairs by the table, other chairs along the walls. The room is gloomy and cheerless; the furniture is old, the armchairs dirty and torn. Within the printing shop, a few compositors are at work; further back a hand press is being worked.

HOVSTAD is sitting at the desk, writing. After a moment or two, BILLING comes in from the right with the DOCTOR'S manuscript in his hand.

BILLING. Well, I must say . . . !

HOVSTAD [*writing*]. Have you read it through ?

BILLING [*puts the manuscript on the desk*]. Yes, I have that.

HOVSTAD. Pretty scathing, isn't he?

BILLING. Scathing! Damn it, it's absolutely devastating! Every word lands—what shall I say?—like a blow from a sledge-hammer.

HOVSTAD. Yes, but they're not the sort you can knock down with one blow.

BILLING. That's true! But then we'll just keep on hitting them . . . time and time again until the whole set-up collapses. Sitting in there reading it, I just felt as though I could see the revolution coming.

HOVSTAD [*turning*]. Hush! Don't let Aslaksen hear that.

BILLING [*lowering his voice*]. Aslaksen is a chicken-hearted little coward. He's got no backbone. But I hope this time you're going to insist? Eh? The Doctor's article will go in?

HOVSTAD. Yes, as long as the Mayor doesn't give in without a fight. . . .

BILLING. Make things damned dull if he does.

HOVSTAD. Well, fortunately we can make something of the situation whatever happens. If the Mayor doesn't accept the Doctor's proposal, then he'll have all the middle class on to him . . . all the Ratepayers Association and the rest. And if he does accept it, then he's got to face a pack of the bigger shareholders in the Baths who have so far been his strongest supporters. . . .

BILLING. Yes, that's right. I dare say it'll cost them a pretty penny. . . .

HOVSTAD. You can be damn' sure it will. Then, you see, once the ring is broken, we can keep pegging away day after day in the paper, pointing out to the public how completely incompetent the Mayor is, and how all the positions of responsibility, in fact the whole council, ought to be handed over to the Liberals.

BILLING. By God, that's good, that is! I can see it . . . I can see it! We're on the brink of revolution!

[*There is a knock on the door.*]

HOVSTAD. Hush! [*Shouts*]. Come in!

[DR. STOCKMANN *comes through the entrance door, back, left.*]

HOVSTAD [*crosses to him*]. Ah, it's you, Doctor. Well?

DR. STOCKMANN. Print it, Mr. Hovstad!

HOVSTAD. Has it come to that?

BILLING. Hurrah!

DR. STOCKMANN. Print away, I tell you. Yes, it *has* come to that. Now they're going to get what's coming to them. This is war, Mr. Billing!

BILLING. War to the knife, I hope! Go ahead and slaughter them, Doctor!

DR. STOCKMANN. This article is only the beginning. Already I've got enough ideas for another four or five of them. Where's Aslaksen?

BILLING [*shouts into the printing shop*]. Can you come here a minute, Aslaksen?

HOVSTAD. Another four or five articles, d'you say? About the same thing?

DR. STOCKMANN. Oh, no! Far from it, my dear fellow. No, they're about quite different things. But they're all bound up with the question of the water-supply and the sewers. You know how one thing leads to another. It's just like what happens when you start tinkering with an old building—just like that.

BILLING. By God, that's true. You pretty soon realize it's all such a shambles that you'll never finish the job properly until you've pulled the whole thing down.

ASLAKSEN [*from the printing shop*]. Pulled the whole thing down! Surely, Doctor, you are not thinking of pulling the Baths down?

HOVSTAD. No, of course not! Don't get alarmed!

DR. STOCKMANN. No, we were referring to something quite different. Well, Mr. Hovstad, what have you got to say about my article?

HOVSTAD. I think it's an absolute masterpiece. . . .

DR. STOCKMANN. Yes, isn't it. . . ? Well, I'm very pleased, very pleased.

HOVSTAD. It's so clear and to the point. You don't need to be an expert to follow it; anybody can understand from it what it's all about. I bet you get every progressively-minded man on your side.

ASLAKSEN. And all the sensible ones as well, I hope.

BILLING. The sensible ones and the other sort too. . . . What I mean is, practically the whole town.

ASLAKSEN. In that case, I think we might venture to print it.

DR. STOCKMANN. I jolly well think so!

HOVSTAD. It will be in tomorrow morning.

DR. STOCKMANN. Yes, by heavens! We mustn't waste any time. By the way, Mr. Aslaksen, that was something I was going to ask you: you'll give the manuscript your own personal attention, won't you?

ASLAKSEN. I will indeed.

DR. STOCKMANN. Take care of it as though it were gold. No misprints, every word is important. I'll look in again later on; perhaps I could check some of the proofs.—Yes, I can't tell you how I'm longing to get this thing in print . . . slam it down . . .

[handwritten: Dr. is feeling angrier, more than oppressed victim]

BILLING. Slam it down, that's right! Like a thunderbolt!

DR. STOCKMANN. . . . to submit it to the scrutiny of every intelligent citizen. Oh, you can't imagine what I've had to put up with today. They've threatened me with all sorts of things; to deprive me of my most basic human rights . . .

BILLING. What! Your human rights!

[handwritten: But it was just the mayor]

DR. STOCKMANN. . . . They tried to degrade me, to rob me of my self-respect, tried to force me to put personal advantage before my most sacred convictions. . . .

BILLING. Damn it, that's going too far!

HOVSTAD. Ah, you can expect anything from that lot.

DR. STOCKMANN. But I'm not going to let them get away with it— I'll make that plain in black and white. Every blessed day I'll be in the *Herald*—lying at anchor, so to speak, and bombarding them with one high-explosive article after another . . .

ASLAKSEN. Oh but, come now. . . .

BILLING. Hurrah! It's war, it's war!

DR. STOCKMANN. . . . I'll batter them to the ground, I'll smash them, I'll blast their defences wide open for all right-thinking men to see! That's what I'll do!

ASLAKSEN. But you will act with moderation, Doctor! Shoot . . . but with moderation. . . .

BILLING. No, no! Don't spare the dynamite!

DR. STOCKMANN [*continues unabashed*]. Because, you see, it's no longer just the water-supply and the sewers now. No, the whole community needs cleaning up, disinfecting. . . .

BILLING. That's what I like to hear!

DR. STOCKMANN. All these dodderers have got to be chucked out! Wherever they are! My eyes have been opened to a lot of things today. I haven't quite got everything sorted out yet, but I will in time. My friends, what we must look for is young and vigorous men to be our standard-bearers. We must have new men in command in all our forward positions.

BILLING. Hear, hear!

DR. STOCKMANN. And if only we hold together, things can't help but go smoothly! We'll launch this whole revolution as smoothly as a ship off the stocks. Don't you think so?

HOVSTAD. For my own part, I think we now have every prospect of placing the control of the council in the proper hands.

ASLAKSEN. And as long as we proceed with moderation, I can't see that there should be any risk.

DR. STOCKMANN. Who the devil cares whether it's risky or not? What I do, I do in the name of truth and in obedience to my conscience.

HOVSTAD. You deserve every support, Doctor.

ASLAKSEN. Yes, it's quite obvious that the Doctor is a true benefactor to the town, a real benefactor to society.

BILLING. By God, Aslaksen, Dr. Stockmann is the people's friend!

ASLAKSEN. I rather think the Ratepayers Association might soon be wanting to use that phrase.

DR. STOCKMANN [*greatly moved, grasps their hands*]. Thank you, thank you, my good friends, for being so loyal. How gratifying it is to hear you say that. That brother of mine called me something quite different. Well, he'll get it all back again, with interest! Well, I must be off now to see a patient of mine, poor devil. But I'll be back, as I promised. Be sure you take good care of that manuscript, Mr. Aslaksen—and, whatever you do, don't go leaving out any of my exclamation marks! If anything, put a few more in! Well, well! Goodbye for now, goodbye!

[*As they show him out, they take leave of each other; he goes.*]

HOVSTAD. There's a man who could be extremely useful to us.

ASLAKSEN. Yes, as long as he keeps to this business of the Baths. But if he gets going on other things, it might not be very wise to follow him.

HOVSTAD. Hm! That all depends on . . .

BILLING. Don't be so damned frightened, Aslaksen.

ASLAKSEN. Frightened? Yes, Mr. Billing, I *am* frightened—when it's a question of local politics. That's something I've learnt in the hard school of experience, you see. But you just put me in high-level politics, even in opposition to the government itself, and you'll see then whether I'm frightened.

BILLING. No, I'm sure you wouldn't be. But that's just what makes you so inconsistent.

ASLAKSEN. It's because I'm a man with a conscience. That's what it is. You can attack the government without really doing society any harm, because you see people like that just don't take any notice—they stay in power as if nothing had happened. But the *local* leaders, they *can* be turned out; and then you might easily get a lot of inexperienced men at the helm, doing immense harm to the interests of the ratepayers and other people.

HOVSTAD. But what about self-government as a factor in the people's education—haven't you thought about *that*?

ASLAKSEN. When a man has acquired a vested interest in something, you can't always expect him to think of everything, Mr. Hovstad.

HOVSTAD. Then I hope to God I never have any vested interests.

BILLING. Hear, hear!

ASLAKSEN [*smiles*]. Hm! [*He points to the desk.*] Your predecessor in that editorial chair was Mr. Steensgaard. He used to be sheriff.

BILLING [*spits*]. Pah! That turncoat.

HOVSTAD. I'm no time-server—and never will be, either.

ASLAKSEN. A politician should never be too certain about anything, Mr. Hovstad. And you, Mr. Billing, hadn't you better draw your horns in just a little these days—seeing you've applied for the post of Secretary to the council?

BILLING. I . . . !

HOVSTAD. *Have* you, Billing?

BILLING. Well . . . Can't you see I'm only doing it to annoy our local bigwigs, damn them.

ASLAKSEN. Well, it's nothing whatever to do with me. But when people accuse me of being cowardly or inconsistent, there's one thing I want to stress: the political record of Aslaksen the printer is an open book. I haven't changed in any way except to become more moderate in my ways. My heart is still with the people. But I'll not deny that my head rather inclines me to support the authorities—the local ones, I mean.

[*He goes into the printing shop.*]

BILLING. Don't you think we'd better finish with him, Hovstad?

HOVSTAD. Do you know anybody else who'd agree to let us have our paper and printing on credit?

BILLING. It's a damned nuisance not having the necessary capital.

HOVSTAD [*sits down at the desk*]. Yes, if only we had *that*. . . !

BILLING. What about approaching Dr. Stockmann?

HOVSTAD [*turning over some papers*]. Oh, what's the use of that? He hasn't anything.

BILLING. No, but he's got a good man up his sleeve—Old Morten Kiil, 'the Badger', as he is called.

HOVSTAD [*writing*]. What makes you so sure *he's* got anything?

BILLING. By God, he's got money all right! And some of it is bound to come to the Stockmanns. Then he'll have to think of providing for . . . for the children, at any rate.

HOVSTAD [*half turning*]. Are you counting on *that*?

BILLING. Counting? I'm not counting on anything.

HOVSTAD. You're right there. And you'd better not count on that job with the council, either. Because I can tell you now—you won't get it.

BILLING. Do you think I don't know that? That's just what I want—not to get it. To be rejected like that is just like adding fuel to the flames —it's like getting a new supply of fresh gall, and you need something like that in a dump like this where nothing really stimulating ever happens.

HOVSTAD [*writing*]. Yes, yes, I know.

BILLING. Well . . . it won't be long now before they hear from me! Now I'm going to sit down and write that appeal to the Ratepayers.

[*He goes into the room, right.*]

HOVSTAD [*sits at his desk, bites his pen shank and says slowly*]. Hm! Aha, so that's it. . . . [*There is a knock at the door.*] Come in!

[PETRA *comes in by entrance door, back, left.*]

HOVSTAD [*rises*]. Well, look who it is! What are you doing here?

PETRA. You must excuse me, but . . .

HOVSTAD [*pulling an armchair forward*]. Won't you have a seat?

PETRA. No, thanks. I can't stay.

HOVSTAD. Is it something from your father, perhaps. . . ?

PETRA. No, it's something from me. [*She takes a book out of her coat pocket.*] Here's that English story.

HOVSTAD. Why have you brought it back?

PETRA. Because I'm not going to translate it.

HOVSTAD. But you promised me faithfully. . . .

PETRA. I hadn't read it then. And you haven't either, have you?

HOVSTAD. No, you know I don't know any English. But . . .

PETRA. Quite. That's why I wanted to tell you that you'll have to look round for something else. [*She puts the book on the table.*] You can never use a thing like this for the *Herald*.

HOVSTAD. Why not?

PETRA. Because it runs completely contrary to everything you believe in.

HOVSTAD. Well, what does that matter. . . ?

PETRA. You don't quite understand. It's all about some supernatural power that's supposed to watch over all the so-called good people, and how everything is for the best . . . and how all the so-called wicked people get punished in the end. . . .

HOVSTAD. Yes, but that's just fine. That's exactly what people want.

PETRA. Can you honestly put stuff like that in front of people? When you yourself don't believe a word of it? You know very well that's not what happens in reality.

HOVSTAD. You're absolutely right, of course. But an editor cannot always do what he wants. You often have to give way to public opinion, in minor things. After all, politics is the most important thing in life—at least, for a newspaper, it is. And if I want to win people over to certain liberal and progressive ideas, it's no good scaring them all off. If they find a nice moral story like this on the back pages of the paper, they are much more ready to accept what we print on the front page—it gives them a sort of feeling of security.

PETRA. Oh, no! Not you, surely! I just can't picture you as a spider spinning a kind of web to trap unwary readers.

HOVSTAD [*smiling*]. Thank you for those few kind words. No, in fact you are right—it was all Billing's idea, not mine.

PETRA. Billing's!

HOVSTAD. Yes, at least he was talking about it just the other day. Billing's really the one who is keen to get that story in. I don't know the book at all.

PETRA. Mr. Billing? A man with all his progressive ideas. . . ?

HOVSTAD. Oh, Billing is a man of parts. I've heard he's also applied for the post of Secretary to the council.

PETRA. I don't believe it, Mr. Hovstad. Whatever makes him think he could stand a job like that?

HOVSTAD. You'd better ask him yourself.

PETRA. I'd never have thought a thing like that of Mr. Billing.

HOVSTAD [*looks at her intently*]. Wouldn't you? Does it come as such a surprise to you?

PETRA. Yes. Or perhaps not. Oh, I don't really know. . . .

HOVSTAD. Journalists like us are not really up to much, Miss Stockmann.

PETRA. Do you really mean that?

HOVSTAD. Now and again I think it.

PETRA. In the ordinary daily routine, perhaps; that I could understand. But when you've taken on something big . . .

HOVSTAD. You mean this business about your father?

PETRA. Yes, exactly. I imagine you must feel like a man with a more worthwhile job than most people.

HOVSTAD. Yes, I do feel a bit like that today.

PETRA. I'm sure you must! Oh, what a splendid calling you have chosen. Blazing a trail for the advancement of truth, and of new and bold ideas. . . ! Or even just to step up and give your support, without fear or favour, to a man who has suffered a great wrong. . . .

idealism

HOVSTAD. Especially when this unfortunate man happens to be . . . hm! . . . I don't really know how to put it. . . .

PETRA. Happens to be so decent and honest, you mean?

HOVSTAD [*quietly*]. Especially when he happens to be your father, is what I meant.

PETRA [*suddenly struck*]. What?

HOVSTAD. Yes, Petra—Miss Petra.

PETRA. Is *that* what you are thinking of first? You're not concerned about the thing itself? Not about truth? Not about Father's public-spirited action?

HOVSTAD. Oh yes, that too, naturally!

PETRA. No thank you, Mr. Hovstad! You have given yourself away this time. And I can never trust you again about anything.

HOVSTAD. I don't see why you want to take it like this when it was mainly for your sake . . . !

PETRA. What makes me cross is that you haven't played straight with Father. You talked to him as though all you cared about was truth and the common good. You made fools of us both. You are not the man you pretended to be. I'll never forgive you . . . never!

HOVSTAD. I shouldn't be too outspoken actually, Miss Petra. Especially not now.

PETRA. Why not now, particularly?

HOVSTAD. Because your father cannot manage without my help.

PETRA [*looking down at him*]. So you're one of those, are you? Pah!

HOVSTAD. No, no, I'm not. I don't know what came over me, saying a thing like that. You mustn't believe a word of it.

PETRA. I know what to believe. Goodbye!

ASLAKSEN [*comes in from the printing shop urgently and with an air of secrecy*]. In Heaven's name, Mr. Hovstad . . . [*He sees* PETRA.] Oh, I'm sorry. I shouldn't . . .

PETRA. There's the book. You'd better give it to somebody else.

[*She walks across to the main door.*]

HOVSTAD [*following her*]. But, Miss Petra . . .

PETRA. Goodbye.

[*She goes.*]

ASLAKSEN. I say, Mr. Hovstad!

HOVSTAD. Well, well . . . what is it?

ASLAKSEN. The Mayor's out there in the printing shop.

HOVSTAD. The Mayor, did you say?

ASLAKSEN. Yes, he wants a word with you. He came in the back way—didn't want to be seen, I suppose.

HOVSTAD. What does he want, I wonder? No, wait here, I'll go myself. . . .

[*He goes over to the door into the printing shop, opens it and invites the* MAYOR *in.*]

HOVSTAD. Aslaksen, keep an eye open to see that nobody . . .

ASLAKSEN. I understand.

[*He goes into the printing shop.*]

MAYOR. I don't suppose you were expecting me here, Mr. Hovstad.

HOVSTAD. No, as a matter of fact I wasn't.

MAYOR [*looking about him*]. You've settled yourself in here nice and comfortably. Very nice.

HOVSTAD. Oh . . .

MAYOR. And here I come without any appointment, and proceed to take up all your precious time.

HOVSTAD. *Please*, Mr. Mayor, I'm only too delighted to be of service. Let me take your things. [*He puts the* MAYOR's *hat and stick on a chair.*] Now, won't you sit down?

MAYOR [*sits at the table*]. Thank you.

[HOVSTAD *also sits down at the table.*]

MAYOR. I have had an extremely disagreeable matter to deal with today, Mr. Hovstad.

HOVSTAD. Really? Of course, with so many things to see to . . .

MAYOR. This particular matter has been raised by the Medical Officer of the Baths.

HOVSTAD. By the Doctor?

MAYOR. He's written a kind of report about a number of alleged shortcomings at the Baths, and sent it to the Board.

HOVSTAD. Has he?

MAYOR. Yes, hasn't he told you? I thought he said . . .

HOVSTAD. Oh yes, that's right! He did mention something about . . .

ASLAKSEN [*coming from the printing shop*]. I'd better have that manuscript. . . .

HOVSTAD [*angrily*]. It's on the desk there.

ASLAKSEN [*finds it*]. Good.

MAYOR. But I say, surely *that's* . . .

ASLAKSEN. Yes, that's the Doctor's article, Mr. Mayor.

HOVSTAD. Oh, is *that* what you were talking about?

MAYOR. Precisely. What do you think of it?

HOVSTAD. I'm no expert, of course, and I've only just glanced at it.

MAYOR. Yet you are printing it?

HOVSTAD. I can't very well refuse a man in his position. . . .

ASLAKSEN. I've got no say in what goes into the paper, Mr. Mayor. . . .

MAYOR. Of course not.

ASLAKSEN. I just print what I'm given.

MAYOR. Quite so.

ASLAKSEN. So if you'll excuse me . . .

[*He walks across towards the printing shop.*]

MAYOR. Just a moment, please, Mr. Aslaksen. With your permission, Mr. Hovstad . . .

HOVSTAD. Please.

MAYOR. Now you are a wise and sensible sort of man, Mr. Aslaksen.

ASLAKSEN. I am very pleased you should think so, Mr. Mayor.

MAYOR. And a man of considerable influence in some circles.

ASLAKSEN. Mainly among the people of moderate means.

MAYOR. The small ratepayers are in the majority—here as everywhere else.

ASLAKSEN. That's right.

MAYOR. And I've no doubt you know what most of them think about things in general. Isn't that so?

ASLAKSEN. Yes, I think I can safely say I do, Mr. Mayor.

MAYOR. Well . . . the fact that this admirable spirit of self-sacrifice is to be found in our town among its less well-endowed citizens . . .

ASLAKSEN. How do you mean?

HOVSTAD. Self-sacrifice?

MAYOR. . . . This shows an admirable public spirit, most admirable. I almost said unexpected, too. But of course you know better than I what people's attitudes are.

ASLAKSEN. But, Mr. Mayor . . .

MAYOR. And in fact it's no small sacrifice that the town will have to make.

HOVSTAD. The town?

ASLAKSEN. But I don't understand. . . . You mean the Baths, surely. . . .

MAYOR. At a rough estimate, the alterations which the Medical Officer considers desirable will come to something like a couple of hundred thousand crowns.

ASLAKSEN. That's a lot of money, but . . .

MAYOR. Of course it will be necessary to raise a municipal loan.

HOVSTAD [*rises*]. Surely it's not the idea that the town . . . ?

ASLAKSEN. It's not going to come out of the rates! Not out of the people's pockets!

MAYOR. My dear Mr. Aslaksen, where else do you see the money coming from?

ASLAKSEN. I think the owners ought to take care of that.

MAYOR. The owners do not see themselves in a position to provide any additional capital.

ASLAKSEN. Is that absolutely certain, Mr. Mayor?

MAYOR. I am assured on that point. If all these extensive alterations are considered desirable, the town itself must pay for them.

ASLAKSEN. But God damn it all—I beg your pardon!—but this puts a completely different light on things, Mr. Hovstad!

HOVSTAD. Yes, it does indeed.

MAYOR. The most ruinous thing is that we'll be forced to close the Baths for a couple of years.

HOVSTAD. Close them? Completely?

ASLAKSEN. For two years?

MAYOR. Yes, the work will take all that long—at least.

ASLAKSEN. Yes, but Heavens! We could never last out that long, Mr. Mayor. What would people like us live on in the meantime?

MAYOR. I regret to say that is an extremely difficult question to answer, Mr. Aslaksen. But what do you expect us to do? Do you think anybody is going to come here if you get people going round making up these stories about the water being polluted, and about the place being a cesspool, and the whole town . . .

ASLAKSEN. Do you think the whole thing might just be imagination?

MAYOR. With the best will in the world, I cannot come to any other conclusion.

ASLAKSEN. Then I must say Dr. Stockmann is being most irresponsible in all this. You must forgive me, Mr. Mayor, but . . .

MAYOR. I regret what you say is quite true, Mr. Aslaksen. My brother has always been rather impetuous, unfortunately.

ASLAKSEN. Are you still prepared to support him after this, Mr. Hovstad?

HOVSTAD. But who would have thought . . . ?

MAYOR. I have drawn up a short statement of the facts, putting a rather more sober interpretation on them; and in it I have suggested some ways in which such defects as may come to light could reasonably be dealt with without going beyond the present resources of the Baths.

HOVSTAD. Have you this statement with you, Mr. Mayor?

MAYOR [*fumbling in his pocket*]. Yes, I brought it with me on the off-chance that . . .

ASLAKSEN [*hastily*]. Heavens above, there he is!

MAYOR. Who? My brother?

HOVSTAD. Where?

ASLAKSEN. He's coming in through the printing shop.

MAYOR. It *would* happen. I don't want to bump into him here, and there was still a lot more I wanted to talk to you about.

HOVSTAD [*points to the door on the right*]. In there for the present.

MAYOR. But . . . !

HOVSTAD. There's only Billing in there.

ASLAKSEN. Quick, quick! He's coming now.

MAYOR. All right. But see if you can't get rid of him quickly.

[*He goes out through the door, right, which* ASLAKSEN *opens, and shuts again behind him.*]

HOVSTAD. Pretend you are doing something, Aslaksen.

[*He sits down and begins to write.* ASLAKSEN *rummages through a pile of newspapers on a chair, right.*]

DR. STOCKMANN [*entering from the printing shop*]. Back again!

[*He puts down his hat and stick.*]

HOVSTAD [*writing*]. Already, Doctor? Hurry up with what we were talking about, Aslaksen. We haven't got a lot of time to spare today.

DR. STOCKMANN. No proofs yet, they tell me.

ASLAKSEN [*without turning round*]. You could hardly expect them yet, Doctor.

DR. STOCKMANN. Well, well, it's just that I'm impatient—as you can well imagine. I can't settle to anything until I've seen the thing in print.

HOVSTAD. Hm! It'll be a good while yet, I fancy. Don't you think so, Aslaksen?

ASLAKSEN. Yes, I'm rather afraid so.

DR. STOCKMANN. Never mind, my dear fellows. I'll look in again. I don't mind coming twice if need be. An important thing like this . . . the welfare of the whole town . . . this is no time for dawdling on. [*About to go, but stops and comes back.*] Actually . . . there was something else I wanted to talk to you about.

HOVSTAD. Excuse me, but couldn't we perhaps make it some other time. . . ?

DR. STOCKMANN. It won't take a second. You see it's just that . . . when people read my article in the paper tomorrow morning, and realize that all through the winter I have been quietly working away in the interests of the town . . .

HOVSTAD. Yes, but Doctor . . .

DR. STOCKMANN. I know what you are going to say. You think I was only damn' well doing my duty . . . my simple duty as a citizen. Of course! I know that as well as you do. But my fellow citizens, you know. . . . Well, I mean, they think rather highly of me, actually, these good people. . . .

ASLAKSEN. Yes, the people have thought very highly of you up to now, Dr. Stockmann.

DR. STOCKMANN. Yes, and that's just what I'm a little bit afraid of. . . . What I mean is . . . a thing like this comes along, and they—especially the underprivileged classes—take it as a rousing call to take the affairs of the town into their own hands in future.

HOVSTAD [*rising*]. Hm! Dr. Stockmann, I don't think I ought to conceal from you . . .

DR. STOCKMANN. Aha! I might have guessed there'd be something in the wind. But I won't hear of it! If anybody's thinking of organizing anything like that . . .

HOVSTAD. Like what?

DR. STOCKMANN. Well, anything at all—a parade or a banquet or a presentation—whatever it is, you must promise me faithfully to put a stop to it. And you too, Mr. Aslaksen! I insist!

HOVSTAD. Excuse me, Doctor, but sooner or later you've got to hear the real truth. . . .

[MRS. STOCKMANN, *in hat and coat, enters by the main door, back, left.*]

MRS. STOCKMANN [*sees the* DOCTOR]. Just as I thought!

HOVSTAD [*goes over to her*]. You here too, Mrs. Stockmann?

DR. STOCKMANN. What the devil do you want here, Katherine?

MRS. STOCKMANN. You know very well what I want.

HOVSTAD. Won't you take a seat? Or perhaps . . .

MRS. STOCKMANN. Thanks, but don't you bother about me. And you must forgive me coming here to fetch my husband; for I'm the mother of three children, I'll have you know.

DR. STOCKMANN. What's all this rubbish! We all know that!

MRS. STOCKMANN. But it doesn't look as if you care very much these days about your wife and children; otherwise you wouldn't be carrying on as you are, bringing us all to rack and ruin.

DR. STOCKMANN. Have you gone stark, staring mad, Katherine? Are you trying to say a man with wife and children has no right to proclaim the truth—has no right to be a useful and active citizen—has no right to be of service to the town he lives in?

MRS. STOCKMANN. Do be reasonable, Thomas!

ASLAKSEN. Just what I say. Moderation in all things.

MRS. STOCKMANN. That's why it's very wrong of you, Mr. Hovstad, to lure my husband away from house and home and fool him into getting mixed up in all this.

HOVSTAD. I don't go about fooling people. . . .

DR. STOCKMANN. Fool me! Do you think I'd let anybody make a fool of *me*!

MRS. STOCKMANN. Yes, you would. I know, I know, you are the cleverest man in town. But you're too easily fooled, Thomas. [*To* HOVSTAD.] Remember, if you print what he's written he loses his job at the Baths. . . .

ASLAKSEN. What!

HOVSTAD. You know, Doctor . . .

DR. STOCKMANN [*laughs*]. Ha ha! Just let them try! Oh no, they wouldn't dare. You see, I have the compact majority behind me.

MRS. STOCKMANN. Yes, worse luck! Fancy having a nasty thing like that behind you.

DR. STOCKMANN. Fiddlesticks, Katherine! Go home and look to your house and let me look to society. Why should you be so afraid; I'm quite confident, and really rather pleased with things. [*Walks up and down, rubbing his hands.*] Truth and the People will prevail, you can take your oath on that. Oh, I see the massed ranks of a great citizen army marching on to victory. . . ! [*Stops by a chair.*] What the devil is *that*?

ASLAKSEN [*turns to look*]. Oh!

HOVSTAD [*similarly*]. Hm!

DR. STOCKMANN. There lies the highest mark of authority.

[*He picks the* MAYOR'S *hat up carefully by the tips of his fingers and holds it aloft.*]

MRS. STOCKMANN. The Mayor's hat!

DR. STOCKMANN. And here the baton of office, too. How in the name of glory . . . ?

HOVSTAD. Well . . .

DR. STOCKMANN. Ah, I see! He's been here trying to talk you over. Ha ha! Came to the right man, eh? Then he must have seen me in the printing shop. [*Bursts into laughter.*] Did he run away, Mr. Aslaksen?

ASLAKSEN [*hurriedly*]. Yes, Doctor, he ran away.

DR. STOCKMANN. Ran away without either his stick or . . . Rubbish, Peter never runs away from anything. But what the devil have you done with him? Ah . . . in there, of course. Now I'll show you something, Katherine!

MRS. STOCKMANN. Thomas . . . please!

ASLAKSEN. Have a care, Doctor!

[DR. STOCKMANN *puts the* MAYOR'S *hat on, takes his stick, walks over and throws open the door, and stands there saluting. The* MAYOR *comes in, red with anger; behind him comes* BILLING.]

MAYOR. What's the meaning of all this tomfoolery?

DR. STOCKMANN. Show some respect, my dear Peter. I'm the one in authority here now.

[*He walks up and down.*]

MRS. STOCKMANN [*near to tears*]. Oh, Thomas, really!

MAYOR [*following him about*]. Give me my hat and my stick!

DR. STOCKMANN [*as before*]. You might be chief constable, but I am the Mayor—I'm head of the whole town, can't you see!

MAYOR. Take that hat off, I tell you. Don't forget it's an official badge of office!

DR. STOCKMANN. Pooh! When a people rises from its slumber like a giant refreshed, do you think anybody's going to be scared by a hat? Because you might as well know, we are having a revolution in town tomorrow. You threatened to dismiss me; well now I'm dismissing you, relieving you of all your official positions. . . . Perhaps you think I can't? Oh yes, I can. Because I can bring irresistible social pressure to bear. Hovstad and Billing will put down a barrage in the *People's Herald*, and Aslaksen will sally forth at the head of the entire Ratepayers Association. . . .

ASLAKSEN. Not me, Doctor.

DR. STOCKMANN. Yes of course you will. . . .

MAYOR. Aha! Then perhaps Mr. Hovstad has decided to associate himself with this agitation after all?

HOVSTAD. No, Mr. Mayor.

ASLAKSEN. No, Mr. Hovstad is not so stupid as to go and ruin both the paper and himself for the sake of some wild idea.

DR. STOCKMANN [*looks round*]. What does this mean?

HOVSTAD. You have represented your case in a false light, Dr. Stockmann; consequently I cannot give it my support.

BILLING. And after what the Mayor was kind enough to tell me in there . . .

DR. STOCKMANN. A false light! You leave that side of things to me. You just print my article—I'm quite ready to stand by everything I say.

HOVSTAD. I'm not going to print it. I cannot and will not and dare not print it.

DR. STOCKMANN. Dare not? What sort of talk is that? You are the editor, aren't you? And it's the editors who control the press, surely?

ASLAKSEN. No, it's the readers.

MAYOR. Fortunately, yes.

ASLAKSEN. It's public opinion, the educated public, the ratepayers and all the others—these are the people who control the press.

DR. STOCKMANN [*calmly*]. And all these forces are against me?

ASLAKSEN. Yes, they are. It would mean total ruin for the town if your article were printed.

DR. STOCKMANN. Indeed.

MAYOR. My hat and my stick!

[DR. STOCKMANN *takes the hat off and puts it on the table, along with the stick.*]

MAYOR [*collecting them both*]. Your term as mayor has come to an abrupt end.

DR. STOCKMANN. This is not the end yet. [*To* HOVSTAD.] So it's quite impossible to get my article in the *Herald*?

HOVSTAD. Quite impossible. And I'm thinking partly also of your family. . . .

MRS. STOCKMANN. Oh, you needn't start worrying about his family, Mr. Hovstad.

MAYOR [*takes a sheet of paper out of his pocket*]. For the guidance of the public, it will be sufficient to print this. It is an official statement.

HOVSTAD [*takes it*]. Good. I'll see that it goes in.

DR. STOCKMANN. But not mine! You think you can gag me and silence the truth! You'll not get away with this so easily. Mr. Aslaksen, will you please take my manuscript and print it for me at once as a pamphlet—at my own expense, and on my authority. I want four hundred copies—no, five . . . six hundred, I want.

ASLAKSEN. Not if you offered me its weight in gold could I let my printing press be used for a thing like that. I daren't offend public opinion. You'll not get anybody in town to print it, I shouldn't think.

DR. STOCKMANN. Give it back to me then.

HOVSTAD [*hands him the manuscript*]. There you are.

DR. STOCKMANN [*takes his hat and stick*]. I'll get it out somehow. I'll call a mass meeting and read it out! All my fellow citizens shall hear the voice of truth!

MAYOR. You'll never get anybody to hire you a hall.

ASLAKSEN. Absolutely nobody, I'm quite certain.

BILLING. No, I'm damned if they will.

MRS. STOCKMANN. But that would be outrageous! Why is everybody against you all of a sudden?

DR. STOCKMANN [*angrily*]. I'll tell you why. It's because all the men in this town are nothing but a lot of old women—like you. All they can think about is their families; they never think about the rest of the community.

MRS. STOCKMANN [*taking his arm*]. Then I'll show them one . . . old woman at least who can be a man . . . for once. I'll stick by you, Thomas!

DR. STOCKMANN. Well said, Katherine. And I *will* have my say, by Heaven! If I can't book a hall, I'll hire a man with a drum to march round town with me, and I'll proclaim it at every street corner.

MAYOR. I can't believe you'd be so absolutely crazy.

DR. STOCKMANN. Oh yes, I would!

ASLAKSEN. You'll not get a single man in the whole of the town to go with you!

BILLING. No, I'm damned if you will!

MRS. STOCKMANN. Don't you give in now, Thomas. I'll get the boys to go with you.

DR. STOCKMANN. That's a wonderful idea!

MRS. STOCKMANN. Morten will love to go; and Ejlif's sure to come along as well.

DR. STOCKMANN. Yes, and then what about Petra! And you too, Katherine?

MRS. STOCKMANN. No, no, not me. But I'll stand in the window and watch, that's what I'll do.

DR. STOCKMANN [*puts his arms round her and kisses her*]. Thank you for that! And now, gentlemen, the gloves are off. We'll see whether you and your shabby tricks can stop an honest citizen who wants to clean up the town.

[*He and his wife go out through the door, back, left.*]

MAYOR [*shakes his head thoughtfully*]. Now he's sent her mad, too.

ACT FOUR

A large, old-fashioned room in the house of CAPTAIN HORSTER. *At the back of the room, double doors open on to an anteroom. On the wall, left, are three windows; against the opposite wall is a dais, on which is a small table, and on it two candles, a water carafe, a glass, and a bell.*

The room is additionally lit by wall lamps between the windows. Downstage left, a table with candles and a chair. Down right is a door, and beside it a couple of chairs.

There is a big crowd of townspeople of all classes. A few women and one or two schoolboys can be seen among them. More and more people keep coming in through the door at the back, filling up the room.

FIRST MAN [*bumping into another man*]. Hello, Lamstad! You here as well?

SECOND MAN. I never miss a public meeting.

THIRD MAN. I expect you've brought your whistle?

SECOND MAN. You bet I have. Haven't you?

THIRD MAN. I'll say I have. Skipper Evensen said he was going to bring his great big cow-horn.

SECOND MAN. Good old Evensen!

[*Laughter in the group.*]

FOURTH MAN [*joining them*]. Here, I say, what's going on here tonight?

SECOND MAN. It's Dr. Stockmann. He's holding a protest meeting against the Mayor.

FOURTH MAN. But the Mayor's his brother!

FIRST MAN. That doesn't matter. Dr. Stockmann's not frightened.

THIRD MAN. But he's got it all wrong. It said so in the *Herald*.

SECOND MAN. Yes, he must be wrong this time, because nobody would let him have a hall for his meeting—Ratepayers Association, Men's Club, nobody!

FIRST MAN. He couldn't even get the Baths Hall.

SECOND MAN. I should think not.

A MAN [*in another group*]. Whose side are we on here, eh?

A SECOND MAN [*in the same group*]. Just you keep an eye on Aslaksen, and do what *he* does.

BILLING [*with a briefcase under his arm, pushing his way through the crowd*]. Excuse me, gentlemen! May I come through, please? I'm reporting for the *Herald*. Thank you . . . thank you!

[*He sits at the table, left.*]

A WORKMAN. Who's he?

SECOND WORKMAN. Don't you know *him*? That's Billing, he's on Aslaksen's paper.

[CAPTAIN HORSTER *conducts* MRS. STOCKMANN *and* PETRA *in through the door, right front.* EJLIF *and* MORTEN *are with them.*]

HORSTER. I thought perhaps the family might like to sit here. You can easily slip out there if anything happens.

MRS. STOCKMANN. Do you really think things might get out of hand?

HORSTER. You never know . . . with all these people here. But you sit here, and don't worry.

MRS. STOCKMANN [*sits down.*] It was very kind of you to offer my husband this room.

HORSTER. Well, since nobody else would . . .

PETRA [*who has also sat down*]. And it was brave of you too, Captain Horster.

HORSTER. Oh, I can't see there was anything particularly brave about it.

[HOVSTAD *and* ASLAKSEN *arrive simultaneously but separately, and make their way through the crowd.*]

ASLAKSEN [*walks over to* HORSTER]. Hasn't Dr. Stockmann arrived yet?

HORSTER. He's waiting in there.

[*Movement in the crowd near the door at the back.*]

HOVSTAD [*to* BILLING]. Look! Here's the Mayor.

BILLING. Yes, damn me if he hasn't turned up after all!

[*The* MAYOR *eases his way through the crowd, bowing politely, and takes up a position by the wall, left. A moment later,* DR. STOCKMANN *enters by the door, right front. He wears a black frock coat and a white cravat. Some people clap uncertainly, which is met by subdued hissing. Then there is silence.*]

DR. STOCKMANN [*in an undertone*]. How do you feel, Katherine?

MRS. STOCKMANN. I'm all right, thanks. [*Lowers her voice.*] Try not to lose your temper, Thomas.

DR. STOCKMANN. Oh, I can control myself. [*Looks at his watch, steps up on the dais, and bows.*] It's now quarter past . . . so I think we can begin. . . .

[*He produces his manuscript.*]

ASLAKSEN. First I think we ought to elect a chairman.

DR. STOCKMANN. No. That's not necessary.

SEVERAL VOICES [*shouting*]. Yes, yes it is!

MAYOR. I should also have thought that we should elect a chairman.

DR. STOCKMANN. But I've called this meeting to deliver a lecture, Peter.

MAYOR. Your lecture might just possibly lead to divergent expressions of opinion.

MANY VOICES [*from the crowd*]. A chairman! A chairman!

HOVSTAD. The consensus of opinion seems to be that we should have a chairman.

DR. STOCKMANN [*controlling himself*]. Very well! Let the 'consensus of opinion' have its way.

ASLAKSEN. Wouldn't the Mayor accept nomination?

THREE MEN [*applauding*]. Bravo! Bravo!

MAYOR. For a number of obvious reasons, I must decline. But fortunately we have here with us a man whom I think we can all accept. I refer, of course, to the chairman of the Ratepayers Association, Mr. Aslaksen.

MANY VOICES. Yes, yes. Good old Aslaksen! Bravo!

[DR. STOCKMANN *gathers up his manuscript and steps down from the dais.*]

ASLAKSEN. If it is the wish of my fellow citizens, I can hardly refuse....

[*Clapping and cheers.* ASLAKSEN *mounts the dais.*]

BILLING [*writing*]. Let's see—'Mr. Aslaksen elected by acclamation...'

ASLAKSEN. And now, perhaps I may be allowed, in this present capacity, to take the opportunity of saying a few brief words. I am a quiet and peace-loving man, who believes in discreet moderation and in ... and in moderate discretion. Everyone who knows me is aware of that.

MANY VOICES. That's right! That's right, Aslaksen!

ASLAKSEN. I have learnt from long experience in the school of life that moderation is the quality that best befits a citizen ...

MAYOR. Hear, hear!

ASLAKSEN. ... and that discretion and moderation are the things whereby society is best served. I might perhaps, therefore, suggest to the honourable gentleman who has called this meeting that he endeavour to keep within the bounds of moderation.

A MAN [*near the door*]. Up the Moderates!

A VOICE. Shut up there!

MANY VOICES. Sh! Sh!

ASLAKSEN. No interruptions, gentlemen, please! Has anybody any comment to make?

MAYOR. Mr. Chairman!

ASLAKSEN. Yes, Mr. Mayor.

MAYOR. In view of the close relationship which, as is doubtless well known, exists between me and the present Medical Officer of the Baths, I should have much preferred not to speak this evening. But my connections with the Baths, to say nothing of my concern for the vital interests of the town, compel me to put forward some sort of proposal. I think I may safely assume that not a single one of us present here today wants to see irresponsible and exaggerated accounts put about concerning the sanitary conditions at the Baths and in the town generally.

MANY VOICES. No, no! Certainly not! We protest!

MAYOR. I should like to propose, therefore, that the Medical Officer be not permitted by this meeting to present his account of the matter.

DR. STOCKMANN [*flaring up*]. Not permitted! What is this . . .?

MRS. STOCKMANN [*coughing*]. Hm! hm!

DR. STOCKMANN [*composing himself*]. Ah! Not permitted, eh!

MAYOR. In my communication to the *People's Herald*, I acquainted the public with the relevant facts, and every right-thinking person can quite well form his own opinion. It clearly shows that the Doctor's proposal—apart from being a vote of censure on the leading citizens of the town—simply means saddling the ratepayers with an unnecessary expenditure of at least several hundred thousand crowns.

[*Cries of disapproval, and whistles.*]

ASLAKSEN [*ringing the bell*]. Order please, gentlemen! I should like to support the Mayor's proposal. I too believe there is some ulterior motive behind the Doctor's agitation. He talks about the Baths, but what he's really after is revolution. He wants to see the control of the council pass into other hands. Nobody doubts but what the Doctor is sincere in his intentions—nobody can be in two minds about that, surely. I too am in favour of self-government by the people, as long as it doesn't fall too heavily on the ratepayers. But that's just what *would* happen here. And that's why I'm damned . . . excuse me, gentlemen . . . why I just can't bring myself to agree with Dr. Stockmann this time. You can pay too dearly even for the best of things sometimes. That's *my* opinion.

[*Animated applause on all sides.*]

HOVSTAD. I feel I ought to make my position clear, too. Dr. Stockmann's agitation seemed in the early stages to be attracting a certain measure of approval and I supported it as impartially as I was able. But then we got wind of the fact that we had allowed ourselves to be misled by an incorrect account. . . .

DR. STOCKMANN. Incorrect. . . !

HOVSTAD. A not wholly reliable account, then. The Mayor's statement has proved that. I trust nobody here doubts my liberal convictions. The policy of the *People's Herald* on the more important political questions must surely be known to everybody. But I have profited from the advice of experienced and thoughtful men that, when it comes to local affairs, a paper should proceed with a certain caution.

ASLAKSEN. I entirely agree with the speaker.

HOVSTAD. And in the matter under discussion it is now undeniably true that Dr. Stockmann has public opinion against him. But what is the first and foremost duty of an editor, gentlemen? Is it not to work in harmony with his readers? Has he not been given, as it were, a tacit mandate to work loyally and unremittingly for the welfare of his fellows? Or am I perhaps mistaken?

MANY VOICES. No, no! Hovstad is right!

HOVSTAD. It has been a sad thing for me to break with a man in whose house I have of late been a frequent guest—a man who until today has enjoyed the undivided goodwill of his fellow citizens—a man whose only . . . or should we say, whose most characteristic failing is to be guided more by his heart than by his head.

A FEW SCATTERED VOICES. That's true! Good old Dr. Stockmann!

HOVSTAD. But my duty to the community compelled me to break with him. There is also one further consideration that impels me to oppose him and, if possible, to prevent him from going any further along this fateful course he has taken. And that is consideration for his family . . .

DR. STOCKMANN. You stick to the water-supply and the sewers!

HOVSTAD. . . . Consideration for his wife and his helpless children.

MORTEN. Is that us he means, Mother?

MRS. STOCKMANN. Hush!

ASLAKSEN. I shall now put the Mayor's proposal to the vote.

DR. STOCKMANN. You needn't bother! I don't intend speaking about all the dirty business at the Baths tonight. No! You are going to hear about something quite different.

MAYOR [*in an undertone*]. Now what's he up to?

A DRUNKEN MAN [*beside the entrance door*]. If I'm entitled to pay rates, I'm also entitled to my own opinion. And it's my entire ... firm ... incomprehensible opinion that ...

SEVERAL VOICES. Be quiet over there!

OTHERS. He's drunk. Chuck him out.

[*The drunken man is put out.*]

DR. STOCKMANN. May I speak?

ASLAKSEN [*rings the bell*]. Dr. Stockmann has the floor!

DR. STOCKMANN. If anybody, even a few days ago, had tried gagging me as they've tried tonight ... they'd have seen me leaping like a lion to the defence of my sacred rights as an individual. But that hardly matters to me now. Now I have more important things to speak about.

[*The crowd presses closer round him.* MORTEN KIIL *can be seen in the crowd.*]

DR. STOCKMANN [*continues*]. I've been doing a lot of thinking in the last few days ... turning so many things over in my mind that in the end my head was buzzing ...

MAYOR [*coughs*]. Hm!

DR. STOCKMANN. ... but I sorted things out in the finish. Then I saw the whole situation very clearly. That's why I am here this evening. I am going to make a great exposure, gentlemen! And the revelation I am going to make to you is incomparably bigger than this petty business about the water-supply being polluted and the Baths standing over a cesspool.

SEVERAL VOICES [*shouting*]. Don't talk about the Baths! We don't want to hear it! None of that!

DR. STOCKMANN. I have said I am going to speak about the tremendous discovery I have made in the last few days ... the discovery that all our *spiritual* sources are polluted and that our whole civic community is built over a cesspool of lies.

DISCONCERTED VOICES [*subdued*]. What's he saying?

MAYOR. Making insinuations. . . !

ASLAKSEN [*his hand on the bell*]. I call upon the speaker to moderate his language.

DR. STOCKMANN. I love my native town as much as ever a man can. I wasn't very old when I left here; and distance and longing and memory lent a kind of enchantment to both the place and the people. [*Some clapping and cheers.*] Then for many a long year I sat up there in the far North, in a miserable hole of a place. Coming across some of the people living here and there in that rocky wilderness, I often used to think they would have been better served, poor half-starved creatures that they were, if they had sent for a vet instead of somebody like me.

[*There is a murmuring in the room.*]

BILLING [*putting his pen down*]. Damn me if I've ever heard . . . !

HOVSTAD. That's a slander on a respectable people!

DR. STOCKMANN. Just be patient a little!—I don't think anybody would want to accuse me of having forgotten my home town up there. I sat brooding—rather like an eider duck—and the thing I hatched out . . . was the plan for the Baths. [*Applause and protests.*] And when fate at long last smiled on me, and it turned out I could come home again—yes, my friends, there didn't seem to be very much more I wanted from life. Just one thing I wanted: to be able to work—eagerly, tirelessly, ardently—for the common good and for the good of the town.

MAYOR [*looking away*]. You choose rather a peculiar way of . . . hm!

DR. STOCKMANN. So there I was—deliriously, blindly happy. Then, yesterday morning—no, actually, it was the evening before—my eyes were opened wide, and the first thing I saw was the colossal stupidity of the authorities. . . .

[*Noises, shouts and laughter.* MRS. STOCKMANN *coughs earnestly.*]

MAYOR. Mr. Chairman!

ASLAKSEN [*rings the bell*]. By virtue of my position . . . !

DR. STOCKMANN. Let's not be too fussy about a word here and there, Mr. Aslaksen! All I mean is I got wind of the colossal botch-up our so-called leaders had managed to make of things down at the Baths. If there's anything I just can't stand at any price—it's leaders! I've just about had enough of them. They are just like a lot of goats in a young forest—there's damage everywhere they go. Any decent man and they just get in his way, they're under his feet wherever he turns. If I had my way I'd like to see them exterminated like any other pest. . . .

[*Uproar in the room.*]

MAYOR. Mr. Chairman, is it in order to make remarks like this?

ASLAKSEN [*his hand on the bell*]. Dr. Stockmann . . . !

DR. STOCKMANN. I can't understand why it has taken me till now to wake up to what these gentlemen really are, when practically every day I've had a perfect specimen of them right in front of my very eyes—my brother Peter—slow on the uptake and set in his ideas. . . .

[*Laughter, noise and whistles.* MRS. STOCKMANN *sits coughing.* ASLAKSEN *rings his bell violently.*]

THE DRUNKEN MAN [*who has come in again*]. Are you referring to me? Because they do call me Petersen . . . but I'll be damned if . . .

ANGRY VOICES. Throw that drunk out! Get rid of him!

[*The man is again thrown out.*]

MAYOR. Who was that person?

A BYSTANDER. Don't know him, sir.

A SECOND MAN. He doesn't belong here.

A THIRD MAN. It must be that timber merchant over from . . . [*The rest is inaudible.*]

ASLAKSEN. The man had obviously had too much to drink. Proceed, Doctor, but do please remember—with moderation.

DR. STOCKMANN. Very well, gentlemen, I shall say no more about our leaders. If anyone imagines from what I've just said that I'm out after these gentlemen's blood this evening, then he's wrong—quite definitely wrong! Because I am happily convinced that all these old dodderers, these relics of a dying age, are managing very nicely to see themselves off—they don't need to call in a doctor to hasten the end. And besides they are not the people who constitute the greatest danger to society. *They* are not the ones who do most to pollute our spiritual life, or to infect the ground beneath us. *They* are not the ones who are the worst enemies of truth and freedom in our society.

SHOUTS FROM ALL SIDES. Who then? Who is, then? Name them!

DR. STOCKMANN. Yes, I'll name them, don't you fret! Because *that's* precisely the great discovery I made yesterday. [*Raises his voice.*] The worst enemy of truth and freedom in our society is the compact majority. Yes, the damned, compact, liberal majority. *That's* what! Now you know.

[*Tremendous commotion in the room. Most of the crowd are shouting, stamping and whistling. Some of the more elderly men exchange glances, and seem to be enjoying things.* MRS. STOCKMANN *anxiously gets to her feet.* EJLIF *and* MORTEN *advance threateningly on some schoolboys who are misbehaving.* ASLAKSEN *rings his bell and shouts for order.* HOVSTAD *and* BILLING *are both trying to speak, but cannot be heard above the noise. At last quiet is restored.*]

ASLAKSEN. As Chairman, I must request the speaker to withdraw his wild remarks.

DR. STOCKMANN. Not on your life, Mr. Aslaksen. It is that majority here which is robbing me of my freedom and is trying to prevent me from speaking the truth.

HOVSTAD. The majority is always right!

BILLING. And it damn' well always stands for the truth too!

DR. STOCKMANN. The majority is never right. Never, I tell you! That's one of these lies in society that no free and intelligent man can help rebelling against. Who are the people that make up the biggest proportion of the population—the intelligent ones or the fools? I think we can agree it's the fools, no matter where you go in this world, it's the fools that form the overwhelming majority. But I'll be damned if that means it's right that the fools should dominate the intelligent. [*Uproar and shouting.*] Yes, yes, shout me down if you like, but you can't deny it! The majority has the *might* —more's the pity—but it hasn't *right*. *I* am right—I and one or two other individuals like me. The minority is always right.

[*Renewed uproar.*]

HOVSTAD. Ha! ha! In the last day or two Dr. Stockmann has turned aristocrat!

DR. STOCKMANN. I've already said I'm not going to waste any words on that bunch of narrow-chested, short-winded old has-beens. They've no longer anything to give to the red-blooded life of today. I'm thinking of the few, the genuine individuals in our midst, with their new and vigorous ideas. These men stand in the very forefront of our advance, so far ahead that the compact majority hasn't even begun to approach them—and it's *there* they fight for truths too newly-born to have won any support from the majority.

HOVSTAD. Aha! So now he's a revolutionary.

DR. STOCKMANN. Yes, by God, I am, Mr. Hovstad! I'm plotting revolution against this lie that the majority has a monopoly of the truth. What are these truths that always bring the majority rallying round? Truths so elderly they are practically senile. And when a truth is as old as that, gentlemen, you can hardly tell it from a lie. [*Laughter and jeers.*] All right, believe it or not! But truths are not by any means the tough old Methuselahs people imagine. The life of a normally constituted truth is generally, say, about seventeen or eighteen years, at most twenty; rarely longer. But truths as elderly as that have always worn terribly thin. But it's only *then* that the majority will have anything to do with them; then it will recommend them as wholesome food for thought. But there's no great food-value in that sort of diet, I can tell you—as a doctor, I know what I'm talking about. All these majority truths are just like salt meat that's been kept too long and gone bad and mouldy. That's at the root of all this moral scurvy that's going about.

ASLAKSEN. It appears to me that the honourable gentleman is straying rather a long way from his subject.

MAYOR. I concur very much with what the Chairman says.

DR. STOCKMANN. You must be mad, Peter. I'm sticking as close to my subject as I can. For that's just what I'm trying to say: that the masses, this damned compact majority—*this* is the thing that's polluting the sources of our spiritual life and infecting the very ground we stand on.

HOVSTAD. And this is what happens, you say, just because the great majority of thinking people are sensible enough to keep their approval for recognized and well-founded truths?

DR. STOCKMANN. My dear Mr. Hovstad, don't talk to me about well-founded truths. The truths the masses recognize today are the same truths as were held by advanced thinkers in our grandfathers' day. We who man the advanced outposts today, we don't recognize them any more. In my opinion, only one thing is certain: and that is that no society can live a healthy life on the old dry bones of that kind of truth.

HOVSTAD. But instead of you standing there and giving us all this airy talk, it would be interesting to hear a bit more about these old, dry bones of truth we are supposed to be living on.

[*Approval from several quarters.*]

DR. STOCKMANN. Oh, I could draw up a whole list of these horrors. But for the moment I'll restrict myself to *one* recognized truth, which is actually a rotten lie but which nevertheless Mr. Hovstad and the *People's Herald* and all the *Herald's* supporters live by.

HOVSTAD. And that is?

DR. STOCKMANN. A doctrine inherited from your forefathers which you fatuously go on spreading far and wide—the doctrine that the general public, the common herd, the masses are the very essence of the people—that they *are* the people—that the common man, and all the ignorant and immature elements in society have the same right to criticize and to approve, to govern and to counsel as the few intellectually distinguished people.

BILLING. Well I'll be damned. . . .

HOVSTAD [*shouting at the same time*]. Citizens, take note of this!

ANGRY VOICES. So we are not the people, eh? Only the top people are to have any say, eh?

A WORKMAN. Chuck him out, saying things like that!

OTHERS. Out with him!

A MAN [*shouting*]. Let's have a blast of it now, Evensen!

[*Great blasts on a horn, along with whistles and tremendous uproar.*]

DR. STOCKMANN [*after the noise has died down somewhat*]. Be reasonable! Can't you bear to hear the voice of truth just for once? I don't expect you all to agree with me straight off. But I must say I expected Mr. Hovstad to admit I was right when he'd got over his first shock. Mr. Hovstad claims to be a free-thinker. . . .

VOICES [*in astonished undertones*]. Free-thinker, did he say? What? Mr. Hovstad a free-thinker?

HOVSTAD [*shouting*]. Prove it, Dr. Stockmann! Have I ever said so in black and white? *embarrassed to be called a free thinker*

DR. STOCKMANN [*reflectively*]. No, damn it, you are right. You've never had the guts. Well, I don't want to embarrass you, Mr. Hovstad. Let's say it's me who's the free-thinker, then. What I'm going to do is prove to you, scientifically, that when the *People's Herald* tells you that you—the general public, the masses—are the real essence of the people, it's just a lot of bunkum. Don't you see it's just a journalistic lie? The public is only the raw material from which a people is made. [*Murmurs, laughter and general disturbance in the room.*] Well, isn't that the way it is with life generally. Look at the difference between pedigree and cross-bred animals. Look at an ordinary barn-yard hen, for instance—fat lot of meat you get off a scraggy old thing like that! And what about the eggs it lays? Any decent, self-respecting crow could do as well. But take a pure-bred Spanish or Japanese hen, or take a pheasant or a turkey—ah! what a difference! Or I might mention dogs, which are so like humans in many ways. Think first of an ordinary mongrel—I mean one of those filthy, shaggy rough dogs that do nothing but run about the streets and cock their legs against all the walls. Compare a mongrel like that with a poodle whose pedigree goes back many generations, who has been properly fed and has grown up among quiet voices and soft music. Don't you think the poodle's brain will have developed quite differently from the mongrel's? You bet it will! That kind of pedigree dog can be trained to do the most fantastic tricks—things an ordinary mongrel could never learn even if it stood on its head.

[*Uproar and laughter.*]

A MAN [*shouts*]. Are you trying to make out we are dogs now?

ANOTHER MAN. We're not animals, Doctor!

DR. STOCKMANN. Ah, but that's just exactly what we *are*, my friend! We are as good animals as any man could wish for. But you don't find all that many really outstanding ones. Oh, there's a tremendous difference between the poodles and the mongrels amongst us men. And the funny thing is that Mr. Hovstad fully agrees with me as long as we are talking about four-footed animals. . . .

HOVSTAD. Yes, it's all right for *them*.

DR. STOCKMANN. All right. But as soon as I apply the principle to two-legged creatures, that's the end of it for Mr. Hovstad. He hasn't the courage of his convictions, he doesn't take things to their logical conclusion. So he turns the whole theory upside down and proclaims in the *Herald* that the barn-yard hen and the street-corner mongrel—that these are the finest exhibits in the menagerie. But that's always the way, and always will be as long as a man still remains infected by the mass mind, and hasn't worked his way free to some kind of intellectual distinction.

HOVSTAD. I make no claim to any kind of distinction. I came from simple peasant stock, and I am proud that my roots go deep into that common people he is insulting.

SOME WORKMEN. Good old Hovstad! Hurrah! Hurrah!

DR. STOCKMANN. The sort of common people I'm talking about are not found simply among the lower classes; they are crawling and swarming all round us—right up to the highest social level. You've only got to look at that nice, pretty Mayor of yours. My brother Peter is as mass-minded a person as anything you'll find on two legs. . . .

[*Laughter and hisses.*]

MAYOR. I must protest against these personal remarks.

DR. STOCKMANN [*imperturbably*]. . . . and that's not because he's descended, like me, from some awful old Pomeranian pirate or something—because that's what we are . . .

MAYOR. An absurd story. I deny it!

DR. STOCKMANN. . . . but because he thinks what his superiors think, and believes what his superiors believe. And anybody who does that is just one of the masses in spirit. You see, that's why my magnificent brother Peter is so terribly lacking in natural distinction—and consequently has so little independence of mind.

MAYOR. Mr. Chairman . . . ! ·

HOVSTAD. So in this country it seems it's the distinguished people who are the liberals! That's a new one!

[*Laughter.*]

DR. STOCKMANN. Yes, that's another part of my discovery. And along with that goes the fact that free-thinking is almost exactly the same as morality. That's why I call it downright irresponsible of the *Herald* to keep putting out this distorted idea, day in day out, that it's the masses, the compact majority that has the monopoly of morality and liberal principles—and that vice and corruption and every kind of depraved idea are an overflow from culture, just as all the filth in our Baths is an overflow from the tannery up at Mölledal! [*Uproar and interruptions.* DR. STOCKMANN, *unperturbed, smiles in his eagerness.*] And yet this same *Herald* can preach about raising the standards of the masses! Good Lord, if what the *Herald* says is right, raising the level of the masses would amount precisely to toppling them straight over the edge to perdition. But fortunately it's just one of those old lies we've had handed down—this idea that culture is demoralizing. No, stupidity and poverty and ugliness are the things that do the devil's work! A house that isn't aired and swept every day—and my wife Katherine says it ought to be scrubbed as well, but that's a debatable point—anybody living for more than two or three years in *that* kind of house will end up by having no moral sense left whatsoever. No oxygen, no conscience! And there must be an awful lot of houses in this town short of oxygen, it seems, if the entire compact majority is so irresponsible as to want to build the prosperity of the town on a quagmire of lies and deceit.

ASLAKSEN. I cannot allow such abusive remarks to be directed at the entire community.

A MAN. I move that the Chairman rule the speaker out of order!

ANGRY VOICES. Yes, yes! That's right. Out of order!

DR. STOCKMANN [*flaring up*]. Then I'll shout the truth on every street corner! I'll write to all the other newspapers! I'll see that the whole country gets to know what's going on here!

HOVSTAD. It might almost seem that Dr. Stockmann is set on ruining the town.

DR. STOCKMANN. I love this town so much that I'd rather destroy it than see it prosper on a lie.

ASLAKSEN. That's putting it pretty strongly.

[*Uproar and whistles.* MRS. STOCKMANN *coughs in vain; the* DOCTOR *no longer hears her.*]

HOVSTAD [*shouting above the din*]. Any man who wants to destroy a whole community must be a public enemy.

DR. STOCKMANN [*with rising temper*]. When a place has become riddled with lies, who cares if it's destroyed? I say it should simply be razed to the ground! And all the people living by these lies should be wiped out, like vermin! You'll have the whole country infested in the end, so that eventually the whole country deserves to be destroyed. And if it ever comes to that, then I'd say with all my heart: let it all be destroyed, let all its people be wiped out!

A MAN [*in the crowd*]. That's the talk of an enemy of the people!

BILLING. That, God damn me, was the voice of the people!

THE WHOLE CROWD [*shouting*]. Yes! Yes! He's an enemy of the people. He hates his country. He hates his people.

ASLAKSEN. As a citizen of this country, and as an individual, I am profoundly shocked by what I have just had to listen to. Dr. Stockmann has betrayed himself in a way I should never have dreamt possible. I must therefore, with great regret, associate myself with the opinion that has just been expressed by my honourable fellow citizens, and I propose we embody that opinion in the form of a resolution. I suggest something like this: 'This meeting declares that it considers Dr. Thomas Stockmann, Medical Officer to the Baths, to be an enemy of the people.'

[*A storm of applause and cheers. A number of people crowd round* DR. STOCKMANN, *cat-calling.* MRS. STOCKMANN *and* PETRA *have risen.* MORTEN *and* EJLIF *fight with the other schoolboys who have also been booing. Some of the grown-ups separate them.*]

DR. STOCKMANN [*to those whistling*]. You fools! I tell you that . . .

ASLAKSEN [*ringing his bell*]. Dr. Stockmann is out of order. A formal vote must be taken; but so as not to hurt anybody's feelings, we will do it by secret ballot. Have you any paper, Mr. Billing?

BILLING. There's both blue and white. . . .

ASLAKSEN [*stepping down*]. That's fine. We can do it quicker that way. Cut it into strips . . . there we are, now. [*To the meeting.*] Blue means no, white means yes. I'll come round myself to collect the votes.

[*The* MAYOR *leaves the room.* ASLAKSEN *and one or two others carry round the slips of paper in their hats.*]

ONE MAN [*to* HOVSTAD]. What's come over the Doctor? What are you to make of it?

HOVSTAD. Well, you know how impetuous he is.

SECOND MAN [*to* BILLING]. Tell me—you've been in their house quite a bit. Does the man drink, have you noticed?

BILLING. I'm damned if I know really what to say. They always bring the toddy out when anybody calls.

THIRD MAN. No, I think it's more likely he's a bit crazy.

FIRST MAN. Ah, I wonder if there's any insanity in the family.

BILLING. Could very well be.

FOURTH MAN. No, it's just spite, that's what it is. Wants to get his own back about something.

BILLING. He did say something secretly about wanting a rise; but he didn't get it.

ALL THE MEN TOGETHER. Well, there you are then!

THE DRUNKEN MAN [*in the crowd*]. I want a blue one. And I want a white one an' all.

VOICES. Is that that drunk again? Chuck him out!

MORTEN KIIL [*approaches the* DOCTOR]. Well, Stockmann, now you see where these monkey tricks of yours have landed you!

DR. STOCKMANN. I have simply done my duty.

KIIL. What was that you said about the tanneries at Mölledal?

DR. STOCKMANN. You heard. I said that was where all the muck came from.

KIIL. From *my* tannery as well?

DR. STOCKMANN. I'm afraid so. Yours is the worst.

KIIL. Are you going to print *that* in the papers?

DR. STOCKMANN. I'm not hiding anything.

KIIL. You might find that costly, Stockmann.

[*He leaves.*]

A FAT MAN [*goes up to* HORSTER, *ignoring the ladies*]. So, Captain Horster, so you lend your house to enemies of the people, eh?

HORSTER. I think I can do what I like with my own property, Mr. Vik.

THE FAT MAN. So you won't mind if I do the same with mine.

HORSTER. What do you mean?

THE FAT MAN. You'll hear from me in the morning.

[*He turns and goes.*]

PETRA. Isn't he the owner of your ship, Captain Horster?

HORSTER. Yes, that's Mr. Vik.

ASLAKSEN [*mounts the platform with the ballot papers; he rings the bell*]. Gentlemen, let me announce the result. With only one vote to the contrary . . .

A YOUNG MAN. That's the drunk!

ASLAKSEN. With only one drunken man's vote to the contrary, the resolution of this meeting was carried unanimously: that Dr. Thomas Stockmann is an enemy of the people. [*Shouting and applause.*] Three cheers for our ancient and honourable community! [*More cheers.*] Three cheers for our able and efficient Mayor, for putting duty before family! [*Cheers.*] The meeting is adjourned.

[*He steps down.*]

BILLING. Three cheers for the chairman!

THE WHOLE CROWD. Good old Aslaksen!

DR. STOCKMANN. My hat and coat, Petra! Captain, have you any room aboard for passengers for the New World?

HORSTER. For you and your family we'll make room, Doctor.

DR. STOCKMANN [*as* PETRA *helps him on with his coat*]. Good! Come on, Katherine! Come along, lads!

[*He takes his wife by the arm.*]

MRS. STOCKMANN [*in a low voice*]. Thomas dear, let's go out by the back way.

DR. STOCKMANN. No back way for me, Katherine. [*Raises his voice.*] You'll hear again from this enemy of the people before he shakes the dust off his feet. I'm not as sweet-tempered as a certain person I could mention. I'm not saying: 'I forgive you, for you know not what you do.'

ASLAKSEN [*shouts*]. That comparison is blasphemous, Dr. Stockmann!

BILLING. Well I'll be . . . ! What dreadful things to say in the presence of decent people.

A COARSE VOICE. And what about those threats he made!

ANGRY SHOUTS. Let's go and break his windows! Duck him in the fjord!

A MAN [*in the crowd*]. Give us another blast, Evensen! Blow! Blow!

[*The sound of a horn and whistles and wild shouts. The* DOCTOR *and his family make for the exit, and* HORSTER *clears a way for them.*]

THE WHOLE CROWD [*howling after them*]. Enemy of the people! Enemy of the people! Enemy of the people!

BILLING [*tidying his papers*]. Well I'm damned if I would want to drink toddy at the Stockmanns' tonight!

[*The crowd makes for the exit; the noise is continued outside; shouts from the street of 'Enemy of the people! Enemy of the people!'*]

ACT FIVE

DR. STOCKMANN'S *study. Along the walls are bookcases and medicine cupboards. On the back wall is the door to the hall; left front is the door to the living-room. On the right wall are two windows, all the glass panes of which are smashed. In the centre of the room is the* DOCTOR'S *desk, covered with books and papers. The room is in disorder. It is morning.*

DR. STOCKMANN, *in dressing-gown, slippers and skull-cap, is bending down and raking under one of the cupboards with an umbrella. Finally he manages to rake out a stone.*

DR. STOCKMANN [*calling through the open door into the sitting-room*]. I've found another one, Katherine.

MRS. STOCKMANN [*from the living-room*]. Oh, you'll find a lot more yet, I'm sure.

DR. STOCKMANN [*adding the stone to a pile of others on the table*]. I'm going to keep these stones—like relics. Ejlif and Morten must see them every day, and when they grow up, they'll inherit them. [*Rakes under a bookcase.*] Hasn't—what the devil's her name again—you know, that girl—hasn't she gone for the glazier yet?

MRS. STOCKMANN [*comes in*]. Yes, but he said he didn't know if he could come today.

DR. STOCKMANN. He daren't—you'll see.

MRS. STOCKMANN. Yes, that's what Randina thought too—he was afraid of what the neighbours might say. [*Calls into the living-room.*] What's that you want, Randina? I see. [*She goes out and comes back at once.*] It's a letter for you, Thomas.

DR. STOCKMANN. Let me see. [*He opens it and reads.*] Aha!

MRS. STOCKMANN. Who's it from?

DR. STOCKMANN. From the landlord. He's given us notice.

MRS. STOCKMANN. Has he really? But he was such a nice man. . . .

DR. STOCKMANN [*looking at the letter*]. He daren't do anything else, he says. He's very sorry, but he daren't do anything else . . . because of the others . . . public opinion . . . not his own master . . . dare not risk putting certain people's backs up. . . .

MRS. STOCKMANN. There you see, Thomas.

DR. STOCKMANN. Yes, yes, I see all right. They are all cowards, the whole lot of them here. Nobody dares do anything because of all the others. [*Flings the letter on the table.*] But that doesn't make any difference to us, Katherine. We are leaving for the New World, and then . . .

MRS. STOCKMANN. But, Thomas, have you really thought about it properly, this business about leaving. . . ?

DR. STOCKMANN. You wouldn't want me to stay here, would you? Not after the way they've taken it out of me, branding me as an enemy of the people, and smashing all my windows! And look here, Katherine! I've even got a tear in my black trousers through them.

MRS. STOCKMANN. So you have! And they are the best pair you've got!

DR. STOCKMANN. You should never have your best trousers on when you turn out to fight for freedom and truth. Well, it's not that I care all that much about the trousers—you can always put a stitch in them for me. But what gets me is the idea of that mob going for me as though they were my equals—*that's* what I can't stomach, damn it!

MRS. STOCKMANN. Yes, they've really been horrid to you here, Thomas. But do we have to go so far as to leave the country for *that*?

DR. STOCKMANN. Don't you think you would get the same insolence from the masses in the other towns as you do here? Of course you would! They're all the same! Oh, to hell! Let them yap! That's not the worst; the worst thing is that all over the country everybody's got to toe the party line. Not that it's likely to be very much better out West either; it will be the same there too, with your liberal public opinions and your compact majorities and all the rest of the rigmarole. But things are on a bigger scale there, you see. They might kill, but they don't torture. They don't take a free man and put the screws on his soul, as they do here. And if the worst comes to the worst, you can get away from it all. [*Walks up and down.*] If only I knew where there was a primeval forest or a little South Sea island going cheap. . . .

MRS. STOCKMANN. But, Thomas, what about the boys?

DR. STOCKMANN [*halts*]. You are funny, Katherine! Would you rather the boys grew up in a society like this? You saw yourself last night how half the population is absolutely mad; and if the other half haven't lost their wits, it's only because they are such thickheads they haven't any wits to lose.

MRS. STOCKMANN. Now then, Thomas dear, you ought to watch what you are saying.

DR. STOCKMANN. Hah! You don't think I'm telling you the truth? Don't they turn every single idea upside down? Don't they make a complete hotch-potch of what's right and what's wrong? Don't they go and call lies what I know perfectly well is the truth? But the craziest thing of the lot is to see all these grown-up men going round calling themselves liberals and imagining they are men of independent minds! Have you ever heard anything like it, Katherine?

MRS. STOCKMANN. Yes, yes, of course that's quite stupid, but . . . [*PETRA comes in from the living-room.*] Back from school already?

PETRA. Yes. I've been given my notice.

MRS. STOCKMANN. Your notice?

DR. STOCKMANN. You too!

PETRA. Mrs. Busk gave me notice. And I thought it was better to leave at once.

DR. STOCKMANN. How right you were!

MRS. STOCKMANN. Who would have thought Mrs. Busk was that sort!

PETRA. Oh, Mother, Mrs. Busk isn't bad, really. I could see quite well she didn't like doing it. But she daren't do anything else, she said. So I have to leave.

DR. STOCKMANN [*laughs and rubs his hands*]. So she didn't dare do anything else, either! That's great!

MRS. STOCKMANN. Oh well, I dare say after that awful scene last night . . .

PETRA. It wasn't just *that*. Listen, Father!

DR. STOCKMANN. Well?

PETRA. Mrs. Busk showed me no less than three letters she'd had this morning. . . .

DR. STOCKMANN. Anonymous, of course?

PETRA. Yes.

DR. STOCKMANN. You see they *daren't* put their names to them, Katherine!

PETRA. And in two of them it said that a certain gentleman, who has been a frequent visitor here, had been talking in the club last night and saying that I had extremely advanced ideas about all sorts of things. . . .

DR. STOCKMANN. Which I hope you didn't deny?

PETRA. You know very well I wouldn't. Mrs. Busk has got one or two pretty advanced ideas herself, when she talks to me privately. But now that this has come out about me, she daren't keep me.

MRS. STOCKMANN. Fancy! A frequent visitor here! You see what you get for your hospitality, Thomas.

DR. STOCKMANN. We are not going to live in this stinking hole any longer. Pack up as quick as you can, Katherine. The sooner we get away the better.

MRS. STOCKMANN. Be quiet—I think there's somebody in the hall. Go and see, Petra.

PETRA [*opens the door*]. Oh, it's you, Captain Horster? Do come in.

HORSTER [*from the hall*]. Good morning. I thought I'd just look in to see how things were.

DR. STOCKMANN [*shaking his hand*]. Thank you. That's very kind of you.

MRS. STOCKMANN. And thank you for your help last night, Captain Horster.

PETRA. But how did you get back home again?

HORSTER. Oh, I managed. I'm pretty tough, you know. The only thing those people are good for is shooting off their mouths.

DR. STOCKMANN. Yes, isn't it astonishing, this sickening cowardice? Here, I want to show you something! Look, here are all the stones they chucked at us last night. Just look at them! Not more than a couple of honest-to-goodness lumps in the whole lot—the rest are just pebbles, bits of gravel! And yet they went on standing out there, shouting and yelling and swearing they were going to beat me up. But as for *doing* anything—no, there isn't much of that in this town.

HORSTER. It was just as well this time, Doctor.

DR. STOCKMANN. I dare say you're right. But it makes you angry all the same. Because if it ever comes to the point where the country really *has* to fight in earnest, then you'll see how public opinion is all for clearing out fast, and the whole of the compact majority will make for the woods like a great flock of sheep, Captain Horster. That's the saddening thing; that's what really upsets me. . . . Oh, what the hell . . . it's all just a lot of nonsense, really. If they've called me an enemy of the people, I might as well be an enemy of the people.

MRS. STOCKMANN. That's something you'll never be, Thomas.

DR. STOCKMANN. I shouldn't bet on it if I were you, Katherine. To be called some nasty name is just like getting a pinprick in the lung. And this blasted name they've called me—it's lodged here under the heart, embedded deep, griping me as if it were acid. And it's no use taking magnesia for *that*!

PETRA. Puh! I should just laugh at them, Father!

HORSTER. They'll come round to other ways of thinking in time, Doctor.

MRS. STOCKMANN. They will, you know, Thomas, as sure as you're standing here.

DR. STOCKMANN. When it's too late, perhaps. Well, serve them right! Then, as they wallow in their filth, they'll wish they hadn't been so ready to drive a patriot into exile. When do you sail, Captain Horster?

HORSTER. Well, actually that was what I came to talk to you about. . . .

DR. STOCKMANN. Well? Something wrong with the ship?

HORSTER. No, only that I'm not sailing with her.

PETRA. Surely you haven't been given notice?

HORSTER [*smiles*]. Yes, I have.

PETRA. You too.

MRS. STOCKMANN. There you are, you see, Thomas.

DR. STOCKMANN. And all in the cause of truth! Oh, if I'd thought for one moment that . . .

HORSTER. Don't you worry about that! I'll get a job all right with some company away from here.

DR. STOCKMANN. So that's our Mr. Vik . . . a man of means, beholden to nobody. . . ! It's a damned shame!

HORSTER. He's very decent otherwise. And he said himself he would have liked to keep me on, if only he dared. . . .

DR. STOCKMANN. But he didn't dare? No, of course not.

HORSTER. He said it wasn't so easy when you belonged to a party. . . .

DR. STOCKMANN. He never spoke a truer word, that fine friend of ours! A party's just like a mincing machine, grinding people's brains up into a kind of hash, and churning out a lot of thickheaded clots.

MRS. STOCKMANN. Oh, Thomas, really!

PETRA [*to* HORSTER]. If only you hadn't walked home with us, things might not have gone so far.

HORSTER. I don't regret it.

PETRA [*holds out her hand*]. Thank you!

HORSTER [*to the* DOCTOR]. What I really wanted to say was this: that if you are set on leaving, I've another idea. . . .

DR. STOCKMANN. Fine! As long as we can get away quickly.

MRS. STOCKMANN. Hush! Wasn't that a knock?

PETRA. That'll be Uncle, for sure.

DR. STOCKMANN. Aha! [*Shouts.*] Come in!

MRS. STOCKMANN. Thomas, dear, promise me . . .

> [*The* MAYOR *comes in from the hall.*]

MAYOR [*in the doorway*]. Oh, you are busy. In that case I'd better . . .

DR. STOCKMANN. No, no! Come in.

MAYOR. But I wanted to speak to you alone.

MRS. STOCKMANN. We'll go into the living-room for the time being.

HORSTER. And I'll look in again later.

DR. STOCKMANN. No, you just go next door with them, Captain Horster. I want to know a bit more about . . .

HORSTER. Very well, I'll wait then.

> [*He goes with* MRS. STOCKMANN *and* PETRA *into the living-room. The* MAYOR *says nothing but glances at the windows.*]

DR. STOCKMANN. Perhaps it's a bit draughty for you in here today. Put your hat on.

MAYOR. Thank you, if I may. [*Does so.*] I think I must have caught a cold yesterday. I stood there shivering. . . .

DR. STOCKMANN. Really? Things seemed warm enough to me.

MAYOR. I regret I was unable to prevent the excesses of last night.

DR. STOCKMANN. Is there anything particular you want to tell me besides that?

MAYOR [*produces a big envelope*]. I have this document for you, from the directors.

DR. STOCKMANN. My notice?

MAYOR. Yes, from today. [*Lays the letter on the table.*] We don't like doing this, but—to be perfectly frank—we daren't do anything else, in the light of public opinion.

DR. STOCKMANN [*smiles*]. Daren't? I seem to have heard that word before, today.

MAYOR. I want you to realize your position. You can't count on any kind of practice in this town in future.

DR. STOCKMANN. To hell with the practice! But what makes you so certain?

MAYOR. The Ratepayers Association is circulating a list, urging all respectable citizens to have nothing to do with you. And I am pretty confident that not a single man will dare refuse to sign it. They simply wouldn't *dare*.

DR. STOCKMANN. I don't doubt. But what then?

MAYOR. If I may give you some advice, it's this: go away for a while....

DR. STOCKMANN. Yes, I had actually been thinking of going away.

MAYOR. Good. And after you'd had six months or so to think things over, and if after mature consideration you then felt you were ready to write a few words of apology, admitting your mistake ...

DR. STOCKMANN. Then I might perhaps get my job back again, you mean?

MAYOR. Perhaps. It's not altogether impossible.

DR. STOCKMANN. But what about public opinion? Surely you won't dare, in the light of public opinion.

MAYOR. Opinion is an extremely variable thing. And, in point of fact, it's rather important that we get some sort of admission from you along those lines.

DR. STOCKMANN. Yes, I can see how you'd come slobbering after that. But, by God, surely you haven't forgotten already what I've told you before about dirty tricks like this!

MAYOR. At that time your position was quite different. At that time you had reason to suppose you had the whole town at your back....

DR. STOCKMANN. Yes, and now I'm supposed to feel as though I had the whole town *on* my back.... [*Flares up.*] I wouldn't care if I had the devil himself *and* his old woman on my back.... Never, I tell you! Never!

MAYOR. A man with a family has no right to be carrying on as you are. You have no right, Thomas.

DR. STOCKMANN. Haven't I? There's only one thing in this world a free man has no right to do. Do you know what that is?

MAYOR. No.

DR. STOCKMANN. Of course not. But *I'll* tell you. A free man has no right to get messed up with filth; things should never reach the stage where he feels like spitting in his own eye.

MAYOR. This all sounds extremely plausible. And if there weren't some other explanation for your obstinacy . . . But then, of course, there is. . . .

DR. STOCKMANN. What do you mean by *that*?

MAYOR. You know perfectly well what I mean. Speaking as your brother and as one who understands these things, let me give you some advice: don't build too much on certain expectations or prospects that might so terribly easily fall through.

DR. STOCKMANN. What on earth are you getting at?

MAYOR. You don't really expect me to believe that you are ignorant of the terms of Morten Kiil's will?

DR. STOCKMANN. I know that what little he has is to go to an Old People's Home. But what's that got to do with me?

MAYOR. In the first place, it's not so little. Morten Kiil is a pretty wealthy man.

DR. STOCKMANN. I had absolutely no idea . . .

MAYOR. Hm . . . really? And you have no idea, I suppose, that a not inconsiderable part of his fortune is to be left to your children, and that you and your wife are to have the interest on this money during your lifetime? Did he never tell you that?

DR. STOCKMANN. Blessed if he did! On the contrary, he's done nothing the whole time but grouse about the impossibly high taxes he had to pay. Are you quite sure about this, Peter?

MAYOR. I have it from a completely reliable source.

DR. STOCKMANN. But, Heavens, that means Katherine's taken care of —and the children too! I must tell them. . . . [*Shouts.*] Katherine, Katherine!

MAYOR [*holds him back*]. Hush! Don't say anything yet!

MRS. STOCKMANN [*opens the door*]. What is the matter?

DR. STOCKMANN. Nothing, my dear. Just go back in again. [MRS. STOCKMANN *shuts the door; he walks up and down.*] Provided for! To think they're all provided for! And for life! It's a wonderful feeling to know that one has that security!

MAYOR. Yes, but that's just it! You can't be sure. Morten Kiil can alter his will any time he likes.

DR. STOCKMANN. But he won't, my dear Peter. The old boy is tickled to death at the way I've gone for you and your precious friends.

MAYOR [*starts, and looks intently at him*]. Aha, that puts a lot of things in a different light.

DR. STOCKMANN. What things?

MAYOR. So the whole thing has been a combined operation. These violent, ruthless attacks you have made—all in the name of truth— against the leading men of the town. . . .

DR. STOCKMANN. What about them?

MAYOR. Just your part of the bargain in exchange for being included in that vindictive old man's will.

DR. STOCKMANN [*almost speechless*]. Peter . . . of all the scum I ever met, you are the worst.

MAYOR. Things are finished now between us. Your dismissal is final . . . for now we have a weapon against you.

[*He goes.*]

DR. STOCKMANN. Well I'll be . . . ! Of all the . . . ! [*Shouts.*] Katherine! I want the floor swilled down after him. Get her to bring her bucket in . . . what's her name . . . damn it, you know . . . that girl who's always got a dirty nose. . . .

MRS. STOCKMANN [*in the living-room doorway*]. Hush, Thomas, please!

PETRA [*also in the doorway*]. Father, Grandfather's here. He wants to know if he can have a word with you alone.

DR. STOCKMANN. Yes, of course he can. [*At the door.*] Come in, Father-in-law. [MORTEN KIIL *comes in; the* DOCTOR *shuts the door after him.*] Well now, what can I do for you? Do sit down.

MORTEN KIIL. I won't sit. [*Looks round him.*] It's looking very nice in here today, Stockmann.

DR. STOCKMANN. It is, isn't it?

KIIL. Very nice indeed it looks. And lots of fresh air too; plenty of that oxygen stuff you were talking about yesterday. Your conscience must be in pretty good shape today, I imagine.

DR. STOCKMANN. Yes, it is.

KIIL. I imagined it would be. [*Tapping his breast pocket.*] Do you know what I've got here?

DR. STOCKMANN. A good conscience too, I should hope.

KIIL. Puh! Something much better than that.

[*He brings out a fat wallet, opens it, and produces a bundle of papers.*]

DR. STOCKMANN [*looks at him in amazement*]. Shares in the Baths?

KIIL. They weren't difficult to come by today.

DR. STOCKMANN. You mean to say you've gone and bought . . . ?

KIIL. As many as I could afford.

DR. STOCKMANN. But, my dear Father-in-law—with things at the Baths in the state they are in now . . . !

KIIL. If only you behave like a sensible man, you'll soon have the place on its feet again.

DR. STOCKMANN. Well, you can see for yourself, I'm doing all I can, but . . . The people in this town are mad!

KIIL. You said yesterday that the worst of the filth came from my works. But if this happened to be true, then my grandfather, and my father before me, to say nothing of myself, have been slowly poisoning the town all these years—like three unclean spirits. You don't think I'm going to take this lying down, do you?

DR. STOCKMANN. I'm afraid you can't help it.

KIIL. No thank you. My good name means a lot to me. I'm told people call me an old badger; and a badger's a kind of pig, isn't it? But I'm not going to let them say 'I told you so'. I want to live and die with my reputation clear.

DR. STOCKMANN. And how are you going to manage that?

KIIL. You are going to clear me, Stockmann.

DR. STOCKMANN. *I* am!

KIIL. Do you know where I got the money to buy all these shares? No, how could you? But I'll tell you. This is the money that Katherine and Petra and the boys are to inherit from me. Because, you see, I've managed to put quite a bit aside, after all.

DR. STOCKMANN [*flaring up*]. You mean you've gone and taken Katherine's money for *this*?

KIIL. Yes, every bit of the money is tied up now in the Baths. And I just want to see now if you really are completely and absolutely stark raving mad, Stockmann. If you are still going to have it that creepy, crawly things are coming from my works, you might as well be flaying Katherine alive, for all the difference it makes—*and* Petra, *and* the boys as well. But then no decent father would do that—not unless he was a madman.

DR. STOCKMANN [*pacing up and down.*] But I *am* a madman! I *am* a madman!

KIIL. But you couldn't be so stark, staring mad as all that, not when it affects your wife and children.

DR. STOCKMANN [*halts in front of him*]. Why couldn't you have talked to me first before going and buying all that trash!

KIIL. What's done can't be undone—it's got to be faced.

DR. STOCKMANN [*walks about restlessly*]. If only I wasn't so certain . . . ! But I'm absolutely convinced I'm right.

KIIL [*weighing his wallet in his hand*]. If you persist with these stupid ideas, then these things will not be worth much, you know.

[*He puts his wallet in his pocket.*]

DR. STOCKMANN. Damn it, surely science could find *some* sort of prophylactic, some preventive or other. . . .

KIIL. You mean something to kill off the animals?

DR. STOCKMANN. Yes, or to render them harmless, at least.

KIIL. Couldn't you try with a bit of rat poison?

DR. STOCKMANN. Oh, don't talk rubbish! But then everybody keeps telling me it's just my imagination. Well, let's make it that then! Let them have it the way they want it! These ignorant little mongrels—calling me an enemy of the people! And tearing the very clothes off my back!

KIIL. And smashing all your windows!

DR. STOCKMANN. And then there's this business of my duty towards my family. I'll have to talk to Katherine about it. She's better than I am at things like that.

KIIL. Fine! She's a sensible woman—and just you pay attention to what she says.

DR. STOCKMANN [*turning on him*]. You're a fine one, too, behaving in this stupid way! Fancy gambling with Katherine's money—and putting me in this dreadful dilemma! When I look at you, it's just like looking at the devil himself. . . !

KIIL. I think I'd better go. But I want to hear from you by two o'clock at the latest. Yes or no. If it's no, the shares go to charity—this very day.

DR. STOCKMANN. And what does Katherine get then?

KIIL. Not a penny. [*The hall door opens;* HOVSTAD *and* ASLAKSEN *can be seen outside.*] Well, look who's here!

DR. STOCKMANN [*stares at them*]. What's this! You dare come to my house?

HOVSTAD. Yes, we do.

ASLAKSEN. You see, we want to talk to you about something.

KIIL [*whispers*]. Yes or no—by two o'clock.

ASLAKSEN [*with a glance at* HOVSTAD]. Aha!

[MORTEN KIIL *leaves.*]

DR. STOCKMANN. Well! What do you want with me? Make it snappy!

HOVSTAD. I can well understand that you are not very well disposed towards us as a result of our attitude at the meeting yesterday. . . .

DR. STOCKMANN. Attitude, you call it! A fine attitude that was! Of all the spineless exhibitions . . . ! Like a couple of old women! God damn it!

HOVSTAD. Call it what you like; but we *couldn't* do anything else.

DR. STOCKMANN. You daren't do anything else, you mean! Well?

HOVSTAD. Yes, if you like.

ASLAKSEN. But why didn't you drop us a hint beforehand? All it needed was a word to Mr. Hovstad or me.

DR. STOCKMANN. A hint? What about?

ASLAKSEN. About what was behind it all.

DR. STOCKMANN. I don't understand you at all.

ASLAKSEN [*nods confidentially*]. Oh yes you do, Dr. Stockmann.

HOVSTAD. There's no need to make a mystery of it any longer.

DR. STOCKMANN [*looks from one to the other*]. For God's sake, won't somebody tell me. . . !

ASLAKSEN. If you don't mind my asking—isn't it true that your father-in-law is going round town buying up all the shares in the Baths.

DR. STOCKMANN. Yes, he's been and bought some shares today. But . . . ?

ASLAKSEN. It might have been wiser if you had picked somebody else to do that—somebody not quite so closely related.

HOVSTAD. And you shouldn't have done all this in your own name, either. There wasn't any need for people to know that the attack on the Baths came from you. You should have approached me, Dr. Stockmann.

DR. STOCKMANN [*looks fixedly ahead; the truth seems to dawn on him, and he says as though thunderstruck*]. But this is incredible! Are such things possible?

ASLAKSEN [*smiles*]. Evidently they are. But they ought preferably to be done with finesse, you know.

HOVSTAD. And it's best to have one or two others in on it, too. Because then the individual responsibility is always reduced if there are several people.

DR. STOCKMANN [*composedly*]. Come to the point, gentlemen. What is it you want?

ASLAKSEN. Perhaps Mr. Hovstad had better . . .

HOVSTAD. No, you do it, Aslaksen.

ASLAKSEN. Well, the thing is that—now that we know how things really are—we think we might venture to put the *People's Herald* at your disposal.

DR. STOCKMANN. So *now* you dare do it? But what about public opinion? Aren't you afraid of having to face a storm of protest.

HOVSTAD. We must try to ride that storm.

ASLAKSEN. And then you must be ready to change your tack quickly, Doctor. As soon as your campaign has had its effect. . . .

DR. STOCKMANN. You mean as soon as my father-in-law and I have bought the shares up cheap . . . ?

HOVSTAD. I suppose it's mainly for research purposes you are anxious to get control of the Baths.

DR. STOCKMANN. Of course. It was with an eye on my research that I managed to get the old Badger to come in on it with me. Then we'll patch up the pipes a bit, and dig up a bit of the beach, and it won't cost the town a penny. Don't you think that'll work? Eh?

HOVSTAD. I think so—if you've got the *Herald* with you.

ASLAKSEN. In a free society, the press has great power, you know, Doctor.

DR. STOCKMANN. Yes, indeed. And so has public opinion. And you, Mr. Aslaksen, will take responsibility for the Ratepayers Association, I suppose?

ASLAKSEN. The Ratepayers Association *and* the Temperance Society. You may depend on that.

DR. STOCKMANN. But, gentlemen—I feel ashamed putting a question like this—but . . . what do *you* get out of this. . . ?

HOVSTAD. Actually, we'd rather not take anything at all for our help, really. But in fact the *Herald* is a bit shaky at the moment; it just can't quite make ends meet, and I should be most reluctant to wind the paper up now, just when there's such a lot of political work to be done.

DR. STOCKMANN. Of course. That would be a sad blow for a friend of the people like yourself. [*Flares up.*] But *I* am an enemy of the people. [*Rushes about the room.*] Where's my stick? Where the devil's my stick?

HOVSTAD. What does this mean?

ASLAKSEN. Surely you don't . . . !

DR. STOCKMANN [*stops*]. And what if I didn't give you a single brass farthing out of all my shares? It's not easy to get money out of us rich people, don't forget.

HOVSTAD. And *you* mustn't forget that this business about the shares can be presented in two very different ways.

DR. STOCKMANN. Yes, and you are just the man to do it. If I don't come to the aid of the *Herald*, then you'll take a pretty poor view of things. The hunt will be up, I dare say. . . . You'll be after my blood . . . you'll be on to me like a dog on to a hare!

HOVSTAD. That's the law of nature. Every animal must fight for survival.

ASLAKSEN. You've got to take your food where you find it, you know.

DR. STOCKMANN. Then let's see if you can find anything out in the gutter. [*Rushes about the room.*] Because now we are damned well going to see who is the strongest animal amongst us three. [*Finds his umbrella and waves it.*] Now, watch out. . . !

HOVSTAD. You wouldn't dare attack us!

ASLAKSEN. Watch what you are doing with that umbrella!

DR. STOCKMANN. Out of the window with you, Mr. Hovstad.

HOVSTAD [*near the hall door*]. Have you gone completely mad?

DR. STOCKMANN. Out of the window, Mr. Aslaksen! Jump, I tell you. And quick about it!

ASLAKSEN [*running round the desk*]. Moderation, Dr. Stockmann! I'm not very strong, I can't stand very much of this. . . . [*Shouts.*] Help! Help!

[MRS. STOCKMANN, PETRA and HORSTER *come in from the living-room.*]

MRS. STOCKMANN. Heavens above, Thomas, what's going on?

DR. STOCKMANN [*swinging the umbrella*]. Jump! Down into the gutter!

HOVSTAD. Unprovoked assault! You're a witness of this, Captain Horster.

[*He hurries out through the hall.*]

ASLAKSEN [*bewildered*]. Anybody who knew the lie of the land about here . . .

[*He slinks out through the living-room.*]

MRS. STOCKMANN [*clinging to her husband*]. Control yourself, Thomas!

DR. STOCKMANN [*throws the umbrella down*]. Damn them, they got away after all.

MRS. STOCKMANN. But what did they want with you?

DR. STOCKMANN. I'll tell you later. I've got other things to think about now. [*He goes to his desk and writes on a visiting card.*] Look, Katherine, what does this say?

MRS. STOCKMANN. 'No', three times. What's that for?

DR. STOCKMANN. That's something else I'll tell you later. [*Hands the card to* PETRA.] *There*, Petra. Get little dirty-face to run over to the Badger's with it, as quick as she can. Hurry! [PETRA *takes the card and goes out through the hall.*] Well, if this hasn't been a hell of a day for callers, I don't know what is. But now I'm going to sharpen up my pen; I'll impale them on it; I'll dip it in venom and gall; I'll chuck the inkpot right in their faces!

MRS. STOCKMANN. Yes, but we're leaving, aren't we, Thomas?

[PETRA *comes back.*]

DR. STOCKMANN. Well?

PETRA. She's taken it.

DR. STOCKMANN. Good! Leaving, did you say? No, I'm damned if we are. We're staying where we are, Katherine!

PETRA. We're staying?

MRS. STOCKMANN. In this town?

DR. STOCKMANN. Yes, just here. The battlefield is here; here the fight will be fought and here I shall triumph! As soon as I've had my trousers stitched, I'm off to town to look for somewhere to live. We've got to have a roof over our heads this winter.

HORSTER. You are welcome to share my house.

DR. STOCKMANN. Can I?

HORSTER. Yes, of course you can. I've plenty of room, and I'm hardly ever at home.

MRS. STOCKMANN. How very kind of you, Captain Horster.

PETRA. Thank you!

DR. STOCKMANN [*shaking his hand*]. Thank you! Thank you! That's that worry off my mind. Now I can get straight down to work in real earnest. Oh, there's no end to the things here that need going into, Katherine! But it's grand that I can give all my time to this now. Because—I was going to tell you—I've got my notice from the Baths, you know. . . .

MRS. STOCKMANN [*sighing*]. Yes, I was expecting that.

DR. STOCKMANN. . . . And they want to take my practice away as well. Well, let them! I won't lose the poor people anyway—those who don't pay anything. And, heavens, they are the ones who need me most. But, by God, they are going to listen to what I have to say. I'll read them a lesson, both in and out of season, as it says somewhere.

MRS. STOCKMANN. But, Thomas dear, surely you've seen now that reading them a lesson doesn't do much good.

DR. STOCKMANN. Don't be so ridiculous, Katherine. D'you think I'm going to let public opinion and the compact majority and all that rigmarole get the better of me? No, thank you! And anyway, what I want to do is so simple and clear and straightforward. I just want to take these mongrels and knock it into their heads that the Liberals are the worst enemies of freedom . . . that the party programmes grab hold of every young and promising idea and wring its neck . . . and that policies of expediency are turning all our standards of morality and justice upside down, so that life's just not going to be worth living. Surely I can make people understand that, Captain Horster? Don't you think so?

HORSTER. Very likely. I don't know very much about these things myself.

DR. STOCKMANN. Well, look here—I'll tell you what I mean! It's the party bosses you've got to get rid of. A party boss is just like a wolf, you see . . . a ravenous wolf who needs so and so many victims every year to keep him going. Just look at Hovstad and Aslaksen! How many do you think *they* haven't seen off in their time? Or else they worry them and maul them about so badly that they are no use for anything except to join the Ratepayers Association and subscribe to the *Herald*! [*Sits on the edge of the table.*] Come over here, Katherine . . . look how beautifully the sun is shining in here today. And this glorious, fresh, spring air that's been let in.

MRS. STOCKMANN. If only we could live on sun and fresh air, Thomas.

DR. STOCKMANN. Well, you'll just have to skimp and scrape a bit on the side—we'll manage all right. That's my least worry. No, the worst thing is this: I don't know of anybody with enough independence of mind to feel like taking on my work after me.

PETRA. Oh, you mustn't think about that, Father. You've plenty of time yet.—Why, here are the boys already.

[EJLIF *and* MORTEN *come in from the living-room.*]

MRS. STOCKMANN. Have you got a holiday today?

MORTEN. No, but we went for the others at playtime. . . .

EJLIF. That's not true. They started fighting us.

MORTEN. And then Mr. Rörlund said we'd better stay away for a few days.

DR. STOCKMANN [*snaps his fingers and jumps down from the table*]. I've got it! I've got it, by Heaven! You are not going to set foot in that school again!

THE BOYS. No more school!

MRS. STOCKMANN. Thomas, really . . . !

DR. STOCKMANN. Never, I say! I'll teach you myself—what I mean is, you'll not learn a blessed thing. . . .

MORTEN. Hurrah!

DR. STOCKMANN. . . . but I'll make decent and independent-minded men of you both. . . . And you must help me, Petra.

PETRA. You can count on me, Father.

DR. STOCKMANN. And we'll have the school in the very room where they called me an enemy of the people. But there ought to be a few more of us. I must have at least a dozen boys to start with.

MRS. STOCKMANN. You're not likely to get them here, not in this town.

DR. STOCKMANN. We'll see about that. [*To the boys.*] What about some of the street-corner lads . . . the real guttersnipes. . . ?

MORTEN. Yes, Father. I know plenty of them!

DR. STOCKMANN. That's fine! Get hold of one or two for me, will you? Just for once, I'm going to try an experiment on these mongrels. You never know what you might find amongst them.

MORTEN. But what are you going to do, when we've grown up into decent and independent-minded men?

DR. STOCKMANN. Then you can drive all the wolves out, lads—make sure that they all go west!

[EJLIF *looks rather doubtful;* MORTEN *jumps and shouts for joy.*]

MRS. STOCKMANN. Oh, just so long as it isn't the wolves who go chasing you, Thomas.

DR. STOCKMANN. You must be mad, Katherine! Chase *me! Now!* When I'm the strongest man in the town!

MRS. STOCKMANN. The strongest. . . ? *Now?*

DR. STOCKMANN. Yes, and I could even go so far as to say that *now* I'm one of the strongest men in the whole world.

MORTEN. Honestly?

DR. STOCKMANN [*dropping his voice*]. Sh! You mustn't say anything about it yet. But I've made a great discovery.

MRS. STOCKMANN. What, again?

DR. STOCKMANN. Yes I have. [*He gathers them about him and says confidentially.*] The thing is, you see, that the strongest man in the world is the man who stands alone.

MRS. STOCKMANN [*smiles and shakes her head*]. Oh, Thomas, Thomas. . . !

PETRA [*bravely, grasping his hands*]. Father!

THE WILD DUCK
[Vildanden]

PLAY IN FIVE ACTS
(1884)

CHARACTERS

HAAKON WERLE, businessman, industrialist, etc.

GREGERS WERLE, his son

OLD EKDAL

HJALMAR EKDAL, his son, a photographer

GINA EKDAL, Hjalmar's wife

HEDVIG, their fourteen-year-old daughter

MRS. SÖRBY, housekeeper to Haakon Werle

RELLING, a doctor

MOLVIK, a one-time theological student

PETTERSEN, Haakon Werle's servant

GRAABERG, the book-keeper

JENSEN, a hired waiter

A fat gentleman

A balding gentleman

A short-sighted gentleman

Six other gentlemen, Haakon Werle's guests

Several hired servants

The first act is at the home of Haakon Werle, and the four following acts at Hjalmar Ekdal's

ACT ONE

At HAAKON WERLE's *house. The study, expensively and comfortably appointed, with bookcases and upholstered furniture; in the middle of the room a desk with papers and documents; the room is softly lit by green-shaded lamps. Folding doors at the back of the room are standing open, and the curtains are drawn back. The sitting-room, spacious and elegant, can be seen within, brilliantly lit by lamps and candelabra. In the study, right front, a baize-covered door leads to the offices. Left front, a fireplace with a glowing coal fire; and further back, a double door into the dining-room.*

PETTERSEN, WERLE's *servant, in livery, and* JENSEN, *the hired waiter in black, are putting the study in order. In the sitting-room, two or three other hired servants are busy arranging the room and lighting candles. A buzz of conversation can be heard from the dining-room, and the laughter of many voices; somebody taps a knife on a glass; silence follows and a toast is proposed; cheers, and again the buzz of conversation.*

PETTERSEN [*lights a lamp on the mantelpiece and puts on the shade*]. Aye, just listen to them, Jensen. There's the old man at it now, off on a long toast to Mrs. Sörby.

JENSEN [*moving an armchair forward*]. Is it right what people say—that there's something between them?

PETTERSEN. God knows.

JENSEN. 'Cos he's been a bit of a lad in his day, hasn't he?

PETTERSEN. Maybe.

JENSEN. They say he's giving this dinner for his son.

PETTERSEN. Yes. His son came home yesterday.

JENSEN. I never knew old Werle had a son.

PETTERSEN. Oh, he's got a son, all right. But you could never get him to leave the works up at Höidal. In all the years I've worked in this house, he's never once been to town.

A HIRED WAITER [*at the door into the sitting-room*]. Here, Pettersen, there's an old fellow here who . . .

PETTERSEN [*muttering*]. Oh, damn. Who wants to come here at *this* time!

[OLD EKDAL *appears in the sitting-room from the right. He is wearing a shabby greatcoat with a high collar, and woollen mittens. He is carrying in his hand a stick and a fur cap, and under his arm a brown-paper parcel. He is wearing a dirty auburn wig and has a little grey moustache.*]

PETTERSEN [*goes towards him*]. Good Lord! What are *you* doing in here?

EKDAL [*in the doorway*]. I just *have* to get into the office, Pettersen.

PETTERSEN. The office shut an hour ago, and . . .

EKDAL. That's what they told me round at the gates, old man. But Graaberg's still in there. Be a good sort, Pettersen, and let me in *this* way. [*He points to the baize door.*] I've been this way before.

PETTERSEN. All right, then, you might as well. [*Opens the door.*] But mind you don't forget to go the proper way out. We've got company.

EKDAL. I can see that . . . hm! Thanks Pettersen, old man. Good old friend. Thanks! [*Mutters to himself.*] Silly old fool! [*He goes into the office;* PETTERSEN *shuts the door after him.*]

JENSEN. Does *he* work in the office as well.

PETTERSEN. No, they just farm some of the copying out to him at rush times. Not but what he hasn't been somebody in his time, Old Ekdal.

JENSEN. Yes, he seemed to have something about him.

PETTERSEN. You're right there. What would you say if I told you that he'd been a lieutenant!

JENSEN. Get away—him a lieutenant!

PETTERSEN. So help me, he was. But then he switched over to the timber business or whatever it was. Supposed to have done the dirty on Old Werle once, or so they say. They were both in on the Höidal works together, you see. Oh, I know Old Ekdal well enough, I do! Many's the time we have had a nip and a bottle of beer together down at Ma Eriksen's.

JENSEN. I don't suppose he's got much money to throw about, has he?

PETTERSEN. Good Lord, man, it's me that does the paying, believe you me. I think people ought to show a bit of respect to those who have known better days.

JENSEN. Did he go bankrupt, then?

PETTERSEN. No, it was worse than that. He was given hard labour.

JENSEN. Hard labour?

PETTERSEN. Or imprisonment, anyway—[*Listens.*] Hush! They are leaving the table now.

[*A couple of servants open the dining-room doors from within. MRS. SÖRBY comes out, in conversation with two gentlemen, followed gradually by all the other guests and HAAKON WERLE. HJALMAR EKDAL and GREGERS WERLE come last.*]

MRS. SÖRBY [*to the servant, in passing*]. Pettersen, will you have coffee served in the music room, please.

PETTERSEN. Very good, Mrs. Sörby.

[*She and the two gentlemen go into the sitting-room and out of it to the right. PETTERSEN and JENSEN go out the same way.*]

A FAT GUEST [*to a BALDING GUEST*]. Whew! What a dinner! Took a bit of getting through!

THE BALDING GUEST. Oh, if you put your mind to it, it's incredible what you can manage in three hours.

THE FAT GUEST. Yes, but afterwards, my dear sir, afterwards!

A THIRD GUEST. I hear they are serving coffee and liqueurs in the music room.

THE FAT GUEST. Splendid! And perhaps Mrs. Sörby will play something for us.

THE BALDING GUEST [*in a low voice*]. As long as she doesn't try playing anything *on* us.

THE FAT GUEST. Oh, I hardly think so. Bertha isn't the sort to go back on her old friends. [*They laugh and go into the sitting-room.*]

WERLE [*in a low, irritable voice*]. I don't think anybody noticed, Gregers.

GREGERS [*looks at him*]. Noticed what?

WERLE. Didn't you notice either?

GREGERS. What was there for me to notice?

WERLE. There were thirteen of us at table.

GREGERS. Really? Were there thirteen?

WERLE [*with a glance towards* HJALMAR EKDAL]. There are twelve of us as a rule. [*To the rest.*] Come along in here, gentlemen. [*He and the rest of the guests, except* HJALMAR *and* GREGERS, *go out at the back to the right.*]

HJALMAR [*who has heard what was said*]. You shouldn't have sent me that invitation, Gregers.

GREGERS. What! They say the party's for me. Am I not allowed to invite my best and only friend. . . .

HJALMAR. But I don't think your father is very pleased. I never come near the house any other time.

GREGERS. So I hear. But I had to see you and have a talk, because I dare say I'll be leaving again soon.—Yes, here we are, two old school friends, and drifted far, far apart, haven't we? We can't have seen each other now for sixteen or seventeen years.

HJALMAR. Is it as long as all that?

GREGERS. It is indeed. Well now, how are you getting along? You are looking well. You've put on a bit of weight, I might almost call you stout.

HJALMAR. Well, I don't know that I would call it stout exactly; but I dare say I look a bit more of a man now than I did then.

GREGERS. Yes, you do. Outwardly you don't seem to have suffered much harm.

HJALMAR [*in a rather gloomy voice*]. Ah, but inwardly, Gregers. It's different there, I can tell you. Of course, you know about the terrible things that have happened to me and my family since we last saw each other.

GREGERS [*softer*]. How are things now with your father?

HJALMAR. My dear fellow, don't let's talk about *that*. My poor unfortunate father is of course living in with me. He has nobody else in the whole world to turn to. But it's so desperately hard for me to talk about all this, you know.—Tell me instead how you have been getting on up at the works.

GREGERS. Delightfully lonely, that's how I've been. Plenty of opportunity to think about all sorts of things. Come over here; let's make ourselves comfortable. [*He sits down in an armchair by the fire and draws* HJALMAR *down into another beside him.*]

HJALMAR [*with feeling*]. Thank you all the same, Gregers, for asking me to your father's dinner-party. For now I can see that you don't hold anything against me any more.

GREGERS [*in surprise*]. What made you think I had anything against you?

HJALMAR. You did have the first few years.

GREGERS. What first few years?

HJALMAR. After the big crash came. And it was only natural you should. It was only by a hair's breadth that your own father missed being dragged into all that . . . that dreadful affair.

GREGERS. And you think I should have held that against you? Whoever gave you that idea?

HJALMAR. I know you *did*, Gregers. Your father told me himself.

GREGERS [*amazed*]. My father! Indeed. Hm! Was that the reason I never heard from you . . . not a single word?

HJALMAR. Yes.

GREGERS. Not even when you went and became a photographer?

HJALMAR. Your father said there was no point in writing to you about anything.

GREGERS [*absently*]. Well, well . . . perhaps he was right. But now Hjalmar, tell me . . . are you reasonably satisfied with things as they are now?

HJALMAR [*with a gentle sigh*]. Oh yes, I think so, pretty well. Can't really complain. As you might expect, it was a bit strange for me, in a way, to begin with. The circumstances I found myself in were so completely changed, of course; but then everything else was completely changed as well. The terrible calamity to Father . . . the shame and the disgrace, Gregers. . . .

GREGERS [*feelingly*]. Yes, indeed, indeed.

HJALMAR. I couldn't possibly think of continuing my studies; there wasn't a penny left, if anything just the opposite, in fact. There were debts. Mostly to your father, I think.

GREGERS. Hm!

HJALMAR. Well, I thought it best to make a clean break, you know . . . leave all the old life and its ways behind. Your father in particular advised me to do that. And since he had put himself out to be so helpful to me . . .

GREGERS. My father?

HJALMAR. Yes, surely you know that? Where could I have found the money to learn photography and set up a studio and establish myself? That sort of thing costs money, I can tell you.

GREGERS. And my father paid for all that?

HJALMAR. Yes, Gregers, didn't you know? I understood from him he had written and told you.

GREGERS. Not a word that it was *him*. He must have forgotten. We have never exchanged anything but business letters. So it was my father, was it!

HJALMAR. Yes, it was him all right. He never wanted anybody to know. But it *was* him. And it was him, too, who made it possible for me to get married. But maybe you didn't know anything about that either?

GREGERS. No, I certainly didn't. [*Clapping him on the arm.*] But my dear Hjalmar, I can't tell you how delighted I am to hear all this . . . yet a bit worried as well. Perhaps I *have* been rather unjust to my father about certain things. For this does reveal a certain kindness of heart, doesn't it? Almost in a way as though he had a conscience. . . .

HJALMAR. Conscience!

GREGERS. Well, well, whatever you care to call it then. No, I can't tell you how glad I am to hear this about my father.—So you are married, then, Hjalmar! That's more than I'm ever likely to be. Well then, I hope you find married life suits you?

HJALMAR. Yes, I do. She's as good and capable a wife as ever a man could wish for. Nor is she altogether without education.

GREGERS [*a little surprised*]. No, I don't suppose she is.

HJALMAR. Life is a great teacher, you see. Contact with me every day . . . and then we have pretty regular visits from one or two most intelligent people. You wouldn't know Gina again, I assure you.

GREGERS. Gina?

HJALMAR. Yes, my dear Gregers, don't you remember she was called Gina?

GREGERS. Who was called Gina? I haven't the slightest idea what . . .

HJALMAR. But don't you remember her being in service in this house for a time.

GREGERS [*looks at him*]. Is it Gina Hansen?

HJALMAR. Yes, of course it's Gina Hansen.

GREGERS. . . . who kept house for us in the last year of Mother's illness?

HJALMAR. That's right. But my dear friend, I know for certain your father wrote and told you I had got married.

GREGERS [*who has risen*]. Yes, he did actually; but he didn't say . . . [*Walks up and down.*] But wait a minute . . . perhaps after all he did . . . now that I think about it. But my father always writes me such short letters. [*Sits on the arm of the chair.*] Listen, Hjalmar, tell me— this is really rather amusing—how did you happen to meet Gina . . . meet your wife?

HJALMAR. Oh, it was quite straightforward. Gina didn't stay very long here in the house. There was a lot of upset here at the time, what with your mother's illness. . . . Gina couldn't put up with it all, so she gave notice and left. That was the year before your mother died . . . or it might have been the same year.

GREGERS. It was the same year. I was up at the works at the time. But what about afterwards?

HJALMAR. Well, Gina went to live at home with her mother, a Mrs. Hansen, a very capable and hard-working woman who ran a little café.. She also had a room to let, as well, a really nice, comfortable room.

GREGERS. And you, I take it, were lucky enough to land it?

HJALMAR. Yes. Actually it was your father who put me on to it. And it was *there*, you see, that I really got to know Gina.

GREGERS. So you got engaged?

HJALMAR. Yes. You know how it is with young people, they very soon get attached to each other. Hm. . . .

GREGERS [*rises and walks about*]. Tell me . . . when you got engaged . . . was it then that my father got you to . . . I mean, was it then that you began to take up photography?

HJALMAR. That's right. Because I was very keen on settling down to something, and the quicker the better. And both your father and I felt that this idea of photography was the best. And Gina thought the same. Besides, there was another reason as well, you see; it just so happened that Gina had taken up retouching.

GREGERS. That fitted in extraordinarily well.

HJALMAR [*pleased, rises*]. Yes, didn't it Gregers! It *did* fit in extraordinarily well, don't you think?

GREGERS. Yes it did, I must say. My father seems almost to have acted the part of Providence for you.

HJALMAR [*moved*]. He did not forsake his old friend's son in the hour of need. For he *is* good-hearted, you see.

MRS. SÖRBY [*enters, arm in arm with* HAAKON WERLE]. Now, my dear Mr. Werle, please don't argue. You mustn't stay in there any longer staring at all those lights. It's not good for you.

WERLE [*letting go her arm and running his hand over his eyes*]. I rather believe you are right.

[PETTERSEN *and* JENSEN, *the hired waiter, enter with trays.*]

MRS. SÖRBY [*to the guests in the other room*]. Punch is served, gentlemen; if anybody wants any, he'll have to come in here and get it.

THE FAT GUEST [*walks over to* MRS. SÖRBY]. But, I say, is it true you have abolished our precious freedom to smoke?

MRS. SÖRBY. Yes, my dear sir. Here, in Mr. Werle's private domain, it is forbidden.

THE BALDING GUEST. And when did you introduce this harsh clause into our smoking regulations, Mrs. Sörby?

MRS. SÖRBY. After the previous dinner-party, my dear sir. For there were certain people who over-stepped the mark.

THE BALDING GUEST. And is one not allowed to overstep the mark just the tiniest bit, Bertha? Seriously?

MRS. SÖRBY. Not in any circumstances, Mr. Balle.

[*Most of the guests are now assembled in* WERLE'S *room; the servants hand round punch.*]

WERLE [*to* HJALMAR, *who is standing over at table*]. What are *you* standing there looking at, Ekdal?

HJALMAR. It's just an album, Mr. Werle.

THE BALDING GUEST [*strolling about*]. Ah! Photographs! That's obviously something for you.

THE FAT GUEST [*in an armchair*]. Haven't you brought along any of your own?

HJALMAR. No, I haven't.

THE FAT GUEST. You should have done. It's good for the digestion to sit and look at pictures.

THE BALDING GUEST. And it always adds something to the general entertainment, don't you know!

A SHORT-SIGHTED GUEST. All contributions gratefully received.

MRS. SÖRBY. What they mean is that, if you are invited out, you are expected to work for your supper, Mr. Ekdal.

THE FAT GUEST. And *that*, where the food is good, is just sheer pleasure, of course!

THE BALDING GUEST. Good Lord, if it's a matter of keeping body and soul together, I must say . . .

MRS. SÖRBY. You are right there!

[*They continue laughing and joking.*]

GREGERS [*quietly*]. You must join in, Hjalmar.

HJALMAR [*with a shrug*]. What do you expect me to say?

THE FAT GUEST. Don't you think, Mr. Werle, that Tokay can be regarded as relatively kind to the stomach?

WERLE [*by the fireplace*]. I can certainly vouch for the Tokay you had today, at any rate; it was one of the very finest vintages. Of course you must have seen that yourself.

THE FAT GUEST. Yes, it had a wonderfully delicate bouquet.

HJALMAR [*uncertainly*]. Does the vintage make any difference?

THE FAT GUEST [*laughing*]. By Heavens, that's good!

WERLE [*smiling*]. There's obviously not much point in putting good wine in front of *you*.

THE BALDING GUEST. It's the same with Tokay as with photographs, Mr. Ekdal. There has to be sunlight. Or am I wrong?

HJALMAR. No, indeed. Sunlight certainly plays a part.

MRS. SÖRBY. Well then it's exactly the same with you court officials. You have got to have a place in the sun as well, as the saying goes.

THE BALDING GUEST. Come, come, that joke's a bit ancient.

THE SHORT-SIGHTED GUEST. Mrs. Sörby is showing her paces. . . .

THE FAT GUEST. . . . And at our expense. [*Threateningly.*] Bertha! Bertha!

MRS. SÖRBY. Well, but it's perfectly true that the different vintages can vary enormously. The old vintages are the best.

THE SHORT-SIGHTED GUEST. Do you reckon *me* among the old ones?

MRS. SÖRBY. Oh, far from it.

THE BALDING GUEST. Listen to her! But what about *me* then, my dear Mrs. Sörby.

THE FAT GUEST. Yes, and me! What vintages do you class us among?

MRS. SÖRBY. I count you among the sweet vintages, gentlemen.

[*She sips a glass of punch; the guests laugh and joke with her.*]

WERLE. Mrs. Sörby always finds a way out . . . when she wants to. But you are not drinking, gentlemen. Pettersen, would you mind. . . ! Gregers, I think we might take a glass together. [GREGERS *does not move.*] Won't you join us, Ekdal? I didn't get a chance of drinking to you at table.

[GRAABERG, *the book-keeper, looks through the baize door.*]

GRAABERG. Excuse me, Mr. Werle, but I can't get out.

WERLE. What, you locked in again?

GRAABERG. Yes, and Flakstad's gone off with the keys. . . .

WERLE. Well, you had better come through this way.

GRAABERG. But there's somebody else as well. . . .

WERLE Come on, come on, both of you. Don't be shy.

[GRAABERG *and* OLD EKDAL *come out of the office.*]

WERLE [*involuntarily*]. Ah!

[*The laughter and chatter of the guests die away.* HJALMAR *starts up at the sight of his father, puts down his glass and turns towards the fireplace.*]

EKDAL [*without looking up, making a series of little bows to each side as he walks, mumbling*]. Excuse me. Came the wrong way. The gate's locked . . . gate's locked. Excuse me.

[*He and* GRAABERG *go out at the back, right.*]

WERLE [*with clenched teeth*]. Damn that Graaberg.

GREGERS [*staring open-mouthed, to* HJALMAR]. Surely that was never . . . !

THE FAT GUEST. What was that? Who was it?

GREGERS. Oh, nobody. Just the book-keeper and another man.

THE SHORT-SIGHTED GUEST [*to* HJALMAR]. Did you know the man?

HJALMAR. I don't know . . . I didn't notice. . . .

THE FAT GUEST [*rises*]. What the devil's wrong? [*He walks over to some of the others who are talking in lowered voices.*]

MRS. SÖRBY [*whispers to the servant*]. Slip him something outside, something really good.

PETTERSEN [*nodding*]. Certainly. [*Goes out.*]

GREGERS [*in a low, shocked, voice to* HJALMAR]. Then it really *was* him.

HJALMAR. Yes.

GREGERS. And yet you stood here and denied that you knew him!

HJALMAR [*in an urgent whisper*]. How could I . . . ?

GREGERS. . . . acknowledge your own father?

HJALMAR [*bitterly*]. Oh, if you were in my shoes, you . . .

[*The conversation among the guests, which has been conducted in low voices, now changes over to a forced conviviality.*]

THE BALDING GUEST [*approaching* HJALMAR *and* GREGERS *in friendly fashion*]. Ah! Standing here and reviving old student memories, eh? Don't you smoke, Mr. Ekdal? Want a light? Oh, no! That's right, we mustn't . . .

HJALMAR. No, thank you! I don't want . . .

THE FAT GUEST. Couldn't you recite us a nice piece of poetry, Mr. Ekdal? There was a time once when you used to do that so prettily.

HJALMAR. I'm afraid I can't remember any.

THE FAT GUEST. Oh, what a pity. Well, Balle, what do you think we had better do now?

[*The two guests walk across the room and out into another room.*]

HJALMAR [*gloomily*]. Gregers—I must go. When once a man has felt the crushing blows of fate, you know. . . . Say goodbye to your father for me.

GREGERS. Yes, of course. Are you going straight home?

HJALMAR. Yes. Why?

GREGERS. Nothing . . . just that I might drop in afterwards.

HJALMAR. No, don't do that. Not at my home. My house is a sad place, Gregers . . . especially after a brilliant banquet like this. We can always meet somewhere in town.

MRS. SÖRBY [*comes across and speaks in a low voice*]. Are you leaving, Mr. Ekdal?

HJALMAR. Yes.

MRS. SÖRBY. Give my regards to Gina.

HJALMAR. Thank you.

MRS. SÖRBY. And tell her I'll look in one of these days.

HJALMAR. Thanks, I will. [*To* GREGERS.] Stay here. I want to slip out unnoticed. [*He sidles across the room, into the next room, and out to the right.*]

MRS. SÖRBY [*softly, to the servant who has returned*]. Well, did the old fellow get anything?

PETTERSEN. Yes, I slipped him a bottle of brandy.

MRS. SÖRBY. Oh, you might have found him something a bit better than that.

PETTERSEN. Not at all, Mrs. Sörby. Brandy is the best thing he knows.

THE FAT GUEST [*in the doorway, with a sheet of music in his hands*]. Do you think we might play something together, Mrs. Sörby?

MRS. SÖRBY. Yes, let's do that.

THE GUESTS. Bravo, bravo!

[*She and all the guests go through the room and out to the right.* GREGERS *remains standing by the fire.* HAAKON WERLE *is searching for something in the writing-desk and seems to want* GREGERS *to leave. As the latter does not move,* WERLE *crosses to the doorway.*]

GREGERS. Just a moment, Father.

WERLE [*stops*]. What is it?

GREGERS. I want a word with you.

WERLE. Can't it wait till we are alone?

GREGERS. No, it can't. Because we might very easily never find ourselves alone.

WERLE [*approaching him*]. What do you mean by *that*?

[*During what follows, a piano is distantly heard from the music room.*]

GREGERS. How could people here let that family go to the dogs like that?

WERLE. I presume you mean the Ekdals?

GREGERS. Yes, I mean the Ekdals. Lieutenant Ekdal was such a close friend of yours once.

WERLE. Yes, he was a bit too close, I'm afraid. And I wasn't allowed to forget it either for years afterwards. He's the one I have to thank for the fact that *my* reputation also suffered.

GREGERS [*quietly*]. Was *he* in fact the only guilty one?

WERLE. Who else do you imagine there could be?

GREGERS. Well, the two of you were both in on the big timber deal together . . . weren't you?

WERLE. But was it not Ekdal who drew up the survey map of the area, that dubious map? He was the one who felled all that illegal timber on state land. It was he who was responsible for running the whole thing up there. I had no idea what Lieutenant Ekdal was up to.

GREGERS. Lieutenant Ekdal didn't seem to have much idea himself what he was up to.

WERLE. That might well be. But the fact remains he was found guilty and I was acquitted.

GREGERS. Yes, I know well enough there was no proof.

WERLE. Acquittal is acquittal. Why do you go raking up all these old and dreadful stories that turned my hair grey before its time? Are these the things you have been brooding about all these years up there? I can tell you one thing, Gregers: here in town all these stories have been forgotten long ago, as far as they concern *me*.

GREGERS. And the poor Ekdals?

WERLE. What do you really expect me to do for these people? When Ekdal was let out, he was a broken man, past helping. Some people in this world only need to get a couple of slugs in them and they go plunging right down to the depths, and they never come up again. You can take my word for it, Gregers, I have gone just as far as I ever could, short of laying myself open to all sorts of suspicion and gossip. . . .

GREGERS. Suspicion? Yes, indeed.

WERLE. I've put Ekdal on doing some copying for the office, and I pay him far, far more for his work than it is worth. . . .

GREGERS [*without looking at him*]. Hm! I don't doubt *that*.

WERLE. You smile? Perhaps you think I'm not telling you the truth? I admit there's nothing in my books to account for it; I never enter expenses of that kind.

GREGERS [*smiles coldly*]. No, there are some expenses better not accounted for.

WERLE [*startled*]. What do you mean by *that*?

GREGERS [*summoning up his courage*]. Have you accounted for what it cost to have Hjalmar Ekdal taught photography?

WERLE. I . . . Why should that be accounted for?

GREGERS. I know now that it was you who paid for it. And now I also know it was you who saw him so nicely settled.

WERLE. Well, and you still want to say I've done nothing for the Ekdals! Those people have involved me in quite enough expense, I can tell you.

GREGERS. Have you entered any of those expenses?

WERLE. What are you asking me about *that* for?

GREGERS. Oh, there are good reasons. Listen, tell me . . . that time you were ready to take such a warm interest in your old friend's son . . . wasn't that just when he was about to get married?

WERLE. Come now . . . how the devil do you expect me, after all these years . . . ?

GREGERS. You wrote me a letter at the time—a business letter, of course, and in the postscript it said, quite briefly, that Hjalmar Ekdal had married a Miss Hansen.

WERLE. Yes, and that was quite right. That's what she was called.

GREGERS. But what you didn't say was that Miss Hansen was Gina Hansen, our housekeeper as was.

WERLE [*with a scornful, but forced laugh*]. No, because it never struck me you were particularly interested in our one-time housekeeper.

GREGERS. No more I was. But . . . [*Lowers his voice.*] . . . there were others in this house who *were* particularly interested in her.

WERLE. What do you mean by *that*? [*Flaring up.*] You are not referring to me, I hope!

GREGERS [*quietly, but firmly*]. Yes, I am referring to you.

WERLE. You have the impertinence to . . . ! How dare you . . . ! And as for this . . . this photographer, the ungrateful . . . how dare he have the nerve to make accusations of this kind!

GREGERS. Hjalmar has never said a single word about this. I don't think he has the slightest suspicion of anything of the kind.

WERLE. Where have you got it from, then? Who could have said a thing like that?

GREGERS. My poor, unhappy mother said it. And that was the last time I saw her.

WERLE. Your mother! Yes, I might have known. The two of you were always pretty thick. She was the one who set you against me from the start.

GREGERS. No, it was all the things she had to put up with, till in the end she gave way and went completely to pieces.

WERLE. Oh, she hadn't anything to put up with at all, no more than plenty of other people, anyway. But what can you do with people that are sick and overwrought? That's something *I* found out. And then along you come harbouring suspicions like this, raking up all sorts of old rumours and nasty gossip about your own father. Listen now, Gregers, I honestly think that at your age you might find something a bit more useful to do.

GREGERS. Yes, perhaps the time has come.

WERLE. Then perhaps you wouldn't take things quite so seriously as you tend to do now. What's the point in you sitting up there at the works, year in and year out, slaving away like any ordinary clerk and not taking a penny more than the standard wage. It's sheer stupidity.

GREGERS. Oh, if only I were quite sure about that.

WERLE. I think I understand you. You want to be independent, don't want to be under any obligation to me. But now is just the opportunity for you to get your independence, be your own master.

GREGERS. Really? And in what way?

WERLE. When I wrote to you saying it was essential you came to town at once . . . hm . . .

GREGERS. Yes, what is it actually you wanted me for? I have been waiting all day to hear.

WERLE. I propose offering you a partnership in the firm.

GREGERS. Me? In your firm? As a partner?

WERLE. Yes. There would be no need for us always to be on top of each other. I thought you might take over the business here in town, and I should move up to the works.

GREGERS. *You* would?

WERLE. Yes. I haven't the capacity for work I once had, you know. And I have to watch my eyes, Gregers, they have started getting a bit weak.

GREGERS. They have always been that way.

WERLE. Not as bad as they are now. And besides—circumstances might make it desirable for me to live up there—at any rate for a time.

GREGERS. I had never imagined anything like that.

WERLE. Listen now, Gregers. There are many things where we don't exactly hit it off. But all the same we are father and son. I think we should be able to reach some kind of understanding between us.

GREGERS. To outward appearances, I suppose you mean?

WERLE. Well, at least that would be something. Think it over, Gregers. Don't you think something like that could be done? Eh?

GREGERS [*looking at him coldly*]. There's something behind all this.

WERLE. What do you mean?

GREGERS. There must be something you want to use me for.

WERLE. When two people are as closely connected as we are, one always has some use for the other, surely.

GREGERS. Yes, that's what they say.

WERLE. I should like to have you at home now for a while. I'm a lonely man, Gregers; I've always felt lonely, all my life; but especially now that I'm getting on a bit in years. I need somebody near me.

GREGERS. You've got Mrs. Sörby.

WERLE. Yes, I have. And she's become pretty nearly indispensable. She's bright, she's easy-going, she livens the place up. And that I can do with pretty badly.

GREGERS. Quite. But in that case you have got what you want.

WERLE. Yes, but I'm afraid it won't last. With a woman in a situation like this, it's so easy for the world to put a false interpretation on things. Indeed, you might say it doesn't do the man very much good, either.

GREGERS. Oh, when a man gives the sort of dinner-parties you give, he can risk a fair amount.

WERLE. Yes, but what about her, Gregers? I'm afraid she won't put up with it much longer. And even if she did—even if she disregarded all the gossip and the back-biting and things like that, out of devotion to me . . . ? Wouldn't you think, then, Gregers, you with your strong sense of justice . . .

GREGERS [*interrupts him*]. Without beating about the bush, tell me one thing. Are you thinking of marrying her?

WERLE. And if I were, what then?

GREGERS. Yes. That's what I'm asking, too. What then?

WERLE. Would you be so completely dead set against it?

GREGERS. No, not at all. By no means.

WERLE. I didn't know whether, perhaps out of respect for the memory of your late mother . . .

GREGERS. I am not neurotic.

WERLE. Well, whether you are or not, you have taken a great weight off my mind. I am delighted I can count on your support in this matter.

GREGERS [*looks steadily at him*]. Now I see what you want to use me for.

WERLE. Use you for? What an expression!

GREGERS. Oh, let's not be too particular in our choice of words—not when we are alone, at any rate. [*Laughs shortly.*] So that's it! That's why I damn' well had to turn up here in town in person. A bit of family life had to be organized in the house all for Mrs. Sörby's sake. A little tableau: father and son! That's something new, that is.

WERLE. How dare you speak like that!

GREGERS. When has there ever been any family life here? Never as long as I can remember! But now, if you please, there's a sudden need for something in that line. Think of the good impression it must create when it is known how the son hurried home—on wings of devotion—to his ageing father's wedding feast. What will be left then of all the stories about the things the poor dead wife had to put up with. Not a whisper! Her own son kills them all stone dead.

WERLE. Gregers, I don't think there's any man in the world you hate as much as me.

GREGERS [*quietly*]. I have seen you at too close quarters.

WERLE. You have seen me with your mother's eyes. [*Drops his voice a little.*] But you mustn't forget that those eyes were . . . clouded, now and again.

GREGERS [*trembling*]. I understand what you are getting at. But who bears the blame for my mother's unhappy disability. It's you, and all these. . . ! The last of them was this female who was palmed off on Hjalmar Ekdal when you no longer . . . ugh!

WERLE [*shrugging his shoulders*]. Word for word, as though I were listening to your mother.

GREGERS [*without paying any attention to him*]. ... and now there he sits, so tremendously trusting and innocent, in the midst of deceit, living under the same roof with a woman like that and not knowing that what he calls his home is built on a lie. [*Comes a step nearer.*] When I look back on everything you've done, it's as if I looked out over a battlefield strewn with shattered lives.

WERLE. I almost think the gulf between us is too wide.

GREGERS [*with a stiff bow*]. So I have observed; I shall therefore take my hat and go.

WERLE. Go? Leave the house?

GREGERS. For now at last I see an objective I can live for.

WERLE. What sort of objective is that?

GREGERS. You would only laugh if I told you.

WERLE. Laughter doesn't come so easily to a lonely man, Gregers.

GREGERS [*pointing out to the back*]. Look, Father, your guests are playing Blind Man's Buff with Mrs. Sörby. Good night and goodbye.

[*He goes out at the back to the right. Laughter and banter are heard from the guests, who come into view in the outer room.*]

WERLE [*muttering scornfully after* GREGERS]. Huh! Poor fellow. And he says he's not neurotic!

ACT TWO

HJALMAR EKDAL'S *studio. The room, which is quite large, is recognizably an attic. On the right is a pitched roof with big skylights, half covered by a blue curtain. In the corner, top right, is the entrance-hall door; downstage, on the same side, a door leads into the living-room. Similarly there are two doors on the left wall, and between them an iron stove. On the rear wall are broad double sliding doors. The studio is cheaply but pleasantly furnished. Between the doors on the right, off the wall a little, stands a sofa, with a table and some chairs; on the table, a lighted lamp, shaded; in the corner by the stove, an old armchair. Various pieces of photographic apparatus and equipment are disposed about the room. On the rear wall, left of the double doors, is a bookcase containing a few books, some boxes and bottles of chemicals, various kinds of instruments, tools and other objects. Photographs and one or two little things like brushes, paper and so on are lying on the table.*

   GINA EKDAL *is sitting at the table, sewing.* HEDVIG *is sitting reading a book on the sofa, shading her eyes with her hands, her thumbs in her ears.*

GINA [*after glancing several times at her, as though secretly worried*]. Hedvig!

[HEDVIG *does not hear.*]

GINA [*louder*]. Hedvig!

HEDVIG [*takes her hands away and looks up*]. Yes, Mother?

GINA. Hedvig dear, you mustn't sit reading any longer.

HEDVIG. Oh, but Mother, can't I read a little bit more? Just a little!

GINA. No, no, you must put the book away now. Your father doesn't like it; he never reads himself in the evenings.

HEDVIG [*shuts the book*]. No, Daddy isn't such a great one for reading.

GINA [*putting her sewing down and taking a pencil and a little note-book on the table*]. Can you remember what we paid for the butter today?

HEDVIG. It was one crown sixty-five.

GINA. That's right. [*Makes a note.*] The amount of butter we go through in this house! And then there was the salami and the cheese . . . let me see. . . . [*Notes it down.*] Then there was the ham . . . hm. . . . [*Adds it up.*] Yes, that already comes to . . .

HEDVIG. And then there was the beer.

GINA. Yes that's right. [*Notes it down.*] It soon mounts up. But there's nothing you can do about it.

HEDVIG. But then Daddy was going to be out, so there was no need to cook a dinner just for the two of us.

GINA. Yes, that was lucky. And then there was that eight crowns fifty I got for the photographs as well.

HEDVIG. Fancy! Was it as much as that?

GINA. Eight crowns fifty exactly.

[*Silence.* GINA *takes up her sewing again.* HEDVIG *takes paper and pencil and begins to draw, shading her eyes with her left hand.*]

HEDVIG. Isn't it lovely to think of Daddy being at a big dinner-party at Mr. Werle's!

GINA. You can't really say he's at Mr. Werle's. It was the son who asked him. [*After a pause.*] We've got nothing to do with Mr. Werle.

HEDVIG. I'm so terribly looking forward to Daddy coming home. Because he promised he'd ask Mrs. Sörby for something nice for me.

GINA. Aye, there's plenty of good things going in *that* house, believe you me.

HEDVIG [*goes on drawing*]. I think I might even be a little bit hungry.

[OLD EKDAL, *with the bundle of papers under his arm and another parcel in his coat pocket, enters by the hall door.*]

GINA. You're very late home today, Grandfather.

EKDAL. They had shut the office. Had to wait in Graaberg's room. And then I came out through . . . hm.

HEDVIG. Did they give you any more copying to do, Grandfather?

EKDAL. All this lot. Just look!

GINA. That was nice.

HEDVIG. And you've got another parcel in your pocket as well.

EKDAL. Eh? Nonsense! That isn't anything. [*Stands his walking stick in the corner.*] This will keep me busy for a long time, Gina, this will. [*Draws one of the sliding doors in the rear wall a little to one side.*] Hush! [*Peeps into the room for a moment or two and then carefully shuts the door again.*] Heh! heh! The whole lot's asleep. And *she's* gone to sleep in the basket. Heh! heh!

HEDVIG. Are you sure she'll not be cold in that basket, Grandfather?

EKDAL. Whatever gives you that idea! Cold? In all that straw? [*Walks over to the door, upper left.*] Are there any matches?

GINA. The matches are on the chest of drawers.

[EKDAL *goes into his room.*]

HEDVIG. It was jolly good, Grandfather getting all that copying to do.

GINA. Yes, poor old soul; now he can earn himself a bit of pocket-money.

HEDVIG. And besides, he'll not be able to sit all morning down at that horrid Ma Eriksen's place.

GINA. Yes, that's another thing.

[*Short silence.*]

HEDVIG. Do you think they'll still be having their dinner?

GINA. Lord knows. I dare say they could be.

HEDVIG. Think of all the lovely things Daddy will be getting to eat! I'm sure he'll be in a good mood when he comes home. Don't you think so, Mother?

GINA. Yes, I do. But just think, if only we could tell him we'd managed to let the room.

HEDVIG. But that's not necessary tonight.

GINA. Oh, it would come in very handy, you know. It's just standing there doing nothing.

HEDVIG. No, what I meant was we don't need it tonight because Daddy will be in a good temper anyway. It's better if we leave the business about the room for some other time.

GINA [*looks across at her*]. Do you like having something nice to tell your father when he comes home at night?

HEDVIG. Yes, because it makes things a bit more cheerful.

GINA [*thoughtfully*]. Oh yes, there's something in that.

[OLD EKDAL *comes in again and makes for the door, front left.*]

GINA [*half turning on her chair*]. Do you want something in the kitchen, Grandfather?

EKDAL. Yes, I do. Don't get up. [*Goes out.*]

GINA. I hope he isn't messing about with the fire in there! [*Waits a moment.*] Just go and see what he's up to, Hedvig.

[EKDAL *comes in again with a little jug of hot water.*]

HEDVIG. Have you been getting some hot water, Grandfather?

EKDAL. Yes, I have. I want it for something. I've got some writing to do, and the ink's gone all thick like porridge . . . heh!

GINA. But you ought to have your supper first, Grandfather. It's all set.

EKDAL. I can't be bothered with any supper, Gina. I'm terribly busy, I tell you. I don't want anybody coming into my room. Nobody at all . . . hm!

[*He goes into his room.* GINA *and* HEDVIG *look at each other.*]

GINA [*in a low voice*]. Where do you suppose he got the money from?

HEDVIG. He must have got it from Graaberg.

GINA. No, never. Graaberg always sends the money to me.

HEDVIG. Then he must have got a bottle on tick somewhere.

GINA. Nobody will give him anything on tick, poor old soul.

[HJALMAR EKDAL, *wearing a topcoat and a grey felt hat, enters right.*]

GINA [*throws down her sewing and gets up*]. Why, Hjalmar! Are you back already!

HEDVIG [*at the same time jumping up*]. Fancy coming now, Daddy!

HJALMAR [*putting down his hat*]. Well, most of them were coming away.

HEDVIG. So early?

HJALMAR. Yes, it was a dinner party, you know.

[*About to take off his topcoat.*]

GINA. Let me help you.

HEDVIG. And me.

[*They help him off with his coat,* GINA *hangs it up on the rear wall.*]

HEDVIG. Were there many there, Daddy?

HJALMAR. Oh no, not many. There were about twelve or fourteen of us when we sat down.

GINA. And did you manage to talk to them all?

HJALMAR. Oh yes, a little. But it was Gregers who monopolized me in the main.

GINA. Is Gregers still as awful as ever.

HJALMAR. Well, he's not particularly good-looking. Hasn't the old man come home?

HEDVIG. Yes, Grandfather's in there writing.

HJALMAR. Did he say anything?

GINA. No, what about?

HJALMAR. Didn't he say anything about . . . ? I thought I heard he'd been to see Graaberg. I'll look in on him for a minute.

GINA. No, no, it's hardly worth . . .

HJALMAR. Why not? Did he say he didn't want me to go in?

GINA. He didn't want *anybody* going in tonight. . . .

HEDVIG [*making signs*]. Sst! sst!

GINA [*does not notice*]. . . . he's been and got himself some hot water. . . .

HJALMAR. Ah! Is he sitting there. . . ?

GINA. Yes, that's just what he is doing.

HJALMAR. Ah, well . . . my poor, white-haired, old father. . . ! Yes, let him get what little pleasure he can out of life.

[OLD EKDAL, *in a dressing-gown, his pipe lit, comes in from his room.*]

EKDAL. You back? I thought it was you I heard talking.

HJALMAR. I've just this minute come.

EKDAL. You didn't see me, did you?

HJALMAR. No, but they said you'd gone through. And I thought I'd walk home with you.

EKDAL. Hm! Nice of you, Hjalmar! Who were all the people there?

HJALMAR. Oh, all sorts. There was Mr. Flor, he's something at Court, and Mr. Balle and Mr. Kaspersen and Mr. . . . . What's-his-name. . . . I can't remember . . . all of them people in Court circles. . . .

EKDAL [*nods*]. Do you hear *that*, Gina? He's been mixing with high society.

GINA. Yes, things are pretty posh in that house now.

HEDVIG. Did any of them sing, Daddy? Or give a recitation?

HJALMAR. No, they just burbled on. They wanted to get me to recite to them, but I wasn't having any.

EKDAL. You weren't having any, eh?

GINA. You could easily have done it, if you wanted to.

HJALMAR. No. You haven't to be at everybody's beck and call. [*Walking up and down.*] I'm not, anyway.

EKDAL. No, no. You don't catch Hjalmar as easily as that.

HJALMAR. I don't see why *I* should be expected to provide the entertainment when I happen to have an evening out. Let the others put themselves out a little. That sort does nothing but go from one house to the next, eating and drinking, day in and day out. Let them jolly well do something in return for all the good food they get.

GINA. But I hope you didn't tell them that?

HJALMAR [*hums*]. Hm . . . hm . . . hm. They were told quite a number of things. . . .

EKDAL. What! All those Court people!

HJALMAR. That doesn't make them any different. [*Casually.*] After that we had a little argument about the Tokay.

EKDAL. Tokay, eh? That's a good wine, that!

HJALMAR [*pauses*]. It *can* be. But, you know, the different vintages are not always equally good; it all depends on how much sunshine the grapes have had.

GINA. Why, Hjalmar, the things you know!

EKDAL. And that's what they started arguing about?

HJALMAR. They tried it on; but then they were given to understand that it was exactly the same with Court officials. It was pointed out that not all *their* vintages were equally good either.

GINA. Really, the things you think of!

EKDAL. Heh, heh! So they had to put that in their pipes and smoke it!

HJALMAR. They got it, straight to their faces!

EKDAL. There you are, Gina. He let them have it straight to their faces, these people at Court.

GINA. Well, fancy! Straight to their faces.

HJALMAR. Yes, but I don't want it talked about. It's not the sort of thing to pass on. And it was all taken in good part, of course. They were nice, pleasant people. Why should I want to hurt them? No!

EKDAL. But straight to their faces . . .

HEDVIG [*ingratiatingly*]. What fun it is to see you in evening dress. You look so nice in evening dress, Daddy!

HJALMAR. Yes, I do, don't I! And this one is really an impeccable fit. Almost as though it had been made for me . . . a bit tight under the arms, perhaps. Help me off, Hedvig. [*Takes the coat off.*] I'll put my jacket on instead. Where have you put my jacket, Gina?

GINA. Here it is.

[*Brings the jacket and helps him on with it.*]

HJALMAR. There we are! Don't forget to let Molvik have the coat back first thing tomorrow morning.

GINA [*puts it aside*]. We'll see to that all right.

HJALMAR [*stretching himself*]. Ah, that feels a bit more like home. And I think it's rather more my line to wear a few casual things like this about the house. Don't you think so, Hedvig?

HEDVIG. Yes, Daddy, I do!

HJALMAR. And if I pull out my tie like this so that the ends can flap about. . . . Look! Eh?

HEDVIG. Yes, it goes well with your moustache and your curly hair.

HJALMAR. I wouldn't exactly call it curly; more wavy, you might say.

HEDVIG. Yes, because it has such soft curls.

HJALMAR. Waves, actually.

HEDVIG [*after a pause, tugs at his coat*]. Daddy!

HJALMAR. Well, what is it?

HEDVIG. Oh, you know as well as I do.

HJALMAR. No, honestly I don't.

HEDVIG [*laughing and crying*]. Oh yes you do, Daddy. You mustn't tease me any longer.

HJALMAR. But what is it?

HEDVIG [*shaking him*]. Oh, stop it now and come on, Daddy. You remember all those nice things you promised me.

HJALMAR. Oh, there now! Fancy me forgetting!

HEDVIG. Now you are just making fun of me, Daddy. Oh, it's horrid of you! Where have you put them?

HJALMAR. But just a minute! I've got something else for you, Hedvig.

[*Walks across and feels in the pockets of the coat.*]

HEDVIG [*jumping and clapping her hands*]. Oh, Mother, Mother!

GINA. Look, you see! Just give him time. . . .

HJALMAR [*with a piece of paper*]. Look, here it is.

HEDVIG. This thing? It's just a piece of paper.

HJALMAR. That's the menu, Hedvig, the complete menu. There it says 'Bill of fare', that means menu.

HEDVIG. Haven't you got anything else?

HJALMAR. I forgot the rest, I tell you. But believe me—it's no great treat having to eat all those things. Go and sit over at the table now, and read what it says on the card, and afterwards I'll tell you what the different courses taste like. There you are, Hedvig.

HEDVIG [*swallows her tears*]. Thanks.

[*She sits down, but does not read;* GINA *makes a sign to her, which* HJALMAR *notices.*]

HJALMAR [*pacing up and down*]. It's incredible all the things a man is supposed to think about; he's only to forget the slightest thing, and straight away all he gets is a lot of sour looks. Well, that's another thing you get used to. [*Pauses near the stove, beside the old man.*] Have you peeped in this evening, Father?

EKDAL. Yes, you bet I have. She's gone in the basket.

HJALMAR. Has she really? In the basket! She must be getting used to it.

EKDAL. Yes, I told you she would. But now, you know, there are still a few other things. . . .

HJALMAR. One or two improvements, you mean.

EKDAL. They've *got* to be done, you know.

HJALMAR. Yes, let's have a little chat about these improvements, Father. Come on, we'll sit on the sofa.

EKDAL. Yes, fine. Hm! Think I'll just fill my pipe first. . . . Must clean it out as well. Hm!

[*He goes into his room.*]

GINA [*smiles to* HJALMAR]. Cleaning his pipe!

HJALMAR. Well, well, Gina, just let him be . . . he's just a poor, old wreck of a man. . . . Yes, those improvements. . . . We'd best get them done tomorrow.

GINA. You'll not have any time tomorrow, Hjalmar.

HEDVIG [*breaking in*]. Yes he will, Mother!

GINA. . . . Don't forget those prints that need retouching; they've been asked for ever so many times.

HJALMAR. What! Those prints again? They'll be ready all right. Have there been any new orders?

GINA. No, worse luck. Tomorrow I've nothing but those two sittings, you know.

HJALMAR. Is that all? Oh well, if you are not ready to put yourself out, then . . .

GINA. But what more am I supposed to do? I'm putting as many adverts in the papers as we can afford, I reckon.

HJALMAR. Oh, the papers, the papers. You can see what use *that* is. And I suppose nobody's been to look at the room either?

GINA. No, not yet.

HJALMAR. Just what you might expect. If people don't show any initiative . . . well! We must pull ourselves together, Gina!

HEDVIG [*going over to him*]. Wouldn't you like me to fetch you your flute, Daddy?

HJALMAR. No, no flute, thank you. *I* don't need any of life's little pleasures! [*Paces about.*] Oh yes, I'll be working tomorrow all right, don't you fret. Working till I'm fit to drop. . . .

GINA. But, my dear Hjalmar, I didn't mean it that way.

HEDVIG. Daddy, what, about bringing you a bottle of beer?

HJALMAR. No, certainly not. There's no need to bring out anything for me. . . . [*Pauses.*] Beer? Was it beer you said?

HEDVIG [*gaily*]. Yes, Daddy. Nice cool beer.

HJALMAR. Well . . . if you really want to, you might bring a bottle.

GINA. Yes, go on. It'll cheer things up a bit.

[HEDVIG *runs over towards the kitchen door.*]

HJALMAR [*stops her by the stove, looks at her, takes her head in his hands and draws her to him*]. Hedvig! Hedvig!

HEDVIG [*smiling through her tears*]. Daddy dear!

HJALMAR. No, don't call me that. There I've been sitting indulging myself at the rich man's table . . . stuffing myself at the festive board. . . ! And I couldn't even . . .

GINA [*sitting at the table*]. Oh, don't talk so silly, Hjalmar.

HJALMAR. It's true. But you mustn't think too badly of me. You know I love you, all the same.

HEDVIG [*throws her arms around him*]. And we love you so much, too, Daddy!

HJALMAR. And even if I am a bit unreasonable now and again, well . . . heavens above! You mustn't forget I'm a man beset by a whole host of troubles. Well, now! [*Dries his eyes.*] This is not the moment for beer. Bring me my flute.

[HEDVIG *runs to the shelves and gets it.*]

HJALMAR. Thanks! There we are. With flute in hand, and both of you close to me . . . ah!

[HEDVIG *sits down at the table beside* GINA; HJALMAR *walks up and down and begins resolutely on a rendering of a Bohemian folk dance, but in a slow elegiac tempo with much 'feeling'.*]

HJALMAR [*breaks off the tune, holds out his left hand to* GINA *and says with emotion*]. What though we have to pinch and scrape in this place, Gina! It's still our home. And this I will say: it is good to be here.

[*He starts to play again; at once there is a knock at the door.*]

GINA [*gets up*]. Hush, Hjalmar! I think somebody's coming.

HJALMAR [*placing the flute back on the shelf*]. Isn't that just like it!

[GINA *walks over and opens the door.*]

GREGERS WERLE [*outside in the passage*]. Excuse me, but . . .

GINA [*shrinking back*]. Oh!

GREGERS. . . . doesn't Mr. Ekdal the photographer live here?

GINA. Yes, he does.

HJALMAR [*walks over to the door*]. Gregers! Is that you again! Come along in.

GREGERS [*comes in*]. I told you I'd be looking in, didn't I?

HJALMAR. But tonight . . . ? Have you left the party?

GREGERS. Both the party and my father's house. Good evening, Mrs. Ekdal. I'm not sure if you recognize me again?

GINA. Oh yes. It's not difficult to recognize you again, Mr. Werle.

GREGERS. No, they say I take after my mother, and I expect you remember her all right.

HJALMAR. Did you say you've left the house?

GREGERS. Yes, I've moved to a hotel.

HJALMAR. Have you now! Well, now that you're here, you might as well take your things off and sit down.

GREGERS. Thanks.

[*Takes off his topcoat. He has changed into plain grey country tweeds.*]

HJALMAR. Here, on the sofa. Make yourself comfortable.

[GREGERS *sits down on the sofa,* HJALMAR *on a chair at the table.*]

GREGERS [*looking round*]. So this is your place, Hjalmar. This is where you live.

HJALMAR. This, as you see, is the studio. . . .

GINA. But it's a bit more roomy here, so we like being in here best.

HJALMAR. We had a nicer place before; but there's one great advantage about this flat, and that's all the extra space. . . .

GINA. And we've also got another room on the other side of the passage, and we can let that.

GREGERS [*to* HJALMAR]. Well, well . . . so you've got lodgers as well?

HJALMAR. No, not yet. It's not as easily done as all that, you know. It needs initiative. [*To* HEDVIG.] Now what about that beer!

[HEDVIG *nods and goes out to the kitchen.*]

GREGERS. So that's your daughter?

HJALMAR. Yes, that's Hedvig.

GREGERS. And she's an only child?

HJALMAR. She's the only one, yes. She's our greatest joy in life, and . . . [*Drops his voice.*] . . . she's also our deepest sorrow, Gregers.

GREGERS. What do you mean?

HJALMAR. Yes, Gregers. She is in grave danger of losing her sight.

GREGERS. Going blind!

HJALMAR. Yes. So far there's only been the first signs, and things might still be all right for quite some time yet. But the doctor has warned us. It's inevitable.

GREGERS. How terribly sad. How did she get like that?

HJALMAR [*sighs*]. Apparently, it's hereditary.

GREGERS [*with a start*]. Hereditary!

GINA. Hjalmar's mother also had poor sight.

HJALMAR. Yes, that's what Father says. I can't remember her myself.

GREGERS. The poor child. And how does she take it?

HJALMAR. Oh, can't you see we haven't the heart to tell her. She doesn't suspect anything. Happy and carefree, just like a little singing bird, there she goes fluttering into a life of eternal night. [*Overcome.*] Oh, it's quite heart-breaking for me, Gregers!

[HEDVIG *enters carrying a tray with beer and glasses which she puts on the table.*]

HJALMAR [*strokes her head*]. Thank you, Hedvig.

[HEDVIG *puts her arms round his neck and whispers in his ear.*]

HJALMAR. No, no sandwiches just now. [*Looks across.*] Unless perhaps Gregers would like some?

GREGERS [*declining*]. No, no thank you.

HJALMAR [*still sadly*]. Well, perhaps you might fetch a few, after all. If you've a crust, that would be all right. But mind you see there's plenty of butter on.

[HEDVIG *nods happily and goes out again into the kitchen.*]

GREGERS [*who has been following her with his eyes*]. She looks strong and healthy enough to me in other respects.

GINA. Yes, there's nothing much else wrong with her, thank God.

GREGERS. She's going to be like you in time, Mrs. Ekdal. How old might she be now?

GINA. Hedvig is just fourteen; it's her birthday the day after tomorrow.

GREGERS. She's a big girl for her age.

GINA. Yes, she's just shot up this last year.

GREGERS. It makes you realize your own age when you see all the young people growing up. How long is it you've been married now?

GINA. We've been married now . . . yes, close on fifteen years.

GREGERS. Fancy, is it so long?

GINA [*suddenly attentive, watching him*]. Yes, that's what it is all right.

HJALMAR. Yes, it must be all that. Fifteen years all but a few months. [*Changing the subject.*] It must have seemed a long time for *you*, Gregers, sitting up there at the works.

GREGERS. It seemed long at the time. But looking back now, I hardly know where it's all gone to.

[OLD EKDAL *comes out of his room, without his pipe, but wearing his old officer's cap; his gait is a bit unsteady.*]

EKDAL. Now then, Hjalmar, now we can sit down and talk about that . . . er . . . what was it again?

HJALMAR [*goes across to him*]. Father, there's somebody here, Gregers Werle . . . I don't know if you remember him.

EKDAL [*looks at* GREGERS, *who has risen*]. Werle? Is that the son? What does he want with me?

HJALMAR. Nothing. It's me he's come to see.

EKDAL. Ah! So there isn't anything the matter?

HJALMAR. No, nothing at all.

EKDAL [*waving his arms*]. Not that I care, you know; I'm not frightened, but . . .

GREGERS [*walks over to him*]. All I wanted was to bring greetings from your old hunting grounds, Lieutenant Ekdal.

EKDAL. Hunting grounds?

GREGERS. Yes, up there by the Höidal works.

EKDAL. Oh, there! They knew me well enough up there at one time.

GREGERS. You were a great one for shooting in those days.

EKDAL. Yes, I dare say you're right there. You are looking at my uniform. I don't have to ask anybody if I can wear it here in the house. So long as I don't go out in the street with it on . . .

[HEDVIG *brings in a plate of sandwiches which she puts on the table.*]

HJALMAR. Sit down now, Father, and have a glass of beer. Help yourself, Gregers.

[EKDAL *staggers mumbling over to the sofa.* GREGERS *sits on the chair nearest him,* HJALMAR *on the other side of* GREGERS. GINA *sits sewing a little way from the table;* HEDVIG *stands beside her father.*]

GREGERS. Can you remember, Lieutenant Ekdal, how Hjalmar and I used to come up in the summer and at Christmas to visit you?

EKDAL. Did you? No, no, no, I can't remember that. But I was a pretty crack shot, although I say it myself. I've even shot bears . . . nine of them, no less.

GREGERS [*looks sympathetically at him*]. And have you given up shooting now?

EKDAL. Oh no, I wouldn't say *that*, my dear sir. Still manage a bit of shooting now and again. Not *that* sort, of course. Because the forest, you know . . . the forest . . . the forest . . . ! [*Drinks.*] Is the forest in good shape up there now?

GREGERS. Not as fine as it was in your day. There's been a lot of felling.

EKDAL. Felling, eh? [*Lowers his voice, as if afraid.*] That's a dangerous business, that. That brings trouble. The forests avenge themselves.

HJALMAR [*fills up his glass*]. A little more, Father?

GREGERS. How is it possible for a man so fond of the outdoor life as you are to live cooped up here in town, hemmed in by these four walls?

EKDAL [*gives a short laugh and glances at* HJALMAR]. Oh, it's not bad here. Not bad at all.

GREGERS. But what about all those things that came to be so much a part of you at one time? The cool, caressing breezes, the open-air life in the forest and on the moors, among the beasts and the birds. . . .

EKDAL [*smiling*]. Hjalmar, shall we show him?

HJALMAR [*quickly, and a little embarrassed*]. Oh, no, no, Father. Not tonight.

GREGERS. What does he want to show me?

HJALMAR. Oh, it's only a sort of . . . You can see it another time.

GREGERS [*continues talking to the old man*]. Now what I had in mind, Lieutenant Ekdal, was that you ought to come back with me up to the works; I'll be returning there very soon. You could quite easily get copying to do up there as well. And there's really nothing here to keep you amused or liven things up for you.

EKDAL [*staring at him in astonishment*]. *Me?* Nothing here for *me*. . . ?

GREGERS. Oh yes, you have Hjalmar. But then he's got his own family. And a man like yourself who's always felt the call of the wild . . .

EKDAL [*strikes the table*]. Hjalmar, he *must* see it now.

HJALMAR. But, Father, is it worth it? It's dark. . . .

EKDAL. Nonsense! It's moonlight. [*Gets up.*] I tell you he *must* see it. Let me past. Come on and help me, Hjalmar!

HEDVIG. Oh yes, go on, Daddy.

HJALMAR [*gets up*]. Very well.

GREGERS [*to* GINA]. What is it?

GINA. Oh, you mustn't expect anything very special.

[EKDAL *and* HJALMAR *have gone to the back wall, and each pushes one of the sliding doors to one side;* HEDVIG *helps* OLD EKDAL; GREGERS *remains standing by the sofa;* GINA *sits unperturbed, sewing. Through the door can be seen a long irregularly shaped loft, with recesses and a couple of free-standing stove-pipes. There are skylights through which bright moonlight shines on some parts of the loft, leaving the rest in deep shadow.*]

EKDAL [*to* GREGERS]. You'd best come right over.

GREGERS [*walks over to them.*] But what *is* it, then?

EKDAL. Look and see. Hm!

HJALMAR [*rather embarrassed*]. All this belongs to Father, you understand.

GREGERS [*beside the door, looks into the loft*]. So you keep poultry, Lieutenant Ekdal!

EKDAL. I'll say we keep poultry. They've gone to roost now. But you should just see *this* poultry in daylight!

HEDVIG. And then there's . . .

EKDAL. Hush! hush! Don't say anything yet.

GREGERS. You've got pigeons as well, I see.

EKDAL. Oh yes! Sure, we have pigeons! They have their nesting boxes up under the eaves. Pigeons like best being up high, you know.

HJALMAR. They're not all ordinary pigeons, though.

EKDAL. Ordinary! No, I should just say not! We've got some tumblers, and we've also a pair of pouters. But come over here! Can you see that hutch over there by the wall?

GREGERS. Yes. What do you use that for?

EKDAL. That's where the rabbits sleep at night, my dear fellow.

GREGERS. Well! So you've got rabbits as well?

EKDAL. Yes, I should damn' well think we have got rabbits! He's asking if we've got rabbits, Hjalmar! Ha! But *now* we really do come to something! *Now* it comes! Out of the way, Hedvig! Come and stand here, that's right; now look down there. Can you see a basket with straw in?

GREGERS. Yes, I can. And I can see a bird sitting in the basket.

EKDAL. Ha! 'A bird!'

GREGERS. Isn't it a duck?

EKDAL [*hurt*]. Yes, obviously it's a duck.

HJALMAR. But what *kind* of duck do you think it is?

HEDVIG. It isn't an ordinary duck. . . .

EKDAL. Hush!

GREGERS. And it isn't one of those foreign breeds either.

EKDAL. No, Mr. . . . Werle; that's no foreign breed; that's a wild duck.

GREGERS. No, is it really? A wild duck?

EKDAL. Yes, that's just what it is. That 'bird' as you call it . . . that's a wild duck. Our wild duck, my dear sir.

HEDVIG. *My* wild duck. Because it belongs to *me*.

GREGERS. And can it really live up here in the loft? Does it get on all right here?

EKDAL. Of course she's got a trough of water to splash about in, you understand.

HJALMAR. Clean water every other day.

GINA [*turning to* HJALMAR]. Hjalmar, my dear, it's getting absolutely freezing in here now.

EKDAL. Hm, let's shut it up then. It's not good to disturb them when they're settled for the night, either. Go on, Hedvig, help!

[HJALMAR *and* HEDVIG *push the doors of the loft closed.*]

EKDAL. You can come and see her properly another time. [*Sits in the armchair by the stove.*] Oh, very remarkable birds, wild ducks are, I can tell you.

GREGERS. But how did you manage to catch it, Lieutenant Ekdal?

EKDAL. It wasn't me who caught it. There's a certain gentleman here in town whom we can thank for that.

GREGERS [*with a slight start*]. That gentleman wouldn't happen to be my father, would it?

EKDAL. You've got it! Precisely! Your father! Hm!

HJALMAR. Funny your guessing *that*, Gregers.

GREGERS. You told me before that you owed such a lot to my father, and so I thought . . .

GINA. But we didn't get the duck from Mr. Werle personally. . . .

EKDAL. It's Haakon Werle we have to thank for her just the same, Gina. [*To* GREGERS.] You see, he was out in a boat, and he let fly at her. But his sight isn't so good now, your father's isn't. Hm! So she was only winged.

GREGERS. Aha! She got a slug or two in her, did she!

HJALMAR. Yes, two or three maybe.

HEDVIG. It was in the wing, so she couldn't fly.

GREGERS. And then she dived right down to the bottom, eh!

EKDAL [*sleepily, his voice thick*]. She did that. Always do that, wild ducks do. Go plunging right to the bottom . . . as deep as they can get, my dear sir . . . hold on with their beaks to the weeds and stuff—and all the other mess you find down there. Then they never come up again.

GREGERS. But, Lieutenant Ekdal, *your* wild duck came up again.

EKDAL. He had such an absurdly clever dog, your father. . . . And that dog, he dived in and fetched the duck up again.

GREGERS [*turning to* HJALMAR]. And then you got it?

HJALMAR. Not straight away. First it was taken to your father's, but it didn't seem to thrive there; so Pettersen was told to do away with it. . . .

EKDAL [*half asleep*]. Ha! Pettersen! That old fool. . . .

HJALMAR [*in a lower voice*]. That was the way we got it, you see, with Father knowing Pettersen; when he heard all the business about the wild duck, he managed to get it turned over to him.

GREGERS. And now it's thriving perfectly well in the loft.

HJALMAR. Yes, incredibly so. It's got quite fat. Well, it's been so long there now it's forgotten what real wild life is like. And that's all that counts.

GREGERS. I'm sure you are right, Hjalmar. So long as it never catches sight of sea and sky. . . . But I mustn't stay any longer. I think your father's asleep.

HJALMAR. Oh, don't you worry about that. . . .

GREGERS. But, by the way . . . didn't you say you had a room to let . . . a vacant room?

HJALMAR. Yes, what of it? Perhaps you know somebody . . . ?

GREGERS. Can *I* have the room?

HJALMAR. You?

GINA. What, *you*, Mr. Werle. . . ?

GREGERS. Can I have the room? I'd move in first thing tomorrow morning.

HJALMAR. Yes, with the greatest pleasure. . . .

GINA. Oh, but Mr. Werle, that's not the sort of room for the likes of you, really.

HJALMAR. But, Gina, what are you saying?

GINA. Well, I mean, that room isn't big enough or light enough, and . . .

GREGERS. I'm not fussy about that, Mrs. Ekdal.

HJALMAR. Myself I'd have said it was rather a nice room; and not badly furnished either.

GINA. But don't forget about those two living underneath.

GREGERS. Who are they?

GINA. Oh, one of them's been a private tutor . . .

HJALMAR. That's Mr. Molvik.

GINA. . . . and then there's a doctor called Relling.

GREGERS. Relling? I know him slightly; he was in practice up in Höidal for a while.

GINA. They're a right pair of wasters, them two. As often as not they're off on a binge in the evenings, and they don't come back till late at night, and then they're not always quite . . .

GREGERS. You soon get used to things like that. I hope I shall be like the wild duck and . . .

GINA. Well, I think you'd better sleep on it first, all the same.

GREGERS. I don't think you're very keen on having me in the house, Mrs. Ekdal.

GINA. Heavens, whatever gives you that idea?

HJALMAR. Yes, really you are behaving very strangely, Gina. [*To* GREGERS.] But tell me, does this mean you are thinking of staying on in town for the time being?

GREGERS [*putting on his topcoat*]. Yes, now I'm thinking of staying.

HJALMAR. But not at your father's? What do you intend doing with yourself?

GREGERS. Ah, if only I knew *that*, my dear Hjalmar . . . it wouldn't be so bad. But when you are burdened with a name like 'Gregers'. . . ! 'Gregers!' And followed by 'Werle'! Have you ever heard anything so hideous?

HJALMAR. Oh, I don't know. . . .

GREGERS. Ugh! I feel I would want to spit at anybody with a name like that. But when once you have the burden of being 'Gregers . . . Werle' in this life, as I have . . .

HJALMAR [*laughs*]. Ha! ha! And if you weren't 'Gregers Werle', what would you want to be?

GREGERS. If I had the choice, I should like most of all to be a clever dog.

GINA. A dog!

HEDVIG [*involuntarily*]. Oh, no!

GREGERS. Yes, a really absurdly clever dog; the sort that goes in after wild ducks when they dive down and bite on to the weeds and tangle in the mud.

HJALMAR. You know, Gregers . . . I don't understand a word of what you are saying.

GREGERS. Oh, well, I dare say there's nothing much to it, anyway. Well then, first thing tomorrow . . . and I'll move in. [*To* GINA.] I'll not cause you much bother; I'll do for myself. [*To* HJALMAR.] We'll talk about the rest tomorrow. Good night, Mrs. Ekdal. [*Nods to* HEDVIG.] Good night!

GINA. Good night, Mr. Werle.

HEDVIG. Good night.

HJALMAR [*who has lit a candle*]. Just a minute, I'll bring a light. It's sure to be dark on the stairs.

[GREGERS *and* HJALMAR *leave by the hall door.*]

GINA [*staring vacantly, her sewing on her lap*]. Wasn't that funny, him talking about wanting to be a dog?

HEDVIG. I'll tell you what, Mother . . . I think he meant something else.

GINA. What else could he mean?

HEDVIG. I don't know. But all the time it was just as though he meant something different from what he was saying.

GINA. Do you think so? It was certainly very funny.

HJALMAR [*comes back*]. The lamp was still on. [*Snuffs the candle and puts it down.*] Ah, at last a man can get a bite to eat. [*Begins to eat a sandwich.*] There you are, you see, Gina . . . see what you can do with a bit of initiative. . . .

GINA. What do you mean 'initiative'?

HJALMAR. Well, wasn't it lucky getting the room let at last. And then imagine! . . . to somebody like Gregers . . . an old friend.

GINA. Really, I don't know what to say, I don't.

HEDVIG. Oh Mother, it'll be lovely, you'll see.

HJALMAR. You are funny, you know. First you were keen on getting it let, and now you don't like it.

GINA. Oh, yes, Hjalmar. If only it had been somebody else. . . . But what do you suppose Mr. Werle's going to say?

HJALMAR. Old Werle? It's no concern of his.

GINA. But you can see they've fallen out about something again, what with him moving out of the house. You know what those two are like with each other.

HJALMAR. Yes, that may be, but . . .

GINA. And now perhaps Mr. Werle will think you are behind it all. . . .

HJALMAR. Let him think! Good God, I admit Mr. Werle's done a great deal for me. But that doesn't mean I've got to go on for ever doing what he wants me to do.

GINA. But, Hjalmar dear, it might also affect Grandfather. Perhaps he'll lose the little bit of money he makes working for Graaberg.

HJALMAR. I could almost wish he would! Isn't it rather humiliating for a man like me to see his grey-haired father being treated like an outcast? But soon we shall know what time in its fullness will bring, I should think. [*Helps himself to another sandwich.*] As truly as I have a mission in life, so shall I fulfil it!

HEDVIG. Oh yes, Daddy, do!

GINA. Hush! Mind you don't wake him.

HJALMAR [*in a lower voice*]. I *will* fulfil it, I tell you. The day will come, when . . . And that's why it's a good thing we managed to let the room; it gives me a bit more independence. And *that's* something a man with a mission in life must have. [*Over by the armchair, greatly moved.*] My poor white-haired old father! Trust in your Hjalmar! He has broad shoulders . . . strong shoulders, anyway. One fine day you'll wake up and . . . [*To* GINA.] You believe that, don't you?

GINA [*getting up*]. Of course I believe it. But let's see about getting him to bed first.

HJALMAR. Yes, let's.

[*They lift the old man carefully.*]

ACT THREE

HJALMAR EKDAL'S *studio. It is morning; the daylight comes through the big window in the sloping roof; the curtain is drawn back.*

HJALMAR *is sitting at the table busy retouching a photograph; several other pictures are lying in front of him. After a while* GINA *comes in by the hall door, in her hat and coat, carrying on her arm a covered basket.*

HJALMAR. Is that you back already, Gina?

GINA. Oh, yes. Have to look slippy. [*She puts the basket on a chair and takes off her things.*]

HJALMAR. Did you look in on Gregers?

GINA. Yes, I did. And a bonny sight it is in there. He's no sooner here but what he's got the whole room in a right rare state.

HJALMAR. Oh?

GINA. Yes, he wanted to manage for himself, he said. Decided to light the fire, so what did he do but screw the damper down so the whole room was filled with smoke. Ugh, the stink! Just like . . .

HJALMAR. Oh dear!

GINA. But you haven't heard the best bit. Because then he wanted to put it out, so he just took a whole jug of water off the washstand and poured it all into the stove, and now there's the most awful wet mess all over the floor.

HJALMAR. What a nuisance!

GINA. I've got the woman downstairs to come and clean up after him— the pig. But the place won't be fit to go into again until this afternoon.

HJALMAR. What's he doing with himself in the meantime?

GINA. He was going out for a bit, he said.

HJALMAR. I looked in on him as well for a minute. Just after you'd gone out.

GINA. So I heard. And you've asked him to lunch.

HJALMAR. Just for a bit of a bite of something, you know. Seeing it's his first day . . . we can't really get out of it. You've always got something in the house.

GINA. I'd better see what I can find.

HJALMAR. But let's not be too stingy about it. Because I think Relling and Molvik are also coming up. I happened to run into Relling on the stairs, you see, so I more or less had to . . .

GINA. So we're going to have them two an' all.

HJALMAR. Good Lord . . . one or two more or less . . . that's surely neither here nor there.

OLD EKDAL [*opens his door and looks out*]. I say, Hjalmar . . . ! [*Notices* GINA.] Oh . . . ah . . .

GINA. Is there something you want, Grandfather?

EKDAL. Oh no, it doesn't matter. Hm! [*Goes in again.*]

GINA [*takes the basket*]. Just keep an eye on him and see he doesn't go out.

HJALMAR. Yes, yes, I will. . . . I say, Gina, a little bit of herring salad would be nice. Because Relling and Molvik were out on the tiles last night.

GINA. As long as they don't land on me before . . .

HJALMAR. No, of course they won't. Take your time.

GINA. Yes, all right. And in the meantime you can get a bit of work done.

HJALMAR. I *am* working! I'm working as hard as I can.

GINA. Because then it means you'll have *that* off your hands, you see.

[*She takes the basket and goes out to the kitchen.* HJALMAR *sits a while working on the photograph with a brush, with obvious distaste and reluctance.*]

EKDAL [*peeps out, looks round the studio and says in a low voice*]. Busy, Hjalmar?

HJALMAR. Yes, can't you see I'm sitting here slaving away at these portraits. . . .

EKDAL. Oh well, of course, if you're all *that* busy. . . . Hm! [*Goes in again: the door remains standing open.*]

HJALMAR [*continues for a while in silence; then he puts down his brush and walks over to the door*]. Are you busy, Father?

EKDAL [*from within, grumbling*]. If *you're* so busy, then *I'm* busy too. Hm!

HJALMAR. All right.

[*Goes back to his work.*]

EKDAL [*after a short pause, appears again at his door*]. Hm! Look, Hjalmar, I'm not *really* as busy as all that.

HJALMAR. I thought you were busy with your copying.

EKDAL. Oh, hell! Surely Graaberg can wait a day or two, can't he? I don't suppose it's a matter of life and death.

HJALMAR. No, and besides you're no slave.

EKDAL. Then there was that thing, you know, for in there . . .

HJALMAR. Yes, precisely. Do you want to go in? Shall I open up for you?

EKDAL. That's maybe not such a bad idea.

HJALMAR [*getting up*]. And then we'd have *that* off our hands.

EKDAL. Exactly. It has to be ready for first thing tomorrow morning. It is tomorrow, isn't it? Eh?

HJALMAR. Yes, it's tomorrow all right.

[HJALMAR *and* EKDAL *take a door each and push; the morning sun is shining in through the skylights; a few pigeons are flying about, others sit cooing on the rafters; occasionally, hens can be heard cackling from further back in the loft.*]

HJALMAR. Well, you'd better get on with it now, Father.

EKDAL [*goes in*]. Aren't you coming?

HJALMAR. Yes, do you know . . . I rather think . . . [*Sees* GINA *at the kitchen door.*] Who me? No, I haven't time. I have to work. But what about our little gadget . . . ? [*He pulls a string and inside a curtain*

*falls, the bottom part of which consists of a strip of old sail cloth, and the
upper part of a piece of fishing net stretched taut. As a result the floor of
the loft is no longer visible.*]

HJALMAR [*walks over to the table*]. There now! Perhaps I can get on in
peace for a while now.

GINA. Is he fiddling about in there again?

HJALMAR. Would you rather see him running off to Ma Eriksen's?
[*Sits down.*] Do you want something? You said . . .

GINA. I just wanted to ask if you thought we could lay the table in
here?

HJALMAR. Yes. I take it we haven't got anybody booked for as early
as that.

GINA. No, the only people I'm expecting are that couple that wanted
to be taken together.

HJALMAR. Why the devil couldn't they have been taken together some
other day!

GINA. Now, Hjalmar my dear, I booked them specially for after
dinner when you are having your sleep.

HJALMAR. Oh well, that's all right then. Yes, we'll eat in here.

GINA. All right. But there's no hurry about laying the table. There's
nothing to stop you from using it for a good while yet.

HJALMAR. Surely you can see I'm using the table just about as hard
as I can go.

GINA. And then you'll be free later, won't you? [*Goes out into the
kitchen again. Short pause.*]

EKDAL [*appears at the loft door, behind the net*]. Hjalmar!

HJALMAR. Well?

EKDAL. I'm afraid we'll have to move the water trough after all.

HJALMAR. Yes, that's just what I've been saying all along.

EKDAL. Hm, hm, hm!

[*Moves away from the door again.* HJALMAR *does a little work, glances over at the loft and half gets up.* HEDVIG *comes in from the kitchen.*]

HJALMAR [*sits down again quickly*]. What do you want?

HEDVIG. I just wanted to be beside you, Daddy.

HJALMAR [*after a moment*]. What do you want to come sniffing round like this for? Are you supposed to be keeping an eye on me, or something?

HEDVIG. No, of course not.

HJALMAR. What's your mother up to now out there?

HEDVIG. Oh, she's right in the middle of making herring salad. [*Walks over to the table.*] Isn't there anything I could help you with, Daddy?

HJALMAR. No, no. I'd best see to it all myself . . . as long as my strength lasts. There's no need, Hedvig; provided your father manages to keep his health. . . .

HEDVIG. Oh, no, Daddy! You mustn't say horrid things like that.

[*She wanders round, stops by the opening and looks into the loft.*]

HJALMAR. What's he doing, Hedvig?

HEDVIG. Looks like a new way up to the water trough.

HJALMAR. He'll never manage *that* by himself, never in this world! Yet here am I condemned to sit here. . . !

HEDVIG [*goes across to him*]. Let *me* have the brush, Daddy. I *can* do it, you know.

HJALMAR. Nonsense. You'll just ruin your eyes.

HEDVIG. Really I shan't. Come on, give me the brush.

HJALMAR [*gets up*]. Well, I don't suppose it'd take more than a minute or two.

HEDVIG. Pooh! What if it did! [*Takes the brush.*] There now. [*Sits down.*] And here's one I can copy from.

HJALMAR. But don't ruin your eyes! D'you hear? I'm not taking any responsibility; you have to take the responsibility yourself. Understand?

HEDVIG [*retouching*]. Yes, yes, I will.

HJALMAR. You are a clever little girl, Hedvig. Just for a couple of minutes, then.

[*He slips past the edge of the curtaining into the loft.* HEDVIG *sits at her work.* HJALMAR *and* EKDAL *can be heard discussing things inside.*]

HJALMAR [*appears behind the netting*]. Oh, Hedvig, hand me those pincers off the shelf, will you? And the chisel as well. [*Turns to face into the loft.*] Now I just want you to see something, Father. Just give me the chance to show you what I mean first.

[HEDVIG *fetches the tools he wanted from the shelf and hands them in to him.*]

HJALMAR. Thanks. Yes, it was a good thing I came, you know.

[*Moves away from the opening; hammering and talking are heard within.* HEDVIG *stands there watching them. A moment later there is a knock on the hall door which she does not notice.* GREGERS WERLE *comes in and stands near the door; he is bare-headed and without a topcoat.*]

GREGERS. Hm?

HEDVIG [*turns and walks over to him*]. Good morning! Please come in.

GREGERS. Thanks. [*Looks over at the loft.*] Sounds as though you've got workmen in the house.

HEDVIG. No, it's only Daddy and Grandfather. I'll go and tell them.

GREGERS. No, no, don't do that. I'll just wait a minute or two instead.

[*He sits down on the sofa.*]

HEDVIG. Everything's in such a mess. . . .

[*Begins to clear away the photographs.*]

GREGERS. Oh, just leave it. Are these photographs waiting to be finished?

HEDVIG. Yes, it's just a little job I was helping Daddy with.

GREGERS. Please don't let me disturb you.

HEDVIG. All right.

[*She arranges the things around her again and settles down to work;* GREGERS *watches her in silence.*]

GREGERS. Did the wild duck sleep well last night?

HEDVIG. Yes, thank you, I think so.

GREGERS [*turning towards the loft*]. It looks quite different in daylight from what it did last night by moonlight.

HEDVIG. Yes, it can change such a lot. In the mornings it looks different from in the afternoons; and when it's raining it looks different from when it's fine.

GREGERS. Have you noticed that?

HEDVIG. Yes, you can't help seeing it.

GREGERS. Do you like being in there too beside the wild duck.

HEDVIG. Yes, when it can be managed. . . .

GREGERS. But I dare say you haven't a great deal of spare time. You have to go to school, haven't you?

HEDVIG. No, I don't go now any more. Daddy is afraid I'll spoil my eyes.

GREGERS. So he probably helps you with your lessons himself.

HEDVIG. Daddy's promised to do some lessons with me, but he hasn't been able to find the time just yet.

GREGERS. But isn't there anybody else who could help you a little?

HEDVIG. Yes, there's Mr. Molvik; but he's not always quite . . . not properly . . . er . . .

GREGERS. You mean, he's drunk?

HEDVIG. Yes, he is.

GREGERS. Well then, you've got time for all sorts of things. And inside there, it must just be like a world of its own, I should think?

HEDVIG. Yes, all of its own. And such a lot of strange things, too.

GREGERS. Really?

HEDVIG. Yes, big cupboards with books in, and a lot of the books have pictures.

GREGERS. Aha!

HEDVIG. And then there's an old cabinet with drawers and compartments in, and a big clock with figures that are supposed to pop in and out. But the clock doesn't go any more.

GREGERS. So time stands still in there . . . beside the wild duck.

HEDVIG. Yes. And then there are old paint boxes and things like that. And all the books.

GREGERS. And do you read these books?

HEDVIG. Oh yes, when I can manage it. But most of them are in English, and I don't understand that. But then I look at the pictures. There's a great big book called *Harryson's History of London*—it must be easily a hundred years old—and that has an enormous number of pictures in. In the front there's a picture of Death with an hour glass, and a girl. I think that's awful. But then there's also all the other pictures of churches and palaces and streets and big ships sailing on the sea.

GREGERS. But tell me, where did you get all these rare things from?

HEDVIG. Oh, an old sea captain used to live here once, and he brought them back with him. They used to call him 'the Flying Dutchman'. That was funny, because he *wasn't* a Dutchman at all.

GREGERS. Wasn't he?

HEDVIG. No. But then in the end he never came back; and all these things were just left here.

GREGERS. Listen now, tell me—when you sit in there looking at the pictures, don't you ever feel you want to get out into the big wide world itself and see something of it?

HEDVIG. Not me! I'm always going to stay at home and help my father and mother.

GREGERS. Touching up photographs?

HEDVIG. No, not just that. Best of all I'd like to learn how to engrave pictures like those in the English books.

GREGERS. Hm! What does your father say to that?

HEDVIG. I don't think Daddy likes it; Daddy's funny that way. Just think, he keeps on at me about learning basket-weaving and wicker-work! But I can't see there can be anything much in *that*.

GREGERS. Oh, no! I don't think so either.

HEDVIG. But Daddy's right when he says if I'd learnt basket-work, I could have made the new basket for the wild duck.

GREGERS. Yes, you could; and you would have been the proper person to do it.

HEDVIG. Because it's my wild duck.

GREGERS. Of course, it is.

HEDVIG. Yes, it belongs to *me*. But Daddy and Grandfather can have the loan of it as often as they like.

GREGERS. Indeed, and what do they do with it?

HEDVIG. Oh, they look after it, and build things for it, and things like that.

GREGERS. I suppose they do; because the wild duck is the most important of all the things in there.

HEDVIG. Yes, she is; because she's a *real* wild bird. It's such a shame, poor thing, she hasn't anybody to keep her company.

GREGERS. No family, like the rabbits.

HEDVIG. No. There's plenty of hens too, and they have grown up together from being chickens. But she's completely cut off from her friends. And then everything about the wild duck is so mysterious. Nobody really knows her; and nobody knows where she's from either.

GREGERS. And the fact that she's been down in the briny deep.

HEDVIG [*glances quickly at him, suppresses a smile and asks*]. What makes you say 'the briny deep'?

GREGERS. What do you expect me to say?

HEDVIG. You could say 'the bottom of the sea' or 'the sea bed'.

GREGERS. But can't I just as well say 'the briny deep'?

HEDVIG. Yes. But it sounds so strange when I hear other people say 'briny deep'.

GREGERS. Why is that? Tell me.

HEDVIG. No, I don't want to. It's just silly.

GREGERS. Oh, I'm sure it isn't. Tell me why you smiled?

HEDVIG. It's because every time I catch myself wondering about things in there—suddenly, you know without thinking—it always strikes me that the whole room and everything in it should be called 'the briny deep'. But that's just silly.

GREGERS. No, you mustn't say that.

HEDVIG. Yes, of course, because it's really only a loft.

GREGERS [*looking hard at her*]. Are you so certain?

HEDVIG [*astonished*]. That it's a loft?

GREGERS. Yes. Do you know for sure?

[HEDVIG *looks at him, open-mouthed and silent.* GINA *enters from the kitchen with a tablecloth.*]

GREGERS [*gets up*]. I'm afraid I've come too early.

GINA. Oh, well, I suppose you've got to be somewhere. Anyway, it will soon be ready. Clear the table, Hedvig.

[HEDVIG *clears up; she and* GINA *lay the table during the following dialogue.* GREGERS *sits down in the easy-chair and glances through an album.*]

GREGERS. I hear you can do retouching, Mrs. Ekdal.

GINA [*with a sidelong glance*]. Yes, I can that.

GREGERS. That was very lucky.

GINA. What do you mean, 'lucky'?

GREGERS. After Hjalmar took up photography, I mean.

HEDVIG. Mother can do photography too.

GINA. Oh yes, I've managed to pick *that* up, all right.

GREGERS. I dare say you're the one that runs the business.

GINA. Yes, when Hjalmar hasn't the time himself. . . .

GREGERS. I imagine his time's pretty well taken up with his old father.

GINA. Yes. And besides it's no job for a man like Hjalmar taking pictures all day long.

GREGERS. I quite agree. But once he's gone in for that kind of thing . . .

GINA. Hjalmar's not like any of your ordinary photographers, Mr. Werle, I can tell you.

GREGERS. Quite. But all the same . . .

[*A shot is fired inside the loft.*]

GREGERS [*starts up*]. What's that!

GINA. Huh! They're shooting again!

GREGERS. Do they shoot, too?

HEDVIG. They go out hunting.

GREGERS. They what! [*Walks over to the loft door.*] Are you hunting, Hjalmar?

HJALMAR [*behind the netting*]. You here? I didn't know. I was so busy. . . . [*To* HEDVIG.] Why didn't you tell us? [*Comes into the studio.*]

GREGERS. Do you go shooting in the loft?

HJALMAR [*shows him a double-barrelled pistol*]. Oh, only with this.

GINA. Yes, and the two of you will finish up by having an accident one of these fine days with that gun.

HJALMAR [*irritated*]. How many times do I have to tell you a weapon like this is called a pistol.

GINA. Well, I can't see that's much better myself.

GREGERS. So you've taken up hunting too, Hjalmar?

HJALMAR. Just a bit of rabbit shooting, now and again. Mostly for Father's sake, you know.

GINA. Funny creatures, men! Always have to have something to deviate themselves with.

HJALMAR [*angrily*]. That's right, yes. We always have to have something to divert ourselves with.

GINA. Yes, *that's* what I said.

HJALMAR. Oh, well! [*To* GREGERS.] Yes, you see, we are lucky the loft is so placed that nobody can hear us when we shoot. [*Places the pistol on the top shelf.*] Don't touch the pistol, Hedvig! One of the barrels is loaded, don't forget.

GREGERS [*looks in through the netting*]. I see you've also got a sporting gun.

HJALMAR. That's Father's old gun. You can't fire it any more, there's something wrong with the lock. But it's fun to have it all the same, because we can take it to pieces and clean it every now and then and grease it and put it together again. . . . Of course, it's mainly my father who tinkers about with these things.

HEDVIG [*over beside* GREGERS]. Now you can see the wild duck properly.

GREGERS. I'm just looking at it now. She seems to be dragging one wing a bit, I think.

HJALMAR. Well, that's not surprising; after all, she's been wounded.

GREGERS. And she's trailing one foot too. Or am I mistaken?

HJALMAR. Perhaps ever so slightly.

HEDVIG. Well, that was the foot the dog bit.

HJALMAR. Otherwise there's absolutely nothing wrong with her; and that's really rather remarkable when you consider she's had a load of shot in her and been chewed about by a dog. . . .

GREGERS [*with a glance at* HEDVIG]. . . . and been down in the briny deep . . . for so long.

HEDVIG [*smiles*]. Yes.

GINA [*arranging the table*]. That blessed wild duck! All the carrying-on there is about that bird!

HJALMAR. Hm! . . . Will lunch soon be ready?

GINA. Any minute now. Hedvig, you must come and help me now.

[GINA *and* HEDVIG *go out into the kitchen.*]

HJALMAR [*in an undertone*]. I don't think there's any point in standing and watching Father. He doesn't like it.

[GREGERS *walks away from the loft door.*]

HJALMAR. And I'd better shut it up before the others arrive. [*Waving his hands to chase the birds away.*] Shoo! Shoo! Get away. [*Speaking as he draws up the curtaining, and pulls the doors together.*] These gadgets here are my own invention. Really it's great fun having something like this to look after, and mending it when it gets broken. And besides it's absolutely necessary, you know, because Gina doesn't like having the rabbits and hens in the studio.

GREGERS. Of course not. And I suppose it's your wife who has the running of it?

HJALMAR. The routine jobs I generally leave to her; then I can retire to the living-room and give my attention to more important things.

GREGERS. What sort of things, actually, Hjalmar?

HJALMAR. I'm surprised you haven't asked me about *that* before. Or perhaps you haven't heard about the invention?

GREGERS. Invention? No.

HJALMAR. Really? Haven't you? Oh, of course, being stuck out there in the wilds, up in the forest. . . .

GREGERS. So you've made an invention!

HJALMAR. Haven't quite managed it yet, but I'm busy on it. When I decided to devote myself to photography, you don't suppose it was with the idea of doing nothing but take pictures of anybody who happened to come along?

GREGERS. No, no, your wife's just been saying the same thing.

HJALMAR. I swore that if I was going to dedicate my powers to this calling, I would raise it to the level where it was both an art and a science. So I decided to make this remarkable invention.

GREGERS. And what does the invention consist of? What's the purpose of it?

HJALMAR. Ah, my dear Gregers, you mustn't ask for details yet. It all takes time, you know. And you mustn't think it's vanity that's urging me on. I'm not thinking of myself in the least. Oh no, night and day I see before me what must be my life's work.

GREGERS. What life's work?

HJALMAR. Have you forgotten that dear old, silver-haired man?

GREGERS. Your poor old father? Yes, but what can you in fact do for him?

HJALMAR. I can restore his own self-respect by raising once more the name of Ekdal to a place of honour and dignity.

GREGERS. So that is your life's work, then?

HJALMAR. Yes, I will rescue this poor castaway, shipwrecked as he was from the moment the storm broke over him. During that terrible inquiry he was no longer himself. That pistol over there, Gregers . . . the one we use to shoot rabbits with . . . it has played its role in the tragedy of the House of Ekdal.

GREGERS. The pistol? Really?

HJALMAR. When judgement had been pronounced and he was about to be sent to prison . . . he had the pistol in his hand. . . .

GREGERS. He had the . . . ?

HJALMAR. Yes, but he didn't dare. He was a coward. He was already so demoralized, so broken in spirit by then. Oh, can you imagine it? Him a soldier, a man who had shot no less than nine bears, who was descended from two lieutenant-colonels . . . not both at the same time of course. . . . Can you imagine it, Gregers?

GREGERS. Yes, I can imagine it very well.

HJALMAR. I can't. But then the pistol figured a second time in our family history. When they had taken him away, and he sat there under lock and key—oh, that was a terrible time for me, I can tell you. I kept the blinds lowered at both windows. When I looked out and saw the sun shining the same as usual, I couldn't understand it. I saw people walking about the streets, laughing and talking about things of no importance. I couldn't understand it. I felt that all creation ought to have come to a standstill, like an eclipse.

GREGERS. I felt just the same when Mother died.

HJALMAR. It was in such a moment that Hjalmar Ekdal held the pistol to his own breast.

GREGERS. You too thought of . . . !

HJALMAR. Yes.

GREGERS. But you didn't shoot?

HJALMAR. No. At the crucial moment I won a great victory over myself. I went on living. But as you can quite understand, it takes some courage to choose life on *those* terms.

GREGERS. Well, it depends how you look at it.

HJALMAR. No, my dear fellow, there's no doubt about it. But it was all for the best, because soon now I shall have my invention ready. And Dr. Relling thinks—as I do too—that Father will then be able to wear his uniform again. I ask for no other reward than that.

GREGERS. So *that's* how it is with the uniform he . . . ?

HJALMAR. Yes, *that's* what he longs and yearns for more than anything else. You have no idea how my heart bleeds for him. Every time we have a little family party—like Gina's and my wedding anniversary, or whatever it might be—in comes the old chap dressed in his lieutenant's uniform of happy memory. But if there's so much as a knock on the front door—because he daren't show himself in front of strangers—away he's off into his room again as fast as his poor old legs will carry him. It's heart-breaking for a son to have to see things like that, Gregers.

GREGERS. Roughly, when do you think the invention will be ready?

HJALMAR. Good Lord, you mustn't ask me about details like dates. An invention is something you can never be completely master of. It's largely a matter of inspiration . . . of intuition . . . and it's pretty nearly impossible to predict when that will come.

GREGERS. But it's making good progress?

HJALMAR. Certainly it's making good progress. Not a day goes by but what I do something on the invention; I'm absorbed in it. Every day after dinner I shut myself up in the living-room, where I can concentrate in peace. But it's no good people trying to rush me, that's no good. Relling says the same.

GREGERS. And you don't feel all these things going on in the loft take you away from your work . . . distract you too much?

HJALMAR. No, no. On the contrary. You mustn't get that idea at all. I can't always go on poring over the same old exhausting problems. I've got to have something else as well to keep me occupied. Inspiration, revelation, you know—when it comes, it comes, that's all.

GREGERS. My dear Hjalmar, I almost believe you've a bit of the wild duck about you.

HJALMAR. The wild duck? How do you make that out?

GREGERS. You have gone plunging down and bitten fast to the weeds.

HJALMAR. You are referring, I suppose, to the blow that crippled my father and very nearly killed him . . . and me too?

GREGERS. Not primarily to that. I wouldn't say you're lamed exactly; but you've landed up in a poison swamp, Hjalmar; you've picked up some insidious disease, and you've gone down to die in the dark.

HJALMAR. Me? Die in the dark? Look, Gregers, you really must stop this kind of talk.

GREGERS. But don't upset yourself. I'll see we get you up again. For now, you see, I too know what my life's work is to be. I found out yesterday.

HJALMAR. That's all very well; but will you please keep *me* out of it. I can assure you that, apart from feeling naturally rather depressed, I am as well as any man could wish.

GREGERS. The very fact that you are, also comes from the poison.

HJALMAR. Please now, my dear Gregers, let's have no more of this talk about diseases and poisons; I'm just not used to that kind of conversation; in my house people never talk to me about unpleasant things.

GREGERS. That's something I can well believe.

HJALMAR. No, it isn't good for me. And this place *doesn't* smell like a swamp, as you keep saying. I know it's only the humble home of a poor photographer of modest means . . . and the place is not very grand. But I am an inventor, you know . . . and a breadwinner too. That's what keeps me above all these petty things.—Ah! Here they are with the lunch!

[GINA *and* HEDVIG *carry in bottles of beer, a decanter of brandy, glasses and other things for the table; at the same time,* RELLING *and* MOLVIK *enter from the hallway; both are without hats or topcoats;* MOLVIK *is dressed in black.*]

GINA [*putting the things on the table*]. Trust them two to be here in time.

RELLING. Molvik got the idea he could smell herring salad, and then there was no holding him. Good morning for the second time, Ekdal.

HJALMAR. Gregers, may I introduce Mr. Molvik, and Doctor . . . ah, but of course you know Relling?

GREGERS. Yes, slightly.

RELLING. Oh, it's Mr. Werle, junior. Yes, we came up against each other once or twice up at the Höidal works. You've just moved in?

GREGERS. I moved in this morning.

RELLING. Molvik and I live just underneath, so if ever you need a doctor or a parson, you don't have far to go.

GREGERS. Thanks, it could happen. Yesterday there were thirteen of us at table.

HJALMAR. Oh, let's not get on to that horrid business again!

RELLING. You needn't worry, Ekdal, it's not going to affect you.

HJALMAR. I hope not, if only for my family's sake. But now let's sit down, and eat, drink and be merry.

GREGERS. Shouldn't we wait for your father?

HJALMAR. No, he'll have his in his room afterwards. Come along!

[*The men sit down at the table, and eat and drink.* GINA *and* HEDVIG *go in and out, waiting on them.*]

RELLING. Molvik was filthy drunk last night, Mrs. Ekdal.

GINA. What, again last night?

RELLING. Didn't you hear him when I brought him home during the night?

GINA. No, can't say I did.

RELLING. Just as well. Because last night Molvik was pretty dreadful.

GINA. Is this true, Mr. Molvik?

MOLVIK. Let us draw a veil over the events of last night. Such things bear no relation to my better self.

RELLING. It just comes over him like a sort of revelation, and then there's nothing for it but to take him out on a binge. Mr. Molvik, you see, is a demonic.

GREGERS. A demonic?

RELLING. Molvik is a demonic, yes.

GREGERS. Hm!

RELLING. And demonic natures are not made for the straight and narrow; they've got to kick over the traces now and then. . . . So you still manage to stick it up there at those nasty, filthy works?

GREGERS. I have until now.

RELLING. And did you get anywhere with that 'claim' you were always coming out with?

GREGERS. Claim? [*Understands him.*] Oh, that!

HJALMAR. What's all this about 'claims', Gregers?

GREGERS. Oh, it's nothing.

RELLING. Ah, but there *was* something. He used to go the rounds of all the labourers' cottages serving up what he called 'the claim of the ideal'.

GREGERS. I was young then.

RELLING. You're right there; you were very young. And this 'claim of the ideal'—you never got anybody to honour it as long as *I* was there.

GREGERS. Nor afterwards, either.

RELLING. Well, I suppose you've had the sense to mark the price down a bit.

GREGERS. Never when I'm dealing with a man who *is* a man.

HJALMAR. Well, that strikes me as being pretty reasonable.—Butter please, Gina.

RELLING. And a slice of pork for Molvik.

MOLVIK. Ugh, not pork!

[*There is a knock on the loft door.*]

HJALMAR. Open up, Hedvig. Father wants to be let out.

[HEDVIG *goes and opens the door a little;* OLD EKDAL *enters carrying a fresh rabbit skin; she shuts the door after him.*]

EKDAL. Good morning, gentlemen! Had some good hunting today. Bagged a big 'un.

HJALMAR. Have you gone and skinned it without *me*. . . !

EKDAL. Salted it, too. It's good tender meat, rabbit-meat. And sweet. Tastes like sugar. Enjoy your lunch, gentlemen!

[*Goes into his room.*]

MOLVIK [*rising*]. Excuse me . . . I can't . . . I must run downstairs at once. . . .

RELLING. Have some soda-water, man!

MOLVIK [*hurrying*]. Ugh! Ugh!

[*Leaves by the hall door.*]

RELLING [*to* HJALMAR]. Let's drink to the grand old sportsman.

HJALMAR [*touching glasses with him*]. Yes, to the sportsman, standing on the brink of the grave.

RELLING. To the grey-haired. . . . [*Drinks.*] But tell me, is it grey hair he has, or is it white?

HJALMAR. Actually, it's somewhere in between. As a matter of fact, he hasn't got all that much hair left.

RELLING. Ah well, people still manage to get by with a wig. Yes, Ekdal, you're really a very lucky man, devoting your life to this splendid mission.

HJALMAR. And I *do* devote myself to it, too, I can tell you.

RELLING. And then you've also got your clever little wife to look after you, pottering about in her slippers all nice and cuddlesome, and making the place all cosy.

HJALMAR. Yes, Gina. . . . [*Nods to her.*] You are a great helpmate to have on life's way, my dear.

GINA. Oh, I wish you wouldn't sit there weighing me up and down.

RELLING. Then what about your Hedvig, eh, Ekdal?

HJALMAR [*moved*]. The child, yes! More than anything else, the child. Come to me, Hedvig. [*Strokes her hair.*] What day is it tomorrow?

HEDVIG. Oh, no, you mustn't say anything, Daddy!

HJALMAR. It's like a knife plunged into my heart when I think how little there will be. Just a small party there in the loft. . . .

HEDVIG. Oh, but that will be simply lovely!

RELLING. Just you wait till this amazing invention sees the light of day, Hedvig.

HJALMAR. Ah yes, then you'll see! Hedvig, I've decided I must make your future secure. You shall not want for anything as long as you live. I shall insist on your having . . . something or other. That shall be the humble inventor's only reward.

HEDVIG [*with her arm round his neck, whispers*]. Oh, my dear, dear Daddy!

RELLING [*to* GREGERS]. Well now, don't you think *this* makes a nice change, to sit at a well-filled table in a happy family circle.

HJALMAR. Yes, I really appreciate these meal-times.

GREGERS. Personally I don't thrive in a poisoned atmosphere.

RELLING. Poisoned atmosphere?

HJALMAR. Oh, let's not have that nonsense all over again!

GINA. God knows there aren't any bad smells in here, Mr. Werle. I give the place a good airing every blessed day.

GREGERS [*rising from the table*]. No amount of airing will get rid of the stench *I* mean!

HJALMAR. Stench!

GINA. Well, what do you think of that, Hjalmar!

RELLING. Excuse me . . . I suppose *you* couldn't be the one who has brought the stench in, from the mines up there?

GREGERS. It's just like you to call what I bring into this house a stench.

RELLING [*walks across to him*]. Listen, Mr. Werle, junior! I strongly suspect you are still carrying this 'claim of the ideal' about with you in full, in your back pocket.

GREGERS. I carry it in my breast.

RELLING. Well, carry the thing where the devil you like; but I wouldn't advise you to try and cash in on it here as long as *I'm* about the place.

GREGERS. And if I do?

RELLING. Then you'll find yourself going head-first down the stairs. Now you know.

HJALMAR [*getting up*]. I say, Relling!

GREGERS. Yes, you just try throwing me out and . . .

GINA [*coming between them*]. You mustn't do that, Mr. Relling. But *this* I will say, Mr. Werle—anybody who can make such an awful mess as the one in your stove has no right coming to me and talking about smells.

[*There is a knock at the hall door.*]

HEDVIG. Mother, somebody's knocking.

HJALMAR. Oh, really! There's just no end to all these comings and goings.

GINA. Let me go. [*Walks over and opens the door, starts, shudders and draws back.*] Oh!

[HAAKON WERLE, *wearing a fur coat, takes a step into the room.*]

WERLE. I beg your pardon, but I believe my son is supposed to be living here.

GINA [*gulping*]. Yes.

HJALMAR [*coming forward*]. Won't you be so good, Mr. Werle, as to . . .

WERLE. Thanks. All I want is to speak to my son.

GREGERS. Yes, what is it? Here I am.

WERLE. I wish to speak to you in your room.

GREGERS. In my room . . . very well.

[*He turns to go.*]

GINA. Good Lord, no! It's in no state for . . .

WERLE. Well, out in the passage, then; I wish to speak to you privately.

HJALMAR. You can do that here, Mr. Werle. Relling can come into the living-room.

[HJALMAR *and* RELLING *go out right;* GINA *leads* HEDVIG *out into the kitchen.*]

GREGERS [*after a short pause*]. Well, now we are alone.

WERLE. You passed a number of remarks last night. . . . And since you've now moved in on the Ekdals, I can only assume that you have in mind something against me.

GREGERS. What I have in mind is to open Hjalmar Ekdal's eyes. He shall see the situation as it is . . . that's all.

WERLE. Is *this* the life's work you were talking about yesterday?

GREGERS. Yes. You haven't left me any other.

WERLE. Is it my fault, then, if your ideas are all mixed up, Gregers?

GREGERS. You've messed up my whole life. I'm not thinking of all the business with Mother. . . . But it's thanks to you that I now suffer the torment of a desperately guilty conscience.

WERLE. Aha! So it's your conscience that's a bit queer, eh?

GREGERS. I should have stood up to you at the time the trap was laid for Lieutenant Ekdal. I should have warned him. For I had a pretty good idea how things would turn out in the end.

WERLE. Yes, you really should have spoken out then.

GREGERS. I didn't dare. I was scared . . . too much of a coward. I can't tell you how frightened of you I was then and for a long time after, too.

WERLE. It would seem that that fear is past now.

GREGERS. Fortunately it is. The wrong that's been done to Old Ekdal, both by me and by . . . others, can never be put right. But what I can do now is free Hjalmar from all the lies and deceit that are causing his ruination.

WERLE. Do you think *that's* likely to do any good?

GREGERS. I'm convinced it will.

WERLE. Do you really think Hjalmar Ekdal is the sort of man who would thank you for that kind of favour?

GREGERS. Yes. He *is* that sort.

WERLE. Hm! We'll see.

GREGERS. And besides, if I'm to go on living, I must find something to cure my sick conscience.

WERLE. It will never recover. From being a child, you've always had a sickly conscience. It's a heritage from your mother, Gregers . . . one thing she did leave you.

GREGERS [*with a contemptuous smile*]. That must have been a bitter pill to swallow when you found you had miscalculated, after expecting her to bring you a fortune.

WERLE. Let us keep to the point.—Are you set on this scheme of putting Ekdal on what you imagine to be the right track?

GREGERS. Yes, I'm quite set on it.

WERLE. Well, in that case I might have saved myself a journey. For I suppose it's no use asking you now if you'll come home again?

GREGERS. No.

WERLE. And you won't come into the firm either?

GREGERS. No.

WERLE. Very well. But as I now intend to marry again, the estate will be divided between us.

GREGERS [*quickly*]. No. I don't want that.

WERLE. You don't want that?

GREGERS. No. My conscience won't let me.

WERLE [*after a pause*]. Are you going back up to the works again?

GREGERS. No. I regard myself as having left your service.

WERLE. But what will you do now?

GREGERS. I shall fulfil my mission, that's all.

WERLE. But what about afterwards? What are you going to live on?

GREGERS. I've saved a bit out of my pay.

WERLE. But how long will *that* last!

GREGERS. I think it will last my time out.

WERLE. What do you mean by that?

GREGERS. I'm not answering any more questions.

WERLE. Goodbye, then, Gregers.

GREGERS. Goodbye.

[HAAKON WERLE *goes.*]

HJALMAR [*peeps in*]. Has he gone?

GREGERS. Yes.

[HJALMAR *and* RELLING *enter;* GINA *and* HEDVIG *come in from the kitchen.*]

RELLING. That's put paid to *that* lunch.

GREGERS. Put your things on, Hjalmar. You are coming for a long walk with me.

HJALMAR. Yes, with pleasure. What did your father want? Anything to do with me?

GREGERS. Just come with me. We must have a little talk. I'll go and get my coat.

[*He goes out by the hall door.*]

GINA. I wouldn't go out with him if I was you, Hjalmar.

RELLING. No, don't do it, old man; stay where you are.

HJALMAR [*takes his hat and topcoat*]. What, when an old friend feels the need to open up his heart to me. . . !

RELLING. Damn it, man! Can't you see the man's mad, barmy, off his head!

GINA. There you are! Now just you be told! His mother sometimes used to have bouts just the same as that.

HJALMAR. All the more reason for him to need a friend's watchful eye. [*To* GINA.] See that dinner's ready in good time, won't you? Goodbye for now.

[*He leaves by the hall door.*]

RELLING. What a pity the man didn't get to hell out of it down one of those mines at Höidal.

GINA. Good Lord! Why d'you say that?

RELLING [*muttering*]. Oh, I've got my reasons.

GINA. D'you think young Werle is really mad?

RELLING. No, worse luck! He's no madder than most. But one kind of ailment he is suffering from, all the same.

GINA. What's wrong with him, then?

RELLING. I'll tell you, Mrs. Ekdal. He's an acute case of inflamed scruples.

GINA. Inflamed scruples?

HEDVIG. Is that a sort of illness?

RELLING. Yes. It's a national illness. But it only occurs sporadically. [*Nods to* GINA.] Thanks for lunch!

[*He goes out by the hall door.*]

GINA [*walking restlessly about the room*]. Ugh, that Gregers Werle. He's always been a queer fish.

HEDVIG [*stands by the table and looks inquiringly at her.*] I think this is all very strange.

ACT FOUR

HJALMAR EKDAL's *studio. A photograph has obviously just been taken; a camera covered with a cloth, a stand, a few chairs, a whatnot and similar things are standing about the floor. Late afternoon light, with the sun about to set; after a little while it begins to get dark.*

GINA *is standing at the open door, in her hand a little container and a wet photographic plate; she is speaking to somebody outside.*

GINA. Yes, absolutely certain. I always keep my promises. The first dozen will be ready for Monday. Good afternoon, good afternoon!

[*Somebody can be heard going downstairs.* GINA *shuts the door, puts the plate into the container and puts that in the shrouded camera.*]

HEDVIG [*enters from the kitchen*]. Have they gone now?

GINA [*tidying up*]. Yes, thank heavens. I've got rid of them at last.

HEDVIG. I wonder why Daddy hasn't come back yet?

GINA. Are you sure he's not down at Relling's?

HEDVIG. No, he's not there. I slipped down the back stairs just now and asked.

GINA. And his dinner's standing here getting cold.

HEDVIG. Yes, fancy! And Daddy's generally home for his dinner on the dot.

GINA. Oh, don't fret, he'll be here soon.

HEDVIG. Oh, I do wish he'd come; because everything seems so strange now.

GINA [*calls out*]. There he is!

[HJALMAR EKDAL *comes in through the hall door.*]

HEDVIG [*going to meet him*]. Daddy! We've been waiting and waiting for you.

GINA [*glancing across*]. There's a long time you've been, Hjalmar.

HJALMAR [*without looking at her*]. Yes, I have, rather.

> [*He takes off his topcoat; GINA and HEDVIG go to help him; he waves them away.*]

GINA. Have you had something to eat with Gregers Werle?

HJALMAR [*hangs up his coat*]. No.

GINA [*going towards the kitchen door*]. Then I'll bring your dinner in for you.

HJALMAR. No, don't bother about any dinner. I don't want anything to eat now.

HEDVIG [*going closer*]. Aren't you feeling well, Daddy?

HJALMAR. Feeling well? Oh yes, not so bad. We went for a rather tiring walk, Gregers and I.

GINA. You shouldn't have, Hjalmar; you're not used to it.

HJALMAR. Huh! There are many things a man's got to get used to in this world. [*Walks up and down.*] Has anybody been here while I've been out?

GINA. Only that engaged couple.

HJALMAR. No new orders?

GINA. No, not today.

HEDVIG. There'll be some more tomorrow all right, Daddy, you'll see.

HJALMAR. I hope you're right. Because tomorrow I'm going to get down to things in real earnest.

HEDVIG. Tomorrow! You haven't forgotten what day it is tomorrow?

HJALMAR. Oh, that's right. . . . Well, the day after, then. After this I'm doing everything myself; I want to do the work all on my own.

GINA. But, Hjalmar, what's the good of *that*? You'll only make your life a misery. I can still manage the photographing; and then you can get on with the invention.

HEDVIG. And then there's the wild duck, Daddy . . . and all the hens and rabbits. . . .

HJALMAR. Don't speak to me about all that nonsense! I'm never going to set foot in that loft again after today.

HEDVIG. But Daddy, you promised me there'd be a party tomorrow. . . .

HJALMAR. Hm, that's right. . . . Well, starting the day after tomorrow, then. That damned wild duck, I'd like to wring its neck.

HEDVIG [*with a scream*]. The wild duck!

GINA. Well, I never did!

HEDVIG [*shaking him*]. But Daddy . . . it's *my* wild duck!

HJALMAR. That's the only thing that's stopping me. I haven't the heart. . . . For your sake, Hedvig, I haven't the heart. But deep down inside me I ought to. I can't see why I should have any creature under my roof that's been in *that* man's hands.

GINA. But, good Lord, just because it was that rogue Pettersen Grandfather got it off, that's no . . .

HJALMAR [*walking about*]. There are certain demands . . . what should I call them? Let us say, demands of the ideal . . . certain claims that a man can't disregard without doing violence to his own soul.

HEDVIG [*following him about*]. But think of the wild duck . . . the poor little wild duck!

HJALMAR [*halts*]. I've told you I'm not going to touch it . . . for your sake. Not a hair of its . . . well, as I said, I'm not going to touch it. There are things of much greater importance to be undertaken. But it's time you had your evening walk, Hedvig; it's nicely dusk for you now.

HEDVIG. No, I can't be bothered to go out now.

HJALMAR. Yes, go on. You seem to be blinking a lot. It's not good for you, all these fumes in here. The air's thick here, under this roof.

HEDVIG. All right, I'll run down the back stairs and go for a little walk. Where's my hat and coat? Oh, they're in my room. But mind, Daddy . . . you mustn't do anything to the wild duck while I'm out.

HJALMAR. Not a feather of its head shall be touched. [*Hugging her.*] You and I, Hedvig . . . we two! Now, run along, my dear.

[HEDVIG *waves to her parents and goes out through the kitchen.*]

HJALMAR [*walks up and down without looking up*]. Gina.

GINA. Yes?

HJALMAR. As from tomorrow—or the day after, let us say—I think I would like to keep the household accounts myself.

GINA. You want to keep the accounts as well?

HJALMAR. Yes, or keep a check on what comes in, at any rate.

GINA. Oh, *that's* not a big job, so help me.

HJALMAR. Ah, I'm not so sure of *that*; you seem to make the money stretch a remarkably long way. [*Halts and looks at her.*] How does that happen?

GINA. It's because Hedvig and me don't need very much.

HJALMAR. Is it true Father gets paid pretty lavishly for the copying he does for Mr. Werle?

GINA. I don't know that it's *so* lavish. I don't know what the rates are for things like that.

HJALMAR. Well, roughly what does he get? Tell me!

GINA. It varies; roughly the cost of his board, and a bit extra for pocket money.

HJALMAR. The cost of his board! You never told me that before!

GINA. Well, really I couldn't. You liked to think he got everything from you.

HJALMAR. And instead he gets it all from Werle!

GINA. Oh well, he's not likely to miss it.

HJALMAR. Light the lamp!

GINA [*lights it*]. Besides, we don't really know if it actually comes from him. It might easily be Graaberg. . . .

HJALMAR. Why are you trying to shift things on to Graaberg?

GINA. Well, I don't know. I just thought . . .

HJALMAR. Huh!

GINA. It wasn't me that got Grandfather his copying to do. It was Berta, that time she was here.

HJALMAR. Your voice seems to be trembling.

GINA [*putting on the shade*]. Is it?

HJALMAR. And your hands are shaking. Aren't they?

GINA [*firmly*]. Tell me straight, Hjalmar. What's he gone and told you about me?

HJALMAR. Is it true . . . *can* it really be true . . . that there was something between you and Old Werle when you were in service there?

GINA. It's not true. Not then, there wasn't. Mr. Werle pestered me plenty, that I will say. And his wife thought there was something in it. What a fuss she kicked up! She just went for me, played merry hell, she did. So I left.

HJALMAR. But then afterwards?

GINA. Well, then I went home. And my mother . . . she wasn't quite what you thought she was, Hjalmar. She kept on at me, about one thing and another. . . . Because Werle was a widower by then.

HJALMAR. Well, what then?

GINA. Well, you might as well know it. He wouldn't be satisfied till he'd had his way.

HJALMAR [*clasping his hands together*]. Is this the mother of my child! How could you keep a thing like that hidden from me!

GINA. Yes, it was wrong of me. I should have told you long ago.

HJALMAR. You should have told me at the time—then I'd have known what sort of woman you were.

GINA. But would you have married me just the same?

HJALMAR. However can you think that?

GINA. There you are! That's why I didn't dare say anything at the time. Because I'd come to like you so very much, you know. I couldn't go and make my whole life a misery. . . .

HJALMAR [*walking about*]. Is this my Hedvig's mother! To think that everything I see around me here . . . [*Kicks a chair.*] My entire home, all of it I owe to your previous lover. Ah, that lecherous old Werle!

GINA. Do you regret the fourteen or fifteen years we have lived together?

HJALMAR [*standing in front of her*]. Tell me this. Haven't you—every day, every hour—regretted this web of deceit you've spun around me like a spider? Answer me that! Haven't you in fact been suffering agonies of worry and remorse?

GINA. Oh, my dear Hjalmar, really I've had far too many other things to think of, what with running the house and everything. . . .

HJALMAR. And this past of yours, do you never give it a thought now?

GINA. No. God knows, I'd pretty nearly forgotten all that old business.

HJALMAR. Oh, how can you stand there so calm and unconcerned! That's what I find so absolutely outrageous. Imagine—not the slightest sign of regret.

GINA. But tell me now, Hjalmar—where would you have been now if you hadn't had somebody like me for a wife?

HJALMAR. Like you!

GINA. Yes, because I've always been as you might say a bit more down-to-earth and business-like than you. Well, that's understandable— I'm a year or two older, after all.

HJALMAR. Where would I have been?

GINA. You were in a pretty bad way all round when you first met me. You can hardly deny that.

HJALMAR. You call that being in a bad way? Oh, you don't understand what it means when a man is weighed down with worry and despair—especially a man with my fiery temperament.

GINA. Well, well, have it as you will. I don't want to make too much of a song and dance about it, either, because you turned out to be a right good husband once you'd got your own house and home.— And we'd made things so nice and cosy, and Hedvig and me were just starting to manage a little bit extra for ourselves in the way of food and clothes.

HJALMAR. Yes, in this swamp of deceit.

GINA. Ugh! That horrible man! What did he have to go and shove his nose in here for!

HJALMAR. I too used to think our home was a good place. What a mistake that was. Now where am I going to find the stimulus I need to make my invention a reality? Perhaps it will die with me; and your past, Gina, will be what's killed it.

GINA [*close to tears*]. Oh Hjalmar, you mustn't say things like that. When all my days I've spent only doing what I thought was best for you.

HJALMAR. I ask you—what about the breadwinner's dream now? When I used to lie in there on the sofa turning the invention over in my mind, I vaguely knew it would drain the very last bit of my strength. I had the feeling that the day I held the patent in my hands, would mark my own . . . last hour. And it was my dream that you should be left comfortably settled, to take your place as the widow of the one-time inventor.

GINA [*drying her tears*]. No, Hjalmar you *mustn't* talk like that. God forbid I should ever live to see the day I'm left a widow!

HJALMAR. Oh, it's all the same either way. Everything's over and done with now. Everything!

[GREGERS WERLE *cautiously opens the hall door and looks in.*]

GREGERS. May I come in?

HJALMAR. Yes, come in.

GREGERS [*advances, his face beaming with joy and holds out his hands to them*]. Well now, my dear people. . . ! [*Looks from one to the other and whispers to* HJALMAR.] Haven't you done it yet, then?

HJALMAR [*aloud*]. I *have* done it.

GREGERS. You *have*?

HJALMAR. I have experienced the bitterest moment of my life.

GREGERS. But also the most sublime, I should think.

HJALMAR. Well, we've got it off our chests, anyway.

GINA. May God forgive you, Mr. Werle.

GREGERS [*greatly astonished*]. But I don't understand.

HJALMAR. What don't you understand?

GREGERS. Now that you have laid bare your souls—this exchange on which you can now build a completely new mode of life—a way of living together in truth, free of all deception. . . .

HJALMAR. Yes, I know; I know all that.

GREGERS. I was absolutely convinced when I came in through that door that I should be greeted by the light of radiant understanding on the faces of husband and wife alike. And all I see is this dull, gloomy, miserable . . .

GINA. Very well then. [*She takes the shade off the lamp.*]

GREGERS. You're not trying to understand me, Mrs. Ekdal. Well, well; in your case perhaps with time . . . But *you* now, Hjalmar? Surely this passage of arms has brought you to some higher resolve.

HJALMAR. Yes, of course it has. That is . . . in a sort of way.

GREGERS. For there is surely no joy in life comparable with that of forgiving one who has sinned, and of raising her up again in love.

HJALMAR. Do you think a man so easily gets over the bitter draught I have just drunk?

GREGERS. No! No *ordinary* man, I dare say. But a man like you. . . !

HJALMAR. Yes, I know, I know. But you mustn't rush me, Gregers. It takes time you know.

GREGERS. There's a *lot* of the wild duck about you, Hjalmar.

[RELLING *has come in by the entrance door.*]

RELLING. What's this now! Is the wild duck on the go again?

HJALMAR. The poor maimed victim of Mr. Werle's sport, yes.

RELLING. Mr. Werle? Is it *him* you're talking about?

HJALMAR. Him and . . . the rest of us.

RELLING [*to* GREGERS *under his breath*]. God damn you!

HJALMAR. What do you say?

RELLING. I was merely expressing the pious wish that this quack here would pack himself off where he belongs. If he stops here, he's just as likely to be the ruination of the pair of you.

GREGERS. Neither of them is being ruined, Mr. Relling. I needn't say anything about Hjalmar; him we know. But she too, deep down within her, surely has something trustworthy, something sincere. . . .

GINA [*near to tears*]. Then you should have just let me be as I was.

RELLING [*to* GREGERS]. Would it be impertinent if I asked what exactly it is you want in this house?

GREGERS. I want to lay the foundation of a true marriage.

RELLING. Don't you think the Ekdals' marriage is good enough as it is?

GREGERS. It's probably as good a marriage as most, I regret to say. But it has never been a *true* marriage.

HJALMAR. You've never given much attention to the claims of the ideal, Relling.

RELLING. Don't talk rubbish, my lad! Mr. Werle, just let me ask you how many—at a rough guess—how many true marriages you have seen in your life?

GREGERS. I hardly think I've seen a single one.

RELLING. Nor have I.

GREGERS. But I've seen innumerable marriages of the opposite kind. And I've had the chance of seeing at close quarters the havoc a marriage like that can wreak on both parties.

HJALMAR. The whole moral basis of a man's life can crumble beneath his feet—*that* is the terrible thing.

RELLING. Well, I've never actually been married myself, so I can't really judge these things. But one thing I do know: that the *child* is also part of the marriage. And you should leave the child in peace.

HJALMAR. Ah, Hedvig! My poor Hedvig!

RELLING. Yes, you'd better just see that you keep Hedvig out of all this. You are both grown people; God knows you can please yourself how much you want to muck up your own personal affairs. But I'm telling you this: just you be careful the way you treat Hedvig, or else you'll perhaps end up by doing her serious harm.

HJALMAR. Harm?

RELLING. Yes, or else she'll do herself some harm—and maybe others with her.

GINA. But how can you tell a thing like that, Mr. Relling?

HJALMAR. There's no immediate danger for her eyes, is there?

RELLING. None of this has got anything to do with her eyes. But Hedvig is at a difficult age. She might get hold of all sorts of funny ideas.

GINA. Why, that's just what she does do! I don't like the way she's started playing with the fire out in the kitchen. She calls it playing houses on fire. Many a time I'm frightened she *will* set the house on fire.

RELLING. There you are, you see. I knew it.

GREGERS [*to* RELLING]. But how do you explain a thing like that?

RELLING [*disdainfully*]. She's reached the age of puberty, my dear sir.

HJALMAR. As long as the child has *me* . . . ! As long as I can keep body and soul together . . . !

[*There is a knock at the door.*]

GINA. Hush, Hjalmar! There's somebody in the hall. [*Calls.*] Come in.

[MRS. SÖRBY, *in outdoor clothes, comes in.*]

MRS. SÖRBY. Good evening!

GINA [*walks over to her*]. Why, Berta, it's you!

MRS. SÖRBY. Yes, it's me. But perhaps I've come at an awkward time?

HJALMAR. Not at all. A messenger from *that* house. . . !

MRS. SÖRBY [*to* GINA]. To be quite honest, I hoped I'd find the menfolk out at this time of day; I just thought I'd pop in for a little chat and say goodbye.

GINA. Oh? Are you leaving?

MRS. SÖRBY. Yes, first thing tomorrow morning . . . up to Höidal. Mr. Werle left this afternoon. [*Casually to* GREGERS.] He sends his regards.

GINA. Well fancy!

HJALMAR. Mr. Werle's gone, d'you say? And you are going to follow him?

MRS. SÖRBY. Yes. What have you got to say to *that*, Mr. Ekdal?

HJALMAR. Watch out, that's all I've got to say.

GREGERS. Let me explain. My father and Mrs. Sörby are going to be married.

HJALMAR. Going to be married!

GINA. Oh, Berta! At last!

RELLING [*with a tremor in his voice*]. Surely this is never true?

MRS. SÖRBY. Yes, my dear Mr. Relling, it's perfectly true.

RELLING. You want to marry again?

MRS. SÖRBY. Yes, that's what it amounts to. Mr. Werle got a special licence, and we'll just have a quiet wedding up at Höidal.

GREGERS. Then I must wish you every happiness, like a good stepson.

MRS. SÖRBY. Thank you, if you really mean it. I can only hope it's going to bring happiness both for me and Mr. Werle.

RELLING. You are safe in hoping that. Mr. Werle never gets drunk— as far as *I* know, at any rate. And I don't suppose he's in the habit of knocking his wives about either, like our late lamented horse doctor.

MRS. SÖRBY. Oh, let Sörby rest in peace, now. He had his good points too, like everybody else.

RELLING. Mr. Werle has some even better points, I dare say.

MRS. SÖRBY. At any rate he hasn't gone and squandered what was best in him. Any man who does *that* must take the consequences.

RELLING. Tonight I am going to go out with Molvik.

MRS. SÖRBY. You shouldn't, Mr. Relling; please don't—for my sake.

RELLING. There's nothing else for it. [*To* HJALMAR.] You can come too, if you want.

GINA. No thank you. Hjalmar's not going out with you to *them* kind of places.

HJALMAR [*angrily in an undertone*]. Oh, shut up!

RELLING. Goodbye, Mrs.—— Werle.

[*He goes out through the hall door.*]

GREGERS [*to* MRS. SÖRBY]. It seems as though you and Dr. Relling know each other pretty well.

MRS. SÖRBY. Yes, we've known each other for years. Once upon a time it looked as if we might have made something of it, the two of us.

GREGERS. Just as well for you that you didn't.

MRS. SÖRBY. Yes, you might well say that. But I've always taken care not to act on impulse. A woman can't just throw herself away, either.

GREGERS. And you're not the least bit afraid I might drop my father a hint about this old affair?

MRS. SÖRBY. You may take it I've already told him myself.

GREGERS. Indeed?

MRS. SÖRBY. Your father knows every conceivable thing that anybody could truthfully think of saying about me. I've told him everything. It was the very first thing I did, when he began to make his intentions plain.

GREGERS. Then I think you must be more than usually frank.

MRS. SÖRBY. Frank is something I've always been. It's the best policy for us women.

HJALMAR. What do you say to that, Gina?

GINA. Oh, we women are so different—some one way, and some another.

MRS. SÖRBY. Well, Gina, I think it's wisest to do things the way I've done them now. And for his part, Mr. Werle hasn't tried to hide anything either. And that's mainly what's brought us together. Now he can sit and talk to me quite openly, just like a child. The whole of his youth and the best years of his manhood, all he heard was a lot of sermonizing about his sins—a healthy and vigorous man like him. And many's the time, from what I've heard, those sermons were about entirely imaginary offences.

GINA. Yes, it's true enough what you say.

GREGERS. If you ladies are going to start on *that* topic, it would no doubt be best if I went.

MRS. SÖRBY. There's no need to go on that account. I won't say another word. But I wanted to make it quite clear to you that nothing's been hushed up and everything's been above board. It might seem as though this is a great piece of luck for me; and so it is, in one way. But at the same time I don't think I'm taking more than I'm giving. I'll never let him down. And I can look after him and take care of him, as nobody else can, now that he'll soon be helpless.

HJALMAR. Be helpless?

GREGERS [*to* MRS. SÖRBY]. Yes, yes. Don't talk about it here.

MRS. SÖRBY. There's no point in hiding it any longer, however much he would like to. He's going blind.

HJALMAR [*with a start*]. Going blind? That's very strange. He's going blind too?

GINA. Lots of people in the same position.

MRS. SÖRBY. And you can imagine what that means for a businessman. Well, I shall try to use my eyes for him as best I can. But now I mustn't stay any longer; I've got so many things to see to at the moment.—Oh yes, something I had to tell you, Mr. Ekdal: if there was anything Mr. Werle could do for you, would you please just approach Graaberg about it.

GREGERS. An offer Hjalmar Ekdal will certainly decline.

MRS. SÖRBY. Indeed? I don't seem to remember him in the past . . .

GINA. No, Berta! Hjalmar doesn't have to take anything from Mr. Werle now.

HJALMAR [*slowly and weightily*]. Give my regards to your future husband and tell him from me that in the near future I intend to call on Graaberg . . .

GREGERS. What! You mean that!

HJALMAR. . . . As I was saying, to call on Graaberg and ask for a statement of the amount I owe his employer. I will pay this debt of honour—ha! ha! debt of honour, that's good! But enough of that. I will repay everything, with five per cent interest.

GINA. But, Hjalmar dear, heaven knows we haven't any money to do that.

HJALMAR. Tell your *fiancé* I am working away steadily at my invention. Tell him the thing that sustains me in this exhausting task is the desire to be rid of a painful burden of debt. That is why I am working on the invention. All the proceeds from it will go towards discharging those obligations imposed on me by your future husband's pecuniary outlay.

MRS. SÖRBY. Something's happened in this house.

HJALMAR. Yes, it has.

MRS. SÖRBY. Very well, goodbye, then! I still had a few things I'd have liked to talk to you about, Gina, but they'd better wait now till another time. Goodbye!

[HJALMAR *and* GREGERS *bow silently.* GINA *accompanies* MRS. SÖRBY *to the door.*]

HJALMAR. Not across the threshold, Gina!

[MRS. SÖRBY *goes;* GINA *shuts the door after her.*]

HJALMAR. There now, Gregers. Now I've got that load of debt off my shoulders.

GREGERS. Soon you will, anyway.

HJALMAR. I think it must be said that my behaviour was most correct.

GREGERS. You are the man I always took you for.

HJALMAR. In certain cases it is impossible to disregard the claim of the ideal. As head of a family there's nothing I can do but grin and bear it. Believe me it's no joke for a man without private means to have to pay off a debt from many years ago, on which, as it were, the dust of oblivion had already settled. But that makes no difference— I have certain human rights, too, that crave satisfaction.

GREGERS [*placing a hand on his shoulder*]. My dear Hjalmar, wasn't it a good thing I came?

HJALMAR. Yes.

GREGERS. So you saw quite clearly how things were—wasn't that a good thing?

HJALMAR [*a little impatiently*]. Yes, of course it was a good thing. But there is one thing that offends my sense of justice.

GREGERS. And what is that?

HJALMAR. The fact that . . . Well, I don't really know if I ought to speak so freely about your father.

GREGERS. Don't mind me at all.

HJALMAR. Well then. . . . You see, what I think is so distressing is the fact that it's now not me who is founding a true marriage, but him.

GREGERS. How can you say that!

HJALMAR. But it's true. Your father and Mrs. Sörby are entering upon a marriage based on full confidence, based on complete and unqualified frankness on both sides; they are not keeping anything back; there's no deception underneath it all. If I might so put it, it's an agreement for the mutual forgiveness of sin.

GREGERS. What of it?

HJALMAR. Well, *there* it all is. But from what you said, you had to go through all this difficult business before you could found a true marriage.

GREGERS. But that's something quite different, Hjalmar. Surely you're not going to compare either yourself or her with those two. . . ? You see what I mean, don't you?

HJALMAR. But I can't get over the fact that there's something in all this that offends my sense of justice. It looks for all the world as though there were no justice at all in things.

GINA. Good gracious, Hjalmar! You mustn't say things like that.

GREGERS. Hm, let's not get ourselves involved in questions like that.

HJALMAR. Yet, on the other hand, I might almost claim to see the guiding finger of fate. He is going blind.

GINA. Oh, perhaps it's not so certain.

HJALMAR. There's no doubt about it. At least we *ought* not to doubt it, for that is precisely what makes it a just retribution. He at one time has blinded a trusting fellow creature. . . .

GREGERS. He has, I regret to say, blinded many.

HJALMAR. And now comes this mysterious implacable power and demands the man's own eyes.

GINA. Ugh, how can you say such awful things! You make me feel scared.

HJALMAR. It profits a man occasionally to immerse himself in the darker things of life.

[HEDVIG, *in her hat and coat, comes in through the hall door, happy and breathless.*]

GINA. You back again already?

HEDVIG. Yes, I didn't want to go any further. And it was just as well, because I met somebody at the door.

HJALMAR. That must have been Mrs. Sörby.

HEDVIG. Yes.

HJALMAR [*walking up and down*]. I'd like to think you'd seen her for the last time.

[*Silence.* HEDVIG *looks shyly from one to the other as though trying to estimate their mood.*]

HEDVIG [*going over to* HJALMAR, *coaxingly*]. Daddy!

HJALMAR. Well—what is it, Hedvig?

HEDVIG. Mrs. Sörby had something for me.

HJALMAR [*halts*]. For you?

HEDVIG. Yes. It's something for tomorrow.

GINA. Berta has always had some little thing for your birthday.

HJALMAR. What is it?

HEDVIG. Oh, you mustn't know what it is yet. Mother has to bring it to me in bed first thing in the morning.

HJALMAR. Oh, all this secrecy, and me being kept in the dark!

HEDVIG [*hastily*]. But you can see it if you like. A big letter.

[*She takes a letter out of her coat pocket.*]

HJALMAR. A letter, too?

HEDVIG. There's only the letter. I suppose the rest is to come later. But just imagine, a letter! I've never had a letter before. And it says 'Miss' on the front. [*Reads.*] 'Miss Hedvig Ekdal.' Fancy, that's me.

HJALMAR. Let me see the letter.

HEDVIG [*hands it to him*]. There, you see.

HJALMAR. That's old Mr. Werle's writing.

GINA. Are you sure, Hjalmar?

HJALMAR. Look yourself.

GINA. Oh, you don't think I would know, do you?

HJALMAR. Hedvig, may I open the letter ... and read it?

HEDVIG. Yes, of course you may, if you want to.

GINA. Please, not tonight, Hjalmar. You know it's meant for tomorrow.

HEDVIG [*softly*]. Oh, please let him read it! It's sure to be something nice. And then Daddy will be pleased and we'll all be happy again.

HJALMAR. I may open it, then?

HEDVIG. Yes, Daddy, please do. It will be fun to find out what it is.

HJALMAR. Very well. [*He opens the letter, reads it, and seems a little taken aback.*] What's this. . . ?

GINA. What does it say?

HEDVIG. Yes, Daddy, do tell us.

HJALMAR. Be quiet. [*Reads it through again; he has turned pale, but controls himself.*] It is a deed of gift, Hedvig.

HEDVIG. Well, fancy that! What am I getting?

HJALMAR. Read it yourself.

[HEDVIG *walks over to the lamp and reads for a moment or two.*]

HJALMAR [*in an undertone, clenching his hands*]. The eyes, the eyes . . . and now this letter.

HEDVIG [*interrupts her reading*]. Yes, but it looks to me as though it's Grandfather who is getting it.

HJALMAR [*takes the letter from her*]. Gina—can you understand this?

GINA. I don't know the first thing about it. Tell me what it is.

HJALMAR. Mr. Werle writes to Hedvig to say that her old grandfather needn't bother about doing any more copying, and that in future he can draw one hundred crowns a month straight from the office. . . .

GREGERS. Aha!

HEDVIG. A hundred crowns, Mother. I read that bit.

GINA. That will be nice for Grandfather.

HJALMAR. . . . a hundred crowns, for as long as he needs it. That means, of course, until he's passed away.

GINA. Well, that's him provided for, poor old soul.

HJALMAR. That's not all. You didn't read far enough, Hedvig. After that, it's to come to you.

HEDVIG. To me? All that?

HJALMAR. You are assured a like amount for the rest of your life, he writes. Do you hear that, Gina?

GINA. Yes, I heard.

HEDVIG. Fancy—all that money I'm going to get! [*Shakes him.*] Daddy, Daddy, aren't you glad?

HJALMAR [*moving away from her*]. Glad! [*Walks up and down.*] Oh, this puts quite a new perspective on things! It opens my eyes to all sorts of possibilities. It's Hedvig. She's the one he's being so generous to!

GINA. Yes, because she's the one who's having the birthday. . . .

HEDVIG. You shall have it, all the same, Daddy. You know I'll give all the money to you and Mother.

HJALMAR. To your mother, yes. That's just it.

GREGERS. Hjalmar, this is a trap that's being set for you.

HJALMAR. Could it be another trap, do you think?

GREGERS. When he was here this morning, he said: 'Hjalmar Ekdal is not the man you take him to be.'

HJALMAR. Not the man . . . !

GREGERS. 'Just wait, you'll see,' he said.

HJALMAR. See that I'd let myself be bought off for a price. . . !

HEDVIG. Mother, what is all this about?

GINA. Go and take your things off.

[*Near to tears,* HEDVIG *goes out by the kitchen door.*]

GREGERS. Yes, Hjalmar. Now we'll see who's right, him or me.

HJALMAR [*slowly tears the document in two, and places the pieces on the table*]. There's my answer.

GREGERS. As I expected.

HJALMAR [*goes over to* GINA *who is standing by the stove and says in a low voice*]. Now let's have no more pretence. If this affair was over and done with when you . . . 'got fond' of me as you put it . . . why did he go and arrange things so that we could afford to get married?

GINA. I suppose he thought he'd be able to come and go here as he liked.

HJALMAR. Is that all? Wasn't he afraid of a certain possibility.

GINA. I don't know what you mean.

HJALMAR. I want to know if . . . your child has a right to live under my roof.

GINA [*drawing herself up, her eyes flashing*]. *You* ask me that!

HJALMAR. I want a straight answer. Is Hedvig mine . . . or . . . ? Well!

GINA [*looking at him coldly and defiantly*]. I don't know.

HJALMAR [*trembling slightly*]. You don't know!

GINA. How should *I* know? A person like *me*. . . .

HJALMAR [*quietly turning away from her*]. This house is no place for me any more.

GREGERS. Think well what you are doing, Hjalmar!

HJALMAR [*putting on his topcoat*]. There's no need to think here, not for a man like me.

GREGERS. Yes there is. There's a tremendous lot to think about. The three of you must remain together if you, Hjalmar, are to win through to that sublime mood of magnanimity and forgiveness.

HJALMAR. I don't *want* to. Never, never! My hat! [*Takes his hat.*] My home has collapsed in ruins about my ears! [*Bursts into tears.*] Gregers, I have no child!

HEDVIG [*who has opened the kitchen door*]. What are you saying? [*Crosses to him.*] Daddy! Daddy!

GINA. There, there.

HJALMAR. Don't come near me, Hedvig! Go away! I can't bear to look at you. Oh, those eyes. . . ! Goodbye.

[*He makes for the door.*]

HEDVIG [*clings tight to him and screams*]. No! No! Don't leave me.

GINA [*shouts*]. Look at the child, Hjalmar! Look at her!

HJALMAR. I will not! I cannot! Let me go. I must get away from all this.

[*He tears himself free of* HEDVIG *and goes out by the hall door.*]

HEDVIG [*with despair in her eyes*]. He's leaving us, Mother! He's leaving us. He's never coming back any more!

GINA. Don't cry, Hedvig. Your father's coming back all right.

HEDVIG [*throws herself sobbing on the sofa*]. No, no, he's never coming back to us again.

GREGERS. You do believe I meant it all for the best, Mrs. Ekdal?

GINA. Yes, I dare say you did. But may God forgive you, all the same.

HEDVIG [*lying on the sofa*]. Oh, I just feel as though I want to die! What have I done? Mother, you must get him to come home again!

GINA. Yes, yes. Be quiet now, and I'll just go out and see if I can see him. [*Puts on her outdoor things.*] He might have gone into Relling's. But you mustn't lie there crying, now. Promise?

HEDVIG [*sobbing convulsively*]. Yes, I'll stop crying. As long as Daddy comes back.

GREGERS [*to* GINA, *who is about to leave*]. Wouldn't it perhaps be better to let him fight his bitter fight to the end.

GINA. Oh, he can do that afterwards. The first thing is to get the child quietened down.

[*She goes out through the hall door.*]

HEDVIG [*sits up and dries her eyes*]. Now you must tell me what's the matter. Why doesn't Daddy want me any more?

GREGERS. You mustn't ask *that* until you've grown up into a big girl.

HEDVIG [*sobbing*]. But I can't go on feeling as awful and miserable as this all the time till I'm grown-up.—I know what it is.—Perhaps I'm not really Daddy's.

GREGERS [*uneasily*]. How could *that* be?

HEDVIG. Mother could have found me, maybe. And now perhaps Daddy's found out. I've read about things like that.

GREGERS. Well, but even so . . .

HEDVIG. Then I think he might have been just as fond of me. Even more. After all, we got the wild duck sent to us as a present, and I'm awfully fond of that.

GREGERS [*leading her off the subject*]. Yes, the wild duck, that's right. Let's talk a bit about the wild duck, Hedvig.

HEDVIG. Poor little wild duck! He can't bear the sight of it, either. D'you know he wanted to wring its neck.

GREGERS. Oh, I'm sure he wouldn't do that.

HEDVIG. No, but that's what he said. And I thought it was rather horrid of Daddy to say that. Because I say a prayer for the wild duck every night, and I ask for it to be delivered from death and all evil.

GREGERS [*looking at her*]. Do you always say your prayers?

HEDVIG. Yes.

GREGERS. Who taught you that?

HEDVIG. I taught myself. It was once when Daddy was very ill, and had to have leeches on his neck. And he said he was at death's door.

GREGERS. Well?

HEDVIG. So I said a prayer for him, after I'd gone to bed. And I've done it ever since.

GREGERS. And now you pray for the wild duck as well?

HEDVIG. I thought I'd better include the wild duck, too. She was so poorly to begin with.

GREGERS. Do you say your prayers in the morning, too?

HEDVIG. Oh no, I don't.

GREGERS. Why don't you say your prayers in the morning as well?

HEDVIG. Well, it's light in the mornings; there's nothing to be afraid of any more.

GREGERS. And the wild duck you are so terribly fond of—your father wants to wring its neck.

HEDVIG. No, he said if *he* had his way, he'd do it. But he said he'd spare it for my sake. That was sweet of him.

GREGERS [*coming closer*]. Supposing you offered to sacrifice the wild duck for *his* sake?

HEDVIG [*rising*]. The wild duck!

GREGERS. Suppose you were ready to sacrifice for him the most precious thing you had in the world?

HEDVIG. Do you think *that* would help?

GREGERS. Try it, Hedvig.

HEDVIG [*quietly, with shining eyes*]. Yes, I will try it.

GREGERS. Have you the proper strength of mind, do you think?

HEDVIG. I'll ask Grandfather to shoot the wild duck for me.

GREGERS. Yes, do that. But not a word to your mother about this!

HEDVIG. Why not?

GREGERS. She doesn't understand us.

HEDVIG. The wild duck. I'll try it first thing tomorrow morning.

[GINA *enters through the hall door.*]

HEDVIG [*goes to meet her*]. Did you find him, Mother?

GINA. No, but I heard he'd called and gone out with Relling.

GREGERS. Are you sure?

GINA. Yes, the caretaker's wife said so. Molvik was with them too, she said.

GREGERS. At a time like this, when his soul desperately needs solitude to win through. . . !

GINA [*takes her things off*]. Yes, men are funny, they are that. God alone knows where Relling has dragged him off to! I rushed over to Ma Eriksen's, but they weren't there.

HEDVIG [*fighting her tears*]. Oh! What if he never comes back home again!

GREGERS. He will come back. I shall take a message to him in the morning, and you'll see he'll come. Sleep well and rest assured about *that*, Hedvig. Good night. [*Goes out through the hall door.*]

HEDVIG [*throws her arms round* GINA'S *neck, sobbing*]. Mother! Mother!

GINA [*pats her on the back and sighs*]. Ah yes. Relling was right. This is what happens when you get these stupid idiots coming round with their fancy demands.

ACT FIVE

HJALMAR EKDAL'S *studio, in the cold grey light of morning; wet snow is lying on the large panes of the skylight.* GINA, *wearing an overall, comes in from the kitchen carrying a brush and a duster and walks over towards the living-room door. At that moment,* HEDVIG *rushes in from the hall.*

GINA [*stops*]. Well?

HEDVIG. Yes, Mother, I think he's very likely in with Relling . . .

GINA. You see, now!

HEDVIG. . . . because the caretaker's wife said she heard two other people come in with Relling last night.

GINA. I fancied as much.

HEDVIG. But that doesn't help very much if he won't come back here.

GINA. At least I can pop down and talk to him.

[OLD EKDAL, *in dressing-gown and slippers and smoking a pipe, appears at the door of his room.*]

EKDAL. Hjalmar! Isn't Hjalmar at home?

GINA. No, he's gone out.

EKDAL. So early? When it's snowing as heavily as this? Oh well, all right, I can go this morning by myself.

[*He pulls the loft door aside;* HEDVIG *helps him; he goes in and she shuts the door behind him.*]

HEDVIG [*in an undertone*]. Oh, Mother, what will poor Grandfather say when he hears Daddy's going to leave us.

GINA. Oh, rubbish! Grandfather mustn't hear anything about it. What a godsend he wasn't around yesterday when all that business was going on.

HEDVIG. Yes, but . . .

[GREGERS *enters through the hall door.*]

GREGERS. Well? Found any trace of him?

GINA. As like as not, he's down there in with Relling, they say.

GREGERS. In with Relling! Has he really been out with those fellows?

GINA. He has that.

GREGERS. But how *could* he? When he desperately needed solitude and a chance to collect himself. . . .

GINA. Ah, you might well say that.

[RELLING *enters from the hall.*]

HEDVIG [*crosses to him*]. Is Daddy in with you?

GINA [*at the same time*]. Is he there?

RELLING. Indeed he is.

HEDVIG. And you never told us!

RELLING. Yes, I'm a bea . . . east. But I had to see to that other bea . . . east first, the demonic one, I mean, of course. And then I fell right off to sleep, so I . . .

GINA. What's Hjalmar got to say today?

RELLING. He doesn't say anything.

GINA. Hasn't he said anything at all?

RELLING. Not a blessed word.

GREGERS. Ah no, I understand that so well.

GINA. What's he doing with himself, then?

RELLING. He's lying on the sofa, snoring.

GINA. Is he? Yes, Hjalmar's pretty good at snoring.

HEDVIG. Is he asleep? Can he really sleep?

RELLING. It certainly looks like it.

GREGERS. Quite understandable! Torn as he was by the conflict in his soul. . . .

GINA. And him not used to late nights.

HEDVIG. Perhaps it's best for him to get some sleep, Mother.

GINA. That's what I'm thinking too. There's no point then in waking him up too soon. Thanks, Mr. Relling. Now I'd better get the house tidied up a bit first . . . then . . . come and help me, Hedvig.

[GINA *and* HEDVIG *go into the living-room.*]

GREGERS [*turns to* RELLING]. Have you any views on the spiritual turmoil going on in Hjalmar Ekdal?

RELLING. I'm damned if I can see any spiritual turmoil going on in him.

GREGERS. What! At a crisis like this, when his whole life has been put on a completely new basis. . . ? How do you suppose a personality like Hjalmar's . . . ?

RELLING. Personality? Him! If he ever showed any signs of anything as abnormal as a personality, it was all thoroughly cleared out of him, root and branch, when he was still a lad—that I can assure you.

GREGERS. That would seem very strange . . . after being brought up with such affectionate care, as he was.

RELLING. By those two crazy, hysterical maiden aunts of his, you mean?

GREGERS. Let me tell you they were women who never shut their eyes to the claim of the ideal.—Ah, I suppose you are just trying to be funny again.

RELLING. No, I'm in no mood for that. Besides, I know all about it. The amount of rhetoric he's brought up about these two 'soul-mothers' of his! But I don't think he has much to thank them for. Ekdal's misfortune is that in his own little circle he's always been considered a shining light. . . .

GREGERS. And don't you think he is? Deep down within, I mean.

RELLING. *I've* never seen any sign of it. Whether his father thought that—that might well be. The dear Lieutenant has always been a bit of a blockhead, all his life.

GREGERS. He's always been a man with the spirit of a child. *That's* what you don't understand.

RELLING. All right, all right! But when our dear, sweet little Hjalmar began as a student of sorts, he was immediately regarded by his fellow-students too as a man with a brilliant future. He was handsome, too, quite captivating—pink and white—the sort the girls all fall for. And because he was the sentimental sort, and there was something appealing in his voice, and because he learned the knack of reciting other people's poetry and other people's ideas . . .

GREGERS [*indignantly*]. Is this Hjalmar Ekdal you are talking about?

RELLING. It is, with your permission. For that's the inside view of this little demi-god you are grovelling to.

GREGERS. I wouldn't have said I was as completely blind as all that.

RELLING. Oh yes, you are. Pretty well, anyway. You see, *you* are a sick man, too.

GREGERS. You are right there.

RELLING. Well then. In your case there are complications. First there are these troublesome inflamed scruples. But then there's something much worse: you are subject to serious fits of hero-worship. You've always got to go round finding something to admire that's not really any of your business.

GREGERS. I must indeed look for something beyond my own self.

RELLING. But then you go and make such tremendous blunders about these wonderful beings you imagine you see and hear around you. Now you are at it again, coming to another labourer's cottage with that claim of the ideal. There just aren't any solvent people living here.

GREGERS. If you haven't any higher opinion of Hjalmar Ekdal than that, I wonder you find any pleasure at all in being everlastingly in his company.

RELLING. Good God, I'm supposed to be a doctor of sorts, aren't I, though I'm ashamed to say it? I have to do something in the way of looking after the sick who are living in the same house as me, poor things.

GREGERS. Really! Is Hjalmar Ekdal sick too?

RELLING. Pretty nearly everybody's sick, unfortunately.

GREGERS. And what treatment are you giving Hjalmar?

RELLING. The usual. I try to keep his life-lie going.

GREGERS. Life . . . lie? I don't think I quite caught . . . ?

RELLING. That's right. That's what I said: the life-lie. You see, the life-lie is the stimulating principle.

GREGERS. May I ask what sort of a life-lie Hjalmar has been inoculated with?

RELLING. I'm afraid not; I don't give secrets like that away to quacks. You would just be in a position to mess him up even worse for me. But it's a tried and tested method; I have used it on Molvik as well. I have made him a 'demonic'. That's the particular cure I had to apply to him.

GREGERS. Isn't he demonic?

RELLING. What the devil do you think being demonic means? It's just a bit of silly nonsense I thought up to keep him alive. If I hadn't done that, the poor devil would have succumbed to mortification and despair years ago. Same with the old Lieutenant there. But he's managed to find his own course of treatment.

GREGERS. Lieutenant Ekdal? What about him?

RELLING. Well, what do you think? Him, the great bear-hunter, shooting rabbits there in the loft? There isn't a happier sportsman in the world than that old man when he gets a chance of raking round in there among all the rubbish. He's collected up four or five withered old Christmas trees, and there's no difference for him between them and the whole tremendous living forest of Höidal. The cocks and the hens are the game birds in the tree tops; and the rabbits hopping about the floor, they are the bears that this intrepid he-man goes in pursuit of.

GREGERS. Poor old, unhappy Lieutenant Ekdal. He certainly has had to relinquish a lot of his youthful ideals.

RELLING. While I remember, Mr. Werle junior—don't use this fancy word 'ideals'; we've got a plain word that's good enough: 'lies'.

GREGERS. Are you trying to say the two things are related?

RELLING. Yes, not unlike typhus and putrid fever.

GREGERS. Dr. Relling, I shall not rest until I have rescued Hjalmar Ekdal from your clutches!

RELLING. So much the worse for *him*. Take the life-lie away from the average man and straight away you take away his happiness. [*To* HEDVIG, *who comes in from the living-room.*] Well, now my little wild duck mother, I'll pop down now and see whether that father of yours is still lying there thinking about his wonderful invention.

[*He goes out through the hall door.*]

GREGERS [*approaches* HEDVIG]. I can see from your face nothing's been done.

HEDVIG. What? Oh, the wild duck. No.

GREGERS. Your courage failed you, I imagine, when it came to the point.

HEDVIG. No it isn't that. But when I woke up early this morning and remembered what we'd talked about, it seemed so strange.

GREGERS. Strange?

HEDVIG. Yes, I don't know. . . . Last night when I first heard it, it seemed such a lovely idea; but when I thought about it again after I had slept on it, it didn't seem much of an idea.

GREGERS. Ah no. You could hardly be expected to grow up here without being the worse for it in some way.

HEDVIG. Oh, what do I care about that. If only Daddy would come. . . .

GREGERS. Ah, if only you'd had your eyes opened to what really makes life worth while! If you had the genuine, joyous, courageous spirit of self-sacrifice, then you would see how quickly he would come back to you. But I still have faith in you, Hedvig.

[*He goes out through the hall door.* HEDVIG *wanders about the room; she is about to go into the kitchen when there is a knocking from within the loft.* HEDVIG *goes over and opens the door slightly.* OLD EKDAL *comes out; he pushes the door to again.*]

EKDAL. Huh! It's not much fun having to go for your morning walk by yourself.

HEDVIG. Didn't you fancy going shooting, Grandfather?

EKDAL. It's not the weather for it today. So dark you can hardly see anything.

HEDVIG. Don't you ever feel like shooting anything else but rabbits?

EKDAL. Aren't the rabbits good enough, then, eh?

HEDVIG. I mean, what about the wild duck?

EKDAL. Ha! ha! Are you frightened I'll go and shoot your wild duck. Not for the world, my dear! I'd never do that!

HEDVIG. No, I dare say you couldn't. It's supposed to be very difficult to shoot wild duck.

EKDAL. Couldn't I? I should jolly well think I could.

HEDVIG. How would you set about it, Grandfather? I don't mean with *my* wild duck, but with others.

EKDAL. I'd try to make sure I shot them in the breast, you know. That's the best place. And then you have to shoot them *against* the lie of the feathers, you see—never with the feathers.

HEDVIG. Do they die then, Grandfather?

EKDAL. I'll say they do . . . if you shoot them properly. Well, I'd better go and tidy myself up. Hm . . . you see . . . hm!

[*He goes into his room.* HEDVIG *waits a moment, glances towards the living-room door, walks across to the bookcase and, standing on tiptoe, she takes the double-barrelled pistol down off the shelf and looks at it.* GINA *with her brush and duster, enters from the living-room.* HEDVIG *quickly replaces the pistol without being noticed.*]

GINA. Don't go upsetting your father's things, Hedvig.

HEDVIG [*moving away from the bookcase*]. I was just tidying up a bit.

GINA. Go into the kitchen instead and see if the coffee is still hot. I'll take a tray of something down with me when I go and see him.

[HEDVIG *goes out.* GINA *begins dusting up the studio. A moment later the passage door is hesitantly opened and* HJALMAR EKDAL *looks in. He has his topcoat on, but no hat; he is unwashed, his hair is ruffled and untidy; he looks heavy and dull about the eyes.*]

GINA [*stops what she is doing, her broom in her hand and looks at him*]. Oh, Hjalmar . . . so you've come back?

HJALMAR [*enters and answers in a dull voice*]. I've come ... but I'm leaving again at once.

GINA. Yes, yes, I suppose that's all right. But good Lord, there's a sight you look!

HJALMAR. A sight?

GINA. Just look at your good winter coat! Not much use for any thing now.

HEDVIG [*at the kitchen door*]. Mother, shall I ... ? [*Sees* HJALMAR, *screams with joy and runs across to him.*] Oh, Daddy! Daddy!

HJALMAR [*turns aside and waves her away*]. Go away, go away! [*To* GINA.] Take her away from me, I tell you!

GINA [*in a low voice*]. Go into the living-room, Hedvig.

[HEDVIG *goes in silently.*]

HJALMAR [*busying himself pulling out the table drawer*]. I must have my books with me. Where are my books?

GINA. What books?

HJALMAR. My scientific works, of course—the technical periodicals I use for my invention.

GINA [*looks in the bookcase*]. Are these them, without any backs on.

HJALMAR. Of course they are.

GINA [*putting a pile of unbound books on the table*]. Shouldn't I get Hedvig to cut the pages for you?

HJALMAR. I don't need any cutting doing.

[*Short silence.*]

GINA. So you haven't changed your mind about moving out and leaving us, Hjalmar.

HJALMAR [*rummaging among the books*]. I should have thought that was pretty evident.

GINA. Ah, well.

HJALMAR [*angrily*]. I can't stay on here having a knife twisted in my heart every hour of the day.

GINA. God forgive you for thinking I could be that bad.

HJALMAR. Prove to me that . . . !

GINA. Strikes me *you're* the one that should think about proving.

HJALMAR. With a past like yours? There are certain claims . . . I might almost be tempted to call them claims of the ideal. . . .

GINA. What about Grandfather? What's to be done with *him*, poor old fellow?

HJALMAR. I know my duty. The helpless old man will come along with me. I shall go to town and make the necessary arrangements. . . . Hm! [*Hesitates.*] Has anybody seen my hat on the stairs?

GINA. No, have you lost your hat?

HJALMAR. There's no doubt I had it on when I got back last night. But I couldn't find it again today.

GINA. Lord! Wherever did you land up with them two old soaks?

HJALMAR. Oh, don't ask questions about things that don't matter. Do you think I'm in a mood to remember details?

GINA. As long as you haven't caught cold, Hjalmar.

[*She goes out into the kitchen.*]

HJALMAR [*talking angrily to himself in an undertone as he empties the table drawer*]. You are a blackguard, Relling. Nothing but a scoundrel, a shameless rake. If only I could get somebody to do you in!

[*He puts some old letters to one side, finds the torn document of the day before, picks it up and looks at the pieces. As* GINA *comes in he quickly puts them down again.*]

GINA [*puts a breakfast tray on the table.*] Just a drop of something to warm you up, if you can fancy it. And some bread and butter and some cold meat.

HJALMAR [*glances at the tray*]. Meat? Never again under this roof! I don't care if I haven't had a bite for nearly twenty-four hours.— My notes! The start of my autobiography! Where's my diary and all my important papers? [*He opens the living-room door, but draws back.*] There she is again.

GINA. Heavens above, the child has to be somewhere!

HJALMAR. Come out.

[*He stands back; and* HEDVIG, *terrified, comes into the studio.*]

HJALMAR [*his hand on the door handle, speaks to* GINA]. As I spend these last moments in what was once my home, I wish to remain undisturbed by those who have no business to be here. . . .

HEDVIG [*runs across to her mother and asks in a low trembling voice*]. Does he mean me?

GINA. Stay in the kitchen, Hedvig. Or no—go into your own room instead. [*Speaking to* HJALMAR, *as she goes in to where he is.*] Just a minute, Hjalmar. Don't upset everything in that chest of drawers. *I* know where everything is.

[HEDVIG *stands motionless for a moment, frightened and confused; she bites her lip to stop herself from crying, and clenches and unclenches her hands.*]

HEDVIG [*softly*]. The wild duck!

[*She creeps across and takes the pistol from the shelf, opens the loft door a little way, slips in and pulls the door behind her.* HJALMAR *and* GINA *begin to argue in the living-room.*]

HJALMAR [*comes out carrying some exercise books and old sheets of paper, which he puts on the table*]. Oh, that old valise isn't much use. There are thousands of things I've got to hump away with me.

GINA [*follows with the valise*]. Well, leave the other things for the time being; just take a shirt and a pair of pants with you now.

HJALMAR. Phew! All these exhausting preparations!

[*He takes off his topcoat and throws it on the sofa.*]

GINA. Your coffee's getting cold.

HJALMAR. Hm!

[*He takes a mouthful without thinking, and then another.*]

GINA [*dusting the backs of the chairs*]. Your worst job now will be finding another loft big enough for the rabbits.

HJALMAR. What! Have I to drag all those rabbits along with me as well?

GINA. Yes, you know Grandfather couldn't live without his rabbits.

HJALMAR. He'll damn' well have to get used to the idea. There are more important matters in life than rabbits among the things *I'm* having to do without.

GINA [*dusting the bookcase*]. Shall I put your flute in your valise?

HJALMAR. No. I don't want any flute. But give me the pistol.

GINA. You want to take that pistol!

HJALMAR. Yes. My loaded pistol.

GINA [*looks for it*]. It's gone. He must have taken it in with him.

HJALMAR. Is he in the loft?

GINA. Oh, he's bound to be.

HJALMAR. Hm. Poor lonely old fellow.

[*He takes a piece of bread and butter, eats it, and drinks up the coffee.*]

GINA. If only we hadn't let that room, you could have moved in there.

HJALMAR. Me live under the same roof as . . . ! Never! Never!

GINA. But couldn't you shake down for a day or two in the living-room? You could be all on your own there.

HJALMAR. Never within these walls!

GINA. Well, what about going in with Relling and Molvik?

HJALMAR. I don't want to hear their names. Just thinking of them is enough to put me off my food, nearly. . . . Ah no! I must out into the storm and the snow . . . go from house to house seeking shelter for my father and myself.

GINA. But, Hjalmar, you haven't any hat. You've lost your hat, remember?

HJALMAR. Oh, the scum. Can't trust them with anything! I'll have to get myself a hat on the way. [*He takes another piece of bread.*] The necessary arrangements will have to be made. I've no desire to go risking my life as well.

[*He looks for something on the tray.*]

GINA. What are you looking for?

HJALMAR. Butter.

GINA. I'll get some straight away. [*Goes out into the kitchen.*]

HJALMAR [*calls after her*]. Oh, you needn't bother. I can just as well eat it dry.

GINA [*brings a butter dish*]. There you are, now. Supposed to be freshly churned.

[*She pours him a fresh cup of coffee; he sits down on the sofa, spreads more butter on the bread, eats and drinks in silence for a moment or two.*]

HJALMAR. Would I, without being disturbed by anybody—anybody at all—be able to move into the living-room for a day or two?

GINA. Yes, you could very nicely, and for as long as you wanted to.

HJALMAR. Because I can't see much likelihood of moving all Father's things out very fast.

GINA. There's something else as well. You'll have to tell him first about not wanting to live here with the rest of us any longer.

HJALMAR [*pushes his coffee cup away*]. Yes, that's another thing. All these complicated arrangements to be revised. I must consider things first, I must have a breathing space. I can't take all these burdens on in one single day.

GINA. No, and when it's such awful weather, too, on top of everything.

HJALMAR [*fingers Werle's letter*]. I see this paper's lying about here still.

GINA. Yes, *I* haven't touched it.

HJALMAR. Not that this bit of paper's got anything to do with me . . .

GINA. Well, I've got no use for it.

HJALMAR. . . . but there's not much point in letting it get destroyed, all the same. In all the upset when I move, it could so easily . . .

GINA. I'll take care of it, Hjalmar.

HJALMAR. After all, this letter belongs in the first place to Father; and it will have to be for him to decide whether he wants to make use of it or not.

GINA [*sighs*]. Yes, poor old Father.

HJALMAR. Might as well be on the safe side. . . . Where will I find the paste?

GINA [*goes to the bookcase*]. Here's the paste pot.

HJALMAR. And a brush?

GINA. Here's the brush as well.

[*She brings him the things.*]

HJALMAR [*taking the scissors*]. Just needs a strip of paper along the back. . . . [*He cuts and pastes.*] Far be it from me to lay hands on anybody else's property, least of all on a penniless old man's. And not on . . . the other person's, either, for that matter. . . . There we are. It can stay there for the present. And when it's dry, put it away. I don't want to see that document ever again. Never!

[GREGERS WERLE *comes in from the hall.*]

GREGERS [*a little surprised*]. What! You here, Hjalmar?

HJALMAR [*gets up quickly*]. I had sunk down from exhaustion.

GREGERS. I see you've had some breakfast.

HJALMAR. The body too makes known its claims on us at times.

GREGERS. What have you decided to do?

HJALMAR. For a man such as me there is but one way open. I am in the process of collecting together the more important of my possessions. But it takes time, you understand.

GINA [*a little impatiently*]. Shall I get the room ready for you, or shall I pack the valise?

HJALMAR [*with an irritated glance at* GREGERS]. Pack . . . and get the room ready.

GINA [*takes the valise*]. All right, I'll put the shirt and the other things in, then.

[*She goes into the living-room and shuts the door behind her.*]

GREGERS [*after a short silence*]. I would never have thought that it would end like this. Is it really essential that you should leave house and home?

HJALMAR [*walking about restlessly*]. What do you expect me to do, then? —I am not made for unhappiness, Gregers. Everything around me has got to be nice and secure and peaceful.

GREGERS. But can't that be done? Try. To my mind you've got a firm foundation to build on . . . just begin at the beginning. Remember you've got your invention to live for, too.

HJALMAR. Oh, shut up about the invention. That's probably pretty far away.

GREGERS. Really?

HJALMAR. Good Lord, what in fact do you expect me to invent? Practically everything's been invented by other people already. It gets more and more difficult every day.

GREGERS. After you've put such a lot of work into it!

HJALMAR. It was that devil Relling who put me up to it.

GREGERS. Relling?

HJALMAR. Yes, he was the one who first suggested I was capable of making some special invention in photography.

GREGERS. Aha! . . . It was Relling!

HJALMAR. It's a thing that's made me intensely happy. Not so much because of the invention itself, as because Hedvig believed in it— believed in it with all the passion of a child. . . . What I mean is that I, like a fool, went and imagined that she believed in it.

GREGERS. Do you really suppose Hedvig went out of her way to deceive you!

HJALMAR. I'm ready to think anything now. Hedvig's the stumbling block now. She'll finish up by taking all the sunshine out of my life.

GREGERS. Hedvig! D'you mean Hedvig! How could *she* ever do anything like that?

HJALMAR [*without answering*]. I can't tell you how I loved that child. I can't tell you how happy I felt every time I came home to my modest room and she would come running across to me, with her poor sweet, strained little eyes. Oh, gullible fool that I was! I was so inexpressibly fond of her . . . and I deluded myself into imagining she was equally fond of me, too.

GREGERS. Can you say that *that* was merely a delusion?

HJALMAR. How should I know? I cannot get anything out of Gina. And anyway she has absolutely no understanding of the element of idealism in this situation. But I feel the need to unburden myself to you, Gregers. There's this terrible uncertainty—perhaps Hedvig never really loved me at all.

GREGERS. That is something you might very well get proof of. [*Listens.*] What's that? I thought I heard the wild duck cry.

HJALMAR. It's the wild duck quacking. Father is in the loft.

GREGERS. Is he! [*Joy lights up his face.*] What I was saying is that you might well have proof that poor misunderstood Hedvig does love you!

HJALMAR. Oh, what proof can she give me! I can hardly place any reliance on anything she says.

GREGERS. I'm sure there's nothing deceitful about Hedvig.

HJALMAR. Oh, Gregers, that's just what isn't so certain. Who knows what Gina and that Mrs. Sörby have sat here whispering and gossiping about? And Hedvig's got long ears. Perhaps that deed of gift wasn't so unexpected. I fancy I noticed something of the sort.

GREGERS. What's this that's got into you?

HJALMAR. I have had my eyes opened. You just watch—you'll see this deed of gift is only a beginning. Mrs. Sörby has always been specially fond of Hedvig, and now she has the power to do whatever she wants for the child. They can take her away from me any time they like.

GREGERS. Hedvig will never, never leave *you.*

HJALMAR. Don't you be so sure. What if they stand there with full hands beckoning to her. . . ? Oh, and I can't tell you how much I loved her! How it would have given me supreme happiness just to have taken her by the hand and led her along, as one leads a child that is afraid of the dark through a great empty room! I'm now convinced that the bitter truth is that the poor photographer up in his attic flat never really meant anything to her at all. All she did in her cunning was to take care that she kept on good terms with him until the right moment came.

GREGERS. You don't really believe that yourself, Hjalmar.

HJALMAR. That's the terrible thing, of course. I just don't know what to believe . . . and I'll never know. But surely you don't doubt it's as I say? Ha! ha! You rely too much on people's idealism, my dear Gregers! Suppose the others came along, their hands full, and they called to the child: 'Come away from him. With us, life is at your feet. . . .'

GREGERS [*quickly*]. Well, what then, d'you think?

HJALMAR. If I then asked her: 'Hedvig, are you willing to give up this life for my sake?' [*Laughs scornfully.*] Oh, yes! I must say. You would soon hear the sort of answer I would get!

[*A pistol shot is heard within the loft.*]

GREGERS [*shouts with joy*]. Hjalmar!

HJALMAR. Look at that, now. He has to go shooting!

GINA. Oh, Hjalmar, I think Grandfather's banging away there in the loft by himself.

HJALMAR. I'll look in.

GREGERS [*quickly, excitedly*]. Wait a minute! Do you know what that was?

HJALMAR. Of course I know what it was.

GREGERS. No, you don't. But *I* do. That was the proof!

HJALMAR. What proof?

GREGERS. That was the child's sacrifice. She's got your father to shoot the wild duck.

HJALMAR. Shoot the wild duck!

GINA. Well . . . !

HJALMAR. What's *that* for?

GREGERS. She wanted to sacrifice the most precious thing she had in the world, for your sake. Then, she thought, you couldn't help loving her again.

HJALMAR [*softly, with emotion*]. Oh, that child!

GINA. The things she thinks of!

GREGERS. All she wanted was for you to love her again, Hjalmar; she didn't think she could live without that.

GINA [*fighting back her tears*]. There you see, Hjalmar.

HJALMAR. Gina, where is she?

GINA [*sniffing*]. Poor little thing, she's sitting out in the kitchen, I expect.

HJALMAR [*crosses, and throws open the kitchen door*]. Hedvig, come out! Come to me! [*Looks round.*] No, she's not here.

GINA. Then she must be in her own room.

HJALMAR [*from outside*]. No, she isn't here either. [*Comes in.*] She must have gone out.

GINA. Well, you wouldn't have her anywhere in the house.

HJALMAR. Oh, if only she'd come back home again soon . . . so that I can tell her properly. . . . Everything's going to be all right, Gregers. Now I really believe we can begin life all over again.

GREGERS [*quietly*]. I knew it—knew that redemption would come through the child.

[OLD EKDAL *appears at the door of his room, dressed in full uniform and busy trying to buckle on his sword.*]

HJALMAR [*astonished*]. Father! Are you there!

GINA. Were you shooting in your room, Father?

EKDAL [*indignantly, coming into the room*]. What d'you mean by going shooting alone, Hjalmar?

HJALMAR [*tense, bewildered*]. Wasn't it you who fired that shot in the loft?

EKDAL. Me? A shot? Huh!

GREGERS [*calls to* HJALMAR]. She's shot the wild duck herself!

HJALMAR. What's all this! [*He rushes to the door of the loft, pulls it to one side, looks in and screams.*] Hedvig!

GINA [*running to the door*]. Dear God, what's the matter!

HJALMAR [*goes in*]. She's lying on the floor!

GREGERS. Hedvig! On the floor!

[*He goes in to* HJALMAR.]

GINA [*at the same time*]. Hedvig! [*She goes into the loft.*] Oh no! No!

EKDAL. Aha! *She's* gone off shooting too, eh?

[HJALMAR, GINA, *and* GREGERS *carry* HEDVIG *into the studio; her right hand hangs down, her fingers still gripping the pistol.*]

HJALMAR [*desperately*]. The pistol's gone off. She's been shot. Call for help! Help!

GINA [*runs into the hall and shouts down*]. Relling! Relling! Dr. Relling! Come up as fast as you can!

[HJALMAR *and* GREGERS *lay* HEDVIG *down on the sofa.*]

EKDAL [*quietly*]. The forest's revenge!

HJALMAR [*beside her on his knees*]. She'll come round soon. She'll come round. . . . Yes, yes.

GINA [*who has come in again*]. Where's she been shot? I can't see anything. . . .

[RELLING *hurries in, followed closely by* MOLVIK; *the latter has neither waistcoat nor collar, and his coat is flying open.*]

RELLING. What's going on here?

GINA. They say Hedvig has shot herself.

HJALMAR. Come here and help!

RELLING. Shot herself! [*He shifts the table to one side, and begins examining her.*]

HJALMAR [*looking anxiously up at him*]. It can't be anything serious, eh, Relling? She's hardly bleeding. Surely it can't be serious?

RELLING. How did this happen?

HJALMAR. Oh, how do I know. . . !

GINA. She wanted to shoot the wild duck.

RELLING. The wild duck?

HJALMAR. The pistol must have gone off.

RELLING. Hm! Indeed!

EKDAL. The forest's revenge. Still I'm not frightened.

[*He goes into the loft and shuts himself in.*]

HJALMAR. Well, Relling . . . why don't you say something?

RELLING. The bullet hit her in the breast.

HJALMAR. Yes, but she'll be coming round.

RELLING. Can't you see Hedvig is dead?

GINA [*bursts into tears*]. Oh my little one!

GREGERS [*huskily*]. In the briny deep . . .

HJALMAR [*springing up*]. No, no, she *must* live! Oh, for God's sake, Relling . . . just for a moment, just long enough for me to tell her how infinitely I loved her all the time!

RELLING. She was hit in the heart. Internal hæmorrhage. She died instantaneously.

HJALMAR. And I drove her away from me like some animal. And in terror she crept into the loft and died, for love of me. [*Sobbing.*] I can never make it up to her again! Never be able to tell her . . . ! [*He clenches his hands and cries to heaven.*] Oh, God on high . . . if Thou *art* there! Why hast Thou done this to me?

GINA. Hush, hush, you mustn't say such terrible things. We had no right to keep her, I dare say.

MOLVIK. The child is not dead; it sleeps.

RELLING. Rubbish!

HJALMAR [*more composed, goes over to the sofa and looks down on* HEDVIG *with folded arms*]. There she lies, stiff and still.

RELLING [*trying to free the pistol*]. It's so tight, so tight.

GINA. Please, Relling, don't force her little fingers. Leave the pistol there.

HJALMAR. She shall take it with her.

GINA. Yes, let her. But she mustn't lie out here for everybody to see. She shall go into her own little room, she shall. Help me with her, Hjalmar.

[HJALMAR *and* GINA *take* HEDVIG *between them.*]

HJALMAR [*as they carry her out*]. Oh, Gina, can you bear this?

GINA. We must help one another. For *now* she's as much yours as mine, isn't she?

MOLVIK [*stretches out his arms and mutters*]. Praised be the Lord. Earth to earth . . . earth to earth. . . .

RELLING [*whispers*]. Shut up, man! You are drunk!

[HJALMAR *and* GINA *carry the body out by the kitchen door.* RELLING *shuts it after them.* MOLVIK *sneaks out into the hall.*]

RELLING [*crosses to* GREGERS]. Nobody's ever going to persuade me this was an accident.

GREGERS [*who has stood horror-stricken, his face twitching*]. Nobody can say how this dreadful thing happened.

RELLING. There was a powderburn on her dress. She must have pressed the pistol right against her breast and fired.

GREGERS. Hedvig has not died in vain. Didn't you see how grief brought out what was noblest in him?

RELLING. Most people feel some nobility when they stand grieving in the presence of death. But how long do you suppose this glory will last in *his* case?

GREGERS. Surely it will continue and flourish for the rest of his life!

RELLING. Give him nine months and little Hedvig will be nothing more than the theme of a pretty little party piece.

GREGERS. You dare say that about Hjalmar Ekdal!

RELLING. We can discuss it again when the first grass starts showing on her grave. Then he'll bring it all up, all about 'the child so untimely torn from a loving father's heart'. Then you'll see him wallowing deeper and deeper in sentimentality and self-pity. Just you watch!

GREGERS. If *you* are right and *I* am wrong, life will no longer be worth living.

RELLING. Oh, life wouldn't be too bad if only these blessed people who come canvassing their ideals round everybody's door would leave us poor souls in peace.

GREGERS [*staring into space*]. In that case I am glad my destiny is what it is.

RELLING. If I may ask—what is your destiny?

GREGERS [*turning to leave*]. To be thirteenth at table.

RELLING. The devil it is!

ROSMERSHOLM
[Rosmersholm]

PLAY IN FOUR ACTS
(1886)

CHARACTERS

JOHANNES ROSMER, of Rosmersholm, a former clergyman

REBECCA WEST, resident at Rosmersholm

KROLL, Rosmer's brother-in-law, a headmaster

ULRIK BRENDEL

PETER MORTENSGAARD

MRS. HELSETH, housekeeper at Rosmersholm

The action takes place at Rosmersholm, an old family estate near a small coastal town in Western Norway

ACT ONE

The living-room at Rosmersholm, spacious, old-fashioned and comfortable. Against the wall, right front, is a stove decorated with fresh birch twigs and wild flowers. Further back is a door. On the back wall, folding doors open on to the entrance hall. On the wall, left, is a window in front of which is a stand with flowers and plants. Near the stove is a table with a sofa and easy chairs. The walls are hung with past and recent portraits of clergymen, officers and officials in their robes and uniforms. The window is open, so also is the hall door and the outer door. Outside can be seen an avenue of ancient trees leading to the estate. It is a summer evening; the sun has set.

REBECCA WEST is sitting in an easy-chair near the window, crocheting a large white woollen shawl which is nearly finished. From time to time she peeps out of the window from behind the flowers. Presently MRS. HELSETH enters from right.

MRS. HELSETH. Hadn't I better start laying the table for supper now, miss?

REBECCA. Yes, please. The pastor will probably be back soon.

MRS. HELSETH. Isn't there an awful draught where you are sitting, miss?

REBECCA. Yes, there is rather. Perhaps you would shut the window.

[MRS. HELSETH *goes over and shuts the door to the hall, then she crosses to the window.*]

MRS. HELSETH [*about to shut the window, looks out*]. But isn't that the pastor coming over there?

REBECCA [*quickly*]. Where? [*Rises.*] Yes, that's him. [*Behind the curtain.*] Come away from there. Don't let him see us.

MRS. HELSETH [*away from the window*]. Well, fancy that, miss! He is starting to use the path by the mill again.

REBECCA. He came by the mill-path a couple of days ago, too. [*Peeping from behind the curtain.*] But now we'll see whether . . .

MRS. HELSETH. Will he dare come across the footbridge?

REBECCA. That's just what I want to see. [*Pause.*] No, he's turning off. He's going round the top again today. [*Away from the window.*] It's a long way round.

MRS. HELSETH. Lord, so he is. I suppose it can't be easy for the pastor to face crossing *that* bridge again. Not after what happened there. . . .

REBECCA [*gathering up her crochet work*]. They cling long to their dead here at Rosmersholm.

MRS. HELSETH. It's my belief it's the dead that cling to Rosmersholm, miss.

REBECCA [*looking at her*]. The dead?

MRS. HELSETH. Yes, as though they couldn't tear themselves away from the ones they left behind, as you might say.

REBECCA. What makes you think that?

MRS. HELSETH. Well, otherwise that White Horse thing wouldn't keep coming around here, I'm sure.

REBECCA. Now, Mrs. Helseth, what *is* all this about the White Horse?

MRS. HELSETH. Oh, there's no point in talking about it. *You* wouldn't believe any of it anyway.

REBECCA. Do you believe in it then?

MRS. HELSETH [*goes and shuts the window*]. Oh, I'm not going to let you try to make me look a fool, miss. [*Looks out.*] Isn't that surely the pastor again, down on the path by the mill?

REBECCA [*looks up*]. Over there? [*Goes to the window.*] Of course not, it's the headmaster!

MRS. HELSETH. So it is of course, the headmaster.

REBECCA. Well, isn't that nice! He'll be on his way to visit us, you'll see.

MRS. HELSETH. Straight over the footbridge for him. Even though it *was* his own sister. Well, I'll go and lay the supper table now, miss.

[*She goes out to the right.* REBECCA *stands a moment at the window, then she waves, smiling and nodding. It is beginning to get dark.*]

REBECCA [*crosses to the door on the right and calls through it*]. Oh, Mrs. Helseth! You will try to find something special for supper please, won't you? You know what the headmaster likes best.

MRS. HELSETH [*outside*]. All right, miss. I'll see what can be done.

REBECCA [*opens the door to the entrance hall*]. Fancy, after all this time...! How delightful to see you again, Mr. Kroll. Do come in.

KROLL [*in the entrance hall, puts down his stick*]. Thank you. I hope I am not disturbing you?

REBECCA. You! For shame, Mr. Kroll, saying a thing like that!

KROLL [*comes in*]. You are always very kind. [*Looks about him.*] Is Rosmer up in his room by any chance?

REBECCA. No, he is out for a walk. He is rather later than usual. But he is bound to be back any minute now. [*Points to the sofa.*] Won't you sit down till he comes?

KROLL [*puts down his hat*]. Thank you very much. [*Sits down and looks round the room.*] How nice and gay you have got this old room looking. Flowers everywhere!

REBECCA. Mr. Rosmer is very fond of having fresh flowers about the place.

KROLL. And you are too, I imagine.

REBECCA. Yes, I find their fragrance so wonderfully soothing. That was a pleasure we had to deny ourselves earlier, of course.

KROLL [*nods sadly*]. Poor Beata couldn't bear the scent of flowers.

REBECCA. Nor the colours either. They used to upset her.

KROLL. Yes, I remember only too well. [*In a brisker tone.*] Well now, and how are things going on out here?

REBECCA. Oh, it's all very quiet and uneventful. One day very much like another. And how are things with you? Is your wife...?

KROLL. Ah, my dear Miss West, don't let's talk about my affairs. In a family there's always something or other that's not quite as it should be. Especially in times like these.

REBECCA [*after a pause, sits in an easy-chair near the sofa*]. You haven't once been out to see us during the vacation. Why is that?

KROLL. Well, you can't always be knocking on people's doors . . .

REBECCA. If you only knew how we had missed you. . . .

KROLL. . . . and apart from that I have been away, you know.

REBECCA. Yes, but just for a week or two. You have been going round all the political meetings, I gather?

KROLL [*nods*]. And what do you say to that? Did you ever imagine I would turn political agitator in my old age? Eh?

REBECCA [*smiles*]. You have always been *something* of an agitator, now, Mr. Kroll.

KROLL. Well yes, but just for my own private amusement. From now on, however, it's going to be in real earnest, I can tell you. Do you ever read any of these Radical papers?

REBECCA. Well, Mr. Kroll, I won't deny that . . .

KROLL. My dear Miss West, there can be no objection to that. Not in *your* case.

REBECCA. That's what I think, too. I have to keep up with things, find out what's going on. . . .

KROLL. Well now, I should never expect you . . . as a woman, I mean . . . to get mixed up in this dispute—this civil war, I might almost call it—that is raging here. But doubtless you have read the abusive things these 'men of the people' have been pleased to say about me? The outrageous insults they thought they could get away with?

REBECCA. Yes, but I thought you bit back pretty sharply.

KROLL. Indeed I did, although I say it myself. And now I have tasted blood, I'll show them that I'm not the sort of man to take things lying down. [*Breaks off.*] But there—don't let us go into that unpleasant and distressing business this evening.

REBECCA. No indeed, my dear Mr. Kroll.

KROLL. Tell me instead, how are you getting along here at Rosmersholm, now that you are on your own? Now that our poor Beata . . . ?

REBECCA. Oh, I get on quite well here, thank you. Of course, in many ways the place seems very empty now that she's gone. She is greatly missed, and greatly mourned . . . naturally. But otherwise . . .

KROLL. Do you intend staying on here? More or less permanently, I mean?

REBECCA. My dear Mr. Kroll, I haven't really thought about it, one way or the other. I have become so used to the place now, I almost feel I belong here.

KROLL. And so you do, I should say.

REBECCA. And as long as Mr. Rosmer feels that I can be of any use or comfort to him—well then, I'll be only too happy to stay, I suppose.

KROLL [*looks at her with some emotion*]. You know . . . there's something rather splendid about that—a woman giving up the best years of her young life, sacrificing them for the sake of others.

REBECCA. Oh, what else would I have had to live for?

KROLL. First, there was the constant strain of looking after your crippled foster-father who was so difficult. . . .

REBECCA. You mustn't think Dr. West was so difficult when we lived up in Finmark. It was those terrible sea voyages that finally broke him. But after we had moved down here . . . well yes, it was hard going for a year or two before he finally went to rest.

KROLL. And those years that followed, weren't they even harder for you?

REBECCA. No indeed, how can you say such a thing! When I was so genuinely fond of Beata. . . . And she, poor thing, so desperately in need of care and friendly sympathy.

KROLL. Thank you for speaking so charitably of her; it does you much credit.

REBECCA [*moves a little closer*]. Dear Mr. Kroll, you said that so sweetly and sincerely that I am sure you don't hold anything against me after all.

KROLL. Hold anything against you? What do you mean?

REBECCA. Well, it wouldn't really be very surprising if it upset you to see a stranger like me running things here at Rosmersholm.

KROLL. What on earth . . . ?

REBECCA. But it seems you don't. [*Holds out her hand.*] Thank you, Mr. Kroll, thank you for that.

KROLL. But what on earth made you think a thing like that?

REBECCA. When you didn't come out as often as before, I began to get a bit worried.

KROLL. Then, believe me, Miss West, you have been on the wrong track entirely. And besides, there's been no real change in things here. Towards the end, and while poor Beata was still alive, you were already in charge of things here. You and you alone.

REBECCA. But I was only acting on her behalf, in the wife's name, as it were.

KROLL. Well, anyway . . . do you know, Miss West . . . I shouldn't at all object, speaking personally, if ever you . . . But perhaps it doesn't do to say things like that.

REBECCA. What things?

KROLL. If it should ever happen that you were to take over the vacant place. . . .

REBECCA. I have the place I want, Mr. Kroll.

KROLL. Yes, in one sense perhaps. . . .

REBECCA [*interrupts him earnestly*]. For shame, Mr. Kroll. How can you sit there and joke about such things?

KROLL. Ah well, I dare say our good Johannes Rosmer thinks that he has had more than enough of matrimony. But all the same . . .

REBECCA. You know, I can't help smiling at you.

KROLL. All the same . . . Tell me, Miss West, if you don't mind my asking: how old are you, in fact?

REBECCA. Twenty-nine, I'm ashamed to say, Mr. Kroll. Going on for thirty.

KROLL. Quite so. And Rosmer . . . let me see, how old is he? He is five years younger than me, so he must be about forty-three. I think it would be very suitable.

REBECCA [*rises*]. Yes, yes. Eminently suitable I'm sure. . . . Will you stay for a cup of tea with us this evening. . . ?

KROLL. Thank you. I *had* thought of staying on a while. There's something I must talk to our good friend about.—Well now, Miss West, just so that you won't start getting any more wrong ideas, I must look out here a bit more often—as I did in the old days.

REBECCA. Oh yes, you *must*. [*Takes both his hands.*] Thank you, thank you. You really are awfully kind after all.

KROLL [*gruffly*]. Am I? That's more than they tell me at home.

[JOHANNES ROSMER *comes in by the door on the right.*]

REBECCA. Mr. Rosmer! Do you see who's sitting here?

ROSMER. Mrs. Helseth told me.

[KROLL *has risen.*]

ROSMER [*in a low choking voice, taking his hands*]. Welcome to this house again, my dear Kroll. [*Places his hands on* KROLL's *shoulders and looks into his eyes.*] My dear old friend! I felt sure things would come all right again between us.

KROLL. But my dear fellow! Don't say you also had this silly idea that something was wrong!

REBECCA [*to* ROSMER]. Isn't it marvellous! It was just our imagination.

ROSMER. Was it really, Kroll? But why were you so obviously keeping away from us?

KROLL [*earnestly and quietly*]. Because I didn't want to appear as a living reminder of those unhappy years . . . and of her who met her end in the millstream.

ROSMER. How good of you to think like that. You always were considerate. But it was quite unnecessary for you to stay away on that account. Come along now, let us sit down on the sofa. [*They sit.*] No, it really doesn't upset me to think about Beata. We talk about her every day. We feel as though she still belonged to the house.

KROLL. Do you really?

REBECCA [*lights the lamp*]. Yes, we really do.

ROSMER. It's rather what you might have expected. We were both so devoted to her. And both Reb . . . both Miss West and I, we know ourselves that we did everything in our power for the poor thing in her affliction. We have nothing to reproach ourselves with. That is why I find myself thinking quite calmly and tenderly about Beata now.

KROLL. You dear, good people! From now on I shall come out to see you every day.

REBECCA [*sits down in an easy-chair*]. Yes, and now all we've got to do is to see that you keep your word.

ROSMER [*rather hesitantly*]. Kroll, my dear fellow . . . I honestly wish there hadn't been this break between us. Ever since we first knew each other, it seemed the obvious thing that you should be the one I always turned to for advice. Ever since I was a student.

KROLL. I know, and it is something that I value very highly. Is there anything in particular now by any chance. . . ?

ROSMER. There are a great many things I would dearly like to talk over frankly with you. A sort of heart to heart talk.

REBECCA. Yes, there are, aren't there, Mr. Rosmer? I think it would be such a good thing . . . two old friends together. . . .

KROLL. And I have even more to talk to you about, believe me. Because I have now become an active politician, as you probably know.

ROSMER. Yes, I know you have. How did that happen?

KROLL. I had to, you know! Had to, whether I liked it or not. You just can't stand idly looking on any longer. Now that these wretched Radicals have got into power . . . it's high time . . . That's why I've persuaded our little circle of friends in town to get together. And not before time, I can tell you.

REBECCA [*with a faint smile*]. Yes, but isn't it a bit late, perhaps?

KROLL. I don't deny it would have been better to have stemmed the torrent a bit earlier. But who could have foreseen what was to come? Not me, anyway. [*Rises and walks up and down.*] Yes, now I've really had my eyes opened. For now these subversive ideas have found their way even into the school.

ROSMER. Into the school? But surely not into your school?

KROLL. Yes they have, I tell you. Into my own school! And what do you think? It has come to my knowledge that the sixth-form boys—or some of them, I should say—have been holding secret meetings for the past six months, and they have been taking Mortensgaard's paper!

REBECCA. Ah, the *Beacon*!

KROLL. Yes, there's a nice thing for future civil servants to feed their minds on, isn't it? But the saddest thing about the affair is that it's all the *clever* lads in the class who have banded together in this conspiracy against me. Only the duffers and the thickheads have kept out of it.

REBECCA. Do you feel very badly about it, Mr. Kroll?

KROLL. Very badly! When I see all my life's work thwarted and undermined like this! [*Lower.*] Yet I might almost have said I was ready to bear even *that*. But that's not the worst. [*Looks round.*] I suppose nobody is likely to be listening at the door?

REBECCA. No, of course not.

KROLL. Then you ought to know that this spirit of defiance and revolt has intruded even into my own home. Into the quiet of my own home! Destroying the peace and quiet of my family life!

ROSMER [*gets up*]. What's that you say? In your own home. . . ?

REBECCA [*goes over to* KROLL]. But my dear Mr. Kroll, what has happened?

KROLL. Would you believe that my own children . . . ? To put it in a nutshell, Lauritz is the ringleader of the group at school. And Hilda has embroidered a red cover to keep the *Beacon* in.

ROSMER. I would never have dreamt such a thing . . . to *you* . . . in your own house. . . .

KROLL. Quite! Who ever would have dreamt a thing like that was possible? In my own house, where obedience and order have always been the rule . . . where until now we've all thought and acted with one mind. . . .

REBECCA. How does your wife take all this?

Kroll: Conservative

KROLL. Now that is the most incredible thing of all. All her life she has shared my opinions and agreed with my views—in big things as well as small. Yet even she tends sometimes to take the children's side in some things. And then she puts the blame on *me* for what has happened. She says I domineer the children, bully them. . . . As though it weren't necessary to. . . . Well, that's the sort of upset going on at home. But naturally I talk about it as little as possible. Things like that are best hushed up. [*Wanders about the room.*] Yes, indeed.

[*He stops at the window, hands behind back, and looks out.*]

REBECCA [*goes over to* ROSMER *and speaks quickly in a low voice so that* KROLL *does not hear*]. Go on, do it!

ROSMER [*in the same tone*]. Not tonight.

REBECCA [*as before*]. Yes, do it now!

[*She moves away and busies herself with the lamp.*]

KROLL [*comes forward*]. Yes, my dear Rosmer, now you know how the spirit of the age has cast its shadow over both my domestic life and my professional activities. And these pernicious, demoralizing, disruptive ideas, don't you think I should fight them with all the weapons I can lay my hands on? Of course, my friend, that is what I mean to do. With the written as well as the spoken word.

ROSMER. And do you have any hopes of achieving anything that way?

KROLL. I can at least do my bit as a citizen, anyway. And I think it is incumbent on every patriotic and right-minded man to do the same. In fact, that is mainly why I have come to see you tonight.

ROSMER. But my dear friend, what do you mean? What do you want me to . . . ?

KROLL. You are going to stand by your old friends. Do as the rest of us are doing. Lend a hand as best you can.

REBECCA. But Mr. Kroll, you know how Mr. Rosmer dislikes that sort of thing.

KROLL. He must try and get over that dislike now. You don't keep properly abreast of things, Rosmer, sitting out here and burying yourself in this historical research of yours. Heavens above, man!

Family trees and things like that are all very well, but unfortunately
this just isn't the time for pursuits of that kind. You simply can't
imagine the state things are in up and down the country. Hardly a
single idea but what it hasn't been turned upside down. And what
an enormous job that's going to be, putting all these things right
again.

ROSMER. That I can well believe. But that kind of job isn't in my line
at all.

REBECCA. And besides I rather think that Mr. Rosmer has come to see
things with a clearer vision than before.

KROLL [*with a start*]. Clearer vision!

REBECCA. Yes, or more independent then. Less prejudiced.

KROLL. What is the meaning of this? Rosmer, surely you are not going
to let yourself be taken in so easily by this snap victory the mob
politicians have won.

ROSMER. My dear fellow, you know very well how little understanding I have of politics. But I certainly feel that in recent years people
have shown a rather greater measure of independence in their ways
of thinking.

KROLL. Indeed! And I suppose you obviously regard that as a good
thing! Anyway, you are vastly mistaken, my friend. Just you try
making a few inquiries about the views that are current among the
Radicals, both out here and in town. There's not a scrap of difference
between them and the precious words of wisdom the *Beacon* keeps
putting out.

REBECCA. Yes, Mortensgaard has a great deal of influence over people
in these parts.

KROLL. Yes, think of him too. A man with his murky past. A person
sacked from his teaching post for immoral conduct! A creature like
that setting himself up as a leader of the people. And he carries it off!
Actually carries it off! He's going to expand his paper, I hear. I
know on good authority he is looking for a capable assistant.

REBECCA. I'm only surprised that you and your friends don't set up
in opposition to him.

KROLL. That's precisely what we are now thinking of doing. We bought the *County Times* today. There was no difficulty about money. But . . . [*turns to* ROSMER] now I come to the real point of my visit to you. Our difficulty is going to be running it, you see . . . on the editorial side. Tell me, Rosmer, don't you feel in a way it's up to you to take it on, for the sake of the cause?

ROSMER [*in consternation*]. Me?

REBECCA. Whatever makes you think a thing like that!

KROLL. I can quite understand your horror of public meetings, not wanting to face all the heckling and things that go on there. But the more sequestered work of an editor, or is it more correct to say . . . ?

ROSMER. No, no, my dear friend. You must not ask me to do it.

KROLL. I would dearly love to have a shot at a thing like that myself, too. But it would be far too much for me. I have taken on such a mass of other things as it is. . . . But you, on the other hand, now that you are no longer burdened with any official duties . . . The rest of us will help you, of course, as best we can.

ROSMER. I can't, Kroll. I would be no good at it.

KROLL. No good at it! You said the same thing when your father got you your living. . . .

ROSMER. I was right. That was why I gave it up.

KROLL. Oh, if you are no worse an editor than you were a clergyman, we'll be content.

ROSMER. My dear Kroll . . . I must insist, once and for all, I cannot do it.

KROLL. All right. But anyway you will let us use your name.

ROSMER. My name?

KROLL. Yes, the name of Johannes Rosmer will in itself be an asset to the paper. The rest of us are looked on as distinct party men. I am told they are even trying to brand me personally as some desperate fanatic. So that if we use our own names for the paper, we cannot count on much of a circulation among the poor misguided masses. You, on the other hand, have always held yourself aloof from the fray. You are known as a tolerant and fair-minded man; your fine brain, your indisputable integrity are appreciated by everybody in the district. Then there's the esteem and respect that come from your once having been a clergyman. And on top of all there's the family name and all that that means.

ROSMER. Oh, the family name . . .

KROLL [*points to the portraits*]. The Rosmers of Rosmersholm . . . clergymen and soldiers . . . high officials . . . men of the highest principles, all of them . . . the foremost family in the district with its seat here now for nearly two hundred years. [*Lays his hand on* ROS-MER'S *shoulder*.] Rosmer, you owe it to yourself and to the traditions of your family to join in the fight to defend those things that have hitherto been held sacred in our community. [*Turns round*.] What do you say, Miss West?

REBECCA [*with a faint laugh*]. Mr. Kroll . . . I can't tell you how ludicrous all this sounds.

KROLL. What's that! Ludicrous!

REBECCA. Yes. For now I'm going to tell you straight. . . .

ROSMER [*quickly*]. No, no, don't! Not now!

KROLL [*looks from one to the other*]. But, my dear friends, what on earth . . . ? [*Breaks off*.] Hm!

[MRS. HELSETH *comes in by the door on the right*.]

MRS. HELSETH. There's a man at the kitchen door. He says he wants to see you, sir.

ROSMER [*relieved*]. Oh, is there? Ask him to come in, then.

MRS. HELSETH. In *here*, sir?

ROSMER. Certainly.

MRS. HELSETH. But he hardly looks the sort of person you would want in the living-room.

REBECCA. What does he look like, then, Mrs. Helseth?

MRS. HELSETH. Well, he's not all that much to look at, miss.

ROSMER. Didn't he tell you his name?

MRS. HELSETH. Yes, I think he said he was called Hekman or something like that.

ROSMER. I don't know anybody by that name.

MRS. HELSETH. He also said his name was Uldrik.

ROSMER [*with a start*]. Ulrik Hetman! Was that it?

MRS. HELSETH. Yes, Hetman, that was it.

KROLL. I seem to have heard that name before. . . .

REBECCA. Surely that was the name he used to write under, wasn't it, that strange man. . . ?

ROSMER [*to* KROLL]. It is Ulrik Brendel's pen-name.

KROLL. That waster Ulrik Brendel. So it is.

REBECCA. So he is still alive.

ROSMER. I thought he was on tour with some theatrical company.

KROLL. The last I heard of him he was in the workhouse.

ROSMER. Ask him to come in, Mrs. Helseth.

MRS. HELSETH. Very good, sir. [*She goes out.*]

KROLL. You are not really going to let this man into your house?

ROSMER. He was once my tutor, you know.

KROLL. Yes, I know that he went and crammed your head full of revolutionary ideas, and that your father drove him out of the house with a horsewhip.

ROSMER [*rather bitterly*]. Even at home Father was very much the major.

KROLL. You should thank him for that in his grave, my dear Rosmer. Well!

[MRS. HELSETH *opens the door on the right for* ULRIK BRENDEL *and then goes out, shutting the door. He is an impressive figure, with grey hair and beard, rather gaunt, but alert and vigorous. He is dressed like a common tramp. Threadbare frock-coat, down at heel, no sign of a shirt. He is wearing old black gloves, and carries a dirty soft hat crumpled under his arm and a walking stick in his hand.*]

BRENDEL [*first hesitates, then walks quickly over to* KROLL *with his hand outstretched*]. Good evening, Johannes!

KROLL. I beg your pardon. . . .

BRENDEL. You never expected to see me again, did you? Not inside these hated walls?

KROLL. I beg your pardon, but . . . [*points*] . . . over there.

BRENDEL [*turns round*]. Quite right. There we have him. Johannes . . . my boy . . . my well-beloved. . . .

ROSMER [*shakes his hand*]. My dear old teacher!

BRENDEL. In spite of certain memories, I felt I could not pass Rosmersholm without paying you a fleeting visit.

ROSMER. You are heartily welcome here now. Of that you may be sure.

BRENDEL. And this charming lady? [*Bows.*] Your lady wife, of course.

ROSMER. Miss West.

BRENDEL. A close relative, presumably. And yonder gentleman whom I do not know? A colleague, I see.

ROSMER. Mr. Kroll, headmaster of the grammar school.

BRENDEL. Kroll? Kroll? Wait a moment. Did you do languages when you were a student?

KROLL. Certainly I did.

BRENDEL. *Donnerwetter*, then I know you!

KROLL. I beg your pardon. . . .

BRENDEL. Weren't you . . .

KROLL. I beg your pardon. . . .

BRENDEL. . . . one of those paragons of virtue that had me thrown out of the Debating Society?

KROLL. That may well be. But I disclaim any closer acquaintance with you.

BRENDEL. All right! *Nach Belieben, Herr Doktor*. It doesn't make the slightest difference to me. Ulrik Brendel will remain the man he is, just the same.

REBECCA. I take it you are on your way to town, Mr. Brendel?

BRENDEL. Exactly, my good lady. At certain recurrent intervals I am compelled to exert myself in the battle for life. That is not something I enjoy doing; but ... *enfin* ... compelling necessity. ...

ROSMER. But my dear Mr. Brendel, won't you please let me give you something to help you out? Help you in some way or other, I mean. ...

BRENDEL. Ha! The very idea! Do you want to defile the bond that links us? Never, Johannes, never!

ROSMER. But what were you thinking of doing in town? Believe me, you won't find it easy. ...

BRENDEL. Leave that to me, my boy. The die is cast. What you see standing before you is one who has embarked on a great campaign, greater by far than all my previous enterprises put together. [*To* KROLL.] May I be allowed to inquire of the Herr Professor—*unter uns*—is there any reasonably decent and respectable and capacious meeting hall in your esteemed town?

KROLL. The biggest is in the Working Men's Institute.

BRENDEL. And has my learned friend any inside influence in this no doubt admirable institution?

KROLL. I have nothing whatever to do with it.

REBECCA [*to* BRENDEL]. You'll have to apply to Peter Mortensgaard.

BRENDEL. *Pardon, madame* ... and what sort of idiot is he?

ROSMER. What makes you think he is an idiot?

BRENDEL. Can't I tell straight away from his name that he is nothing but a plebeian.

KROLL. That's an answer I hadn't expected.

BRENDEL. But I shall control my feelings. There's nothing else for it. When one comes—as I have come—to a turning point in one's

career. . . . That's settled. I shall make contact with this individual
. . . initiate direct negotiations. . . .

ROSMER. Are you in earnest about having reached a turning point?

BRENDEL. Does my young friend not know that no matter where
Ulrik Brendel is, he is always in earnest? Yes, Johannes, I am going
to put on a new man . . . throw off this modesty and reserve I have
hitherto observed.

ROSMER. How. . . ?

BRENDEL. I shall lay hold on life with eager hands . . . I shall step forth
. . . mount up. It is the air of a tempestuous, cataclysmic age we
breathe. . . . I intend now to place my mite on the altar of liberty.

KROLL. You too?

BRENDEL [*to them all*]. Is the general public here in any way acquainted
with my occasional writings?

KROLL. No, quite frankly I must admit that . . .

REBECCA. I have read quite a number of them. My foster-father had
them.

BRENDEL. Then, my dear lady, you have been wasting your time. They
are just so much trash, I tell you.

REBECCA. Really?

BRENDEL. Those you have read, yes. My really important works are
known to nobody, man or woman. Not a soul . . . except myself.

REBECCA. How is that?

BRENDEL. Because they are unwritten.

ROSMER. But my dear Mr. Brendel . . .

BRENDEL. You know, my dear Johannes, that I am a bit of a sybarite,
a gourmet. Have been all my days. I like to take my pleasures in
solitude. For then I enjoy them twice as much. So you see, whenever
golden dreams came over me . . . enveloping me . . . whenever new
ideas were born within me, dazzling, audacious . . . when I felt the
rush of their beating wings . . . these things I formed into poems
and visions and images. In rough outline, as it were, you understand.

ROSMER. Yes, of course.

BRENDEL. Oh, what passions, what rapture have I known in my time, Johannes! The mysterious bliss of creation . . . in rough outline, as I said . . . the applause, the gratitude, the eulogies, the laurel crowns . . . all this I have abundantly gathered in with glad and trembling hands. Indulged myself in secret fantasies that my mind reeled with ecstasy. . . .

KROLL. Hm!

ROSMER. But you never wrote it down?

BRENDEL. Not a word! I have always felt quite nauseated at the thought of solemnly writing it all out. And anyway, why should I profane my own ideals when I could enjoy them in all their purity, and keep them to myself? But now they shall be sacrificed. In truth, I feel like a mother who gives her young daughters into the arms of their husbands. But sacrifice them I shall—sacrifice them on the altar of liberty. A series of well-conceived lectures . . . over the whole country. . . !

grandiose

REBECCA [*animatedly*]. How splendid of you, Mr. Brendel! You are giving the most precious thing you have.

ROSMER. The only thing.

REBECCA [*looks significantly at* ROSMER]. How many are there who do that? *Dare* do that?

ROSMER [*returns the look*]. Who knows?

BRENDEL. My audience is touched. That comforts my heart . . . and strengthens my will. And with that I thereby proceed to action. Yet there is *one* thing. . . . [*To* KROLL.] Can you tell me, my dear sir, whether there is such a thing as a Temperance Society in town? For total abstainers? Yes, of course, there must be.

KROLL. Yes, there is. I am its president, at your service.

BRENDEL. As if I couldn't tell by looking at you! Well, it is not impossible that I may look in on you and enrol myself for a week.

KROLL. You must forgive me—but we don't accept members by the week.

BRENDEL. *A la bonne heure*, my good sir! Ulrik Brendel never comes knocking round the door of societies of that kind. [*Turns.*] But I must not outstay my welcome in this house, so rich in memories. I must go to town and select a suitable lodging. There is, I presume, a decent hotel?

REBECCA. Won't you have a drink to warm you up before you go?

BRENDEL. How do you mean, gracious lady—to warm me up?

REBECCA. A cup of tea, or . . .

BRENDEL. To my generous hostess, my thanks. But I cannot impose any longer on private hospitality. [*Waves his hand.*] Farewell, good people. [*Goes towards the door but turns.*] Oh, by the way . . . Johannes . . . Pastor Rosmer, could you for old time's sake do your former tutor a favour?

ROSMER. With the greatest of pleasure.

BRENDEL. Good. Could you . . . for a day or two . . . lend me a clean dress shirt?

ROSMER. Is that all!

BRENDEL. You see I am travelling on foot . . . this time. My trunk is being sent on.

ROSMER. Of course. But is there nothing else, then?

BRENDEL. Well, as a matter of fact, there is. . . . Perhaps you could spare an old overcoat you have done with?

ROSMER. Yes, yes, certainly I can.

BRENDEL. And if there happened to be a decent pair of boots to go with the overcoat. . . .

ROSMER. We'll manage that too. We'll send them on as soon as we know your address.

BRENDEL. I wouldn't dream of it! All that inconvenience on my account. I can easily take these few odd things along with me.

ROSMER. Very well. Just come upstairs with me.

REBECCA. Let me go. Mrs. Helseth and I will see to it.

BRENDEL. I could never think of allowing this distinguished lady to . . .

REBECCA. Oh nonsense. Come along, Mr. Brendel.

[*She goes out to the right.*]

ROSMER [*holds* BRENDEL *back*]. Tell me . . . isn't there anything else I can do for you?

BRENDEL. I can't imagine what else there *could* be. Ah, yes, damn it all, there is . . . now that I think about it. . . ! Johannes . . . you haven't by any chance got eight crowns on you?

ROSMER. Let me see. [*Opens his purse.*] I have a couple of ten crown notes.

BRENDEL. Well, well, never mind. I'll just take those. I can always get them changed in town. Meanwhile, thanks very much. Don't forget, it was two ten crowns I got. Good night, Johannes, my own dear boy! And a respectful good night to you, sir!

[*He goes out to the right, where* ROSMER *takes leave of him and shuts the door behind him.*]

KROLL. Good God. . . . So that is the Ulrik Brendel people once believed would make something of himself in the world.

ROSMER [*quietly*]. At least he has had the courage to live his life in his own way. I don't think *that's* such a small thing after all.

KROLL. What! A life like his! I almost believe he's the sort who could turn your ideas upside down all over again.

ROSMER. Oh, no. Now I have got all my ideas straightened out.

KROLL. If only I could believe that, my dear Rosmer. You are so terribly impressionable in many ways.

ROSMER. Let us sit down. I want to talk to you.

KROLL. By all means.

[*They sit down on the sofa.*]

ROSMER [*after a pause*]. Don't you think it is nice and comfortable out here?

KROLL. Yes, it certainly is nice and comfortable—and peaceful. Yes, you have got yourself a home, Rosmer. And I have lost mine.

ROSMER. My dear friend, don't say that. The wound will always heal again.

KROLL. Never, never, the sting will always rankle. Things can never be as they were before.

ROSMER. I want you to listen to me, Kroll. We two have been close friends for many, many years now. Can you ever imagine our friendship finishing up on the rocks?

KROLL. I can't imagine anything in the world ever coming between us. Whatever has put this into your mind?

ROSMER. Because obviously it's immensely important to you to have your friends holding the same views and opinions as you.

KROLL. Well, yes. But we two are pretty well agreed. On the big questions, at any rate.

ROSMER [*quietly*]. No, not any longer.

KROLL [*makes to jump up*]. What is that!

ROSMER [*restraining him*]. You must sit still. I beg you, Kroll.

KROLL. What is all this? I don't understand you. Tell me straight.

ROSMER. In my mind, it is high summer once more. I see with a new youthful vision. And therefore I have taken my stand. . . .

KROLL. Where? Where do you stand?

ROSMER. Where your children stand.

KROLL. You? You! Surely it is impossible! Where, do you say?

ROSMER. I take my stand on the same side as Lauritz and Hilda.

KROLL [*bows his head*]. A renegade! Johannes Rosmer a renegade!

ROSMER. I ought to have been so glad, so sublimely happy, being what you call a renegade. But I suffered greatly, all the same, because I knew well enough it would come as a bitter disappointment to you.

KROLL. Rosmer . . . Rosmer! I shall never get over this. [*Looks sadly at him.*] Oh, to think that even you should want to lend yourself to the work of corrupting and perverting this unhappy country.

ROSMER. It is the work of liberation I want to take part in.

KROLL. Oh yes. That's what it's called both by those at the top and their poor dupes. But do you really think any sort of liberation can be expected from the doctrines now busy poisoning our whole social life?

ROSMER. I am no supporter of any prevailing doctrine, nor indeed of either side in the dispute. I want to try to bring men together from all sides. As many and as sincerely, as I can. I will devote my life and all my strength to this one thing: to create a true democracy in this land.

KROLL. Don't you think we have enough democracy already? For my part I think the whole lot of us are well on the way to being dragged down into the mud where the only ones to thrive are the common people.

ROSMER. That is precisely what makes me define the true aim of democracy.

KROLL. What is that?

ROSMER. To make all my countrymen noblemen.

KROLL. All. . . .

ROSMER. As many as possible, anyway.

KROLL. By what means?

ROSMER. By liberating their minds and purifying their wills, I should say.

KROLL. Rosmer, you are a dreamer. Are *you* going to liberate them? Are *you* going to purify them?

ROSMER. No, my dear friend. I only want to try and rouse them to it. As for *doing* it, that is their own affair.

KROLL. And you think they can?

ROSMER. Yes.

KROLL. And by their own power?

ROSMER. Exactly! By their own power! There is no other.

KROLL [*rises*]. Are these words that befit a clergyman?

ROSMER. I am no longer a clergyman.

KROLL. Yes, but . . . the religion you were brought up to. . . ?

ROSMER. Is no longer mine.

KROLL. No longer . . . !

ROSMER [*rises*]. I have given it up. I *had* to give it up, Kroll.

KROLL [*controlling his agitation*]. Indeed. Yes, yes. The two things doubtless go together. . . . Was that the reason you left the service of the church?

ROSMER. Yes. As soon as I had straightened out my ideas . . . when I was absolutely certain that it wasn't just some temporary aberration but instead something that I could not and would not escape from—then I left.

KROLL. And it has been working up inside you all this time. And we, your friends, were given no hint of it. Rosmer, Rosmer, how could you hide the sorrowful truth from us!

ROSMER. Because I thought it was something that concerned nobody but myself. And I didn't want to cause you or any of my other friends any unnecessary sorrow. I thought I could go on living here as before, quietly and happily. I wanted to read and to bury myself in all those works that had previously been closed books to me. To make myself thoroughly familiar with that great world of truth and freedom that has now been revealed to me.

KROLL. Apostasy! Every word proves it. But what makes you want to confess this secret apostasy at all? And why *now* exactly?

ROSMER. You yourself made me do it, Kroll.

KROLL. *I* made you. . . !

ROSMER. When I heard how violently you had been carrying on at the public meetings . . . when I read about all the uncharitable speeches you made there . . . all the hateful things you said about the people on the other side . . . the sneers, the contempt of your opponents . . . Oh, Kroll . . . how could you turn like that! There was no escaping my duty. In the present struggle men are growing evil. Their minds must be given a sense of peace and happiness and conciliation. That is why I now stand forth and openly confess to being what I am. I too want to try out my powers. Couldn't you . . . from your side . . . stand by me, Kroll?

KROLL. Never as long as I live will I compromise with these subversive forces in society.

ROSMER. Then let us at least fight with honourable weapons—since fight we must.

KROLL. Any man who is not with me in these critical matters, I want nothing whatever to do with. Nor do I owe him any consideration.

ROSMER. Does that also mean me?

KROLL. It is you who have broken with me, Rosmer.

ROSMER. *Is* this a breach then?

KROLL. This! It is a breach with all those who have previously stood by you. Now you must take the consequences.

[REBECCA WEST *comes in from the right and opens the door wide.*]

REBECCA. There we are. He is on his way now to his great sacrificial feast. Now we can have our supper. Won't you come in, Mr. Kroll?

KROLL [*takes his hat*]. Good night, Miss West. There is nothing more to keep me here.

REBECCA [*eagerly*]. What is this? [*Shuts the door and goes nearer.*] Have you told him. . . ?

ROSMER. Now he knows.

KROLL. We will not let you get away, Rosmer. We will force you back on our side again.

ROSMER. I shall never come back.

KROLL. We shall see. You are not the man to hold out alone.

ROSMER. I shall not be entirely alone, after all. There are two of us to bear the loneliness.

KROLL. Ah. . . ! [*A suspicion seems to cross his mind.*] Even that too! Beata's very words!

ROSMER. Beata. . . ?

KROLL [*dismissing the thought*]. No, no . . . that wasn't nice. . . . Forgive me.

ROSMER. What? What wasn't nice?

KROLL. No, let us not talk about it. Ugh! Forgive me. Goodbye!

[*He goes towards the hall door.*]

ROSMER [*follows him*]. Kroll! Things must not end like this between us. I'll look in on you tomorrow.

KROLL [*in the entrance hall, turns*]. You shall not set foot in my house.

[*He takes his stick and goes.* ROSMER *stands for a moment in the open door, then he shuts it and goes over to the table.*]

ROSMER. Never mind, Rebecca. We'll manage all right, we two firm friends. You and I.

REBECCA. What do you think he meant, Johannes, when he said 'That wasn't nice'?

ROSMER. Don't worry about that, my dear. He himself didn't really believe what he thought. But I'll look in and see him tomorrow. Good night!

REBECCA. You are not going up early again tonight? After this?

ROSMER. Tonight, as every night. I feel so relieved now that it is all over. You see, I am quite calm. And you, my dear Rebecca, you mustn't get upset either. Good night!

REBECCA. Good night, my dear. Sleep well.

[ROSMER *goes out by the hall door, and is then heard climbing the stairs.* REBECCA *walks over and pulls a bell-pull beside the stove. Shortly after* MRS. HELSETH *comes in from the right.*]

REBECCA. You might as well clear the table again, Mrs. Helseth. The pastor doesn't want anything . . . and the headmaster has gone home.

MRS. HELSETH. The headmaster gone! What was the matter with him, then?

REBECCA [*takes her crochet work*]. He thought it was blowing up for a storm. . . .

MRS. HELSETH. That's funny. There isn't a cloud in the sky tonight.

REBECCA. As long as he doesn't meet the White Horse, that's all. Because I am afraid it won't be long before we hear again from some of these spooks of yours.

MRS. HELSETH. God forgive you, miss! Don't say such dreadful things.

REBECCA. Well, well. . . .

MRS. HELSETH [*in a lower voice*]. Do you really think that somebody here is meant to go soon?

REBECCA. Of course not! I don't think anything of the sort. But there are so many kinds of White Horses in the world, Mrs. Helseth. Well, good night, I'm going to my room now.

MRS. HELSETH. Good night, miss.

[REBECCA *takes her crochet work and goes out right.*]

MRS. HELSETH [*turns down the lamp, shakes her head and mutters to herself*]. Lord! . . . Lord! . . . That Miss West. The things she says sometimes.

ACT TWO

JOHANNES ROSMER's *study. The way into it is through a door, left. At the back is a doorway with a curtain drawn back, leading to his bedroom. Right, a window, and in front of it a writing-table covered with books and papers. Bookshelves and cupboards line the walls. Simply furnished. Left, an old-fashioned sofa, with a table in front of it.* ROSMER, *in a smoking-jacket, is sitting on a high-backed chair at the writing-table. He is cutting the pages of a periodical, pausing now and again to read it. There is a knock on the door on the left.*

ROSMER [*without turning round*]. Come in.

[REBECCA WEST *enters, in a dressing-gown.*]

REBECCA. Good morning.

ROSMER [*thumbing through his book*]. Good morning, my dear. Was there something you wanted?

REBECCA. I just wanted to ask if you had slept well.

ROSMER. Oh, I had such a lovely deep sleep. No dreams. . . . [*Turns.*] And you?

REBECCA. Yes, thanks . . . eventually, in the early hours of the morning. . . .

ROSMER. I can't remember feeling as light-hearted as this for a long time. Oh, what a good thing I got it off my chest.

REBECCA. Yes, you shouldn't have kept it to yourself so long, Johannes.

ROSMER. I can't understand how I could be such a coward.

REBECCA. Well, it wasn't exactly cowardice. . . .

ROSMER. Oh yes, it was. When I look closely at things, I can see it was partly cowardice.

REBECCA. All the more courageous of you then to make a clean break. [*Sits down on a chair beside him at the writing-table.*] But now I want to tell you something I've done . . . but you mustn't be angry with me about it.

ROSMER. Angry? My dear, whatever makes you think . . . ?

REBECCA. Yes, because I did perhaps rather take it upon myself.

ROSMER. Well, let me hear it then.

REBECCA. Last night, when this man Ulrik Brendel was leaving . . . I wrote him two or three lines to give to Mortensgaard.

ROSMER [*rather doubtfully*]. But, my dear Rebecca. . . . Well, what did you say then?

REBECCA. I said that if he could do anything for this unfortunate man, and help him in any way, he would be doing you a service.

ROSMER. My dear, you shouldn't have done that. You won't have done Brendel any good by it. And Mortensgaard is a man I would much rather keep away from. You remember the business I had with him once before.

REBECCA. But don't you think it might be as well to be on good terms with him again?

ROSMER. Me? With Mortensgaard? Whatever makes you think that?

REBECCA. Well, because things might be a bit uncertain now, you know . . . now this business has arisen between you and your friends.

ROSMER [*looks at her and shakes his head*]. You don't really imagine that Kroll or the others would feel in any way vindictive. . . ?

REBECCA. In their first flush of anger, my dear . . . nobody can be sure. After the way Mr. Kroll took it . . .

ROSMER. Oh, you know him better than that, surely. Kroll is every inch a gentleman. I am going to town this afternoon to have a talk with him. I want to talk to them all. Oh, it will all be all right, you'll see. . . .

[MRS. HELSETH *appears at the door, left.*]

REBECCA [*gets up*]. What is it, Mrs. Helseth?

MRS. HELSETH. Mr. Kroll is downstairs in the hall.

ROSMER [*gets up quickly*]. Kroll!

REBECCA. Mr. Kroll! Well!

MRS. HELSETH. He asked if he could come up and have a word with the pastor.

ROSMER [*to* REBECCA]. What did I tell you! Of course he can. [*Goes to the door and shouts down the stairs.*] Do come up, my dear fellow. I am delighted to see you.

[ROSMER *stands holding the door open.* MRS. HELSETH *goes.* REBECCA *draws the curtain over the doorway, then tidies up the room a little.* KROLL *enters, carrying his hat.*]

ROSMER [*quietly, with emotion*]. I knew it . . . knew it couldn't be the last time. . . .

KROLL. Today I see things in an altogether different light from yesterday.

ROSMER. Yes, of course you do, Kroll, don't you? Now that you have had time to give it more thought. . . .

KROLL. You completely misunderstand me [*Puts his hat on the table near the sofa.*] It is important I talk to you alone.

ROSMER. Why can't Miss West . . . ?

REBECCA. No, no, Mr. Rosmer. I'll go.

KROLL [*looks her up and down.*] You must excuse me, Miss West, for calling so early in the morning . . . for catching you unawares before you had time to . . .

REBECCA [*surprised*]. What do you mean? Do you think it's not right I should wear a dressing-gown about the house?

KROLL. Heaven forbid! I have, of course, no idea what the done thing is now at Rosmersholm.

ROSMER. But, Kroll . . . you are like a different person today.

REBECCA. Good morning to you, Mr. Kroll.

[*She goes out left.*]

KROLL. If you will allow me. . . . [*He sits down on the sofa.*]

ROSMER. Yes, my dear fellow, let's sit down together comfortably and talk things over. [*He sits down in a chair facing* KROLL.]

KROLL. I didn't sleep a wink last night. I lay awake the whole night, thinking and thinking.

ROSMER. And what do you say today?

KROLL. It's a long story, Rosmer. Let me begin with a sort of introduction. I can give you a short report about Ulrik Brendel.

ROSMER. Has he been to see you?

KROLL. No. He settled himself in a low public house, in the lowest of company, of course, drinking and standing drinks as long as his money lasted. Then he began abusing the whole company as a lot of riff-raff—in which incidentally he was quite right—whereupon they set on him and threw him out into the gutter.

ROSMER. It seems he is quite incorrigible.

KROLL. He had also pawned your coat, but they say that has been redeemed for him. Can you guess by whom?

ROSMER. By you yourself, perhaps?

KROLL. No. By our worthy Mr. Mortensgaard.

ROSMER. Indeed.

KROLL. I have been given to understand that Mr. Brendel's first call was upon this 'idiot' and 'plebeian'.

ROSMER. Well, it was very lucky for him. . . .

KROLL. Indeed it was. [*Leans over the table towards* ROSMER.] But that brings us to something which—for the sake of our old . . . our former friendship—it is my duty to warn you about.

ROSMER. My dear fellow, whatever can *that* be?

KROLL. I'll tell you: some game or other is going on in this house behind your back.

ROSMER. What makes you think that? Is it Reb . . . is it Miss West you are referring to?

KROLL. Exactly. I can well understand her point of view. She's been used to having her way so long now in this place. But all the same . . .

ROSMER. My dear Kroll, you are completely mistaken about this. She and I—we have no secrets from each other about anything in the world.

KROLL. Has she confessed, then, that she has been in correspondence with the editor of the *Beacon*?

ROSMER. Oh, you are referring to the few lines she wrote for Ulrik Brendel to take.

KROLL. So you are on to that. And do you approve of her thus forming an association with that scandalmonger who week after week sets out to make a laughing stock of me, both as a schoolmaster and as a public figure?

ROSMER. My dear Kroll, I am sure that side of things never once occurred to her. And in any case, she is a completely free agent, of course, just as I am.

KROLL. Indeed? I take it that's another of these new ideas you have gone in for. I suppose Miss West takes the same view of things as you?

ROSMER. She does. We two have advanced together, trusting in each other.

KROLL [*looks at him and slowly shakes his head*]. Oh, you poor, blind, dupe!

ROSMER. Me? What makes you say a thing like that?

KROLL. Because I dare not . . . *will* not think the worst. No, no, let me finish. You really do value my friendship, don't you, Rosmer? And my respect, too? Don't you?

ROSMER. Surely I don't have to answer that question.

KROLL. All right. But there are other things that do demand an answer . . . a full explanation from you. Would you be willing to submit to a sort of interrogation. . . ?

ROSMER. Interrogation?

KROLL. Yes . . . to let me ask some questions about one or two things that you might find it painful to be reminded of? For instance, this business of your apostasy . . . well, your emancipation, as you like to call it. . . . It's all bound up with so many other things that you must, for your own sake, try to explain.

ROSMER. My dear Kroll, ask about whatever you like. I have nothing to hide.

KROLL. Tell me then . . . what do you think in fact was the *real* reason why Beata went and put an end to her life?

ROSMER. Can you be in any doubt about that? Or rather is it possible to inquire into the reasons why a sick unhappy woman of unsound mind does what she does?

KROLL. Are you certain that Beata really was of unsound mind? The doctors at any rate thought perhaps it wasn't certain.

ROSMER. If the doctors had ever seen her as I so often saw her, day and night, they would never have had any doubt.

KROLL. Nor had I, then.

ROSMER. Oh, no! There wasn't a shadow of doubt, I regret to say. I told you, didn't I, about her wild fits of sensual passion . . . which she expected me to respond to. Oh! how she appalled me. And then there was the way she used to reproach herself quite unnecessarily about certain things towards the end.

KROLL. Yes, when she had been told that she would never have any children.

ROSMER. Well, I put it to you. . . . All this dreadful agony of mind about something that wasn't her fault at all. . . ! And is she really supposed to have been in her right mind?

KROLL. Hm! Can you remember if you had any books in the house at the time dealing with the institution of marriage, giving the modern, advanced view.

ROSMER. I remember Miss West did lend me a book of that sort. She inherited Dr. West's library. But my dear Kroll, you could never imagine we were so thoughtless as to let the poor ailing creature get hold of ideas like that? I give you my solemn assurance we are not to blame. It was her own disordered mind that drove her to those wild aberrations.

KROLL. One thing, however, I can now tell you. And that is that poor Beata, tormented and over-wrought, put an end to her own life so that you might be happy . . . and free to live your own life as you wanted.

ROSMER [*half rising from his chair*]. What do you mean by that?

KROLL. Listen to me quietly, Rosmer. Now I can speak about it. Twice in the last twelve months before her death she came to see me, and she poured out all her feelings of agony and despair.

ROSMER. About what you just said?

KROLL. No, the first time she came, she declared you were well on the way to apostasy. That you were going to abandon the faith of your fathers.

ROSMER [*eagerly*]. What you are saying is impossible, Kroll. Quite impossible! You must be mistaken.

KROLL. Why is that?

ROSMER. Because while Beata was alive I was still wrestling with my own doubts. It was a fight I fought alone and in utter secrecy. I don't even believe that Rebecca . . .

KROLL. Rebecca?

ROSMER. Well, then . . . Miss West. I call her Rebecca for convenience.

KROLL. So I have noticed.

ROSMER. That's why I find it quite incomprehensible that anything of the kind should ever have occurred to Beata. And why didn't she talk to me about it? She never did, never a single word.

KROLL. Poor soul. She begged and implored me to speak to you.

ROSMER. And why didn't you?

KROLL. Do you think at that time I doubted for one moment that she might not have been out of her mind. An accusation of that kind against a man like you! And then . . . it must have been about a month after . . . she came again. This time she looked a bit calmer.

But as she was leaving she said: 'They can expect to see the White Horse at Rosmersholm again soon.'

ROSMER. Yes, yes. The White Horse—she was always talking about that.

KROLL. And when I tried to distract her from these morbid ideas, she just answered: 'I haven't much time left. Because now Johannes must marry Rebecca at once.'

ROSMER [*almost speechless*]. What did you say? I marry . . . !

KROLL. That was the Thursday afternoon. On the Saturday evening she threw herself off the bridge into the millstream.

ROSMER. And you never warned us!

KROLL. You knew yourself how often she used to make remarks about not having long to live.

ROSMER. I know. But all the same, you *should* have warned us!

KROLL. I did think of it. But by then it was too late.

ROSMER. And all this time you didn't . . . ? Why have you kept quiet about all this?

KROLL. What was the good of coming here and worrying you and upsetting you still more. Naturally I took it all as a mere figment of her disordered brain. Until yesterday evening.

ROSMER. And now you think differently?

KROLL. Didn't Beata see things clearly enough when she said you were going to abandon the faith you were brought up to?

ROSMER. Yes, that I don't understand. I find that absolutely incomprehensible.

KROLL. Incomprehensible or not, there it is. And now I ask you, Rosmer, how much truth is there in that other accusation of hers? In the last one, I mean?

ROSMER. Accusation? Was that an accusation?

KROLL. Perhaps you didn't notice how it was phrased. She wanted to go, she said. . . . Why? Well?

ROSMER. So that I might marry Rebecca. . . .

KROLL. That wasn't quite the way it was put. Beata expressed herself rather differently. She said, 'I haven't much time left. Because now Johannes must marry Rebecca at once.'

ROSMER [*looks at him for a moment, then rises*]. Now I understand you, Kroll.

KROLL. Well, then? What is your answer?

ROSMER [*quietly and controlled*]. To anything so absolutely unheard-of. . . ! The only proper answer would be to point to the door.

KROLL [*rises*]. Very well.

ROSMER [*stands facing him*]. Listen to me. For over a year now—in fact ever since Beata died—Rebecca West and I have lived on here at Rosmersholm alone. All that time you have known of Beata's charge against us. But never at any time have I observed the slightest sign that you disapproved of Rebecca and me living here together.

KROLL. I didn't know until last night that it was a question of an apostate and . . . an emancipated woman living under one roof.

ROSMER. Ah. . . ! So you don't think there is any sense of virtue to be found among free-thinkers? Doesn't it strike you they might have a natural instinct for morality?

KROLL. I don't place much reliance on any kind of morality that is not rooted in the faith of the Church.

ROSMER. And you include Rebecca and me in that too? My relations with Rebecca. . . !

KROLL. I cannot bring myself, merely on your account, to abandon my view that there is no tremendous gulf between free-thinking and . . . hm!

ROSMER. And what?

KROLL. . . . and free-love, if you must have it.

ROSMER [*gently*]. And you have no shame in saying that to me? You who have known me since I was a boy.

KROLL. That's exactly why. I know how easily you are influenced by those you associate with. And this Rebecca of yours . . . well, Miss West, then . . . we don't really know very much about her. I tell

you straight, Rosmer, I'm not letting you go. And you yourself . . .
you must try and save yourself while there's time.

ROSMER. Save myself? What . . . ?

[MRS. HELSETH *looks in through the door on the left.*]

ROSMER. What do you want?

MRS. HELSETH. I wanted to ask Miss West if she would come downstairs.

ROSMER. Miss West is not up here.

MRS. HELSETH. Isn't she? [*Looks about her.*] That's funny. [*She goes.*]

ROSMER. You were saying . . . ?

KROLL. Listen. Whatever went on here in secret while Beata was still
alive . . . and whatever is still going on here . . . I don't want to
inquire into any further. Your marriage was admittedly a very
unhappy one. And in one way that might well be taken as an
excuse. . . .

ROSMER. Oh, how little you really know me. . . !

KROLL. Don't interrupt me. What I want to say is this: if you *must* go
on living here with Miss West, then it's absolutely essential that
this change of heart of yours—this tragic defection she has led you
into—is kept hushed up. Let me speak! Let me speak! What I say
is this: if this madness must go on, then in Heaven's name go ahead
and *think* whatever you like . . . about anything under the sun. But
see that you keep your opinions to yourself. After all it's a purely
personal affair. There's no necessity to go shouting a thing like that
all over the countryside.

ROSMER. But there *is* a necessity for me to extricate myself from a
false and ambiguous position.

KROLL. But you have a duty towards the traditions of your family,
Rosmer. Remember that. Since time immemorial Rosmersholm has
been like a stronghold of order and high thinking . . . of respect and
esteem for all those things which are accepted and acknowledged by
the best people in our society. If ever the rumour got about that
you yourself had abandoned what I might call the Rosmer tradition,
it would lead to disastrous and irreparable confusion.

ROSMER. My dear Kroll, I cannot bring myself to see the matter in that light. To me it seems I have a bounden duty to bring a little light and happiness into those places where the Rosmers have spread gloom and oppression all these long years.

KROLL [*looks sternly at him*]. Yes, that would indeed be an undertaking worthy of the man who is the last of his line. Leave such things alone, Rosmer. You are not cut out for that sort of work. You were made for the academic life.

ROSMER. Yes, that may be so. But now I also want to take part in the battle of life.

KROLL. The battle of life . . . do you know what that will mean for you? It means a fight to the death against every one of your friends.

ROSMER [*quietly*]. I don't suppose they are all such fanatics as you.

KROLL. You are a gullible creature, Rosmer. Inexperienced, that's what you are. You have no idea of the fury of the storm that will break over your head.

[MRS. HELSETH *puts her head through the door, left.*]

MRS. HELSETH. Miss West would like to know . . .

ROSMER. What is it?

MRS. HELSETH. There's a man downstairs who would like a word with the pastor.

ROSMER. Is it the man who was here last night?

MRS. HELSETH. No, it's Mortensgaard.

ROSMER. Mortensgaard!

KROLL. Aha! So it's come to that, has it? Already!

ROSMER. What does he want with me? Why didn't you send him away?

MRS. HELSETH. Miss West told me to ask if he was to come up.

ROSMER. Tell him there's somebody here. . . .

KROLL [*to* MRS. HELSETH]. Let him come up.

[MRS. HELSETH *goes.*]

KROLL [*takes his hat*]. I quit the field—for the time being. But the main action is still to be fought.

ROSMER. As true as I stand here, Kroll . . . I have nothing to do with Mortensgaard.

KROLL. I don't believe you any more. Not in anything. Not on any matter at all can I believe you after this. Now it is war to the knife. We must see if we cannot render you harmless.

ROSMER. Oh, Kroll . . . how low you have sunk!

KROLL. I? You can talk! Remember Beata!

ROSMER. Are you going to bring that up all over again?

KROLL. No. The mystery of the millstream you must try to solve in the light of your own conscience . . . if you still have one.

[PETER MORTENSGAARD *enters softly and quietly through the door on the left. He is a small, slightly-built man with reddish hair and beard.*]

KROLL [*with a look of hate*]. So! The *Beacon*, eh! Burning at Rosmersholm. [*Buttons his coat.*] Well, now I can have no doubt about what course to steer.

MORTENSGAARD [*quietly*]. The *Beacon* will always be burning to guide Mr. Kroll home.

KROLL. Yes, you have given plenty of evidence of your good will. Actually, one of the Commandments does tell us that we shouldn't bear false witness against our neighbour. . . .

MORTENSGAARD. You don't have to teach me about the Commandments, Mr. Kroll.

KROLL. Not even the Seventh?

ROSMER. Kroll!

MORTENSGAARD. If anybody had to do it, then the obvious person would be the pastor here.

KROLL [*with suppressed scorn*]. The pastor? Yes, Pastor Rosmer is without doubt the obvious person for *that*. I wish you a profitable discussion, gentlemen.

[*He goes out, slamming the door after him.*]

ROSMER [*stares fixedly at the door, and speaks to himself*]. Well, well. . . . So be it then. [*Turns.*] Now will you tell me, Mr. Mortensgaard, what brings you out here to see me?

MORTENSGAARD. Actually, it was Miss West I was looking for. I felt I had to thank her for the kind letter I got from her yesterday.

ROSMER. I know she wrote to you. Have you had a word with her?

MORTENSGAARD. Yes, for a minute. [*With a slight smile.*] I hear that certain ideas have changed out here at Rosmersholm.

ROSMER. My ideas have changed about quite a lot of things. I might almost say . . . about everything.

MORTENSGAARD. That's what Miss West said. And that's why she thought I had better come up and have a little talk with you about certain things.

ROSMER. About what things, Mr. Mortensgaard?

MORTENSGAARD. Can I put it in the *Beacon* about you changing your ideas . . . that you support the radical progressive policy?

ROSMER. Certainly you may. Indeed I'd even go so far as to *ask* you to put it in.

MORTENSGAARD. It will be in first thing in the morning. It's news of considerable importance when Pastor Rosmer of Rosmersholm takes the view that he can seek the light in the other sense as well.

ROSMER. I don't altogether understand you.

MORTENSGAARD. What I mean is that it contributes to the moral backing of our party every time we get a supporter with serious Christian principles.

ROSMER [*in some surprise*]. Then you don't know . . . ? Didn't Miss West tell you *that* as well?

MORTENSGAARD. Tell me what, Pastor Rosmer? Miss West was in rather a hurry. She told me to come upstairs and hear the rest from you.

ROSMER. Then I must tell you that my emancipation is total. In all things. I have severed all connection with the teachings of the Church. From now on, such things are of absolutely no concern to me.

MORTENSGAARD [*looks at him in amazement*]. Never! If the moon fell out of the sky, I couldn't be more . . . ! Even the pastor himself renouncing . . .

ROSMER. Yes, I have reached the same stage that you reached long ago. So you can announce *that* in the *Beacon*, too.

MORTENSGAARD. That too? No, my dear pastor. Forgive me, but there's no point in mentioning that aspect of the thing.

ROSMER. Not mention it?

MORTENSGAARD. Not to begin with, I mean.

ROSMER. But I don't understand. . . .

MORTENSGAARD. Look, Pastor Rosmer. . . . I dare say you are not so familiar with the ins and outs of things as I am. But now that you have come over to the radical cause, and if—as Miss West says— you are thinking of taking an active part in the movement, then I suppose you'll want to do all you possibly can to help.

ROSMER. Yes, I most certainly do.

MORTENSGAARD. Well, I'd better just make clear, Pastor Rosmer, that if you come out with all this about throwing up the Church, it will be like tying your own hands right from the very start.

ROSMER. Do you think so?

MORTENSGAARD. Yes, you can be quite sure there'll not be very much you can do then in these parts. And besides, we've got plenty of free-thinkers already, Pastor Rosmer. I might almost say too many. What the party really needs is Christian elements—something that everybody has to respect. That's what we are badly short of. So the wisest thing for you to do is to keep quiet about any of the things that don't really concern the public. There, that's what I think.

ROSMER. I see. So you wouldn't dare have anything to do with me if I openly confessed my apostasy?

MORTENSGAARD [*shakes his head*]. I wouldn't like to risk it, Pastor Rosmer. Lately I have made it a rule never to support anybody or anything opposed to the Church.

ROSMER. And have you returned to the Church yourself then, of late?

MORTENSGAARD. We needn't go into that.

ROSMER. So that's how it is, then. Yes, now I understand you.

MORTENSGAARD. Pastor Rosmer, you ought to remember that I of all people am not wholly free to act as I wish.

ROSMER. What's stopping you then?

MORTENSGAARD. The thing that stops me is that I am a marked man.

ROSMER. Ah . . . of course.

MORTENSGAARD. A marked man, Pastor Rosmer. You in particular ought to remember that. For you more than anybody else were the person who had me branded.

ROSMER. If I had thought then as I now think, I would have dealt with your transgression much more considerately.

MORTENSGAARD. That I can well imagine. But now it is too late. You have branded me once and for all, branded me for life. I don't suppose you really understand what a thing like that means. But now, perhaps, you will soon see for yourself how painful it feels, Pastor Rosmer.

ROSMER. I?

MORTENSGAARD. Yes, surely you never believe that Kroll and his crowd will show any mercy for the way you have deserted them. And the *County Times* is out for blood, they say. You yourself could quite easily become a marked man, too.

ROSMER. I feel secure against any attack on personal grounds, Mr. Mortensgaard. My conduct cannot be impugned.

MORTENSGAARD [*with a faint smile*]. That's a bold thing to say, Pastor Rosmer.

ROSMER. Perhaps it is. But it is one I feel justified in being so bold about.

MORTENSGAARD. Even if you were to scrutinize your own conduct as thoroughly as you once scrutinized mine?

ROSMER. You say that so strangely. What are you getting at? Is there something specific?

MORTENSGAARD. Yes, there is 'one thing. Just one. But *that* could be bad enough if any of those malicious people on the other side got wind of it.

ROSMER. Be good enough to tell me what this thing is supposed to be.

MORTENSGAARD. Can't you guess, Pastor Rosmer?

ROSMER. No, I can't. I haven't the faintest idea.

MORTENSGAARD. In that case then, I might as well tell you. I have in my possession a strange letter that was written here at Rosmersholm.

ROSMER. Miss West's letter, you mean. Is it so strange?

MORTENSGAARD. No, there's nothing strange about that letter. But I got another letter from this place once.

ROSMER. Also from Miss West?

MORTENSGAARD. No, Pastor Rosmer.

ROSMER. Well, from whom, then? From whom?

MORTENSGAARD. From the late Mrs. Rosmer.

ROSMER. From my wife! *You* got a letter from my wife?

MORTENSGAARD. Yes, I did.

ROSMER. When?

MORTENSGAARD. Not long before she died. It must be about eighteen months ago, now. And that letter is the one that is strange.

ROSMER. You know of course that my wife had had a mental breakdown at that time.

MORTENSGAARD. Yes, I know there were many people who thought that. I doubt if you would think so from the letter. When I say the letter is strange, I mean in a different sense.

ROSMER. And what on earth did my poor wife want to write to you about?

MORTENSGAARD. I have the letter at home. She begins by saying more or less that she is living in fear and trembling; there are so many wicked people in the district, she says; and all these people think about is what harm they can do you.

ROSMER. Me?

MORTENSGAARD. So she said. And then came the strangest bit of all. Shall I go on, Pastor Rosmer?

ROSMER. Of course! Tell me all. Don't keep anything back.

MORTENSGAARD. Your wife begged and implored me to be magnanimous. She was aware, she said, that it was the pastor who had had me dismissed from the school. And she implored me earnestly not to revenge myself.

ROSMER. How did she imagine you might revenge yourself?

MORTENSGAARD. It says in the letter that if I heard any rumours about certain shameful things supposed to be going on at Rosmersholm, I hadn't to pay any attention to them; it would only be things put about by those wicked people in order to distress you.

ROSMER. Does it say that in the letter?

MORTENSGAARD. You can read it yourself, Pastor Rosmer, at any time.

ROSMER. But I don't understand. . . ! What did she imagine these wicked rumours would be about?

MORTENSGAARD. In the first place, that you were supposed to have renounced your religious beliefs. This your wife firmly denied—at that time. And then . . . hm. . . .

ROSMER. Then?

MORTENSGAARD. Yes, then she says . . . it's a bit confused, this . . . that she is quite unaware of any immoral relations at Rosmersholm. That she has never been wronged in any way. And if there ever should be any rumours to that effect, she implores me not to refer to them in the *Beacon*.

ROSMER. No mention of any names?

MORTENSGAARD. No.

ROSMER. Who brought you the letter?

MORTENSGAARD. I promised not to tell. It was brought to me one evening after dark.

ROSMER. If you had taken the trouble to inquire at the time, you would have learned that my poor unfortunate wife was not quite in her right mind.

MORTENSGAARD. I did inquire, Mr. Rosmer. But I must say, I didn't exactly get *that* impression.

ROSMER. You didn't? But why have you chosen this moment to tell me about this old and confused letter?

MORTENSGAARD. As a warning to be extremely careful, Pastor Rosmer.

ROSMER. In my personal affairs, you mean?

MORTENSGAARD. Yes, remember you have now lost any immunity you might have had in the past.

ROSMER. You seem convinced there's something here to hide.

MORTENSGAARD. I don't see any reason why an emancipated man shouldn't live as full a life as possible. But, as I said, just be careful from now on. If any rumours get around that offend against the proprieties, you can be sure the reputation of the whole radical movement will suffer. Goodbye, Pastor Rosmer.

ROSMER. Goodbye.

MORTENSGAARD. I am going straight to my office to put the great news in the *Beacon*.

ROSMER. Put it all in.

MORTENSGAARD. I'll put in everything that the dear public needs to know.

[*Bows and goes out.* ROSMER *remains standing in the doorway whilst* MORTENSGAARD *goes downstairs. The sound of the outer door being shut is heard.*]

ROSMER [*calls softly from the doorway*]. Rebecca! Reb . . . hm. [*Loudly.*] Mrs. Helseth, isn't Miss West down there?

MRS. HELSETH [*is heard downstairs in the hall*]. No, sir, she's not here.

[*The curtain at the back of the room is drawn back.* REBECCA *appears in the doorway.*]

REBECCA. Johannes!

ROSMER [*turns*]. Were you in my bedroom! My dear, what were you doing there?

REBECCA [*goes up to him*]. I was listening.

ROSMER. Oh, Rebecca, but how could you!

REBECCA. Certainly, why not? He was so nasty, the way he spoke about my dressing-gown. . . .

ROSMER. Ah, so you were also in there when Kroll . . . ?

REBECCA. Yes, I wanted to know what he was after.

ROSMER. I would have told you.

REBECCA. You would hardly have told me everything. And certainly not in his own words.

ROSMER. Did you hear everything?

REBECCA. Most of it I think. I had to go downstairs for a moment when Mortensgaard came.

ROSMER. And then you came up again. . . .

REBECCA. Don't take it so badly, my dear.

ROSMER. You must always do what you think is right and proper. You are a free agent. . . . But what do you make of all this, Rebecca. . . ? Oh, never before have I needed you as much as I do now.

REBECCA. But surely we've been prepared for something or other like this happening.

ROSMER. No, no! Not for this.

REBECCA. Not for this?

ROSMER. I did think that perhaps sooner or later our pure and beautiful friendship might be misinterpreted and sneered at. Not by Kroll. I never imagined anything like that of him. But all those others with their coarse minds and their shifty eyes. Oh yes, Rebecca, I had good grounds for keeping the relations between us so jealously concealed. It was a dangerous secret.

REBECCA. Oh, why must we worry about what others think? We know, you and I, that we have no reason to feel guilty.

ROSMER. I? Not feel guilty? Yes, so I thought . . . until today. But now . . . now, Rebecca. . . .

REBECCA. Well, what about now?

ROSMER. How am I to explain Beata's terrible accusation?

REBECCA [*vehemently*]. Oh, stop talking about Beata! Stop thinking about Beata any more! Just when you had begun to put her right out of your mind, now that she's dead.

ROSMER. Since I heard about all this, she seems in some uncanny way to be back among the living again.

REBECCA. Oh no, not that, Johannes, not that!

ROSMER. Yes, I tell you. We must try to get to the bottom of this. Whatever can have led Beata into this ghastly mistake?

REBECCA. Surely *you* are not beginning to doubt she was very nearly insane?

ROSMER. Yes, I am. That's just what I cannot be absolutely certain about any more. And besides . . . even if she were . . .

REBECCA. If she were! Well, what then?

ROSMER. What I mean is . . . where are we to look for the immediate cause that tipped her sick mind over into madness?

REBECCA. Oh, what's the use of going on brooding about it like this!

ROSMER. I can't help it, Rebecca. I can't get rid of this nagging doubt, however much I would like to.

REBECCA. Oh, but that's a dangerous thing to do . . . turning this morbid affair over and over in your mind.

ROSMER [*walks about restlessly, pondering*]. I must have let something slip, one way or another. She must have noticed how happy I began to feel after *you* had come to live here.

REBECCA. Yes, my dear, but even if you did . . . !

ROSMER. I tell you . . . it didn't escape her notice that we read the same books. That we liked to get together and talk about all the recent developments. Yet I don't understand! Because I was so careful to spare her any unpleasantness. When I look back, I think I did my utmost to keep her away from anything we were interested in. Or perhaps that wasn't so, Rebecca?

REBECCA. Yes, yes! You certainly did.

ROSMER. And you too. And yet . . . ! Oh, it's terrible to contemplate! She must have been going about here . . . sick with passion . . . never saying a word . . . watching us . . . noticing everything . . . and misinterpreting everything.

REBECCA [*wringing her hands*]. Oh, I should never have come to Rosmersholm.

ROSMER. To think what she must have suffered in silence! All the horrible things her sick brain must have been capable of believing about us. Did she never say anything to you that might have given you a hint?

REBECCA [*apparently startled*]. To me! Do you think I'd have stayed on here a day longer?

ROSMER. No, no, of course not. Oh, what a battle she must have fought. And fought alone, Rebecca. In despair, and quite alone. And then, in the end, her triumph . . . that agonizing indictment . . . in the millstream. . . .

[*He throws himself down on the chair near the writing-table, rests his elbows on the table and hides his face in his hands.*]

REBECCA [*approaches him cautiously from behind*]. Listen to me, Johannes. If it were in your power to call Beata back . . . to you . . . to Rosmersholm . . . would you do it?

ROSMER. Oh, how do I know what I would or wouldn't do? I can think of nothing but this one thing . . . this one irrevocable thing.

REBECCA. Now you were going to live, Johannes. You had already begun. You had made yourself completely free . . . in all things. You felt so happy and carefree. . . .

ROSMER. I know . . . I really did. And now this crushing weight.

REBECCA [*behind him, with her arms on the back of the chair*]. How lovely it was when we used to sit in the dusk downstairs in the living-room. Helping each other to plan our lives anew. You wanted to lay hold of life—the throbbing life of the day, as you used to say. You wanted to go from house to house like a messenger of deliverance, winning the minds and the wills of men. Creating all about you a nobility . . . in ever wider circles. Noble men.

ROSMER. Happy, noble men.

REBECCA. Yes, happy.

ROSMER. For it is happiness that brings nobility of mind, Rebecca.

REBECCA. Don't you think . . . perhaps suffering too? Great suffering.

ROSMER. Yes . . . so long as you come through . . . get over it . . . rise above it.

REBECCA. That's what *you* must do.

ROSMER [*shakes his head sadly*]. I shall never succeed in rising above this, never completely. There will always be some doubt remaining, some question. I shall never again know the joy of the one thing that makes life so wonderful to live.

REBECCA [*over the back of the chair, softly*]. And what do you think that is, Johannes?

ROSMER [*looks up at her*]. Quiet, happy innocence.

REBECCA [*takes a step back*]. Yes, innocence.

[*Short pause.*]

ROSMER [*with elbows on the table, his head in his hands and looking straight ahead*]. And how she must have worked things out, how systematically she must have pieced things together. Beginning first with suspicions about my faith. . . . However did she come by that idea at that time? Yet she did. And then it grew into certainty. And then . . . yes, it wasn't difficult for her then to suppose all the other things possible. [*Sits up in his chair and runs his hands through his hair.*] Oh, all these wild speculations. I'll never be rid of them. I'm sure of it. I know it. They'll always be there, ready to charge in and remind me of the dead.

REBECCA. Like the White Horse of Rosmersholm.

ROSMER. Exactly. Rushing out of the darkness. Out of the stillness.

REBECCA. So you are going to let life go by just when you had begun to lay hold of it, and all because of these morbid fantasies.

ROSMER. You are right, it's hard. Hard, Rebecca. But the choice isn't mine. How do you suppose I could ever put all this behind me?

REBECCA [behind the chair]. By forming new associations.

ROSMER [starts and looks up]. New associations!

REBECCA. Yes, new associations with the world outside. Living, working, doing things. Not sitting here brooding and stewing over insoluble problems.

ROSMER [gets up]. New associations? [Walks across the room, stops near the door and comes back again.] One question occurs to me. Haven't you asked yourself the same thing, Rebecca?

REBECCA [breathing hard]. Tell me . . . what . . . you mean.

ROSMER. How do you think our association will be after today?

REBECCA. I still think our friendship can endure . . . whatever happens.

ROSMER. Yes, but that wasn't exactly what I meant. I was meaning the thing that first brought us together . . . the thing that unites us so closely . . . the belief we share that a man and a woman can live together simply on terms of friendship.

REBECCA. Yes, yes . . . what of it?

ROSMER. I mean that *that* kind of relationship . . . like ours, in fact . . . doesn't it best go with the sort of life that's lived quietly, serenely, happily. . . .

REBECCA. Well?

ROSMER. But the sort of life I see opening up in front of me is one of strife and unrest and strong passion. For I do mean to live my life, Rebecca! I'm not going to be beaten down by any grim thoughts of what might be. Nobody is going to decide my life for me, neither the living nor . . . anybody else.

REBECCA. No, no, don't let them! Be a free man in all things, Rosmer!

ROSMER. Then do you know what I think? Don't you? Don't you see how I can best rid myself of all those nagging memories . . . from all the misery of the past?

REBECCA. Well?

ROSMER. By confronting it all with a new and living reality.

REBECCA [*feels for the back of a chair*]. A living . . . ? What do you mean?

ROSMER [*comes closer*]. Rebecca . . . if I were to ask you . . . will you be my wife?

REBECCA [*for a moment speechless, then gives a cry of joy*]. Your wife! Your . . . ! Me!

ROSMER. Good. Let us try. We two will be one. The space left here by the dead must remain empty no longer.

REBECCA. Me . . . in Beata's place. . . !

ROSMER. Then that puts her out of the picture. Right out. For good.

REBECCA [*in a soft, trembling voice*]. Do you think so, Johannes?

ROSMER. It must do! It *must*. I will not go through life with a corpse on my back. Help me to throw it off, Rebecca. And let us stifle all memory in freedom, in joy, in passion. You shall be to me the only wife I ever had.

REBECCA [*masters herself*]. Let us have no more talk of this. I will never be your wife.

ROSMER. What! Never! Oh, don't you think you might come to love me? Isn't there already a hint of love in our friendship?

REBECCA [*puts her hands over her ears as if in terror*]. You mustn't talk like that, Johannes! Mustn't say such things!

ROSMER [*seizes her arm*]. It's true! There *is* some tender promise in our feelings for each other. Oh, when I look at you, I see you feel the same. Don't you, Rebecca?

REBECCA [*once again firm and composed*]. Listen to me. I tell you this: if you persist in this, I shall leave Rosmersholm.

ROSMER. Leave! You! You can't. It's impossible.

REBECCA. It's even more impossible for me to become your wife. Never in this world can I be that.

ROSMER [*looks at her in surprise*]. You say 'can'. And you say it so strangely. Why can't you?

REBECCA [*takes both his hands in hers*]. Dear friend . . . for your sake as well as mine . . . don't ask me why. [*Lets go his hands.*] There it is, Johannes.

[*She goes towards the door on the left.*]

ROSMER. After today there can be for me only one question: Why?

REBECCA [*turns and looks at him*]. Then that will be the end.

ROSMER. Between you and me?

REBECCA. Yes.

ROSMER. Never can there be an end to things between us. You will never leave Rosmersholm.

REBECCA [*with her hand on the door latch*]. No, I don't suppose I shall. But if you ever ask me again . . . that's the end of things, all the same.

ROSMER. The end. . . ? What . . . ?

REBECCA. Yes, for then I go the way Beata went. Now you know, Johannes.

ROSMER. Rebecca. . . !

REBECCA [*in the doorway, nods slowly*]. Now you know. [*She goes.*]

ROSMER [*stares in bewilderment at the closed door, and says to himself*]. What . . . is . . . this?

ACT THREE

The living-room at Rosmersholm. The window and the hall door are open. The morning sun is shining outside. REBECCA WEST, *dressed as in Act I, is standing at the window, watering and arranging the flowers. Her crochet-work is lying on the armchair.* MRS. HELSETH *is going round dusting the furniture with a feather mop.*

REBECCA [*after a moment or two of silence*]. Strange that the pastor is staying so long upstairs today.

MRS. HELSETH. Oh, he often does that. He'll be down soon, I should think.

REBECCA. Have you seen anything of him?

MRS. HELSETH. Just for a minute. He was in his bedroom getting dressed when I went up with his coffee.

REBECCA. The reason I ask is because he wasn't feeling quite himself yesterday.

MRS. HELSETH. Yes, he did look a bit off-colour. I was wondering if there wasn't maybe a bit of trouble between him and his brother-in-law.

REBECCA. What sort of trouble do you think?

MRS. HELSETH. That I couldn't say. Perhaps it's this Mortensgaard that's made them fall out.

REBECCA. That's always possible. Do you know anything about Peter Mortensgaard?

MRS. HELSETH. Not me! Whatever gives you that idea, miss? A person like that!

REBECCA. You mean because he's the editor of that awful paper?

MRS. HELSETH. Oh, it's not just *that*. Surely, miss, you must have heard about him having a child by that married woman whose husband had gone away and left her?

REBECCA. Yes, I heard. But that must have been long before I came here.

MRS. HELSETH. Bless me, yes! He was quite young at the time. She at least might have had a bit more sense than him. He wanted to go ahead and marry her, but that just couldn't be done. So he had to suffer pretty heavily for it. But, my goodness, Mortensgaard has got on since those days. There are plenty of people ready to run after *him* now.

REBECCA. Many of the poor turn to him first when there's any trouble.

MRS. HELSETH. It needn't always be just the poor. . . .

REBECCA [*glances at her furtively*]. Really?

MRS. HELSETH [*vigorously dusting the sofa*]. People you would least expect, miss.

REBECCA [*arranging the flowers*]. Now, this is just some idea you have got hold of, Mrs. Helseth. You can hardly be expected to know anything like that for certain.

MRS. HELSETH. So you think I don't know, miss, do you? But I'm telling you I do. If you must know, I once took a letter to Mortensgaard myself.

REBECCA [*turns*]. Never! Did you?

MRS. HELSETH. Yes, that I did. And, what's more, the letter was written here at Rosmersholm.

REBECCA. Really, Mrs. Helseth?

MRS. HELSETH. Yes, that it was. And written on fine paper it was. And sealed with fine red sealing-wax, too.

REBECCA. And you were the one entrusted with taking it? Well then, my dear Mrs. Helseth, it's not difficult to guess who it was from.

MRS. HELSETH. Well?

REBECCA. Naturally it must have been something that poor Mrs. Rosmer, stricken as she was . . .

MRS. HELSETH. It's you who said it, Miss West, not me.

REBECCA. But what was in the letter? No, of course . . . how could you possibly know that?

MRS. HELSETH. Hm, maybe I do know, all the same.

REBECCA. Did she tell you what the letter was about?

MRS. HELSETH. No, she didn't exactly do that. But when Mortensgaard had finished reading it, he started asking me all sorts of questions, going on and on about it, so I had a pretty good idea what it was all about.

REBECCA. What do you think was in it then? Oh, dear, kind Mrs. Helseth, do tell me!

MRS. HELSETH. Certainly not, miss. Not for anything in the world.

REBECCA. Oh, surely you can tell *me*. You and I are such good friends, aren't we?

MRS. HELSETH. Heaven forbid I should tell you anything about *that*, miss. All I can say is it was something not very nice that they had gone and got the poor, sick lady to believe.

REBECCA. Who had got her to believe it?

MRS. HELSETH. Wicked people, Miss West. Wicked people.

REBECCA. Wicked . . . ?

MRS. HELSETH. Yes, I say it again. Downright wicked people it must have been.

REBECCA. And who do you think it could have been?

MRS. HELSETH. Oh, I know all right what I think. But God forbid that I should ever say anything. Not but what there isn't a certain lady in town . . . hm!

REBECCA. I can see you mean Mrs. Kroll.

MRS. HELSETH. Yes, she's a fine one, she is. She's always been so stuck up with me. And she's never been very fond of you, either.

REBECCA. Do you think Mrs. Rosmer was in her right mind when she wrote that letter to Mortensgaard?

MRS. HELSETH. The mind's a funny thing, miss. But I don't think she was completely gone.

REBECCA. But she went a bit queer when she was told she could never have any children. It was *then* the insanity first started.

MRS. HELSETH. Yes, she took that very badly, poor thing.

REBECCA [*takes her crochet-work and sits in a chair near the window*]. All the same, Mrs. Helseth, don't you think *that* was really a good thing for the pastor?

MRS. HELSETH. What was, miss?

REBECCA. That there were no children. Well?

MRS. HELSETH. Hm, I don't really know what to say to that.

REBECCA. Yes, it was, believe me. It was best for him. Pastor Rosmer is not the kind of man who can put up with a lot of crying children.

MRS. HELSETH. Children never cry at Rosmersholm, miss.

REBECCA [*looks at her*]. Never cry?

MRS. HELSETH. No. Children have never been known to cry in this house, not as long as anybody can remember.

REBECCA. That's strange.

MRS. HELSETH. Yes, isn't it strange? But it runs in the family. And there's another strange thing. When they grow up, they never laugh. Never laugh as long as they live.

REBECCA. But that's extraordinary. . . .

MRS. HELSETH. Have you ever seen or heard the pastor laugh, miss?

REBECCA. No, now I come to think about it, I almost believe you are right. But then I don't think people in this part of the world laugh very much at all.

MRS. HELSETH. They don't. People say it began at Rosmersholm. And then I suppose it spread, like a sort of infection.

REBECCA. You are a deep one, you are, Mrs. Helseth.

MRS. HELSETH. Oh, you mustn't sit there making fun of me, miss. . . . [*Listens.*] Hush, hush . . . the pastor is coming down now. He doesn't like seeing mops in here.

[*She goes out through the door, right.* JOHANNES ROSMER, *stick and hat in hand, comes in from the hall.*]

ROSMER. Good morning, Rebecca.

REBECCA. Good morning, my dear. [*After a while, crocheting.*] Are you going out?

ROSMER. Yes.

REBECCA. It's a lovely day.

ROSMER. You didn't come in to see me this morning.

REBECCA. No, I didn't. Not today.

ROSMER. Aren't you going to do it in future, either?

REBECCA. Oh, I don't know yet.

ROSMER. Has anything come for me?

REBECCA. The *County Times* has come.

ROSMER. The *County Times*. . . !

REBECCA. It's lying on the table there.

ROSMER [*puts down his hat and stick*]. Is there anything in about . . . ?

REBECCA. Yes.

ROSMER. Yet you didn't send it up. . . .

REBECCA. You would read it soon enough.

ROSMER. Well. [*Takes the paper and reads it standing at the table.*] What! . . . 'Cannot emphasize too strongly this warning against unprincipled deserters.' [*Looks across at her.*] They call me a deserter, Rebecca.

REBECCA. They mention no names.

ROSMER. That makes no difference. [*Reads on.*] 'Secret traitors to the good cause . . .' 'Judas-like creatures who have the impudence to confess their apostasy as soon as they believe the most opportune and . . . the most profitable moment has arrived.' 'A reckless outrage on the fair name of an honoured family . . .' '. . . in the expectation that those at present in power will not neglect to make some suitable reward.' [*Puts the paper on the table.*] How can they write such things about me! Men who have known me so well and so long. Things they don't even believe themselves. Things they know there isn't a single word of truth in—yet they write them all the same.

REBECCA. There's more yet.

ROSMER [*takes the paper again*]. 'Inexperience and lack of judgement . . .' '. . . pernicious influence, perhaps even extending to matters which for the present we are unwilling to make subjects for public discussion or censure . . .' [*Looks at her.*] What is this?

REBECCA. It's obviously aimed at me.

ROSMER [*puts down the paper*]. Rebecca . . . these are the doings of unscrupulous men.

REBECCA. Yes, I don't think they need talk about Mortensgaard.

ROSMER [*walks about the room*]. There is work for redemption here. Everything that is good in man will be destroyed if this kind of thing is allowed to go on. But it shall not. Oh, how happy I should feel if I could bring a little light into all this murky nastiness.

REBECCA [*gets up*]. Oh, how right you are! That would be something great and glorious for you to live for.

ROSMER. Just think if I could make them see themselves for what they really are. Bring them to a sense of shame and repentance, get them to approach one another in a spirit of tolerance . . . of love, Rebecca.

REBECCA. Yes, if you concentrate everything on this, you'll win—you'll see.

ROSMER. I think it might be done. Oh, what joy then to be alive. No more bitter strife, only friendly rivalry. All eyes fixed on the same goal. Every mind, every will striving on and on . . . up and up . . . each by the path best suited to its nature. Happiness for all . . . created by all. [*Happens to look out through the window, starts and says sadly.*] Ah! Not by me.

REBECCA. Not . . . not by you?

ROSMER. And not *for* me either.

REBECCA. Oh, Johannes, you mustn't let such misgivings get the better of you.

ROSMER. Happiness . . . dear Rebecca . . . happiness is more than anything that serene, secure, happy freedom from guilt.

REBECCA [*stares straight ahead*]. Ah, this question of guilt. . . .

ROSMER. Oh, that's nothing you are likely to know very much about. Whereas I . . .

REBECCA. You least of all!

ROSMER [*points out of window*]. The millstream.

REBECCA. Oh, Johannes. . . !

[MRS. HELSETH *looks in through the door, right.*]

MRS. HELSETH. Miss West!

REBECCA. Later, later. Not now.

MRS. HELSETH. Just one word, miss.

[REBECCA *walks over to the door.* MRS. HELSETH *tells her something. They whisper together for a moment.* MRS. HELSETH *nods and goes.*]

ROSMER [*uneasily*]. Was it anything for me?

REBECCA. No, only household matters. . . . Now you ought to go out for a walk in the fresh air, my dear Johannes. A good long walk, you should make it.

ROSMER [*takes his hat*]. Yes, come on. We'll go together.

REBECCA. No, my dear, I can't just now. You go on your own. But shake off all these gloomy thoughts. Promise me.

ROSMER. I'll never be able to shake them off, I am very much afraid.

REBECCA. Oh, why do you let these empty fears have such power over you. . . !

ROSMER. I am sorry, but they are not so empty as you think, Rebecca. I lay awake all night turning them over in my mind. Perhaps Beata saw straight after all.

REBECCA. What do you mean?

ROSMER. Saw straight when she believed I was in love with you, Rebecca.

REBECCA. You think *that*?

ROSMER [*places his hat on the table*]. One question has been tossing about in my mind. . . . Weren't we all the time simply deceiving ourselves about the way things were between us when we called it 'friendship'?

REBECCA. You mean it might just as well have been called . . . ?

ROSMER. . . . Love. Yes, Rebecca, that is what I mean. Even while Beata was still alive, my thoughts were all for you. It was you alone I longed for. It was with you that I found calm, happy, serene contentment. If we really think about it, Rebecca . . . we began our life together like two children falling sweetly and secretly in love. Making no demands, dreaming no dreams. Didn't you also feel that way about it? Tell me?

REBECCA [*struggling with herself*]. Oh . . . I don't know what to answer.

ROSMER. And it was this life of intimacy, *with* each other and *for* each other, we took for friendship. No, Rebecca, our life together has been a spiritual marriage . . . perhaps from the very first day. That is why the guilt is mine. I had no right to it . . . no right for Beata's sake.

REBECCA. No right to a happy life? Do you believe that, Johannes?

ROSMER. She looked on our relationship through the eyes of *her* love. Judged our relationship by the nature of *her* love. That was only natural. Beata could not have judged otherwise than she did.

REBECCA. But why should you reproach yourself for Beata's wild ideas?

ROSMER. It was for love of me . . . *her* kind of love . . . that she threw herself into the millstream. The fact is inescapable, Rebecca. I can never get away from it.

REBECCA. Oh, you must put everything out of your mind but the great and splendid task you have dedicated your life to.

ROSMER [*shakes his head*]. I fear that is something that can never be done, my dear. Not by me. Not after what I know now.

REBECCA. Why not by you?

ROSMER. There can be no victory for any cause that springs from guilt.

REBECCA [*vehemently*]. Oh, all these doubts, these fears, these scruples— they are just part of the family tradition. The people here talk about the dead coming back in the form of charging white horses. I think this is the same sort of thing.

ROSMER. Maybe it is, but what's the use if I can't escape them now? And believe me, Rebecca, it is just as I said. Any cause that is to win a lasting victory must have at its head a happy and guiltless man.

REBECCA. Is happiness something *you* can't exist without either, then, Johannes?

ROSMER. Happiness? Yes, my dear, it is.

REBECCA. Even though you can never laugh?

ROSMER. That makes no difference. Believe me, I have a great capacity for happiness.

REBECCA. Now you really must have your walk, my dear. A nice long one, really long, do you hear? Here is your hat and here is your stick.

ROSMER [*takes both*]. Thank you. You are not coming with me?

REBECCA. No, no. I can't just now.

ROSMER. Very well. But you'll be with me all the same.

[*He goes out through the hall. After a moment* REBECCA *peeps out after him from behind the open door. Then she goes over to the door on the right.*]

REBECCA [*opens the door and speaks in a low voice*]. All right, Mrs. Helseth. You can let him in now.

[*She goes over to the window. Shortly after,* KROLL *comes in from the right. He bows silently and formally and keeps his hat in his hand.*]

KROLL. Has he gone, then?

REBECCA. Yes.

KROLL. Does he generally stay out long?

REBECCA. Oh, yes. But he is a bit unpredictable today. So if you don't want to meet him . . .

KROLL. No, no. It's you I want to talk to. And quite alone.

REBECCA. Then we had best make the most of our time. Do sit down, Mr. Kroll.

[*She sits down in the easy-chair near the window.* KROLL *sits on a chair beside her.*]

KROLL. Miss West . . . you can hardly imagine how profoundly and how painfully this has affected me . . . this change in Johannes Rosmer.

REBECCA. We expected something of the sort . . . to begin with.

KROLL. Only to begin with?

REBECCA. Mr. Rosmer was quite confident that sooner or later you would join him.

KROLL. *I* should?

REBECCA. You and all his other friends as well.

KROLL. Ah, there you see! That shows you how uncertain he is in his judgement when it concerns his fellow men and their practical affairs.

REBECCA. Furthermore . . . now that he feels he has a duty to himself to carry on what he has begun . . .

KROLL. Yes, but look . . . that's exactly what I do not believe.

REBECCA. And what *do* you believe then?

KROLL. I believe that *you* are the one behind it all.

REBECCA. You got that idea from your wife, Mr. Kroll.

KROLL. It doesn't matter very much where I got it from. What is certain is the strong suspicion I feel . . . the extremely strong suspicion, I might say . . . when I start thinking of the way you have behaved ever since you got here.

REBECCA [*looks at him*]. I seem to remember there was a time when you felt an extremely strong *faith* in me, my dear Mr. Kroll. A warm faith, I might almost say.

KROLL [*in a subdued voice*]. Who is there you couldn't bewitch . . . if you tried?

REBECCA. Are you saying I tried to . . .

KROLL. Yes, you did. I'm no longer such a fool as to imagine you cared anything for me the way you carried on. All you wanted was to get your foot in at Rosmersholm. Get yourself established here. That's what I was supposed to help you with. I can see it all now.

REBECCA. Then you have completely forgotten that it was Beata who begged and prayed me to move out here.

KROLL. Yes, after you had managed to bewitch her as well. Or do you want to call that friendship, the way she came to feel about you? She idolized you, worshipped you. The outcome of it was . . . how shall I put it? . . . a kind of desperate infatuation. Yes, that's the only way to describe it.

REBECCA. You will please remember the state your sister was in. As far as I'm concerned, I don't think I can be said to be particularly highly-strung.

KROLL. No, you are not. But that's what makes you even more dangerous for those you want in your power. You find it easy to calculate all things and act with complete deliberation . . . precisely because you have a cold heart.

REBECCA. Cold? Are you so sure of that?

KROLL. I am absolutely certain of it now. Otherwise you could never have kept it up here year after year, never swerving in the pursuit of what you were after. Well, well . . . you have got what you wanted. You have got him and everything else in your power. But to get your way, you have had no scruples about making him unhappy.

REBECCA. That's not true. It wasn't me. It was *you* who made him unhappy.

KROLL. Me indeed!

REBECCA. Yes, when you allowed him to think he was to blame for Beata's terrible end.] He invented the letter?

KROLL. So that struck home deep, did it?

REBECCA. Surely you must realize that. A mind as sensitive as his . . .

KROLL. I thought these so-called emancipated men knew how to suppress all such scruples. . . . But there it is! Oh yes, I suppose deep down I knew it well enough. The descendant of these men here looking down at us . . . he'll not escape so easily from what has been handed down unbroken from generation to generation.

REBECCA [*looks down thoughtfully*]. Johannes Rosmer has roots that go deep into his ancestry. That is certainly very true.

KROLL. Yes, and you would have thought of that if you had had any pity for him. But I don't suppose you are capable of consideration of that kind. Your background and his are of course poles apart.

REBECCA. What do you mean . . . my background?

KROLL. I was thinking of your family background. Of your antecedents . . . Miss West.

REBECCA. I see. Yes, that's quite true, I do come from quite humble beginnings. But at the same time . . .

KROLL. It is not class or position I am referring to. I am thinking of the moral side of your background.

REBECCA. Of the . . . ? In what way?

KROLL. The very circumstances of your birth.

REBECCA. What's that you say?

KROLL. I mention it of course only because it explains your whole conduct.

REBECCA. I don't understand a word of all this. Tell me exactly what you mean!

KROLL. I thought surely you must know. Otherwise it wouldn't make sense . . . letting yourself be adopted by Dr. West. . . .

REBECCA [*gets up*]. Ah! Now I understand!

KROLL. . . . Taking his name. Your mother's name was Gamvik.

REBECCA [*walks across the room*]. My father's name was Gamvik, Mr. Kroll.

KROLL. Your mother's occupation must have brought her into pretty regular contact with the local doctor.

midwife? probably not prostitute

REBECCA. Yes, it did.

KROLL. And no sooner has your mother died than he takes you into his house. . . . He treats you harshly. Yet you stay with him. You know he won't leave you a penny. All you got was a case full of books. And yet you stick it out, put up with him, look after him right to the very end.

REBECCA [*by the table, looks scornfully at him*]. And what I did you put down to something immoral, something criminal, about the circumstances of my birth!

KROLL. What you did for him I attribute to some intuitive daughterly instinct. Indeed I consider your whole conduct derives from the circumstances of your birth.

REBECCA [*hotly*]. But there's not a word of truth in anything you say. And I can prove it! Dr. West didn't come to Finmark until after I was born.

KROLL. You will forgive me, Miss West, but he was already there the year before. I have gone into that.

REBECCA. You are wrong I tell you. You are completely wrong.

KROLL. You said yourself a couple of days ago that you were twenty-nine. Going on for thirty.

REBECCA. Really? Did I say that?

KROLL. Yes, you did. And from that I can work it out that . . .

REBECCA. Stop! There's no point in working it out. I might as well tell you at once. I am a year older than I pretend to be.

KROLL [*smiles incredulously*]. Really? This is something new. How does that happen?

REBECCA. When I was twenty-five, and still not married, I thought I was getting a bit too old. So I began subtracting a year.

KROLL. You? An emancipated woman. Have you still got old-fashioned ideas about the proper age for marriage?

REBECCA. Yes, it is silly . . . and ridiculous, too. But there's always some little thing or other that sticks and you just can't shake yourself free of it. It's just the way we are made.

KROLL. Just as you say. But my calculations can still be correct, just the same. For Dr. West was up there on a flying visit the year before he was appointed.

REBECCA [*vehemently*]. It's not true!

KROLL. Isn't it?

REBECCA. No. My mother never mentioned it.

KROLL. Didn't she now?

REBECCA. No, never. Nor Dr. West either. Never a word.

KROLL. Might it not be because they both had good reason to skip a year? Just as you did, Miss West. Perhaps it's a family peculiarity.

REBECCA [*walks about wringing her hands*]. It's impossible. It's just something you want to get me to believe. Never in the world is this true. It cannot be true! Never in the world. . . !

KROLL [*gets up*]. But my dear Miss West . . . why in Heaven's name are you taking it like this? You make me feel quite alarmed! What am I to think. . . ?

REBECCA. Nothing. You are not to think anything.

KROLL. Then you really must tell me why you are taking this little matter . . . this possibility . . . so much to heart.

REBECCA [*composes herself*]. It's quite simple, of course, Mr. Kroll. I have no desire to be looked on here as illegitimate.

KROLL. Indeed! Well, well, let's be content with that explanation . . . for the time being. But it seems you also have a certain . . . prejudice on this point, too.

REBECCA. Yes, I suppose I have.

KROLL. Well, I imagine it's pretty much the same with most of what you call your emancipation. You have read up a lot of new ideas and opinions. You have acquired a smattering of various ideas and theories—that somehow seem to upset a good many things that up to now we took for incontrovertible and inviolate. But in your case, Miss West, it never got beyond being anything but an abstraction. Book knowledge. It never got into your blood.

REBECCA [*thoughtfully*]. Perhaps you are right.

KROLL. Yes, just take a good look at yourself and you will see. And if it is like that in your case, it's easy enough to guess how it is with Johannes Rosmer. The very idea of *him* getting up and announcing his apostasy . . . why, it's sheer and utter madness . . . like hurling

...long to destruction. Think . . . a man of his retiring ... Imagine *him* rebuffed . . . hunted by the very circle he ... belonged to. Exposed to ruthless attack from the best ... the community. He's never the man to stand up to that.

He *must* stand up to it! It's too late now for him to draw back.

KROLL. It's not in the least too late. Not by any means. What has happened can be kept dark . . . or at least it can be interpreted as a purely temporary, though regrettable, aberration. But . . . there is in fact *one* measure that is absolutely imperative.

REBECCA. And what is that?

KROLL. You must get him to legalize the relationship, Miss West.

REBECCA. The relationship between us?

KROLL. Yes. You *must* see he does that.

REBECCA. You can't get away from the idea that our relationship needs . . . legalizing, as you put it?

KROLL. I have no wish to go personally into the matter any further. But I have been struck before by the fact that the easiest conventions to break with seem to be those that concern . . . hm!

REBECCA. Concern the relations between a man and a woman, I suppose you mean?

KROLL. Yes . . . speaking candidly . . . that's what I think.

REBECCA [*walks across the room and looks through the window*]. I could almost say . . . I wish you were right, Mr. Kroll.

KROLL. What do you mean by that? You said it so strangely.

REBECCA. Oh, I don't know. Don't let's talk any more about it. . . . Ah! There he comes.

KROLL. Already. Then I'll go.

REBECCA [*turns to him*]. No . . . please stay. There's something I want you to hear.

KROLL. Not now. I don't think I could bear to see him.

REBECCA. Don't go . . . I beg you! Or you will regret it later. It is the last time I shall ask anything of you.

KROLL [*looks at her in surprise and puts down his hat*]. Very well, Miss West. As you wish.

[*There is a moment's silence. Then* ROSMER *comes in from the hall.*]

ROSMER [*sees* KROLL, *stops in the doorway*]. What! Are *you* here!

REBECCA. He would have preferred not to meet you, Johannes, my dear.

KROLL [*involuntarily*]. 'My dear'?

REBECCA. Yes, Mr. Kroll. Johannes and I call each other 'dear'. That's one result of the 'relations' between us.

KROLL. Was it *that* you promised I should hear?

REBECCA. That . . . and a little more.

ROSMER [*comes closer*]. What is the purpose of your visit here today?

KROLL. I wanted to make one last attempt to stop you, to win you back.

ROSMER [*points at the newspaper*]. After what's in there?

KROLL. I didn't write it.

ROSMER. Did you do anything to try and stop it?

KROLL. That would have been unjustifiable interference with the cause I serve. Nor was it in my power.

REBECCA [*tears up the paper, crumples the pieces and throws them behind the stove*]. There. Now it's out of sight. And let it be out of mind as well. For there'll be no more of that sort of stuff, Johannes.

KROLL. Oh yes, if only you could make such things unnecessary.

REBECCA. Come, let's sit down, my dear. All three of us. Then I'll tell you everything.

ROSMER [*sits down involuntarily*]. What's come over you, Rebecca? So unnaturally calm. . . . What is it?

REBECCA. The calmness of resolution. [*Sits.*] You sit down too, Mr. Kroll.

[KROLL *sits on the sofa.*]

ROSMER. Of resolution, you say. What resolution?

REBECCA. I want to give you back again what you need to live your life. You shall have your happy innocence back again, my dear.

ROSMER. But what is all this!

REBECCA. I just want to tell you something. That's all that's necessary.

ROSMER. Well?

REBECCA. When I came down here from Finmark . . . together with Dr. West . . . I felt as though a great, new wide world were opening before me. The doctor taught me most things . . . indeed practically all the odds and ends of knowledge I possessed about life were from him. [*With a struggle, and scarcely audible.*] And then . . .

KROLL. And then?

ROSMER. But Rebecca . . . I know all this.

REBECCA [*collecting herself*]. Yes, yes . . . I suppose in one way you are right. You knew as much as was necessary.

KROLL [*looks hard at her*]. Perhaps I had better go.

REBECCA. No, stay where you are, my dear Mr. Kroll. [*To* ROSMER.] Yes, that was it, you see . . . I wanted to be in at the dawning of the new age, wanted to be in on everything, all the new ideas. One day Mr. Kroll told me about the great influence Ulrik Brendel had once had over you, while you were still a boy. I thought I might manage to pick up again where he left off.

ROSMER. You came here with this ulterior motive. . . !

REBECCA. I wanted us to go forward together in freedom. On and on, ever further. But between you and full and complete freedom was this grim, insurmountable barrier.

ROSMER. What do you mean . . . barrier?

REBECCA. I mean, Johannes, that you could only grow to freedom in the clear light of the sun. But there you were, wilting and sickly in the gloom of a marriage like yours.

ROSMER. Never until today have you spoken to me like that about my marriage.

REBECCA. No, I didn't dare, in case I frightened you off.

KROLL [*nods to* ROSMER]. Do you hear *that*?

REBECCA [*continues*]. But I knew very well where your salvation lay. Your only salvation. So I took action.

ROSMER. What do you mean . . . you took action?

KROLL. Do you mean to say . . . ?

REBECCA. Yes, Johannes. . . . [*Gets up.*] Don't get up. Nor you either, Mr. Kroll. Now it must be told. It wasn't you, Johannes. You are innocent. It was *I* who lured . . . who ended by luring Beata out on the twisted path. . . .

ROSMER [*jumping up*]. Rebecca!

KROLL [*getting up from the sofa*]. . . . The twisted path!

REBECCA. The path . . . that led to the millstream. Now you know, both of you.

ROSMER [*as if stunned*]. But I don't understand. . . . What is she saying . . . I don't understand a single word. . . !

KROLL. Oh yes, Rosmer. I am beginning to understand.

ROSMER. But what did you do? What could you possibly have told her? There was nothing. Not a thing!

REBECCA. She was informed that you were ridding yourself of all your old-fashioned prejudices.

ROSMER. Yes, but I wasn't . . . not then.

REBECCA. I knew you soon would.

KROLL [*nods to* ROSMER]. Aha!

ROSMER. Well, and what else? Now I must know everything.

REBECCA. Shortly after that . . . I begged and implored her to let me leave Rosmersholm.

ROSMER. Why did you want to leave . . . just then?

REBECCA. I didn't want to leave. I wanted to stay here where I was. But I told her it would be best for us all . . . if I left before it was too late. I gave her to understand that if I stayed on . . . certain things . . . might happen.

ROSMER. You actually said that? You did that?

REBECCA. Yes, Johannes.

ROSMER. So that's what you meant when you said you 'took action'.

REBECCA [*in a broken voice*]. That's what I meant.

ROSMER [*after a pause*]. Have you confessed everything now, Rebecca?

REBECCA. Yes.

KROLL. Not everything.

REBECCA [*looks at him in terror*]. What else do you think there is?

KROLL. Didn't you finally give Beata to understand that it was imperative—not just that it would be best, but that it was imperative—for your sake as well as Rosmer's, that you should leave and go somewhere else . . . as quickly as possible. . .? Well?

REBECCA [*in a low, indistinct voice*]. Perhaps I did say something like that.

ROSMER [*sinks into the armchair near the window*]. And the poor sick creature went and believed it, all this web of lies and deceit. Believed every word of it . . . implicitly. [*Looks up at* REBECCA.] And she never turned to me. Never once said a word to me about it. Oh, Rebecca . . . I can see from your face . . . that was because *you* dissuaded her.

REBECCA. She had got it into her head that a childless wife had no right to stay on. So she persuaded herself it was her duty to you to make way for another.

ROSMER. And you . . . you did nothing to remove this idea?

REBECCA. No.

KROLL. Perhaps you even encouraged it? Answer me. Did you or did you not?

REBECCA. That might well have been the impression she got from me, I suppose.

ROSMER. Yes, yes . . . she always gave in when faced with your strength of will. And then she did make way. [*Jumps up.*] How could you . . . how could you play such a horrible game!

REBECCA. I thought it was a choice between two lives, Johannes.

KROLL [*sternly and peremptorily*]. That choice was not for *you* to make.

REBECCA [*vehemently*]. But do you think I set about these things deliberately in cold blood! I was different then from what I am now, standing here talking about it. And besides, it seems to me a person can want things both ways. I wanted to get rid of Beata, one way or another. But I never really imagined it would ever happen. Every little step I risked, every faltering advance, I seemed to hear something call out within me: 'No further. Not a step further!' . . . And yet I could not stop. I *had* to venture a little bit further. Just one little bit further. And then a little bit more . . . always just a little bit more. And then it happened. That's the way things like that do happen.

[*A short silence.*]

ROSMER [*to* REBECCA]. And how do you think things will be for *you* now? After this?

REBECCA. I shall take things as they are. It's not important now.

KROLL. Not the slightest hint of remorse. Perhaps you don't even feel any.

REBECCA [*coldly aloof*]. Forgive me, Mr. Kroll . . . but that's something that concerns nobody but me. That's something I shall settle with myself.

KROLL [*to* ROSMER]. And this is the woman you are living under the same roof with . . . in the closest intimacy. [*Looks round at the portraits.*] Oh, if only they could see you now, these men of the past.

ROSMER. Are you going into town?

KROLL [*takes his hat*]. Yes. And the quicker the better.

ROSMER [*also taking his hat*]. I'm coming with you.

KROLL. You are! Yes, I was sure we hadn't lost you for good.

ROSMER. Come on, Kroll! Come on!

[*They both go out through the hall without looking at* REBECCA. *After a moment,* REBECCA *walks cautiously over to the window and looks out from behind the flowers.*]

REBECCA [*speaks softly to herself*]. Not across the bridge today either. Round by the top. Never across the millstream. Never. [*Moves away from the window.*] Well, well.

[*She crosses the room and pulls the bell-rope. A moment later* MRS. HELSETH *comes in from the right.*]

MRS. HELSETH. What is it, miss?

REBECCA. Mrs. Helseth, would you be so kind as to have my trunk brought down from the loft.

MRS. HELSETH. Your trunk?

REBECCA. Yes, you know, the brown sealskin trunk.

MRS. HELSETH. Certainly. Goodness, but are you going away?

REBECCA. Yes, I'm going away, Mrs. Helseth.

MRS. HELSETH. What! Now?

REBECCA. As soon as I have packed.

MRS. HELSETH. I've never heard the likes of it! But you'll be back again soon, won't you, miss?

REBECCA. I'm never coming back.

MRS. HELSETH. Never! But good heavens! What's it going to be like at Rosmersholm without Miss West here any longer. Just when poor Pastor Rosmer was nice and settled.

REBECCA. Yes, but today I have become afraid, Mrs. Helseth.

MRS. HELSETH. Afraid! Heavens . . . what of?

REBECCA. I thought I caught a glimpse of white horses.

MRS. HELSETH. White horses! In broad daylight!

REBECCA. Oh, they are out at all hours . . . the White Horses of Rosmersholm [*Breaks off.*] Well now, what about that trunk, Mrs. Helseth.

MRS. HELSETH. Yes, of course. The trunk.

[*They both go out to the right.*]

ACT FOUR

The living-room at Rosmersholm. It is late afternoon. A shaded lamp is burning on the table.

REBECCA WEST is standing at the table, packing some things into a hold-all. Her cloak and hat and the white crocheted shawl are hanging over the back of the sofa.

MRS. HELSETH comes in from the right.

MRS. HELSETH [*seems ill at ease and speaks in a low voice*]. All your things have been brought down now, miss. They are in the kitchen passage.

REBECCA. Good. Is the coach ordered?

MRS. HELSETH. Yes. He wants to know what time he has to be here.

REBECCA. I think about eleven o'clock. The boat leaves at midnight.

MRS. HELSETH [*hesitates a little*]. But what about the pastor? Suppose he isn't back by then.

REBECCA. I'll just have to go. If I don't see him, you can tell him I shall write. A long letter. Tell him that.

MRS. HELSETH. Yes, I suppose that's all right . . . writing to him, but . . . poor Miss West . . . I think you ought to try and talk to him just once more.

REBECCA. Perhaps you're right. And yet, perhaps not.

MRS. HELSETH. Oh . . . that I should live to see a thing like this . . . I'd never have thought it!

REBECCA. What *did* you think then, Mrs. Helseth?

MRS. HELSETH. Well, really I thought Pastor Rosmer was more of a man than that.

REBECCA. More of a man?

MRS. HELSETH. Yes, really I did.

REBECCA. But, my dear Mrs. Helseth, what do you mean?

MRS. HELSETH. I mean what's right and proper, miss. He shouldn't be getting out of it like this, he shouldn't.

REBECCA [*looks at her*]. Listen to me, Mrs. Helseth. Tell me the plain, honest truth—why do you think I am going away?

MRS. HELSETH. Good heavens, I suppose because you have to, miss. Well, I mean to say! But really I don't think it's very nice of the pastor. Mortensgaard did have some excuse because *her* husband was still alive. So *they* couldn't get married however much they wanted to. But the pastor . . . well. . . !

REBECCA [*with a faint smile*]. Could you really think a thing like that about me and Pastor Rosmer?

MRS. HELSETH. Never in the world. What I mean is . . . not until today.

REBECCA. But today . . . ?

MRS. HELSETH. Well . . . after all the nasty things there's supposed to be about him in the papers. . . .

REBECCA. Aha!

MRS. HELSETH. What I mean is, you can believe anything of a man who's ready to go over to Mortensgaard's religion.

REBECCA. Oh yes, I suppose so. But what about me? What have you got to say about me?

MRS. HELSETH. Bless me, miss, I can hardly see it's any great fault of yours. When a woman's all on her own, it can't be easy for her to resist, I dare say. We're only human, Miss West, all of us.

REBECCA. That's very true, Mrs. Helseth. We are all only human. . . . What can you hear?

MRS. HELSETH [*in a low voice*]. Oh Lord! I think he's coming.

REBECCA [*starts*]. After all . . . ! [*Firmly.*] Well then, so be it.

[JOHANNES ROSMER *comes in from the hall.*]

ROSMER [*sees the luggage, turns to* REBECCA *and asks*]. What does this mean?

REBECCA. I'm leaving.

ROSMER. Now?

REBECCA. Yes. [*To* MRS. HELSETH.] Eleven o'clock then.

MRS. HELSETH. Very good, miss.

[*She goes out to the right.*]

ROSMER [*after a short pause*]. Where are you going, Rebecca?

REBECCA. North . . . with the boat.

ROSMER. North? What do you want up there?

REBECCA. That's where I came from, wasn't it?

ROSMER. But there's nothing for you up there now.

REBECCA. There's nothing down here either.

ROSMER. What did you think of doing?

REBECCA. I don't know. I just want to have done with everything.

ROSMER. Have done with everything?

REBECCA. Rosmersholm has broken me.

ROSMER [*suddenly attentive*]. What's that you say?

REBECCA. Completely and utterly broken me. When I first came here,
I had some spirit; I wasn't afraid to do things. Now I feel crushed
by a tradition quite foreign to me. I feel after this as though I hadn't
any courage left for anything.

ROSMER. Why not? What do you mean by this tradition you say
you . . . ?

REBECCA. My dear Johannes, let's not talk about that now. How did
you get on with Mr. Kroll?

ROSMER. We have come to terms.

REBECCA. So! So it came to that in the end.

ROSMER. He invited all our old friends to join us at his house. They
made it quite clear that the task of ennobling the minds of men . . .
is not really the thing for me. And you know, it's a pretty hopeless
kind of thing, anyway. I'm giving it up.

Broken too

REBECCA. Yes . . . perhaps it's best that way.

ROSMER. So *that's* what you say now, is it? That's your view *now*?

REBECCA. I've come round to that. In the last few days.

ROSMER. You are lying, Rebecca.

REBECCA. Lying. . . ?

ROSMER. Yes, lying. You have never believed in me. You have never believed I had it in me to carry this thing through successfully.

REBECCA. I believed we two could manage it together.

ROSMER. That's not true! You thought that *you* yourself might be able to do something with your life; and that maybe you could utilize me for your own ends; you thought I might serve you somehow in your schemes. *That's* what you thought.

REBECCA. Listen to me, Johannes. . . .

ROSMER [*sits down wearily on the sofa*]. Oh, what's the use! I see through it all now. I have been like wax in your hands.

REBECCA. Listen to me, Johannes. We must get things straight. It will be our last chance. [*Sits on a chair near the sofa.*] I had thought of writing to you to tell you all about it . . . when I was back up North again. But perhaps it's better if you hear it now.

ROSMER. Is there still more to tell?

REBECCA. You still haven't heard the main thing.

ROSMER. The main thing?

REBECCA. Something you've never even suspected. Something that puts everything else in its true light.

ROSMER [*shakes his head*]. I don't understand you at all.

REBECCA. It's perfectly true I angled for admission here to Rosmersholm. Because I had the feeling I would succeed in doing rather well for myself here. In one way or another, if you see what I mean.

ROSMER. Well, you managed to achieve what you set out to do.

REBECCA. I think I could have achieved any mortal thing—then. For I still had the courage of a free mind. I felt no scruples; I wasn't prepared to give way for anything. But then came the start of something that finally broke my will . . . and turned me from then on into a poor frightened thing.

ROSMER. The start of what? Tell me plainly.

REBECCA. Something that came over me . . . a wild and uncontrollable passion . . . oh, Johannes!

ROSMER. Passion? You. . . ! For what?

REBECCA. For you.

ROSMER [*tries to spring up*]. What's that you say?

REBECCA [*restrains him*]. Stay where you are, my dear. There's more to tell.

ROSMER. Are you trying to tell me . . . you were in love with me . . . in that way?

REBECCA. I felt you couldn't call it anything else but being 'in love'—at that time. I really did think it was love. But it wasn't. It was what I said . . . wild, uncontrollable passion.

ROSMER [*with difficulty*]. Rebecca . . . is this really you . . . you . . . sitting here telling me all this?

REBECCA. Of course, what do you think, Johannes!

ROSMER. And it was as a result of this . . . under the influence of this . . . that you 'took action' as you put it.

REBECCA. It swept over me like a storm at sea. Like one of those storms we sometimes get in the winter up North. It takes hold of you . . . and carries you away with it . . . for as long as it lasts. It never occurs to you to resist.

ROSMER. Then it swept poor Beata into the millstream.

REBECCA. Yes, it was like a fight to the death between Beata and me at that time.

ROSMER. You were certainly the strongest of us at Rosmersholm. Stronger even than Beata and me together.

REBECCA. I knew you well enough to realize there was no way I could reach you until you had been set free . . . in mind and in deed.

ROSMER. But I don't understand you, Rebecca. You yourself . . . and the way you have behaved . . . it's all a complete mystery to me. Now I *am* free . . . in both respects. You are standing right within reach of the goal you set yourself from the very first. And yet . . . !

REBECCA. I have never been further from my goal than I am now.

ROSMER. . . . And yet yesterday, you know, when I asked you . . . begged you . . . to be my wife, you cried out as though in terror, saying it could never be.

REBECCA. I cried out in despair, Johannes.

ROSMER. Why?

REBECCA. Because Rosmersholm has paralysed me. My will-power has been sapped, my spirit crippled. Once I dared tackle anything that came my way; now that time is gone. I have lost the power to act, Johannes.

ROSMER. .Tell me how this has happened.

REBECCA. Through living with you.

ROSMER. But how? How?

REBECCA. When I found myself living alone with you here . . . after you had found your real self . . .

ROSMER. Yes, yes?

REBECCA. . . . Because you were never wholly yourself as long as Beata was alive. . . .

ROSMER. I'm afraid you are right.

REBECCA. But when I began living here with you . . . in peace . . . in solitude . . . when without any kind of reserve you shared all your thoughts with me . . . all your feelings just as they came, so delicate and fine . . . *then* I felt the great transformation taking place. Gradually, you understand. Almost imperceptibly . . . but overwhelmingly in the end, and reaching right to the very depths of my soul.

ROSMER. Oh, what is all this you are saying, Rebecca!

REBECCA. All the rest . . . that horrible, sensual passion . . . faded far, far away. My restless agitation subsided in peace and quiet. A feeling of tranquillity came over me . . . a stillness like that which comes over a colony of sea-birds on the Northern coast under the midnight sun.

ROSMER. Tell me more of this. Everything you know.

REBECCA. There isn't very much more to tell, Johannes. Just that then I felt that this was the beginning of love . . . a great and selfless love that was content with being together as we *have* been together.

ROSMER. Oh, if I had had even the slightest inkling of all this!

REBECCA. It is best as it is. Yesterday . . . when you asked me if I would be your wife . . . I cried out with joy. . . .

ROSMER. Yes, you did, didn't you, Rebecca! I thought that was how it was.

REBECCA. For a moment, yes. I forgot myself. It was my old urgent spirit struggling to free itself again. But now it has no strength left . . . no stamina.

ROSMER. How do you explain what has happened to you?

REBECCA. It is the Rosmer philosophy of life . . . or in any case *your* philosophy . . . that has infected my will.

ROSMER. Infected?

REBECCA. And made it sick. Made it a slave to laws that had meant nothing to me before. You . . . being together with you . . . has given me some nobility of mind. . . .

ROSMER. Oh, if only I could believe that!

REBECCA. You need have no doubts about that. The Rosmer philosophy of life ennobles all right. But . . . [*shakes her head*] . . . but . . . but . . .

ROSMER. But what?

REBECCA. . . . But it kills happiness, Johannes.

ROSMER. Is that what you think, Rebecca?

REBECCA. For me, at least.

ROSMER. Yes, but are you quite certain? If I were to ask you again . . . ? Implore you . . .

REBECCA. Oh, my dear . . . please don't let us ever talk about that again. It's impossible. . . ! I think you ought to know, Johannes, I have . . . a past.

ROSMER. More than what you have already told me?

REBECCA. Yes. Something more, something different.

ROSMER [*with a faint smile*]. Isn't that strange, Rebecca. Do you know, I've occasionally suspected something of the sort.

REBECCA. Have you? And yet . . . in spite of that . . . ?

ROSMER. I never really believed it. I just toyed with the idea, you know.

REBECCA. If you want me to, I'll tell you that now as well.

ROSMER [*remonstrating*]. No! No! I don't want to hear a thing. Whatever it is, I want to forget it.

REBECCA. But I can't.

ROSMER. Oh, Rebecca. . . !

REBECCA. Yes, Johannes . . . that is the terrible thing . . . the very moment when I am being offered all the happiness in life I could wish for . . . it's now I see my own past confronting me like a barrier.

ROSMER. Your past is dead, Rebecca. It hasn't any hold on you any more . . . hasn't any connection with you . . . as you are *now*.

REBECCA. Oh, my dear, these are just empty phrases, you know. What about innocence? Where do I get *that*?

ROSMER [*sadly*]. Ah, yes . . . innocence.

REBECCA. Yes, innocence. Where happiness and contentment are found. Wasn't that after all the idea you wanted to foster in your new generation of happy and noble men. . . ?

ROSMER. Oh, don't remind me of *that*. That is nothing but a broken dream, Rebecca. An impetuous idea I don't believe in any more. . . . You know, people can't be ennobled from the outside.

REBECCA [*quietly*]. Not even by gentle love and affection, you think?

ROSMER [*thoughtfully*]. Yes . . . that could be a tremendous thing, of course. One of the most glorious things in life, I should think . . . if only it were so. [*Restlessly.*] But how can I be sure about a question like that? How can I know for certain?

REBECCA. Don't you believe me, Johannes?

ROSMER. Oh, Rebecca, how *can* I believe you . . . after the furtive way you have gone on here! And now you come along with this new idea. If there's anything behind it, please tell me straight out. If there's anything you want, I'll be only too glad to do all I can.

REBECCA [*wringing her hands*]. Oh, this killing doubt. . . ! Johannes . . . Johannes. . . !

ROSMER. Yes, it is terrible, Rebecca. But there's nothing I can do about it. I shall never be able to free myself from this doubt. Never know for certain that your love is whole-hearted and true.

REBECCA. But doesn't something deep within you tell you of the change that has taken place in me! And that this change is your doing . . . and yours alone!

ROSMER. Oh, Rebecca . . . I have no faith any longer in my power to change people. I have no faith in myself any more. No faith either in myself or in you.

REBECCA [*looks darkly at him*]. Then how are you going to live?

ROSMER. Yes, that I don't know. I simply can't imagine. I don't think I *can* live. . . . Nor can I think of anything in the world it might be worth living for.

REBECCA. Oh, life . . . life brings its own regeneration. Let us hold fast to it, Johannes. . . . We leave it soon enough.

ROSMER [*jumps up restlessly*]. Then give me back my faith again! My faith in *you*, Rebecca! Faith in your love. Proof! I must have proof!

REBECCA. Proof? How can I give you proof. . . ?

ROSMER. You *must*! [*Walks across the room.*] I can't stand this desolation . . . this terrible emptiness . . . this . . . this . . .

[*There is a loud knock on the hall door.*]

REBECCA [*starts up from her chair*]. Ah . . . do you hear that?

[*The door opens, and* ULRIK BRENDEL *comes in. He is wearing a dress shirt, a black coat and a good pair of boots with his trousers tucked in; otherwise he is dressed as on his previous appearance. He looks confused.*]

ROSMER. Oh, it's you, Mr. Brendel!

BRENDEL. Johannes, my boy! Greetings . . . and farewell!

ROSMER. Where are you going so late?

BRENDEL. Downhill.

ROSMER. What. . . ?

BRENDEL. I am going home, my dear pupil. I am homesick for the great void.

ROSMER. Something has happened to you, Mr. Brendel! What is it?

BRENDEL. So you observe the transformation? Yes . . . and well you may. When I last set foot in this room, I stood before you as a man of substance, patting my breast pocket.

ROSMER. Indeed! But I don't quite understand. . . .

BRENDEL. But what you see tonight is a deposed king standing amid the ashes of his burnt-out palace.

ROSMER. If there's anything I can do to help . . .

BRENDEL. You still have the heart of a little child, Johannes. Can you let me have a small loan?

ROSMER. Yes, of course. I'd be glad to.

BRENDEL. Could you manage me an ideal or two?

ROSMER. What did you say you wanted?

BRENDEL. One or two cast-off ideals. That would be doing a good deed. Because I'm cleaned out, my dear boy . . . absolutely flat.

REBECCA. Didn't you give your lecture?

BRENDEL. No, gracious lady. What do you think! Just as I was standing ready to shower out the contents of the cornucopia, I made the painful discovery that I was bankrupt.

REBECCA. But what about all those still unwritten works of yours?

BRENDEL. For twenty-five years I have been like a miser sitting on his padlocked chest. And then yesterday . . . when I opened it up to get at the treasure . . . there was none. . . . The mills of time had ground it all to dust. Not a blessed thing left, *nichts*.

ROSMER. Are you absolutely certain?

BRENDEL. There's no room for doubt, my dear boy. The President convinced me of that.

ROSMER. The President?

BRENDEL. Well . . . His Excellency, then. *Ganz nach Belieben*.

ROSMER. Whom do you mean?

BRENDEL. Peter Mortensgaard, of course.

ROSMER. What?

BRENDEL [*mysteriously*]. Hush, hush! Peter Mortensgaard is lord and master of the future. Never have I been in a more august presence. Peter Mortensgaard possesses the secret of omnipotence. He can do whatever he wants.

ROSMER. Oh, you can't believe that!

BRENDEL. Oh yes, I can, my boy! Because Peter Mortensgaard never wants to do more than he *can*. Peter Mortensgaard is quite capable of living his life without ideals. And it is precisely *that*, don't you see, that is the great secret of practical success. It is the sum of all the world's wisdom. *Basta!*

ROSMER [*in a low voice*]. Now I understand . . . why you are leaving here poorer than you came.

BRENDEL. *Bien!* Then be warned by the example of your old teacher. Cross out everything he ever tried to impress on you. Build not thy house on shifting sand. And watch yourself . . . and look carefully . . . before you build on this charming creature now sweetening life for you here.

REBECCA. Do you mean me?

BRENDEL. I do, my enchanting little mermaid.

REBECCA. And why shouldn't anybody build on me?

BRENDEL [*comes a step nearer*]. I gather that my one-time pupil has a mission to fulfil.

REBECCA. What if he has. . . ?

BRENDEL. His success is assured. But . . . I would have you know . . . on one inescapable condition.

REBECCA. What is that?

BRENDEL [*takes her gently by the wrist*]. That the woman who loves him goes out into the kitchen and gladly chops off her dainty, pink and white little-finger . . . *here*, just here near the middle joint. Furthermore, that the aforesaid woman in love . . . equally gladly . . . cuts off her incomparably formed left ear. [*Lets her go and turns to* ROSMER.] Farewell, my conquering Johannes.

What?

ROSMER. Are you going now? On this dark night?

BRENDEL. The dark night is best. Peace be with you.

[*He goes. There is a moment of silence in the room.*]

REBECCA [*breathes heavily*]. Oh, how close and sultry it is in here!

[*She goes over to the window, opens it and remains standing there.*]

ROSMER [*sits down in the armchair over by the stove*]. There seems nothing else for it, Rebecca. I see that you must leave.

REBECCA. Yes, I can't see that there's any other choice.

ROSMER. Let us make the most of these last few minutes. Come over here and sit beside me.

REBECCA [*goes and sits down on the sofa*]. What is it, Johannes?

ROSMER. First I want to tell you this: you need have no worry about your future.

REBECCA [*smiles*]. Hm! *My* future!

ROSMER. I have prepared for all contingencies, long ago. Whatever happens, you are taken care of.

REBECCA. You even thought of that too, my dear!

ROSMER. That you might have known.

REBECCA. I have never given any thought to that kind of thing for many a long day.

ROSMER. Yes, yes. . . . You probably never imagined things could ever be any different between us from what they were.

REBECCA. Yes, that's what I thought.

ROSMER. I was the same. But if anything were to happen to me now . . .

REBECCA. Oh Johannes . . . you will live longer than me.

ROSMER. It is within my power to do with this miserable life of mine whatever I think best, you know.

REBECCA. What are you saying! Surely you are not thinking of . . . ?

ROSMER. Do you think that would be so strange? After the dismal, pitiful defeat I have suffered! I was going to carry a great cause on to victory . . . and now look! And now I've quit the whole thing . . . before the battle had even started!

REBECCA. Take up the fight again, Johannes! If only you would try . . . you'll see you'll win. Bringing nobility to the minds of hundreds . . . thousands. If only you would try!

ROSMER. Oh, Rebecca . . . when I don't believe any longer in my own cause.

REBECCA. But your cause has already stood the test. One person at least you have certainly ennobled . . . me, as long as I live.

ROSMER. Yes . . . if only I could believe you.

REBECCA [*wringing her hands*]. Oh, but Johannes . . . can't you think of anything . . . anything at all that would make you believe it?

ROSMER [*starts, as if in fear*]. Don't! You mustn't ask me about that! Please don't go on! Don't say another word!

REBECCA. I must. . . . This is just what we must talk about. Can't you think of anything that would wipe out this suspicion? *I* can't think of anything at all.

ROSMER. It's best that you can't . . . best for us both.

REBECCA. No, no, no . . . I'm not going to be put off like that. If you can think of any single thing that would acquit me in your eyes, then I demand as my right that you name it.

ROSMER [*as if impelled against his will*]. Let us see, then. Yours is a great love, you say. That through me you have won nobility of soul. Is it true? Are you sure you have reckoned things out right? Shall we prove it? Eh?

REBECCA. I am ready.

ROSMER. Any time?

REBECCA. Whenever you like. The sooner the better.

ROSMER. Then let me see, Rebecca . . . if you . . . for my sake . . . this very night . . . [*Breaks off.*] Oh no, no, no!

REBECCA. Yes, Johannes. Yes, yes! Tell me and you shall see.

ROSMER. . . . If you have the courage . . . gladly, as Ulrik Brendel said . . . for my sake, tonight . . . gladly . . . to go the same way . . . Beata went?

REBECCA [*rises slowly from the sofa and says almost inaudibly*]. Johannes . . . !

ROSMER. Yes, Rebecca . . . that is the question that will haunt me . . . after you have left. Every hour of the day my thoughts will keep returning to it. I seem to see you clearly in my mind's eye . . . standing right out in the middle of the bridge. Then you lean out over the railing! . . . You sway as the rush of the water draws you down. No . . . you draw back. You dare not do what *she* dared.

REBECCA. But supposing I did have the courage? If I did dare, and gladly. What then?

ROSMER. Then I should have to believe you. Then surely I would get back my faith again in the cause . . . faith in my power to bring nobility into the minds of men . . . faith in man's power to achieve that nobility of mind.

REBECCA [*slowly takes up her shawl, throws it over her head, and says with composure*]. You shall have your faith back again.

ROSMER. Have you the courage and the will . . . for that, Rebecca?

REBECCA. That is something you can judge in the morning . . . or later . . . when they drag me up.

ROSMER [*with his head in his hands*]. There is a horrible fascination in this . . . !

REBECCA. Because I don't want to lie there . . . not any longer than necessary. Make sure they find me.

ROSMER [*jumps up*]. But all this . . . it's sheer madness. Go . . . or else stay! I'll take you at your word . . . once more.

REBECCA. Empty phrases, Johannes. No easy way out now, my dear, no running away. How can you ever take my word for things after today?

ROSMER. But I do not want to see you defeated, Rebecca!

REBECCA. There will be no defeat.

ROSMER. There will. You'll never bring yourself to go the way Beata went.

REBECCA. Don't you think so?

ROSMER. Never. You are not like Beata. You are not in the power of some twisted view of life.

REBECCA. But I am in the power of the Rosmersholm view of life . . . *now*. Where I have sinned . . . it is right that I should atone.

ROSMER [*looks fixedly at her*]. Is *that* how you see it?

REBECCA. Yes.

ROSMER [*resolutely*]. Well then, I give *my* loyalty to our emancipated view of life. There is no judge over us. Therefore we must see to it that we judge ourselves.

REBECCA [*misunderstanding him*]. That's right . . . that too. My going will save what is best in you.

ROSMER. Oh, there's nothing left in me to save.

REBECCA. Oh, yes there is. But as for me . . . from now on I'd only be a drag on you, like some sea-troll slumped over the ship that is to carry you forward. I must go overboard. Do you expect me to go through life dragging behind me a crippled existence? . . . For ever brooding over the happiness I forfeited by my past? I must quit the game, Johannes.

ROSMER. If you go . . . I go with you.

REBECCA [*smiles almost imperceptibly, looks at him and says gently*]. Yes, come with me . . . and be my witness. . . .

ROSMER. I go with you, I said.

REBECCA. As far as the bridge, yes. You know you never dare go out on it.

ROSMER. Have you noticed that?

REBECCA [*sadly and brokenly*]. Yes. That was what made my love hopeless.

ROSMER. Rebecca . . . now I lay my hand on your head . . . [*does so*] and take you to be my truly wedded wife.

REBECCA [*takes both his hands and puts her head on his breast*]. Thank you, Johannes. [*Lets go.*] And now I go gladly.

ROSMER. Man and wife should go together.

REBECCA. Only as far as the bridge, Johannes.

ROSMER. Out on it, too. As far as *you* go . . . I too go with you. For now I dare.

REBECCA. Are you absolutely convinced . . . that this way is the best for you?

ROSMER. I know it's the only way.

REBECCA. Suppose you were only deceiving yourself. . . . Suppose it were all a delusion . . . one of those White Horses of Rosmersholm.

ROSMER. It could well be. We can never escape them, we of this house.

REBECCA. Then stay, Johannes!

ROSMER. The husband shall go with his wife, as the wife with her husband.

REBECCA. Yes, but first tell me this: is it you who goes with me, or I with you.

ROSMER. That is something we shall never fathom.

REBECCA. Yet I should so much like to know.

ROSMER. We go together, Rebecca. I go with you, you with me.

REBECCA. I rather think that too.

ROSMER. For now we two are one.

REBECCA. Yes, now we are one. Come! Let us go gladly.

[*They go out hand in hand through the hall and can be seen turning to the left. The door remains standing open after them. The room stands empty for a few moments. Then* MRS. HELSETH *opens the door on the right.*]

MRS. HELSETH. Miss West . . . the coach is . . . [*Looks about her.*] Not in? Gone out together at this time of night? Well . . . I must say that's . . . hm! [*Goes out into the hall, looks around and comes back in again.*] Not on the seat. Well . . . well . . . [*Goes to the window and looks out.*] Good God! That white thing there. . . ! Bless my soul . . . yes, they are both on the bridge. God forgive the sinful creatures! Putting their arms round each other! [*Screams.*] Oh . . . over the side . . . both of them! Into the millstream! Help! Help! [*Her knees tremble; shaking, she holds on to the back of a chair; she can scarcely utter the words.*] No, no help there . . . the dead woman has taken them.

(handwritten annotations)

"the explained supernatural"

supernatural: white horse
explained: Rebecca's white
crocheted shawl from
act's stage directions

shows up
in Gothic
novels

ANTON CHEKHOV	**Early Stories**
	Five Plays
	The Princess and Other Stories
	The Russian Master and Other Stories
	The Steppe and Other Stories
	Twelve Plays
	Ward Number Six and Other Stories
FYODOR DOSTOEVSKY	**Crime and Punishment**
	Devils
	A Gentle Creature and Other Stories
	The Idiot
	The Karamazov Brothers
	Memoirs from the House of the Dead
	Notes from the Underground and **The Gambler**
NIKOLAI GOGOL	**Dead Souls**
	Plays and Petersburg Tales
ALEXANDER PUSHKIN	**Eugene Onegin**
	The Queen of Spades and Other Stories
LEO TOLSTOY	**Anna Karenina**
	The Kreutzer Sonata and Other Stories
	The Raid and Other Stories
	Resurrection
	War and Peace
IVAN TURGENEV	**Fathers and Sons**
	First Love and Other Stories
	A Month in the Country

The Oxford World's Classics Website

www.worldsclassics.co.uk

- Information about new titles
- Explore the full range of Oxford World's Classics
- Links to other literary sites and the main OUP webpage
- Imaginative competitions, with bookish prizes
- Peruse the Oxford World's Classics Magazine
- Articles by editors
- Extracts from Introductions
- A forum for discussion and feedback on the series
- Special information for teachers and lecturers

www.worldsclassics.co.uk

American Literature

British and Irish Literature

Children's Literature

Classics and Ancient Literature

Colonial Literature

Eastern Literature

European Literature

History

Medieval Literature

Oxford English Drama

Poetry

Philosophy

Politics

Religion

The Oxford Shakespeare

A complete list of Oxford Paperbacks, including Oxford World's Classics, Oxford Shakespeare, Oxford Drama, and Oxford Paperback Reference, is available in the UK from the Academic Division Publicity Department, Oxford University Press, Great Clarendon Street, Oxford OX2 6DP.

In the USA, complete lists are available from the Paperbacks Marketing Manager, Oxford University Press, 198 Madison Avenue, New York, NY 10016.

Oxford Paperbacks are available from all good bookshops. In case of difficulty, customers in the UK can order direct from Oxford University Press Bookshop, Freepost, 116 High Street, Oxford OX1 4BR, enclosing full payment. Please add 10 per cent of published price for postage and packing.